1 MONTH OF
FREE
READING

at
www.ForgottenBooks.com

By purchasing this book you are eligible for one month membership to ForgottenBooks.com, giving you unlimited access to our entire collection of over 1,000,000 titles via our web site and mobile apps.

To claim your free month visit:
www.forgottenbooks.com/free914815

ISBN 978-0-265-95316-7
PIBN 10914815

No. 8140

United States
Circuit Court of Appeals

For the Ninth Circuit.

W. PIERCE, Claimant of the Oil Screw vessel
"TAHOMA" official number 214741, her engines,
tackle, apparel, furniture, dories, gear, cargo,
etc., and J. R. KECKMAN, Surety,

Appellants,

UNITED STATES OF AMERICA, ATLAS EN-
GINE COMPANY, a corporation, and FISH-
ING VESSEL OWNERS MARINE WAYS,
a corporation,

Appellees.

Apostles on Appeal

Upon Appeal from the District Court of the United
States for the Territory of Alaska,
Division Number One

United States
Circuit Court of Appeals

For the Ninth Circuit.

W. PIERCE, Claimant of the Oil Screw vessel "TAHOMA" official number 214741, her engines, tackle, apparel, furniture, dories, gear, cargo, etc., and J. R. HECKMAN, Surety,

Appellants,

vs.

UNITED STATES OF AMERICA, ATLAS ENGINE COMPANY, a corporation, and FISHING VESSEL OWNERS MARINE WAYS, a corporation,

Appellees.

Apostles on Appeal

Upon Appeal from the District Court of the United States for the Territory of Alaska, Division Number One

Parker Printing Company, 545 Sansome Street, San Francisco.

INDEX

[Clerk's Note: When deemed likely to be of an important nature, errors or doubtful matters appearing in the original certified record are printed literally in italic; and, likewise, cancelled matter appearing in the original certified record is printed and cancelled herein accordingly. When possible, an omission from the text is indicated by printing in italic the two words between which the omission seems to occur.]

Page

Answer 9

Assignment of Errors.. 256

Bill of Exceptions, Allowance of............................ 279

Bond for Costs on Appeal....................................... 268

Costs, Stipulation for... 270

Claim of Owner... 277

Certificate of Clerk to Apostles on Appeal........... 280

Certificate of Judge to Bill of Exceptions............. 279

Citation on Appeal... 276

Decree 30

Exceptions of Claimant to Findings and Conclusions 23

Exceptions of Claimant to Decree........................... 32

Findings of Fact requested by Fishing Vessel Owners Marine Ways, Intervenor................12, 19

Findings Requested by Claimant.....................13, 14

Findings of Fact and Conclusions of Law............. 18

Libel 3

Names and Addresses of Counsel............................. 1

Notice of Appeal... 255

Opinion of Court... 242

Index   Page

Order Extending Term of Court for Purpose of
   Settling Bill of Exceptions............................ 252

Order of Release of Attached Property.............. 274

Order Allowing Appeal.................................... 275

Petition for Appeal.. 254

Praecipe for Apostles on Appeal..................... 267

Reporter's Certificate 278

Statement .... a

Stipulation for Costs..................................... 270

Stipulation for Release of Attached Vessel.......... 272

Stipulation in re Captain Monson's testimony... 163

Transcript of Testimony (commencing).............. 32

    Evidence of Libelant:

      Hanson, Capt. Bernard
        —direct 179
        —eross 181

      Heggem, Ingvosld (Deposition)
        —direct 108
        —cross 112

      Hudson, F. G. (Deposition)
        —direct 46
        —cross 50
        —recalled, direct 52
        —cross 52

      Johnson, Albert J. (Deposition)
        —direct 41
        —cross 45

Index   Page

Evidence of Libelant (cont.):

Nickerson, G. W.

—direct 38

—cross 73

—redirect 90

—recross 92

Sunderland, Capt. Louis

—direct 182

Woodward, G. C.

—direct 121

—recalled, cross 149

Wright, M. C. (Deposition)

—direct 93

—cross 98

—redirect 106

Vernon, Paul R.

—direct 118

—recalled, cross 148

Evidence of Respondent:

Nickerson, G. W.

—direct 186

—cross 212

—redirect 223

—recross 226

Pierce, Winnie

—direct 226

—cross 232

—redirect 236

W. Pierce, et al. vs.

Index   Page

Exhibits for Libelant:

1—Letter, The F. E. Hunt, Limited, to Atlas Engine Company................ 54

2—Letter, F. E. Hunt, Limited, to Fishing Vessel Owners Marine Ways 56

3—Letter, Atlas Engine Company to F. E. Hunt, Limited........................... 58

4—Photostatic copy of Letter, F. E. Hunt, Limited, to Atlas Engine Company 60

5—Photostatic copy of Letter, Atlas Engine Company to F. E. Hunt, Limited 63

6—Photostatic copy of Letter, F. E. Hunt, Limited, to Atlas Engine Company 65

7—Photostatic copy of Letter, F. E. Hunt, Limited, to Atlas Engine Company 67

8—Photostatic copy of Letter, F. E. Hunt, Limited, to Atlas Engine Company 68

9—Depositions of Albert J. Johnson, F. G. Hudson, M. C. Wright and Ingvold Heggem 41

10—Statement and Affidavit of Arthur Johnson, dated Oct. 10, 1933.......... 120

Index   Page

Exhibits for Libelant (cont.)

11—Statement of Arthur Johnson dated
   July 21, 1933... 127

12—Bill of Sale.. 135

13—Affidavit

   Rejected 148
   Admitted 163

14—(Identical with "15") 175

15—Report of Confidential Interview...... 175

Exhibits for Claimant:

A—Letter, G. W. Nickerson to Capt.
   Egel Ericksen 196

B—Letter, Egill Eriksen to F. E.
   Hunt, Ltd. 197

In the District Court of the United States for the
Western District of Washington,
Northern Division.
In Admiralty.
No. ....

W. PIERCE, Claimant of the Oil Screw vessel
"TAHOMA" official number 214,741, her engine, tackle, apparel, furniture, dories, gear,
cargo, etc.,

   and

J. R. HECKMAN,

          Appellants,

     vs.

THE UNITED STATES OF AMERICA, ATLAS
ENGINE COMPANY, a corporation, FISH-
ING VESSEL OWNERS MARINE WAYS,
a corporation,

          Appellees.

STATEMENT.

Time of Commencement of Cause, September 17,
1934.

   Names of Parties to Cause:

W. PIERCE, Claimant of the Oil Screw Vessel
 "TAHOMA";
J. R. HECKMAN, Surety,

          Appellants,

THE UNITED STATES OF AMERICA, Libelant,
ATLAS ENGINE COMPANY, a corporation, Intervenor,
FISHING VESSEL OWNERS MARINE WAYS,
 a corporation, Intervenor,

          Appellees.

NAMES AND ADDRESSES OF COUNSEL:

A. H. ZIEGLER, Esq.,
Ketchikan, Alaska,
for Claimant and Surety, Appellant.

WM. A. HOLZHEIMER, Esq.,

G. W. FOLTA, Esq.,
U. S. Attorney and Assistant, respectively,
First Division, Alaska;
Juneau, Alaska,
for Libelant;

LESTER O. GORE, Esq.,
Ketchikan, Alaska,
for Intervenors.

———

DATE OF FILING PLEADINGS:

Libel filed September 17, 1934.

Answer to Libel filed October 6, 1934.

Claim of Owner filed September 24, 1934.

Stipulation for Costs filed September 24, 1934.

Stipulation for Release of Attached vessel filed Sept. 24, 1934.

Order of Release filed September 24, 1934.

———

PROCESS, MONITION AND ATTACHMENT:

Respondent Gas Screw Vessel "TAHOMA" was seized and released upon the Libel of The United States of America.

Time of Trial—June 6-7, 1935.

Name of Judge presiding at Trial—Hon. Geo. F. Alexander, of said District Court.

The trial was upon the merits, upon the Libel and Answer thereto.

Requested Findings of Fact of Intervenor, Fishing Vessel Owners Marine Ways, Inc., filed November 16, 1935.

Claimant's Requested Findings of Fact and Conclusions of Law, filed June 7, 1935.

Claimant's Requested Findings of Fact and Conclusions of Law filed November 16, 1935.

Intervenor Fishing Vessel Owners Marine Ways Requested Findings of Fact and Conclusions of Law filed June 7, 1935.

Findings of Fact and Conclusions of Law filed June 7, 1935. [2*]

Exceptions of Claimant to Findings and Conclusions and to Failure of Court to Find the Fact and Conclusions of Law requested by Claimant, filed December 7, 1935.

Opinion of Court, dated September 7, 1935.

Decree filed November 16, 1935.

Exception of Claimant to Decree filed December 7, 1935.

Assignment of Errors filed December 17, 1935.

Notice of Appeal filed December 17, 1935.

Bond for Costs on Appeal filed December 17, 1935.

Order Allowing Appeal filed December 17, 1935.

Order Extending Term of Court for Purpose of

---

*Page numbering appearing at the foot of page of original certified Transcript of Record.

Settling Bill of Exceptions and Transmitting Apostles on Appeal dated December 17, 1935.

Citation on Appeal filed December 17, 1935. [3]

In the District Court for the District of Alaska, Division Number One, at Ketchikan. In Admiralty.

No. 1778-KA

UNITED STATES OF AMERICA,

Libelant,

vs.

The Oil Screw vessel TAHOMA, official number 214,741, her engine, tackle, apparel, furniture, dories, gear, cargo, etc.,

Respondent.

LIBEL IN ADMIRALTY

Before the Honorable Geo. F. Alexander, Judge of the District Court for the District of Alaska, Division Number One:

On this 17th day of September, 1934, comes Geo. W. Folta, Attorney of the United States for the First Division, Territory of Alaska, who prosecutes here for the said United States, in its behalf, in a cause of forfeiture, civil and maritime, in which the United States of America is concerned, and informs this Honorable Court:

That the United States of America brings suit of forfeiture herein against a certain vessel, to-wit, the oil screw vessel TAHOMA, official number 214741, her engine, tackle, furniture, apparel, dories, gear, cargo and so forth, for breach of the customs, navigation and shipping laws of the United States of America and alleges:

1.

That on March 31, 1925, at the Port of Ketchikan, in the Territory of Alaska, in pursuance of Chapter One Title [4] XLVIII "Regulation of Commerce & Navigation" R. S. U. S. (46 U. S. C. A. 11, et seq.,) the said vessel TAHOMA was duly registered in the United States Customs Service and official number 214741 was duly assigned said vessel, and a certificate of registry was duly issued to and thereafter and during all the time mentioned herein, was used for said vessel, a copy of which certificate is annexed hereto, marked Exhibit "A" and by reference made a part hereof; which said certificate during all the times mentioned herein was and is in full form, force and effect for the uses and purposes for which intended and obtained.

2.

That thereafter, to-wit, on or about May 29, 1933, at a foreign port, to-wit, the Port Of Prince Rupert, Province of British Columbia, Dominion of Canada, the registered sole owner of said oil screw vessel TAHOMA, to-wit, W. Pierce, unlawfully and fraudulently sold and transferred, on whole or in part, by way of trust, confidence and otherwise, to a subject and citizen of a foreign state, to-wit, to F. E.

Hunt, Ltd., of the Dominion of Canada, the said vessel TAHOMA.

3.

That on or about the 17th day of September, 1933, the said vessel TAHOMA cleared from Prince Rupert, Canada, for Alaska, and on the 18th day of September, 1933, arrived within a district of the United States, to-wit, the Collection District of Alaska, and remained in said district until about October 5, 1933, and that neither the master nor the person in charge of said vessel within eight days after said vessel arrived in said District of the United States, or at any other time, surrendered or delivered up to the Collector of Customs [5] for the District of Alaska the said certificate of registry so procured, as aforesaid, by the said W. Pierce.

4.

That on September 13th 1934, the said vessel TAHOMA was seized by Lieutenant Commander F. W. Brown, commanding the United States Coast Guard Cutter Talapoosa, on the high seas in the Gulf of Alaska, and thereafter on the same day was brought within the First Division, Territory of Alaska, in public waters of the United States, within the admiralty and maritime jurisdiction of this court, and the said vessel is now lying at Ketchikan, in said First Division, Territory of Alaska, within the jurisdiction of this court.

5.

That all and singular the matters hereinbefore
secondly and thirdly articulated are contrary to the
provisions of Sections 4146 and 4172 R. S. U. S.
(46 U. S. C. A. 23 and 41). That by reason of the
premises and by virtue of said sections, the said oil
screw vessel TAHOMA, her engine, tackle, apparel,
cargo, etc., became forfeited.

6.

That all and singular the premises are and were
true and within the admiralty and maritime jurisdiction of the United States and this Honorable
Court.

SECOND CAUSE OF ACTION:

For a further and second separate cause for forfeiture of said vessel TAHOMA, her engine, tackle,
apparel, furniture, cargo, etc., for breach of the
customs-navigation-shipping laws of the United
States, libelant realleges all the facts set forth in
the first cause of action and in addition thereto
alleges: [6]

1.

That from the time of the sale and transfer, as
aforesaid, of the said vessel TAHOMA, continuously up to the time of her seizure, said vessel was
unlawfully and fraudulently engaged in foreign
trade and said certificate of registry so granted and
issued, as aforesaid, for said vessel, was knowingly
and fraudulently used for a vessel not entitled to
the benefit thereof, to-wit, the vessel TAHOMA, by

reason of the sale and transfer of said vessel as aforesaid.

2.

That on September 13th 1934, the said vessel TAHOMA was seized by Lieutenant Commander F. W. Brown, commanding the United States Coast Guard Cutter Talapoosa, on the high seas in the Gulf of Alaska, and thereafter on the same day was brought within the First Division, Territory of Alaska, in public waters of the United States, within the admiralty and maritime jurisdiction of this court, and the said vessel is now lying at Ketchikan, in said First Division, Territory of Alaska, within the jurisdiction of this court.

3.

That all and singular the matters hereinbefore firstly articulated are contrary to the provisions of Section 4189 R. S. U. S. (46 U. S. C. A. 60) Section 18 Act of Congress June 5, 1920, 41 Stats. 994 (46 U. S. C. A. 808). That by reason of the premises and by virtue of the said sections, the said oil screw vessel TAHOMA, her engine, tackle, apparel, cargo, etc., became forfeited.

4.

That all and singular the premises aforesaid are and were true and within the admiralty and maritime jurisdiction [7] of the United States and this Honorable Court.

WHEREFORE, the said Attorney of the United States, on behalf of the United States, prays the usual process and monition of this Honorable Court

against the said oil screw vessel TAHOMA, her
engine, tackle, apparel, cargo, etc., and that all persons concerned in such vessel and her engine, tackle,
apparel, cargo, etc., may be cited to appear and
show cause why a forfeiture of the same should not
be decreed, and that all due proceedings being had
therein this Honorable Court may be pleased to
decree for the forfeiture aforesaid, and that the said
vessel TAHOMA, her engine, tackle, apparel, cargo,
etc., may be condemned as forfeited and sold according to the statutes and Acts of Congress in that
behalf provided.

G. W. FOLTA,

Asst. United States Attorney [8]

In the District Court for the District of Alaska,
Division Number, at Ketchikan, in Admiralty

No. 1778-KA

UNITED STATES OF AMERICA,

Libelant,

vs.

The Oil Screw Vessel "Tahoma", official number
214741, her engine, tackle, apparel, furniture,
dories, gear, cargo, etc.,

Respondent,

W. E. PIERCE,

Claimant,

ATLAS ENGINE COMPANY, a corporation,

Intervening Libelant.

ANSWER

Comes now W. E. Pierce, the above named claimant, by his proctor, A. H. Ziegler, and answering the libel on file, admits, denies and alleges as follows:

I.

Answering Paragraph 1 of the libel, claimant admits the same.

II.

Answering Paragraph 2 of the libel, claimant denies the same.

III.

Answering Paragraph 3 of the libel, claimant admits the same, but alleges that the "Tahoma"

and the master in [9] charge were under no obligation to surrender or deliver to the Collector of Customs a certificate of registry of the "Tahoma"
within eight days after the "Tahoma" arrived in
Alaska, or at all.

IV.

Answering Paragraph 4 of the libel, claimant
admits the same.

V.

Answering Paragraph 5 of the libel, claimant
denies the same.

VI.

Answering Paragraph 6 of the libel, claimant
admits the jurisdiction of this Court.

FURTHER ANSWERING said libel and the
second cause of action therein contained, claimant
admits, denies and alleges as follows:

I.

Answering Paragraph 1 of the second cause of
action in the libel, claimant denies the same.

II.

Answering Paragraph 2 of the second cause in
said libel, claimant admits the same.

III.

Answering Paragraph 3 of the second cause in
said libel, claimant denies the same.

IV.

Answering Paragraph 4 of the second cause of
action in said libel, claimant admits the jurisdiction

of this Court and denies the other allegations in said Paragraph contained.

WHEREFORE, claimant prays that he be admitted to defend [10] accordingly; that the libelant take nothing by its suit herein; that the same be dismissed and that claimant have such other further and different relief as to the Court may seem equitable in the premises.

A. H. ZIEGLER

Proctor for Claimant

United States of America
Territory of Alaska—ss.

A. H. ZIEGLER, being first duly sworn, on oath, deposes and says: I am the proctor for W. E. Pierce, the claimant in the foregoing Answer; I have read the foregoing Answer and the contents thereof are true as I verily believe; that I make this verification upon behalf of claimant because he is not at Ketchikan, Alaska, the place where this verification is made.

A. H. ZIEGLER

Subscribed and sworn to before me this 5th day of October, 1934.

[Notarial Seal]   MARGARET OTTESEN,
                  Notary Public for Alaska.
                  My com. ex. 10/23/37

[Endorsed]: "Filed in the District Court Territory of Alaska, First Division Oct 6 1934. Robert E. Coughlin, Clerk By R. Russell, Deputy." [11]

[Title of Court and Cause.]

REQUESTED FINDINGS OF FACT

COMES NOW Lester O. Gore, Proctor for Intervenor, Fishing Vessel Owners Marine Ways, Inc., a corporation, and requests the following finding of fact in the above entitled cause:

That on or about May 29, 1933, F. E. Hunt, Ltd., a foreign corporation, a citizen of Great Britain, took over the active control, management and operation of the "TAHOMA" and the shipment of its catches of halibut to American markets, in payment of the indebtedness of said vessel to said corporation (1) by removing the record owner and master, W. Pierce, from command of the "TAHOMA" and placing him in charge of another American vessel, to-wit: the "WAVE"; (2) by making a colorable appointment of J. A. Johnson, an American citizen, as Master of the "TAHOMA" for the sole purpose of dealing with the libelant in matters pertaining to and [12] arising under the customs, navigation and shipping laws of Great Britain, actually in charge, command and control of said vessel when away from Prince Rupert, and (4) by receiving and distributing the earnings and profits from such operations, and sharing therein. The intervenors herein agreed and consented that F. E. Hunt, Ltd., take over the management and control of the "TAHOMA";

and further findings of fact as follows:

That the intervenors furnished supplies, equipment and machinery and made repairs to said vessel "TAHOMA" necessary to enable said vessel to go to sea, of the reasonable value claimed, prior to the seizure and prior to the date of the transfer of the "TAHOMA" to F. E. Hunt, Ltd.

LESTER O. GORE
Proctor for Intervenor

[Endorsed]: "Filed in the District Court, Territory of Alaska, First Division Nov 16 1935 Robert E. Coughlin Clerk By .... Deputy." [13]

[Title of Court and Cause.]

CLAIMANT'S REQUESTED FINDINGS OF FACT AND CONCLUSIONS OF LAW

The claimant hereby requests the Court to make and enter the following Findings of Fact and Conclusions of Law, which request is filed with the Court before decision is rendered in the above suit.

I.

That W. Pierce, the registered owner of the Oil Screw "TAHOMA", did not, as alleged in the libel, or at all, unlawfully and fraudulently sell, in whole or in part by way of trust, confidence, or otherwise, to a subject and citizen of a foreign state, to-wit, F. E. Hunt, Ltd., the said Vessel "TAHOMA".

II.

That said "TAHOMA" did not, as alleged in the libel, unlawfully or fraudulently engage in foreign trade and the certificate of registry of the "TAHOMA" was not knowingly or fraudulently used for a vessel, to-wit, the vessel "TAHOMA", [14] not entitled to the benefits thereof.

CONCLUSIONS OF LAW

From the foregoing Findings of Fact, the claimant requests the Court to make the following declaration and conclusion of law:

I.

That the American Oil Vessel "TAHOMA", her engine, tackle, apparel, cargo, etc., did not become forfeited by reason of the matters and things set forth in the libel, or at all.

Dated this 7th day of June, 1935.

A. H. ZIEGLER,

Attorney for Claimant.

[Endorsed]: "Filed in the District Court Territory of Alaska, First Division at Ketchikan Jun 7 1935 Robert E. Coughlin, Clerk By _____ Deputy." [15]

———

[Title of Court and Cause.]

CLAIMANT'S REQUESTED FINDINGS OF FACT AND CONCLUSIONS OF LAW.

The claimant hereby requests the Court to make

and enter the following Supplemental Findings of Fact and Conclusions of law:

I.

That the consideration to Pierce, owner of the Tahoma, in permitting F. E. Hunt, Ltd., to take over the operation and management of the Tahoma, was that Pierce should receive the boat Wave, of the value of $500.00, with which to make a living, for which consideration Pierce agreed that the Tahoma should be operated in order that the indebtedness of the Tahoma could be paid off, and it was further agreed between Pierce and F. E. Hunt, Ltd. that if a sale of the Tahoma could be made, Pierce would consent thereto, and the purchase price be applied in payment of Pierce's indebtedness and the remainder, if any, be paid to Pierce.

II.

That F. E. Hunt, Ltd., and the above Intervenors, did [16] not agree to, nor did they at any time, release Pierce from his *his* indebtedness to them, nor did Pierce at any time agree to permit said F. E. Hunt, Ltd., and the Intervenors to take and receive the Tahoma, for the boat "Wave" and payment of his indebtedness to said corporations.

III.

That the arrangement made between Pierce, F. E. Hunt, Ltd., and the Intervenors, for the operation of the Tahoma, by said F. E. Hunt, Ltd., was made in good faith and with the honest belief on the part of all concerned that said arrangement did not constitute a violation of law.

IV.

That there was no evidence in writing of the sale or transfer of the Tahoma, or of any interest therein.

V.

That after F. E. Hunt, Ltd., took over the operation and management of the Tahoma, W. Pierce, Claimant, performed work on the Tahoma, during the winter, or closed fishing season and received no pay therefor.

CONCLUSIONS OF LAW.

From the foregoing Findings of Fact, the Claimant requests the Court to make the following declaration and conclusion of law:

I.

That W. Pierce, did not unlawfully and fraudulently, sell and transfer, in whole or in part, by way of trust, confidence and otherwise, to a subject and citizen of a foreign state, to-wit: to F. E. Hunt, Ltd., of the Dominion of Canada, the said vessel Tahoma.

Dated at Ketchikan, Alaska, November 9th, 1935.

H. L. FAULKNER and

A. H. ZIEGLER

Proctors for Claimant and Intervenor, Atlas Engine Company, a corporation.

[Endorsed]: "Filed [17] in the District Court, Territory of Alaska, First Division Nov 16 1935 Robert E. Coughlin, Clerk By .... Deputy." [18]

[Title of Court and Cause.]

INTERVENOR FISHING VESSEL OWNERS MARINE WAYS' REQUESTED FINDINGS OF FACT AND CONCLUSIONS OF LAW.

From the evidence introduced upon the trial of the above entitled cause, the Court finds the Intervenor, FISHING VESSEL OWNERS MARINE WAYS, a corporation, at the request of the Master and Owner of the Oil Screw Vessel "TAHOMA" sold and delivered to said vessel for the use thereof goods, wares, and merchandise and performed services thereon, which goods, wares and merchandise and services performed were necessary to said vessel to permit her to go upon her intended voyages and were so sold and delivered and services performed on and between December 31, 1929 and January 28, 1930; that the value thereof, including interest to June 30, 1934 is $1203.66 of which $140.00 has been paid, leaving a balance due on said date in the sum of $1063.66.

And as a CONCLUSION OF LAW, the Court finds that said intervenor is entitled to judgment in the sum of $1063.66 with interest thereon at 8% per annum from June 30, 1934, for its costs and disbursements incurred, for an attorney fee in the sum of $................. and that said vessel be condemned and sold to satisfy the demands of intervenor. [19]

Dated at Ketchikan, Alaska, this 7th day of June, 1935.

LESTER O. GORE
Proctor for Intervenor.

[Endorsed]: "Filed in the District Court Territory of Alaska, First Division at Ketchikan Jun 7 1935. Robert E. Coughlin Clerk By .... Deputy." [20]

———

[Title of Court and Cause.]

FINDINGS OF FACT
and
CONCLUSIONS OF LAW

The above entitled cause coming on for trial at the Special April 1935 Term of said court, and having been tried before the court on the 6th and 7th days of June, 1935, Geo. W. Folta, Assistant United States Attorney appearing for the libelant, and A. H. Ziegler, Esq., for claimant and intervenor Atlas Engine Company, and Lester O. Gore, Esq., for intervenor Fishing Vessel Owners Marine Ways; and after hearing the allegations and proofs of the parties, the arguments of counsel and reading briefs for the respective parties and being advised in the premises, the following Findings of Fact and Conclusions of Law, constituting the decision of the court in said action, are hereby made and filed:

FINDINGS OF FACT

1.

That on March 31, 1925, at the Port of Ketchikan, within the Collection District of Alaska, the oil screw vessel [21] "TAHOMA" was duly registered, according to law; that official number 214741 was assigned to said vessel and a certificate of registry issued thereto, entitling the said vessel to engage in foreign trade, which certificate was in full force and effect and used by said vessel during all the times mentioned in the libel herein.

2.

That during all the times mentioned in the libel the said vessel "TAHOMA" was engaged in halibut fishing, plying between American waters and Prince Rupert, Canada, and sold its catches for shipment to American markets, via Prince Rupert, duty free.

3.

That on or about May 29, 1933, F. E. Hunt, Ltd., a foreign corporation, a citizen of Great Britain, (with the consent, knowledge and agreement of intervenors herein) took over the active control, management and operation of the "TAHOMA" and the shipment of its catches of halibut to American markets, in payment of the indebtedness of said vessel to said corporation (1) by removing the record owner and master, W. Pierce, from command of the "TAHOMA" and placing him in charge of another American vessel, to-wit, the "WAVE": (2)

by making a colorable appointment of J. A. Johnson, an American citizen, as master of the "TAHOMA" for the sole purpose of dealing with the libelant in matters pertaining to and arising under the customs, navigation and shipping laws of the United States; (3) by placing Antone Martinson, a citizen of Great Britain, actually in charge, command and control of said vessel when away from Prince Rupert, and (4) by receiving and distributing the earnings [22] and profits from such operations, and sharing therein.

4.

That on February 27, 1934, F. E. HUNT, Ltd., placed B. A. Petterson in charge of the "TAHOMA" as master of record, and that said Petterson continued as such until the date of the seizure.

5.

That on or about the 17th day of September, 1933, the said vessel "TAHOMA" cleared from Prince Rupert, Canada, for Alaska, and on the 18th day of September, 1933, arrived within a district of the United States, to-wit, the Collection District of Alaska, and remained in said district until about October 5, 1933, and that neither the master nor the person in charge of said vessel within eight days after said vessel arrived in said district of the United States, or at any other time, surrendered or delivered up to the Collector of Customs for the District of Alaska the said certificate of registry.

6.

That on September 13, 1934, the said vessel "TAHOMA" was seized by the Coast Guard on the high seas and on the same day brought within the First Judicial Division, Territory of Alaska, and was in the custody of the Coast Guard within the jurisdiction of this court at the time of the filing of the libel.

7.

That during all of the time mentioned herein no duty was paid on the halibut caught by the "TAHOMA", its master and crew, and shipped into the United States via Prince Rupert B. C. [23]

8.

Yhat the intervenors furnished supplies, equipment and machinery and made repairs to said vessel "TAHOMA" necessary to enable said vessel to go to sea, of the reasonable value claimed, prior to the seizure and before the transfer of the "TAHOMA" to F. E. Hunt, Ltd.

CONCLUSIONS OF LAW

I.

That on or about May 29, 1933, at Prince Rupert, B. C. the American vessel "TAHOMA" was transferred in whole or in part, by way of trust, confidence and otherwise, to F. E. Hunt, Ltd., a citizen of Great Britain; and that the said F. E. Hunt, Ltd., thereby became entitled to the whole or part or share of, and became indirectly interested in, such vessel and in the profits and issues thereof, and became the equitable owner of said vessel.

II.

That thereafter and until the seizure of the "TAHOMA" the said vessel was unlawfully and fraudulently engaged in a foreign trade and the said certificate of registry was knowingly and fraudulently used for said vessel when she was no longer entitled to the benefit of said register.

III.

That all the shipments of halibut made by the said vessel or F. E. Hunt, Ltd., during all the times mentioned in the libel were subject to an import duty of two cents a pound under the provisions of the tariff act (19 U. S. C. A. 1001, Par. 717,) and that such shipments were made in fraud of the revenue of the United States. [24]

IV.

That the claims of intervenors constitute maritime liens and are allowed in the sums prayed for, but on account of their conduct are allowed in the principal sums only, without interest or attorneys' fees.

V.

That the vessel "TAHOMA" became forfeited as of May 29, 1933, to the United States under the first cause of action, and as of September 27, 1933, under the second cause of action.

Let judgment be entered accordingly.

Dated at Juneau, Alaska, this 23rd day of November, 1935.

GEO. F. ALEXANDER,
District Judge.

[Endorsed]: Filed in the District Court Territory of Alaska, First Division, at Juneau Nov 23, 1935 Robert E Coughlin, Clerk. [25]

[Title of Court and Cause.]

EXCEPTIONS TO FINDINGS OF FACT AND CONCLUSIONS OF LAW

and

EXCEPTIONS TO FAILURE OF COURT TO FIND THE FACTS AND CONCLUSIONS OF LAW REQUESTED BY CLAIMANT

Comes now W. Pierce, claimant in the above suit, and excepts to the Findings of Fact and Conclusions of Law entered and filed herein on November 23rd, 1935, said Findings of Fact and Conclusions of Law having been proposed by the Respondent, as follows:

I.

Excepts to Finding of Fact No. 3, which reads as follows:

"That on or about May 29, 1933, F. E. Hunt, Ltd., a foreign corporation, a citizen of Great Britian, (with the consent, knowledge and agreement of intervenors herein) took over the active control, management and operation of the "TAHOMA" and the shipment of its catches of halibut to American markets, in payment of the indebtedness of said vessel to said corporation (1) by removing the record owner and master, W. Pierce from command of the "TAHOMA" and placing him in charge of another American vessel, to-wit, the "WAVE": (2) by making [26] a colorable appointment of J. A. Johnson, an American citizen, as master of the "TAHOMA" for the sole purpose of dealing with the libelant in matters pertaining to and arising under the customs, navigation and shipping laws of the United States; (3) by placing Antone Martinson, a citizen of Great Britain, actually in charge, command and control of said vessel when away from Prince Rupert, and (4) by receiving and distributing the earnings and profits from such operations, and sharing therein," as being contrary to and unsupported by the evidence.

II.

Excepts to Findings of Fact No. 4, which reads as follows:

"That on February 27, 1934, F. E. Hunt, Ltd., placed B. A. Petterson in charge of the "TAHOMA" as master of record, and that said Petterson continned as such until the date of the seizure," as being contrary to and unsupported by the evidence.

III.

Excepts to the Court's conclusion of Law No. 1, which reads as follows:

"That on or about May 29, 1933, at Prince
Rupert, B. C., the American vessel "TAHOMA"
was transferred in whole or in part, by way of trust,
confidence and otherwise, to F. E. Hunt, Ltd., a citizen of Great Britian; and that the said F. E. Hunt,
Ltd., thereby became entitled to the whole or part
or share of and became indirectly interested in such
vessel and in the profits and issues thereof, and
became the equitable owner of said vessel.", as being
contrary to and unsupported by the evidence. [27]

IV.

Excepts to Conclusion of Law No. 2, which reads
as follows:

"That thereafter and until the seizure of the
"TAHOMA" the said vessel was unlawfully and
fraudulently engaged in a foreign trade and the
said certificate of registry was knowingly and
fraudulently used for said vessel when she was no
longer entitled to the benefit of said register.", as
being contrary to and unsupported by the evidence.

V.

Excepts to Conclusion of Law No. 3, which reads
as follows:

"That all shipments of halibut made by the said
vessel or F. E. Hunt, Ltd., during all the times
mentioned *the* the libel were subject to an import
duty of two cents a pound under the provisions of
the tariff act (19 U. S. C. A. 1001, par. 717) and
that such shipments were made in fraud of the reve-

nue of the United States.", as being contrary to and unsupported by the evidence.

VI.

Excepts to the Court's Conclusion of Law No. 5, which reads as follows:

"That the vessel "TAHOMA" became forfeited as of May 29, 1933, to the United States under the first cause of action, and as of September 27, 1935, under the second cause of action.", as being contrary to and unsupported by the evidence.

VII.

The Claimant excepts to the failure of the Court to Find the Facts requested by claimant dated June the 7th and November 9th, 1935, respectively as follows: [28]

I.

"That W. Pierce, the registered owner of the Oil Screw "TAHOMA", did not as alleged in the libel, or at all, unlawfully and fraudulently sell, in whole or in part by way of trust, confidence, or otherwise, to a subject and citizen of a foreign state, to-wit F. E. Hunt, Ltd., the said vessel "TAHOMA."

II.

That said "TAHOMA" did not, as alleged in the libel, unlawfully or fraudulently engage in foreign trade, and the certificate of registry of the "TA-HOMA" was not knowingly or fraudulently used for a vessel, to-wit, the vessel "TAHOMA", not entitled to the benefits thereof."

I.

That the consideration to Pierce, owner of the Tahoma in permitting F. E. Hunt, Ltd., to take over the operation and management of the Tahoma, was that Pierce should receive the boat Wave, of the value of $500.00, with which to make a living for which consideration Pierce agreed that the Tahoma should be operated in order that the indebtedness of the Tahoma could be paid off, and it was further agreed between Pierce and F. E. Hunt, Ltd., that if a sale of the Tahoma could be made, Pierce would consent thereto, and the purchase price be applied in payment of Pierce's indebtedness and the remainder, if any, be paid to Pierce.

II.

That F. E. Hunt, Ltd., and the above Intervenors, did not agree to, *no* did they at any time, release Pierce from his indebtedness to them, nor did Pierce at any time agree to permit said F. E. Hunt, Ltd., and the Intervenors to take and [29] receive the Tahoma, for the boat "Wave" and payment of his indebtedness to said corporations.

III.

That the arrangement made between Pierce, F. E. Hunt, Ltd., and the Intervenors, for the operation of the Tahoma, by said F. E. Hunt, Ltd., was made in good faith and with the honest belief on the part of all concerned that said arrangement did not constitute a violation of law.

IV.

That there was no evidence in writing of the sale or transfer of the Tahoma, or of any interest therein.

V.

That after F. E. Hunt, Ltd., took over the operation and management of the Tahoma, W. Pierce, Claimant, performed work on the Tahoma, during the winter, or closed fishing season and received no pay therefor.''

Said requested findings being what the Claimant contended the facts to be and which requested Findings were in accordance with the evidence.

VIII.

Claimant excepts to the Court's failure to enter the Conclusions of Law requested by claimant as follows:

''That W. Pierce did not unlawfully and fraudulently sell and transfer in whole, or in part, by way of trust, confidence, or otherwise, to a subject and a citizen of a foreign state, to-wit, to F. E. Hunt, Ltd., of the Dominion of Canada, the said Vessel ''TAHOMA''

a. ''That the American oil vessel ''TOHAMA'' her engine, tackle, apparel, cargo, etc. did not become forfeited by reason of the matters and things set forth in the libel or at all.'' [30]

Said Conclusions of Law being what the Claimant contended constituted the law to be from the evidence in said suit.

Dated at Ketchikan, Alaska, this 2nd day of December, 1935.

A. H. ZIEGLER & H. L. FAULKNER

Proctors for Claimant

The foregoing exceptions noted and allowed this 17 day of December, 1935.

GEO. F. ALEXANDER

District Judge

[Endorsed]: "Filed in the District Court Territory of Alaska, First Division Dec 7 1935. Robert E. Coughlin Clerk By Peggy D. McLeod Deputy."

[31]

In the District Court for the Territory of Alaska, Division Number One, at Juneau in Admiralty

No. 1778 KA

UNITED STATES OF AMERICA,

Libelant,

vs.

Oil screw vessel TAHOMA, official number 214741, her engine, tackle, apparel, etc.,

Respondent,

W. PIERCE,

Claimant,

ATLAS ENGINE COMPANY, a corporation,

Intervenor,

and

FISHING VESSEL OWNERS MARINE WAYS, INC., a corporation,

Intervenor.

DECREE

The issues in this case having been duly brought on for trial before the Honorable Geo. F. Alexander, United States District Judge, at the Special May 1935 Term this court, at Ketchikan on June 6 and 7 and the allegations and proofs on behalf of the parties having been heard and considered and the court having rendered and filed its opinion and made findings of fact and conclusions of law, now on the motion of Geo. W. Folta, Assistant United States Attorney, proctor for libelant, it is

ORDERED AND DECREED BY THE COURT that the said oil screw vessel TAHOMA, its engines, tackle, apparel, furniture, dories and gear under seizure in the above entitled case be, and the same accordingly are condemned as forfeited to the United States [32] for the reasons stated in the libel; and it is further

ORDERED that the libelant recover of the claimant its costs and that execution issue therefor, and that the intervenors recover the principal amount of their liens as prayed for, without interest or attorneys fees and without costs. It is further

ORDERED AND DECREED that the stipulators for costs and for the release of said vessel TAHOMA shall cause the engagement of their stipulations to be performed within twenty (20) days hereof or that they or either of them show cause why summary judgment should not be entered against them on their respective stipulations for costs and the appraised value of said vessel within four (4) days thereafter.

Done in open court at Juneau, Alaska this 23rd day of November, 1935.

GEO. F. ALEXANDER
U. S. District Judge.

[Endorsed]: "Filed in the District Court Territory of Alaska, First Division Nov 16 1935. Robert E. Coughlin Clerk By .... Deputy." [33]

[Title of Court and Cause.]

EXCEPTION OF CLAIMANT TO DECREE ENTERED HEREIN ON NOVEMBER 23, 1935.

Comes now W. Pierce, Claimant in the above suit and excepts to the entire Decree herein entered on the 23rd day of November 1935 as follows:

Because said Decree is contrary to and unsupported by the evidence and the law in the above entitled suit.

Dated this 2nd day of December, 1935.

A. H. ZIEGLER & H. L. FAULKNER
Proctors for Claimant.

The foregoing exception noted and allowed this 17 day of December, 1935.

GEO. F. ALEXANDER
District Judge

[Endorsed]: "Filed in the District Court Territory of Alaska, First Division Dec 7 1935. Robert E. Coughlin Clerk By Peggy D. McLeod Deputy"

[34]

[Title of Court and Cause.]

REPORTER'S TRANSCRIPT OF TESTIMONY.

BE IT REMEMBERED, That on this 6th day of June, 1935, at the hour of 10 o'clock A. M., the above entitled cause came on for trial before the Court without a Jury, the Honorable GEO. F. ALEXANDER, U. S. District Judge, presiding; the

Libellant appearing by G. W. FOLTA, Esq., Assistant United States Attorney; the Respondent, Claimant and the Intervening Libellant appearing by A. H. ZIEGLER, Esq., their Proctor; the Intervenor appearing by LESTER O. GORE, Esq., its Proctor;

Both sides having announced themselves ready for trial, Mr. Ziegler requested a continuance until 2 o'clock P. M. the same day, because of the recent arrival of his witnesses;

AND THEREUPON the following proceedings were had and done, and testimony taken, to-wit: [35]

Mr. GORE: If the Court please, we might be able to shorten the trial of this case if I can get counsel to agree to certain matters. I am not interested in prosecuting or defending the forfeiture, nor am I interested in contesting the martime lien of the Atlas Engine Company. My only interest is in etsablishing the Marine Ways lien. Mr. Folta took the testimony of my witness at Seattle and established the claim of Nordby. It is all in the deposition and I don't know whether you want those depositions all read or will take them as published, because it is only before the court and not before a jury. It will save a lot of time. How many are there?

Mr. FOLTA: Three.

Mr. GORE: As far as the Marine Vessels Owners Association is concerned you establish the amount of the claim, and establish it was done in the interest of Mr. Pierce who was the owner of the vessel—as far as you can. Have you any objection to agreeing that they are maritime liens and that the amount claimed in the libel is correct?

Mr. FOLTA: No, I am willing to stipulate that the amount they claim is correct; but I don't want to stipulate that they are maritime liens. Of course that is a matter of law anyhow; and it seems to me from the depositions and evidence that the Court could arrive at a conclusion.

Mr. GORE: Yes, I am willing to stand on the deposition as to whether or not the service was done for the vessel and the material went into the vessel. How about [36] you, Mr. Ziegler?

Mr. ZIEGLER: Both claims are in the same status. I think the amounts are correct and I don't think that the United States will contest the correctness of the amounts; just a question—as Mr. Folta says—whether or not they constitute maritime liens, and the ranks that they would be entitled to in the event forfeiture is decreed.

The COURT: I imagine that would be the principal question.

Mr. ZIEGLER: That would dispense with reading those depositions at the trial.

The COURT: Is the Government ready to proceed?

Mr. FOLTA: Yes, the Government is ready.

The COURT: I think we had better go ahead.

Mr. ZIEGLER: That is satisfactory, if the Court please. I will try to do the best I can being no better prepared.

The COURT: I understand there is some disadvantage, but we will save time by it. We will adjourn two hours during the noon recess so you can check up.

Mr. GORE: Do you wish the depositions read?

Mr. FOLTA: There is part of the depositions I would like to have read, but perhaps on another phase—as the matter of the lien—

Mr. GORE: Yes, part is lien and the other part deals with different subject matter.

The COURT: Counsel is entitled to present their case any way they see fit. The depositions may be offered as a whole and then you can read such part of them as [37] *them as* are necessary or you think necessary at the time.

Mr. GORE: There has been an order entered to publish the deposition?

Mr. FOLTA: Yes.

Mr. FOLTA and Mr. ZIEGLER then made opening statements to the Court concerning the issues of the case. The following then occurred:

Mr. FOLTA: To shorten this as much as possible, I think Mr. Ziegler and I can agree to stipulate on a few facts. I have spoken to him this morning about it.

Will you be willing to stipulate, Mr. Ziegler, that from May 29th, 1933 to February 27th, 1934, the name of J. A. Johnson, or Arthur Johnson, was endorsed on the certificate of registry as Master, and that from February 27th, 1934 to the date of the seizure the name of B. A. Peterson or Petterson is endorsed on the certificate of registry as master?

Mr. ZIEGLER: I think I will be willing to stipulate the records in the Customs House show that to be the case and approximately with respect to the date—May 29th to February—although I have not seen the document, but I would want to qualify it by showing the boat was only operated to October 27th, at the close of the halibut season, that is, he was not on the boat then. The Customs House records I presume show that, if you say they do. If you say it is a fact I will be willing to stipulate the records so show;—that between the date of approximately May 29th, 1933 and February 27th, 1934 the name of John Arthur Johnson was endorsed in the Customs House [38] records as master of the "Tahoma" and that on or about October 27th, 1933 the halibut schooner "Tahoma" was tied up and was not operated until after February 27th, 1934.

Mr. FOLTA: From February 27th, 1934 the name of B. A. Petterson is endorsed on the certificate as master?

Mr. ZIEGLER: Yes.

Mr. FOLTA: Another thing—

The COURT: Let's get that other matter—Who else's name is endorsed as master?

Mr. FOLTA: B. A. Petterson, from February 27th, 1934 to the date of the seizure.

Mr. ZIEGLER: We will stipulate that.

The COURT: February 27th 1934 to the date of the seizure?

Mr. FOLTA: Yes; that is in September, 1934 the seizure took place.

Mr. FOLTA: Will you also stipulate all the catches of halibut by the "Tahoma" from May 29th, 1933, to the time of the seizure were shipped to American markets by way of Prince Rupert, duty free?

Mr. ZIEGLER: If the Court please—on that point I would not feel like stipulating on that question, because the view I take of the case it is immaterial, it is not relevant or competent evidence in connection with the libel. I would stipulate such is the case, reserving the right, however, to object to the materiality of that itself.

Mr. FOLTA: All right.

Mr. ZIEGLER: As long as it is understood I have that privilege. [39]

Mr. ZIEGLER: If the Court please,—in regard to that stipulation, I would like that it be part of the stipulation that the owner of the boat, Mr. Pierce, obtained the consent and approval from the Secretary of State at Washington to market his catch of halibut at Prince Rupert. I have a letter from the Secretary of State to that effect. If you agree to stipulate that it will be unnecessary to go into that angle of it.

Mr. FOLTA: I would not mind stipulating anything competent, but no statement of the Secretary of State is more binding than the statement of a man on the street. The Secretary of State cannot give anybody permission to do anything that later on the officers may deem to be fraud on the revenue of the Government, and for that reason it is no more binding than the statement of any other person.

Mr. ZIEGLER: On that point, as I recall, that letter was from the Secretary of the Treasury, who has immediate jurisdiction over shipping and the shipping laws and violations.

The COURT: I think you had better submit it in the regular way. [40]

———

G. W. NICKERSON,

called as a witness on behalf of the Libellant, being first duly sworn, testified as follows:

Direct Examination

By Mr. FOLTA:

Q. Will you state your name, residence and business?

A. George Watson Nickerson, Prince Rupert British Columbia, Canada.

Q. What business are you in?

A. Manager and Director of F. E. Hunt, Ltd., ship's chandlers.

Q. How long have you been such officer?

A. I think about '22·

Q. Since 1922?

A. Yes.

Q. Is Milward F. Nickerson your brother?

A. Nephew.

Q. Also an officer of the corporation?

A. Secretary-Treasurer.

(Testimony of G. W. Nickerson.)

Q. The F. E. Hunt Company is a Canadian corporation?

A. Yes.

Q. Who owns the stock?

A. G. W. Nickerson Ltd. own 24,999 shares, Milward F. Nickerson owns one share.

Q. Who operates or is in charge of G. W. Nickerson Company?

A. I am.

Q. That is a brokerage firm?

A. Yes, financial firm.

Q. You are directly in charge?

A. I am manager and director of it—I own one share of F. E. [42] Hunt, Ltd., to qualify.

Q. You are a citizen and subject of Great Britain?

A. Yes.

Q. And your nephew is also?

A. Yes.

Q. What are your duties, as distinguished from your nephew's duties, in connection with the management or operation of F. E. Hunt, Ltd.?

A. I am the "boss" when it comes down to the final decisions; not all the time—in the ordinary course of events he runs the business.

Q. When something out of the ordinary comes up he refers it to you?

A. Yes.

Q. But in the ordinary conduct of the business he is in charge?

(Testimony of G. W. Nickerson.)

A. Yes.

Q. Mr. Nickerson, you are familiar with the operation of halibut boats, I suppose?

A. Yes.

Q. Are you familiar with the practice of halibut boat captains or masters in docking vessels?

A. Yes.

Q. For instance, it is the practice of the master of a halibut boat to dock it himself?

A. Not necessarily. If he has confidence in one of the crew and for some reason doesn't want to be there, he leaves it to him.

Q. If he is aboard he docks the vessel?

A. I suppose, usually, unless his attention is diverted [42] elsewhere.

Mr. FOLTA: I offer in evidence the depositions in this case, as Libellant's exhibit "1".

The COURT: They may be received.

Mr. ZIEGLER: Subject to any objections we may have to make?

Mr. FOLTA: I ask that this letter be marked Libellant's exhibit number two for identification. Let's see—there is an identifying mark on it. If the court please, that may be confusing, it is marked Libellant's exhibit "1". They are all marked separately.

Mr. ZIEGLER: I think you'd better use the same identifying mark or it will be confusing.

Mr. FOLTA: I think perhaps, if the court

please, I will offer the deposition as Libellant's exhibit "9" to avoid confusion.

The COURT: That is including the exhibits?

Mr. FOLTA: I want to exclude these letters. I want the letters marked separately. They are marked separately as part of the depositions and I want, for the sake of convenience, to use the same mark during the trial.

Mr. ZIEGLER: If you don't use the same mark of identification as in the depositions you wouldn't be able to identify the exhibits.

Mr. FOLTA: I want to use the same mark.

Mr. ZIEGLER: May I see that?

Mr. FOLTA: I haven't offered it yet.

(Depositions were admitted in evidence as Libellant's Exhibit "9") [43]

(Of the four depositions included in Exhibit "9" those of Albert J. Johnson and F. G. Hudson, are as follows; that of M. C. Wright occurs in its order at page 88 hereof [see p. 93 of this printed record] and that of Ingvold Heggem at page 101 hereof [see page 108 of this printed record])

ALBERT J. JOHNSON,

a witness for Intervenor Atlas Engine Co.

Q. (By Mr. BRONSON). Where do you reside?

A. Seattle.

(Deposition of Albert J. Johnson.)

Q. What is your business?

A. Marine Hardware and ship chandlery; outfitters.

Q. *W*ngaged with any company?

A. Yes; Nordby Supply Company.

Q. Is that a corporation.

A. Yes, sir.

Q. What is your position with that company?

A. Secretary.

Q. How long have you been its secretary?

A. The last two years.

Q. And as secretary of that company are you familiar with its books of account and the business of the company?

A. Yes, sir.

Q. It is alleged that the Nordby Supply company had an account and claim against the Gas Screw Tahoma. Tell us whether or not that is correct?

A. Yes, sir.

Q. When did that claim arise and what is the nature of it?

A. From the year 1930 and 1931 and through January, we sold them merchandise from time to time.

Q. What is the basis of that claim?

A. The sale of merchandise. [44]

Q. Can you give us the items, the date of the item and the amount, and the character of the items?

(Deposition of Albert J. Johnson.)

A. We sold them December 17, 1929, paints; a heater; rope and different things like that; and in 1930.

Q. What is the amount of the items and the sale price? Have you a memorandum showing these items?

A. Yes sir.

Q. You have the original books of account here?

A. Yes, sir.

Q. And this memorandum I show you, was that prepared from the original books?

A. Yes.

Q. Have you checked that as to its accuracy with the original entries?

A. Yes.

Mr. BRONSON: It is agreeable to counsel that this statement be used, rather than to submit the ledger sheets?

Mr. FOLTA: That is agreeable to us.

Mr. STEINER: We agree to that.

Q. The Commissioner has marked this sheet exhibit A for identification for intervenor Atlas Engine Co. Is that the compilation that you have mentioned?

A. Yes sir.

Q. And that shows fully and accurately the account of the Nordby Supply company?

A. Yes.

(Deposition of Albert J. Johnson.)

Q. And do you know that the materials listed there were actually sold and delivered on or about the dates indicated?

A. Yes, sir, they were. [45]

Q. And were the prices which are shown on that memorandum and the prices which are also shown on your books of account, the fair and reasonable value of the merchandise at that time?

A. Yes.

Q. What amounts have been paid, if any, on that account?

A. He paid October 3, 1931, $12.00; and August 15, 1934, by check $49.34.

Q. As against the original total of how much?

A. The original total was $131.27.

Q. Leaving a balance of how much?

A. $69.93.

Q. Is any part of that balance paid?

A. No.

Q. Is it all due.

A. It is all due.

Q. Has demand been made for payment of that?

A. Yes, sir.

Mr. BRONSON: We offer this exhibit A for identification in evidence.

Paper marked Intervenor Atlas Engine Co., exhibit A, attached to and returned herewith.

Q. Mr. Johnson, it is a fact, is it not, that the Nordby Supply company sold, transferred and

(Deposition of Albert J. Johnson.)

assigned this particular account that you have been referring to, to the Atlas Engine Company?

A. Yes sir.

Q. Handing you a paper which has been marked exhibit B for identification, I will ask you whether or not that is your signature to that? [46]

A. Yes, sir.

Q. Was that instrument executed and delivered on or about the date it bears?

A. Yes, sir.

Mr. BRONSON: I offer exhibit B for identification in evidence.

Paper marked Intervenor Atlas Engine Co. exhibit B. Attached to and returned herewith.

Cross Examination.

Q. (By Mr. FOLTA). Mr. Johnson, Who ordered these supplies?

A. The captain of the Tahoma, Winnie Pierce, ordered them.

Q. At that time, I suppose, Pierce was the record-owner of the Tahoma?

A. Yes.

Q. And credit was extended on the vessel, not on the credit of Pierce?

A. Well, the vessel and Pierce both.

Q. Were these supplies listed in exhibit A ordered of you, or did you have personal knowledge that they were ordered for the boat?

(Deposition of Albert J. Johnson.)

A. I practically sold all of it, and delivered practically all of it at the same time to the vessel.

Q. Was that at the same time the Tahoma was undergoing alterations and the installation of a diesel engine?

A. At tht time she was painting up at the Fishermens' dock.

(Witness Excused) **[47]**

————

Deposition of

F. G. HUDSON,

a witness for Intervenor Atlas Engine Co.:

Q. (By Mr. BRONSON). Where do you reside?

A. Seattle.

Q. What is your business?

A. Salesman for the Atlas Engine company.

Q. How long have you been in that position?

A. About 11 years.

Q. As salesman are you familiar with the various sales of engines and machine equipment which the Atlas Engine company makes to vessels?

A. Yes, I am.

Q. Are you familiar with any engine equipment sold to the gas boat Tahoma?

A. Yes, sir.

Q. Have you any records here pertaining to that? Ledger sheets?

A. Yes, sir.

(Deposition of F. G. Hudson.)

Q. Will you give us the date of the sale that you have mentioned?

A. The date of the sale was December 18, 1928.

Q. What was sold at that time?

A. A seventy-five horsepower Atlas Imperial Full Diesel engine.

Q. Was the engine delivered to that vessel?

A. Yes.

Q. Where was the vessel at that time?

A. Fishermens' Dock in Ballard.

Q. What was the sale price.

A. The sale price was $6725.00. [48]

Q. Was any amount paid down at that time?

A. There was $500.00 paid down with the order and $1510 was paid down at the time the engine was installed.

Q. What was the date of that sale?

A. December 18.

Q. What year?

A. 1928.

Q. What was the date of the two payments that you have mentioned?

A. The sale might have been made a little before that; the $500.00 was paid on the 18th.

Q. That was a down payment, cash payment?

A. Yes.

Q. Would that be substantially contemporaneous with the purchase itself?

A. Well, there is a contract here, I think, when the engine was ordered.

(Deposition of F. G. Hudson.)

Q. Handing you Atlas Engine company exhibit C for identification, I will ask you whether or not that was the contract that you have referred to?

A. Yes.

Mr. BRONSON: I offer this identification C in evidence.

> Paper marked Intervenor Atlas Engine Co. exhibit C; attached to and returned herewith.

Q. Now were any other arrangements made with these parties as to evidencing this indebtedness?

A. Well, it is our practice to take a first Customs mortgage on a vessel.

Q. Was that done at this time?

A. Yes, it was. **[49]**

Q. I hand you a paper which has been marked D for identification, a series of four promissory notes, a Custom House form of mortgage, and an assignment in writing from O. E. Nelsen to the Atlas Engine company; and there is attached to the exhibit a receipt from the Custom House dated February 11, 1929. Now examine identification D and state whether or not the notes attached to that instrument, and the instrument itself are the respective notes and mortgage you have referred to?

A. Yes, they are.

Q. Now, was anything done to replace the notes that are attached to that instrument, at any time?

A. To replace them?

Q. Yes.

(Deposition of F. G. Hudson.)

A. Well, we tried to collect on it several times; and then there was a new series of notes made out at a later date.

Q. Were the new series of notes executed and delivered to the Atlas Engine company?

A. Yes, sir.

Q. I hand you a paper which has been marked for identification exhibit E and ask you what the several papers are?

A. These are the renewal notes.

Q. This first instrument of this exhibit E is not a note but appears to be advice about the notes attached to it.

A. Yes, sir.

Q. Now will you tell me, Mr. Hudson, just what amounts beyond the two payments that you mentioned, the $500.000 and the $1510.00, have been paid on the account? [50]

A. I believe Mr. *Wig*ht could give you that information better than I can.

Q. Have you got the original ledger sheets?

A. Yes.

Q. You are not familiar with the book-keeping end of it?

A. No.

Mr. BRONSON: I offer identifications D and E in evidence.

Papers marked Intervenor Atlas Engine Co. exhibits D and E, respectivel*t*; attached to and returned herewith.

(Deposition of F. G. Hudson.)

Q.   Was the Tahoma a new vessel at the time of this sale?

A.   No; it was an old vessel.

Q.   It had had an engine in it?

A.   Yes.

Q.   Where was the vessel at the time the sale was made?

A.   Seattle.

Q.   Are you familiar with the Nordby Supply company account?

A.   No, I do not know about that.

Cross Examination.

Q.   (By Mr. FOLTA). You secured the order for this engine did you?

A.   Yes.

Q.   From whom?

A.   Mr. Pierce.

Q.   Did you have anything to do with arranging terms of payment, or anything like that?

A.   Yes, I did.

Q.   Any one else in the office participate or was it left entirely to you. [51]

A.   That was left to me.

Q.   The engine you sold was installed?

A.   Installed, yes.

Q.   And who arranged for credit to be extended through you or someone else?

A.   Well, yes, I believe I was responsible for that at that time.

Q.   You were dealing entirely with Pierce?

A.   Yes.

(Deposition of F. G. Hudson.)

Q. Had you know him before that?

A. Just slightly.

Q. Did you rely on the credit of the vessel or Pierce's credit.

A. On the credit of the vessel.

Q. Now will you look at these papers again and see when the mortgage was executed and also the first notes?

A. The first notes were dated on January 11, 1929.

Q. And the mortgage was dated when, the same time?

A. Second day of February 1929.

Q. The engine was sold in December 1928?

A. Yes. The mortgage was not executed until the installation of the engine was completed.

Q. Did you yourself arrange for the giving of the mortgage and notes, or was it somebody else?

A. I did that myself.

Q. Now the new series of notes were executed and given when?

A. December 16, 1931.

Q. Was that to change the terms somewhat?

A. No.

Q. Extended the time. [52]

A. Extended the time.

Q. The installments were paid the same; it was simply an extension of time.

A. Well, I am not familiar with this; I did not have anything to do with the second series of notes.

(Deposition of F. G. Hudson.)

Q. Did you have anything to do with the attempt to secure payments?

A. No, I did not.

(Witness Excused) [53]

F. G. HUDSON,

being recalled for further direct examination testified as follows:

Q. (By Mr. BRONSON). Mr. Hudson, in making this sale of the engine to the Tahoma, did you handle that transaction in the ordinary way you transact business in the sales of that character, or differently?

A. No, it was the same as in the handling of hundreds of others.

Q. Do you customarily request and take notes and mortgage on vessels at that time?

A. Absolutely.

Q. Was it your intention or was it a particular deviation in this case, to give up a lien claim against the vessel?

A. No, it was not.

Cross Examination.

Q. (By Mr. FOLTA). These notes are signed, I believe, by Winnie Pierce and Margaret Pierce. Do you know who Margaret Pierce is?

(Deposition of F. G. Hudson.)

A. Margaret Pierce is his wife; I am quite sure she is.

Q. Do you know how she happened to sign the notes?

A. Well, we usually have the wife sign, if possible.

Q. That was just a regular practice in all cases.

A. Yes, sir.

Q. When you renewed the notes and took a second series of notes, you still intended to rely on the credit of the vessel, or still intended that your indebtedness should be a lienagainstthevessel?

A. Against the vessel, yes.

(Witness Excused) [54]

[Testimony of G. W. Nickerson, resumed.]

Q. Mr. Nickerson, will you look at that and state whether or not that is your signature?

A. Yes, that is my signature.

Mr. FOLTA: I should state for the purpose of the record he is examining a letter marked Libellant's exhibit "1".

We offer this in evidence as Libellant's exhibit "1". (Showing proctor for claimant).

Mr. ZIEGLER: No objection.

The COURT: It may be received.

(Said letter was admitted in evidence and marked Libellant's exhibit "1"; and is as follows:

(Testimony of G. W. Nickerson.)

"F. E. HUNT, LIMITED
Wholesale Dealers in
Hardware, Ship Chandlery
and Fishing Supplies

Prince Rupert, B. C.
May 18th, 1933.

Can boat Tahoma be sold in
Canada without going thru.
Marshall

Atlas Engine Co.,
Seattle, Wash.
Dear Sirs:—

We are enclosing a copy of a letter to the Fishing Vessel Owners Marine Ways, and would ask you two to get together, and make a prompt decision.

We think the suggestion we have made is very fair, and the only reason that we do not propose cleaning up your accounts, and taking the whole obligation ourselves, is that finances do not permit.

Yours truly,
THE F. E. HUNT, LIMITED
G. W. Nickerson"

GWN/C:
Encl.

[Endorsed]: "Lbls. Exhibit No. 1 Received in [55] evidence Jun 6 1935 in cause No. 1778 KA.

ROBERT E. COUGHLIN,
Clerk.

By _____ Deputy."

(Testimony of G. W. Nickerson.)

Mr. ZIEGLER: That is now known as Libellant's exhibit "1"?

Mr. FOLTA: Yes.

Q. I show you another letter, marked Exhibit "2" for the libellant, and ask you to examine that and state whether or not that is your signature—whether you sent that letter—whether that is the letter that you enclosed with Libellant's exhibit "1" just offered in evidence. You may just examine your signature.

A. No signature on this one.

Q. Do you recognize this as the letter you enclosed?

A. I will read it through and see. —Yes, I wrote that letter.

Mr. FOLTA: If the court please, I offer this as Libellant's exhibit "2".

The COURT: It may be received.

(Said letter was admitted in evidence and marked Libellant's exhibit "2"; and is as follows, to-wit): [56]

(Testimony of G. W. Nickerson.)

"F. E. HUNT, LIMITED
Wholesale Dealers in
Hardware, Ship Chandlery
and Fishing Supplies

Prince Rupert, B. C.
May 18th, 1933.

"Fishing Vessel Owners Marine Ways,
Salmon Bay Terminal,
Seattle, Wash.

Dear Sirs:

Re Captain W. Pierce's gasboat "Tahoma." For some time it has been evident to us that this man is not adapted to carrying on successfully halibut fishing from a boat the size of the "Tahoma", therefore we have about persuaded him to agree to make a trade, taking for his equity a small American boat that would cost about Twenty-five Hundred Dollars ($2,500.00), thus bring the entire obligation, including interest to date, about Eleven Thousand Dollars ($11,000.00), the creditors being You, the Atlas Engine Co., ourselves, and an account of about One Hundred Dollars ($100.00) with the Norvy Supply Co. in Ketchikan.

Before making this deal we require to have assurance from you and the Atlas people that you are willing to wait for your money until it is earned by the boat or she can be sold. We would be agreeable to dividing between you and the Atlas 50% of her earning after insurance and upkeep had been taken off. This, of course, is a much larger percentage

(Testimony of G. W. Nickerson.)

than you would be entitled to on the basis of her obligations, and our security is equal with yours, and better than the Atlas Engine Co. notwithstanding the fact that they have a mortgage.

We have one or two men in sight who might take this boat, but they would not entertain the proposition unless assured, that in the event of them touching at Seattle, no attachment against their trip would be made. If you know of any well qualified Captain in Seattle who would care to operate this boat or anyone who cares to buy her on a down payment of about Three Thousand Dollars ($3,000.00), we would be glad to have you advise us.

We are sending a copy of this letter to the Atlas Engine Co. in Seattle, and would suggest that you get in touch with them, and advise us at once as to your decision, as it is not desirous to have this boat tied up indefinitely.

In the meantime we would appreciate you sending us a statement of your account with interest to date, so that we can arrive at the exact figures outstanding against this boat.

Yours truly,
F. E. HUNT, LIMITED."

GWN/C:

[Endorsed]: "Lbls. Exhibit No. 2 Received in Evidence Jun 6 1935 in cause No. 1778-KA. Robert E. Coughlin, Clerk, by ....Deputy." [57]

(Testimony of G. W. Nickerson.)

Mr. FOLTA: I will read the letters after they are offered.

Q. Mr. Nickerson, I hand you a letter marked Libellant's Exhibit "3" and ask you whether or not that is the reply which you received in answer to Libellant's exhibits "1" and "2"?

A. I think that is.

Mr. FOLTA: I offer this as Libellant's exhibit "3".

> (Said letter was admitted in evidence and marked Libellant's exhibit "3"; and is as follows, to-wit:

"May 31st 1933

F. E. Hunt, Ltd.
Prince Rupert, B. C.
Gentlemen:

We have your letter of May 18th relative to the boat "Tahoma" which is owned by Captain Winnie Pierce, and are pleased to advise that we have gone over your proposition with the Fishing Vessel Owners Marine Ways. As we understand it, you have tied up the "Tahoma" and intend selling or trading it to some other party who will be more adapted to operating the boat than Capt. Pierce. It is also your request that we guarantee that the boat will no be touched by ourselves whenever in Seattle and in return we receive 50% of the boat earnings after insurance and upkeep are deducted.

We will naturally be glad to help you work this thing out but in view of the fact that the boat is in

(Testimony of G. W. Nickerson.)

Prince Rupert and that we must give an unconditional guarantee indicating [58] that we will instigate no action against the boat, we do not feel inclined to accept the proposition as outlined by you. We are perfectly willing to grant a two years extension of our accounts provided certain definite payments be guaranteed by you or we will discount the amounts substantially for a cash settlement at this time, but we do not feel that we should waive our rights against the boat for such an uncertain amount as might be earned by the boat these next two years.

In accordance with your suggestion, we will be on the lookout for someone in Seattle who would be interested in taking the boat out and making a down payment of $3,000.00. We hope that some arrangement may be worked out on the basis of our above suggestion for the settlement of our accounts and that we will have your answer immediately. We are herewith enclosing our statements of account as of June 1st, 1933.

> Very truly yours
> ATLAS ENGINE COMPANY
> FISHING VESSAL OWNERS
> MARINE WAYS"

[Endorsed]: "Lbls. Exhibit No. 3 (Three) Received in Evidence Jun 6 1935 in case No. 1778-KA Robert E. Coughlin Clerk by .... Deputy.''

(Testimony of G. W. Nickerson.)

Q.   Mr. Nickerson, I hand you a photostatic copy of a letter marked Libellant's exhibit "4", and ask you to examine that and state whether that is your signature?

A.   Yes sir.

Mr. FOLTA: I offer this in evidence as Libellant's exhibit "4".

(Photostatic copy of letter was admitted in evidence and marked Libellant's Exhibit "4"; and is as follows, to-wit): **[59]**

"F. E. HUNT, LIMITED
Wholesale Dealers in
Hardware, Ship Chandlery
and Fishing Supplies

Prince Rupert, B. C.
June 5th, 1933.

Atlas Engine Company,
Fishing Vessel Owners' Marine Ways,
Seattle, Wash.

Dear Sirs:—

We have yours of the 31st., and are somewhat surprised that there would be any question re accepting our proposition. The fact that you have declined it leads us to believe that if you occupied the advantageous position that we do, you would look after yourselves, and let us take what is left. We, on the other hand have been willing to take the short end of the stick, in order to clean you up as soon as possible. We wonder if you are aware that under our laws we could attach this vessel for

(Testimony of G. W. Nickerson.)

debt, sell her, and obtain a Canadian register, and you would have no claim, in *order* words that we would be a preferred account. Unless you accept our proposition, we may eventually have to do this, as we cannot afford to have this boat tied up indefinitely, and she cannot be profitably operated, unless she is free to go to Seattle to sell her fish, when she has a reasonable trip. We can obtain a very good man here to take the boat out, and are satisfied that in normal conditions, she would quickly liquidate her debt.

While we failed to state in our previous letter that in the event of your giving a two years extension. we would give the same, yet we assumed that you would realize that we were not asking for any concessions that we were not prepared to give.

If. on receipt of this letter, you are prepared to reconsider, and accept our proposition, please wire; as the quicker the boat goes out, the quicker we will be getting some money in. In the event of you not accepting this, and we [60] should decide to let the boat operate out of here, we do not see where there would be any obligations on us to apply any of the surplus earnings to your account, for if it is a case of everyone for himself, we must naturally look out for No. 1.

We certainly have been very fair and reasonable in connection with this account. We have even paid out of our own pocket insurance premiums in order to keep the boat insured, while we have allowed other boats that owe us money to operate without

(Testimony of G. W. Nickerson.)
insurance, and we probably will drop this policy
when it becomes due, unless you can see your way
clear to fall in line.

Yours truly,

F. E. HUNT, LIMITED

G. W. Nickerson.''

GWN/C:

[Endorsed]: "Libls. Exhibit No. 4 Received in
Evidence Jun 6 1935 in case No. 1778-KA   Robert
E. Coughlin, Clerk   By ....Deputy.''

Q. I also show you photostatic copy of a letter,
Mr. Nickerson, marked Libellant's exhibit "5", and
ask you to examine that and state whether or not
you received that in reply to Libellant's exhibit
"4"?

A. That is the letter, but I don't accept part of
it as being the understanding, where he says Pierce
was to turn the boat over to me.

Mr. ZIEGLER: Any testimony concerning it
will be raised later on. You just identify them—
whether or not they were written.

Mr. FOLTA: I offer that in evidence as Libellant's Exhibit "5".

(Photostatic copy of Letter was admitted in
evidence as Libellant's exhibit "5"; and is as
follows, to-wit) [61]

(Testimony of G. W. Nickerson.)

"Seattle, Washington
June 12, 1933

Mr. F. E. Hunt, Ltd.
Prince Rupert, B. C.
Gentlemen:

We have your letter of the 5th, relative to the boat "Tahoma" and regret to note that none of our suggestions for the liquidating of our accounts against the boat have appealed to you. We hope, however, that you do not feel that we are not willing to cooperate with you in working this boat out of its indebtedness. We have now gone over both of your recent letters on this subject thoroughly, and now believe it wise to work with you.

There are a few features of the proposition made in your letter of May 18th, which are not quite clear to us and in order to expedite matters and remove the necessity of delay through further correspondence, we will accept your offer on the following basis:

It is our understanding that there is now approximately $8500.00 against the boat and that you intend turning over to Captain Pierce a boat worth $2500.00, which will raise the total obligation to about $11,000.00. Captain Pierce is to convey the "Tahoma" to you. The boat will then proceed to work itself out of debt and pay us fifty per cent of the earnings, after the insurance, upkeep and operating expenses are deducted.

You will send us an itemized statement of each trip the boat makes, giving us a detailed statement

(Testimony of G. W. Nickerson.)
of the catch, deductions and the balance, if any, for distribution. This arrangement will continue for a period of two years.

If, during this two year period, any outside party takes action against the boat, we will all retain the right to protect our interests by intervening. [62]

So long as the foregoing are complied with, we agree to operate on the above basis for a period of two years and we will not take action against the boat during that period unless compelled to do so by reason of her seizure by third parties.

We regret the necessity of writing you instead of wiring as you requested, but we believed it better to have a thorough understanding before proceeding. We will appreciate hearing from you as to just what you intend doing in regard to turning over the above vessels, and who the new Captain will be.

Hoping that this will enable you to go ahead and close the deal in time to profit from this season's fishing, we remain

Very truly yours,

ATLAS ENGINE COMPANY

By..

FISHING VESSEL OWNERS

MARINE WAYS

By.."

[Endorsed]: "Lbls. Exhibit No. 5 Received in Evidence Jun 6 1935 in Cause No. 1778-KA   Robert E. Coughlin Clerk, By ....Deputy."

(Testimony of G. W. Nickerson.)

Q. Mr. Nickerson I hand you three more photostatic copies of letters, or three photostatic copies of three additional letters, and ask you to examine them. They are marked Libellant's exhibits "6", "7" and "8",—and state whether or not you and your nephew signed them?

A. I guess that one is signed by me—that is my signature—

Q. Yes.

A. That is my nephew's signature—yes, that is my nephew's signature. [63]

Mr. FOLTA: We offer these, if the court please, as Libellant's exhibits "6", "7" and "8".

(Photostatic copies of letters were admitted in evidence and marked Libellant's exhibits "6", "7" and "8"; and are as follows:)

"F. E. HUNT, LIMITED

Wholesale Dealers in

Hardware, Ship Chandlery

and Fishing Supplies

Prince Rupert, B. C.

June 17th, 1933.

Atlas Engine Company,

Fishing Vessel Owners Marine Ways,

Seattle, Wash.

Dear Sirs:—

In accordance with your decision to cooperate with us, we have arranged with Capt. T. Martinsen, one of the most successful fishing Captains out of here, who recently lost his boat, to take out the Tahoma, and we hope that he will be able to operate

(Testimony of G. W. Nickerson.)

for at least the balance of the season. If this man
were an American citizen, we are satisfied that he
would buy the boat, and it is just possible should
he be able to arrange with some American in whom
he has confidence as a partner, that he might decide to buy it. In any event we think that a good
deal has been made, and we believe that before the
two years are up you will have received your
montey.

The only outside creditor is Nordby, and we may
decide to pay him a little later in the season.

This company's debt against the debtor must remain in exactly the same status as it is now, as
foreigners cannot have an ownership interest in an
American vessel. Possibly we will allow the register
to stay as it is, as there would be nothing that Captain Pierce could do, if he wished. Your mortgage
[64] and our bills are sufficient lien on the ship.
We will, however, have a Bill of Sale signed in
blank, so that it could be used instantaneously if so
desired.

In connection with the boat we are transferring
to Pierce, there is some little work to be done on
her, and as soon as we get our bills, we will send
you a statement of just what the total indebtedness
against the "Tahoma" will be.

Thanking you for your cooperation, we are.

Truly yours,

GWN/C　　　　F. E. HUNT, LIMITED.

G. W. Nickerson"

[Endorsed]: "Lbls Exhibit No. 6 Received in
Evidence Jun 6 1935 in cause No. 1778-KA Robert
E. Coughlin, Clerk. By _____Deputy."

(Testimony of G. W. Nickerson.)

"F. E. HUNT, LIMITED
Wholesale Dealers in
Hardware, Ship Chandlery
and Fishing Supplies

Prince Rupert, B. C.
February, 5/34.

The Atlas Engine Company,
69 Columbia St.,
Seattle, Wash.
Dear Sirs:

Re M.V. "Tahoma" we enclose herewith statement showing the operations for the year 1933. You will note that she did not earn all of her Interest, but we are in hopes that if fish prices improve that she should do considerable better this season. We have arranged to have the same Captain take the Boat that had her since mid season last year, as we have every confidence in him.

While we are not in a position to send you any money [65] just now we will try and send you some as early as possible.

We will mail you a copy of the new Insurance Policy as soon as we receive same.

Yours very truly,
THE F. E. HUNT LIMITED
Encl.(1)   M. G. Nickerson."

[Endorsed]: "Lbls Exhibit No. 7 Received in evidence Jun 6 1935 in cause No. 1778-KA Robert E. Coughlin Clerk   By .... Deputy."

(Testimony of G. W. Nickerson.)

"F. E. HUNT, LIMITED
Wholesale Dealers in
Hardware, Ship Chandlery
and Fishing Supplies

Prince Rupert, B. C.

The Atlas Gas Engine Co.,
Seattle, Wash.

Dear Sirs,

We are enclosing herewith Marine Insurance Policy on the M/V "TAHOMA" for the sum of fifteen hundred dollars, which reads loss if any payable to your Company, as your interest may appear.

Captain Pierce says to inform you that he will start paying on his account just as soon as he possibly can.

Yours very truly,
F. E. HUNT, LIMITED

Encl.(1)   M. G. Nickerson

Sec-Treas."

[Endorsed]: "Lbls. Exhibit No. 8 Received in evidence Jun 6 1935 in cause No. 1778-KA. Robert E. Coughlin, Clerk   By _____Deputy."

———

Mr. FOLTA: If the Court please, to make intelligible the further examination of the witness I want to read these letters now.

(Mr. Folta read Exhibits "1" and "2" to the court and commenced reading "3", during which the following occurred:)

(Testimony of G. W. Nickerson.)

Mr. ZIEGLER: I notice writing on these exhibits introduced. Do you know whose handwriting they are in?

Mr. FOLTA: In the recipient's.

Mr. ZIEGLER: The handwriting on the letters is not Mr. Nickerson's. The addressee makes inquiries by pencil. [66]

Mr. FOLTA: Yes, the court can see that. I didn't read them either.

Mr. ZIEGLER: I just noticed that on the side and didn't know whose handwriting they were in.

The COURT: It may be understood, then, that the memoranda on the face of the letter was not made by Mr. Nickerson and is not part of the exbibit?

Mr. FOLTA: Yes.

Mr. ZIEGLER: I don't think they should be a part of the exhibit, but think it is better to consider them part of it, because the court, in reading the exhibit, can not close its eyes to them; but have the understanding who put them on there. No objection to them.

(Mr. Folta concluded the reading of Exbibit "3")

Mr. FOLTA: I just want to call attention to the fact that the signer of that letter and of the other letters are lienors or intervenors in this case.

(Mr. Folta then read exhibits "4", "5", "6", "7" and "8" to the court)

(Testimony of G. W. Nickerson.)

Q. Mr. Nickerson, it was pursuant to that arrangement, was it, that the "Tahoma" was operated the balance of the year 1933?

A. That she was operated?

Q. Yes.

A. Yes, I think she was operated the balance of that year.

Q. You say pursuant to the arrangement entered into with the Seattle lienor—so far as operating—

A. And applying the profits as suggested, the operating [67] arrangement was this man was to operate her.

Q. The T. Martinson mentioned in one of those exhibits, you say, was to have charge of the vessel, was a Canadian citizen?

A. He is Norwegian; I suppose he is a Canadian citizen.

Q. Do you know that?

A. No, I couldn't swear he is.

Q. How long have you dealt with him?

A. I suppose probably thirteen or fourteen years.

Q. He is the owner of the Canadian vessel "Livingstone"—until it was wrecked?

A. Yes.

Q. Then he would have to be a Canadian citizen?

A. Yes, or he couldn't own her.

Q. Wasn't he a Canadian citizen?

(Testimony of G. W. Nickerson.)

A. I think so, but I couldn't swear he was.

Q. You say you have known him since when?

A. Probably twenty years. He dealt with us probably thirteen years.

Q. Where is Mr. Martinson now?

A. Prince Rupert.

Q. He was employed on the "Tahoma" in 1933?

A. He was on her, yes.

Q. How about 1934—was he on her then?

A. Yes, he was on her in '34·

Q. Up to the time of the seizure, or had he been on her since?

A. Up to the time of the seizure and the balance of '34—made one trip, I think, after the seizure.

Q. By the way, about the first of June, 1933, Mr. Nickerson, [68] who was your bookkeeper—for F. E. Hunt?

A. Capstick.

Q. Do you recall his making out a bill of sale for the "Wave" to Mr. Pierce?

A. To—I don't think he made out any bill of sale. There was a bill of sale made, yes, supposed to be made out to Earnie Pierce—a mistake was made—"Winnie Pierce" was in there—and it was changed.

Q. In the first bill of sale Winnie Pierce was inserted as transferee?

A. Yes, and it was corrected.

Q. Did he prepare that?

A. No, I think it was in my office.

(Testimony of G. W. Nickerson.)

Q. Who prepared it?

A. My stenographer, Miss Cameron.

Q. Acting under your direction?

A. Yes.

Q. You saw it afterwards and noticed there had been an error?

A. Yes.

Q. At that time, Mr. Nickerson, at the time this bill of sale was made out was—who had been in charge of the "Wave"?

A. Peterson. She was tied up—had been all summer.

Q. He is the present master of the "Tahoma"?

A. Yes.

Q. At that time, about June 1st, 1933, was the "Wave"—owned by Petterson—indebted to F. E. Hunt?

A. A Mrs. Elinor Kincaid, an American, held a mortgage on it.

Q. What was her indebtedness, do you know?

A. I think the mortgage was somewhere around $2500.00; I would not be positive; it is a matter of record. [69]

Q. Did you handle the transfer of the "Wave" from Petterson to Pierce yourself?

A. We negotiated the arrangement with Petterson.

Q. You mean F. E. Hunt?

A. As F. E. Hunt, or the agent of Pierce and Petterson.

(Testimony of G. W. Nickerson.)

Q. Nobody else of F. E. Hunt had anything to do with it?

A. Not in the actual doing of it.

Q. After Johnson took charge of the "Tahoma" what did Winnie Pierce do?

A. He was operating the "Wave" part of the time; he was sick for a month during the fishing season.

Q. What was Petterson doing during that period?

A. I don't know, he might have been fishing on some other boat, he wasn't operating any boat.

Mr. FOLTA: I think that is all.

Cross Examination.

By Mr. ZIEGLER:

Q. Mr. Nickerson, as a preliminary question, just explain how long Mr. Pierce has lived in Prince Rupert?

A. About ten years.

Q. Has he a family there?

A. Yes.

Q. An American citizen?

A. Yes, so far as I know.

Q. During that time has he dealt with your store there as an outfitting store for halibut boats?

A. Yes; prior to moving to Prince Rupert he dealt with us.

Q. Has he a family? [70]

A. One child.

(Testimony of G. W. Nickerson.)

Q. One child and his wife?

A. Yes.

Q. They are all living there?

A. Yes.

Q. Just explain to the court the nature of your business there, so the court will know.

A. We carry on a general ship's chandler or shipping boat business, similar to people that carry on and conduct that business here. We loan money to people to buy boats and engines, and give them credit. They get their checks; they turn them over to us. Usually the captain gets his share along with the crew, and if he is indebted to us—unless he is pretty hard up and needs the money—the balance goes to apply on his account. We virtually act as his agent when he is at sea. If he owes us too much we are in a position to tell him what his policy shall be when he is ashore.

Q. It is a fact that both American and Canadian boats fishing out of Prince Rupert do get indebted to your office in large amounts?

A. Yes.

Q. And have to work it out?

A. Yes.

Q. And in order to do that isn't it a fact that you—and stores on this side as well—assume sort of management of the boat?

A. Yes.

Q. To protect your credit to the boat?

A. Yes; we have the final say. [71]

(Testimony of G. W. Nickerson.)

Q. I wish you would—there have been a number of letters read—just tell this court in your own words the entire history of these various transactions mentioned in the correspondence between F. E. Hunt, Ltd., and Mr. Pierce, the owner of the "Tahoma" and the "Wave". I think you can do it by telling the whole story to the court better than me asking you the questions.

A. This goes way back until when Pierce first bought the "Tahoma". I don't know what year it was. Prior to that he operated a boat called the "Wabash". We, through Mrs. Kincaid, arranged with the Bank of Commerce for him to borrow money. Mrs. Kincaid arranged for him borrowing money on the boat. In 1928 he had cleaned that up and financed an engine.

Q. Is that the Atlas engine for which claim is made?

A. Yes. So with the Atlas Engine Company he made some arrangement and wrote or wired us to ask if we could loan him $3200.00. We sent him a check. The check I have with me. We didn't stipulate he was to give us any security or was to put it into an engine, although we assumed the major portion was to be paid the Atlas Engine Company as the first installment on the engine. In 1929. I think, he paid the Atlas Engine Company a little money, and about in 1932 the Atlas Engine Company began to get pretty insistent for their

(Testimony of G. W. Nickerson.)

money. From time to time I sort of constituted myself their representative as well as our own, as we didn't want to see anybody lose money or Pierce lose his boat; we were all in about the same jack-pot at that time—about a step ahead of the sheriff. So we wrote several letters to the Atlas Engine Company [72] trying to pacify them and get them to lay off. In 1933 Mr. Pierce's brother went to M. F. Nickerson, and told him Winnie Pierce had come to the conclusion—

Mr. FOLTA: I think I shall have to object to the hearsay conversation.

The COURT: Yes.

A. It has to be told because Mr. Pierce was at sea when this thing happened.—Anyway the gist of the thing was that Mrs. Kincaid had this mortgage on the "Wave" and while she was in debt for about $2500.00 she was looked on as a total loss. She was on the beach and everything was bad about her, and I guess if somebody had come along and offered Mrs. Kincaid five hundred dollars she would have been tickled to death to have gotten it. Anyway, as Pierce didn't negotiate this himself you merely have to tell the story—his brother did the negotiating. Anyway Pierce was willing to do anything with respect to the "Tahoma" to get some little boat to operate, in which he felt he could make a living. He realized, or believed, he was at the point where the Atlas Engine Company could jump on him.

(Testimony of G. W. Nickerson.)

Mr. FOLTA: I object to his testimony—

The WITNESS: I am coming to the conversation where—

Mr. FOLTA: I ask that Mr. Nickerson eliminate that before he comes to it.

Mr. ZIEGLER: I think any arrangement between—with respect to the "Tahoma"—between Hunt, Ltd. and Pierce, is competent evidence, and any conversation with Mr. Pierce and the claimant, who is now in court, is competent evidence. We are here to explain all the [73] transactions with the "Tahoma." The claimant claims there was no sale made. We have a right to explain the entire deal. Of course it might be more properly a matter of defense. I adopted this procedure to get the facts before the court. We don't want to introduce anything that is not competent.

Mr. FOLTA: I think Mr. Nickerson ought to state the arrangement and not what somebody else believed, or thought or feared.

The COURT: Yes.

The WITNESS: Can I tell the conversation between Earnie Pierce and myself?

Mr. ZIEGLER: No; the court rules that is not competent.

A. When Winnie Pierce came in, I saw him and told him that I didn't want his boat. We were willing to do anything it was possible to do. This "Wave" was there, and I could arrange to buy

(Testimony of G. W. Nickerson.)

Pete Petterson's equity; we thought we could arrange, so far as Mrs. Kincaid was concerned, to turn her over to him and change her mortgage to the "Tahoma". When the "Tahoma" paid out, if she ever did, what she owed originally, and the balance to apply against what I had against the "Wave"—that it would be all right with Mrs. Kincaid. I told him—I said—the question is to make some sort of arrangement with the Atlas Engine Company and the Marine Ways in Seattle. I made it very emphatic to Pierce we didn't want to take advantage of the unique situation in order to take the "Tahoma" away from him. We knew he wouldn't try to steal her from us. So far as we were concerned it could carry on indefinitely. [74] I wrote the Atlas Engine Company.

Q. In this correspondence with the Atlas Engine Company and the Fishing Vessels Marine Ways in what capacity did you write them, with respect to your own interests and Mr. Pierce's also?

A. Yes, and their interests. I thought on account of previous correspondence we had with them they were looking to us to play the game with them, that we were their agents too. I told Mr. Pierce we didn't want to take the boat, but I said, "I will write the Atlas Engine Company telling them what you are prepared to do. You are prepared to turn the 'Tahoma' over to the creditors, provided you can get a different boat or some other boat to

(Testimony of G. W. Nickerson.)

operate and have it charged against the 'Tahoma'."
So I carried on this correspondence with the
Atlas Engine Company, and they were loath to do
anything. I think we bluffed them a little—gave
them to understand we had rights we didn't have.
Whether it was the bluff or a change of heart, they
agreed to our proposition. You will note in one
letter—the next to the last—we were prepared to
give the same extension they were prepared to give,
which would not have been necessary if they were
going to take the boat over. In the final letter I
didn't think it good business to tell them we were
not taking the boat over so I told them it was completed and we would take a blank bill of sale, not
necessarily to F. E. Hunt, Ltd.

Q. At that time, and since you have been in
business there, you knew, as a Canadian subject,
you could not take title to an American boat?

A. Absolutely. I had customers in Seattle if I
wanted to [75] camouflage the deal I could have
done so. At no time was it in my mind I was going
to take the "Tahoma" from Pierce, or see him lose
her. He threw himself on our mercy, and I thought
it best to carry on correspondence with the Atlas
Engine Company on the assumption that would be
done—that they might be more ready to give an
extension if they thought Pierce was clear of it
already. I didn't tell them I had no intention of
taking the "Tahoma" over, or anyone. I repeatedly after that—Captain Pierce was always willing

(Testimony of G. W. Nickerson.)

for us to do whatever would protect the creditors. As long as he had a little boat he was satisfied. I told him the "Tahoma"(?) was there and would make him money. It was not our intention to take the boat. "We have twenty other boats in difficulties, and we are not taking them, so why take yours?"

Q. During the time covered by these letters— 1932, '33 and '34, isn't it a fact that the average halibut boat was a liability rather than an asset?

A. Everyone—

Mr. FOLTA: Object as calling for an opinion and a conclusion. We are not going into that matter anyway.

Mr. ZIEGLER: Don't go into that phase of it.

Q. At the time you had this correspondence with these creditors in Seattle was Pierce and the "Tahoma" indebted to you and to them in a considerable amount?

A. Yes.

Q. Can you give the Court an idea of the amount, how much it was?

A. Roughly about $8500.00, was owed on the "Tahoma" to everybody. That included interest. **[76]**

Q. Her value— what would you say at that time —in comparison with the indebtedness?

A. In May—in a letter to Captain Ingvold Erickson, on behalf of Mr. Pierce, he offered him

(Testimony of G. W. Nickerson.)

the "Tahoma"—I don't know whether it was for $12,000.00 or not. It is in my file. I have forgotten what the price was, but I offered it to him on behalf of Mr. Pierce. I have his answer. Look in my file. May I read the letter?

Mr. FOLTA: I want to see it first.

A. Eleven thousand dollars is the price.

Q. What time was that?

A. September 14th, 1933.

Q. September 14th, 1933?

A. His answer is dated September 19th.

Q. At that time the price was—

A. Eleven thousand dollars.

Q. At a forced sale at that time, Mr. Nickerson, do you think there would be any possibility of realizing that value out of the boat?

A. No.

Mr. FOLTA: Object to that?

The COURT: I don't see as it is material anyway.

Q. Now, Mr. Nickerson on May 18th you wrote a letter to the Atlas Engine Company and stated you were enclosing a copy of a letter to the Fishing Vessels Owners' Marine Ways and "would ask you two to get together and make a prompt decision. We think the suggestion we have made is very fair, and the only reason that we do not propose cleaning up your accounts and taking the whole obligation ourselves is that finances do not permit." [77]

(Testimony of G. W. Nickerson.)

A. We meant we would loan Pierce the money and clean them up and take a chance on getting it out of the "Tahoma" when she made it.

Q. You mean you would advance the money to retire their claims?

A. Have the boat work it out, yes.

Q. Is that customary over there?

A. Yes, quite customary, to pay the outside bills and center all the bills in ourselves, as we have the first crack at the check. Unfortunately that is what outfitting houses have been doing for the past eight or ten years.

Q. On June 5th or June 12th a copy of a letter is here — from the Atlas Engine Company — addressed to you, which acknowledges your letter of the fifth of June with reference to the negotiations concerning the "Tahoma". In this letter they state "there are a few features of the proposition made in your letter of May 18th which are not quite clear to us and in order to expediate matters and remove the necessity of delay through further correspondence, we will accept your offer on the following basis: It is our understanding that there is now approximately $8500.00 against the boat and that you intend turning over to Captain Pierce a boat worth $2500.00, which will raise the total obligation to about $11,000.00. Captain Pierce is to convey the "Tahoma" to you. The boat will then proceed to work itself out of debt and pay us fifty

(Testimony of G. W. Nickerson.)

per cent of the earnings, after the insurance, upkeep and operating expenses are deducted.''

This is a letter written by the Atlas Engine Company. Did you in your letter of June 5th, to which [78] they refer, state in there that you had made any arrangement to have the ''Tahoma'' conveyed to you?

Mr. FOLTA: The letters are in evidence, if the court please.

The COURT: Letters themselves are the best evidence.

Q. I will ask you—your letter of June 5th. In this letter, Mr. Nickerson, did you state in the letter to those Seattle creditors that you would—as they say in the reply—have Captain Pierce convey the ''Tahoma'' to you?

Mr. FOLTA: That is the question to which objection was sustained.

The COURT: I just passed on it; sustained. It isn't for the witness to interpret the letters.

Q. Did you ever tell any of these creditors that you would have Pierce convey the boat to you?

A. Not to my recollection, but when I used the words ''us'' or ''our'' I was occupying the position of the representative of all the creditors. I didn't mean F. E. Hunt, Ltd., or myself. I was acting for the creditors, including the Atlas Engine Company and the Marine Ways.

(Testimony of G. W. Nickerson.)

Q. I will read this letter of June 5th, to which
the letter of June 12th is a reply.

(Mr. Ziegler read Exhibit "4")

Now, in the letter of June 5th which I just read,
you state as follows: "We * * * are somewhat
surprised that there would be any question re accepting our proposition." I would like to have Mr.
Nickerson explain what that proposition was—the
letter itself mentions it.

Mr. FOLTA: I think the .etters here constitute
the entire correspondence between the parties.
Unless [79] he is able to show there is further correspondence, in explanation of this thing, it would be
not only improper but incompetent. One letter is
a reply to another. It constitutes the whole correspondence on the subject.

Mr. ZIEGLER: This letter from Hunt to the
Atlas Engine Company refers to a letter from the
Atlas Engine Company dated May 31st, which is
introduced in evidence. I would like to read that
to call Mr. Nickerson's attention to what arrangement, if any, was made.

The COURT: I think you can shorten it up a
lot by asking the witness whether they had any
other arrangements or contacts with these parties
by letter. Did you?

The WITNESS: No, I don't recall anything. I
discussed the matter in Seattle with them after she
was seized.

(Testimony of G. W. Nickerson.)

Q. Mr. Nickerson in the June 5th letter you wrote to the Atlas Engine Company, it referred to your proposition contained in your letter of the 31st of May, and the 31st of May letter is introduced in evidence and reads as follows:

(Mr. Ziegler read exhibit "3" to the court and witness)

This letter refers to making a down payment of $3,000.00 on the "Tahoma". It doesn't say to whom.

Mr. ZIEGLER: If the court please, I would ask permission to explain the statement. The letter itself doesn't say to whom the money was to be paid. He says here: "In accordance with your suggestion, we will be on the lookout for someone in Seattle who would be interested in taking the boat out and making a down payment of $3000.00. We hope that some arrangement may be worked out [80] on the basis of our above suggestion for the settlement of our accounts.

The COURT: That is pursuant to the suggestion made in the previous letter?

Mr. ZIEGLER: I think it is covered by the previous letter.

Q. Mr. Nickerson, I think the Court asked you this question: Did you make any arrangements, orally or by letters, which are not here, or any overtures or suggestions to the Seattle creditors that you would have the "Tahoma" conveyed to you?

A. No.

(Testimony of G. W. Nickerson.)

Q. Do you know why they made that statement in the letter of June 12th?

A. Unless there was a previous letter they gathered from it.

Q. That would be your explanation, then?

A. Yes, there is only that correspondence.

Q. That you intended to have it conveyed to you?

A. Yes; it must be from some of the correspondence, because I had never seen them until after the boat was seized.

Q. The last letter I read refers to your letter of May 18th of the Fishing Vessel Owners' Marine Ways, containing a proposition with respect to the "Tahoma". On that letter I see several memorandums made in pencil. Do you know who put them there and the explanation of them?

A. You want me to read these memos?

Q. Yes, read them.

A. This is all evidently there is. And the copy of the letter came from them I presume.

Mr. ZIEGLER: This is a copy, is it not. Mr. Folta? [81]

Mr. FOLTA: Yes, it is a photostatic copy. (Exh. "2")

Q. The first one here is, "They taking title from Pierce," the next one "If you are taking title we agree to accept". "Trading another boat and therefore become . . . ." I don't know what that is. Do you know?

(Testimony of G. W. Nickerson.)

A. "Taking another boat and therefore becoming owner." They have it underlined here. I don't know why they connect it up with that there.

Q. They are statements or questions written by them?

A. They wrote them all there. I have never seen that before. It is a copy of a letter I wrote, and those notations were not on when it went.

Q. Did you ever see those notations?

A. No, I never saw them before.

Q. Know nothing about them?

A. No.

The COURT: I think we will make time now by taking an adjournment until 1:30.

(At 11:40 o'clock A.M. Court adjourned until 1:30 o'clock P.M. the same day, reconvening at 1:43 o'clock P. M., whereupon G. W. NICKERSON resumed the witness stand and the cross examination by MR. ZIEGLER proceeded as follows:)

Q. Going back to these letters which have been introduced here as Libellant's exhibits—did you talk to Mr. Pierce himself before writing these letters, and if not—upon what facts did you base your authority to write those letters?

A. If I recall correctly, the first letter was written on the 18th of May. I don't think the "Tahoma" was in then. [82] I think it was written entirely on a conversation Earnest had with my

(Testimony of G. W. Nickerson.)

nephew. I think I also discussed the thing later with Earnest Pierce, after this had been conveyed. It was based entirely on this conversation. Pierce never told me—Winnie Pierce never told me—that he had, nor I never asked him to transfer, by word or letter, the "Tahoma" to me or anybody else.

Q. You assumed then, as I take it, that Mr. Pierce would be willing to consent to these arrangements in the letter following the conversation with his brother?

A. I knew Winnie Pierce was in a state of worry, he was willing to do anything that would give him a chance to earn a living. He felt whatever was best for his creditors was what he would be prepared to do.

Q. In one letter you mention something about taking a bill of sale in blank. I will ask you if you ever did take a bill of sale from Pierce on the "Tahoma"?

A. No.

Q. Did you have any agreement with him of any kind?

A. No.

Q. Ever have any oral arrangement or agreement with him by which he was to convey the "Tahoma" or any interest in it? That is—to sell it to you?

A. No, the oral conversation was we didn't want to use our position to deprive him of the "Tahoma"

(Testimony of G. W. Nickerson.)

if there was anything in her after the bills were paid. We didn't want any boats.

Q. You mentioned a bill of sale in these letters to the Seattle creditors. Did you ever take any bill of sale?

A. No. [83]

Q. What did you have in mind when you said you would take a bill of sale in blank?

A. I never intended to take it unless they forced the issue; if I had taken it I would have taken it in the name of someone entitled to receive it. Naturally I was business man enough not to waive any rights I had; naturally I wouldn't transfer a boat the Canadian Government would not accept or I would have a boat on my hands I couldn't do anything with.

Q. Has your firm taken bills of sale of American boats prior to that time and since?

A. We have been interested in transferring American boats to Canadian registry, yes, and knew the procedure you had to go through to obtain a permit from the American Government before the Canadian Government would give you a register.

Q. After these letters were written to the Seattle creditors and you made this arrangements for handling or the operation of the "Tahoma". as outlined in the letters, did you endeavor to sell the "Tahoma" on behalf of Pierce?

A. Yes: I wrote Ingvold Erickson and told him on behalf of Mr. Pierce I would arrange for him

(Testimony of G. W. Nickerson.)
to buy the "Tahoma" for $11,000.00, or words to that effect.

Q. I hand you a carbon copy of a letter, and ask you if you know what that is, if you can recall it or identify it?

A. That is the letter.

Q. You know what the letter is?

A. Yes, I wrote the letter.

Mr. ZIEGLER: If the court please—

The WITNESS: On that bill of sale I of course felt I was acting for all the creditors.

Mr. ZIEGLER: If the court please, this testimony [84] is not a matter of defense testimony only but it is also cross examination on these particular letters too and we can conclude the thing without recalling him.

(Slight discussion)

Mr. ZIEGLER: I think that is all on this phase of the case.

Redirect Examination.

By Mr. FOLTA:

Q. Who is Mrs. Kincaid?

A. She is my mother-in-law.

Q. What share does a captain get over and above the share of the fisherman on these halibut boats?

A. Usually ten per cent.

Q. You say other boats have been indebted to you. Do you mean other American boats?

A. Yes.

(Testimony of G. W. Nickerson.)

Q. Have you ever acquired title to an American boat as a result of indebtedness?

A. No, I don't think we ever had to take one over.

Q. How about the "Annabel."

A. The "Annabel" was sold in court at Sheriff's sale, I believe.

Q. Didn't you assign the claim to Mr. Ziegler?

A. That was handled by M. F. Nickerson.

Q. Don't you know that?

A. I think it was assigned.

Q. Wasn't that the purpose of assigning the claim—so you could get judgment here against him?

A. Only way to get the money. [85]

Q. Mr. Ziegler got a permit from the Shipping Board to sell it to you?

A. She was sold to us for a man named Peterson.

Q. When was that?

A. Last year, probably the last two months.

Q. After the seizure of the "Tahoma"?

A. I don't know when the "Annabel" was seized. I think it was a year ago last winter, no —a year ago last fall—the fall of '34 or '33.

Mr. ZIEGLER: '33 it was.

Q. It is since that the conveyance of the "Annabel" was made to you?

A. I don't know when the "Annabel" was seized.

Q. She wasn't seized.

(Testimony of G. W. Nickerson.)

A. She was seized by the Sheriff; I am not sure what month she was seized in.

Q. I am referring, of course, to action by the Government. Was it since the seizure of the "Tahoma" you assigned your claim to the "Annabel"?

A. I wouldn't say; I am not sure. As a matter of fact I was in Seattle, or the States, when this arrangement was made.

Mr. FOLTA: I think that is all.

Recross Examination.

By Mr. ZIEGLER:

Q. You say that was done by your nephew?

A. Yes.

Q. You don't remember the dates?

A. No, I was in the States when he came to Juneau.

Q. As near as you recall, if you don't know anything about [86] the facts of it, the "Tahoma" was seized last year along in the latter part of the year?

Mr. FOLTA: No, 1933.

A. Not the "Tahoma."

Q. You know — from your recollection, the "Annabel" was sold over at Juneau or Sitka?

A. It was in the fall of 1933. I think she came into Prince Rupert in the fall—Christmas 1933 or New Years Day 1934.

(Testimony of G. W. Nickerson.)

Q. When that suit was brought the "Annabel" was not within the jurisdiction of this court—that was for supplies furnished the boat, and you sent your claim over here?

A. Yes.

Mr. ZIEGLER: That is all.

Mr. FOLTA: That is all.

(Witness Excused)

Mr. FOLTA: If the Court please, I offer to read the cross examination of Wright and Heggem, two witnesses whose depositions were taken on the forfeiture side of this case. The cross examination bears on the nature of the liens as well as the forfeiture, but I offer them now.

The COURT: These depositions are all in evidence now, aren't they, in toto?

Mr. FOLTA: Yes.

WHEREUPON the witness M. C. WRIGHT, by deposition testified as follows:

(Mr. FOLTA read to the court the cross examination of Mr. WRIGHT and from thence to the end of the deposition) [87]

"M. C. WRIGHT,

a witness for Intervenor Atlas Engine Co.:

Q. (By Mr. BRONSON). You reside in Seattle, Mr. Wright?

A. Yes, sir.

(Deposition of M. C. Wright.)

Q. What is your connection with the Atlas Engine Company?

A. Vice-president.

Q. When did you first have connection with the Atlas Engine company?

A. July 1932.

Q. That was here in Seattle?

A. Before that I was in Oakland.

Q. You have been in charge of the Atlas Engine company office here in Seattle since the date given.

A. Yes.

Q. And as such you are actively engaged in conducting its affairs.

A. Yes, sir.

Q. And have had direct connection with its transactions and collections since that time?

A. Yes.

Q. You were not familiar, I understand, with the original transaction between the owners of this boat Tahoma and the Atlas Engine company and Mr. O. E. Nelson.

A. I had nothing to do with that.

Q. Will you refer to the books of account of the Atlas Engine Company—you have them here, have you?

A. Yes.

Q. Will you refer to the ledger sheets and whatever other records of the Atlas Engine company that you have here, and tell us the condition of that

(Deposition of M. C. Wright.)

account as it appears [88] by the books, as to payments from the inception of that account?

A. The original account on the deferred payments is $4440; and against that we have received $540.00 on the principal; on the interest we have received payments regularly until December 1, 1930; I haven't that totaled up.

Q. Have you prepared a copy of the ledger sheets?

A. Yes, sir.

Q. These are the original sheets?

A. Yes.

Q. And you have prepared copies?

A. Yes, sir. (Producing sheets).

Q. I now hand you these sheets which have been marked for identification as Atlas Engine company's exhibits F and G, and ask you what these are?

A. These are copies of our note ledger of this account, covering the different balances that we have been carrying on the account, showing a list of the payments on the principal as well as payments on the interest.

Q. Are these two exhibits accurate and complete copies of your ledger sheets?

A. They are identical copies.

Q. Have you checked them to ascertain that?

A. Yes, I have.

(Deposition of M. C. Wright.)

Q. Do these ledger sheet copies correctly reflect the transactions that have occurred since your connection with the business here in Seattle?

A. Yes, they do, with the exception of certain agreements as to the extending time for payments. [89]

Q. But for the payments.

A. Yes.

Q. Anything which would be shown in the ledger, the book account.

A. Yes, sir.

Q. Can you give us the total amount which was due the first day of October, 1934?

A. The total amount here is $861.66; that is exclusive of certain attorneys fees that we had put in there.

Q. And does that figure which you have given us include anything on behalf of the Nordby Supply company?

A. It does not.

Q. Does it include anything other than this original purchase of the engine?

A. It is the balance that remains on the original purchase and interest.

Q. There is an amount of interest which has been included?

A. Interest $321.66.

Q. That is interest from what date to what date?

A. The interest from the beginning was paid to December first 1930; this amount is interest accruing since that date.

(Deposition of M. C. Wright.)

Q. When was the last payment of any kind that was received?

A. We received $200.00 the first part of this year; I believe it was February; I think that was through Hunt & Co.; that was supposed to be a disbursement of the earnings of the boat last year.

Q. Did you also have an open account with this vessel, Mr. Wright, which is not shown in the account of the engine purchase? [90]

A. No, we did not. The only open account is the item of attorneys fees shown here amounting to $52.75.

Q. You took that out of the account?

A. Yes; it was suggested that we leave that out.

Q. Then this figure of $861.66 has not this $52.00 item in it.

A. No, that was taken out.

Q. Has that item of $861.66 anything beside the principal and interest in it?

A. Nothing at all.

Q. Is that amount now due and owing?

A. Yes.

Q. And I take it it is unpaid.

A. That is correct.

Q. Have you made demands for that balance or any preceding balance?

A. At intervals of probably three weeks or a month, for the last three years.

Mr. BRONSON: I do not know whether it will be contested as to whether the Atlas Engine com-

(Deposition of M. C. Wright.)

pany is a corporation and has paid its last annual
'license fee?

Mr. FOLTA: Not on the part of the government.

Mr. STEINER: We do not raise that question.

Q. The Atlas Engine company is a corporation,
is it?

A. Yes.

Q. Do you know whether it has paid its annual
license fee for the period from June 1, 1934 to June
1, 1935?

A. I know it has.

Q. Do you know anything about the purchase
of the account of the Nordby Supply company? [91]

A. Yes, I handled that.

Q. Did the Atlas Engine company purchase that
account from the Nordby Supply company?

A. Yes, sir, we did.

Q. On or about what date?

A. It was last fall, as I recollect the 18th of September.

Q. Is the Atlas Engine company owner of that
account receivable now?

A. Yes.

Q. Has any part of that been paid since the date
of assignment?

A. No part.

Cross-Examination:

Q. (By Mr. FOLTA). Mr. *Wi*ght, when did Mr.
Nilsen retire?

A. Approximately the time I arrived here. He
left in May and I arrived in July.

(Deposition of M. C. Wright.)

Q. Of 1932.

A. Yes, 1932.

Q. Now, at the time you arrived here, or any time after you arrived, did you ever see Mr. Pierce?

A. I have never seen him; he has never been down.

Q. As far as you know the vessel operated out of Prince Rupert all the time?

A. I have no evidence that he did not operate out of there.

Q. These payments that you have received were received from whom?

A. They were received from Pierce. At times they would be on the F. E. Hunt check; whether that was disbursement money paid to him by them or payment direct, I could [92] not say, but supposedly they were from Pierce direct.

Q. But the check would be an F. E. Hunt check.

A. Yes.

Q. Do you recollect who signed the checks?

A. These checks were signed by Hunt; I have a notation that they were signed by Hunt.

Q. The notation was made where?

A. We have the old deposit books indicate that the checks came from Hunt; but that was not a hundred per cent all the way through; it would vary.

Q. But most of them were from Hunt & Co.?

A. Yes.

Q. You have seen them yourself?

(Deposition of M. C. Wright.)

A.   I have never seen the checks. The only check we received was one that came in this spring for $200.00. That was from Hunt; all the others came before I arrived. The only record we have is in the deposit books and the ledger sheets.

Q.   After you received the payment in February from Hunt, were any payments received on your indebtedness from F. E. Hunt or Pierce?

A.   No payments after that.

Q.   Did you experience any difficulty in collecting any part of this indebtedness because of further indebtedness to F. E. Hunt & Co.?

A.   Well, we were completely stalled; their account was supposed to be in a lien claim; and the position of the boat in Prince Rupert, a lien claim subsequently arose and would naturally come ahead.

Q.   Well, you people and F. E. Hunt & Co., made some kind [93] of an arrangement where Hunt would send you a certain portion of the earnings of the Tahoma?

A.   We entered into that agreement together with the Fishing Vessel Owners'; we were to participate in an amount of money—fifty per cent of any amount of money over and above the expenses of the boat. I believe the $200. received last February was from that.

Q.   And that is how you came to receive the checks from F. E. Hunt?

A.   No, that agreement was dated in 1933, about a year after I arrived.

(Deposition of M. C. Wright.)

Q. Since that agreement what payments you have received have been on F. E. Hunt & Co. checks?

A. That is the only check we have gotten.

Q. Did they send you statements of the vessel's operation?

A. We received no detailed statement; but we did get a statement showing that the earnings had been only ten dollars above expenses and they would not be able to send a check for that—we had a bill for $500.00 interest.

Q. This arrangement was made between the Atlas Engine Co. and the Fishing Vessel Owners' Marine Ways and F. E. Hunt; and you acted for the Atlas Engine Co.

A. Yes, G. W. Nickerson acted for the Hunt Co.

Mr. BRONSON: This is not cross examination, but I am willing you continue briefly.

Mr. FOLTA: I will not be long about it.

Q. Mr. Wright, I hand you a letter purporting to be from F. E. Hunt Co. under date of May 18, 1933 addressed to your company inclosing a letter of the same date to the Fishing Vessel Owners' Marine Ways, and ask you [94] if you recollect receiving that letter with the inclosure?

A. I do.

Q. You are familiar with Nickerson's signature?

A. That is his signature, at least we have received several letters from him.

Mr. FOLTA: I offer the two letters in evidence.

Letters marked libelants' exhibits 1 and 2; attached to and returned herewith.

(Deposition of M. C. Wright.)

Q. I hand you now a letter dated May 31, 1933 written jointly by the Atlas Engine company and the Fishing Vessel Owners' *Maine* Ways, in reply to their letter, and ask you if you recollect that?

A. I do.

Mr. FOLTA: I offer the letter in evidence.

Paper marked Libelant's exhibit 3; attached to and returned herewith.

Q. I hand you another letter dated June 5, 1933, addressed to the Atlas Engine Company and the Fishing Vessel Owners' Marine Ways, signed by G. W. Nickerson, and ask you if you remember receiving that letter with reference to the same matter?

A. Yes, sir.

Mr. FOLTA: I offer the letter in evidence.

Letter marked Libelant's exhibit 4; attached to and returned herewith.

Q. Also hand you a letter under date of June 12, 1933, evidently in reply to the letter exhibit 4, and ask you if you recollect that?

A. Yes, sir. [95]

Mr. FOLTA: I offer the letter in evidence.

Letter marked Libelant's exhibit 5; attached to and returned herewith.

Q. Also show you a letter under date of June 17, 1933, with further reference to the same matter, addressed to your company and the Fishing Vessel Owners' Marine Ways, from F. E. Hunt, and ask you if you recollect receiving that letter?

A. Yes.

(Deposition of M. C. Wright.)

Mr. FOLTA: I offer the letter in evidence.

Letter marked Libelant's exhibit 6; attached
to and returned herewith.

Q. One more letter. This is from Hunt & Co.
concerning the operation of 1933, and ask you if
you recall receiving that?

A. I do.

Mr. FOLTA: I offer this letter in evidence.

Letter marked Libellant's exhibit 7; attached
to and returned herewith.

Q. Mr. Wright, in entering into this arrangement for the payment of the debts due by the Tahoma to yourselves and the Fishing Vessel Owners'
Marine Ways and F. E. Hunt & Co., I believe you
stated you acted for the Atlas Engine Company,
and signed the originals of these letters, photostatic
copies of which are now in evidence.

A. I did, yes, sir.

Q. Now since that time there has been one payment received.

A. A payment.

Q. From F. E. Hunt & Co.? [96]

A. It was July of last year that we received that
—June 29th; I thought that it was this spring;
but it was last year.

Q. Have you seen Nickerson? Has he been
here?

A. I have talked to him twice.

Q. Since this arrangement was entered into,
once before and the last time was about three

(Deposition of M. C. Wright.)
or four months ago—it was the last part of December—had there been any other agreement or arrangement succeeding this? Or is that still the arrangement?

A. The arrangement is the same at present.

Q. One was a secondary arrangement; did you
have any further conversations with reference to
the operation of the Tahoma?

A. Nothing more definite. Our position was:
sitting tight at that time; and we did not want to
make any statements that might change things; we
were very satisfied the way things were.

Q. Did Nickerson have anything to say about it?

A. He wanted us to help him out of the hole,
but there was nothing that we could do.

Q. What did he mean by "the hole"?

A. In our last conversation, at the time the boat
had been seized in Ketchikan, he came down and saw
both Heggman and myself, but there was nothing
really done at that time.

Q. When he asked you to try to get him out
of the hole, did he go into details or particulars
about it?

A. As I recollect he suggested that we write to
Washington; that was the only suggestion, that
we write to Washington [97] and ask leniency; but
I really forget what he wanted us to say.

Q. Did he say anything about trying to establish
a lien at Ketchikan in this case?

(Deposition of M. C. Wright.)

A. No, he said nothing to us about any lien in Ketchikan.

Q. All he wanted you to do was to write to Washington?

A. To get this present action dismissed.

Q. Did he suggest any method by which it could be dismissed?

A. No.

Q. Have you had any correspondence since with him with reference to the Tahoma?

A. No, I haven't—well, he has written, I believe, requesting that we write or work on the case in an effort to release the action.

Q. You have that letter, have you?

A. I do not recollect whether he wrote or not: he left a file with us; I do not think he did write. it was just our conversation; we returned his file to him at Prince Rupert.

Q. When was it that you saw him last and had conversations with him with reference to this matter?

A. In the early part of December.

Q. And the first time was shortly after the seizure?

A. No; the first time was before the seizure, in the winter of 1933.

Q. When he was here in the winter of 1933, Mr. Wright, as I understand, you had some conversation about the operation of the Tahoma at

(Deposition of M. C. Wright.)
that time under the arrangement that you entered
into in the summer.

A. That is correct. That was the conversation
that led [98] up to this agreement that we originally decided on in the summer.

Re-Direct Examination:

Q. (By Mr. BRONSON). As far as you know
has the Tahoma been in the state of Washington
or American jurisdiction during the period that you
have been in Seattle?

A. I am sure it has not.

Q. Prior to her presence in Ketchikan?

A. Not that I know of.

Q. And did that absence of the vessel have anything to do with your failure to take any steps
against this vessel sooner than were taken?

A. Yes, it prohibited our doing anything about
it. Hunt's letters show that he has a maritime
lien up there and if we went into his camp our
lien would be secondary to his and we would not
get very far.

Q. Was there any discussion had by you with
Hunt pertaining to that point?

A. Well, his letters state very clearly that he
has the whip-hand and if we do not want to fall in
line we can fall out of line and take what is left.

Q. Over how long a time have you received such
statements?

A. It has been ever since I have been here.

(Deposition of M. C. Wright.)

Q. (By Mr. FOLTA). Mr. Wright, was there any understanding as between the various creditors here named, as to keeping up the insurance on the Tahoma?

A. They have always kept up the insurance; that has been the agreement, to keep up the insurance. [99]

Q. Who has kept it up?

A. F. E. Hunt has kept up the insurance; the insurance policy was made out; but I don't know about the payments.

Q. How do you know that Hunt & Co. paid the premium?

A. We have no evidence to that effect other than we received a copy of the policy.

Q. Do you know who did pay the premium?

A. We had no way of knowing; we always received a copy and that was forwarded by Hunt & Co.

Q. This copy of a letter undated, I assume it has reference to the arrangement that you people made as to the handling of the insurance on the Tahoma?

A. Yes, that was a renewal policy that was forwarded.

Q. That was forwarded to you?

A. Forwarded to us, yes.

Q. Did you ask that the policy be sent to you?

A. Why, it was sent each year; it expired on the 8th of February, and we only had asked for it on one occasion that they slipped up on it.

(Deposition of M. C. Wright.)

Q. Did Hunt and company ever keep the insurance policies or did you people always have it?

A. We merely had a copy; who had the original I do not know.

Mr. FOLTA: I offer this letter in evidence.

Letter marked Libelant's exhibit 8; attached to and returned herewith.

Mr. BRONSON: I offer in evidence Intervenor Atlas Engine Co. identifications exhibits F and G.

Copies of ledger sheets marked Intervenor Atlas Engine Co. exhibits F and G; attached to and returned herewith.''

————

AND THEREUPON the witness ING-VOSLD HEGGEM, by desposition, testified as follows: [100]

"DEPOSITIONS FOR INTERVENOR FISHING VESSEL OWNERS' MARINE WAYS.

Deposition of

INGVOSLD HEGGEM,

a witness for Intervenor Fishing Vessel Owners' Marine Ways:

Q. (By Mr. STEINER). The Fishing Vessel Owners' Marine Ways is a corporation, is it?

A. Yes, sir.

Q. And has paid its annual license fee last due?

A. Yes.

(Deposition of Ingvosld Heggem.)

Q. What has been your connection with it?

A. Management.

Q. How long have you been manager?

A. Twelve years.

Q. Exclusively.

A. Yes, sir.

Q. Did your corporation make any repairs on the vessel Tahoma?

A. Yes sir.

Q. At whose request?

A. The skipper.

Q. Who was the skipper?

A. Captain Pierce.

Q. Was he also the owner at the time?

A. That is what we understood.

Q. What did these repairs consist of?

A. Well we had a contract to do certain work incidental to the installing of the new engine; and after that there was painting and dry docking and repairs.

Q. Such repairs as were necessary for the navigation of [101] the boat.

A. Yes.

Q. What was the amount of your charge?

A. You have a statement before you. $1103.89 is the balance due to date.

Q. Does that represent the reasonable value of the work you did?

A. Yes sir.

(Deposition of Ingvosld Heggem.)

Q. And that bill was submitted to Pierce from time to time?

A. Yes sir.

Q. And he has recognized it and acknowledged it, the amount you state?

A. Yes.

Q. That includes interest?

A. Yes.

Q. What was the original amount of the contract? $644.00?

A. That is the original and there was one more.

Q. $278.47? Making a total of $942.47?

A. Yes.

Q. Now this account of $644.00 is dated Dec. 31, 1929?

A. Yes; the bill was made out shortly after the work was completed.

Q. Substantially the same time, was it?

A. Well, there was a bill before that.

Q. That represents the completion of it?

A. Yes.

Q. Now the bill of January 28, 1930 of $278.47, does that represent the completion, approximately, of the work?

A. Yes.

Q. And a credit of $20.00 on Jan. 28, 1930; that represents [102] the time when the work was done.

A. Yes.

(Deposition of Ingvosld Heggem.)

Q. And these items represent the fair, reasonable value of the work that was done?

A. Yes.

Q. Now you have charged interest from that time to Sept. 19, 1934, amounting to $270.49.

A. I believe that is correct.

Q. Now what if any payments have been made on that?

A. $120.00 in May 1934.

Q. That is the only payment made?

A. There was a credit of $20.00.

Q. What date was that?

A. Jan. 29, 1930.

Q. And then the only other payment is the $120.00.

A. Yes, May 31, 1934.

Q. I hand you five letters which have been marked for identification as Intervenor Fishing Vessel Owners' Marine Ways A-1, and ask you if you received them from Capt. Pierce, except the last one which is from Hunt & Co.?

A. Yes, sir.

Q. These are the original letters, are they?

A. Yes sir.

Mr. STEINER: I offer the letters in evidence. Letters marked Intervenor Fishing Vessel Owners' Marine *Was* exhibit A-1; attached to and returned herewith.

Q. Mr. Heggem where has this vessel been since you made these repairs?

(Deposition of Ingvosld Heggem.)

A. We understood she has been in Canada.

Q. When was she last in this port, so far as you know? [103]

A. As far as I know it was in 1930 when she was at our place.

Q. Since that time she has not been here?

A. I have not seen her.

Cross Examination

Q. (By Mr. FOLTA). During all this time what has been your position with the Vessel Owners' Marine Ways?

A. Manager for the last 12 years.

Q. The work done on the Tahoma was not original construction?

A. No sir; it was repairs.

Q. Repairs or alterations?

A. Alterations.

Q. Alterations and repairs.

A. Yes, sir.

Q. Just what did these alterations consist of? Did it change the type of the vessel?

A. In 1928 they put a new engine in her and the alterations were made about that; in 1929 alterations were made about taking out the donkeys.

Q. You of course know that this work was done?

A. Yes sir.

Q. And did you know Pierce before the work was done?

(Deposition of Ingvosld Heggem.)

A. I don't think I met him before 1928.

Q. That is, he came to you people and made arrangements with you, entered into a contract for doing this work?

A. Yes, sir.

Q. Did you rely on the credit of the vessel or on Pierce's credit?

A. The vessel.

Q. That is the usual course. [104]

A. All our bills are made out to the boat and owners.

Q. Since that time the vessel has been operating out of Prince Rupert, as far as you know?

A. As far as I know.

Q. Have you seen Pierce since that time?

A. No.

Q. And I suppose it was your understanding that the boat got into considerable debt in Prince Rupert?

A. That is what we heard later on.

Q. And F. E. Hunt & Co. sort of used that as a club over you the same as they did the Atlas Engine company?

A. I would not say that.

Q. Mr. Heggem, will you look over these letters Libelant's exhibits 1 to 6, inclusive, and state whether or not you entered into that arrangement on behalf of your company for the operation of the Tahoma?

(Deposition of Ingvosld Heggem.)

A.   I could not swear to every word; we have a copy of them.

Q.   You have seen all of these libelant's exhibits 1 to 6?

A.   Yes.

Q.   Well, these letters signed by the Atlas Engine company and the Fishing Vessel Owners' Marine Ways, included in exhibits 1 to 6 were sent to F. E. Hunt & Co. were signed by you?

A.   Yes.

Q.   Now, Mr. Heggem, since entering into that arrangement has there been any change or other arrangement superseding this one?

A.   No, not that I know of. After the vessel was seized [105] we turned it over to our lawyer, Mr. Steiner.

Q.   Before the vessel was seized, Mr. Heggem, after this arrangement was entered into, from whom did you receive any payments on account?

A.   Hunt & Co.

Q.   On their checks?

A.   I don't remember exactly.

Q.   Would your records show in what form those payments were made?

A.   No. Our record shows it was paid on account of the Tahoma.

Q.   The check would be put through the bank and you would not see it any more.

A.   That is right.

(Deposition of Ingvosld Heggem.)

Q. Did you receive letters with the checks?

A. No, I think not. Just got the check.

Q. Do you remember whether this check was the check of F. E. Hunt & Co.?

A. I am pretty sure it was.

Q. Signed by Nickerson?

A. Nickerson signed.

Q. That is G. W. Nickerson?

A. Yes.

Q. Did you know G. W. Nickerson?

A. I met him.

Q. When did you first meet him, about?

A. About a year ago last December.

Q. And from all the correspondence with him did you become acquainted with his signature?

A. Fairly, yes. [106]

Q. When you met him in December, was it concerning the Tahoma?

A. Yes.

Q. What did he say then?

A. He asked if he could find three thousand dollars to go up and buy the boat to go fishing on.

Q. That is the same thing he said in one of these letters.

A. Yes.

Q. Did he not state, somewhere in these exhibits 1 to 6 that he thought Pierce was not a capable man to operate the Tahoma?

A. Yes.

(Deposition of Ingvosld Heggem.)

Q. And he wanted to put some one else in his place?

A. Yes.

Q. So that the indebtedness to F. E. Hunt & Co., and you people and the Atlas Engine Co., would have at least a better show of being paid off?

A. Yes.

Q. You say that was in December 1933?

A. It was in 1933.

Q. Have you seen him since?

A. Yes, he was out to the yard last winter, around December.

Q. Did you have any further conversation with him about the Tahoma?

A. Yes.

Q. What was said?

A. About releasing the boat. I told him that we had turned it over to Steiner and for him to go and see him.

Q. What did he want you to do?

A. He wanted us to help him release the boat. I told him [107] I did not know anything about it; that we had turned it over to our attorney and he could see him.

Q. What did he want you to do to get the release of the boat?

A. Nothing said about that. He was just talking about getting it released.

Q. Did he make some suggestion of what you should do, the same as the Atlas Engine company,

(Deposition of Ingvosld Heggem.)

write a letter to Washington, something of that kind?

A.   No. I told him I did not know anything about that. It was out of my hands. It was turned over to our attorney and for him to see him.

Q.   Did he say anything about the lien of the F. E. Hunt & company?

A.   Not as far as I remember.

(Witness Excused)

——————

Mr. STEINER: I offer in evidence the statement of account referred to in the testimony of the witness.

Paper marked Intervenor Fishing Vessel Owners' Marine Ways exhibit A-2; attached to and returned herewith." [108]

——————

DEPOSITION OF INGVOLD HEGGEM:

MR. FOLTA then read from the deposition from the cross-examination on page 29 thereof, to the end of said deposition.

PAUL R. VERNON,

called as a witness on behalf of the Libellant, being first duly sworn, testified as follows:

Direct Examination

By Mr. FOLTA:

Q. Will you state your name?

A. Paul R. Vernon.

Q. What is your position?

A. Deputy Collector of Customs at Petersburg. Alaska.

Q. How long have you been connected with the Customs Service?

A. About four and three-quarters years.

Q. Did you know John A. Johnson, sometimes known as Arthur Johnson, that was registered master of the "Tahoma" from May to February, 1934?

A. He came into the offiee as Arthur Johnson.

Q. It is part of your duties, Mr. Vernon, when a boat enters American territory from a foreign port, such as Prince Rupert, do you require an oath as to ownership and operation of the boat, etc.?

A. Yes.

Q. Did you require such of Johnson?

A. Yes.

Q. Master of the "Tahoma". I will ask you if this is the statement or oath you got from Johnson?

A. It is.

Q. Who was present when you took that? [109]

A. Carrol Clausen, who at that time was United States Commissioner at Petersburg.

(Testimony of Paul R. Vernon.)

Mr. FOLTA: We offer this in evidence as Libellant's exhibit "10."

Mr. ZIEGLER: If the Court please, we offer an objection to this statement, signed by the master of the boat, as hearsay testimony. Our position is it comes within the rule of hearsay and is not binding on the registered owner of the boat— Winnie Pierce.

Mr. FOLTA: If the Court please, the master is always the general agent of the owner, and any statement made by him within the scope of his employment is admissible.

Mr. ZIEGLER: I concede that is the rule—the master is the agent of the owner, and while his statements are admissible as evidence they are not binding on the court; that seems to be the rule. However, his testimony can only be admitted so far as anything concerning the owner goes. His statement as to third parties—as to what he said about me or F. E. Hunt Ltd., or someone else who is not the owner, and of which he is not the agent and who is not his principal—he cannot possibly bind him. I have no objection to counsel reading into the record the portion of the statement signed by the master, affecting the ownership of the boat, but with reference to his employment thereon and other matters contained therein I think it is inadmissible, and I think it will be error if admitted, for certainly we cannot be bound, Winnie Pierce cannot be bound by what a master aboard the boat says about some third party pertaining to the scope [110] of his employment.

(Testimony of Paul R. Vernon.)

(Further argument.)

The COURT: I think it is admissible under the allegations of the second cause of action.

Mr. ZIEGLER: I think it is admissible under the allegations but not the proof.

The COURT: In any event it will be received at this time subject to further objections.

(Said statement was admitted in evidence as Libellant's exhibit "10" and is as follows, to-wit:)

"Oct. 10, 1933

STATEMENT & AFFIDAVIT OF
ARTHUR JOHNSON

To Whom It May Concern:

This is to state that on the 29th day of May, 1933, I was employed by F. E. Hunt, Ltd., of Prince Rupert, B. C., to act as master of the Am. Ol. s. TAHOMA, O/N 214,741.

That I was given to understand that Winnie Pierce, of Prince Rupert, B. C. was the owner of the boat as far as I was concerned in answering questions and signing papers pertaining to the vessel was concerned.

That from the beginning of my employment, I was given to understand that I was master of the vessel in name only and that I was to be guided in all matters of the vessel by Tony Martinsen, (a Canadian Citizen) so far, that, on leaving the dock, I was to turn over the navigation of the vessel to

(Testimony of Paul Vernon.)

Tony Martinsen, that I would revert to the position of a fisherman, and that I would perform the duties of such a fisherman.

That I was to be given, and have been given, a regular fishermans share, plus ten per cent of the "BOAT SHARE," this ten per cent of the BOAT SHARE to be in payment for my services for acting as master of the vessel, in order that the aforesaid Tony Martinsen would not have to appear at the U. S. Customs House.

     Signed Arthur Johnson

Witness:

  C. Clausen

[Endorsed]: "Lbls. Exhibit No. 10 Received in Evidence Jun 6 1935 [111] in cause No. 1778-KA. Robert E. Coughlin, Clerk. By............................Deputy."

  Mr. ZIEGLER: No cross-examination.

  (Witness excused.)

G. C. WOODWARD,

called as a witness on behalf of the Libellant, being first duly sworn, testified as follows:

Direct Examination

By Mr. FOLTA:

  Q. Will you state your name and official position, and residence.

  A. G. C. Woodward, American Consul, assigned to Prince Rupert, British Columbia.

  Q. How long have you been assigned to the post at Prince Rupert?

  A. Since October, 1927.

(Testimony of G. C. Woodward.)

Q. Mr. Woodward, just state briefly your duties with reference to the documents and management of American vessels and the shipment of halibut through Prince Rupert, product [112] of American vessels?

A. American vessels are required to enter and clear at the consulate. In the case of Prince Rupert the landing of American halibut, or halibut termed the product of American fisheries was required to be reported at the Consulate and oath taken by the master and two members of the crew.

Q. That entitles the shipment to go through without the payment of duty?

A. Without the payment of duty. Of course we take a record of the landings and shipments; of course in change of masters we require proof of the authorities of the persons authorizing the appointment of the new master. The question of ownership arises sometimes and we are authorized to satisfy the Consulate as to the proper ownership.

Q. During the course of the conduct of your office did you become acquainted with the "Tahoma"?

A. Yes, it has been coming in there regularly since I have been at Prince Rupert.

Q. Were you acquainted with its registered owner and master until May 29th, Mr. Winnie Pierce?

A. Yes, he comes in regularly, has come in regularly, or did.

(Testimony of G. C. Woodward.)

Q. You, of course, have been acquainted with the "Tahoma" since that time?

A. Yes.

Q. Were you acquainted with the registered owner prior to the summer of 1933, B. A. Peterson or Petterson, of the halibut schooner "Wave"? [113]

A. Yes, I was, as owner and master of the boat.

Q. Were you acquainted with John A. Johnston, sometimes known as Arthur Johnson, who was endorsed on the certificate of registry as master, May 29th, 1933?

A. Approximately that date, I would have to verify that, but about the latter part of May.

Q. Were you acquainted during the time his name appeared as master?

A. During the time he appeared on the register as master I know he was placed on there by the Consulate.

Q. Do you know anything about Johnson's qualifications as master of halibut boats?

Mr. ZIEGLER: Object to that as immaterial and incompetent.

Mr. FOLTA: It is preliminary.

Mr. ZIEGLER: If the court please, the fact that the Customs officials and authorities at Prince Rupert endorsed this man as Master would establish the fact of his qualifications. I don't see how counsel can impeach the records of the United States by any testimony of this kind.

Mr. FOLTA: The Consulate doesn't pass on the qualifications of anybody signing up as master. But

(Testimony of G. C. Woodward.)

in this case I don't want counsel to lose sight of the
fact that it is the Government's theory that there
was a conspiracy between the various people
whereby Pierce relinquished his equity in the "Tahoma" and was put in charge of the "Wave" just as
the correspondence indicates, and that they had to
have somebody in charge as master who was an
American. On that theory, that there was a change
of [114] ownership and that Pierce surrendered his
equity in the "Tahoma" so as to make way for somebody else to be put on as master, it becomes competent to show that the person put in charge of the
"Tahoma", while he may have had the necessary
qualifications as to citizenship, did not have the
qualifications of master for management or navigation of vessels, and particularly in view of Johnson's statement in the affidavit received in evidence.

Mr. ZIEGLER: Counsel can't come into court
and state his theory of the case is this and that and,
based on theory alone, pave the way for the introduction of incompetent evidence. If counsel lays the
proper foundation for the reception of this kind of
testimony, that is a different thing, but I never
heard of a theory yet dispensing with the rule of
evidence. I raise the objection that the testimony of
Mr. Woodward concerning this man's qualifications
as master is incompetent, not only is it incompetent,
but if the testimony would be permitted it would be
impeachment of the parties on the record in the
Treasury Department.

(Further argument by counsel.)

(Testimony of G. C. Woodward.)

The COURT: The statement he makes in this letter is plain enough. He says what his duties are and what he did in pursuance of the instructions he was given. The witness may answer, subject to future objections.

Q. You might answer that—whether or not you knew he was qualified.

A. My understanding was he was not qualified as a master of a boat of that size.

Mr. ZIEGLER: I renew the objection, and move the [115] testimony be stricken. It is purely the opinion of the witness here; there is nothing showing he is even qualified.

The COURT: Objection sustained.

Q. Mr. Woodward, you answered before this answer, I think, that Johnson was not qualified. What do you base that on? Just tell the court what you base that on.

Mr. ZIEGLER: My motion to strike his answer was allowed.

Mr. FOLTA: That is another question.

Q. Did you ever have any conversation with Arthur Johnson concerning the operation of the "Tahoma" after May 29th, 1933?

A. If I am permitted—He first came to the Consulate and stated he had the opportunity of being made master of this vessel. He was required to prove his citizenship. It took some little time; then the consulate signed him on. I had a conversation with him regarding the operation of the boat.

Q. What was that conversation?

(Testimony of G. C. Woodward.)

A. My recollection is he was employed by the company—Hunt and Company; and I questioned them as to the length of time he had operated vessels, and he had simply been a fisherman or seaman on a vessel; he had never been master on a vessel before, but the qualifications for being signed on as master was merely American citizenship, consequently I signed him on as such.

Q. Did he himself say whether he was qualified?

A. He said he didn't consider himself qualified.

Q. Did he say what pay he was to receive for acting in this [116] capacity?

A. I don't quite recollect, but it was the usual fisherman's wages and a slight increase.

Q. Mr. Woodward, I will show you a statement—what purports to be a statement signed by Arthur Johnson, and ask you what that is?

A. That is a typewritten statement—a statement made by him to me, which was typed, and signed by him in my presence.

Q. As to what?

A. As to his employment and the amount he was to receive.

Mr. FOLTA: I offer this in evidence as Libellant's exhibit "11".

Mr. ZIEGLER: Object to it on the ground it is immaterial; for this reason—When a man is signed on by the Customs as Master of a vessel, it must be a person presumed to be qualified to be signed on or it would not be done. It looks to me like the

(Testimony of G. C. Woodward.)

American Consulate is attempting to impeach the Customs officials at Prince Rupert.

(Further argument.)

The COURT: It may be received for what it is worth.

Mr. ZIEGLER: Take an exception.

————

(Said statement was admitted in evidence and marked Libellant's exhibit "11"; and is as follows, to-wit:)

"Prince Rupert, B. C., Canada,
July 21, 1933.

"John Arthur Johnson, being questioned, states:

That under arrangement with Messrs. F. E. Hunt, Limited, he agreed to act as master of the Ga. s. "Tahoma" of Ketchikan, Alaska, 16 net tons, Official No. 214,741; [117]

That while it is customary for masters of halibut vessels of the size and type of the "Tahoma" to receive 10 per cent of the boat's share in addition to the share allotted members of the crew, in his case he receives 5 per cent of the boat's share owing to the fact that he is only responsible as a member of the crew and for entering and clearing the vessel as an American citizen while Anton Martinsen receives 10 per cent of the boat's share as well as the share as a member of the crew owing to the fact that he has actual charge of the operations of the vessel:

That so far as he has a personal knowledge his transaction is entirely with Messrs. F. E. Hunt,

(Testimony of G. C. Woodward.)

Limited˜and not with W. Pierce, who appears on the register of the said vessel as owner thereof;

That according to his understanding thereof the reason for such arrangement is that he has had insufficient experience as a halibut fisherman to have charge of the operations of a halibut vessel of the size of the "Tahoma."

ARTHUR JOHNSON

JOHN ARTHUR JOHNSON

[Endorsed]: "Lbls. Exhibit No. 11 RECEIVED IN EVIDENCE Jun 6 1935 in cause No. 1778-KA. Robert E. Coughlin, Clerk. By............................Deputy." (Court Seal)

"United States of America

First District of Alaska—ss.

I, ROBERT E. COUGHLIN, Clerk of the United States District Court in and for the First District of Alaska, do hereby certify that the annexed and foregoing is a true and fully copy of the original Lbls. Exhibit No. 11 United States of America, Libelant, vs. Oil Screw Vessel, Tahoma, etc. Respondent, W. Pierce, Claimant, Atlas Engine Company, and Fishing Vessel Owners Marine Ways, corporation, Intervenors, No. 1117 K.A. now remaining among the records of the said Court in my office. IN TESTIMONY WHEREOF, I have hereunto subscribed my name and affixed the seal of the aforesaid Court at Juneau, Alaska, this 15th day of June, A.D. 1935.

(Court Seal)　　ROBERT E. COUGHLIN, Clerk,

By..Deputy."

[118]

(Testimony of G. C. Woodward.)

Q. Mr. Woodward, are you acquainted with Antone Martin?

A. From his having come to the office, I have a general acquaintanceship, as I have with a majority of the Canadian and American halibut fishermen in Prince Rupert.

Q. Who is Antone Martin?

A. He was formerly owner of the Canadian halibut vessel "Livingstone."

Q. Is that a halibut schooner?

A. That was a halibut schooner. Sometime after its loss he was on the "Tahoma". My first knowledge of this was that all aliens who are employed in Prince Rupert are—on halibut vessels—are required to come to the Consulate and we secure particulars of their origin, as we would from anybody coming from the States, as they really are aliens coming from the States.

Q. After Johnson's name was endorsed as master of the "Tahoma" on the register, do you know where Tony Martin was employed?

A. You mean on the vessel?

Q. Yes; was he employed on the "Tahoma"?

Mr. ZIEGLER: Object as incompetent, irrevelant and immaterial; object as immaterial who was employed on the "Tahoma."

The COURT: I think it would be material whether or not he was employed at that time.

(Testimony of G. C. Woodward.)

Mr. ZIEGLER: Exception, if the court please.

Q. Do you know whether or not he was employed —during the time Johnson was acting as master was Tony Martinson employed aboard the "Tahoma"?

A. My understanding is he was working on the "Tahoma" before Johnson was master.

Q. Did he continue?

A. He continued.

Q. After Johnson was signed on the register as master?

A. Yes.

Q. Did you ever see anyone other than Johnson docking. the [119] schooner "Tahoma"?

A. I saw Captain Martinson in the pilot house handling the wheel as the boat docked on one occasion. I go down to the dock some mornings to get the fisheries statistics.

Q. Did you see Johnson at that time?

A. Johnson was on deck.

Q. Do you know what is the custom or practice of masters of halibut schooners as to docking the halibut schooner?

A. I don't profess to understand halibut fishing, but——

Mr. ZIEGLER: If the court please he doesn't know what the practice is.

Mr. FOLTA: He didn't finish tne answer yet.

Q. Mr. Woodward, have you watched halibut schooners being docked at Prince Rupert many times?

(Testimony of G. C. Woodward.)

A. Yes, it is part of my work.

Q. Ever seen any halibut schooners docked by anybody other than the master?

A. So far as I remember I did not, but of course I might not always know who the master of the boat is; I am not a fisherman.

Q. You say Martinson, previous to going on the "Tahoma" was master of the "Livingstone"?

A. My understanding—general knowledge.

Q. Do you know whether the "Livingstone" was an American or a Canadian vessel?

A. Canadian vessel.

Q. Do you know where Martinson is now?

A. I believe he was in Prince Rupert a short time ago. I understand he is still there.

Q. Do you know how many pounds of fish were shipped through [120] Prince Rupert from the "Tahoma" during the time that—from May 29th, 1933, to the time of the seizure?

A. May I refer to a memorandum?

Q. Yes.

A. This wouldn't necessarily represent the amount landed. It was the amount landed and sent to the United States. In some cases they are taken for home consumption. From the latter part of May, 1933 until the date of the seizure 318,960.

Q. Actually shipped?

A. Yes.

Mr. ZIEGLER: We move the answer be stricken as incompetent, immaterial and irrelevant, how

(Testimony of G. C. Woodward.)
much or how little halibut was brought into Prince
Rupert.

The COURT: Yes, I don't think it is material.

Mr. FOLTA: I offer it to show motive. We alleged fraudulent operation and on that point I think
it is competent to show it was done for gain.

The COURT: I think it is a matter of general
knowledge that a large amount of fish is shipped
through Prince Rupert.

Q. Did you have any dealings with F. E. Hunt,
Ltd., with reference to the payment of duty on
these shipments?

A. At the time the question of the possible alien
ownership in the vessel came up I thought I was
justified, under the instructions I received from the
Department of State, and Congress, to verbally suggest to buyers the possibility that duty might later
be assessed on the landings or shipments through
the United States of the halibut brought in by the
"Tahoma". Some question came up,—possibly [121]
lowering the value of the fish on the exchange,
and I was advised by Messrs. Hunt and Company
that the company would be responsible for any
duty should it be later assessed. In the meantime the
fish went through free of duty, as American fish.

Q. F. E. Hunt assumed the responsibility for
payment of the duty?

A. Should it later on be charged.

Q. Mr. Woodward, do you know about when,

(Testimony of G. C. Woodward.)

with reference to May 29th, 1933, there was a change in the masters on the "Wave"?

A. It was somewhere around that time, but I couldn't state without referring to the record.

Q. About the same time?

A. About the same time.

Q. May 29th, 1933. Mr. Woodward, I think you have already testified that prior to that time Petterson was part owner and master of the "Wave"?

A. He was owner of a half interest, and was master.

Q. After May 29th, 1933, who became the master of the "Wave" in Peterson or Petterson's place?

A. Captain Winnie Pierce.

Q. That is the claimant in this case?

A. Yes.

Q. In connection with the change of masters on the "Wave" let me also ask you whether there was a change in the ownership of the "Wave"?

A. It was transferred by Captain Petterson to Earnest Pierce—I forget the initials. I understand a brother of Captain Winnie Pierce; and later the other half interest was [122] transferred by the estate, or the heir, of the deceased owner of the other half interest.

The COURT: To what Pierce?

The WITNESS: To Earnest Pierce.

The COURT: The whole title, you say, was eventually transferred to Earnest Pierce?

The WITNESS: I don't recollect whether the second half was given to Earnest Pierce or Winnie.

(Testimony of G. C. Woodward.)
It was Earnest Pierce, yes, he took the entire interest and later it was transferred.

Q. I show you what purports to be a bill of
sale, and ask you what that is and whether you
recognize it?

A. The transfer of the half interest by Captain
Petterson was done through the office and they
brought up the bill of sale and it was acknowledged
before the notary, and the practice is that bills of
sale are notaried or acknowledged by a Consul so
they might use any bill of sale and it was made up
before the consul. This was the one which was
brought up first.

Mr. FOLTA: If the court please, we offer this
in evidence as Exhibit "12".

Mr. ZIEGLER: No objection.

(Testimony of G. C. Woodward.)

(Bill of sale was admitted in evidence and marked Libelant's Exhibit "12"; and is as follows, to-wit) : **[123]**

"Cat No. 1340

THE UNITED STATES OF AMERICA
Department of Commerce
Bureau of Navigation

BILL OF SALE OF REGISTERED VESSEL
(Secs. 4170, 4171, 4192, 4193, 4194 and 4196,
Revised Statutes, and Arts. 57 and 61,
Customs Regulations of 1923)

To All to Whom These Presents Shall Come, Greeting:

KNOW YE, That B. A. Petterson, *or* Prince Rupert, British Columbia one-half (½) owner of the Gas Screw or vessel called the Wave of the burden of seven (7) tons, or thereabouts, for and in consideration of the sum of Twenty-five Dollars (25.00) dollars, lawful money of the United States of America, to . . . in hand paid, before the sealing and delivery of these presents, by Earnest George Pierce of Prince Rupert, British Columbia the receipt whereof he does hereby acknowledge and is therewith fully satisfied, contented, and paid, have bargained and sold, and by these presents do bargain and sell, unto the said Ernest George Pierce of Prince Rupert, British Columbia . . . heirs, executors, administrators, and assigns, One-half (½) of the said Gas Screw or vessel, together with

(Testimony of G. C. Woodward.)

One-half (½) the masts, bowsprit, sails, boats, anchors, cables, tackle, furniture and all other necessaries thereunto appertaining and belonging; the latest CERTIFICATE OF REGISTRY of which said Gas Screw or vessel is as follows, viz: **[124]**

A True Copy of the Latest Certificate of Registry

Insert "Permanent" or　　　Official No.　Letters
"Temporary"

Permanent　　　　　　　　220,540
Register No. 27-A

THE UNITED STATES OF AMERICA
Department of Commerce
Bureau of Navigation

Length over all 40 feet　　Radio Call: ....
Measured Ketchikan, 1920 . Service: Fish
Rebuilt at.................... 1........　Number of Crew,
Remeasured :.................. 1........　　excluding Master: 2
　　　　　　　　　　　　　Horsepower: H. P. 25

CERTIFICATE OF REGISTRY

In Pursuance of Chapter One, Title XLVIII, 'Regulation of Commerce and Navigation,' Revised Statues of the United States,

Ben B.A.P. A. Petterson of Prince Rupert, British Columbia having taken and subscribed the oath required by law, and having sworn that he is the half-owner of the vessel called the Wave, of . . . whereof Ernest George Pierce is at present master, and is a citizen of the United States, and that the

(Testimony of G. C. Woodward.)

said vessel was built in the year 1920, at Ketchikan of wood, as appears by P L #3-A issued at Ketchikan September 16, 1920, now surrendered; Trade changed and said license having certified that the said vessel is a Gas Screw; that she has one deck, one mast, a sharp head, and a sharp stern; that her register length is 35.6/10 feet, her registered breadth 9.8/10 feet, her registered depth 4.8/10 feet, her height . . . /10 feet; that she measures as follows:

	Tons	100ths
Capacity under tonnage deck	10	50
Capacity between decks above tonnage deck		.
Capacity of inclosures on the upper deck, viz: Forecastle........; bridge........; poop........; break..........; houses-round..........; side..........; chart..........; radio..........; hatchway 0.21; light and air;		21
Gross Tonnage	10	71

(Testimony of G. C. Woodward.)

Deductions under Section 4153, Revised Statutes, as amended:

Crew space .... Master's cabin ....
Steering Gear................... Anchor gear ....
                               Boatswain's stores...
Chart house................... Donkey engine and
                               boiler ....
Storage of sails........... Radiohouse ....;
                               Propelling power
                               (actual space
                               2.73), 3.42
                               Total Deductions 3   42
                               _____
                               Net Tonnage 7   —

The following-described spaces, and no others, have [125] been omitted, viz; Forepeak..........., aft-peak............., open forecastle..........., open bridge..........., open poop..............., open shelterdeck..............., anchor gear..........., steering gear..........., donkey engine and boiler..........., other machinery spaces..........., light and air space over propelling machinery..........., companions..........., syklights..........., wheelhouse 1.37, galley..........., condenser..............., water-closets..............., cabins...............

_____

and the said...............having agreed to the description and admeasurement above specified, according to law, said vessel has been duly REGISTERED at this PORT.

(Testimony of G. C. Woodward.)

GIVEN under my hand and seal, at the Port of..........................., this..................day of..................., in the year one thousand nine hundred and.................

(Place for Seal...
of Comptroller   Comptroller of
of Customs?   Customs

(Place for Seal..
of Collector   Collector of
                             Customs

      (Seal of the
      Department of...
      Commerce)   Commissioner of
                             Navigation

TO HAVE AND TO HOLD the said Gas Screw or Vessel..........and appurtenances thereunto belonging unto him the said Ernest George Pierce One-half (½) heirs, executors, administrators and assigns, to the sole and only proper use, benefit and behoof of the said Ernest George Pierce one-half (½) his heirs, executors, administrators, and assigns forever; And...........the said.............................has promised, covenanted, and agreed, and by these presents do......... promise, covenant and agree, for himself, his heirs, executors, administrators and assigns to and with the said Ernest George Pierce his heirs, executors, administrators, and assigns to warrant and defend the said Gas Screw or........... vessel and all the other before-mentioned appurtenances against all and every person and persons whomsoever...........

(Testimony of G. C. Woodward.)

IN TESTIMONY WHEREOF, The said B. A. Petterson has hereunto set his hand and seal this 4th day of December, in the year of our Lord one thousand nine hundred and Thirty-three.

B. A. PETTERSON [Seal]

Signed, sealed and [Seal]

delivered in presence of:— [Seal]

G. W. Nickerson

Prince Rupert B. C. Canada.

Province of British Columbia

County of Prince Rupert—ss.

BE IT KNOWN, That on this 7th day of December, 1933, personally appeared before me, B. A. Petterson..................and acknowledged the within instrument to be his free act and deed. [126]

IN TESTIMONY WHEREOF, I have hereunto set my hand and seal this 7th day of December, A. D. 1933.

[Notarial Seal] J. E. COLLART

Notary Public in and for the Province of British Columbia.

(Testimony of G. C. Woodward.)

(Blànk across the back as follows):

Cat. No. 1340

DEPARTMENT OF COMMERCE

BUREAU OF NAVIGATION

BILL OF SALE

of

REGISTERED VESSEL

....

to

....

Called the ....

Customhouse ....

.... 19.........

Received for record.....................h.

.................m. ....M.

Recorded, book....................................

page ....

....

Collector of Customs.''

————

The COURT: Did I understand you to say a moment ago Winnie Pierce became Captain and master of the ''Wave'' after the transfer from Petterson to Pierce, or one of them?

The WITNESS: He became master before the transfer [127] was made. Captain Petterson ceased operating the boat before the transfer was made, and on his authority I appointed Captain Winnie Pierce as master.

(Testimony of G. C. Woodward.)

Q. That is the claimant here?

A. Yes, that is the claimant here.

Q. Mr. Pierce, the claimant, became master of the "Wave"?

A. Yes. That was prior to the transfer of the "Wave", that is on the register of the Customs House, prior to the transfer to Earnest Pierce.

Q. Prior to the record of it?

A. Prior to the record of it in the Customs House.

Q. Mr. Woodward, can you tell by looking at that bill of sale to whom that bill of sale was first made out?

Mr. ZIEGLER: I think it speaks for itself.

A. If I am wrong in what I am stating, stop me; but Captain Petterson told me he had made a bill of sale to Winnie Pierce.

Mr. ZIEGLER: If the court please—what kind of testimony is that—what somebody told him. Objcet to it and move it be stricken.

Mr. FOLTA: It is competent because they are all conspirators. The acts and doings of one is the acts and doings of all, and the transfer of the boat, as evidenced by these letters and what Petterson said and what Winnie Pierce said are part of the res gestae. It is not necessary the conspiracy be alleged before evidence relating to the conspiracy has operation.

Mr. ZIEGLER: I think even if counsel contends this evidence tends to support a conspiracy he must

(Testimony of G. C. Woodward.)

at least lay the foundation for its admission as evidence. All he [128] has is a theory that there was an agreement by all these parties to evade the United States customs laws.

(Further argument) (Mr. Folta cited a case which was brought and shown to the court.)

The COURT: I am not satisfied that this case is in point. It has to do with prohibition cases. I don't know whether it would be applicable to this class of case or not. It is purely a criminal proceeding also. At any rate that, and some other phases of the case, will have to be gone into later, and it is going to be received subject to the right to object further.

Mr. ZIEGLER: That will be satisfactory, if the court please.

(Further slight argument.)

Mr. FOLTA: I think the question was answered.

Q. Mr. Woodward, will you examine Libellant's exhibit "12" and state whether or not you can tell to whom that was first made out, or who the transferree was first named in it?

A. May I state it is part of the duty of the Consul to satisfy himself that a vessel is properly owned. It is part of the duty of the consul the same as a customs officer; in order to show why I checked on this bill of sale. In doing so I found that in the underscoring it had originally been made out to Winnie Pierce in two places and that the date had been changed.

(Testimony of G. C. Woodward.)

Q. What had the date been?

A. I put it under a magnifying glass at the time
and it seemed to be August 30th. I questioned Captain Petterson regarding the transfer, and in order
to satisfy the [129] records I had him make a written statement as to the fact that he had transferred
the vessel.

Q. Did Petterson say under what circumstances
he transferred the "Wave"?

A. That it was for debts he owed Messrs. Hunt
and Company—his understanding was——

(Question read.)

Mr. ZIEGLER: Object to that as hearsay, incompetent, irrelevant and immaterial, and for the
other reasons made to all testimony concerning this
bill of sale.

The COURT: It all goes back to the same question. It may be received on the same basis.

Q. Mr. Woodward, in stating to you that he
made this transfer that is, when Petterson stated
to you he made this transfer of his equity in the
"Wave" to Pierce in payment of his indebtedness
to F. E. Hunt, Ltd., did he say what the amount
of his indebtedness was?

A. It was something like a thousand dollars
which he owed the company for supplies and three
hundred cases—I can't say. I would have to refer
to the statement, but it was something like that.
That was for the half interest that he owned.

Q. Mr. Woodward, is it customary for the master
of a halibut schooner to sign the stock sheets?

(Testimony of G. C. Woodward.)

A. It is a requirement of the Consulate; it is not in the regulations, but I have had that done in order to check with their affidavits. In some cases they would come up before the stock sheet came up and I would check the stock sheet against the affidavit.

Q. Explain what a stock sheet is. [130]

A. A statement of sale of halibut showing the quality, quantity and amount—price per pound and total price. The buyers have it made in duplicate and furnish one to my office, and it is kept on the files until the fish is shipped.

Q. Did you require the master of the boat to sign it?

A. Yes, in order to identify it.

Q. Do you know who signed the stock sheets for the "Tahoma" during the time Johnson was signed on as master?

Mr. ZIEGLER: Object as immaterial. The consul already stated it is not a matter of law but a requirement of his own.

Mr. FOLTA: I am not seeking to give it force. It is only evidence showing who was in charge of the boat.

The COURT: The question is in what capacity he signed it.

Mr. FOLTA: But he testified he required the master to sign the stock sheet.

(Testimony of G. C. Woodward.)

Mr. ZIEGLER: Is an American Consul supposed to protect American subject, to come into court and say he lays down arbitrary rules in a foreign port, which may be used against American citizens. It is purely a personal whim, and I think it will develop how it was laid down before the testimony is through. I object to it as incompetent.

The COURT: I don't think it makes any difference. If he had gone into a grocery store and bought supplies and the owner required him to receipt for them or the clerk in the grocery store, it would not make any difference how it came up. It is a question in what capacity [131] he signed and whether he did. I think he may answer on that theory.

Q. Do you know who signed the stock sheet and in whose handwriting it was?

A. It is left to the discretion of the Consul to carefully check the landing and shipment. It came to my attention that a stock sheet was produced signed by Martinson, Tony Martinson. I referred it back to the buyer, stating it would be necessary to have the master sign it and on checking back and comparing the handwriting I found the stock sheet had been signed—this was when Johnson was first put on as master—that some stock sheets had been signed in the name of Johnson but in the handwriting of Martinson.

Mr. ZIEGLER: I move that the answer be stricken. He is willing to go a long ways, and he is

(Testimony of G. C. Woodward.)

qualifying now as a handwriting expert. The documents are not presented; and he expresses the opinion the signature is in somebody else's writing.

The COURT: I think it is too far afield.

Q. Have you any of those stock sheets with you?

A. No, but I have the affidavits showing the handwriting of Martinson and Johnson. Stock sheets are not kept after the halibut is shipped; only so long as it is on hand.

Q. Will you produce one of the affidavits showing the handwriting of Johnson and the handwriting of Martinson?

A. May I go downstairs.

Q. Yes.

(Recess 10 minutes; reconvened as before with witness Woodward on the stand.) [132]

Q. Mr. Woodward, did you get a sample of the signature of Johnson and Martinson?

A. That is the affidavit that the master makes of the landing.

Q. This is a stock sheet?

A. No; it is the affidavit required by the Treasury Department. The stock sheet is on the buyer's form.

Mr. FOLTA: I offer this in evidence as Libellant's Exhibit "13":

Mr. ZIEGLER: I don't see the materiality of it. I don't have any particular objection to it going in, but I must object to it because it is immaterial.

Mr. FOLTA: It is all corroboration.

(Testimony of G. C. Woodward.)

(Further argument.)

The COURT: I don't think it would be admissible, unless you expect to follow them up with the sheets themselves.

(Further argument.)

The COURT: There is nothing in these that shows that Martinson was the master. That one states Johnson was master and the other that B. A. Petterson was master.

(Further argument.)

The COURT: Of course there is nothing here for a basis of comparison. If there was that would be another matter.

(Exhibit "13" was accordingly rejected as evidence.)

Mr. FOLTA: Note an exception.

Mr. FOLTA: I think that is all.

Mr. ZIEGLER: If the Court please, I would like to have permission for Mr. Woodward to step down a minute so I can recall Mr. Vernon for one question on cross [133] examination.

The COURT: Very well.

PAUL R. VERNON,

recalled, testified further as follows:

Cross-Examination

By Mr. ZIEGLER:

Q. Mr. Vernon, you testified here you had Arthur Johnson sign a statement dated October 10th, 1933, regarding the American oil screw "Ta-

(Testimony of Paul R. Vernon.)

homa" which statement was introduced and marked
Libellant's exhibit "10" dated October 10th, 1933.
Before you had that statement made out, Mr.
Vernon, you received word from Mr. Woodward,
didn't you.

A. No.

Q. Did you receive word from any Customs official?

A. Yes.

Q. Don't you know that came from Mr. Woodward?

A. No.

Q. You don't know that yourself?

A. No.

Q. But it isn't customary for you to have this
kind of a statement made out?

A. Not unless additional circumstances call
for it.

Mr. ZIEGLER: That is all.

(Witness Excused.) [134]

G. C. WOODWARD,

recalled, testified further as follows:

Cross Examination

By Mr. ZIEGLER:

Q. Mr. Woodward, how long have you been
American Consul there at Prince Rupert?

A. Since October, 1927.

(Testimony of G. C. Woodward.)

Q. Since October, 1927; and what are your duties, generally, there, as American Consul?

A. They cover quite a wide range, including invoicing, registering American citizens, looking after distressed seamen, taking care of American vessels. The principal work of the Consulate and the reason for the Consulate being there is checking through the fish produce of the American fisheries.

Q. One of the prime reasons for the creation of your office, or any consulate, is to look after the interests of American citizens, isn't it?

A. Yes.

Mr. FOLTA: Object, as calling for a legal conclusion and not on any phase of the case.

Mr. ZIEGLER: It is preliminary. I want to follow it up to show there is feeling in this case between the gentleman on the stand and the people on the various sides that affects his whole testimony.

The COURT: I think, as a matter of fact, we all know the principal duties of the American Consul are of course to look after the interests of American citizens. We don't need any testimony on that subject.

Q. It is no part of your duty to see that the duty on goods [135] going to Canada, on fish going in there, is paid to Canada, is it?

Mr. FOLTA: Object as incompetent and immaterial.

Mr. ZIEGLER: We claim it is competent as showing his interest in the case, if he has attempted to do that.

(Testimony of G. C. Woodward.)

The COURT: The duty due Canada?

Mr. ZIEGLER: Yes, collectible by the Canadian authorities. If he interests himself, as American Consul, in seeing they get their duties it is beyond his province.

Mr. FOLTA: This man doesn't have anything to do with Canadian duties.

The COURT: Yes. I think it is going a long way afield.

Q. Mr. Woodward before July 21st, 1933, you came to the conclusion in your own mind, didn't you, that the American oil screw "Tahoma" was taken over by F. E. Hunt and Company?

A. Not in my own mind,—from general information I received.

Q. General gossip?

A. It followed other vessels had been handled in the same manner. Part of my duty is to protect the American Government, as well as American citizens.

Q. I concede it is, and I am not criticizing you for that, but you, in one way, determined either by information received in regular channels, or gossip and different round-about ways, that Pierce had sold the "Tahoma" to F. E. Hunt Company, didn't you?

A. I don't know how to answer that. It is part of my duty to protect the American Government. I do that when possible, when it comes to my attention, I do what I can [136] about it.

Mr. ZIEGLER: Withdraw the question.

(Testimony of G. C. Woodward.)

Mr. FOLTA: Object to that.

Q. Isn't it a fact that you suspected—put it this way:—that you suspected that Hunt Company had purchased the "Tahoma" and held an interest in the "Tahoma" before you took this statement from Arthur Johnson?

A. I was given to understand that, as I stated before, from general information. It was general information on the waterfront.

Q. You believed that information, didn't you?

A. I don't believe information that is general. I check. If I get corroborative evidence I furnish the department with it. I don't take hearsay.

Q. From what you heard you really believed, in your own mind, this sale had taken place, didn't you?

A. I don't believe I have authority to believe something I cannot prove.

Q. What is your opinion about it.

Mr. FOLTA: Object to any opinions.

The COURT: I think the witness already explained the whole proposition. He says when information of that kind comes to him it is his duty to investigate, and he did investigate it.

Mr. ZIEGLER: I want to find out what he bases the information on. He stated once it was on waterfront gossip.

Mr. FOLTA: He doesn't have to disclose the source of his information under any circumstances. The only question is whether the information he had is competent. [137]

(Testimony of G. C. Woodward.)

The COURT: The only thing the Court wants to know is whether it was in pursuance of this information he had that he took this affidavit from Johnson.

Q. You had heard this talk around, about the sale of the "Tahoma" to F. E. Hunt, and after hearing that you took the affidavit from Johnson, didn't you?

A. I had a statement from Johnson.

Q. You had a statement from Johnson that was dated July 21st, 1933?

A. It shows here.

Q. That is the correct date, isn't it?

A. If that is the date on the statement.

Q. I understood you to say when you testified that this is the form of statement that you take from masters when they are signed on boats, is that correct?

A. I am afraid——

Mr. ZIEGLER: I withdraw that.

Q. Did you—or do you take a statement from all masters when they sign on American vessels in Canadian ports?

Mr. FOLTA: Object as immaterial—what he does in other cases.

Mr. ZIEGLER: It is cross examination; and we contend we have a right to develop the fact, if true, that Mr. Woodward had an unusual interest in establishing the fact in this case. I am not saying Mr. Woodward is not correct, but it is cross examination of his interest in the matter.

(Testimony of G. C. Woodward.)

Mr. FOLTA: The interest has to be pecuniary; not an interest in seeing the laws are observed.

(Further argument.)

The COURT: He may ask him. [138]

Q. Do you take statements from masters that are signed on these halibut boats, on the American halibut boats, at Prince Rupert?

A. Depending entirely on circumstances. We are given a wide range of discretion in immigration and shipping restrictions, and all cases. Whenever a case comes to our attention that arouses suspicion we have authority to investigate. We do that when necessary. If it is not necessary and there is no occasion for it we don't do it.

Q. Unless there are suspicious circumstances or something that requires investigation on your part in your official capacity, you do not take these statements, do you?

A. It is uniform in so far as when it is needed.

Q. Who determines when it is needed?

A. It lies with the consulate official—part of our duties.

Q. Let's understand each other: You do not take these statements in every case, only in a case where——

A. In the opinion of the consulate it is necessary.

Q. Can't you answer that question "Yes" or "No."

The COURT: He answered the question.

A. I am trying to explain that the matter is left to the discretion of the consulate official. In foreign

(Testimony of G. C. Woodward.)

countries we are allowed a great deal of latitude in matters dealing with registration, passports, immigration, and notarial work—dozens and dozens of different subjects.

Q. I understand that it is entirely in your discretion?

A. Yes. Personality never enters into it; makes additional work.

Q. You had heard these circumstances in connection with the sale of the "Tahoma" so you got hold of Johnson and [139] investigated?

A. I couldn't say I "got hold of Johnson". Johnson voluntarily came to the office and said he had an opportunity to become master of the "Tahoma". Under our regulations he was required to prove American citizenship. There are other statements I secured from him besides that.

Q. When he came to go through the usual formality of signing on as master is that the time you took the statement from him?

A. I would not be able to state unless I saw the date of his signing on.

Q. Any way to determine that?

A. I presume it would be in the records of the consulate.

Q. You haven't them here?

A. I could not fortell this.

Q. What did you say to Johnson when you asked for this statement?

A. It has been quite a while ago. I couldn't state how it came up; purely in conversation; I knew he

(Testimony of G. C. Woodward.)
was only a young lad of twenty. The question of
citizenship never came up before. He had difficulty
proving his citizenship through his parents.

Q.   The law is that is the only qualification necessary to be endorsed on as a master, isn't that correct? In other words, an American subject comes
into your office and proves he is a citizen of the
United States and wants to be signed on a certain
halibut boat. You cannot refuse him that right, can
you?

A.   We can refuse him that right until we have
proper authority [140] from the persons having
charge of the vessel.

Q.   You would not assume he was going to sign
on some boat that would not consent would you?

A.   I have had occasions.

Q.   Did that situation arise in this case?

A.   Not in that case.

Q.   Isn't it a fact, in making this statement you
did it with the idea in mind of establishing the fact
that the "Tahoma" had been sold by Pierce to F.
E. Hunt Company? Wasn't that part of the idea
you had in mind?

A.   It makes no difference to the consulate who
owns the vessel so long as it is owned by an American citizen. The duty of the Consul is to see the
statutes are complied with in regard to ownership
of American vessels. It requires one hundred per
cent American ownership on an American vessel. I
presume that it what you are asking.

(Testimony of G. C. Woodward.)

Q. What I am trying to get at is this. If you hadn't heard anything about these rumors about the sale of the "Tahoma" would you have required this statement from Johnson?

Mr. FOLTA: Object.

The COURT: Sustained.

Q. Prior to the time you got this statement did you have any altercation with F. E. Hunt Company about this boat? Did you discuss it with them prior to the time you got the statement from Johnson?

A. If my recollection serves me right I think the question of duty came up. I think the letter I received from him protecting the Government against——

Q. You insisted, as American Consul, didn't you, that there [141] should be a two cent duty on halibut coming in on the "Tahoma"?

A. No, I didn't insist. I did not have authority to insist. I had nothing to do with the collection of duty. My duty in connection with that class of work ·is to see the export or trans-shipment to the United States,—that the alleged product of American fisheries doesn't exceed the amount landed, as well as the ownership of the vessels by American citizens.

Q. If there was a question about the nationality you would send a memorandum along to the buyers, wouldn't you, about the nationality of the fish? Wouldn't you send a memorandum to the buyers of the fish in Prince Rupert?

(Testimony of G. C. Woodward.)

A.   In ordinary cases the fish is not permitted to be invoiced until proof is furnished to the Consulate. In this case the question arose.

Q.   Did you then send a note to the buyers about the duty on this fish?

A.   No.

Q.   Did you do that at any time?

A.   No.

Q.   Talk to them about it?

A.   I notified them verbally the question might arise.

Q.   What did you say to them?

A.   That was all—that the question might later arise as to the halibut being dutiable.

Q.   You asked Mr. Pierce, prior to this date you questioned him about the ownership of the "Tahoma" and the "Wave", didn't you?

A.   Which Mr. Pierce? [142]

Q.   Winnie Pierce.

A.   I believe I required him to furnish and give me an affidavit as to the ownership. We have a form for that, a customs form.

Q.   Have you that affidavit?

A.   I don't believe it is here.

Q.   You didn't bring that along?

A.   No.

Q.   Do you remember what he said in the affidavit?

A.   It is a form which states that the—words to this eyect—that the ownership as shown on the register is the true ownership.

(Testimony of G. C. Woodward.)

Q. He made such an affidavit?

A. I believe he did.

Q. Didn't you just say he did?

A. My recollection is I required him to make an affidavit, as well as others during that period; it is customary when there is a doubt.

Q. You had Mr. Pierce make one of these affidavits in 1933 didn't you, when Johnson was on the boat?

A. I am sorry I couldn't recollect the date.

Q. You had him make two, didn't you, as to the ownership?

A. I couldn't recollect the dates, whether I required two or not, but I know I required several boats, or the owners or masters of several boats to make these affidavits, as a protection.

Q. For whom?

A. For the Consulate, as to being true ownership.

Q. The one that you demanded, and to which you were entitled from Pierce, was given before you got this statement from [143] Johnson, wasn't it?

A. I couldn't say whether it was before or after. I would not be able to recollect.

Q. I will hand you here a carbon copy of a letter, and ask you if that will refresh your memory?

A. I remember receiving a letter similar to this. I presume this is a copy.

Q. Hadn't you gotten the statement from Pierce before that?

(Testimony of G. C. Woodward.)

A. I could not tell you; I could not remember.

Q. Mr. Pierce complained over there, didn't he, Mr. Woodward, to you and to the Treasury Department, about the treatment he had received at your hands? You knew that, didn't you?

A. No, I didn't know that.

Q. Didn't you receive copies of those letters?

A. From whom?

Q. From the Treasury Department?

A. Not that I am aware of. I think I would remember if I received a complaint, because that is naturally something you do remember.

The COURT: Did you say you did receive such correspondence, or didn't?

The WITNESS: This letter is a copy of a letter I presume I received from Winnie Pierce, yes. I understood him to say it was a letter from the Treasury Department complaining.

Q. You did receive a letter from Pierce?

A. I received a letter from him, that——

Q. In which he complained about you notifying the buyers over there that the fish landed from the "Tahoma" might be dutiable and he notified you he was taking the matter [144] up with the Treasury Department?

A. If that letter says that—I think that is a copy of the letter I received—I have a great deal of work over at the consulate.

Q. Read it over.

(Testimony of G. C. Woodward.)

Mr. FOLTA: I object to questions about the letter, and the witness reading it, as having nothing to do with the case. The fact that Mr. Pierce made a complaint is not relevant.

(Slight argument.)

The COURT: I don't see how it affects the issues in the case.

Mr. ZIEGLER: The only purpose of the testimony is affecting the interest of Mr. Woodward. I might state to the court that we intend to prove that as a result of these conversations had between Mr. Woodward and Mr. Pierce, regarding this ownership and notifying the buyers of these things that Mr. Pierce was obliged to find out where he stood in Prince Rupert with respect to the fish delivered from these boats, that he took it to the proper authority at Washington, the Treasury Department, and that the Treasury Department, after these things happened, wrote him a letter and told him the fish were not dutiable and the manner in which he was operating the "Tahoma" out of that port raised no objection on the part of the Treasury Department of the United States.

The COURT: That raises a lot of collateral issues. If it affected the duty payable to the Canadian Government it would be none of the American Consul's business. If it affected the fish shipped in transit from Prince [145] Rupert to American markets it would be subject to American duty and would be the Consul's business.

(Further argument.)

(Testimony of G. C. Woodward.)

The COURT: It seems to me that is what any sane man would have done under those circumstances, either prove or disprove whether there was any basis for a complaint or not. I don't know what else a man would do under circumstances of that kind.

Q. Now, Mr. Woodward, after receiving this affidavit from Johnson in which he stated that he was employed by F. E. Hunt, and agreed to act as master of the "Tahoma" you then notified the authorities on this side, didn't you?

A. My recollection is I notified the Department at Washington, D. C.

Q. You never sent any word directly to the Customs here?

A. I don't know whether I am permitted to disclose the workings of the office or not.

Mr. FOLTA: Object to the question anyway. It doesn't make any difference what his methods were.

The COURT: I don't think it is material, what he did in pursuance of his employment.

Mr. ZIEGLER: I appreciate that, but I cannot develop the case all at one time. Here is a statement taken by Mr. Woodward in which Johnson signed he was to get ten per cent in addition to the regular share, and one signed by Vernon, or vice versa, in which he says five per cent. We contend they are circumstances to be taken into consideration,—how

(Testimony of G. C. Woodward.)

they were gotten, whether because of suggestions made to them, whether any form of [146] duress or coercion was used to get a statement, and on top of that we propose to show the statement gotten by the Department of Justice from Johnson before he died, which is later than this and repudiates these statements. Isn't it competent evidence to show—investigate that and find out how the statements were gotten, and the circumstances?

Mr. FOLTA: I offer the affidavit of Johnson before he died.

Mr. ZIEGLER: I want it admitted.

Mr. FOLTA: I offer it right now.

The COURT: It may be admitted then.

(Affidavit of Johnson was then admitted in evidence as Libellant's exhibit "13"; and is as follows, to-wit:)

State of Arizona
County of Pima—ss.

I, JOHN ARTHUR JOHNSON, after having been duly sworn, upon oath, depose and say:

I was born at Tacoma, Washington on June 29, 1911 but have lived in the Province of Canada at Prince Rupert, B. C. since I was two years of age. I am a citizen of the United States.

I have been employed as a fisherman on my stepfather's boat, Margaret I, off and on since 1929, which boat is under Canadian registry and has operated out of Prince Rupert and has been engaged in halibut fishing in Hecate Straits.

About May 22, 1933 when I returned from a fishing trip, I heard about fisherman's dock at Prince Rupert that I was to be made the Master of the Tahoma, an oil screw vessel, which I thought belonged to Winnie Pierce, an old but not intimate acquaintance [147] of mine. The next day, May 23, I ran into Mr. Pierce at the wharf and in talking to him I asked him if I was to be made Master of the Tahoma. He replied that he didn't know. Later on in the day I also met Antone Martinson at the Wharf. I had known Mr. Martinson for several years. He asked me if I would act as Master of the Tahoma and clear the boat for him. He did not tell me what his connection with the boat was but I assumed he had been made Master and wanted me to clear the boat because it was under American registry and I was an American Citizen. He did not tell me what my share would be but I also assumed it would be the customary fisherman's share plus ten per cent of the boat's share. Mr. Martinson was very vague at this time and did not tell me definitely about my employment.

On May 23, 1933, I went to see Mr. Woodward, American Consul at Prince Rupert who told me he would give me the papers on the Tahoma and would permit me to clear it. I did not ask for the papers on the boat at that time.

It was very common gossip around Prince Rupert that F. E. Hunt Ltd., had taken over the Tahoma because Pierce could not pay what he owed the company. The F. E. Hunt Ltd. is a Ship's Chandlery. Several days after I talked to Mr. Pierce, Mr. Martinson and the American Consul, I went to see Mr. Milward Nickerson, Manager of the F. E. Hunt Ltd. about my commission on the Tahoma. I had a conversation with him alone at the store in which he told me Mr. Martinson was to be Captain and that I was to act as Master for the purpose of clearing the boat. He said I would receive in addition to a fisherman's share, five percent of the boat's share.

About three weeks after my conversation with Mr. Nickerson and on the date of sailing I obtained the boat's papers from the American Consul at Prince Rupert. I was notified of the sailing date by Mr. Martinson who had been given the commission of [148] Captain. On this trip and on seven other trips I cleared the boat. I gave up my commission about October 27, 1933 at the end of the halibut season.

On five of the above mentioned trips we fished in Hecate Straits. On the last three trips we fished off the coast of Alaska. We fished for Halibut entirely and brought all catches to Prince Rupert and disposed of the fish at the Public market. The check for the fish was made out in my name and I immediately turned it over to Mr. Nickerson, who would pay off the crew in cash. I do not know what he did with the balance of the boat's share after paying Martinson and me.

All provisions for the Tahoma were obtained from F. E. Hunt Ltd., and were paid for out of the proceeds of the sale of the fish which were turned over to Mr. Nickerson. The provisions were charged to the boat. The fuel for the boat was obtained from the Union Oil Company, was also charged to the boat and paid for by The F. E. Hunt Ltd.

At no time did I receive any orders from Mr. Pierce and at no time while I was in command of the boat was Mr. Pierce aboard. All my orders came from Mr. Martinson. Mr. Pierce was not present at any of the times I turned over the checks to Mr. Nickerson and as far as I know never received any part of the boat's share.

I know Mr. Capstick, bookkeeper for the F. E. Hunt Ltd. but I have never talked to him about the Tahoma. I have heard of the Atlas Engine Company and the Fishing Vessel Owners Marine Ways but I do not know and have not talked to anyone connected with these concerns.

I do not know who owns the Tahoma and I have never discussed the boat's ownership with any person.

JOHN ARTHUR JOHNSEN [149]

(Testimony of G. C. Woodward.)

Subscribed and sworn to before me at Tucson, Arizona, this Third day of October, 1934.

L. C. TAYLOR

Special Agent, Division of Investigation, United States Department of Justice, Los Angeles, California.''

[Endorsed]: ''Lbls. Exhibit No. 13 received in evidence Jun 6 1935 in cause No. 1778-KA. Robert E. Coughlin, Clerk. By..Deputy.''

Mr. ZIEGLER: If that is admitted I want a copy of the special investigator's report on this same man, to have all the things before the court.

The COURT: You just asked to have it admitted. I am admitting it on the joint request of both counsel.

Mr. ZIEGLER: I take it they will all be admitted if the Court finally rules the others to which I objected are admissible.

The COURT: It will be received on the same theory.

Q. Mr. Woodward, you testified to something in connection with other qualifications of Johnson as master on the boat. Haven't you seen boats moving around the harbor and docking around Prince Rupert and other waterfront places where people are at the wheel moving the boat around who are not the master? You know that, don't you? [150]

(Testimony of G. C. Woodward.)

A. I think I stated a while ago I was not sufficiently familiar with the masters of the various vessels, and I paid no attention to the Canadian vessels, so I paid no attention to the people at the wheel.

Q. Don't you know down in your own heart, as a matter of fact, the master is not always at the wheel or in the wheel house? You know that don't you?

A. I don't doubt at all there are occasions—but I am not in a position to state truthfully, because I am not familiar with the various captains.

Q. When Mr. Pierce came in to sign on as master of the "Wave", Winnie Pierce, did you ask him about his qualifications to navigate a boat?

A. From conversation with Captain Winnie Pierce I knew he had been fishing halibut for probably twenty-five years. I did not raise the question because I did not know; I would conclude he is a qualified man.

Q. Is it any part of your official business to inquire into the navigational ability of a man who wants to sign on as master? Isn't the only reason you did in this case of Arthur Johnson that you heard this waterfront gossip about the sale of the "Tahoma" and were trying to get something on F. E. Hunt?

A. I have no reason for wanting to get something on F. E. Hunt. My business ends when I prove to my satisfaction that ownership in an

(Testimony of G. C. Woodward.)

American vessel is American. The question of who owns a vessel doesn't concern me at all, if it is alien.

Q. After Mr. Pierce gave you this affidavit of ownership you were not satisfied with it? [151]

A. I cannot recall when I got it.

Q. But he did give it to you?

A. Yes.

Q. You were not satisfied with it?

A. I cannot tell when I received it.

Q. When you did receive it were you satisfied?

A. There are occasions when we have to accept written evidence until we find something to the contrary. We accept a man's oath for what it is until something to the contrary turns up.

Q. Did you believe he committed perjury when he signed it?

Mr. FOLTA: Object as incompetent, irrelevant and immaterial.

A. I don't know whether I am without the bounds of regulations——

. The COURT: I suppose the purpose of all these questions is to develop whether or not there was any feeling on the part of the Consul.

Mr. ZIEGLER: Yes.

The COURT: I don't think the testimony on the whole tends to prove or disprove that issue.

Q. Now, Mr. Woodward, you testified about a bill of sale here and said you used a magnifying glass. You were pretty much interested in this case, weren't you?

(Testimony of G. C. Woodward.)

A. The bill of sale was presented in a changed form.

Q. And you were very much interested on account of your suspicion of irregular ownership of the "Tahoma" weren't you?

A. No more so than any other case which would have come up. I have other cases, several cases. I have no personal [152] feeling in any of those matters.

Q. This bill of sale was never even put through the Customs House was it?

A. If there is no mark on it it would not be.

Q. You know it wasn't; you know it was never used, don't you?

A. I only know it was signed and sent to the office.

Q. They left it in your office—never took it away?

A. They secured a new one.

Q. Why didn't you tell the court about that?

A. I believe I said a while ago—I explained that —a bill of sale of a vessel is sworn to before an American Consul and I stated that at the time.

Q. On all of these bills of sale they don't have to go before the American Consul?

A. If they don't come before the American Consul I have no authority.

Q. Didn't I just understand you to say that all of these bills of sale have to be taken before the Consul?

(Testimony of G. C. Woodward.)

A. Yes, so far as I understand my regulations.

Q. Don't you know as a fact, as a matter of law, they do not have to do that. If I own a boat at Prince Rupert I can go before a notary public and execute a bill of sale and don't have to go before the Consul?

Mr. FOLTA: Object as incompetent, irrelevant and immaterial, no bearing on the case.

The COURT: It is made out before a notary public. He explained that before and told you how it should be properly taken before the consul. As I understand he also stated previously that they never made any subsequent bill of sale before the Consul. Is that the fact? [153]

A. They never acknowledged the bill of sale before me, no.

(The COURT): I think the witness explained that before.

Q. They did make out a bill of sale after this one?

A. Yes, it was acknowledged and accepted by the consulate in place of that one.

Q. And this was acknowledged before a notary public. Do you know why the new bill of sale was made out—a different one?

A. I presume at my suggestion it be acknowlelged before the American Consul. They presented that to me. If a Collector admits a bill of sale on

(Testimony of G. C. Woodward.)

the record without a certificate it doesn't concern
my office, because I have no jurisdiction; it is entirely on the opinion of the Collector.

Q. You stated you had a conversation with Petterson?

A. You mean Captain Petterson?

Q. At the time this bill of sale was made out,
and that he was to receive credit for his indebtedness to Hunt.

A. I didn't say that the statement was made. Do
you mean that bill of sale?

Q. No. I don't recall the time you fixed when
that statement was made?

A. He made the statement to me that on or about
June 15th he made out a bill of sale which was
made out, if I recollect, either by the bookkeeper or
manager of Hunt and Company.

Q. What year?

A. 1933.

Q. What did you say then—he made a bill of
sale?

A. He signed the bill of sale. **[154]**

Q. On what boat?

A. On the "Wave".

Q. What did he say?

A. He stated that——

Q. That was the "Wave"?

A. Yes, it was the "Wave". He was half owner
in the "Wave".

Q. He said he made a bill of sale out to the
bookkeeper?

(Testimony of G. C. Woodward.)

A. No, he signed a bill of sale that had been made out or prepared by the bookkeeper or manager, I just don't recollect; and signed it. I can't tell whether he signed it in blank or by someone else.

Q. You haven't that statement here?

A. Is it with those papers—I believe it is there.

Q. Mr. Woodward, Johnson went on the "Tahoma" about May 29th, 1933, didn't he?

A. I believe there is a statement there showing when he was made master; whatever the date is it would be somewhere around there.

Q. Do you recall when he went out?

A. I recall when he went out, but as to the exact date I don't know.

Q. Was it about that time, was it in May?

A. I would imagine it would be. I think,—I can't recall offhand.

Q. It was sometime—he went on the boat as master quite sometime before you got this statement from him dated July 21st, didn't he?

A. I couldn't tell the date, because it has been quite sometime. We handle a number of vessels in the office. I could not verify the date unless it is in the papers there. [155]

Q. Do you know whether or not it is a fact that he went out actually as the master on the boat quite sometime before you got the statement from him?

A. He may have, but I could not say without verifying.

(Testimony of G. C. Woodward.)

Q. You didn't get this statement from him the day he came to see you, to sign on as master, did you?

A. I think I have two statements from him and just when the dates were I can't tell you, whether before he signed as master or after. If I had the records here I could turn to it.

Q. Where is the other paper?

A. If it is not among the papers I presume it is in the consulate.

Q. Did you take two statements from him concerning the work on the "Tahoma", his capacity on the "Tahoma"?

A. Two statements, but I couldn't tell you what they are about.

Q. Why didn't you bring the other statement with you?

A. Is the other statement there?

Mr. FOLTA: I don't know.

Mr. ZIEGLER: I wish you would investigate and find out. I want to find out if he has made another different statement.

A. I imagine that is what I referred to.

Q. You got another statement from him then, did you?

A. It was simply a conversation I wrote down when I was there. Later I had him sign that statement. It is dated July 20th.

Q. Read what it says.

Mr. FOLTA: I think it should be offered in [156] evidence first.

Mr. ZIEGLER: We offer it in evidence, if the court please. We are not in our defense yet.

The COURT: It may be received.

(Said paper was received in evidence and marked Libellant's Exhibit "15" and is as follows, to-wit:)

"Prince Rupert, B. C., Canada, July 20, 1933.

Confidential interview with John Arthur Johnson in connection with ownership of the American halibut schooner "Tahoma" of Ketchikan.

He admitted that his experience as a halibut fisherman, as indicated below, is not sufficient to warrant his being employed as the master of a halibut fishing vessel the size of the "Tahoma" and that his American citizenship was the reason for his employment;—that Anton (Tony) Martinsen, formerly owner of the Canadian halibut vessel "Livingston," recently sunk, is really in charge of the "Tahoma" during the fishing operations.

When inquiry was made as to who employed him while at first he intimated that W. Pierce, appearing as owner of the "Tahoma" on the register thereof, employed him as master of the vessel, upon being closely questioned he admitted that he had no dealings with Pierce but that he was employed by Messrs. F. E. Hunt, Limited;

His experience as a halibut fisherman is as follows: Fished on Canadian vessels in 1929 and

1930 and part of 1931; from June, 1931 during that year he fished on American halibut vessels "Eclipse" and "Attu," two and three months, respectively. He fished on Canadian vessels in 1932 and in 1933 until he was given an opportunity of being master of the American halibut schooner "Tahoma" on account of his American citizenship and that he received his position on account of such citizenship. GCA/ael

[Endorsed]: "Lbls. Exhibit No. 15 RECEIVED IN EVIDENCE Jun 6 1935 in cause No. 1778-KA, Robert E. Coughlin, Clerk, By............................Deputy." (Court Seal)

United States of America
First District of Alaska—ss:

I, ROBERT E. COUGHLIN, Clerk of the United States District Court in and for the First District of Alaska, do hereby certify that the annexed and foregoing is a full and true copy of the original Lbls. Exhibit No. 15, United States of America, Libelant, vs. Oil Screw Vessel, TAHOMA., etc. Respondent, W. Pierce, Claimant, Atlas Engine Company and Fishing Vessel Owners Marine Ways, corporation, Intervenors, No. 1117 KA. now remaining among the records of the said Court in my office. IN TESTIMONY WHEREOF I have hereunto subscribed my name and affixed the seal of the aforesaid Court at Juneau, Alaska this 15th day of June AD 1935.
Robert E. Coughlin, Clerk. By...
(Court Seal)   Deputy Clerk." [157]

(Testimony of G. C. Woodward.)

Mr. ZIEGLER: I have not read it myself. If the court please, I will read it out loud.

(Mr. Ziegler then read the Respondent's exhibit "A" to the Court.)

Q. When you took this statement Mr. Woodward, at first he stated Mr. Pierce had employed him as master, didn't he?

A. Does it say there that——

Q. Yes. "When inquiry was made as to who employed him, at first he intimated that Winnie Pierce, appearing as owner of the "Tahoma" on the register thereof, employed him as master of the vessel, upon being closely questioned he admitted that he had no dealings with Pierce but that he was employed by Messrs. F. E. Hunt, Ltd." You closely questioned him?

A. I did.

Q. What did you say to him?

A. I could not remember.

Q. Did you use any coercion?

A. Why should I threaten anyone; I have no reason.

Q. I am not saying you did. I am asking you if you did.

A. Certainly didn't.

Q. What do you mean by "closely questioned"?

A. I put that crudely, but I imagine I re-questioned him; went over the matter with him again.

[158]

(Testimony of G. C. Woodward.)

Q. Isn't it a fact at the time you were trying to get Johnson to give you information that would confirm the rumors you had about the boat having been sold?

A. The matter was a matter for investigation. I was investigating. It was done officially.

Q. Mr. Woodward, suppose Johnson had refused to give you these statements. Could you have compelled him to give them?

Mr. FOLTA: Object to that as calling for a matter of opinion on an immaterial matter.

Mr. ZIEGLER: I want to find out whether or not that is a statement that the Consul is required to make, that the law provides he must make, or gives him authority to take. It all goes to his interest, if the court please.

A. I confess I don't know how much of the consulate business I should disclose. I can state this— anything offered by me here has been sent to the Department and the Department, so far, has not said anything to me adversely about it.

Q. I shouldn't think they would. Do your regulations require you to take these statements?

A. I have explained before, the regulations give us a wide range of discretion in all matters. When in doubt we ask instructions of the department. When not in doubt we proceed, and submit it to the Department.

(Testimony of G. C. Woodward.)

Q. Does the law require you to take these statements?

A. I am stating under the consulate regulations we are allowed certain discretion and to use our judgment.

Q. Does the law give you authority to take these statements?

Mr. FOLTA: Object as a matter of law.

The COURT: This matter has been gone into now to almost interminable length. I think I understand it. [159]

Mr. ZIEGLER: I think that is all.

(Witness Excused)

(Short recess)

CAPT. BERNARD HANSON,

called as a witness on behalf of the Libellant, being first duly sworn, testified as follows:

Direct Examination

By Mr. FOLTA:

Q. Will you state your name, Captain?

A. Bernard Hanson.

Q. What is your occupation?

A. I am a halibut fisherman, skipper of a boat.

Q. Ever acted as master of a halibut boat?

A. Yes.

Q. How long?

A. Since 1920—fifteen years.

(Testimony of Capt. Bernard Hanson.)

Q. Captain, will you state what is the practice as to docking a halibut schooner in the halibut fishing trade coming in to dock, particularly with a load of fish, like into Prince Rupert, if the master is aboard and up who docks the boat?

Mr. ZIEGLER: Object to this testimony and this entire line as incompetent, irrelevant and immaterial. I don't see, even under counsel's theory, how this has any bearing on the issues of the case, of proving a sale of the "Tahoma" was made by Mr. Pierce to F. E. Hunt, Ltd.; incompetent, immaterial and irrelevant. [160]

Mr. FOLTA: Just one of the circumstances that go to show who was in charge of the boat.

(Further argument.)

The COURT: It would not be immaterial right now. It seems to me we are ahead of ourselves. There is no issue on that question.

(Further argument.)

Mr. FOLTA: Object—and renew the objection as incompetent, irrelevant and immaterial. Even if it were true that Johnson was to act as master while Martinson operated the boat it is immaterial and has no bearing on the issues in the case.

The COURT: This is a trial before the court anyway. It will be received subject to the objection that the other testimony has been received under.

Mr. ZIEGLER: I ask for an exception, if the court please.

(Testimony of Capt. Bernard Hanson.)

Q. Captain, will you answer the question?

A. It depends. Of course if the master is on deck coming in to the port naturally he would land the boat. Of course in case he is sleeping sometimes you have a man who knows how to handle the boat you would not cause him to get up, but if he is on deck he lands his own boat.

Mr. FOLTA: You may cross examine.

Cross Examination

By Mr. ZIEGLER:

Q. Pretty near all your boats you have in addition to the captain some man competent to dock the boat if necessary don't you? [161]

A. Yes.

Mr. FOLTA: Object. The question here is what is the practice and not whether somebody else can do it.

Q. However, if the master is asleep, or below. or playing a game of pinochle and doesn't want to come up he doesn't come up does he, to land the boat?

A. Well, it depends on the——

Q. On the man he has there?

A. On the man he has there. Take down at the dock here, taking a boat up to the dock, I should be there, but I have a man I can trust, I wouldn't always have to dock the boat.

(Testimony of Capt. Bernard Hanson.)

Q. It is more a matter of convenience than anything else?

A. Yes.

(Witness Excused)

———

CAPT. LOUIS SUNDERLAND,

called as a witness on behalf of the Libellant, being first duly sworn, testified as follows:

Direct Examination

By Mr. FOLTA:

Q. Captain, will you state your name?

A. Louis Sunderland.

Q. What is your occupation?

A. Fisherman.

Q. Have you ever maneuvered a halibut schooner as captain? [162]

A. Yes.

Q. How long?

A. Since '17·

Q. And you are master of a halibuter now, are you?

A. Yes.

Q. Do you know what the practice is of masters of halibut schooners in landing a loaded boat at a dock, as to whether the master does it if he is up on deck or up or whether somebody else does it?

(Testimony of Capt. Louis Sunderland.)

A. Ordinarily the master lands it, that is when he is up anyway.

Mr. FOLTA: You may cross examine.

Mr. ZIEGLER: No questions.

(Witness Excused)

Mr FOLTA: Call Captain Monson.

Mr. ZIEGLER: We will stipulate he will testify the same way.

Mr. FOLTA: Very well.

I think that is the Government's case, if the court please.

Mr. ZIEGLER: Now, if the court please, at this time the claimant moves for judgment in its behalf and moves for a dismissal of the complaint for the reason and on the ground that the allegations of the libel have not been sustained, and on the further ground that the evidence as introduced by the United States, uncontradicted, does not establish in the degree of proof required by law in forfeiture cases beyond a reasonable doubt, or at [163] all that, as alleged in the libel, Winnie Pierce, sold by way of trust, confidence or otherwise, in whole or in part, any part of the oil screw vessel "Tahoma" as alleged in the libel.

The COURT: The motion will be denied.

Mr. ZIEGLER: Exception.

(At 4:40 o'clock P. M. Court adjourned until 10 o'clock A. M. June 7, 1935.)

JUNE 7, 1935, 10 o'clock A. M., Court reconvened pursuant to adjournment, with all parties present as heretofore, whereupon the trial proceeded as follows:

Mr. ZIEGLER: At this time I would like permission from the court to make a motion with regard to the testimony to which I objected. The court reserved its ruling on that testimony until later, and I think in order to preserve my rights I should make a motion again before I start my case.

The claimant now moves that all testimony introduced by the Libellant which was objected to on the ground of immateriality and not a proper foundation laid for its reception, be stricken and disregarded by the court.

The COURT: The motion will be denied, with the understanding of course on which the evidence was received.

Mr. ZIEGLER: Note an exception, please.

The COURT: Yes.

Mr. ZIEGLER: With the court's permission, I would like to make another motion going to the sufficiency of the evidence. [164]

The claimant now moves for the dismissal of the libel on the ground of the insufficiency of the evidence offered by the United States to support the allegations of the libel, and upon the further ground that the evidence introduced is not sufficient to establish a sale of the vessel "Tahoma" or any interest therein which would constitute a violation of the law of Alaska or of the United States, in view of Section 4319 Compiled Laws of Alaska. (Reads section 4319).

(Argument by respective counsel on the motion.)

The COURT: Well, I don't think the Court would be justified in sustaining the motion at this time; overruled.

Mr. ZIEGLER: Exception.

The COURT: Exception allowed.

Mr. FOLTA: For the purpose of the record, so there will be no confusion, I would like to have the record show that libellant's exhibits 1 to 8, consisting of letters exchanged between F. E. Hunt and the intervenors are the same letters and exhibits to which reference is made in the cross examination of witnesses or deponents Wright and Heggem, and that the letters received as exhibits in connection with the cross examination in taking the depositions of those two witnesses, and identified by the deponents in cross examination, are the same letters as were received in evidence on the trial here and numbered libellant's exhibits "1" to "8".

Mr. GORE: If there is any doubt in Mr. Folta's mind relative to the exhibits,—I understood the Court accepted the depositions and exhibits as evidence in this case. Is that correct? [165]

Mr. FOLTA: Yes. But in reading the cross examination of the two witnesses, neither Mr. Ziegler

nor I read that part of the cross examination that
stated the letter questioned about from time to time
was number so and so, and I thought in order to
make it plain we should show that the letters identified by the intervenors in testifying in Seattle were
the same letters included in exhibits "1" to "8".

Mr. GORE: You gentlemen will stipulate with
me that the evidence or exhibits introduced by
Heggem, Fishing Vessels Oowners' Association, are
the same exhibits now before the court and in evidence.

Mr. ZIEGLER: Yes.

Mr. FOLTA: Yes.

Mr. GORE: I will not introduce it separately.

The COURT: I understood the depositions, with
the exhibits attached, had been introduced.

Mr. GORE: Yes.

The COURT: Let the record so show. [166]

RESPONDENT'S TESTIMONY.

G. W. NICKERSON,

recalled in behalf of the Respondent, testified
as follows:

Direct Examination

By Mr. ZIEGLER:

Q. I think when you were on the stand before
you stated how long you had been engaged in business at Prince Rupert?

A. Yes.

(Testimony of G. W. Nickerson.)

Q. That business is ship's chandlery business?

A. Yes.

Q. Explain quickly and briefly what that business is.

A. We deal mostly with halibut and salmon boats, sell them supplies—if they owe any money take the boat's share to apply on account; sometimes when we feel that the man who owns the boat has not made enough on his share and needs some of the boat's share to carry him along we are as generous as possible.

Q. Do you act as agents for a boat?

A. I do. I am a ship's broker and agent for ships, F. E. Hunt, Ltd. and G. W. Nickerson Company, Ltd.

Q. Are those two companies G. W. Nickerson Company, Ltd. and F. E. Hunt Company related?

A. G. W. Nickerson owns all but two shares of Hunt, Ltd.

Q. Mr. Wright, of the Atlas Engine Company, gave his evidence in Seattle. I will read a portion of his testimony.

(Reading from p. 20, line 20 of deposition of M. C. Wright.)

"Question: Mr. Wright, in entering into this arrangement for the payment of the debts due by the 'Tahoma' to yourselves [167] and the Fishing Vessel Owners' Marine Ways and F. E. Hunt & Co., I believe you stated you acted for

(Testimony of G. W. Nickerson.)

the Atlas Engine company, and signed the originals of these letters, photostatic copies of which are now in evidence?

Answer: I did, yes, sir.

Question: Now since that time there has been one payment received?

Answer: A payment.

Question: From F. E. Hunt & Co.?

Answer: It was July of last year that we received that—June 29th; I thought that it was this spring; but it was last year.

Question: Have you seen Nickerson? Has he been here?

Answer: I have talked to him twice.

Question: Since this arrangement was entered into, once before and the last time was about three or four months ago—it was the last part of December—had there been any other agreement or arrangement succeeding this? Or is that still the arrangement?

Answer: The arrangement is the same at present.

Question: One was a secondary arrangement; did you have any further conversations with reference to the operation of the 'Tahoma'?

Answer: Nothing more definite. Our position was: sitting tight at that time; and we did not want to make any statements that might

(Testimony of G. W. Nickerson.)

change things; we were very satisfied the way things were.

Question: Did Nickerson have anything to say about it?

Answer: He wanted us to help him out of the hole, but [168] there was nothing that we could do.

Question: What did he mean by 'the hole'?

Answer: In our last conversation, at the time the boat had been seized in Ketchikan, he came down and saw both Heggem and myself, but there was nothing really done at that time.

Question: When he asked you to try to get him out of the hole, did he go into details or particulars about it?

Answer: As I recollect he suggested that we write to Washington; that was the only suggestion, that we write to Washington and ask leniency; but I really forget what he wanted us to say."

Do you recall having a conversation with Mr. Wright with reference to the "Tahoma" along the line he has testified here?

A. Not exactly as he—I had a conversation with him.

Q. You did have a conversation about the "Tahoma" and her having been seized?

A. Yes.

(Testimony of G. W. Nickerson.)

Q. Explain to the court just what the conversation was.

Mr. FOLTA: Object, unless it is limited to the very statement that appears in the deposition. He can't, by mere device of explaining one simple isolated statement put in a lot of self-serving declarations or make any explanation he sees fit.

Mr. ZIEGLER: I certainly object to counsel using the word "device." It indicates suspicion or trying to impress the court we are trying to use a "device". I don't think he means that. Addressing myself to the objection: Mr. Wright testified to a certain conversation in Seattle. We have a right to state whether or not it was [169] had and if not what Mr. Nickerson's version of it was.

The COURT: Yes, he can give his own version, restricting himself——

Mr. ZIEGLER: To the sale of the "Tahoma".

A. The last time I saw him, in the fall of 1934, after the "Tahoma" was seized—I saw Mr. Wright, and not as owner of the "Tahoma" but the three of us, his company, the Fishing Vessels Owners Association, were all vitally interested in the seizure. I didn't say, "Help me out of the hole." I suggested to Wright they were American citizens, and went on to say if this were a case in Canada I would be able to make representations to the Ottawa Government and get her without expense and if our contentions were correct it would

(Testimony of G. W. Nickerson.)

be dismissed. I said to him, "Do the same thing. Go to your Senators and Congressmen, see what they can do for you, your interest is not as much as mine. They owe you more money, but you want your money. If there are any wires to be pulled do it. I can't do it. I am a Canadian citizen."

Q. Did you, in that conversation state to him in the words he used, that you wanted him to try to "get you out of the hole"?

A. No, I don't think the word "hole" was used.

Q. You can see how he got impatient?

A. Yes, but I don't see why he should, because the last letter we wrote him on this thing is to the effect that we could not take an equity in the "Tahoma" and were to make an extension of the account for two years.

Q. In discussing this with him did he give you any definite answer then? [170]

A. He said to go out to see Heggem at the Marine Ways, and we will try to get together later and go into the thing. I went and saw Heggem and he told me the same thing—going to turn it over to the lawyers. Mr. Wright says, "We will get together later, no need of me chasing him around any longer."

Q. Did you go to Seattle especially on this matter?

A. No, I was on a vacation.

(Testimony of G. W. Nickerson.)

Q. Did you leave your files with Mr. Wright or
Mr. Heggem, about the "Tahoma"?

A. Yes, I think after our conversation with Mr.
Wright, I went into his office Monday morning.
That is the last I heard of Mr. Wright. He sent
my files back by mail.

Q. I ask you if this is a letter pertaining to
that same matter?

A. Yes, that is the letter.

Mr. ZIEGLER: I desire to introduce the letter
in evidence in corroboration of the witness' explanation of his motive in going to Seattle and
what occurred there with Mr. Wright.

Mr. FOLTA: It has no tendency to corroborate
anything except he left the file down there.

(Further slight argument)

The COURT: It could not be more than corroboration of a very immaterial matter. I don't
see that it adds anything to the case one way or
the other.

Mr. ZIEGLER: All right.

Q. Mr. Nickerson, Libellant's exhibit "10" is a
letter dated October 10th, 1933, at Petersburg,
Alaska, or a statement signed by Arthur Johnson,
witnessed by Mr. Clausen, which [171] reads as
follows. (Reads exhibit "10") I will ask you
whether or not that statement is substantially correct, or otherwise.

A. In a general way.

(Testimony of G. W. Nickerson.)

Mr. FOLTA: Object as wholly improper; reading a letter and asking if it is substantially correct. I think that the question should be more specific.

Mr. ZIEGLER: I read it to avoid his reading the letter.

Q. You heard the statement made by Johnson master of the boat and I think you read it yourself.

A. Yes.

The COURT: I think that is proper.

Q. Just explain to the court what arrangement it was you had with Johnson for going on the "Tahoma".

A. In a general way this statement is correct. I think he is wrong when he says the ten per cent. It was five per cent I think. When the boat went to sea Martinson was the man we looked to to get the fish. It was not Johnson, it was Martinson. Johnson was nominally captain of the boat. When she was in port he had to be on the boat at Prince Rupert when she moved from one dock to another. but Martinson was the man we looked to for the fish. We would not have given Johnson the boat without a competent man with him.

Q. The last part of it says, "Johnson states he was to get ten per cent in payment for his services in order that Tony Martinson would not have to appear before the United States Customs House."

A. No, we didn't have that; that was whatever the law [172] required. I don't know whether Mar-

(Testimony of G. W. Nickerson.)

tinson would have to appear or not; they had to find that out with the consul.

Q. In making the arrangements, which Johnson stated in his letter, with him and Martinson, did you violate any Canadian laws or United States laws that you know anything about?

Mr. FOLTA: Object as calling for a legal conclusion.

The COURT: You ask if he did violate the law.

Mr. ZIEGLER: Withdraw that.

Q. Mr. Nickerson, as far as you know was there anything illegal in the manner in which you handled the operation of the "Tahoma"?

Mr. FOLTA: Object, as a question of fact for the court.

(Slight argument.)

The COURT: He may answer.

A. We were, we felt, in the position of a creditor of a foreign boat and representing two other creditors who were Americans the same as the boat; that was our position. We tried to work out something where we would all get our money and possibly Mr. Pierce would have something left at the end.

Q. In this arrangement was there anything illegal about it, so far as you knew at the time?

Mr. FOLTA: Object to that.

Mr. ZIEGLER: Correct, ignorance of the law does not excuse one, but in matters of this kind people's intention is one of the principal things.

Mr. FOLTA: He is asking if his own acts were illegal. [173]

(Testimony of G. W. Nickerson.)

Mr. ZIEGLER: It is not binding the court. We simply desire to show it was done and the reason for it.

The COURT: I think he already answered, as far as it is proper.

Mr. ZIEGLER: All right.

Q. Mr. Nickerson, I show you a statement made by Arthur Johnson before Mr. Woodward, which has been introduced in evidence. I think you have read it. Glance over it; I would like to ask you about that.

A. I think this statement is probably the nearest correct of the three statements Johnson made, and is substantially the arrangement.

Q. In this statement Johnson states he was employed by F. E. Hunt and Company to act as master of the "Tahoma".

A. Yes.

Q. He got that impression?

A. Yes, I don't think all the details were gone into. I think Martinson and Johnson arranged the details, but we were cognizant of what was going on.

Q. Mr. Nickerson, after you had made the arrangement with the Seattle creditors for the disposition or operation or whatever you might call it, of the "Tahoma", did you endeavor on behalf of Mr. Pierce, to negotiate a sale of the "Tahoma"?

A. Yes.

Q. I hand you a letter and reply and ask you if you can identify those?

(Testimony of G. W. Nickerson.)

A.   Yes, I wrote this letter to Erickson; this is his reply. I had previously taken it up with the Atlas and Vessel Owners to try and sell the boat. **[174]**

Mr. ZIEGLER: I offer it in evidence.

Mr. FOLTA: Object on the ground it has no bearing on any of the issues in the case, and is not the same as the admission of letters on behalf of the Libellant because they constitute admissions. It has no bearing on any issue in the case and is incompetent and immaterial.

(Further argument.)

The COURT: It may be received.

(Letter and reply were admitted in evidence and marked Respondent's exhibits "A" and "B" and are as follows, to-wit:)

"COPY"

"Prince Rupert, B. C.
Sept. 14th, 1933

Capt. Egel Ericksen,
C/O Fishing Vessel Owners Assn.,
Seattle.

We understand that you have had the misfortune to lose your boat. In the event of your contemplating the purchase of another boat, we offer you on behalf of Captain Pierce, the "Tahoma" at Eleven Thousand ($11,000.00) Dollars.

She is equipped with a 75 H. P. Atlas engine, installed either three or four years ago. The exact

(Testimony of G. W. Nickerson.)

date could be ascertained from the agents of this engine in Seattle. She is in very good shape and the engine would not have to be re-bored for at least and other year. Capt. Pierce has never run this boat to the capacity of her power. I do not know her exact measurements but do know she is capable of packing forty-five (45,000#s) thouzand pounds of fish from the Estward.

She was, I believ. built around Se ttle. and it is quite possible that you could obtain all the particulars from some one there.

Yours very truly

(signed) G. W. NIFKERSON,

Managing Director of F. E. Hunts Ltd.''

''EGILL ERIKSEN
1908 N. 36th St.
Seattle

Sept 19 193

F. E. HUNT, Ltd.
Prince Rupert B. C.
Dear Sir:

Received your letter of Sept 14-33 regarding M/S Tahoma. [175]

I am not interested in the M/S Tahoma at the price you are asking. Not at this time. However if the price was somewhere right I might consider

(Testimony of G. W. Nickerson.)
a buy, but the price would have to be considerably
reduced.

Thanking you for the offer

Yours truly

EGILL ERIKSEN

Is the Tahoma under
American register?''

[Endorsed]: ''Respondent's Exhibit No. A received in evidence Jun 7 1935 in cause No. 1778-KA.

ROBERT E. COUGLHIN

Clerk

By ————————————— Deputy''

Mr. FOLTA: To which we except on the ground
it is immaterial on any issue in the case, and particularly as it has not been identified it constitutes
purely hearsay.

Q. Did you receive a reply from the addressee
of your letter, Egill Eriksen?

A. Yes.

Q. You know him?

A. Yes.

Q. You know that is his signature?

A. I have seen his signature before.

Mr. FOLTA: I still object for the same reason—
not identified.

Mr. ZIEGLER: I think if there is any doubt what
it is—the signature of the letter—the court will take
into consideration—the Court knows the circum-

(Testimony of G. W. Nickerson.)

stances and can determine what it is. I think it has been sufficiently identified.

The COURT: Overruled.

Q. I direct your attention to the testimony of Mr. Heggem, of the Fishing Vessel Marine Ways, given at Seattle in [176] the deposition which has been introduced in court here. I will read a question or two ahead of the matter I want to direct your attention to. First he mentions here he received checks from Hunt and Company—were they from Hunt?

A. Signed by M. F. Nickerson.

Q. They were, however, Hunt's checks?

A. Yes, Hunt Ltd., I think is what he means.

Q. And he goes on: (p. 31 line 28 of Heggem deposition).

(Reading) "From all the correspondence with him did you become acquainted with his signature?

Answer: Fairly, yes.

Question: When you met him in December, was it concerning the Tahoma?

Answer: Yes.

Question: What did he say then?

Answer: He asked if he could find three thousand dollars to go up and buy the boat to go fishing on.

Question: That is the same thing he said in one of these letters?

Answer: Yes.

(Testimony of G. W. Nickerson.)

Question: Did he not state, somewhere in these exhibits '1' to '6' that he thought Pierce was not a capable man to operate the 'Tahoma'?

Answer: Yes.

Question: And he wanted to put someone else in his place?

Answer: Yes.

Question: So that the indebtedness to F. E. Hunt & Company, and you people and the Atlas Engine Company would have at least a better show of being paid off? [177]

Answer: Yes.

Question: You say that was in December, 1933?

Answer: It was in 1933

Question: Have you seen him since?

Answer: Yes. He was out to the yard last winter, around December.

Question: Did you have any further conversation with him about the 'Tahoma'?

Answer: Yes.

Question: What was said?

Answer: About releasing the boat. I told him that we had turned it over to Steiner and for him to go and see him.

Question: What did he want you to do?

Answer: He wanted us to help him release the boat. I told him I did not know anything about it; that we had turned it over to our attorney and he could see him.

(Testimony of G. W. Nickerson.)

Question: What did he want you to do to get the release of the boat?

Answer: Nothing said about that. He was just talking about getting it released.

Question: Did he make some suggestion of what you should do, the same as the Atlas Engine Company, write a letter to Washington, something of that kind?

Answer: No. I told him I did not know anything about that. It was out of my hands. It was turned over to our attorney and for him to see him.

Question: Did he say anything about the lien of the F. E. Hunt & Company?

Answer: Not as far as I remember."

You were down to Seattle in the fall of '34· after [178] the seizure?

A. Yes.

Q. Were you down in the fall of '33?

A. Yes.

Q. Shortly after this letter was written to Egill Erickson about selling the boat?

A. Yes.

Q. At the time you were there he stated you asked him if he could find three thousand dollars to buy the boat to go fishing on?

A. In '34·

Q. Did you make any such statement?

A. No, I didn't.

(Testimony of G. W. Nickerson.)

Q.   Are you fishing yourself or did you ever fish?

A.   When I was a kid about fourteen I was supposed to start as a fisherman?

Q.   You didn't make that statement then?

A.   No.

Q.   But you did discuss selling the boat?

A.   Yes.

Q.   Explain to the court what the discussion was.

Mr. FOLTA: Object as not being limited to the
statement in the deposition that——

The COURT: Reframe the question.

Q.   Now just state to the court what your conversation with Mr. Heggem was at that time with
reference to finding a purchaser for the boat and
also about having the boat released.

Mr. FOLTA: Object, two questions in one.

The COURT: The rule does not permit throwing
the [179] gates wide open.

Mr. ZIEGLER: Mr. Heggem testified to the conversation. We are entitled to show our version of
the conversation.

The COURT: Certainly; but restrict it to the——

Mr. ZIEGLER: To the conversation testified by
Mr. Heggem,—getting a purchaser for the boat and
releasing the boat.

Q.   You understand that?

A.   Yes; with the exception of me going to buy
the boat and go fishing Mr. Heggem's statement is
about correct.

(Testimony of G. W. Nickerson.)

Q. What was said?

A. We were talking about somebody to buy the boat. Pete Petterson was mentioned. He had seen Pete Petterson and said "Pete wants to get this boat." I think that is where he gets the three thousand in. With that exception that statement is substantially correct. We discussed the thing in a general way—that they could get the boat released or make a try to get it released. He had had experience in getting fines lifted on American boats in Canada.

Q. Mr. Nickerson, Mr. Woodward testified, as I recall it, Johnson was a man about twenty years of age. Do you know what his age was at the time?

A. Pretty well.

Q. What was his age?

A. Well, the boy—I have known him there about twenty-three years. He must have been a lad of five or six years when he came from the States. I would say twenty-five years of age. [180]

Q. Did you see his death notice in the paper?

A. Yes sir.

Mr. FOLTA: Object to that.

The COURT: It is in now, go ahead.

Mr. FOLTA: Move it be stricken.

Mr. ZIEGLER: I consent that it be stricken and the court disregard it.

The COURT: Very well.

Q. Mr. Nickerson, do you know whether or not Johnson was fishing on big halibut boats as early as 1926 or 1927?

(Testimony of G. W. Nickerson.)

A. I would have to be guided by the statements read yesterday. I knew he had been fishing out of Ketchikan and Prince Rupert, but I don't know the boats.

Q. Do you know the time?

A. I know he had been fishing a good many years, way back six or seven, seven or eight years.

Q. Lived in Prince Rupert a great many years before he died?

A. Yes.

Q. He died in Arizona?

A. Yes.

Q. Mr. Nickerson, I show you Libellant's exhibit "12" which is a bill of sale testified to by Mr. Woodward. Did you see that? Have you looked it over?

A. I think this bill of sale was made in my office by my stenographer on information given her by me. I saw it because I signed it as a witness.

Q. Do you have any distinct recollection of a change in the bill of sale from Earnest Pierce, as testified?

A. I have a dim recollection, through my fault or the stenographer's fault Winnie Pierce's name got there and [181] was erased; there was no effort to conceal.

Q. Was this bill of sale finally made by the parties conveying it—the "Wave"?

A. No, there was another made out.

Q. To whom?

(Testimony of G. W. Nickerson.)

A. Earnest Pierce, as I recall it. That is the way it went through.

Q. Mr. Nickerson, I just called your attention to a letter, being part of the negotiations between you and the Seattle creditors, which has been introduced in evidence. This letter is from the Atlas Engine Company, dated June 12th, in which they accepted a proposition. It has been introduced in evidence.— accepted a proposition made by you for the future management or conduct of the "Tahoma". In that letter they state that they accepted your proposition on the following conditions and named certain conditions, one of which was Captain Pierce is to convey the "Tahoma" to you. I will ask you if you ever complied with that condition of their letter?

A. No.

Q. You answered that letter on June 17th and accepted the arrangement made in their letter and stated in your letter: "This company's debt against the debtor must remain in exactly the same status as it is now, as foreigners cannot have an ownership interest in an American vessel"?

A. Yes.

Q. Was that applying to the proposition that you had an interest in the boat?

Mr. FOLTA: Object. I think that is a matter for the [182] Court to pass on.

Q. You stated on previous examination that you didn't take conveyance of the boat from Pierce?

A. Yes.

(Testimony of G. W. Nickerson.)

Q. Did you ever have an agreement that you would take a conveyance?

A. No; mental or otherwise. We always felt that if it was necessary for ourselves and the other creditors that Pierce would give us a conveyance to be used for the advantage of the creditors. We could force him.

Q. In these letters which have been introduced you stated in one of them as part of your negotiations that you would be willing to take the same extension that you were giving them with reference to the time to be allowed to pay. If you were going to take title to the boat would you have to give them any extension or would you be entitled to any extension then?

Mr. FOLTA: Object.

The COURT: Sustained.

Mr. ZIEGLER: I don't care to take up the court's time, but I want to get the facts before the court, and Mr. Nickerson's and Mr. Pierce's view of the matter before the court.

Q. Now, Mr. Nickerson, Mr. Woodward testified Mr. Petterson made an affidavit in which he stated that in consideration of his turning over the "Wave" to you, or Pierce, he was to be released from the store bill of Nickerson.

A. I think that was the understanding—never got it in writing, but it was substantially true. We didn't think we had anything in the first place. [183]

Q. Did you value the "Wave"?

(Testimony of G. W. Nickerson.)

A. No, we thought she was a loss, because——

Q. What was the value of the boat when you took her over?

A. I don't think we could get anything for her.

Q. Do you know the value of halibut boats at Prince Rupert?

A. Pretty well.

Q. You have been in business quite a while?

A. Yes.

Q. Did you at that time know the reasonable value of the "Wave"?

A. Yes.

Q. What, in you opinion would be a reasonable fair value of the "Wave"?

Mr. FOLTA: Object, he is not qualified yet.

The COURT: He said, as I understand it, he knows something about the valuation of boats.

The COURT: He may answer.

Mr. FOLTA: Exception.

A. If anyone had offered me three hundred dollars I would have thought he was crazy.

Q. After the boat was acquired by "Pierce" did he do work on the boat himself?

A. Yes.

Mr. FOLTA: Pierce or Petterson?

Mr. ZIEGLER: Pierce.

Mr. FOLTA: On the "Wave"?

Mr. ZIEGLER: Yes.

Q. Did he do work?

A. Yes, he repaired her and it was possible to go out on her—in haywire shape. [184]

(Testimony of G. W. Nickerson.)

Q. In making your arrangements, Mr. Nickerson, regarding the obtaining of the "Wave" and operation of the "Tahoma" with whom did you make most of those arrangements?

A. The first conversation was with his brother. When he came in we sort of confirmed it.

Q. At that time what was Mr. Pierce's general condition with reference to transacting any normal business?

Mr. FOLTA: I think this is speculative.

The COURT: I don't know what that may be.

Mr. ZIEGLER: I think it might be pertinent to determine why arrangements were made with Mr. Pierce's brother rather than himself.

The COURT: Do you mean Pierce himself was not able?

Mr. ZIEGLER: I do. I think it will come out when the court hears Mr. Pierce on the stand.

The COURT: I don't think we are going into any matters of that kind.

Mr. ZIEGLER: Does the court mean the fact, if it can be substantiated, honestly, that Mr. Pierce was in bad physical and nervous state and not competent to transact ordinary business affairs, that it would not have any bearing on this court with reference to arrangements between the "Tahoma" and the "Wave".

The COURT: All that involves is whether or not Pierce was competent to do business then the question arises whether or not his brother had authority to transact business for him.

(Testimony of G. W. Nickerson.)

(Further argument)

The COURT: It raises too many collateral questions.

Mr. ZIEGLER: I will not insist on it, but I am sure [185] it will be brought out by counsel on cross examination.

(Recess five minutes)

Q. Mr. Nickerson, just state to the court, in conclusion, your exact arrangement with Mr. Pierce and his brother with reference to the "Wave" and "Tahoma", taking over the "Tahoma". Just tell the court just what that arrangement was you actually made when you came to a final arrangement, or the status of the matter.

A. When this thing was first suggested we thought from every angle it was best to get the thing in a position where it could be liquidated by the creditors for their own consideration first, and, if there was anything—for Pierce; Accordingly I wrote a letter that way. In that, Hunt was gong to take a bill of sale or get an equity in the "Tahoma" otherwise than an interest in her earnings, to pay the bills she owed, not her profits. Along that line we were willing to give them the "Wave" under any consideration.

Q. In your letter to the Seattle creditors you stated he wanted a small boat to use—Did you get him a small boat?

A. Yes, we got him the "Wave".

Q. With respect to the "Tahoma" did you have any conversation with Mr. Pierce about that,

(Testimony of G. W. Nickerson.)

whether you wanted to take it away from him or
wanted or would take it away from him?

A. No, I told Mr. Pierce all the way through I
felt he would eventually get something out of the
"Tahoma" but we wanted—

Mr. FOLTA: Object to all this. The agreement
is evidenced by the letter. I do not think they can
be varied by oral evidence.

Mr. ZIEGLER: Those letters indicate what Mr.
Pierce [186] was willing to do to solve the situation. Just the mere proof of the letters wouldn't
prove that was done. We are entitled to show what
was actually done with respect to the boats, that is,
whether there was a sale made. Counsel doesn't want
to preclude us from testifying as to the arrangements between Mr. Pierce and Hunt.

Mr. FOLTA: The objection is based on the fact
that one of his answers is directly contrary to the
statement in the letter signed by him.

Mr. ZIEGLER: Assuming that to be the case,
there is no rule of law by which he can contradict
them if the negotiations with Mr. Pierce were not
made in accordance with what he said they would
be in the letter. Does counsel mean we must be
bound by those letters?

The COURT: He can state what arrangement
was made.

Mr. FOLTA: Exception.

A. There was no arrangement with Mr. Pierce,
either conversation or writing, whereby the boat was
transferred to us. I never said in my letter I was

(Testimony of G. W. Nickerson.)

going to. I said what Pierce was prepared to do and did say I would take a blank bill of sale, not for F. E. Hunt, Ltd., but it would have to be decided from a legal standpoint who could take the bill of sale. From the time I wrote that letter nothing was ever done. Never approached Pierce for a bill of sale; in fact, I told him several times, ''Hold onto the boat.'' I felt there would be something in it for him.

Q. You never took a bill of sale?

A. Never took a bill of sale, never agreed to take over the boat.

Q. Ever have any understanding with Pierce he should sell the [187] boat to you or transfer or mortgage it to you or anything?

A. Not to us.

Q. What has been your connection with the boat then since these letters were written?

A. Acting as the agent of Pierce and the creditors.

Q. Have you accounted to Seattle creditors for any earnings of the ''Tahoma''?

A. Yes.

Q. Have you received the same proportions—more or less?

A. Not any more; we tried to split it on the same basis.

Q. Was that for any interest you had in the boat or payment of your obligations to Pierce?

(Testimony of G. W. Nickerson.)

A. He owed us. We felt if we wanted to we could have sued Pierce and attached the boat. We didn't want to do that.

Mr. ZIEGLER: That is all.

Cross Examination

By Mr. FOLTA:

Q. If you had done that—sought to enforce your lien against the boat sooner, the first thing you would have to do would be to pay twenty-five per cent duty?

A. Yes.

Q. Of course that would be considerable?

A. Not much, it would be what she brought.

Q. Were your relations or dealings with the "Tahoma" any different from your dealings with any other boat?

A. No.

Q. That applies, of course, to the "Wave"?

A. Yes, she owed us money. [188]

Q. There is no difference in your dealings with these two particular boats?

A. No, we didn't handle it any different.

Q. Did you appoint a captain for any other boat?

A. No.

Q. How is it, if your dealings were the same, you didn't appoint a captain?

A. We didn't.

Q. Didn't you say Johnson's statement—you appointed him—was correct?

(Testimony of G. W. Nickerson.)

A. He had legal authority from Pierce, if you want to put it we appointed him.

Q. You say the "Wave" was worth three hundred dollars—must have been in pretty bad shape?

A. Yes, she was.

Q. You, if you were selling her, wouldn't expect to get over three hundred dollars?

A. No.

Q. At that time how much money did she owe you?

A. Between Mrs. Kincaid and ourselves, somewhere around $2200.00 including interest.

Q. In addition to $2600.00 owed you you paid $150.00 for a half interest?

A. To get the title, yes.

Q. Why did you pay anything if she owed you $2600.00?

A. It was cheaper than going to court; two mortgages against her; we had to seize her; it was the cheapest way out.

Q. Did you hear that the question of the ownership of the "Tahoma" and "Wave" was being investigated?

A. We heard the Consul was taking affidavits.

[189]

Q. You heard it about the time of the affidavits?

A. Yes, we heard it; Johnson discussed it with me and going to the consulate to make the affidavit.

Q. You were aware of what was going on?

A. Yes.

(Testimony of G. W. Nickerson.)

Q.　Since that time you have become the owner of the "Wave"?

A.　Yes. I am the owner of the "Wave".

Q.　You assigned your claim to Mr. Ziegler?

A.　No, not the "Wave", the "Annabel".

Q.　You are the owner of the "Wave"?

A.　Yes.

Q.　When?

A.　About a month ago.

Q.　How much duty then did you pay on her?

A.　We paid $110.00, I think, 25% on $500.00 and 6% sales tax.

Q.　She brought $500.00?

A.　Valued at $500.00.

Q.　How long ago did you say you got her?

A.　About a month or so.

Q.　When did you bring proceedings against her?

A.　I didn't bring proceedings against her.

Q.　How did she happen to be sold to you?

A.　Bought the equity out.

Q.　Whose equity did you buy?

A.　$2500.00 to Peterson, Mrs. Thomas $150.00 I think. Besner, or a fellow named Morrie held a mortgage of $2,000.00. We paid him $200.00.

Q.　Why did you buy it?

A.　Because we sort of undertook to Pierce to get him a boat [190] to operate; we did get him a boat to operate.

Q.　Wasn't the real reason why you acquired title to the "Wave" because you were afraid the "Wave" would be seized?

(Testimony of G. W. Nickerson.)

A.   No, there was nothing to seize the "Wave" for.

Q.   (The COURT)   Who was the actual owner of the "Wave" at the time of the transfer to Winnie Pierce?

A.   The Thomas estate and Ben Petterson. It was registered in their name half and half.

Q.   (The COURT)   The bill of sale was made by whom?

A.   Petterson—his half is all he was selling.

Q.   (The COURT)   It was an absolute transfer?

A.   Yes, of his half interest.

Q.   (The COURT)   Was the other half interest subsequently transferred?

A.   Yes.

Q.   (The COURT)   To whom?

A.   Earnest Pierce.

Q.   (The COURT)   For whom?

A.   By the heir of the estate.

Q.   (By Mr. FOLTA—resuming): Mrs. Irvington.

A.   I think so.

Q.   (The COURT)   That was an absolute transfer?

A.   Yes, subject to the mortgages.

Q.   (The COURT)   What mortgages?

A.   I think Mrs. Kincaid's mortgage was somewhere around a couple of thousand dollars, might have been $2500.00, and the Richardson mortgage was two thousand dollars.

(Testimony of G. W. Nickerson.)

By Mr. FOLTA:

Q. The Kincaid mortgage, you handled that transfer entirely?

A. We arranged to have the mortgage; M. F. arranged with [191] Petterson and I arranged with Mrs. Kincaid.

Q. You handled the entire transaction?

A. Yes.

The COURT: There is no recitation made in the bill of sale about mortgages or liens.

A. That is one reason why this bill of sale. I didn't think it was necessary. When we came to transfer to Canadian registry the mortgages had to be cleaned up.

The COURT: In any transfer of this kind isn't it customary to recite any mortgages or liens against the property?

A. They should be on the face of the transfer, but it wasn't done.

The COURT: These bills, you knew all about them?

A. Bill of sale?

The COURT: Yes:

A. Yes.

The COURT: You also knew about the mortgages or liens?

A. I knew about the Kincaid mortgages, but not about Besner until we came to transfer to Canadian registry.

Q. Did she know?

A. No.

(Testimony of G. W. Nickerson.)

Q. You were acting for her?

A. We sent the mortgage over here; they did not file it; if there was another one previously filed.

Q. You made no inquiry as to the Customs House records?

A. I handled it just the same as our own Customs House records.

Q. You say it was either your mistake or the stenographer's [192] that the name Winnie Pierce was typed into the bill of sale?

A. I am satisfied it was.

Q. Do you know whose fault it was?

A. I could not swear to it.

Q. But you do know one of you made the mistake?

A. No, I wouldn't say whether I gave the wrong notes, or what happened, I think when it went up to the Consul's office——

Q. When you went up to the Consul's office or before?

A. Earnie Pierce, as I recall, came to me——

Q. You answered the question.

A. All right.

Q. You think, now, you discovered the mistake?

A. It must have been a mistake.

Q. You directed "Winnie Pierce" be typed out?

A. Yes, or erased.

Q. Will you examine the month on the last page here, in the line that says, "In Testimony Whereof the said B. A. Petterson has hereunto set his hand

(Testimony of G. W. Nickerson.)

and seal this 4th day of December" the month originally inserted there was it not August—visible
through the month of December?

A. I don't know that.

Q. Do you know when it was made out?

A. No.

Q. Was it made in December?

A. According to that it was.

Q. The first one?

A. I don't remember which month it was.

Q. Can you see that then—the month of "August"?

A. No, I can't. [193]

Q. Is it your recollection, Mr. Nickerson, that
this was made out in December?

A. I think there has been an erasure there; I
don't know—it looks—

Q. I am asking you your recollection.

A. I don't know the month.

Q. You don't know when it was made out?

A. No, I will have to take it as I find it there.

Q. Now, you say you never had any agreement
with Winnie Pierce, the claimant, as to taking over
the "Tahoma" or putting him on the "Wave"?

A. I say we never consummated the agreement.

Q. But he was taken off the "Tahoma" and put
on the "Wave"?

A. Not "taken off".

Q. How did he happen to relinquish the "Tahoma",.do you know?

A. If you will let me—

(Testimony of G. W. Nickerson.)

Q   Withdraw the question.

Did you effect his transfer from the "Tahoma" to the "Wave"?

A   Only voluntarily on his part.

Q.   It was you who was responsible for that change?

A.   After he volunteered it.

Q.   After he was willing to make the change?

A.   Yes.

Q.   In order to put him on the "Wave" you had to get Petterson off?

A.   The "Wave" had been tied up since last summer, no correspondence from anybody; we had to get Petterson to agree.

Q.   So the arrangement was made just as you outlined in your letter to the Seattle lienors?

A.   That we got a boat for Pierce to operate, which was the [194] "Wave".

Q.   Do you remember when you acquired title to the "Annabel"?

A.   I think the thing must have been wound up —she arrived in Prince Rupert either Christmas or New Years Day, if it was Christmas it was 1933 I think, and if it was New Years Day it would be 1934 she arrived in Prince Rupert.

Q.   Don't you know as a matter of fact the bill of sale was recorded in March of this year?

A.   Of the "Annabel"?

Q.   Yes.

(Testimony of G. W. Nickerson.)

A. That was the transfer; that was when she was transferred to Canadian registry, to us. I thought you meant when we seized her.

Q. Do you recall this—that the bill of sale was reported in the Customs House here in March of this year?

A. I think it was probably about that time.

Q. If the Customs House records show it was March 23d you would not dispute that?

A. No, I would not.

Q. Do you know if Mr. Ziegler wired afterwards, April 5th or 6th to the Consulate, authorizing the appointment of Johnson as master?

A. Yes.

Q. Do you know how he come to do that if you were the owner of the boat?

A. Yes.

Q. How?

A. Some delay about the transfer; wanted to go out as an American boat one trip; it was arranged for Arthur Johnson to take her, as the application was in the Customs they [195] had no authority to give.

Mr. ZIEGLER: I have no objection to this, but just want to state it is immaterial and taking up unnecessary time. If the court wants to hear it I have no objection.

(Slight discussion)

The COURT: I do want to know for my own satisfaction right now thought about this transfer

(Testimony of G. W. Nickerson.)

of the "Wave". The "Wave" you say, was transferred to Earnie Pierce?

A. Yes, but it was for the benefit of Winnie Pierce. We felt Winnie Pierce was to get the "Wave" eventually.

Q. (The COURT):You knew he was to get it right then, as far as the transfer was concerned didn't you?

A. Couldn't until the mortgage was cleaned up.

Q. (The COURT): The mortgage had to be recited in this bill of sale, in order to have any validity, didn't it?

Mr. ZIEGLER: I hesitate to rise, but I don't believe that is the procedure. There is nothing in the Customs House that—

Mr. FOLTA: But a mortgage has to be recorded on documents of the vessel and cannot be lost sight of in any transfer.

By Mr. FOLTA:

Q. Mr. Nickerson, you say at the time you wrote this letter of June 17th to the Atlas Engine Company and the Fishing Vessel Owners Marine Ways, Libellant's exhibit "6", that you did have an intention of having a bill of sale signed in blank?

A. Not to F. E. Hunt, Ltd.

Q. Just answer the question.

A. No. [196]

Q. But one was to be signed?

A. By the owner, Pierce.

Q. What were you going to use it for?

(Testimony of G. W. Nickerson.)

A. `So that if we got a chance to sell the boat or clean it up it could be done without delay.

Q. You were going to have him sign a blank bill of sale and if you got a chance to sell the boat or clean it up it could be done without delay?

A. Yes.

Q. What was Pierce doing after May 29th, 1933? Was he going out regularly on the "Wave"?

A. Three trips.

Q. Do you know when he made the first trip?

A. I think after the date here he returned from his trip June 12th, 1933.

Q. Do you know when he went out on that trip?

A. I imagine he was gone about 12 days.

Q. Is that the usual trip?

A. Depends on how you find the fish, the usual trip is about ten days.

Q. He continued operating the "Wave" until when?

A. Until July when he was taken sick.

Q. What has he been doing since?

A. With the exception of the time he was sick he operated the "Wave" during the halibut season.

Q. Until when?

A. Right now.

Q. Still operating?

A. Still operating.

Q. You say here, "Will have bill of sale signed in blank so [197] it could be used instantaneously if desired".

(Testimony of G. W. Nickerson.)

A. Yes.

Q. Why?

A. So we could sell it at once; if a fisherman wanted a boat he would want it then.

Q. It wasn't the purpose to have a bill of sale blank so if seized it could be signed by Pierce?

A. I don't think it has to be on the boat.

Q. If that boat were sold in Prince Rupert and you had a bill of sale it would have to be recorded in the Customs House here?

A. Yes.

Q. Certainly?

A. Yes.

Mr. FOLTA: I think that is all.

Re-direct Examination

By MR. ZIEGLER:

Q. When you acquired the "Wave" for Mr. Pierce, how long had she been lying up on the beach before that?

A. At the time Petterson returned from about two months trip, probably about the middle of August, and we said "No more credit" and the boat was tied to the dock.

Q. That was what year?

A. Thirty-two.

Q. Then did she lay on the beach there or tied to the dock for until you acquired her for Pierce next year?

A. Yes.

(Testimony of G. W. Nickerson.)

Q. You were asked about mortgages and liens against the "Wave" [198] when you took the bill of sale. If you bought the "Wave" you realized you had to pay the mortgages off to get her clear?

A. Yes.

Q. Was there any necessity for mentioning them in the bill of sale, that you knew of?

Mr. FOLTA: Object as calling for an opinion.

Mr. ZIEGLER: The court interrogated on that point. I want his understanding.

The COURT: It is not for Mr. Nickerson to interpret the law.

(Slight discussion)

Q. Mr. Nickerson, when you acquired this boat for Mr. Pierce, you say you knew there was one mortgage on there to Mrs. Kincaid?

A. Yes.

Q. And later on you discovered there was another mortgage too?

A. Richardson Moore mortgage.

Q. And were those mortgages cleaned off the boat?

A. They are now.

Q. How much did it cost you to pay off all those mortgages?

Mr. FOLTA: Object.

A. Two hundred dollars to Besner.

Q. And Mrs. Kincaid agreed to release?

A. Yes.

(Testimony of G. W. Nickerson.)

Q. After the boat was fixed up by Mr. Pierce her value was fixed at $500.00?

A. Yes, and duty paid on that basis. [199]

By the COURT:

Q. I don't understand yet about the "Wave". Was it your intention when the "Wave" was transferred to Pierce that it should be transferred to him free and clear of all incumbrances?

A. Yes, we had in mind giving him the "Wave".

Q. I understood you a while ago, at the time you made the transfer of the "Wave" to Pierce, that was in consideration of any claims he might have against the "Tahoma"?

A. That is he was agreeable to that.

Q. Wasn't that the understanding?

A. In relinquishing his equity, by letting someone else operate the boat.

Q. What was the actual consideration at the time of the transfer?

A. The consideration was he would let us operate the "Tahoma" for the benefit of creditors as agents; if there was an opportunity to sell her legally, why sell her.

Q. For whose benefit?

A. Creditors; if there was anything left he would get it.

The COURT: That is all.

Mr. ZIEGLER: That is all.

(Testimony of G. W. Nickerson.)

Re-cross Examination

By Mr. FOLTA:

Q. You said that because he let you operate the "Tahoma" for the benefit of creditors?

A. Yes.

Q. Did you make any such arrangement as that with any other boat? [200]

Mr. ZIEGLER: Object to that as incompetent and immaterial.

The COURT: Objection sustained.

Q. Was that a legal method of dealing with boats; transfer somebody from one boat to another?

Mr. ZIEGLER: Object as immaterial; it will try out the facts in each particular case.

A. When I get in a jack-pot I have to make the best deal I can.

Mr. FOLTA: That is all.

Mr. ZIEGLER: No further questions.

(Witness Excused)

––––––

WINNIE PIERCE,

of the Respondent, and claimant herein, called as a witness on his own behalf, being first duly sworn, testified as follows:

Direct Examination

By Mr. ZIEGLER:

Q. State your name, Mr. Pierce.

A. Winnie Pierce.

(Testimony of Winnie Pierce.)

Q. Where do you live?

A Prince Rupert.

Q. How long have you lived there?

A. Since '23·

Q. When?

A. Twenty-three.

Q. Nineteen twenty-three?

A. Nineteen twenty-three. [201]

Q. Are you a married man?

A. Yes.

Q. Have you a family?

Mr. FOLTA: Object as immaterial.

The COURT: Yes, let's don't take up time with those matters.

Q. Have you been living in Prince Rupert, Mr. Pierce, since that time?

A. Yes sir.

Q. You are an American citizen?

A. Yes sir.

Q. How did it happen you were living in Prince Rupert then?

A. For several reasons.

Mr. FOLTA: I think perhaps that is immmaterial too. I think we should shorten it up.

(Slight discussion).

The COURT: I don't know how it can be material.

Q. Mr. Pierce, what is your business?

A. Fishing.

(Testimony of Winnie Pierce.)

Q. What kind of fishing?

A. Halibut fishing.

Q. Have you owned any boats yourself?

A. Yes.

Q. What boats?

A. I owned the "Wabash" previous to the "Tahoma".

Q. When did you stop fishing on the "Tahoma"?

A. I came in the trip about the middle of May I think.

Q. What year?

A. Thirty-three, I would not be sure of the date.

Q. Did you have any arrangement with F. E. Hunt Company [202] concerning the "Tahoma" and the "Wave"?

A. Yes, we had sort of an agreement.

Q. Explain to the court how you happened to leave the "Tahoma" and take over the "Wave"?

A. Well, I hadn't been very well in the spring and talking it over with my brother, what I would like to do, and one thing and another, really I didn't have nerve enough—I sort of asked if he would.

Q. Did you ask him to make arrangements for you?

A. Yes, I told him what I would like to do and asked him if he would.

Q. Did he make those arrangements for you?

A. Yes.

Q. Who did he make the arrangements with?

A. Nickerson.

(Testimony of Winnie Pierce.)

Q. Of F. E. Hunt and Company?

A. Yes, manager I suppose.

Q. What were those arrangements?

Mr. FOLTA: He could not know what the arrangements were if somebody else made them.

Mr. ZIEGLER: He left the "Tahoma" and went on the "Wave" so he should know.

The COURT: He should know.

Mr. FOLTA: The question is what arrangements were made by somebody else.

The COURT: We are not interested in long-winded negotiations. I want to know what was done.

Q. I asked what arrangements were made or what arrangements did you have yourself with F. E. Hunt Company about the "Wave" and the "Tahoma"? [203]

A. After my brother talked to them he told me. Then when I come in he asked if I was agreeable to those arrangements. He said——

Q. What was that arrangement?

A. The arrangement was I thought I would get somebody in the boat that would make more money than I could.

Q. What was the idea in getting someone else on the "Tahoma"?

A. I wasn't very lucky making money with her, thought someone else could.

Q. Say anything about getting you another boat to operate?

A. Yes, he agreed to get me one.

(Testimony of Winnie Pierce.)

Q. Did they later get you one?

A. Yes.

Q. What was that, what boat?

A. The "Wave".

Q. After they got the "Wave" for you did you go out and operate it?

A. I went for a while that season. I didn't do very well. I was sick.

Q. What was it made you sick?

Mr. FOLTA: Object as immaterial.

The COURT: Sustained.

Mr. ZIEGLER: At this time I would like to offer proof by the witness at the time the negotiations were conducted he was in a nervous state, was not well, didn't feel like transacting his own business and had his brother do so for him.

The COURT: That was already stated in substance.

Q. Mr. Pierce, as I understand, you made one or two trips on the "Wave" and tied up on account of sickness? [204]

A. Yes.

Q. After that did you continue to operate the "Wave"?

A. I made one more trip that season.

Q. Did you operate her at the present time?

A. Yes.

Q. What was your arrangement about the "Tahoma" with F. E. Hunt Company—put it the other way around—did you ever sign any papers, agreements or bill of sale with Nickerson on the "Tahoma"?

(Testimony of Winnie Pierce.)

A. No, there never was any talk about a bill of sale.

Q. Ever talk to you about buying the "Tahoma" or taking it over to own it themselves?

A. No, nobody did.

Q. Did you ever agree there at any time to sell the "Tahoma" to them or anybody or any part of the "Tahoma"? Was there ever any talk between any people of F. E. Hunt Company relating to sale of the "Tahoma" to them or anybody else?

A. No.

Q. Did Mr. Nickerson here, or Milward Nickerson, ever ask you to sign a bill of sale to the "Tahoma"?

A. No.

Q. Did you sign a bill of sale or any paper in blank conveying any interest in the "Tahoma"?

A. No.

Q. Who owns the "Tahoma" at the present time?

A. I do.

Q. Since they took over the "Tahoma" and operated her have you kept any track of or tried to find out what she was earning or how she was paying off?

A. We do. [205]

Q. None of the boats have made very much have they?

A. No.

Q. Mr. Pierce, while you were operating the "Tahoma"—she was an American ship—still is?

A. Yes sir.

(Testimony of Winnie Pierce.)

Q. Did you obtain permission or consent of the Treasury Department at Washington to the manner in which you were operating the boat and fishing with her?

Mr. FOLTA: Object to that as not binding on the court.

(Argument.)

The COURT: I cannot see how it would be competent.

Mr. ZIEGLER: Our position is the letter from the United States is binding on the United States no different than if they were private litigants.

The COURT: No, a letter of that kind raises a multitude of collateral issues. You wrote a letter. What was the occasion? What information did they act on, and a dozen collateral issues.

Mr. ZIEGLER: We make the offer.

The COURT: Offer refused, exception allowed.

Mr. ZIEGLER: You may cross examine.

Cross Examination

By Mr. FOLTA:

Q. Since you were transferred to the "Wave" you have confined your operations entirely to the "Wave"—you haven't interested yourself in the operation of the "Tahoma"?

A. Oh, yes, I did.

Q. How? [206]

A. I do overhauling of the engine, take care of the engine.

Q. Have you taken care of the engine since?

A. Every winter I go over it.

(Testimony of Winnie Pierce.)

Q. So far as the navigation of the vessel is concerned, you haven't anything to do with it?

A. No.

Q. You have never directed when she should be sent out, what trips or where?

A. I can't.

Q. And of course you didn't put up any money to cover the operations of the "Tahoma" since you got off of it, did you?

A. To cover the operations?

Q. Yes, for any purpose?

A. No, her own earnings.

Q. Ever go aboard her after May 29th 1933 to give orders to anybody?

A. I go aboard her often.

Q. To give orders to anybody?

A. No.

Q. Who put up the money for the bond for the release of the "Tahoma"?

A. I don't know.

Q. You didn't?

A. No.

Q. Did you wire to me in this case?

A. Yes.

Q. You did?

A. Through Mr. Nickerson.

Q. What do you owe F. E. Hunt Company now?

[207]

A. I don't know exactly.

Q. Have any idea—don't you get statements?

A. I don't know exactly.

(Testimony of Winnie Pierce.)

Q. `Don't you get a statement?

A. Yes, but I don't know.

Q. Do you remember from these statements what your indebtedness is?

A. Roughly.

Q. What is it?

A. I wouldn't say for sure. I think it would be close to five thousand dollars, four and a half or five thousand.

Q. Any particular reason why you don't re- member?

A. No.

Q. Have you any personal indebtedness besides that?

A. No.

Q. To F. E. Hunt Company?

A. No.

Q. You had an agreement with them that they would operate the "Tahoma" for any particular length of time?

A. No, no particular length of time.

Q. It was just indefinite?

A. Until that we would try to pay her bills, keep somebody in until she could pay her bills.

Q. Do you know when the "Tahoma" made her first trip with Johnson as master?

A. I know the approximate time. I would not say the exact date, but somewhere about the last of May.

Q. Who distributed the earnings of the "Wave" since you have been in charge of her?

(Testimony of Winnie Pierce.)

A. The earnings, so far as I imagine, were for upkeep: she [208] was in a run-down condition.

Q. Who got the money she earned?

A. Went for upkeep.

Q. To whom was the money paid she received for fish?

A. As soon as it was made it had to be paid.

Q. To whom did the earnings go or proceeds from the sale of the fish?

A. I was promised the earnings of the "Wave" after she was fixed up.

Q. I am speaking of the time you took charge of the "Wave" from the beginning; to whom did the proceeds of the sale of the fish go?

A. To me first.

Q. Then where?

A. To pay for fixing up.

Q. Pay for fixing her up?

A. Yes sir.

Q. Who was that, fixed her up?

A. She was in a very run-down condition.

Q. To whom did you make payments for fixing her up?

A. Several.

Q. F. E. Hunt?

A. No, they didn't fix her.

Q. Didn't have anything to do with it?

A. No, I would have whoever I could get.

Q. Did you pay any money to F. E. Hunt from the earnings of the "Wave"?

A. No.

(Testimony of Winnie Pierce.)

Q. You have made some money, however?

A. Made some. [209]

Q. It was a profitable operation to a certain extent?

A. No sir, not yet.

Q. Although you have made some money?

A. Yes.

Q. When you were on the "Tahoma" Mr. Pierce, before May 29th, 1933 who got the proceeds from the sale of the fish?

A. You mean who took the check?

Q. Yes.

A. I did.

Q. Did you turn it over to somebody?

A. No, I settled a trip as we always do.

Q. With whom?

A. We always settle with F. E. Hunt.

Q. Did you pay off the men?

A. Yes, and expenses of the trip.

Q. And pay F. E. Hunt what was left?

A. Let it go towards the bills.

Q. How long had you known Martinson at the time he was put aboard the "Tahoma"?

A. About ten or fifteen years.

Q. How long had you known Johnson?

A. Probably about five years.

Re-direct Examination

By Mr. ZIEGLER:

Q. You were asked by Mr. Folta about the earnings from the "Tahoma". Up to the time you went

(Testimony of Winnie Pierce.)

off the "Tahoma", as I understand it, your accounts were settled through the F. E. Hunt and Company?

Mr. FOLTA: Object as leading.

Mr. ZIEGLER: It is leading. [210]

The COURT: Just ask him.

Q. You know how the accounts in halibut boats are handled by the stores on this side, in Ketchikan?

A. Yes sir.

Mr. FOLTA: Object as immaterial, no foundation laid.

Mr. ZIEGLER: I wanted to find out, if possible, whether the accounts were handled any different from on this side.

The COURT: I don't think it is material.

Mr. ZIEGLER: That is all.

(Witness Excused)

Mr. ZIEGLER: That is the Claimant's case, if the court please.

Mr. FOLTA: No rebuttal.

————

(Court thereupon recessed until 2 o'clock P. M. the same day, reconvening as per recess, with all parties present as heretofore, whereupon the cause proceeded as follows):

Mr. ZIEGLER: Before the argument commences I want to ask the court for a ruling on the various portions of evidence to which an objection was interposed. This testimony was received subject to the objection that was then made, and in order that

the record will be straight and clear on that point
I ask the court to make a ruling on all the objections upon which the court reserved its ruling. I
can't point those out to the court without going
through the record, but the objections cover all the
testimony concerning statements made by the master
of the boat and by the Consul, as I recall it, in all
those cases where the evidence was sought to be admitted by the [211] United States on the theory
that a conspiracy had been proven and which fact
rendered the testimony admissible.

Mr. FOLTA: If the court please, when Mr. Ziegler consented and asked that the affidavit of Johnson
be introduced in evidence as an exhibit and when
Mr. Nickerson got on the stand and testified freely
and voluntarily as to the arrangement with Johnson
and said Johnson's statement to the Deputy Collector of Customs at Petersburg, October 10th, 1933,
was generally true, with the exception of the amount
of extra payment he was to get, he waived every objection he had made.

Mr. ZIEGLER: I distinctly recall the additional
affidavits were stipulated to be admitted with the
understanding we had the right to have those objections urged on the court, and of course I did not
waive the objections I made by cross examining
other witnesses, because I could not anticipate the
court's ruling; in other words, I could not take the
position I am absolutely right and therefore am not
going to cross examine witnesses because if the court
admits them it is error. That is not the law or the
rule. I recall distinctly, however, these affidavits

were stipulated to be admitted with that under-standing.

(Further slight argument.)

The COURT: The testimony will be admitted for what it is worth.

Mr. ZIEGLER: Note an exception.

The COURT: Exception allowed.

(Respective counsel then addressed the Court in argument.) [212]

After argument of counsel, the following occurred:

Mr. ZIEGLER: I would like to call attention to the fact, in regard to sharing in the profits in this case. there is no profit shown until the bills are paid.

Mr. FOLTA: How about the $200.00 sent to Seattle?

Mr. ZIEGLER: That is receipts from the fish trap. But it is not a profit until the bills are paid.

Mr. FOLTA: Before the case is finally sub-mitted, the Circuit Court Rules have been changed which require parties to present their findings be-fore the decision, and I offer the findings on behalf of the Libellant.

Mr. GORE: I offer findings on behalf of the Intervenor.

Mr. ZIEGLER: I also represent the Atlas En-gine Company, and will prepare the findings for them.

Mr. GORE: The testimony of the intervenor, of course, is all in the depositions. I don't believe anyone has answered to the petition in intervention where we set forth that the property was delivered, service performed and reasonable value so much, and that the work was done. It went into the boat for the use of the boat at the request of the master and owner. That being the case the intervenor is entitled to its demand.

Mr. FOLTA: The only thing it seems to me that is wrong with that is that applied to the ordinary civil case, but in admiralty no answer is required to the petition in intervention except when it is ordered by the court. There is no such order here. While I feel sort of sorry for the lienors, because they acted rather openly about the thing, [213] as far as the United States is concerned, the evidence discloses their participation and knowledge of these acts we contend work a forfeiture. Of course, if they had such knowledge, they lose their lien.

Mr. GORE: I don't know of any such law. You don't wait until you file the intervention before you are subject to maritime lien.

Mr. FOLTA: Sure; but I mean loss by the fact that they subsequently assented to any violation of the law.

Mr. GORE: They didn't consent to any violation of the law. The evidence does not show that. The evidence only shows so far as they are concerned the transfer could be made. You cannot presume they knew of any illegal transfer.

Mr. FOLTA: That may be.

Mr. GORE: I am willing to stand on the testimony.

Mr. ZIEGLER: The same situation exists with reference to the Atlas Engine Company. It is not contested, practically admitted by the owner here. I will prepare findings and decree on their claim.

Mr. GORE: Do you think it necessary to file a separate decree?

Mr. ZIEGLER: I don't think so, unless the Court desires it.

The COURT: That rule only covers findings. The Court is going to take this matter under advisement. I would like to have the benefit of such briefs as the parties care to file, although I do not want it to drag on interminably. I will give you two weeks to prepare and present such briefs as you care to file, and will also have to have a transcript of the record I think to check up on [214] some other matters on which I am in doubt.

Mr. ZIEGLER: That will be satisfactory to us, to file our authorities that we desire to submit, in two weeks. I will try to get it before.

The COURT: I think you understand my position generally. It is this,—whether or not the facts and circumstances, as proven, are such as would work a forfeiture, that is the real question in the case as I view it. And also while we are at it the Court is going to have to consider the question— What effect those facts may have upon the lien claimants here, in their participation. I don't think that there is any question but what, aside from that,

the lien claimants, as they stand uncontested, will
be entitled to be allowed. If there is any question
about priority——

Mr. GORE: There is no question of priority
is there?

Mr. ZIEGLER: No, it is destroyed by virtue of
what Mr. Folta claims.

Mr. FOLTA: Unless it is affected with knowledge or something of that kind and comes ahead of
the forfeiture.

Mr. GORE: Yes, we all agree on that.

The COURT: Very well.

(Adjourned at 4:03 o'clock P. M.) [215]

———

[Title of Court and Cause.]

OPINION.

This cause arises on a libel filed by the United
States against the oil screw vessel "Tahoma." The
libel is in two counts. The first count charges that
on or about May 29th, 1933, at a foreign port, to-wit
the port of Prince Rupert, Province of British
Columbia, Dominion of Canada, W. Pierce, the
registered sole owner of said vessel unlawfully and
fraudulently sold and transferred in whole or in
part, by way of trust, confidence and otherwise
to a subject and citizen of a foreign state, to-wit,
F. E. Hunt, Ltd., of the Dominion of Canada, said
vessel "Tahoma."

It is further alleged that on or about the 17th
day of September, 1933 said vessel "Tahoma"

cleared from Prince Rupert, Canada, for Alaska, and on the 18th day of September, 1933, arrived within a district of the United States, to-wit: [216] the Customs Collection District of Alaska, and remained in said district until about October 5th, 1933, and that neither the master nor the person in charge of said vessel, within eight days after said vessel arrived in said district of the United States, or any other time, surrendered or delivered up to the Collector of Customs for said District of Alaska the certificate of registry so procured as aforesaid by the said W. Pierce.

The second count alleges that from the time of the sale and transfer as aforesaid on or about May 29th, 1933, and continuously up to the time of her seizure as aforesaid said vessel was unlawfully and fraudulently engaged in foreign trade, and said certificate of registry so granted and issued as aforesaid for said vessel was knowingly and fraudulently used for a vessel (the "Tahoma") not entitled to the benefit thereof by reason of the sale and transfer of said vessel as aforesaid. That all and singular the matters aforesaid are contrary to the provisions of the laws of the United States regulating the sale, transfer and operation of vessels under its registry and that by reason of the premises and by virtue of the laws of the United States the said vessel "Tahoma," her engine, tackle, apparel, cargo, etc. became forfeited.

Following the seizure of said vessel under said libel the defendant, W. Pierce, filed a claim to said vessel as the owner thereof and moved that she be released under bond, which was subsequently done.

Thereafter libels of intervention were filed by the above named intervenors and an answer filed by claimant, and after issues joined as to all the parties in interest trial [217] was had thereon.

It is undenied that on March 31st, 1925 at the port of Ketchikan and within the collection district of Alaska the oil screw vessel "Tahoma" was duly registered according to law and the official number 214,741 was assigned to her, and the certificate of registry issued entitling said vessel to engage in foreign trade, which certificate was in full force and effect and used by said vessel during all the times mentioned in the libel. It further appears that during all the time mentioned in the libel said vessel "Tahoma" was engaged in halibut fishing, plying between American waters and Prince Rupert, Canada, and sold its catches for shipment to American markets via Prince Rupert duty free.

It is contended by the Government that on or about May 29th, 1933 F. E. Hunt, Ltd., a foreign corporation and citizen of Great Britain, took over the active control, management and operation of the "Tahoma" and the shipment of its catches of halibut to American markets, and applied the proceeds thereof in payment of the indebtedness of said vessel to said foreign corporation and to bills owed by said vessel to the intervenors.

The evidence shows that by May, 1933, the "Tahoma" became so heavily indebted to F. E.

Hunt, Ltd., that said corporation made a deal with W. Pierce, the registered owner of the vessel, whereby said corporation turned over the American halibut schooner "Wave" to said claimant for his equity in the "Tahoma" and thereafter assumed the active management, control and operation of the "Tahoma" and collected and disbursed the earnings of the "Tahoma" for the benefit of itself and the intervenors. The agreement is set [218] forth in Libellant's exhibits "1" to "8". The libellant contends that this agreement constitutes a conspiracy to defraud the United States of its revenue and of the function, authority and right to have vessels documented under the laws of the United States owned wholly by and in command of masters who are citizens of the United States. The Libellant further claims that F. E. Hunt, Ltd., G. W. Nickerson, W. Pierce, B. A. Petterson, John A. Johnson, Antone Martinsen and the intervenors became parties to this conspiracy and that in pursuance thereof the claimant Pierce was forced to transfer his equity in the "Tahoma" to F. E. Hunt. Ltd., for Petterson's equity in the "Wave" while Antone Martinsen, a foreigner, was placed in command of the "Tahoma," the name of John A. Johnson, an American, twenty-two years old, being endorsed on the certificate of registry of the "Tahoma" as master. The libellant, however, contends that this appointment of Johnson was made for the sole purpose of facilitating the evasion of the shipping and customs laws of the United States and continuing the operation of the "Tahoma" under American registry to secure exemption from the payment of the duty on its catches; that Johnson was only master in name and for the purposes aforesaid but had and exercised no authority over the operation of said vessel, but that the real master of said vessel was Martinsen, a British subject acting by appointment of and under the orders of F. E. Hunt, Ltd.

The claimant Pierce contends that such operation of the "Tahoma" was not inconsistent with his ownership thereof; that there was no transfer nor change of ownership; and that he consented to such a change in her operation for the benefit of the creditors and lienors of said vessel. [219]

The libellant contends that the evidence, viewed in the light of all the attendant circumstances, shows such a change of ownership or transfer of interest in the "Tahoma" as to work a forfeiture of claimant's interest. It claims that F. E. Hunt, Ltd., in effect coerced the intervenors under threat of enforcing its superior lien (Libellant's exhibit No. 4) to assent to the arrangement outlined for the removal of Pierce, the then record owner and master and claimant herein, from the "Tahoma" and placing him on the "Wave", giving him Petterson's equity in the "Wave" in exchange for claimant's equity in the "Tahoma," and this appears to be borne out by the evidence. It is of no avail to say that there was no formal transfer, no recording with American customs officials of formal documents as pointed out by the claimant, for such documents could not be recorded unless such sale was first made known to and authorized by the United States Shipping Board and sale authorized in conformity with our law. On the other hand it is quite apparent that the ownership status of the "Tahoma" and "Wave" did not remain as before the agreements, evidenced by exhibits numbers "1" to "8" inclusive, were put into effect. The question in this case is not whether there was a record transfer of the vessel in question, but rather whether there was such an actual or equitable transfer as to be subversive of our statutes. The object of the law is to give to American ship owners and to them only, a preference by allowing fish, etc. caught by them to enter this country duty free, and of course at the same time to deny such preference to foreigners. That being the object, the law should be so interpreted as to effectuate its object, and if anyone other than an American [220] citizen profited through evasion of the customs by any arrangement, no matter what its character, by or through the catch of the "Tahoma" it was a fraud on both the letter and spirit of the law. In the instant case, even the method of operation of the vessel was a fraud on the customs laws of the United States, and a studied effort at their evasion. F. E. Hunt, Ltd. appointed an American master (on paper) who was not the actual master at all but merely a puppet of their

own, appointed because he was a citizen of the
United States, in an effort to circumvent the law,
and because the real master could not qualify as
master under our law.

The F. E. Hunt Company, Ltd. seeks to justify
its conduct in taking over and operating the "Tahoma" under the guise of a creditors, rather than
enforcing its right as a creditor under Canadian
laws, by contending that the "Tahoma" could have
been libelled under the Canadian laws at Prince
Rupert and sold and placed under Canadian registry, but the reason for not having done so is
very apparent. To have done so would have en-
tailed the initial outlay of twenty-five per cent of
her sale price as duty before she could be put
under Canadian registry, and a six per cent sales
tax and loss of the exemption from the payment
of a duty of two cents a pound on the halibut
shipped to her principal market, viz. the United
States. The desire to avoid these consequences furnished the motive to attempt to continue the operation of the "Tahoma" under her American registry and take their chances on being discovered
in their operation.

In June, 1933, Captain Petterson, master of the
"Wave" told the American consul at Prince Rupert
(Tp. 120) that at the request of F. E. Hunt, Ltd.
he transferred his [221] equity in the "Wave" to
F. E. Hunt, Ltd. in payment of the boats' indebtedness to that firm. G. W. Nickerson, the manager
of F. E. Hunt, Ltd. testified to the same effect

(Tp. 183). He further said that F. E. Hunt, Ltd. bought the "Wave" "in order to get a boat for W. Pierce to operate." In F. E. Hunt's letter to the intervenors on June 17, 1933 (Libellant's exhibit No. 6) Nickerson says "In connection with the boat we are transferring to Pierce there is some little work to be done on her and as soon as we get 'our' bills we will send you a statement of just what the total indebtedness against the 'Tahoma' will be," which indicates pretty conclusively that F. E. Hunt, Ltd. was not acting as Pierce's agent and flatly contradicts the testimony of Nickerson as to the capacity in which he acted. Nickerson further testified (Tp. 186) that when the matter of the indebtedness of the "Tahoma" came up in the spring of 1933 "Hunt was going to take a bill of sale or get an equity in the 'Tahoma'" and (Tp. 187) that Hunt decided they would take a blank bill of sale to the "Tahoma", not for themselves, but that "it would have to be decided from a legal standpoint who could take the bill of sale." All of this goes to show what the real transaction was and that the principal concern of F. E. Hunt, Ltd. was to cover its own tracks so effectually that in case anything should happen it would not be caught in its own trap.

The Court finds that the evidence in this case is sufficient to warrant a finding of probable cause for the institution of the proceedings under both the first and second counts of the libel, and we so find. "Probable cause" as used in this connection, means

no more than present [222] circumstances creating
suspicion. (U. S. vs. Certain Jewelry, 59 Fed. 684;
and Feathers of Wild Birds vs. U. S. 267 Fed.
964-966). Having found that there was probable
cause for the institution of the libel, the burden of
proof is thereby cast on the claimant, but has not
been sustained by him.

The explanation offered by the claimant and F.
E. Hunt, Ltd. of the taking over of the "Tahoma"
are both unsatisfactory and unconvincing. It is admitted by claimant's answer that the "Tahoma"
and her master in charge failed to surrender or deliver to the Collector of Customs for the Alaska
District the certificate of her registry within eight
days after the arrival in Alaskan waters or at all.

I believe from the testimony in this case that
there was such a transfer of the "Tahoma" as the
law in question seeks to guard against. I was confirmed in that opinion by the actions and testimony
on the stand of both Nickerson, the Hunt Company
manager, and of Pierce, the pseudo claimant, both
of whom were halting, evasive and generally unsatisfactory witnesses. Pierce didn't seem to have
any intelligent idea of what had transpired regarding his interest in the "Tahoma" or its transfer,
and had little or no conception of what occurred,
after his transfer to the "Wave", and admitted
blandly that he knew little or nothing about the
operations of the "Tahoma" after his transfer to
the "Wave" nor what she made or to whom her
earnings were disbursed, except that he knew that he

didn't participate in them, except by a possible application of them to his indebtedness, and no statement of that had ever been furnished to him, while Nickerson, though glib enough, was generally evasive on the [223] vital points of his testimony. I am therefore forced to the conclusion that there has been an unlawful and fraudulent transfer of the "Tahoma" to F. E. Hunt, Ltd., a British subject, in contravention of our law.

It follows that if there was an unlawful or fraudulent transfer, as found, that the certificate of registry of the "Tahoma" was unlawfully and fraudulently used in a foreign trade by the "Tahoma" after she was no longer entitled to the benefits thereof by reason of the alleged transfer in violation of Sections 60 and 808, Title 46, U. S. C. A., because it is admitted that the "Tahoma" was engaged in halibut fishing and in the sale of her catch to American markets during the entire period of time up to the date of her seizure.

We therefore find that the allegations of the libel have been sustained and judgment for forfeiture is hereby ordered.

Regarding the intervenors, there is some evidence to the effect that they understood something of what was being done by the F. E. Hunt Company, but in their eagerness to collect their claims they were either ignorant or careless of the results of their own conduct. It appears, however, that their claims are based on work done and supplies furnished for the vessel long preceding any connection

with F. E. Hunt, Ltd. and long before any violation
of the law took place and it can hardly be said that
they knowingly participated in the fraudulent transfer or operation of the vessel "Tahoma" by F. E.
Hunt, Ltd., and as their liens are good maritime
liens and accrued prior to the illegal acts complained
of, their claims will be allowed in the principal [224]
sums prayed for but on account of their conduct,
without costs or counsel fees to any of the intervenors.

Findings and judgment may be prepared in accordance with this opinion.

Dated at Juneau, Alaska, September 7th, 1935.

GEO. F. ALEXANDER,

Judge.

[Endorsed]: Filed in the District Court, Territory
of Alaska, First Division, Sep. 7, 1935. Robert E.
Coughlin, Clerk. [225]

[Title of Court and Cause.]

ORDER EXTENDING TERM OF COURT FOR PURPOSE OF SETTLING BILL OF EXCEPTIONS AND TRANSMITTING APOSTLES ON APPEAL.

Now on this day, upon motion of appellants Proctor, the court being fully advised in the premises,

IT IS HEREBY ORDERED that the time for
the return of the Citation on appeal herein be, and

the same hereby is extended until March 20th, 1936; and,

IT IS HEREBY FURTHER ORDERED, that the time for the filing, allowance and settlement of appellant's Bill of Exceptions herein be, and the same is enlarged and extended to February 20th, 1936; and,

IT IS HEREBY FURTHER ORDERED, That the present term of the District Court for the District of Alaska, Division Number One, in which term the decree appealed from, was entered, be, and the same hereby is kept alive and open and extended to March 20th, 1936, for the purposes above mentioned and in order to enable appellants to cause to be transmitted to the Circuit Court for the Ninth Circuit the Apostles on Appeal, which time [226] is accordingly hereby allowed to the appellants, and that the bond for release of the vessel be considered as a supersedeas bond.

Dated at Juneau, Alaska, December 17, 1935.

GEO. F. ALEXANDER,
District Judge.

[Endorsed]: Filed in the District Court, Territory of Alaska, First Division, Dec. 17, 1935. Robert E. Coughlin, Clerk. By Peggy D. McLeod, Deputy. [227]

[Title of Court and Cause.]

`   PETITION FOR APPEAL:

W. Pierce, Claimant, and J. R. Heckman, Surety, herein, conceiving themselves aggrieved by the final Decree of the Court entered herein on November 23rd, 1935, forfeiting the OIL SCREW VESSEL "TAHOMA", etc., to the United States, and having filed their assignments of error herein, pray the Court to allow an appeal to the Honorable United States Circuit Court of Appeals for the Ninth Circuit and to fix the amount of cost bond on appeal, and to allow the Bond heretofore filed in the above suit for the Release of the OIL VESSEL TAHOMA etc., to serve as a supersedeas.

Dated this 14th day of December, 1935.

A. H. ZIEGLER

Proctor for Appellants.

Copy received and service admitted before the filing of this Petition with the Clerk of the Court, this 17th day of Dec. 1935.

G. W. FOLTA, Asst. U. S. Atty.

Proctor for United States of America

LESTER O. GORE

Proctor for Intervenors.

[Endorsed]: "Filed in the District Court Territory of Alaska, First Division, Dec. 17, 1935. Robert E. Coughlin, Clerk. By Peggy D. McLeod, Deputy." [228]

[Title of Court and Cause.]

NOTICE OF APPEAL

To: The United States of America, and Its Proctor, W. A. Holzheimer, Atlas Engine Company and Fishing Vessel Owners Marine Ways, corporations, and their Proctor, L. O. Gore:

You and each of you will please take notice that the undersigned, W. Pierce and J. R. Heckman, appeal from the final decree made, entered and signed by the Honorable George F. Alexander, Judge of the District Court for the District of Alaska, in the above entitled cause, on the 23rd day of November, 1935, whereby the said court ordered and decreed the forfeiture to the United States the OIL SCREW VESSEL TAHOMA, etc., and rendered judgment against J. R. Heckman, as surety on the bond for release of attached property in the above suit, and from each and every order, decree, ruling, finding, step and proceeding had, made, rendered and entered in the above entitled cause, taking and making such appeal to the Circuit Court of Appeals for the Ninth Circuit. [229]

Dated at Ketchikan, Alaska, December 14th, 1935.

A. H. ZIEGLER,
Proctor for Appellants.

Copy received and service admitted before the filing of this Notice with the Clerk of the above court, this 17th day of Dec. 1935.

G. W. FOLTA
Proctor for the United States
of America
LESTER O. GORE
Proctor for Intervenors.

[Endorsed]: "Filed in the District Court Territory of Alaska, First Division Dec 17 1935. Robert E. Coughlin Clerk. By Peggy D. McLeod, Deputy." [230]

[Title of Court and Cause.]

ASSIGNMENT OF ERRORS.

W. Pierce and J. R. Heckman, Claimant and Surety, respectively, appellants herein, say that in the record Findings of Fact and Conclusions of Law, Final Decree, Opinion, orders and proceedings of the District Court for the District of Alaska, there are manifest and material errors, and said W. Pierce and J. R. Heckman now make, assign and present the following Assignment of Errors therein, on which they rely, to-wit:

I.

The district court erred in receiving in evidence, over claimant's objection, libelant's Exhibit No. 10.

II.

The District Court erred in admitting in evidence the following testimony given by G. C. Woodward, a witness upon behalf of libelant, to-wit:

"Q. After Johnson's name was entered as master of the "TAHOMA" on the register, do you know where Tony Martin was employed?

A. You mean on the vessel? [231]

Q. Yes, he was employed on the "TA-HOMA", do you know whether or not he was employed—during the time Johnson was acting as master was Tony Martinson employed aboard the "TAHOMA"?

A. My understanding is he was working on the "TAHOMA" before Johnson was master."

Because said testimony was incompetent, irrelevant and immaterial, and to which testimony an objection was duly made and exception allowed.

III.

The District Court erred in receiving in evidence, over claimant's objection, the following testimony given by G. C. Woodward, a witness upon behalf of libelant, to-wit:

"Q. Mr. Woodward, can you tell by looking at that Bill of Sale to whom that Bill of sale was first made out?

A. If I am wrong in what I am stating, stop me; but Captain Petterson told me he had made a Bill of Sale to Winnie Pierce."

Because said testimony was hearsay and no foundation was alleged or made for its admission and to which testimony claimant duly objected and moved be stricken and to which ruling the Court in receiving said evidence an exception was duly allowed.`

IV.

The District Court erred in receiving in evidence, over claimant's objection, the following testimony:

"Q. Did Petterson say under what circumstances he transferred the "WAVE"?

A. That it was for debts he owed Messrs. Hunt & Co.—his understanding was——"

Because said testimony was hearsay and incompetent and no proper foundation plead or laid for the reception of said testimony in evidence. To the introduction of such evidence an exception was duly noted by the Court. [232]

V.

The Court erred in receiving in evidence the following testimony offered by Bernard Hansen, a witness upon behalf of libelant, to-wit:

"Q. Captain, will you state what is the practice as to docking a halibut schooner in the halibut fishing trade coming into dock, particularly with a load of fish, like into Prince Rupert, if the master is aboard and up, who docks the boat?

A. It depends. Of course, if the master is on deck coming into the port naturally he would land the boat. Of course, in case he is sleeping, sometimes you have a man who knows how to handle the boat, he would not call him to get up, but if he is on deck he will land his own boat."

Because said testimony was immaterial and to the introduction of which testimony claimant objected.

VI.

The District Court erred in failing to permit claimant to testify in answer to the following question, to-wit:

"Q. Did you obtain permission or consent of the Treasury Department to the manner in which you were operating the boat and fishing with her?"

And in refusing to receive in evidence the following letter from the Treasury Department of the United States to W. Pierce, to-wit:

"TREASURY DEPARTMENT
Bureau of Customs
Washington

August 29, 1933

Mr. Winnie Pierce,
P. O. Box 396
Prince Rupert, B. C.
Sir:

The Bureau is in receipt of your letter of July 29, 1933, in regard to the operation of the gas ship TAHOMA as an American fishery.

[233]

The Bureau, after a careful consideration of the matter, perceives no objection to the Consul issuing the free entry documents for the fish taken by the TAHOMA at the present time.

The State Department has been advised to this effect.

By direction of the Commissioner:

Respectfully,

(Signed) H. A. HAYWARD

Assistant General Counsel

VII.

The District Court erred at the conclusion of the libelant's case in failing to dismiss the libel and granting judgment for claimant which was based on the ground that the allegations of the libel had not been sustained and on the further ground that the evidence of libelant uncontradicted failed to establish a degree of proof required by law to warrant a forfeiture of the "TAHOMA".

VIII.

The District Court erred in failing to grant claimant's motion for a dismissal of the action upon the ground that the evidence introduced was not sufficient to constitute a violation of law of Alaska or the United States.

IX.

The District Court erred in finding as it did in Finding of Fact No. 2 entered by the Court as follows:

That during all the times mentioned in the libel the said vessel "TAHOMA" was engaged in halibut fishing, plying between American waters and Prince Rupert, Canada, and sold its catches for shipment to American markets, via Prince Rupert, duty free.

X.

The District Court erred in finding as it did in Finding of Fact No. 3 entered by the Court as follows:

> That on or about May 29, 1933, F. E. Hunt, Ltd., a foreign corporation, a citizen of Great Britain, [234] (with the consent, knowledge and agreement of intervenors herein) took over the active control, management and operation of the "TAHOMA" and the shipment of its catches of halibut to American markets, in payment of the indebtedness of said vessel to said corporation (1) by removing the record owner and master, W. Pierce from command of the "TAHOMA" and placing him in charge of another American vessel, to-wit, the "WAVE": (2) by making a colorable appointment of J. A. Johnson, an American citizen, as master of the "TAHOMA" for the sole purpose of dealing with the libelant in matters pertaining to and arising under the customs, navigation and shipping laws of the United States; (3) by placing Antone Martinson, a citizen of Great Britain, actually in charge command and control of said vessel when away from Prince Rupert, and (4) by receiving and distributing the earnings and profits from such operations, and sharing therein.

XI.

The District Court erred in finding as it did in Finding of Fact No. 7 entered by the Court as follows:

That during all of the time mentioned herein no duty was paid on the halibut caught by the "TAHOMA", its master and crew, and shipped into the United States via Prince Rupert, B. C.

XII.

The District Court erred in making the Conclusions of Law it did in the above suit which were as follows:

I.

That on or about May 29, 1933, at Prince Rupert B. C. the American vessel "Tahoma" was transferred in whole or in part, by way of trust, confidence and otherwise, to F. E. Hunt, Ltd., a citizen of Great Britain; and that the said F. E. Hunt, Ltd., thereby became entitled to the whole or part or share of and became indirectly interested in such vessel and in the profits and issues thereof, and became the equitable owner of said vessel.

II.

That thereafter and until the seizure of the "TAHOMA" the said vessel was unlawfully and fraudulently engaged in a foreign trade and the said certificate of registry was knowingly and fraudulently used for said vessel when she was no longer entitled to the benefit of said register. [235]

III.

That all the shipments of halibut made by the said vessel or F. E. Hunt, Ltd., during all the times mentioned in the libel were subject to an import duty of two cents a pound under the provisions of the tariff act (19 U. S. C. A. 1001, par. 717) and that such shipments were made in fraud of the revenue of the United States.

V.

That the vessel "TAHOMA" became forfeited as of May 29, 1933, to the United States under the first cause of action, and as of September 27, 1933, under the second cause of action.

Because the Conclusions so made by the Court were contrary to the evidence and law in the case and unsupported by the facts, the evidence, and the law applicable thereto.

XIII.

The District Court erred in not making the following Findings of Fact requested by claimant.

I.

That W. Pierce, the registered owner of the Oil Screw "TAHOMA" did not, as alleged in the libel, or at all, unlawfully and fraudulently sell, in whole or in part by way of trust, confidence, or otherwise, to a subject and citizen of a foreign state, to-wit, F. E. Hunt, Ltd., the said vessel "TAHOMA".

II.

That said "Tahoma" did not, as alleged in the libel, unlawfully or fraudulently engaged in foreign trade, and the certificate of registry of the "TAHOMA" was not knowingly or fraudulently used for a vessel, to-wit, the vessel "TAHOMA", not entitled to the benefits thereof.

III.

That the consideration of Pierce, owner of the "TAHOMA" in permitting F. E. Hunt, Ltd., to take over the operation and management of the "TAHOMA", was that Pierce should receive the boat "WAVE," of the value of $500.00, with which to make a living, for which consideration Pierce agreed that the "TAHOMA" should be operated in order that the indebtedness of the "TAHOMA" could be paid off, and it was further agreed between [236] Pierce and F. E. Hunt, Ltd., that if a sale of the "TAHOMA" could be made, Pierce would consent thereto, and the purchase price be applied in payment of Pierce's indebtedness and the remainder. if any, be paid to Pierce.

IV.

That F. E. Hunt, Ltd., and the above Intervenors, did not agree to, nor did they at any time. release Pierce from his indebtedness to them, nor did Pierce at any time agree to permit said F. E. Hunt. Ltd., and the Intervenors to take and receive the "TAHOMA," FOR the boat "WAVE" and payment of his indebtedness to said corporations.

V.

That the arrangement made between Pierce, F. E. Hunt, Ltd., and the Intervenors, for the operation of the "TAHOMA", by said F. E. Hunt, Ltd., was made in good faith and with the honest belief on the part of all concerned that said arrangement did not constitute a violation of law.

VI.

That there was no evidence in writing of the sale or transfer of the "TAHOMA," or of any interest therein.

V.

That after F. E. Hunt, Ltd.. took over the operation and management of the "TAHOMA," W. Pierce, Claimant, performed work on the "TAHOMA", during the winter, or closed fishing season and received no pay therefor.

XIV.

The District Court erred in refusing to find as a Conclusion of Law that the American Oil Vessel "TAHOMA," her engine, tackle, apparel, cargo, etc., did not become forfeited by reason of the matters and things set forth in the libel or at all.

XV.

The District Court Erred in entering its Decree in the above suit decreeing that the Oil Screw Vessel "TAHOMA", etc. [237] was subject to forfeiture and should be forfeited.

XVI.

The District Court erred in finding and deciding that there was probable cause for the seizure of the Oil Screw Vessel "TAHOMA", etc.

XVII.

The District Court erred in finding and deciding that the burden of proof was cast on the claimant to prove that the Oil Screw Vessel "TAHOMA." etc. had not become subject to forfeiture.

WHEREFORE, the appellants pray that said Final Decree be reversed and that such other decrees and orders as may be just and proper in the premises be made herein.

A. H. ZIEGLER,

Proctor for Appellants.

Copy received and service admitted this 17 day of December, 1935.

G. W. FOLTA,

Proctor for Libelant.

Copy received and service admitted this 16 day of December, 1935.

LESTER O. GORE,

Proctor for Intervenors.

[Endorsed]: "Filed in the District Court, Territory of Alaska, First Division, Dec. 17, 1935. Robert E. Coughlin, Clerk. By Peggy D. McLeod, Deputy."

[238]

[Title of Court and Cause.]

PRAECIPE FOR APOSTLES ON APPEAL.

To Robert E. Coughlin, Clerk of the above entitled
Court:

Please prepare transcript of record in this cause
on Appeal to the United States Circuit Court of
Appeals for the Ninth Circuit, and include in said
transcript the following:

Statement required by Admiralty Rule 4,
Sec. 1, subdivision (a), (b) and (c) of said Circuit Court of Appeals, Ninth Circuit.

The following pleadings:

Libel.

Answer to Libel.

Claim of Owner.

Stipulation for Costs.

Stipulation for Release of Vessel.

Order of Release (of Vessel).

Requested Findings of Fact of Fishing Vessel Owners Marine Ways (2); Claimant's Requested Findings of Fact and Conclusions (2);

Findings of Fact and Conclusions of Law.

Exceptions of Claimant to Findings and Conclusions, etc.

Opinion of Court.

Decree.

Exception of Claimant to Decree.

Assignment of Errors.

Notice of Appeal and Petition for Appeal.

Bond for Costs on Appeal.

Order Allowing Appeal.

Order Extending Term of Court, etc.

Citation on Appeal.

Libelant's exhibits 1 to 15 except 14, Respondent's Exhibits A and B.

A. H. ZIEGLER,
Proctor for Claimant W. Pierce,
and Surety, J. R. Heckman.

[Endorsed]: Filed in the District Court, Territory of Alaska, First Division at Ketchikan, Feb. 24, 1936. Robert E. Coughlin, Clerk. [239]

———

[Title of Court and Cause.]

BOND FOR COSTS ON APPEAL.

KNOW ALL MEN BY THESE PRESENTS: That the undersigned, W. Pierce and J. R. Heckman, as principals, and N. R. Walker, Ketchikan, Alaska, as surety, are held and firmly bound unto the United States of America, the libelant, in the sum of Two Hundred Fifty ($250.00) Dollars to be paid to the said United States of America, for the payment of which well and truly to be made we bind ourselves, our successors and assigns, by these presents.

Sealed with our seals and dated this 14th day of December, 1935.

WHEREAS, W. Pierce and J. R. Heckman, as appellants have appealed to the United States Cir-

cuit Court of Appeals for the Ninth Circuit from a
Final Decree entered in the above entitled cause
bearing date of the 23rd of November, 1935.

NOW, THEREFORE, the condition of this obligation is such that if the above named appellants,
W. Pierce and J. R. Heckman [240] shall prosecute said appeal with effect, and pay all costs which
may be awarded against them as such appellants if
said appeal is not sustained, then this obligation
shall be void, otherwise the same shall be and remain in full force and effect.

> W. PIERCE and J. R. HECKMAN
> By A. H. ZIEGLER, their Proctor
> N. R. WALKER, Surety

Subscribed and sworn to before me this 14th day
of December, 1935.

[Notarial Seal]   LESTER O. GORE,
Notary Public for Alaska. My commission expires
> Nov. 27, 1938.

United States of America,
Territory of Alaska—ss.

N. R. WALKER, being first duly sworn on oath
deposes and says: That I am a resident of the Territory of Alaska, and am worth the sum of Five
Hundred ($500.00) Dollars over and above all my
just debts and liabilities and exclusive of property
exempt from execution, and that I am not a coun-
sellor or attorney at law, marshal, deputy marshal,
clerk of court, or other officer of any court.

> N. R. WALKER

Subscribed and sworn to before me this 14th day
of December, 1935.

[Notarial Seal]   LESTER O. GORE,
Notary Public for Alaska. My commission expires
    Nov. 27, 1938.

O.K.   LESTER O. GORE
                    Proctor for Intervenors.

[Endorsed]: Filed in the District Court Territory
of Alaska, First Division Dec. 17, 1935. Robert E.
Coughlin Clerk By Peggy D. McLeod Deputy. [241]

[Title of Court and Cause.]

STIPULATION FOR COSTS

WHEREAS, a libel has been filed in this Court
on the 17th day of September, 1934, against the Oil
Screw Vessel TAHOMA, official number 214741, her
engine, tackle, apparel, furniture, dories, gear, cargo,
etc., for the reasons and causes in said libel mentioned, and

WHEREAS, a claim has been filed in this cause
by Winnie Pierce, and the said F. J. CHAPMAN
of Ketchikan, Alaska, by occupation Laundryman,
surety, and the said claimant hereby consenting and
agreeing that in case of default or contumacy on
the part of the claimant or his surety, execution
for the sum of Five Hundred ($500.00) Dollars,
may issue against their goods, chattels and lands.

NOW, THEREFORE, IT IS HEREBY STIPU-
LATED AND AGREED for the benefit of whom it
may concern, that the stipulators undersigned are,

and each of them is hereby bound in the sum of [242] Five Hundred ($500.00) Dollars, conditioned that the claimant above named shall pay all costs and expenses which shall be awarded against him by the final decree of this Court, or upon appeal, by the Appellate Court.

WINNIE PIERCE, Claimant, Principal
By A. H. ZIEGLER, Proctor.
F. J. CHAPMAN, Surety.

United States of America,
Territory of Alaska—ss.

F. J. CHAPMAN, being a party to the above stipulation, being first duly sworn on oath, deposes and says: That he resides as above set forth and is worth the sum of One Thousand ($1000.00) Dollars over and above all just debts and liabilities; that he is not a counselor or attorney at law, marshal, deputy marshal, clerk of the court, or other officer of any court.

F. J. CHAPMAN

Subscribed and sworn to before me this 22nd day of September, 1934.

[Seal]   MARGARET OTTESEN
Notary Public for Alaska. My Com. ex. 10/23/37.

[243]

[Title of Court and Cause.]

STIPULATION FOR RELEASE OF ATTACHED VESSEL

KNOW ALL MEN BY THESE PRESENTS, that we, WINNIE PIERCE, principal, and J. R. HECKMAN, Ketchikan, Alaska, occupation Banker, are held and firmly bound in the penal sum of Eight Thousand ($8,000.00) Dollars, unto William T. Mahoney, United States Marshal for the First Division of the District of Alaska, his executors, administrators, successors or assigns, for the payment of which well and truly to be made, we bind ourselves and each of us and each of our heirs, executors, administrators and assigns, jointly and severally, firmly by these presents.

Sealed with our seals and dated this 22nd day of September, 1934.

> WINNIE PIERCE, Claimant and Principal
> By A. H. ZIEGLER, Proctor
> J. R. HECKMAN Surety

WHEREAS, a libel has been filed in the District Court of the United States for the First Division of Alaska on the 17th [244] day of September, 1934, by the United States of America, libelant, against the Oil Screw TAHOMA, official number 214741, he rengine, tackle, apparel furniture, dories, gear, cargo, etc., on which process of attachment has issued and the said ship is in the custody of the United States Marshal under the said atachment and the said Winnie Pierce having applied for a discharge of said ship from the custody of the Marshal and having filed a claim claiming the said property as owner, and having filed a stipulation for claimant's costs pursuant to the rules and practices of the said Court,

NOW, THEREFORE, the condition of this obligation is such that if the above bounden shall abide by and perform the decree of this Court and the appellate court, then this obligation shall be void, otherwise the same shall be a— remain in full force and virtue.

> WINNIE PIERCE, Claimant and principal
> By A. H. ZIEGLER, Proctor
> J. R. HECKMAN, Surety

United States of America,
Territory of Alaska—ss.

J. R. HECKMAN, being first duly sworn, on oath, deposes and says: That I am a resident and inhabitant of the Territory of Alaska, but no marshal, counselor at law, clerk of court, or other officer of any court, and that I am worth the sum of Sixteen Thousand ($16,000.00) Dollars over and above all just debts and liabilities and exclusive of property exempt from execution.

> J. R. HECKMAN

Subscribed and sworn to before me this 22nd day of September, 1934.

[Notarial Seal]   MARGARET OTTESEN
Notary Public for Alaska. My com. ex. 10/23/37

[Endorsed]: Filed in the District Court Territory of Alaska, First Division Sep. 24, 1934, Robert E. Coughlin, Clerk. By R. Russell, Deputy." [245]

[Title of Court and Cause.]

ORDER OF RELEASE OF ATTACHED PROPERTY

Winnie Pierce, having filed his claim of ownership to the above described property, and a motion to release the same from the seizure and attachment by the U. S. Marshal for the First Division of the District of Alaska, and,

It appearing the value of said property has been stipulated in the sum of $8,000.00; and, the said claimant having filed his stipulation for costs and a stipulation in the sum of $8,000.00, for the redelivery or return of said attached property, as required by law,

NOW, THEREFORE, It is hereby ordered that the above property be, and the same hereby is, ordered released, and surrendered by the U. S. Marshal, to the claimant, or to his proctor, A. H. Ziegler.

Dated at Ketchikan, Alaska, September 24th, 1934.

GEO. F. ALEXANDER,
District Judge.

[Endorsed]: "Filed in the District Court Territory of Alaska, First Division, Sept. 24, 1934. Robert E. Coughlin, Clerk. By R. Russell, Deputy."
[246]

[Title of Court and Cause.]

ORDER ALLOWING APPEAL

W. E. Pierce, Claimant, and J. R. Heckman, Surety, appellants, having filed herein their petition for an order allowing an appeal to the Circuit Court of Appeals for the Ninth Circuit and it appearing from the records and files in this cause that they are entitled to an appeal and that the same should be allowed.

NOW, THEREFORE, IT IS HEREBY ORDERED that an appeal be, and the same hereby is allowed the said appellants, W. E. Pierce and J. R. Heckman, to the Circuit Court of Appeals for the Ninth Circuit in the above entitled suit and from the judgment and decree of this court entered and filed in the above entitled suit on the 23rd day of November, 1935, and

IT IS FURTHER ORDERED that the amount of the cost bond on appeal be, and same hereby is fixed at $250.00, and the cost bond filed with this order is hereby approved; and,

IT IS FURTHER ORDERED that the Bond for Release of [247] attached property filed herein shall operate as a supersedeas and execution hereby is stayed.

Dated at Juneau, Alaska, December 17th, 1935.

GEO. F. ALEXANDER,

District Judge.

[Endorsed:] "Filed in the District Court Territory of Alaska, First Division December 17, 1935. Robert E. Coughlin, Clerk. By Peggy McLeod, Deputy." [248]

[Title of Court and Cause.]

CITATION ON APPEAL.

The President of the United States to the United
    States of America, Atlas Engine Company, a
    corporation, and Fishing Vessel Owners Marine
    Ways, a corporation and to their Proctors, W.
    A. Holzheimer and L. O. Gore:

You are hereby cited and admonished to be and
appear in the United States Circuit Court of Appeals for the Ninth Circuit to be holden at San
Francisco, State of California, within thirty days
from the date of this citation pursuant to a petition
and order allowing appeal and this citation filed in
the office of the District Court, Division Number
One, Territory of Alaska, in a cause wherein W. E.
Pierce and J. R. Heckman are appellants and you
appellees, and then and there to show cause, if any
there by, why the Final Decree in said petition,
order allowing appeal and this citation on appeal
mentioned should not be corrected on appeal and
speedy justice done to the parties in that behalf,

WITNESS the Honorable Charles Evans Hughes,
Chief Justice of the United States this 17th day
of December, 1935.

                    GEO. F. ALEXANDER,
                                Judge.

Due service of the above Citation admitted.
Dec. 17, 1935.

G. W. FOLTA,
Proctor for the United States.
LESTER O. GORE,
Proctor for Intervenors.

[Endorsed:] Filed in the District Court Territory of Alaska, First Division. Dec. 17, 1935. Robert E. Coughlin, Clerk. By Peggy L. McLeod, Deputy.

[249]

———

[Title of Court and Cause.]

CLAIM OF OWNER

Comes now Winnie Pierce, by his proctor, A. H. Ziegler, and appears before this Honorable Court, and makes claim to the said Oil Screw Vessel TAHOMA, official number 214741, her engine, tackle, apparel, furniture, dories, gear, cargo, etc., as the same are attached and seized by the United States Marshal for the District of Alaska, Division Number One, and avers that he is the true and bona fide owner of the said Oil Screw TAHOMA and that no one else is the owner thereof.

WHEREFORE claimant prays to defend accordingly.

A. H. ZIEGLER

Subscribed and sworn to before me this 22nd day of September, 1934.

[Notarial Seal]   MARGARET OTTESEN
Notary Public for Alaska.
My com. ex. 10/23/37.

[Endorsed:] "Filed in the District Court, Territory of Alaska, First Division, Sep. 24, 1934. Robt. Coughlin, Clerk. By Ruth Russell, Deputy." [250]

[Title of Court and Cause.]

United States of America,
Territory of Alaska—ss.

I, JOHN H. NEWMAN, the Official Court Reporter who reported the proceedings and testimony in the trial of the above entitled cause, hereby certify that the foregoing is a full, true and correct transcript of all the proceedings and testimony, both oral and documentary (save for some argument omitted) offered and introduced in the trial of the foregoing action, and also of all exceptions taken and noted, and of the exhibits offered and admitted in said trial (with the exception of exhibit "14" which is a duplicate of exhibit "13"); and I now certify the foregoing consisting of pages numbered from 35 to 215 inclusive, to be such transcript.

IN TESTIMONY WHEREOF, I have hereunto signed my name at Juneau, Alaska, this 1st day of February, 1936.

JOHN H. NEWMAN,
U. S. Court Reporter.   [251]

And now on this 20th day of February, 1936, and within the time allowed therefor, the
duly and regularly presents this his Bill of Exceptions to the Court.

A. H. ZIEGLER,

Attorney for Appellants.

Service admitted Feb. 20th, 1936.

G. W. FOLTA,

Asst. United States Attorney.

LESTER O. GORE,

Proctor for Intervenors.

And the same having been examined by the Court and the counsel on both sides, and the Court having found the same to be correct and to speak the truth in every particular; to contain a full and complete record of all the proceedings had in this cause, and a statement of all the material evidence adduced at the trial thereof, signs, settles and allows this bill of exception.

GEO. F. ALEXANDER,

U. S. District Judge.

Dated February 20th, 1936.

CERTIFICATE OF JUDGE TO BILL OF EXCEPTIONS:

And I, the undersigned, the Judge before whom this cause was tried, do hereby certify that the above and foregoing bill of exceptions so signed, settled and allowed by me speaks the truth in every particular, contains all the material evidence ad-

mitted at the trial of this cause and an accurate
and complete record of all the proceedings had
and that the same is in all respects, full, accurate
and complete and I hereby order that this bill of
exceptions be and the same is hereby made a part
of the record in this cause.

DONE this 20th day of February, 1936.

GEO. F. ALEXANDER,

U. S. District Judge.

[Endorsed:] Filed in the District Court, Territory of Alaska, First Division at Ketchikan, Feb.
20, 1936. Robert E. Coughlin, Clerk. [252]

In the District Court for the Territory of Alaska,
Division Number One, at Ketchikan

United States of America,
Territory of Alaska, Division No. 1—ss.

I, ROBERT E. COUGHLIN, Clerk of the District Court for the Territory of Alaska, Division
Number One, hereby certify that the foregoing and
hereto attached 253 pages of typewritten matter,
numbered from 1 to 253, both inclusive, constitute
a full, true, and complete copy, and the whole
thereof, of the record prepared in accordance with
the praecipe of attorneys for defendant-appellants,
on file in my office and made a part hereof, in cause
No. 1778-KA, wherein the United States of America
is plaintiff-appellee and W. PRICE, Claimant of
the Oil Screw Vessel "TAHOMA" and J. R.
HECKMAN are defendant-appellants.

I further certify that said record is by virtue of an appeal and citation issued in this cause, and the return thereof in accordance herewith.

I further certify that this transcript was prepared by me in my office, and that the cost of preparation, examination and certificate, amounting to Eighty-three and 00/100 ($83.00) Dollars, has been paid to me by counsel for defendant-appellants.

IN WITNESS WHEREOF, I have hereunto set my hand and the seal of the above-entitled court this 28th day of February, 1936.

[Seal]   ROBERT E. COUGHLIN,

Clerk.

———

[Endorsed]: No. 8140. United States Circuit Court of Appeals for the Ninth Circuit. W. Pierce, Claimant of the Oil Screw vessel "Tahoma" official number 214741, her engines, tackle, apparel, furniture, dories, gear, cargo, etc., and J. R. Heckman, Surety, Appellants, vs. United States of America, Atlas Engine Company, a corporation, and Fishing Vessel Owners Marine Ways, a corporation, Appellees. Apostles on Appeal. Upon Appeal from the District Court of the United States for the Territory of Alaska, Division Number One.

Filed March 9, 1936.

PAUL P. O'BRIEN,

Clerk of the United States Circuit Court of Appeals for the Ninth Circuit.

United States Circuit Court of Appeals
For the Ninth Circuit

W. PIERCE, Claimant of the Oil Screw
  vessel "TAHOMA" official number
  214741, her engines, tackle, apparel,
  furniture, dories, gear, cargo, etc.,
  and J. R. HECKMAN, Surety,
                                    Appellants.

vs.

UNITED STATES OF AMERICA, ATLAS
  ENGINE COMPANY, a corporation,
  and FISHING VESSEL OWNERS
  MARINE WAYS, a corporation,
                                    Appellees.

UPON APPEAL FROM THE DISTRICT COURT
OF THE UNITED STATES FOR THE
TERRITORY OF ALASKA, DIVISION
NUMBER ONE.

FILE

SEP 28 19

A. H. ZIEGLER,
Proctor for Appellant.   PAUL P. O'BRI

INDEX

Page

Statement of the Case 1

Assignment of Errors 3

Argument 10

Proposition Number One 10

Proposition Number Two 19

Proposition Number Three 29

Proposition Number Four 30

TABLE OF CASES CITED

THE BURDETT, 9 Peters, 681 34

THE CHIQUITA, 44 Fed. (2nd) 302-303 20

THE CHIQUITA, 41 Fed. (2nd) 842 31

THE CHIQUITA, 44 Fed. (2nd) 302 31

THE CHIQUITA, 19 Fed. (2nd) 417 33

THE PILOT, 42 Fed. (2nd) 290 33

THE WINNIE, 58 Fed. (2nd) 653 34

STATUTES CITED

ACTS OF CONGRESS:

R.S.U.S. Sections 4146-4172 30

R.S.U.S. Section 4189 31

41 Statutes (46 U.S.C.A. 808) 31

United States Circuit Court of Appeals
For the Ninth Circuit

W. PIERCE, Claimant of the Oil Screw
vessel "TAHOMA" official number
214741, her engines, tackle, apparel,
furniture, dories, gear, cargo, etc.,
and J. R. HECKMAN, Surety,

Appellants.

vs.

UNITED STATES OF AMERICA, ATLAS
ENGINE COMPANY, a corporation,
and FISHING VESSEL OWNERS
MARINE WAYS, a corporation,

Appellees.

UPON APPEAL FROM THE DISTRICT COURT
OF THE UNITED STATES FOR THE
TERRITORY OF ALASKA, DIVISION
NUMBER ONE.

BRIEF OF APPELLANTS

STATEMENT OF THE CASE

This is a forfeiture procedure against the American schooner Tahoma for violation of shipping and customs laws of the United States. (46 U.S.C.A.

23, 41, 46, 60 & 808). The case was tried June 6-7, 1935.

The Tahoma was engaged in a foreign trade, namely; transporting her catches of halibut from the high seas and Territorial waters of the United States to the foreign port of Prince Rupert and shipping the fish through Canada to American markets duty free. She was operated under a certificate of registry issued to her then sole owner and master, W. Pierce, the claimant and appellant, at the Port of Ketchikan, Alaska, in 1925.

On September 13, 1934, the Tahoma was seized by the Coast Guard on the high seas and brought within the jurisdiction of the District Court of Alaska, libeled for violation of the laws afore-mentioned and released on bond to W. Pierce, Claimant.

The first cause of action, set forth in the libel, alleges unlawful and fraudulent transfer, on or about May 29, 1933, of the said vessel by Pierce to F. E. Hunt, Ltd., a citizen and subject of a foreign state, and the failure to surrender her certificate of registry to the Collector of Customs for the District of Alaska, in violation of Sections 23 and 41, Title 46, U.S.C.A.

The second cause of action alleges that the said certificate of registry was unlawfully and fraudulently used in a foreign trade by the Tahoma after she was no longer entitled to the benefit thereof by reason of the alleged transfer in violation of Sections 60 and 808, Title 46, U.S.C.A.

W. Pierce appeared as claimant and filed his answer to the libel, admitting all the allegations of the libel except those as to the transfer of the vessel to F. E. Hunt, Ltd., and the fraudulent use of the certificate of registry.

The intervenors named claimed maritime liens against the Tahoma.

The District Court rendered its decision in the suit, decreeing forfeiture of the Tahoma. W. Pierce, Claimant and Appellant, and J. R. Heckman, Surety on the bond for the release of the Tahoma sued out their appeal to this Court.

The evidence shows that the Tahoma, prior to May 1933 became heavily indebted to F. E. Hunt, Ltd., and the intervenors, and that on or about said time the said Corporation agreed with the intervenors and W. Pierce to operate the Tahoma for the benefit of all concerned, pursuant to which agreement John A. Johnson became the Master of record of the Tahoma and W. Pierce became the Master in charge of the American halibut schooner WAVE. The agreement is set forth in libelants Exhibits 1 to 8. (P.R. pp. 54-68).

ASSIGNMENT OF ERRORS

VI.

The District Court erred in failing to permit

claimant to testify in answer to the following
question, to-wit:

> "Q. Did you obtain permission or consent
> of the Treasury Department to the manner in
> which you were operating the boat and fishing
> with her?"

And in refusing to receive in evidence the following letter from the Treasury Department of the
United States to W. Pierce, to-wit:

"TREASURY DEPARTMENT
Bureau of Customs
Washington

August 29, 1933

Mr. Winnie Pierce
P. O. Box 396
Prince Rupert, B. C.

Sir:

The Bureau is in receipt of your letter of
July 29, 1933, in regard to the operation of the
gas ship TAHOMA as an American fishery.

The Bureau, after a careful consideration
of the matter, perceives no objection to the
Consul issuing free entry documents for the
fish taken by the TAHOMA at the present time.

The State Department has been advised to
this effect.

By direction of the Commissioner:

Respectfully,

(Signed) H. A. HAYWARD

Assistant General Counsel"

(P.R. pp. 259-260)

VII.

The District Court erred at the conclusion of the libelant's case in failing to dismiss the libel and granting judgment for claimant which was based on the ground that the allegations of the libel had not been sustained and on the further ground that the evidence of libelant uncontradicted failed to establish a degree of proof required by law to warrant a forfeiture of the "TAHOMA." (P.R. p. 260).

X.

The District Court erred in finding as it did in Finding of Fact No. 3 entered by the Court as follows:

> That on or about May 29, 1933, F. E. Hunt, Ltd., a foreign corporation, a citizen of Great Britain, (with the consent, knowledge and agreement of intervenors herein) took over the active control, management and operation of the "TAHOMA" and the shipment of its catches of halibut to American markets, in payment of the indebtedness of said vessel to said corporation (1) by removing the record owner and master, W. Pierce, from command of the "TAHOMA" and placing him in charge of another American vessel, to-wit; the "WAVE": (2) by making a colorable appointment of J. A. Johnon, an American citizen, as master of the "TAHOMA" for the sole purpose of dealing with the libelant in matters pertaining to and arising under the customs, navigation and shipping laws of the United States; (3) by placing Anton Martinson, a citizen of Great Britain,

actually in charge, command and control of said vessel when away from Prince Rupert, and (4) by receiving and distributing the earnings and profits from such operations, and sharing therein.
(P.R. p. 261).

XII.

The District Court erred in making the Conclusions of Law it did in the above suit which were as follows:

I.

That on or about May 29, 1933, at Prince Rupert, B. C., the American vessel "Tahoma" was transferred in whole or in part, by way of trust, confidence and otherwise, to F. E. Hunt, Ltd., a citizen of Great Britain; and that the said F. E. Hunt, Ltd., thereby became entitled to the whole or part or share of and became indirectly interested in such vessel and in the profits and issues thereof, and became the equitable owner of said vessel.

II.

That thereafter and until the seizure of the "TAHOMA" the said vessel was unlawfully and fraudulently engaged in a foreign trade and the said certificate of registry was knowingly and fraudulently used for said vessel when she was no longer entitled to the benefit of said register.

III.

That all the shipments of halibut made by the said vessel or F. E. Hunt, Ltd., during all the times mentioned in the libel were subject to an import duty of two cents a pound under the provisions of the tariff act (19 U.S.C.A. 1001, par. 717) and that such shipments were made in fraud of the revenue of the United States.

V.

That the vessel "TAHOMA" became forfeited as of May 29, 1933, to the United States under the first cause of action, and as of September 27, 1933, under the second cause of action.

Because the Conclusions so made by the Court were contrary to the evidence and law in the case and unsupported by the facts, the evidence, and the law applicable thereto. (P.R. pp. 262-263).

XIII.

The District Court erred in not making the following Findings of Fact requested by claimant.

I.

That W. Pierce, the registered owner of the Oil Screw "TAHOMA" did not, as alleged in the libel, or at all, unlawfully and fraudulently sell, in whole or in part by way of trust, confidence, or otherwise, to a subject and citizen of a foreign state, to-wit, F. E. Hunt, Ltd., the said vessel "TAHOMA."

II.

That said "TAHOMA" did not, as alleged in the libel, unlawfully or fraudulently engaged in foreign trade, and the certificate of registry of the "TAHOMA" was not knowingly or fraudulently used for a vessel, to-wit, the vessel "TAHOMA," not entitled to the benefits thereof.

III.

That the consideration of Pierce, owner of the "TAHOMA" in permitting F. E. Hunt, Ltd., to take over the operation and management of the "TAHOMA," was that Pierce should receive the boat "WAVE" of the value of $500.00, with which to make a living, for which consideration Pierce agreed that the "TAHOMA" should be operated in order that the indebtedness of the "TAHOMA" could be paid off, and it was further agreed between Pierce and F. E. Hunt, Ltd., that if a sale of the "TAHOMA" could be made, Pierce would consent thereto, and the purchase price be applied in payment of Pierce's indebtedness and the remainder, if any, be paid to Pierce.

IV.

That F. E. Hunt, Ltd., and the above Intervenors, did not agree to, nor did they at any time, release Pierce from his indebtedness to them, nor did Pierce at any time agree to permit said F. E. Hunt, Ltd., and the Intervenors to take and receive the "TAHOMA" for the boat "WAVE" and payment of his indebtedness to said corporations.

V.

That the arrangement made between Pierce, F. E. Hunt, Ltd., and the Intervenors, for the operation of the "TAHOMA" by said F. E. Hunt, Ltd., was made in good faith and with

the honest belief on the part of all concerned
that said arrangement did not constitute a violation of law.

VI.

That there was no evidence in writing of the
sale or transfer of the "TAHOMA," or of any
interest therein.

V.

That after F. E. Hunt, Ltd., took over the
operation and management of the "TAHOMA,"
W. Pierce, Claimant, performed work on the
"TAHOMA," during the winter, or closed fishing season and received no pay therefor. (P.R.
pp. 263-264-265).

XIV.

The District Court erred in refusing to find as a
Conclusion of Law that the American Oil Vessel
"TAHOMA," her engine, tackle, apparel, cargo, etc.,
did not become forfeited by reason of the matters
and things set forth in the libel or at all. (P.R. p.
265).

XV.

The District Court erred in entering its Decree in
the above suit decreeing that the Oil Screw Vessel
"TAHOMA," etc., was subject to foreifture and
should be forfeited. (P.R. p. 265).

XVI.

The District Court erred in finding and deciding
that there was probable cause for the seizure of the

Oil Screw Vessel "TAHOMA," etc. (P.R. p. 266).

XVII.

The District Court erred in finding and deciding that the burden of proof was cast on the claimant to prove that the Oil Screw Vessel "TAHOMA," etc., had not become subject to forfeiture. (PR. p. 266).

ARGUMENT

PROPOSITION NUMBER ONE

At the conclusion of the testimony for libellant claimant moved the Court to dismiss the libel on the ground that the allegations of the libel had not been sustained and that the uncontradicted evidence of libellant failed to establish the degree of proof required by law to warrant the forfeiture of the Tahoma. This motion raised the sufficiency of the evidence and also the question of whether there was probable cause for the seizure. In order to decide that question, it is necessary to determine whether the agreement established in libellant's Exhibits 1 to 8 worked a forfeiture of the Tahoma. At the conclusion of the testimony (P.R. p. 241) the Court stated: "I think you understand my position generally. It is this,—whether or not the facts and circumstances, as proven are such as would work a forfeiture, that is the real question in the case as I view it."

So that the sufficiency of the evidence may be determined, we feel it necessary to set forth the agreement contained in libellant's Exhibits 1 to 8, respecting the Tahoma. The agreement entered into, as shown by those letters, is that on May 18, 1933, it was evident that Pierce was not adapted to carrying on successfully fishing from a boat the size of the Tahoma. F. E. Hunt, Ltd., persuaded Pierce to make a trade, taking for his equity a small American boat that would cost about $2,500.00, which would bring the entire indebtedness against the Tahoma to about $11,000.00. F. E. Hunt, Ltd., stated they had one or two men in sight who would take the Tahoma, providing the intervenors did not disturb the Tahoma when marketing the catches at Seattle. The intervenors stated in their letter of May 31, 1933, (P.R. p. 58) they understood F. E. Hunt, Ltd., had tied up the Tahoma and intended selling or trading it to some other party who would be more adapted to operating the Boat than Capt. Pierce. The intervenors stated that, acting on the suggestion of F. E. Hunt, Ltd., they would be on the lookout for someone in Seattle who would be interested in taking the Boat and making a down payment of $3,000.00. June 5, 1933, F. E. Hunt, Ltd., again wrote a letter to the intervenors (P.R. p. 60), indicating surprise that the intervenors had not accepted its proposition. It stated in the letter it would be willing to give the same extension for payment of debts that the intervenors would give. June 12, 1933, intervenors wrote to F. E. Hunt, Ltd., (P.R. p. 63), stating that they hoped F. E. Hunt,

Ltd., would not feel the intervenors were unwilling to cooperate in working the boat out of its indebtedness, and stated further that their understanding was there is now approximately $8,500.00 against the Boat and that you intended turning over to Capt. Pierce a boat worth $2,500.00 which would raise the total obligation to about $11,000.00. Capt. Pierce to convey the Tahoma to you. The boat would then proceed to work itself out of debt. And on June 17, 1933, F. E. Hunt, Ltd., addressed another letter to the intervenors (P.R. p. 65), stating that in accordance with decision of the intervenors to cooperate with F. E. Hunt, Ltd., it had arranged with Capt. T. Martinsen to take out the Tahoma, and stating further that the debt of F. E. Hunt, Ltd., against the debtor must remain in exactly the same status as it now is since foreigners could not have an ownership interest in an American vessel and, stating further, we will have a bill of sale signed in blank, so that it could be used instantaneously if so desired and, further, that as soon as work was done on the boat which Pierce was to receive, F. E. Hunt, Ltd., would send a statement to the intervenors, showing what the total indebtedness against the Tahoma would be.

In addition to the foregoing agreement, Mr. G. W. Nickerson, of F. E. Hunt, Ltd., who was called as a witness by libellant testified further, (P.R. p. 76); "From time to time I sort of constituted myself their representative as well as our own, as we didn't want to see anybody lose money or Pierce lose his boat; we were all about in the same jackpot at that time—about a step ahead of the sheriff"; (P.R. p. 77) "When Winnie Pierce came in I saw him and told him I didn't want his boat. We were willing to do anything it was possible to do. This 'Wave' was there, and I could arrange to buy (P.R. p. 78) Pete Petterson's equity; we thought we could arrange, so far as Mrs. Kincaid was concerned, to turn her over to him and change her mortgage to the Tahoma. When the Tahoma paid out, if she ever did, what she owed originally, and the balance to apply against what I had against the Wave— that it would be all right with Mrs. Kincaid. I told him—I said—the question is to make some sort of arrangement with the Atlas Engine Company and the Marine Ways in Seattle. I made it very emphatic to Pierce we didn't want to take advantage of the unique situation in order to take the Tahoma away from him. We knew he wouldn't try to steal her from us. So far as we were concerned it could carry on indefinitely. I wrote the Atlas Engine Company (P.R. pp. 77-78). Then Mr. Nickerson told Mr. Pierce they didn't want to take the boat, but said, "I will write the Atlas Engine Company telling them what you are prepared to do. You are prepared to turn the Tahoma over to the creditors, provided you can get this boat or some other boat to operate and have it charged to the Tahoma." That, it said then, he knew, as a Canadian subject, he could not take title to an American boat; that he had customers in Seattle; if he wanted to camouflage the deal, he could have done so but at no time was it in his mind that he was going to take the Tahoma from Pierce or see him lose it; that Pierce threw himself on the mercy of the F. E. Hunt, Ltd.; that they had twenty other boats in difficulty and were not taking them so why take the Tahoma; (P.R. pp. 78-79-80); that in May F. E. Hunt, Ltd., wrote a letter to Captain Ingvold Erickson, on behalf of Pierce, and offered the Tahoma for sale for $12,000.00, (P.R. pp. 80-81); that F. E. Hunt, Ltd., might loan Pierce the money for the intervenors claims and take chances on getting it out of the Tahoma when she made it (P.R. p. 82).

Mr. Nickerson testified that he made no arrangement orally or by letters or overtures or suggestions to the Seattle creditors that he would have the Tahoma conveyed to him, (P.R. p. 85); that his first negotiations for taking over the operation of the Tahoma was with the brother of claimant; that the arrangement was based entirely on a conversation with the brother; that claimant never told him that he would transfer the Tahoma, nor did Nickerson ever ask claimant to transfer the Tahoma by word or letter; that Pierce was in a state of worry, that he was willing to do anything that would give him chances to earn a living; that he felt whatever was best for his creditors was what he would be prepared to do; that Nickerson never took a bill of sale from Pierce on the Tahoma; that he never had any oral arrangement or agreement with Pierce by which he was to convey the Tahoma or any interest in it; that the conversation with Pierce was that F. E. Hunt, Ltd., did not want to use their position to deprive him of the Tahoma, that if there was anything in the boat after the bills were paid; that F. E. Hunt, Ltd., did not want any boats; that F. E. Hunt, Ltd., did not take any bill of sale to the boat; that it never intended to take a bill of sale unless they forced the issue; that if a bill of sale had to be taken, it would be in the name of someone entitled to receive it; that Nickerson, as agent of F. E. Hunt, Ltd., would not transfer a boat the Canadian Government would not accept, because the Company would have a boat on its hands it could not do anything with; that his firm had been interested in transferring Canadian boats to American registry and knew the procedure which had to be gone through to do so; that after the arrangements mentioned in libellant's Exhibits 1 to 8 had been nego-tiated, Nickerson, on behalf of Pierce, endeavored to sell the Tahoma for $11,000.00. (P.R. pp. 87-88-89-90).

The foregoing constitutes what was purported to be done by the F. E. Hunt, Ltd., and the intervenors, as was shown by the letters, *and shows what was actually done.*

The testimony for libellant further shows that after F. E. Hunt, Ltd., had assumed the management of the Tahoma, it placed one Johnson on the boat as Master and one Antone Martinson aboard to actually do the navigating and fishing with the vessel. The testimony further shows that a bill of sale was executed by F. E. Hunt, Ltd., for the Wave, on which alterations had been made, but that said bill of sale was never used to actually pass title.

Claimant contends that the circumstances of the proposed agreement and what actually occurred in pursuance to the proposed agreement was, F. E. Hunt, Ltd., took over the management of the Tahoma, furnished the Wave to Pierce with which he might make a living, transferred the indebtedness against the Wave to the Tahoma and thereafter managed the fishing operations of the Tahoma, accounting to the intervenors for the earnings thereof.

The appointment of Johnson, as Master, under the circumstances shown by libellant's testimony was legal. For the purpose of determining the sufficiency of the evidence to show probable cause, or substantiating the allegations of the libellant, it can be assumed that Johnson was appointed master in name only; that the real master was Martinson. The shipping and navigation laws on boats of this type, provide the only qualifications of masters to be—a citizen of the United States, over the age of twenty-one years. Therefore, the appointment of Johnson was in compliance with the law and an act

which either Pierce or F. E. Hunt, Ltd., could legally
do.

Apparently the theory of the Proctor of Libellant,
and which was adopted by the Court, was that a
mortgage or transfer of the earnings of a maritime
bottom to a foreigner was tantamount to a violation of the statute under which the suit has been
brought. This theory is untenable. The statute
only prohibits the transfer or sale of an interest in
or sale of the boat itself. Giving testimony of libellant its most favorable construction would show
absolutely no transfer or sale of the Tahoma in
violation of the statute. The arrangement clearly
shows that the creditors did what they had a perfect
right to do, and that is, with the consent and acquiescence of Pierce, they took over the management
of the Tahoma and the distribution of its earnings.
The theory of the prosecution, which was adopted
by the Court in its Findings, was a conspiracy was
entered into between F. E. Hunt, Ltd., the intervenors, Johnson, Martinson, Pierce and Petterson—
the former Master of the Wave—to defraud the
Revenue Laws of the United States by operating
the Tahoma under her American registry. Unless
a transfer or sale of the Tahoma were established
under the proof of libellant in violation of law,
there could not possibly be anything unlawful in
any of the acts of the parties mentioned with respect to the actual operation of the Tahoma. If no
sale in violation of law had been made, there could

be no violation of the Revenue Laws in failing to pay the duty on the halibut delivered by the Tahoma. In other words, in the absence of positive proof that an American vessel had changed ownership, every single act of all parties concerned was legal in every respect and they violated no law whatsoever. The actions in appointment of the Master of the Tahoma and the operation of the vessel at worst can only be considered suspicious, had there been an actual sale of the Tahoma in violation of statute. There is nothing in the evidence presented by libellant to prove that Pierce was ever released from his indebtedness against the Tahoma, including the increased indebtedness by reason of furnishing him the fishing boat Wave. The evidence shows conclusively that no bill of sale was taken; that Nickerson never discussed the transfer of the boat with Pierce but on the contrary shows that F. E. Hunt, Ltd., insisted, through Nickerson, that the status of its claim against the Tahoma must remain as it was because of the statute forbidding ownership of an American vessel by a foreign person or corporation.

We contend that at the conclusion of the case of libellant, the libel should have been dismissed for the reasons herein mentioned and because the facts proven did not work a forfeiture of the Tahoma. The Trial Court was not justified, even, in finding probable cause, because the testimony for libellant, construed in its most favorable light, shows no more than that Pierce agreed that the earnings of the Tahoma could be received by the creditors in payment of his indebtedness. It could not be contended that Pierce would not have the right to assign the earnings from the Tahoma in payment of his indebtedness, both to his American and foreign creditors.

The motive ascribed by the Court to Hunt, Ltd., in connection with the arrangement proven, was a desire or intent to defraud the United States of its duty on the halibut. That is the inference drawn by the Trial Court, and we submit that is is more reasonable to infer that the motive was to enable F. E. Hunt, Ltd., to transfer its indebtedness against the Wave to the Tahoma and by controlling the fishing operations of the boat have a better chance of collecting its claim, consisting of prior indebtedness, and the claims of intervenors. That was an honest motive in the exercise of good business and surely the courts are not inclined to impute an improper motive where an honest one is equally or more susceptible of being inferred.

The motion to dismiss, as requested in claimants assignment of errors (VIII. P.R. p. 260) should have been granted.

PROPOSITION NUMBER TWO

I shall treat assignment of errors X., and XII., (P.R. pp. 261-262-263) in connection with assignment of errors XIII, XIV, XV, XVI and XVII (P.R. pp. 263, 264, 265 and 266), since they all relate to the findings and conclusions of the Trial Court and the failure of the Court to make the findings and conclusions requested by claimant.

Should the Court determine that seizure was made with probable cause and the motion to dismiss not properly taken, we respectfully contend that the testimony was insufficient to warrant the decree of forfeiture and that claimant has by his testimony established that no sale or transfer of the Tahoma occurred in violation of the Statute.

We desire to point out to the Court our position with respect to the general rule in equity and admiralty cases on appeal. The rule is that findings of fact made by the Court in admiralty cases on conflicting evidence will not be disturbed on appeal. The Trial Court took the position that the only question before it was whether the facts proven were sufficient to work a forfeiture of the Tahoma. We respectfully point out that the evidence in this case is not one of conflicting testimony but entirely one going to the sufficiency of the evidence. This Court in the case of CHIQUITA (44 Fed. 2nd 302 p. 303) stated: "The testimony in this case was indefinite and not conclusive rather than conflicting." This case is one that comes within the same rule; therefore, this Court under the law can determine whether or not the findings made by the Trial Court were supported by the evidence.

It is respectfully contended that the finding made by the Trial Court, assignment of errors X, (P.R. p. 261) was not and could not possibly be supported by the evidence. In that finding, the Court found that F. E. Hunt, Ltd., took over the active control, management and operation of the Tahoma; first by removing the record owner and master W. Pierce from the command of the Tahoma and placing him in charge of another American vessel, the Wave; and, by making a colorable appointment of J. A. Johnson as Master of the Tahoma for the sole purpose of dealing with libellant in matters pertaining to and arising under the customs, navigation and shipping laws of the United States. The testimony does not show that Pierce was removed from the command of the Tahoma. The record discloses that this was done freely and voluntarily by Pierce, that it was entirely satisfactory with him and that no force or coercion whatsoever was used. The portion of the finding, with reference to making a colorable appointment of Johnson as Master, is entirely unwarranted and unjustified and not in accordance with the facts. In connection with this finding of the Court, it must be borne in mind that the act of placing Johnson on the Tahoma, as Master, was entirely within the law and legal in every respect, and the Court by using the word "colorable" ascribed to that act a suspicious or fraudulent motive, which is entirely outside of the evidence. (P.R. p. 261). Thus it is seen that the finding of the Court when the two portions thereof, above-mentioned, are taken from it, shows nothing irregular, unlawful or contrary to law, and the Court was in error in making the conclusion it did, namely; (XII, P.R. pp. 262, 263) to the effect that the Tahoma was transferred in whole or in part by way of trust, confidence or otherwise; that the vessel was unlawfully and fraudulently engaged in trade and became forfeited as of May, 1933, to the United States.

It is further respectfully contended that the findings of the Court should have been as requested by the claimant in assignment XIII, (P.R. p. 264) subdivision III thereof.

The claimant requested the Court to find, in subdivision IV of the XIII assignment (P.R. p. 264), that there was no agreement between Pierce, F. E. Hunt, Ltd., and the intervenors to take and receive the Tahoma for the boat Wave plus the indebtedness of Pierce to said corporation and that the arrangement made between Pierce, F. E. Hunt, Ltd., and intervenors was made in good faith and with an honest belief on the part of all concerned that said arrangement would not constitute a violation of law; that there was no evidence in writing of the sale or transfer of the Tahoma, or any interest therein, and that after F. E. Hunt, Ltd., took over the operation and management of the Tahoma,

Pierce, the claimant, performed work on the Tahoma without pay therefor.

In support of the foregoing contention we will detail briefly the testimony of G. W. Nickerson and W. Pierce, given after the close of libellant's case. Mr. Nickerson testified that after the Tahoma was seized, he was in Seattle and spoke with Mr. Wright, an officer of one of the intervenors; that he did not ask Mr. Wright to help him out of the hole but suggested that Mr. Wright and the other interested parties were American citizens and that if the contentions of Mr. Nickerson were correct, the case should be dismissed; that those gentlemen should go to their Senators and Congressmen and see what they could do; (P.R. pp. 190-191) that in September of the year 1933 he addressed a letter to Captain Egil Erickson, Seattle, offering on behalf of Captain Pierce the Tahoma at $11,000.00, to which Erickson replied, substantially, that if the price were somewhere right, he might consider a buy; (P.R. p. 196-197-198) that he never requested any officer of the intervenors in Seattle to find $3,000.00 to buy the boat to go fishing on and that he was not a fisherman; (P.R. pp. 201-202) that Nickerson had a dim recollection of the change in the bill of sale for the Wave to Earnest Pierce, that through his fault or the stenographer's Winnie Pierce's name got there and was erased; there was no effort to conceal; that the first bill of sale, being one of libellant's exhibits, on which the erasure appeared, was not used; that there was another one made up; (P.R. p. 204) that he never complied with the conditions mentioned in a letter from the Atlas Engine Company, dated June 12th, which was that Captain Pierce was to convey the Tahoma to F. E. Hunt, Ltd.; that on June 17th he answered the letter of June 12th and stated "This Company's debt against the debtor must remain in exactly the same status as it is now, as foreigners cannot have an ownership interest in an American vessel"; (P.R. p. 205) that he never had an agreement with Pierce that he would take a conveyance—mental or otherwise; that he felt if it was necessary for his Company and the other creditors that Pierce would give a conveyance to be used for the advantage of the creditors; he could be compelled to do so; (P.R. p. 206) that there was no arrangement with Mr. Pierce, either by conversation or writing, whereby the boat was transferred to us; he never said in his letter he was going to; that what he did say was what Pierce was prepared to do and did say he would take a blank bill of sale, not for F. E. Hunt, Ltd., but it would have to be decided from a legal standpoint who could take the bill of sale; that from the time he wrote the letter to the intervenors nothing was ever done; that Pierce was never approached for bill of sale; that, in fact, he told Pierce several times "Hold on to the boat"; that he felt there would be something in it for Pierce; that he never took a bill or sale; never agreed to take over the boat; that he had accounted to the Seattle creditors for the earnings of the Tahoma; that his Company tried to split the earnings on the same basis; (P.R. pp. 210-211) that he felt if his Company wanted to, they could have sued Pierce and attached the boat; that they did not want to do that; (P.R. p. 212) that it was cheaper to acquire the Wave for Pierce the way it was done than going to Court; (P.R. p. 213) that he effected the transfer from the Tahoma to the Wave voluntarily on the part of Pierce; (P.R. p. 219) that a bill of sale was to be signed by Pierce so that if they got a chance to sell the boat, or clean it up, it could be done without delay; that the bill of sale could be used instantaneously if desired so it could be sold at once; if a fisherman wanted a boat he would want it then; (P.R. pp. 222-223) that the consideration for taking over the operation of the Tahoma was that it would be operated by F. E. Hunt, Ltd., for the benefit of the creditors, as agents, and if there was an opportunity to sell her legally, to sell her for the benefit of the creditors and if there was anything left, Pierce would get it. (P.R. p. 225).

Winnie Pierce testified that he had lived in Prince Rupert since 1923; that he was a married man; an American citizen; that his business was fishing; that he hadn't been very well in the spring and talked the matter of the Tahoma over with his brother; that he told his brother what he would like to do and asked him to make the arrangements;

that he made the arrangement with Nickerson; that the arrangement was—Pierce wanted to get somebody in the boat who would make more money than he could; (P.R. p. 227-228-229) that he never signed any paper, agreements or bill of sale with Nickerson on the Tahoma; that there never was any talk about a bill of sale; that there never was any talk about buying the Tahoma or taking it over to own themselves; that he never agreed at any time to sell the Tahoma or any part; that there was never any talk with anybody from F. E. Hunt, Ltd., relating to the sale of the Tahoma or anybody else; that no one ever asked him to sign a bill of sale to the Tahoma; that he did not sign a bill of sale or any paper in blank, conveying any interest in the Tahoma; that he owned the Tahoma at the time of the trial; (P.R. pp. 230-231) that since Pierce was transferred to the Wave he interested himself in the operation of the Tahoma; that he did overhauling of the engine and took care of the engine every winter; (P.R. p. 232) that he went aboard the Tahoma often; that he didn't know exactly how much he owed F. E. Hunt, Ltd. (P.R. p. 233); that the agreement with F. E. Hunt, Ltd., was that they would operate her to try to pay her bills and keep somebody on her until she could pay her bills. (P.R. p. 234).

Pierce did not impress the Trial Court as a good witness. There are often reasons appearing in taking testimony why a witness creates an unfavor-

able impression. In the case of Pierce it might
have been that he was not a well man; that he was
careless in his affairs or that he was heavily involved during the depression which existed so that
he did not keep an accurate record of the transaction in his mind of the exact indebtedness. His
testimony, however, is positive: That he never
agreed to or did execute any agreement whereby
any interest in the Tahoma, or any share or any
portion thereof, was sold or was to be sold to F. E.
Hunt, Ltd. We do not feel that the Trial Court was
justified in utterly disregarding the positive statements of Pierce. It is true he had an interest in the
case, yet it is equally true that a man is not to be
disbelieved because he has an interest in litigation.
The testimony of Nickerson is equally positive
throughout the entire record: That no such sale or
transfer of the Tahoma occurred as alleged in the
libel. It is true that a proposal was made by Nickerson to take a blank bill of sale—this appeared in
the letters exchanged between Nickerson and the
intervenors. Nickerson explained his reason in
considering taking a blank bill of sale which was
that if a ready sale presented itself for the Tahoma,
the deal could be closed promptly. The salient
feature of the testimony of both Nickerson and
Pierce is that no sale was ever made and no agreement ever signed. On the contrary, the testimony
discloses that Nickerson advised Pierce to hold on
to the boat for he felt there would be something in
it for him.

Mr. Woodward, the American Consul at Prince Rupert, whose investigation of this matter sprang from waterfront gossip, introduced a bill of sale from one B. A. Petterson to Ernest George Pierce, being libellant's Exhibit XII, (P.R. p. 135), which the testimony discloses was never used to convey the Wave to Pierce. The theory of libellant, with reference to this bill of sale, was that it cast suspicion on the part of F. E. Hunt, Ltd., because of erasures or alterations in the bill of sale. It must be borne in mind that this bill of sale was not used or never recorded. The fact that there might have been alterations or erasures in it, which Nickerson could not readily explain, should cast no suspicion on the motive of him. This Court knows that legal documents are oft-times changed before recording and if every document could be impugned on account of alterations or erasures, a great per cent of recorded documents would be subject to the same suspicion.

We earnestly contend that had F. E. Hunt, Ltd., desired to acquire title to the boat, it could have libeled the same in the usual manner at the Port of Prince Rupert, B. C., and foreclosed the Seattle lienors out of their claims against the boat. The amount of money thereby saved would greatly exceed the Court costs or any other cost incident thereto. We feel that the true test of the question, as to whether or not the Tahoma was sold or transferred to F. E. Hunt, Ltd., is this: Could F. E. Hunt,

Ltd., on the testimony as disclosed by the record have brought a suit against Pierce to compel Pierce to execute a bill of sale to them for the Tahoma? Could F. E. Hunt, Ltd., prevail in a suit for specific performance, based on the agreement to sell, claimed to have been entered into by libellant as shown by the exhibits and the testimony? Certainly no one would claim that F. E. Hunt, Ltd., could or should prevail in such a suit against Pierce. If not, the entire case of libellant falls. This appears to us to be the gist of the whole controversy. Because some of the acts of the parties appear to have been irregular, the Court should not view them all with suspicion. However, we contend that none of the acts should be so viewed unless they are actually unlawful. The Trial Court, we contend, was in error in making the findings and conclusions it did and decreeing the forfeiture of the Tahoma. It is our opinion that the Trial Court failed to distinguish the difference between an assignment, mortgage or transfer of the earnings of the boat from an actual sale or transfer of the boat itself.

PROPOSITION NUMBER THREE

The Court erred in failing to admit and receive in evidence the letter set forth in assignment of errors VI, (P.R. p. 259), which was a letter received by Winnie Pierce August 29, 1933, after the alleged sale occurred in May, 1933. This was a letter from the Treasury Department to Pierce, the claimant, relative to the manner in which the Tahoma was being operated out of Prince Rupert. The Court refused to receive the letter in evidence, to which refusal an exception was taken and allowed. (P.R. p. 232). It is the contention of the libellant that the letter is admissible, not only because it shows the United States, libellant in the suit, sanctioned the operation of the Tahoma but because it shows conclusively that several times after the alleged sale occurred Pierce was manifesting an active interest in the operation of the Tahoma while engaged in halibut fishing. If, as claimed by the libellant, Pierce actually sold the Tahoma in May, 1933, how can his actions be explained in interesting himself in the operations of the boat? If he sold the Tahoma, as alleged and found by the Court, he should have no interest whatsoever in the Tahoma.

PROPOSITION NUMBER FOUR

The District Court erred in finding and deciding that the burden of proof was cast on the claimant to prove that the oil vessel Tahoma had not become subject to forfeiture. It is our contention that the evidence taken as a whole does not warrant the decree of forfeiture and that the burden of proof did not rest with the claimant.

It must be borne in mind that the first cause of action of the libel is for Sections 4146 and 4172 R.S.U.S. (46 U.S.C.A. 23 and 41). These statutes prohibit the sale of an American vessel to a citizen of a foreign state, and require that when a sale be made, the certificate be surrendered within seven days, etc.

The second cause of action is based on violation of provisions of Section 4189 R.S.U.S. (46 U.S.C.A. 60) and 41 Statutes (46 U.S.C.A. 808), in that the Tahoma was unlawfully and fraudulently engaged in foreign trade and the certificate of registry was knowingly and fraudulently used for a vessel not entitled to the benefit thereof, by reason of the sale and transfer of said vessel, as alleged in the first cause of action of the libel.

Obviously the second cause of action falls if the first cause of action has not been proven. Because if no sale occurred in violation of law, the second cause of action likewise could not be sustained by the evidence.

This is not such a case as the CHIQUITA 41 Fed. (2nd) 842, and affirmed in the CHIQUITA 44 Fed. (2nd) 302. In the CHIQUITA CASE, the libel was for violation of Sec. 325 (46 U.S.C.A.) for engaging in unlicensesd trade.

In this case the Court stated:

> "But even assuming that the procedure similar to that authorized by said section 615 of the Tariff Act of 1922 is applicable in libels under Section 4377 of the Revised Statutes, nevertheless, I think it is not imperative to disagree

with the Commissioner in his determination as
to the sufficiency of the evidence to justify
forfeiture of this yacht. It may be that a strong
suspicion which justifies a finding of probable
cause at the conclusion of libelant's evidence
could be enlarged in the mind of the Commissioner so as to constitute a preponderance of
the evidence at the conclusion of the hearing,
but such is not necessarily the case, because it
may also appear that, although at the conclusion of libelant's evidence probable cause is
shown, yet, when the adverse party goes forward with his proof, even though it may not
be convincing, it may nevertheless be sufficient to render forfeiture unwarranted. In
other words, the quantum of proof sufficient
to show probable cause may be lacking in that
probative force which justifies forfeiture of
property * * *"
41 Fed. (2nd) 843.

The decision inthis case was affirmed in 44 Fed.
(2nd) 302, and this court stated in deciding the case:

"In reaching this conclusion we have assumed that there was probable cause for the
seizure and that the burden of proof rested
upon the appellee" and "The testimony on the
part of the government gives rise to little more
than a suspicion at best." and, "The testimony
in the case was indefinite and inconclusive
rather than conflicting."

In the case at bar the Tahoma was not libeled for
engaging in unlicensed trade.

We contend that the law as announced in the
Chiquita Case therefor does not apply with reference to the burden of proof.

The CHIQUITA CASE supra, cites the case of the Pilot 42 Fed. (2nd) 290, decided in 1930, long after the passage of the Tariff Act, wherein the Court stated:

> "I prefer, however, to decide the case upon the plain question of fact involved in the record, and I am constrained to find that the government has not met the burden of proving affirmatively that there was completed sale and transfer within the meaning of the act."

The Pilot case was one wherein the boat was charged with being sold to persons not citizens without approval of the Shipping Board, and the Court stated further:

> "It seems to me clear that the purchaser could not have proceeded against the buyer for breach of contract if there had been a failure to deliver the boat."

We have heretofore contended in this brief, that F. E. Hunt, Ltd., could not have compelled Pierce to deliver title or bill of sale to the Tahoma.

Again, the Circuit Court of Appeals, Fifth Circuit, in the case of the CHIQUITA, 19 Fed. (2nd) 417, which was a libel for sale to persons not citizens, the Court in refusing to forfeit the vessel, stated:

> "The frequent changes of name and ownership may give rise to the suspicion that the ship's true ownership was sought to be concealed, but property may not be declared for-

feit on mere suspicion. It was incumbent upon the government to show with reasonable certainty that the CHIQUITA was an American vessel when proceeded against. That burden has not been sustained."

"In forfeiture proceeding the government has burden of proving false oath was made in connection with application for license for boat," see

The WINNIE, 58 Fed. (2nd) 653.

This was a libel instituted under the same Sections as in the Tahoma case.

The Court said:

"We are asked, however, to make a judicial finding from the evidence that the libelant has legally proven that a false oath was made when the boat was registered. This we cannot do. Moreover, if the burden was on the claimant to prove the verity of the oath taken, we would not find that he had met this burden. It must, however, be carried by the libelant, and in this it has failed."

THE BURDETT, 9 Peters, page 681, states the rule of law in forfeiture cases as follows:

"If a fair construction of the acts and declarations of an individual do not convict him of an offense, if the facts may be admitted as proved, and the accused be innocent, should he be held guilty of an act which subjects him to the forfeiture of his property, on a mere presumption? He may be guilty, but he may be innocent. If the scale of evidence does not preponderate against him—if it hang upon a

> balance, the penalty cannot be enforced; no individual should be punished for a violation of law, which inflicts a forfeiture of property, unless the offense shall be established beyond reasonable doubt. This is a rule which governs a jury in all criminal prosecutions; and the rule is no less proper for the government of the court, when exercising a maritime jurisdiction."

This rule is set forth in the CHIQUITA 19 Fed. (2nd) supra. The CHIQUITA case is cited in the Notes of Decisions in 46 U.S.C.A., paragraph 41, being the identical section which it is claimed the TAHOMA violated. The Burdett case is also cited under Section 60 46 U.S.C.A. at page 42 under Sub-Paragraph 8, as follows:

> "Procedure for Forfeiture. a Prosecution under this section is a penal one and the penalty may not be inflicted unless the violation of the law is established beyond a reasonable doubt."

This reference was made in the compilation long after the passage of the Tariff Act.

We respectfully contend that the circumstances do not even reveal suspicion, but even if this Court decides otherwise, that no individual should be punished for a violation of law which inflicts a forfeiture of property. It is our contention that all the facts and circumstances proven in the case at bar are equally as consistent with innocence as they are with guilt. Surely Pierce could have operated the TAHOMA himself, and agreed that the earnings of the boat be paid to creditors on its indebtedness, which is no more than the evidence discloses was actually done.

As stated before in this brief, the Trial Court failed to distinguish the difference between what was proposed to be done by the creditors, as shown by the letters, and *what was actually* done as shown by all the evidence.

F. E. Hunt, Ltd., should not even be censored and Mr. Pierce deprived of his property merely because they all deemed it expedient and good business to have the boat operated by some one other than Pierce in order that the creditors would have a better opportunity to collect their indebtedness, and in the end, as stated by Nickerson, turn back the management of the TAHOMA to Pierce after the bills were paid. The Court's attention is directed to the fact that the letters exchanged between Nickerson and the Intervenors were written in the usual course of business, and no effort made to conceal the arrangement which was proposed, and what was actually done thereafter.

CONCLUSION

We respectfully urge that for the reasons mentioned the decree of the lower Court should be reversed, and the suit dismissed so far as it pertains to the forfeiture.

Respectfully submitted,

A. H. ZIEGLER,
Proctor for Claimant and Appellants.

ASSIGNMENT OF ERRORS UPON WHICH APPELLANTS RELY.

(1)   Assignment of Error VI, PR PP 259-260, set forth in verbatim at PP 3-4 herein and presented in Proposition Number Three at PP 29-30 of this brief.

(2)   Assignment of Errors VII and XVI PR PP 260-266, set forth in verbatim herein at PP 5-9-10 and presented in Proposition Number One of this brief at PP 10 to 19 inclusive.

(3)   Assignment of Errors X, XII, XIII, XIV, XV, XVI and XVII, PR PP 261-266 inclusive, set forth in verbatim at PP 5-10 inclusive herein and presented in Proposition Number Two of this brief at PP 19-29 inclusive.

(4)   Assignment of Error XVII, PR 266, set forth in verbatim at P. 10 herein and presented in Proposition Number Four of this brief at PP 30-36 in- clusive.

STATUTES INVOLVED.

R. S. SECTION 4146.

"* * * and if any foreigner, or any person for the use and benefit of such foreigner, shall purchase or otherwise become entitled to the whole or any part or share of, or interested in such vessel, the same being within a district of the United States, the certificate shall, within seven days after such purchase * * * and if such purchase, change or transfer of property shall happen when such vessel shall be at any

NO. 8140

IN THE

United States
Circuit Court of Appeals

For the Ninth Circuit

W. PIERCE, Claimant of the Oil
Screw Vessel TAHOMA, official
number 214741, her engines, tackle,
apparel, furniture, dories, gear cargo, etc., and J. R. HECKMAN,
Surety,

Appellants,

vs.

UNITED STATES OF AMERICA,
ATLAS ENGINE COMPANY, a
corporation, and FISHING VES-
SEL OWNERS MARINE WAYS,
a corporation,

Appellees.

---

*Upon Appeal from the District Court of the
United States, for the Territory of
Alaska, Division Number One.*

Brief on Behalf of United States

FILED

OCT 21 19::

WM. A. HOLZHEIMER,
United States Attorney

GEO. W. FOLTA,
Asst. United States Attorney

PAUL P. O'BRIEN,
CLERK

INDEX

Pages

Statement of Facts.. 1- 4
Scope of Argument.. 4- 6
Questions Presented.. 6- 7
Argument 7-44

    I. The Court did not err in denying motion to dismiss the libel at the close of libelant's case for insufficiency of evidence to sustain the libel.. 7

    II. Evidence is sufficient to show such a transfer of ownership or interest in the TAHOMA to an alien as to sustain the forfeiture: 8

        1. Formation of Conspiracy to Transfer TAHOMA to Alien.................................... 8-14

        2. Transfer and Operation of TAHOMA........14-20

        3. Transfer of Wave in Exchange for TAHOMA 20-21

        4. Evidence on Behalf of Appellants...........21-27

        5. Meaning of Transfer by Way of Trust, Confidence or Otherwise.......................28-39

    III. A letter from a legal officer of the United States Customs Bureau to the Claimant dated Aug. 29, 1933, purporting to be in reply to one from him which was not produced and to prove the contents of which no offer was made, and stating that the "Bureau perceives no objection to the Consul issuing free entry documents for the fish taken by the TAHOMA at the present time," is inadmissible................39-42

Pages

IV. Section 1615, Title 19 U. S. C. A., by virtue of the provisions of Sec. 328, Title 46 U. S. C. A., is applicable and casts burden of proof on claimant after a showing of probable cause for the seizure..42-44

Conclusion 44-45

CASES CITED

American Film Co. v. Reilly, 278 F. 147-148.... 7

Bull v. New York, 167 F. 792................................ 7

The Burdette, 9 Pet. 681-682................................ 44

Central Vermont Trans. Co. v. Durning 71 F
    (2) 273.. 37

Dayton Rubber Co. v. Sabra, 63 F (2) 865........ 5

Eastern Oil Co. v. Holcomb, 212 F. 126, 129...... 4

Greenway v. U. S. 67 F (2) 738........................ 5

Lilienthal's Tobacco v. U. S. 97 U. S. 237, 272.. 44

The Chiquita, 19 F (2) 417-418........................ 43

The Margaret, 9 Wheat. 419-424............ 19-20, 35 38

The Persian, 158 F. 912.................................... 7

The Pilot, 42 F (2) 290.................................... 38

Union Pac. Ry. Co. v. Daniels, 152 U. S.
    684, 688.. 7

U. S. v. Davidson, 50 F (2) 517........................ 43

U. S. v. Regan, 232 U. S. 37............................ 44

Wilber v. National Bank, 294 U. S. 120............ 41

TEXTBOOKS CITED

65 C. J. 1276, Sec. 38.. 41

1 R. C. L. 432, Sec. 40...................................... 7

Pages

STATUTES CITED

Sec. 4146 R. S., 46 U. S. C. A. 23............ ...... 2-3, 18

Sec. 4172 R. S., 46 U. S. C. A. 41............................ 2

Sec. 4189 R. S., 46 U. S. C. A. 60 .... 2- 3

Sec. 808 Title 46 U. S. C. A.............................. 2- 3

Sec. 4173 R. S., 46 U. S. C. A. 42...................... 15

Sec. 4380 R. S., 46 U. S. C. A. 328..................... 42

Article 34 Chapter 2, Customs Regulations 1931 15

STATUTES INVOLVED

Sec. 1 Merchant Marine Act, June 5, 1920, 46
    U. S. C. A. 861................................... 28

Sec. 1, Merchant Marine Act May 22, 1928, 46
    U. S. C. A. 891.................................. 29

Sec. 4142, R. S., 46 U. S. C. A. 19.................... .29-30

Sec 4143 R. S., 46 U. S. C. A. 21....................... 30

Sec. 4146 R. S., 46 U. S. C. A. 23....................30-31

Sec. 4171 R. S., 46 U. S. C. A. 40..................... 31

Sec. 4172 R. S., 46 U. S. C. A. 41....................31-32

Sec. 4173, R. S., 46 U. S. C. A. 42..................32-33

Sec. 4131 R. S., 46 U. S. C. A. 221....................33-34

Sec. 4189 R. S., 46 U. S. C. A. 60..................... 34

Sec. 808, 46 U. S. C. A.............................. 34

Article 34, Chapter 2, Customs Regulations of
    the U. S. 1931.................................34-35

Sec. 1615, 19 U. S. C. A.............................. 42

Sec. 4380 R. S., 46 U. S. C. A. 328..................... 43

IN THE

United States
Circuit Court of Appeals

For the Ninth Circuit

W. PIERCE, Claimant of the Oil
Screw Vessel TAHOMA, official
number 214741, her engines, tackle,
apparel, furniture, dories, gear cargo, etc., and J. R. HECKMAN,
Surety,

Appellants,

vs.

UNITED STATES OF AMERICA,
ATLAS ENGINE COMPANY, a
corporation, and FISHING VES-
SEL OWNERS MARINE WAYS,
a corporation,

Appellees.

NO. 8140

Brief on Behalf of United States

This is an appeal from a decree of forfeiture
and condemnation entered against the American
schooner TAHOMA and W. Pierce, claimant, by the
District Court for the Territory of Alaska, Division
Number One, at Juneau, in November, 1935, for

violation of the shipping and custom laws (46 U. S. C. A. 23, 41, 60 and 808, infra, pp. 30, 31, 34).

STATEMENT OF FACTS

On March 31, 1925, at the port of Ketchikan, Alaska, the American fishing schooner TAHOMA, through her then sole owner and master, W. (Winnie) Pierce, claimant herein, received a certificate of registry. Thereafter and until her seizure by the Coast Guard on the high seas off the coast of Alaska, on Sept. 13, 1934, she was engaged in a foreign trade, to wit, transporting her catches of halibut from the high seas to the foreign port of Prince Rupert, Canada, for transhipment by rail through Canada to American markets, duty free.

The TAHOMA continued in command of the claimant Pierce, as master, until May, 1933. By that time she had become so heavily indebted to F. E. Hunt, Ltd., a Canadian corporation, managed and controlled by G. W. Nickerson and M. F. Nickerson, subjects and citizens of Great Britain, that said corporation induced or coerced the intervenors, the Atlas Engine Co., and the Fishing Vessel Owners' Marine Ways, both of Seattle, Wash., to agree to its taking over the management, operation and control of the TAHOMA. In pursuance of this agreement, F. E. Hunt, Ltd., removed Pierce from command of the TAHOMA, replacing him with an American citizen, one John Arthur Johnson, also known as Arthur Johnson, and appointed Pierce master of the American schooner Wave, which was similarly indebted to it. F. E. Hunt, Ltd., also placed aboard the TAHOMA Antone Martinsen, a Canadian, who had been recently master of the Canadian schooner Livingstone until she was wrecked, and who was actually in charge of the TAHOMA until her seizure.

On Sept. 17, 1934, the United States instituted suit against the TAHOMA, alleging two grounds of forfeiture in its libel, to wit, 1, an unlawful and fraudulent transfer, in whole or in part, of said vessel, by way of trust, confidence or otherwise, on or about May 29, 1933, by Pierce to F. E. Hunt, Ltd., a citizen and subject of a foreign state, and failure to surrender her certificate of registry to the Collector of Customs for the district of Alaska; and, 2, the unlawful and fraudulent use of said certificate of registry in a foreign trade by the TAHOMA after she was no longer entitled to the benefit thereof by reason of the alleged transfer (Secs. 4146, 4189 R. S., 46 U. S. C. A. 23, 60 and 808, infra, pp. 30, 31, 34). Pierce filed his claim of ownership and answered, admitting all the allegations of the libel except those as to the transfer of the vessel and the unlawful and fraudulent use of its certificate of registry. The TAHOMA was released on bond.

The Atlas Engine Co. and Fishing Vessel Owners' Marine Ways intervened, asserting maritime liens. All the witnesses, except those whose testimony was taken by intervenors to establish their claims of liens, were heard in open court. The court found for the libellant. The claimant Pierce excepted to the findings on the ground that they are "contrary to and unsupported by the evidence," and in addition excepted generally to the decree.

Appellee contends that the evidence shows that the TAHOMA was transferred to F. E. Hunt, Ltd., an alien. Appellants contend that such transfer was merely in pursuance of an arrangement with Pierce under which Hunt, Ltd., was to manage and operate the vessel until her indebtedness was paid off. The questions raised concern the admissibility of evidence and its sufficiency.

SCOPE OF THE ARGUMENT:

An explanation as to the scope of appellee's argument is deemed necessary because of the failure of appellants to observe the rules of this court in the preparation of their brief. The brief sets forth no specification or errors and does not clearly present the questions and points of law relied on. There is an improper grouping and argument (*Eastern Oil Co. v. Holcomb*, 212, F. 126, 129, CCA-8) under the heading of "Proposition Number Two" (brief p. 19) of six of the nine assignments of error relied on. These six assignments predicate error on exceptions to the court's findings on the ground that they are "contrary to and unsupported by the evidence," to the court's refusal to make findings and to its decree. Moreover, to add to the difficulty of extracting the precise questions presented under this cryptic heading, the court's findings and appellants' requested findings deal largely with probative instead of ultimate facts. Apparently these assignments are all directed to the question of the sufficiency of the evidence to support the decree, except assignment XV (R. p. 265), which is based on a general objection to the decree. As it is well settled that such an objection presents nothing for review no further question is presented under "Proposition No. Two":

Dayton Rubber Co. v. Sabra 63 F (2) 865 (CCA-9)

Greenway v. U. S. 67 F (2) 738 (CCA-10)

Eliminating the probative facts we find that the ultimate and essential facts found by the court and to which the argument under "Proposition Number Two" must be deemed to be directed are,—

1. That there was a transfer by way of trust, confidence or otherwise of the TAHOMA to an alien, with a consequent interest in her profits;

2. That there was no surrender of her certifi-

cate to the Collector of Customs within eight days after her arrival in the United States following such transfer; and

3. That after such transfer the TAHOMA was engaged in a foreign trade under her original cer-certificate of registry. The conclusion of law is that the TAHOMA became forfeited under the first and second causes of action.

QUESTIONS PRESENTED:

I.

Did the court err in denying claimant's motion to dismiss the libel at the close of libelant's case on the ground that the evidence to sustain the libel was insufficient?

II.

Does the evidence show such a transfer of the TAHOMA, in whole or in part, by way of trust, confidence or otherwise, to an alien, as to sustain the forfeiture?

III.

Is a letter from a legal officer of the U. S. Customs Bureau to the claimant, dated Aug. 29, 1933, purporting to be in reply to one from him which was not produced and to prove the contents of which no offer was made, and stating that the

"Bureau perceives no objection to the consul issuing free entry documents for the fish taken by the TAHOMA at the present time," admissible?

IV.

Is Section 1615, Title 19 U. S. C. A., by virtue of the provisions of Sec. 328, Title 46, U. S. C. A., applicable so as to cast the burden of proof on claimant after a showing of probable cause for seizure?

ARGUMENT

1. THE COURT DID NOT ERR IN DENYING MOTION TO DISMISS THE LIBEL AT THE CLOSE OF LIBELANT'S CASE FOR INSUFFICIENCY OF EVIDENCE TO SUSTAIN THE LIBEL

A motion to dismiss a libel at the conclusion of the libelant's case for an insufficiency of the evidence to sustain the libel is improper in admiralty (1 R. C. L. 432, Sec. 40; *The Persiana* 158 F. 912, DC; *Bull v. New York*, 167 F. 792, cert. den. 214 U. S. 526). Moreover, the objection was waived by the subsequent introduction of evidence and the failure to renew the motion at the conclusion of all the evidence.

Union Pac. Ry. v. Daniels 152 U. S. 684, 688
American Film Co. v. Reilly 278 F. 147, 148
(CCA-9)

II: EVIDENCE IS SUFFICIENT TO SHOW SUCH A TRANSFER OF OWNERSHIP OR INTEREST IN THE TAHOMA TO AN ALIEN AS TO SUSTAIN THE FORFEITURE

A determination of the question of the sufficiency of the evidence to sustain the forfeiture necessitates a rather lengthy review of the evidence, in the light of the rules that the evidence for the appellee must be viewed most favorably and every reasonable inference deduced therefrom; and that unless the finding of the trial court is clearly wrong or there is no substantial evidence tending to support such finding, the decree must be affirmed. Notwithstanding these rules appellants confine their argument to a discussion of evidence introduced on their behalf, which merely presents a conflict.

1. Formation of Conspiracy to Transfer TAHOMA to Alien.

Until May 29, 1933, the American fishing schooners TAHOMA and WAVE were owned and commanded by B. A. Petterson and W. Pierce, respectively. By that time both vessels became heavily involved in debt, principally to F. E. Hunt, Ltd., of Prince Rupert, Canada, an alien corporation (R. pp. 38-39). The TAHOMA was also indebted to the Atlas Engine Co., and the Fishing Vessel Owners' Marine Ways of Seattle, Washington, intervenors herein. F. E. Hunt, Ltd., acting through its manager, G. W. Nickerson, conceived the idea of taking over the WAVE and TAHOMA, replacing Pierce with Tony Martinsen, an alien, as master of the TAHOMA, securing the endorsement of the name of John A. Johnson, an American, as master on her certificate of registry to give the transaction the appearance of compliance with the laws of the United States, and continuing her operation under American registry in order to secure exemption from the payment of the duty of 2c a pound on her catches of halibut.

Before putting this plan into effect, F. E. Hunt, Ltd., sought the acquiescence of the intervenors, and on May 18, 1933, wrote them outlining the plan (Libelant's exhibit No. 2, R. pp. 54-57). Of especial significance is the following extract from that letter (R. p. 56):

> "*We have about persuaded him* (*Pierce*) *to make a trade, taking for his equity* (*in the Tahoma*) *a small American boat* (the Wave) that would cost about $2500, thus bringing the entire obligation, including interest to date, to about $11,000.

> "*We would be agreeable to dividing between you and the Atlas Engine Co., 50% of her earnings after insurance and upkeep has been taken care of.*"

F. E. Hunt, Ltd., also indicated in this letter its willingness to sell the TAHOMA.

The intervenors considered this proposal, and wrote in the margin of this letter, Exhibit No. 2, supra, the following:

> *"They taking title from Pierce."*
>
> *"If you are taking title we agree to accept."*
>
> *"Trading another boat and therefore become owner."*

indicating the construction placed upon this letter by them. These notations, for some reason, were improperly omitted from the printed record, but their existence is established by the testimony (R. pp. 86-87). On May 31, 1933, intervenors answered (Libelant's Exhibit No. 3, R. pp. 58-59) evincing an unwillingness to enter into the proposed arrangement and stating:

> *"As we understand it, you have tied up the TA-HOMA and intend selling or trading it to some other party who will be more adapted to operating the boat than Pierce."*

This construction in view of the circumstances and the object sought to be attained, was entirely reasonable and was neither denied nor corrected by Hunt in subsequent correspondence on the subject. On the contrary, in its reply of June 5, 1933, Hunt, Ltd., threatens intervenors with the possibility of proceeding against the TAHOMA under Canadian law, which would result in the loss of their liens, and continues:

"In the event of you not accepting this and *we should decide to let the boat operate out of here,* we do not see where there would be any obligation on us to apply any of the surplus earnings to your account." (Libelant's exhibit No. 4, R. pp. 60-62).

After receiving this threatening letter, the intervenors became tractable and signified a willingness to agree, for in their letter of June 12, 1933 (Libelant's Exhibit No. 5, R. pp. 63-64) they state:

"*It is our understaning* that there is now approximately $8500 against the boat and **that** *you intend turning over to Capt. Pierce a boat worth $2500,* which will raise the total obligation to $11,000. *Capt. Pierce is to convey the TAHOMA to you.* The boat will then proceed to work itself out of debt.

"We will appreciate hearing from you as to just what you intend doing *in regard to turning over the above vessels* and who the new captain will be.

"Hoping this will enable you to go ahead and close the deal in time to *profit* from the season's fishing, we remain."

The power to "turn over vessels," appoint masters and the right to share in the profits implies dominion and control that is absolutely inconsistent with the absence of ownership.

F. E. Hunt, Ltd., under date of June 17, 1933, (Libelant's Exhibit No. 6, R. p. 65), replied:

"We have arranged with Capt. T. (Tony) *Martinsen,* one of the most successful of fishing captains, who recently lost his boat, *to take out the Tahoma. If this man were an American citizen,* we are satisfied he would buy the boat, and it is just possible, should he be able to arrange with some American in whom he has confidence as a partner that he might decide to buy it."

Here is an admission that Martinsen, an alien, was to be master. Nickerson testified that Martinsen was in command of the TAHOMA because of Johnson's inexperience (R. p. 193)

That the placing of Martinsen aboard the TAHOMA was not done in ignorance of law is apparent from the following extract from the same letter, supra:

"This company's (F. E. Hunt, Ltd.,) debt must remain in exactly the same status as it is now, as foreigners cannot have an ownership in an American vessel. *Possibly we will allow the register to stay as it is, as there is nothing Pierce could do if he wished. We will however, have a bill of sale, signed in blank, so that it could be used instantaneously, if so desired.*

"In connection with the boat (American schooner Wave) *we are transferring to Pierce* there is some little work to be done on her and as soon as *We* get *our* bills we will send you a statement of just what the total indebtedness against the Tahoma will be."

The foregoing correspondence reveals the illegality of the entire scheme. To the eyes of the American customs officers, "the debt must remain in exactly the same status." The language that "possibly *we* will allow the register to stay as it is, as there is nothing Pierce could do if he wished," is not that of a mere lienor or creditor. As a precaution against Pierce's doing anything about it, a bill of sale would be taken *in blank* so that it could be used instantaneously. Pierce could not complain without disclosing his part in the conspiracy. If, however, he rebelled, a stroke of Nickerson's pen would have completed the instrument conveying title from Pierce to Hunt. It should be noted that it is stated a boat "was being *transferred*" to Pierce. It is difficult to see why the Wave should be transferred to Pierce if the TAHOMA had not been taken from him. What other consideration could Pierce, an insolvent, give for the Wave?

The foregoing amply shows a conspiracy between F. E. Hunt, Ltd., claimant Pierce, B. A. Pettersen, John A. Johnson, Antone Martinsen and the intervenors to defraud the United States of its revenue and of the function, authority and right to have its vessels owned and commanded by its citizens. The evidence also shows that in pursuance of this conspiracy Pierce transferred his

equity in the TAHOMA to F. E. Hunt, Ltd.; that
Antone Martinsen, an alien, was secretly placed
in command as master; John A. Johnson openly
placed aboard the TAHOMA as dummy master to
facilitate the evasion of the laws of the United
States; the TAHOMA was operated in foreign
trade as before and 318,000 pounds of halibut shipped, via Canada, into the United States as the
product of American fisheries on which the duty
of $6,300 was not paid (R. p. 131).

2. Transfer and Operation of Tahoma.

So much for the evidence of the formation of
the conspiracy. The scene now shifts to its execution, principally in the operation of the TAHOMA.
It was necessary for Johnson, the pseudo-master
of the TAHOMA to appear at the consulate in connection with his appointment (R. p. 155), and
later to clear the vessel for American waters. Upon
doing so Johnson told the consul that he had had
no experience as a master and did not consider
himself qualified to act as such (R. pp. 125-126).
But since Johnson was able to satisfy the consul
that he possessed the one essential qualification
of citizenship, his name was endorsed on the TA-
HOMA'S certificate of registry as master. It was
now common gossip along the Prince Rupert waterfront that F. E. Hunt, Ltd., had taken over the
TAHOMA for debt (R. pp. 152, 164-165). It eventu-

ally reached the ears of the American consul, who deemed it his duty to investigate. Even though he had not been apprised of such gossip, he was authorized by law to inquire into the ownership status of American vessels, particularly in the event of a change of masters (R. pp. 122, 143, 154, 156) and it was his duty to ascertain what halibut was the product of American fisheries and entitled to exemption from the duty (R. pp. 122, 150, 157-158). He questioned Johnson and reduced his statements to writing (Libelant's Exhibits Nos. 11, 15, R. pp. 127, 175). In them Johnson states that he was employed by F. E. Hunt, Ltd., ostensibly as master but actually to enter and clear the vessel because of his American citizenship; that for this he received extra pay, but that Antone Martinsen, a Canadian citizen, was actually the master and received the pay of master. G. W. Nickerson testified that one of these two statements is the nearest correct of the three written statements made by Johnson, but failed to identify the statement to which he thus referred (R. p. 195).

On October 10, 1933, when the TAHOMA entered the port of Petersburg, Alaska, Deputy Collector of Customs Vernon, secured an oath of the master as to the ownership of the TAHOMA, as required by Sec. 42, Title 46 U. S. C. A., and Article 34, Chapter 2 Customs Regulations, infra pp. 32, 34, 35) which was received in evidence as Libelant's exhibit No. 10 (R. p. 120). In it Johnson states that he was employed by F. E. Hunt, Ltd., as master of the TAHOMA and given to understand that W. Pierce was the owner *"so far as I was concerned in answering questions and signing papers pertaining to the vessel,"* and

> "That from the beginning of my employment, I was given to understand that *I was master of the vessel in name only* and that I was to be guided in all matters of the vessel by Tony Martinsen, *a Canadian citizen,* so far *that on leaving the dock I was to turn over the navigation of the vessel to Tony Martinsen,* that I would revert to the position of fishermen, and that I would perform the duties of such a fisherman,"

and that he (Johnson) would receive extra pay for acting as master in order that Tony Martinsen would not have to appear before the U. S. Customs officials.

On the cross-examination of Woodward, American consul, proctor for claimant announced that he would demand that the affidavit of John A. Johnson taken just before he died be introduced (R. p. 163). Proctor for libelant immediately offered it in evidence, and this otherwise inadmissible affidavit was received in evidence and appears as libelant's exhibit No. 13 (R. pp. 163-166). In it Johnson deposed that he heard on the waterfront about May 22, 1933, that he was going to be made

master of the TAHOMA; that the next day Antone
Martinsen asked him if he would act as master
of the TAHOMA and clear the boat for him; that it
was common gossip that Hunt had taken over the
TAHOMA. Milward Nickerson, Secretary-Treasurer of F. E. Hunt, Ltd., (who with G. W. Nickerson, ran the business of F. E. Hunt, Ltd., R. p. 30)
told him that Martinsen was to be the captain and
affiant was to act as master for the purpose of
clearing the boat, for which he would receive 5%
extra. Three weeks later affiant was notified of
the sailing date by Martinsen. The check for the
fish sold by the TAHOMA was made out in affiant's name and turned over to *Nickerson who
paid off the crew in cash;* that *fuel for the TA-
HOMA was paid for by F. E. Hunt, Ltd.;* that
affiant never received any orders from Pierce;
that Pierce was never aboard the TAHOMA and
that all of affiant's orders came from Martinsen
(R. pp. 164-165).

Moreover, Martinsen was seen docking the
TAHOMA at Prince Rupert, while Johnson was
on deck (R. pp. 129-130). Testimony of the witnesses Hanson, Sonderland, and Monson established
the fact that a master himself docks his vessel if
he is on watch or on deck (R. pp. 179-183).

When the American consul notified prospective
fish buyers at Prince Rupert of the possibility that

the duty of 2c a pound on halibut would be assessed against the catches of the TAHOMA, it was F. E. Hunt, Ltd., who guaranteed payment of the duty (R. p. 132).

After the close of the 1933 fishing season, and just before the 1934 season commenced, F. E. Hunt, Ltd., rendered an accounting of the TAHOMA'S earnings to intervenors and stated, (Libelant's Exhibit No. 7, R. p. 67):

> "*We have arranged to have the same captain* (Martinsen) *take the boat out that had her since midseason last year,* as we have every confidence in him. While *we* are not in a position to send you any money just now, *we* will try to send you some as early as possible.
>
> "We will mail copy of new insurance policy."

The TAHOMA'S new owner kept up the insurance (R. pp. 61-67), made an accounting of her earnings and later distributed her profits (R. pp. 99-100-101, 114). The statute prohibits aliens from becoming interested in the profits of American vessels (46 U. S. C. A. 19, 23, infra, pp. 29, 30).

Appellants point to the failure of the appellee to produce documentary evidence of the transfer of the TAHOMA. But a violation of law is seldom attended with the execution and delivery of formal documents, and guilt is not yet made to depend on the production of documents attesting that fact.

The argument is made that the appointment of Johnson as master under the supervision of Martinsen was lawful. By a parity of reasoning it would be lawful for an alien to own and operate an American vessel by the device of a dummy owner possessing the requisite citizenship. The appointment of a dummy master is a plain violation and would not have been resorted to had the TAHOMA not been transferred to Hunt, Ltd. For no other reason would a dummy master be hired at considerable expense for a vessel trying to work herself out of debt.

A like situation was involved in the *Margaret*, 9 Wheat. 421, arising under the same statute. The real master masqueraded as a passenger. Since the TAHOMA was not authorized to carry passengers, Martinsen, her real master, masqueraded as a fisherman. The language of the court in that case is particularly appropriate to the case at bar:

> "The Legislature foresaw that it would be impossible for the officers of the government to ascertain the secret intention of parties, or the object of ostensible transfers or ownership. Whether such transfers were bona fide, or colorable, for meritorious or illegal purposes, were matters of private confidence, and could rarely be ascertained by competent and disinterested proof. To admit secret transfers of ownership to any person, and especially to

foreigners, and allow at the same time, to the ships, the full benefit of the American character, would be hazarding the main objects of the act; it would invite all sorts of contrivances to evade the laws and disable the government from possessing means to detect frauds'' (9 Wheat. 419, 424).

3. Transfer of Wave in Exchange for TAHOMA.

The transfer of the American vessel Wave by F. E. Hunt, Ltd., to Pierce necessarily throws light on the transfer of the TAHOMA to F. E. Hunt, Ltd. Prior to May 29, 1933, B. A. Petterson, an American citizen, was owner and master of the Wave (R. p. 133). At about that time F. E. Hunt, Ltd., transferred the Wave to Pierce free and clear of all incumbrances (R. p. 225) and Pierce became its master. Petterson however, found himself without employment (R. p. 73) but on February 27, 1934, after the resignation of Johnson as nominal master of the TAHOMA because of ill health, Petterson was appointed master of the TAHOMA in order that the evasion of the shipping, customs and revenue laws of the United States might be continued. Petterson told the American consul that he had transferred the Wave to F. E. Hunt, Ltd., for her debt (R. p. 144) and Nickerson testified that this was substantially true (R. p. 206). Petterson had executed a bill of sale of the Wave that had been made out by F. E. Hunt, Ltd., (R. p. 173) which was delivered in May or June, 1933. Although possessed of the legal title to the Wave from that time, F. E. Hunt, Ltd., did not record the bill of sale or obtain a Canadian registry until in May, 1935 (R. pp. 214-216). Undoubtedly the seizure of the TAHOMA made it appear too hazardous to continue the operation of the Wave under American registry.

It should be noted that while appellants frankly admit the Wave transaction (Brief p. 16-17) they contend that this "couldn't happen" to the TAHOMA.

4. Evidence on Behalf of Appellants.

In addition to the claimant, the only witness produced for the defense is G. W. Nickerson, manager of F. E. Hunt, Ltd. Neither Petterson nor Martinsen appeared nor was their absence accounted for. It is clear that they were in a position to testify fully upon the issues. The attitude and demeanor of Nickerson and the claimant while testifying were such as to evoke unfavorable criticism on the part of the court. In its opinion (R. pp. 250-251) they are characterized as halting, evasive and generally unsatisfactory witnesses.

Moreover, as already pointed out, Nickerson admitted that the statements of Johnson made to the consulate, to the deputy collector of customs at Petersburg, and to the Department of Justice before his death in Arizona, are substantially correct. He also admitted the genuineness of the correspondence between F. E. Hunt, Ltd., and the intervenors (Libelant's Exhibits Nos. 1 to 8) but seeks to avoid the implications of these exhibits by asserting that he deliberately misled the intervenors in order to insure the final acceptance of his proposal to take over and operate the TAHOMA. Thus, with reference to libelant's exhibit No. 6, written in answer to intervenors letter (Libelant's exhibit No. 5, R. pp. 63-64) he testified:

> "In the final letter (Libelant's exhibit No. 6, supra,) I didn't think it good business to tell them (intervenors) that we were not taking the boat (Tahoma) over, so I told them it (the transfer) was completed and we would take a blank bill of sale. He (Pierce) threw himself on our mercy and I thought it best to carry on correspondence with the Atlas Engine Co., on the assumption that would be done —that they might be more ready to give an extension if they thought Pierce was clear of it (the Tahoma) already." (R. p. 79).

Thus, it appears that Nickerson who asserts that he is merely a creditor, was perfectly willing to brand himself as dishonest and to assume the character of a knave if by doing so he could only deceive the court into believing that the illegality with which the entire transaction appears tainted, is strictly confined to his person.

But it is now argued in the brief (p. 36) that as these inculpatory letters were written in the usual course of business, without any attempt to conceal their object, that in itself is proof that the acts which were done were innocent. It will thus be perceived that first there is an attempt to explain away their character by the confession that Nickerson was deceiving intervenors; then in their brief the inconsistent position is taken that they are true, but that since there was no attempt to conceal, they must be above suspicion. Of course, Hunt, Ltd., never dreamed that this correspondence would come under the scrutiny of U. S. Customs Agents.

The remainder of Nickerson's testimony is so self-contradictory and inconsistent that it is entitled to but little credence. Early in his testimony he attempted to testify that he did not know whether Tony Martinsen was a Canadian citizen (R. pp. 70-71) in the face of his statement in Libelant's exhibit No. 6 (R. pp. 65-66) to the intervenors:

> "We have arranged with Capt. T. Martinson, one of the most successful fishing captains, who recently lost his boat, to take out the Tahoma. *If this man were an 'American citizen* * * *

In this exhibit he also states that "there is nothing Pierce could do if he wished" about the taking over of the TAHOMA, so completely was he in Hunt's power. But on the stand Nickerson testified that Pierce "was willing to do anything with the TAHOMA to get some little boat to operate in which he felt he could make a living" (R. p. 76).

In a further attempt to disclaim an ownership interest Nickerson testified that his connection with the TAHOMA was merely that of agent for Pierce, F. E. Hunt, Ltd., and the intervenors (R. pp. 72, 194, 211). This all-encompassing agency and attempt to represent sharply conflicting interests necessarily resulted in eventually swallowing one of the principals. The existence of any such relationship is negatived not only by the probabilities but the evidence. In Libelant's exbibit No. 4 (R. pp. 60-62) we have the spectacle of the agent threatening two of his principals with the loss of the security for their liens, and of "bluffing" them into submission (R. p. 79), and indeed Wright, Vice President of the Atlas Engine Company, testified that they (the intervenors) were completely stalled and that F. E. Hunt, Ltd., held the whip hand (R. pp. 100-106).

In December, 1934, after the seizure of the TAHOMA, G. W. Nickerson went to Seattle and asked the intervenors to help *him* "out of the hole"

he had gotten into (referring to the seizure of the
TAHOMA). Wright, of intervenors Atlas Engine
Co., testified that "he (Nickerson) suggested that
we write to Washington and ask leniency. He
wanted us to do what we could to get the action
dismissed" (R. pp. 104-105, 116). Nickerson himself admitted that he suggested to intervenors that
they go to their congressmen and "pull wires" to
get the action against the TAHOMA dismissed (R.
pp. 189-191).

Can it be contended that Nickerson was still
acting as agent when he asked his "principals"
to get *him* out of the hole *he* had gotten into? Such
statements and acts show a consciousness of guilt.
Nickerson attempted to justify his actions in this
respect by testifying that "when I get into a jack-
pot I have to make the best deal I can" (R. p.
226).

In Libelant's Exhibit No. 2 Nickerson states
that the Wave which he was to turn over to Pierce
would cost $2500 (R. pp. 56-57). On the stand he
testified "If anyone had offered me $300 for the
Wave, I would have thought he was crazy" (R. p.
207). In his testimony concerning Libelant's Exhibit No. 5 he testified that he "didn't think it
good business to tell the intervenors that we were
not taking the boat over, so I told them it was
completed and we would take a blank bill of

sale" (R. p. 79). Later he testified that the reason for taking the bill of sale was so that she could be sold without delay (R. pp. 222-223); that he thought it best to get the thing in a position where it could be liquidated by the creditors and that accordingly he wrote them that Hunt would take a bill of sale, or acquire an equity in the TA-HOMA and that "along that line we were willing to give him (Pierce) the Wave under any consideration (R. p. 209).

The source of this unusual power over the Wave was identical with the source of his power over the TAHOMA. If he could barter with the Wave, he could do likewise with the TAHOMA. By virtue of such bill of sale Hunt's title to the TAHOMA was complete. Even without it he had acquired an equitable title that would be undoubtedly cognizable and enforceable in the Canadian courts. He acquired similar title to the Wave in the spring of 1933, but it was not till two years later that she was placed under Canadian registry (R. p. 214). It is probable that he would have continued operating the Wave under her original certificate of registry to obtain the duty exemption, but he had heard that the American consul was investigating the ownership status of the Wave and TAHOMA (R. p. 213), and, after the TA-HOMA was seized he must have feared that the

Wave would meet a similar fate. No explanation is offered as to why, if the TAHOMA was to be operated by Hunt temporarily only, for the benefit of creditors, it was necessary to buy the Wave for Pierce.

During the entire period the interest of Nickerson and his acts are those of an owner and operator and not those of a lienor. It is conceded that F. E. Hunt., could have proceeded against the TAHOMA in their local courts and obtained title to her and thereafter operated her under Canadian registry. It was from no altruistic motive that this was not done, but from a desire to avoid the payment of the duty of 25% and a sale tax of 6% upon such a transfer, as well as the duty of 2c a pound on her catches of halibut.

By comparison, the testimony of claimant Pierce is so short and of such little value that one is immediately impressed with the thought that it is the testimony of one who no longer has a vessel at stake; that the real claimant is F. E. Hunt, Ltd., and that Pierce, like Johnson, is merely a dummy. Pierce testified that since May, 1933, he had nothing further to do with the operation or management of the TAHOMA *did not know who furnished the bond for her release after her seizure, or how much he owed F. E. Hunt, Ldt., on the TAMOHA.*

5. Meaning of "Transfer by way of Trust, Confidence or Otherwise."

It is submitted that the term "transfer by way of trust, confidence or otherwise" is very comprehensive and contemplates any transfer whereby the requirements as to the manning and ownership of American vessels are evaded, regardless of the means or device employed to accomplish such evasion. An examination of the statutes in pari materia sheds light on the intent of Congress in the use of the term under consideration.

Sec. 1 of the merchant marine act of June 5, 1920 (46 U. S. C. A. 861) declares:

> "It is necessary for the national defense and for the proper growth of its foreign and domestic commerce that the United States shall have a merchant marine of the best equipped and most suitable types of vessels sufficient to carry the greater portion of its commerce and serve as a naval or military auxiliary in time of war or national emergency, *ultimately to be owned and operated privately by citizens of the United States; and it is declared to be the policy of the United States to do whatever may be necessary to develop and encourage the maintenance of such a merchant marine,* and, insofar as may not be inconsistent with the express provisions of this act, the United States Shipping Board shall, in the disposition of vessels and shipping property as hereinafter provided, in the making of

rules and regulations, and in the administration of shipping laws keep always in view this purpose and object as the primary end to be attained."

This policy is reaffirmed in Sec. 1 of the merchant marine act of May 22, 1928 (46 U. S. C. A. 891) in this language:

"The policy and primary purpose declared in section 1 of the merchant marine act of 1920 are hereby confirmed."

It is clear that statutes having any tendency to give effect to this policy must be construed in the light of this express declaration of national policy. Of first importance are those statutes designed to restrict the ownership and manning of American vessels to citizens and providing means to promote this end and penalties for their violation, to wit:

Sec. 4142 R. S., 46 U. S. C. A. 19:

"In order to the registry of any vessel, an oath shall be taken and subscribed by the owner, or by one of the owners thereof, before the officer authorized to make such registry, declaring * * * that the person so swearing is a citizen of the United States, AND THAT THERE IS NO SUBJECT OR CITIZEN OF ANY FOREIGN PRINCE OR STATE, DIRECTLY OR INDIRECTLY, BY WAY OF TRUST, CONFIDENCE, OR OTHERWISE, INTERESTED IN SUCH VESSEL OR IN THE PROFITS OR ISSUES THEREOF; AND THAT THE MASTER THEREOF IS A

CITIZEN, NAMING THE MASTER, AND STATING THE MEANS OR MANNER IN WHICH HE IS A CITIZEN."

Sec. 4131 R. S., 46 U. S. C. A. 21:

"If any of the matters of fact alleged in the oath taken by an owner to obtain the registry of any vessel, which within the knowledge of the party so swearing are not true, there shall be a forfeiture of the vessel, together with her tackle, apparel, and furniture, in respect to which the oath shall have been made, or of the value thereof to be recovered, with the costs of suit, of the person by whom the oath was made."

Sec. 4146 R. S., 46 U. S. C. A. 23:

"A certificate of registry shall be solely used for the vessel for which it is granted, and shall not be sold, lent, or otherwise disposed of, to any person whomsoever; * * * and if any foreigner, or any person for the use and benefit of such foreigner, shall purchase or otherwise become entitled to the whole, or any part or share of, or interest in such vessel, the same being within a district of the United States, the certificate shall, within seven days after such purchase, change or transfer of property, be delivered up to the collector of the district; and if any such purchase, change, or transfer of property shall happen when such vessel shall be at any foreign port or place, or at sea, then the master or person having the charge or command thereof shall, within eight days after his arrival within any district of the United States, deliver up the certificate to the collector of such district."

* * *

Sec. 4171 R. S., 46 U. S. C. A. 40:

"When the master or person having the charge or command of a registered vessel is changed, the owner, or one of the owners, or the new master of such vessel, shall report such change to the collector of the district where the same has happened, or where the vessel shall first be after the same has happened, and shall produce to him the certificate of registry of such vessel, and shall make an oath, showing that such new master is a citizen of the United States, and the manner in which or means whereby he is so a citizen. Thereupon the collector shall indorse upon the certificate of registry a memorandum of such change, specifying the name of such new master, and shall subscribe the memorandum with his name; and if other than the collector of the district by whom the certificate of registry was granted, shall transmit a copy of the memorandum to him, with notice of the particular vessel to which it relates; and the collector of the district, by whom the certificate shall have been granted, shall make a like memorandum of such change in his book of registers, and shall transmit a copy thereof to the Commissioner of Navigation. If the change is not reported, or if the oath is not taken, as above directed, the registry of such vessel shall be void, and the master or person having the charge or command of her shall be liable to a penalty of $100."

Sec. 4172 R. S., 46 U. S. C. A. 41:

"If any vessel registered as a vessel of the United States shall be sold or transferred, in whole or in part, by way of trust, confidence or otherwise, to a subject or citizen of any foreign prince or state, and such sale or transfer shall not be made known, as hereinbefore directed, such vessel, together with her tackle, apparel, and furniture, shall be forfeited. If such vessel, however, be so owned in part only, and it is made to appear to the jury before whom the trial for such forfeiture is had that any other owner of such vessel, being a citizen of the United States, was wholly ignorant of the sale or transfer to or ownership of such foreign subject or citizen, the share or interest of such citizen of the United States shall not be subject to such forfeiture, and the residue only shall be so forfeited."

Sec. 4173 R. S., 46 U. S. C. A. 42:

"Upon the entry of every vessel of the United States from any foreign port, if the same shall be at the port at which the owner or any of the part owners reside, such owner or part owner shall make oath that the register of such vessel contains the name or names of all the persons who are then owners of the vessel; or if any part of such vessel has been sold or transferred since the granting of such register, that such is the case, and that no foreign subject or citizen has, to the best of his knowledge and belief, any share, by way of trust, confidence or otherwise, in such vessel. If the owner or any part owner does not reside at the port at which such vessel enters, the master shall make oath to the like effect. If the owner, or part owner, where there is one, or the master, where there is no owner, refuses so to swear ,such vessel shall not be entitled to the privileges of a vessel of the United States.''

Sec. 4131 R. S., U. S. C. A. 221:

''Vessels registered pursuant to law and no others, except such as shall be duly qualified according to law for carrying on the coasting or fishing trade, shall be deemed vessels of the United States, and entitled to the benefits and privileges appertaining to such vessels; but no such vessel shall enjoy such benefits and privileges longer than it shall continue to be wholly owned by a citizen or citizens of the United States or a corporation created under the laws of any of the States thereof, and be commanded by a citizen of the United States. And all the officers of vessels of the United States who shall have charge of a watch, including pilots, shall in all cases be ciitzens of the United States. The word ''officers'' shall include the chief engineer and each assistant engineer in charge of a watch on vessels propelled wholly or in part by steam; and no person shall be qualified to hold a license as a commander or watch officer of a merchant vessel of the United States who is not a native born citizen, or whose naturalization as a citizen shall not have been completed. In cases where on a foreign voyage, or on a voyage from an Atlantic to a Pacific port of the United States, any such vessel for any reason deprived of the services of an officer below the grade of master, his place, or a vacancy caused by the promotion of another officer to such place, may be supplied by a person not a citizen of the United States until the first return of such vessel to its home port; and such vessel shall not be liable to any penalty or penal tax for such employment of an alien officer."

Sec. 4189 R. S., 46 U. S. C. A. 60:

"Whenever any certificate of registry, to any vessel is knowingly and fraudulently obtained or used for any vessel not entitled to the benefit thereof, such vessel, with her tackle, apparel and furniture shall be liable to forfeiture."

Sec. 808, Title 46 U. S. C. A.;

* * *"It shall be unlawful *to sell, transfer or mortgage,* or, except under regulations prescribed by the board, *to charter,* any vessel purchased from the board or documented under the laws of the United States to any person not a citizen of the United States, or to put the same under a foreign registry or flag, without first obtaining the board's approval.

"Any vessel *chartered, sold, transferred, or mortgaged* to a person not a citizen of the United States or placed under a foreign registry or flag, or operated in violation of any provision of this section shall be forfeited to the United States" * * *.

Article 34, Chapter 2, Customs Regulations of the United States, 1931

"*Evidence of Citizenship of Owners and officers*: In addition to the oaths of citizenship specified, a collector of customs may require the production of such further evidence as may be necessary to satisfy him that the person is a citizen of the United States and a proper notation of the evidence produced should be made on the papers retained in the collector's office, such as the number, date and office of issue of officer's license or a seaman's passport or a citizen's passport, or the same date as to a birth certificate or a naturalization certificate.''

In the *Margaret*, 9 Wheat. 419, 421, a forfeiture was decreed under the same statute as in the case at bar. There was a transfer, in Cuba, to a Spanish subject. The vessel thereafter sailed for the United States under American documents. The Spanish documents were in the custody of its Spanish master, who posed as a passenger. Of the transfer, the court said:

"It was completely within the words of the law, a transfer 'by way of trust and confidence' to a foreign subject; the trust and confidence being that the vessel should be reconveyed to the American owner when the special purposes of the transfer were entirely consummated. * * * The case is brought within the very terms of the act of congress, which does not require a beneficial or bona fide sale, but a transmutation of ownership 'by way of trust, confidence or otherwise.' ''

On the question of policy, the court said:

"But it is said that the case is not within the policy of the act. What the policy of the act is can be known only by its provisions; and

every section of it betrays a strong solicitude
on the part of the legislature, to trace and in-
spect every change of ownership; and for this
purpose, to require a public avowal of it, and
an alteration of the ships documents, so as to
exhibit, at all times, the names of all persons
who are the legal owners. *The policy evinced by
this course of legislation is the encouragement
of American navigation and American ship-
building to the exclusion of foreign navigation
and foreign ownership and securing to American registered ships a preference, in all our
revenue transactions,* over all vessels which
were not strictly entitled to the character. The
legislature foresaw that it would be impossible
for the officers of government to ascertain the
secret intentions of parties or the object of os-
tensible transfers of ownership. Whether such
transfers were bona fide, or colorable, for meri-
torious or illegal purposes, were matters of
private confidence, and could rarely be ascertained by competent and disinterested proof.
To admit secret transfers of ownership to any
person, and especially to foreigners and allow at the same time, to the ships, the full
benefit of the American character, would be
hazarding the main objects of the act; it would
invite all sorts of contrivances to evade the
laws, and disable the government from possessing means to detect frauds. The correct course
of legislation was, therefore, obvious. It was
to lay down a strict and plain rule, requiring
all transfers to be made known from time to
time, as they occurred; and a surrender of the
American documents when the legal ownership passed to a foreigner, whatever might be
the secret trusts with which it was accompanied. The words of the section now under
consideration, are direct to this purpose; and

so far from contravening, they support, in the
fullest manner, the general policy of the act.
They are not, then, to be construed in a more
limited sense than their obvious purport indicates.''

See also *Central Vermont Transportation Co. v.
Durning,* 71 F. (2) 273, affirmed in 294 U. S. 33,
for discussion of legislative history of this policy.

It is submitted that the transfer of the possession of an American vessel to an alien, for any
length of time, and her operation and management
by the transferee, with or without a right to the
profits, with an understanding, oral or written,
that upon the performance of a certain condition
or occurrence of some event, there would be a redelivery of the vessel to the transferor, would be
a transfer "by way of trust and confidence" within the purview of the statutes using that term.

A transfer "otherwise" than by way of trust
or confidence necessarily implies something less,
and was undoubtedly intended to embrace all transfers, devices or means that might be resorted to
for the purpose of evading the law. The assignment
or mortgaging of the earnings of the TAHOMA, accompanied by a change of possession, operation
and management, would certainly constitute a
transfer by way of trust and confidence or otherwise, the trust and confidence being that upon the

payment of her debt, the vessel would be returned to her record owner.

Viewed in the light of these statutes and the national policy, can it be contended that the transfer, or the delivery of the possession and operation, management and control of the TAHOMA by an alien, with an interest in her profits, does not fall squarely within the terms of the statute? Whether the judicial enforcement of such a transaction could be had in the courts of Canada is not the test to be applied. But it is apparent that it would be enforceable. Can it be doubted that an agreement for the transfer of the TAHOMA from Pierce to Hunt, accompanied by a corresponding change in her possession could not be enforced? As was said of a similar transfer by the court in *Margaret*, 9 Wheat. 421, the fact that it was a fraud on the laws of one country did not make it the less binding as between the parties.

The case of the *Pilot* 42 F (2) 290, D. C. cited by the appellants' brief (p. 33) not only fails to support their contention on this point, but is distinctly favorable to that of the appellee. In that case there was an agreement to sell an American vessel to a foreigner, but the vessel had not been delivered to the purchaser, and in fact was at another place. The court held that since there had been no delivery, there was no sale, and

that in any event ample time remained before the
contemplated delivery in which the seller could
have obtained the consent of the Shipping Board to
the sale.

The conclusive answer to the appellants' contention as to the nature of the transaction is that
Johnson, who had no reason to favor appellee, reaffirmed his previous three statements on his
deathbed and that Nickerson admitted their truth-
fulness.

The evidence is amply sufficient to show such
a transfer of the TAHOMA, with an attendant
right to her profits, as to sustain the forfeiture.
It is rare that so much evidence can be obtained
of an illicit transaction in a foreign country, necessarily shrouded in secrecy. The transfer of the
TAHOMA is not reasonably susceptible of any
greater degree of proof. To require more would
completely nullify the law and make impossible
the attainment of the end intended by Congress.
The ease with which such a transfer can be hid-
den points to the probability that such transfers are
common and that the United States is defrauded
of much revenue.

III.   A LETTER FROM A LEGAL OFFICER
OF THE UNITED STATES CUSTOMS BUREAU
TO THE CLAIMANT DATED AUG. 29, 1933,

PURPORTING TO BE IN REPLY TO ONE
FROM HIM WHICH WAS NOT PRODUCED
AND TO PROVE THE CONTENTS OF WHICH
NO OFFER WAS MADE, AND STATING THAT
THE "BUREAU PERCEIVES NO OBJECTION
TO THE CONSUL ISSUING FREE ENTRY
DOCUMENTS FOR THE FISH TAKEN BY THE
TAHOMA AT THE PRESENT TIME" IS INAD-
MISSIBLE:

When the claimant Pierce was on the stand, his
proctor asked him (R. p. 232) "Did you obtain permission or consent of the Treasury Department at
Washington to the manner in which you were operating the boat and fishing with her?" to which
an objection was interposed and sustained. An offer was then made of the following letter:

TREASURY DEPARTMENT
Bureau of Customs
Washington.

August 29, 1933

Mr. Winnie Pierce,
P. O. Box 396,
Prince Rupert, B. C.

Sir:

The Bureau is in receipt of your letter of July
29, 1933, in regard to the operation of the gas
ship TAHOMA as an American fishery.

The Bureau after careful consideration of the
matter, perceives no objection to the Consul

issuing free entry documents for the fish taken by the TAHOMA at the present time.

The State Department has been advised to this effect.

By direction of the Commissioner:

Respectfully,

(Signed) H. A. HAYWARD

Assistant General Connsel."

Standing alone this letter is meaningless. No offer was made to produce a copy or prove the contents of the letter which elicited the reply from Washington. It appears to be wholly incompetent on and irrelevant to any issue. If it is sought to be implied that Pierce was given permission to transfer the TAHOMA to Hunt, or allow Hunt to operate it as the evidence shows, the answer is that no one short of a dictator could authorize such acts. It is well settled that the United States is not bound or estopped by the mistakes, negligence or laches of its officers, or their acts, if such acts are not within the scope of their authority (Wilber v. National Bank, 294 U. S. 120, 123; 65 C. J. 1276, Sec. 38). If the Secretary of the Treasury is vested with any such authority or discretion appellants have failed to point it out. They do not even discuss the point or cite a single authority on this point or on the question of the admissibility of such a communication.

It is argued that the offered letter shows that Pierce was still interested in the operation of the boat. The answer to this is that Hunt, Ltd., used Pierce just as it used Johnson in dealing with the government of the United States—merely as a dummy.

IV.   SECTION 1615, TITLE 19, U. S. C. A., BY VIRTUE OF THE PROVISIONS OF SEC. 328, TITLE 46 U. S. C. A., IS APPLICABLE AND CASTS BURDEN OF PROOF ON CLAIMANT AFTER A SHOWING OF PROBABLE CAUSE FOR THE SEIZURE.

Sec. 1615, Title 19, U. S. C. A., provides:

> "In all suits or actions brought for the forfeiture of any vessel, vehicle, merchandise or baggage seized under the provisions of any law relating to the collection of duties or imports or tonnage, where the property is claimed by any person, the burden of proof shall lie upon such claimant; and in all suits or actions brought for the recovery of the value of any vessel, vehicle, merchandise or baggage because of violation of any such law, the burden of proof shall be upon the defendant. Provided that probable cause shall be first shown for the institution of such suit or action, to be judged of by the court."

Appellee contends that this section is appropriated to the case at bar by the provisions of Sec. 4380, R. S. (46 U. S. C. A. 328), providing:

"All penalties and forfeitures which shall be incurred by virtue of this chapter may be sued for, prosecuted and recovered as penalties and forfeitures incurred by virtue of the laws relating to the collection of duties and shall be appropriated in like manner, except when otherwise provided."

U. S. v. Davidson, 50 F (2) 517, CCA-2; The Chiquita 41 F (2) 842 (D. C.), affirmed by this court in 44 F (2) 302. Appellants seek to distinguish these cases on the ground that they each involve the use of a vessel in a trade other than that for which she was licensed. No reason is apparent why the statute should not apply to suits involving the use by a vessel of a certificate of registry to which she is no longer entitled.

The Chiquita case (19 F (2) 417, 418, CCA-5) is not in point. There the vessel was seized and sold under admiralty process to satisfy a maritime lien in a foreign country, and thereafter registered as a British vessel. She was seized and proceeded against by the United States on the theory that she was still an American vessel. The court held that her nationality had been completely divested by a foreign court and that the burden to prove she was an American vessel was on libelant. The decision is absolutely silent on the question of the burden of proof *after a showing of probable cause for seizure.*

Under this heading appellant insists that to sustain the forfeiture the proof must be beyond a reasonable doubt, and cites the *Burdett*, 9 Pet. 681, 682. However in *Lilienthal Tobacco v. U. S.* 97 *U. S.* 237, 272, the court modified or at least distinguished its decision in the Burdett case, and in *United States v. Regan*, 232 U. S. 37, expressly disapproved it and declared that "the true measure of persuasion is not proof beyond a reasonable doubt but the preponderating weight of the evidence" (*U. S. v. Regan*, supra, p. 50).

CONCLUSION

Appellee respectfully submits that the forfeiture should be sustained because the evidence clearly shows:

1. An agreement to take over the TAHOMA from Pierce;

2. An execution of the agreement by the transfer of the TAHOMA for the Wave;

3. Operation, control and management of the TAHOMA by Hunt, Ltd., an alien;

4. A distribution of the earnings and profits from the operation of the TAHOMA;

5. That Martinsen, an alien, was in command of the TAHOMA as master, while Johnson was master in name only;

6. Admissions by Hunt, Ltd., through the witness Nickerson, its general manager, that the statements of Johnson are substantially true.

WM. A. HOLZHEIMER,
United States Attorney

GEO. W. FOLTA,
Asst. United States Attorney

United States

Circuit Court of Appeals

For the Ninth Circuit.

GEORGE F. COVELL, GEORGE H. McKAIG,
E. A. COVELL, NELLIE L. COVELL,
N. O. BOWMAN, ALICE DENNETT and
ELEANOR DENNETT,

Appellants,

vs.

WATERFORD IRRIGATION DISTRICT,

Appellee.

Transcript of Record

Upon Appeal from the District Court of the United
States for the Northern District of California,
Northern Division

FILED

APR 10 1936

PAUL P. O'BRIEN,

PARKER PRINTING COMPANY, 545 SANSOME STREET, SAN FRANCISCO

No. 8141

United States
Circuit Court of Appeals

For the Ninth Circuit.

GEORGE F. COVELL, GEORGE H. McKAIG,
E. A. COVELL, NELLIE L. COVELL,
N. O. BOWMAN, ALICE DENNETT and
ELEANOR DENNETT,

Appellants,

vs.

WATERFORD IRRIGATION DISTRICT,

Appellee.

Transcript of Record

Upon Appeal from the District Court of the United
States for the Northern District of California,
Northern Division

INDEX

[Clerk's Note: When deemed likely to be of an important nature, errors or doubtful matters appearing in the original certified record are printed literally in italic; and, likewise, cancelled matter appearing in the original certified record is printed and cancelled herein accordingly. When possible, an omission from the text is indicated by printing in italic the two words between which the omission seems to occur.]

Page

Agreed Statement for Appeal 70

Answer to petition for confirmation of plan
of readjustment of debts 97

Order 159

Order of reference to a Special Master 105

Petition for confirmation on plan of read-
justment of debts 71

Exhibits attached to petition for confirmation:

A—Copy of resolution of Reconstruction Finance Corporation of January
29, 1934, authorizing the loan 78

B—Copy of resolution of Board of Directors of petitioner adopting a plan
for the refunding and readjustment
of its indebtedness 87

C—Copy of Order 12 of the California
Districts Securities Commission ap-
proving the plan 94

Index   Page

Exhibits for Petitioner—(cont.):

D-1 to D-107, inclusive—Acceptances in writing of the plan by certain creditors of said district named in Exhibit F... 94

E—List of all creditors of petitioner, their addresses and a description of their claim, consisting of the known bondholders of petitioner........................... 94

F—Separate list of the creditors mentioned in Exhibit E who had accepted the plan, together with their addresses 95

G—Form of letter of transmittal and deposit used by the consenting creditors 95

H—Itemization of the expenses incident to carrying out the readjustment plan in the total sum of $4,674.00 95

I—Copy of an order of the California Districts Securities Commission approving the filing of the aforesaid petition 95

J—Copy of a resolution of the Board of Directors of the Waterford Irrigation District, authorizing the filing of said petition and accepting and approving said plan of readjustment 95

Index   Page

Exhibits for Petitioner:

1 to 15—Various pleadings, papers and
documents on file in the proceeding... 127

16—Map of the Waterford district............ 127

17—Tabulation of figures showing the
amount that it would be necessary to
levy for 1935, if the levy were made
in accordance with Section 39 of the
California Irrigation District Act...... 127

18—Form of tax receipt used by the
district 127

19—Statement of the Stanislaus
County Auditor showing the tax rate
in the county to be $1.70 per hun-
dred and showing also the rate of assessments for the Oakdale High
School bonds and for the Waterford
and other school districts within the
Waterford Irrigation District............... 127

20—Chart showing the loss and gain
statement of the Waterford Development Company for the years 1913 to
1933 127

21—Graph illustrating the losses of the
Waterford Development Company
during this period.............................. 127

22 and 23—Quotation sheets by Elworthy & Co. quoting prices for
Waterford District bonds.................... 128

Index   Page

Exhibits for Petitioner—(cont.):

24—Schedule of county taxes and irrigation district assessments from 1924 to 1933 on property of various witnesses 128

25—Copy of order establishing the Waterford Irrigation District by the supervisors of Stanislaus County........ 128

26—Copy of the resolution of the board of directors of the district authorizing the first bond issue of $465,000.00 128

27—Same with reference to the second bond issue of $205,000.00............................. 128

28—Resolution changing the denomination of the bonds of the second issue... 128

29 and 30—Petition for, and order of California Securities Commission approving a former plan to refinance the indebtedness of the district............... 128

31—Application of the Waterford Irrigation District to the R. F. C. requesting a loan.. 128

32—Amended resolution of the Reconstruction Finance Corporation granting the district a loan upon which the present plan is based............................... 128

33 and 34—Transcript of various resolutions, agreements and letters of the district issued in pursuance of its efforts to **refinance**............................ 128

Index Page

Exhibits for Petitioner—(cont.):

35—Order of the District Securities
Commission approving the present
plan of refinancing.................................... 129

36, 37, 38, 39, 40, 41, 42—Copies of letters to the bondholders urging them
to accept the plan and reporting the
progress thereof 129

43—Resolution of the directors, July
14, 1934, authorizing the filing of the
petition 129

44—Order of the District Securities
Commission authorizing the filing of
the petition 129

45—Itemized statement of expenses in-
curred in the proceeding.......................... 129

46—Resolution of the directors of May
13, 1933, requesting the District
Securities Commission to approve a
rate of assessment for 1933 under
Section 11 of the California District
Securities Act.. 129

47—Order of the Commission approv-
ing said assessment rate for 1933........... 129

48—Resolution of the directors adopted
August 11, 1934, applying to the
Commission under Section 11 for ap-
proval of the same rate for 1934........... 129

Index   Page

Exhibits for Petitioner—(cont.):

49—Tabulation showing the assessments levied and statement of deliuquent tax rolls of the district.................. 129

50—Tabulation showing properties deeded to district.................. 130

51—Tabulation showing the two bond issues of the district and the amounts maturing and delinquent each year 130

52—Trial balance sheet of the district for September 30, 1934.................. 130

53—Statement showing cash on hand and estimated revenues and total liabilities for the year 1934/35.......... 130

54—Copy of resolution of Board of Directors of Waterford Irrigation District fixing the assessment rate for the year 1931/32.................. 131

55—Resolution for the year 1932/33, fixing the tax rate.................. 131

56—Copy of resolution of Board of Directors of Waterford Irrigation District adopted September 9, 1933, levying assessments for the year 1933/34 131

57—Copy of resolution of Board of Directors of Waterford Irrigation District fixing the assessment rate for the year 1934/35.................. 132

Index   Page

Exhibits for Petitioner—(cont.):

58 to 61, inclusive—Affidavits of publication of delinquent list for the years 1930 to 1933 and delinquent lists for those years.. 132

62—Tabulation showing the original expenditures of the district of the moneys obtained from its bond issue 132

63—Classification of the lands of the district 132

64—Graph showing a cross section of the district giving underground water level 132

65—Tabulation showing the crops grown in the district for the years 1919 to 1934.. 132

66—Map No. 2 showing the irrigated area of the district in 1933.................... 133

67—Graph showing the development of irrigated areas in the district................. 133

68—Tabulation showing the real estate holdings in the district from 1918 to 1934, the figures showing 1932, 323; 1933, 336; 1934, 318............................ 133

69—Tabulation showing the acreage and various sized holdings in the district on November 1, 1934.................... 133

70—Tabulation showing the payment that would become due under the old

Index   Page

Exhibits for Petitioner—(cont.):

bond issue upon final maturity and
the necessary tax rate assuming a
15% delinquency.. 134

71—Map No. 3 showing in color the
condition of delinquency on March
1, 1934 134

72—District crop report for 1934............ 134

73—Tabulation showing the estimated
amount required for operation, maintenance and replacement for July 1,
1934 to July 1, 1935.................................... 134

74—Tabulation showing the same for
the calendar year 1935................................ 134

75—Tabulation showing the assessments that have been levied and paid
on land which had never been irri-
gated 134

76—Two certificates of extension of es-
crow by two bondholders............................ 134

77—Certificate by escrow agent setting
forth a list of creditors represented
by the American Trust Company......... 135

78—Photostatic copy of a bond of the
first issue of the district............................ 135

79—Photostatic copy of a bond of the
second issue of the district...................... 138

80—Communication from Emil Schram
of the Reconstruction Finance Cor-

Index   Page

Exhibits for Petitioner—(cont.):

poration extending the time of the
loan to January 31, 1935.................................... 139

Exhibits for Respondents:

A and B—Reconnaissance Soil Survey
of the lower San Joaquin Valley to-
gether with map... 139

C—Report by the District Securities
Commission showing the crop report
for 1933 139

D—Statement from the Stanislaus
County Auditor's office showing the
outstanding bonded indebtedness of
the county and of various school districts overlapping Waterford Irri-
gation District 139

E—Bulletin 21 of the Division of
Water Resources of the State of
California, page 177, containing a
short history of the Waterford Irri-
gation District dated 1929.............................. 139

F—List of mortgages and deeds of
trust of record against lands in the
Waterford Irrigation District............................ 146

G—Letter from George F. Covell, respondent, explaining his opposition
to the plan.. 146

H—Report of the County Agricultural
Extension Service 146

Index	Page
State Controller's Certificate	138
Stipulation	158
Supplemental answer	100

Witnesses for petitioner:

Beard, W. F.	108
Cressy, Albert	110
Galt, Amos A.	110
Lehmkuhl, William	112
Quinley, C. W.	122
Rodden, William	111
Taylor, Arch L.	110
Whitmore, R. K.	112

Witnesses for respondents:

Covell, George F.	124
Mason, J. R.	126
Pitts, M. R.	124
Assignment of Errors	55
Certificate of Clerk U. S. District Court to Transcript on Appeal	160
Citation on Appeal	161
Decree Confirming Plan of Readjustment	39
Findings of Fact and Conclusions of Law	5
Names and Addresses of Attorneys	1
Order Continuing Proceeding in Effect	2

Order Allowing Appeal.. 55

Order Amending Minutes of Court.................................... 3

Petition for Appeal.. 53

Praecipe for Transcript on Appeal.............................. 159

Undertaking on Appeal.. 66

PROCEEDINGS IN UNITED STATES CIRCUIT COURT OF APPEALS.

Assignment of errors.. 174

Citation on appeal.. 176

Decree confirming plan of readjustment...................... 172

Order allowing appeal.. 175

Petition for appeal.. 164

Stipulation as to record on appeal................................ 177

In the Matter of
WATERFORD IRRIGATION DISTRICT,
An Insolvent Taxing District.

> George F. Covell
> George H. McKaig
> E. A. Covell
> Nellie L. Covell
> N. O. Bowman
> Alice Dennett
> Eleanor Dennett
>> Respondents and Objecting
>> Creditors

Attorneys for Appellee
HANKINS & HANKINS, Esqs.
Pacific Bldg.
San Francisco, Calif.

Attorney for Appellants
W. COBURN COOK, Esq.
Berg Bldg.
Turlock, Calif.

In the Northern Division of the United States
District Court for the Northern District of
California.

IN BANKRUPTCY.

No. 5552

In the Matter of

WATERFORD IRRIGATION DISTRICT,
An Insolvent Taxing District.

ORDER CONTINUING PROCEEDING
IN EFFECT

The petition of Waterford Irrigation District,
the taxing District above-named, for an order continuing the above-entitled proceeding in effect to
and until the 24th day of May, 1936, unless it shall
have sooner been terminated by final decree entered
herein, having been heard in open court this day and
Counsel for all of the creditors of said District who
have appeared herein having stipulated with Counsel for said Petitioner that said matter might be
heard without notice, and it appearing to the satisfaction of the Court that no formal decree confirming the plan of readjustment of the indebtedness
of said District set forth in its original petition on
file herein has been entered and that more than one
year has elapsed since the filing of said original
petition, and said District having filed herein various consents in writing, signed by creditors of said
District holding outstanding bonds of said District
and unpaid interest coupons appertaining thereto
in an amount greater than one-half of the total

amount of all claims of creditors of said District affected by said plan of readjustment, and it further appearing to the satisfaction of the Court that creditors of said District holding more than one-half in amount of all claims affected by said plan of readjustment have consented in writing to such continuance; now, therefore,

IT IS HEREBY ORDERED that the above-entitled proceeding be, and hereby is, continued in effect to and until the 24th [1*] day of May, 1936, unless sooner terminated by final decree of this Court entered herein.

Done in open court this 4th day of February, 1936.

> HAROLD LOUDERBACK
> Judge of the above-entitled Court.

[Endorsed]: Filed Feb. 5, 1936. [2]

[Title of Court and Cause.]

ORDER AMENDING MINUTES OF THE COURT AND AUTHORIZING ENTRY OF FINDINGS OF FACT AND CONCLUSIONS OF LAW AND FORMAL DECREE AS OF JULY 30, 1935.

WHEREAS, this Court did on the 3rd day of July, 1935, after due consideration of the Report of the Special Master herein, overrule certain Exceptions to said Report and did affirm said Report

---

*Page numbering appearing at the foot of page of original certified Transcript of Record.

as made by said Special Master and, in making
said order, it was the purpose and intent of this
Court to, and this Court did, confirm the plan of
readjustment of the outstanding indebtedness of
Waterford Irrigation District, the Petitioner herein, as said plan is set forth in the petition of said
District on file herein, but the record of said order
in the minutes of the Court does not clearly express
the intent and purpose of the Court and the terms
and scope of said order; and

WHEREAS, it was further ordered on said 3rd
day of July that the fees of the Special Master
should be determined thereafter by the Court and
thereafter the Court did fix the amount of said fees
at the sum of $500 in addition to the amounts shown
in said Report to have been expended in said Special
Master for necessary expenses in connection with
said matter; and

WHEREAS, the parties herein have stipulated
in open Court that the matters covered by this order
may be considered at this time; now, therefore,

IT IS HEREBY ORDERED that the minutes
of this Court for the 3rd day of July, 1935, insofar
as they relate to said matter, be, and hereby are,
amended so as to read as follows:

"Special Master's report and exceptions
there-[3]to having been submitted and being
now fully considered, it is ordered that the said
report be and same is hereby affirmed and exceptions thereto are hereby overruled, and that
the plan of readjustment of the outstanding indebtedness of Waterford Irrigation District,

the Petitioner herein, be and same is hereby confirmed, Further ordered that fees of Special Master shall be determined by Court at hearing to be had thereon, said hearing to be noticed to all parties interested.''

AND IT IS FURTHER ORDERED that findings of fact and conclusions of law in accordance with the facts found and reported in said Special Master's report and in accordance with this order, and a formal decree showing the confirmation of said plan of readjustment and other pertinent matters and prescribing the procedure to be taken for the consummation of said plan may be entered herein as of the 30th day of July, 1935, and that said decree may include a judgment for costs in the amount of $5.00 for each of said Exceptions overruled.

Done in open court this 4th day of February, 1936.

HAROLD LOUDERBACK
Judge of the above-entitled Court

[Endorsed]: Filed Feb. 5, 1936. [4]

[Title of Court and Cause.]

FINDINGS OF FACT AND CONCLUSIONS OF LAW

At a stated term of the Northern Division of the United States District Court for the Northern District of California, held at the Court Room thereof, in the City and County of San Francisco, on the

3rd day of July, in the year of our Lord one thousand nine hundred and thirty-five, the above-entitled proceeding came on regularly for hearing before the Honorable Harold Louderback, District Judge, upon the report of Stephen N. Blewett Esq., Special Master theretofore appointed by the Court to take testimony in support of and in opposition to the petition of Waterford Irrigation District filed herein; said petitioning irrigation district being represented by Messrs. Hankins and Hankins of San Francisco, California, and certain creditors of said district, to-wit, George F. Covell, George H. McKaig, David F. Selby, E. A. Covell, Nellie L. Covell, and N. O. Bowman, having appeared herein in opposition to said petition and being represented by W. Coburn Cook, Esq., of Turlock, California, and certain other creditors of said petitioning district, to-wit, Alice Dennett and Eleanor Dennett, having appeared herein in opposition to said petition and being represented by Messrs. Dennett & Zion of Modesto, California, which said creditors so appearing are hereinafter referred to as "the Respondents"; and Counsel for the Respondents having duly filed herein Twelve Exceptions to said report of said Special Master and having presented to the Court a motion that said report be amended by striking therefrom [5] the summary of testimony contained in said report and inserting in lieu thereof a certain summary of testimony attached to said exceptions, and the Court having duly and fully considered said report of said Special Master and said exceptions thereto and said motion, and having on said 3rd

day of July, by order orally made, affirmed said
report of said Special Master and confirmed said
plan of readjustment and overruled all of the exceptions thereto, except that the Court took under
further consideration the matter of fees to be allowed to said Special Master for his services in said
matter, and the Court having thereafter determined
that the amount to be allowed as such fees should
be Five Hundred Dollars, and the making of Findings of Fact and Conclusions of Law and the entry
of a formal decree herein having been unavoidably
delayed beyond the expiration of one year from
the date of the filing of the original petition herein,
and said proceeding having, by order of this court
made on the 4th day of February, 1936, pursuant to
the written consent of creditors of said District holding more than one-half in amount of all claims
affected by said plan, been duly continued in effect
to and until the 24th day of May 1936 unless sooner
terminated by entry of a final decree herein, and
the court having, by order duly made on said 4th
day of February 1936, amended the minutes of the
court for said 3rd day of July, 1935, to show the
confirmation of said plan of readjustment and authorized the signing and filing of Findings of Fact
and Conclusions of Law and a final decree herein as
of the 30th day of July, 1935; now therefore,

THE COURT NOW MAKES herein the following Findings of Fact:

I.

That Petitioner, Waterford Irrigation District, is
an irrigation district duly organized September 15,

1913, under and by virtue of that certain statute of the State of California entitled "An act to provide for the organization and government of [6] irrigation districts and to provide for the acquisition or construction thereby of works for the irrigation of the lands embraced within such districts, and, also, to provide for the distribution of water for irrigation purposes," approved March 31, 1897, as said statute had been amended and was in effect on said 15th day of September,. 1913, which said statute, as amended from time to time, is known as and is hereinafter called, the "California Irrigation District Act," and that said district has, ever since its organization, existed under and been subject to and governed by said statute as the same has been from time to time amended and has been subject to and governed by all other statutes supplementary thereto; that said district comprises approximately 14,110 acres of land, all of which is located in the County of Stanislaus, State of California, and within the Northern Division of the Northern Judicial District of California.

II.

That in the year 1916, said district duly authorized the issuance of its bonds in the sum of $465,000, which said bonds were designated as the First Issue of the bonds of said district and were dated January 1, 1917, and thereafter were all sold; that each of said bonds provided that it was to bear interest at the rate of 6 per cent per annum, payable January 1st and July 1st of each year of the life of the respective bonds, at the office of the Treasurer of said district at Waterford, California, and that said bonds were made payable serially in various amounts on the 1st day of January of each of the years from 1928 to 1947, both inclusive; that at the time of said hearing before said Special Master certain of the bonds of said First Issue of the face value of $18,600 had matured and had been paid by said district, and there were then, and now are, outstanding bonds of said First Issue of the total face value of $446,400; that when said bonds were issued the semi-annual interest to accrue thereon was evidenced by [7] coupons attached thereto.

That in the year 1919, said district duly authorized the issuance of its bonds in the sum of $205,000, which said bonds were designated as the Second Issue of the bonds of said district and were dated July 1, 1919, and thereafter were all sold; that each of said bonds provided that it was to bear interest at the rate of 5½% per cent per annum, payable January 1st and July 1st of each year of the life of the respective bonds at the office of the Treasurer of said district at Waterford, California, and evidenced by coupons attached to the respective bonds; that said bonds were made payable serially in various amounts on the 1st day of July of each of the years from 1927 to 1946, both inclusive; that at the time of said hearing before said Special Master certain of the bonds of said Second Issue of the face value of $19,475, had matured and had been paid by said district, and there were then, and now are, outstanding bonds of said Second Issue of the total face value of $185,525.

That said district has paid, or made provision for the payment of, all of its said bonds and interest coupons maturing on or prior to the 1st day of January, 1932, but none of such bonds or interest coupons which have matured since January 1, 1932, has been paid; that the total face value of the outstanding bonds of said district is $631,925; that on the 3rd day of July, 1935, certain of said bonds and interest coupons had matured and had not been paid, to-wit:

	Matured and Unpaid Bonds	Matured and Unpaid Coupons	Totals
First Issue	$65,100.00	$86,490.00	$151,590.00
Second Issue	29,725.00	33,740.41	63,465.41
TOTALS	$94,825.00	$120,230.41	$215,055.41

That the amounts of bonds and interest coupons maturing or to mature on the respective dates of payment are as follows: [8]

	First Issue		Second Issue		
	Bonds	Unpaid Coupons	Bonds	Unpaid Coupons	Total
1,	$13,950	——	——	——	$13,950.00
1,	——	$12,973.50	$5,125	$5,101.93	23,200.43
1,	13,950	12,973.50	——	4,961.00	31,884.50
1,	——	12,555.00	6,150	4,961.00	23,666.00
1,	18,600	12,555.00	——	4,791.87	35,946.87
1,	——	11,997.00	8,200	4,791.87	24,988.87
1,	18,600	11,997.00	——	4,566.37	35,163.37
1,	——	11,439.00	10,250	4,566.37	26,255.37

| First Issue | | Second Issue | | |
Bonds	Unpaid Coupons	Bonds	Unpaid Coupons	Total
23,250	11,439.00	——	4,284.50	38,973.50
——	10,741.50	12,300	4,284.50	27,326.00
25,575	10,741.50	——	3,946.25	40,262.75
——	9,974.25	12,300	3,946.25	26,220.50
25,575	9,974.25	——	3,608.00	39,157.25
——	9,207.00	12,300	3,608.00	25,115.00
27,900	9,207.00	——	3,296.75	40,376.75
——	8,370.00	13,325	3,296.75	24,964.75
27,900	8,370.00	——	2,903.31	39,173.31
——	7,533.00	14,350	2,903.31	24,786.31
27,900	7,533.00	——	2,508.68	37,941.68
——	6,696.00	14,350	2,508.68	23,554.68
27,900	6,696.00	——	2,114.06	36,710.06
——	5,859.00	14,350	2,114.06	22,323.06
27,900	5,859.00	——	1,719.43	35,478.43
——	5,022.00	15,375	1,719.43	22,116.43
32,550	5,022.00	——	1,296.62	38,868.62
——	4,045.50	15,375	1,296.62	20,717.12
37,200	4,045.50	——	873.81	42,119.31
——	2,929.50	15,375	873.81	19,178.31
46,500	2,929.50	——	451.00	49,880.50
——	1,534.50	16,400	451.00	18,385.50
51,150	1,534.50	——	——	52,684.50
$446,400	$241,753.50	$185,525	$87,691.23	$961,369.73

[9]

III.

That the governing body of said district is a
Board of Directors, as provided in said act where-
under said district was organized and, by order of
said Board, said district duly filed herein on the
6th day of August, 1934, a petition stating that
it was insolvent and unable to meet its debts as
they matured and that it desired to effect a plan
of readjustment of its debts; that said petition
was accompanied by payment to the Clerk of this
Court of the filing fee required by law, and said
petition did state that a plan of readjustment had
been prepared and was filed and submitted with
said petition, and that creditors of said district owning not less than 66-2/3 per centum in amount of
the bonds of the Petitioner, excluding bonds, notes,
or certificates of indebtedness owned, held, or controlled by the Petitioner in a fund or otherwise,
had accepted it in writing; that said written acceptances were attached to and filed with said petition; that said district had theretofore prepared a
plan of readjustment of its indebtedness and said
plan was filed and submitted with said petition;
that said plan provided for the purchase of the
outstanding bonds of said district with money to
be obtained by a loan to said district from the
Reconstruction Finance Corporation, an agency of
the United States of America, as was set forth
in a certain resolution of said Reconstruction
Finance Corporation authorizing a loan of not exceeding $312,500 to or for the benefit of said district
on certain terms and conditions set forth in said

resolution, whereof a copy was attached to said petition; that there was also attached to said petition a resolution duly adopted by the Board of Directors of said district accepting said loan for and on behalf of said district on the terms and conditions set forth in said resolution of said Reconstruction Finance Corporation; that said resolution of said Reconstruction Finance Corporation recited that the indebtedness of said district as of February 1, 1933, consisted of [10] its outstanding bonds in the principal amount of $634,925, and unpaid interest thereon in the sum of $53,525.93, and the bonds and coupons evidencing such indebtedness were referred to in said resolution, and are hereinafter referred to, as the "Old Securities"; that said statement of indebtedness included bonds of the face value of $3,000 which matured prior to January 1, 1932, and have since been paid and included certain interest coupons which matured January 1, 1932, or prior thereto, which have since been paid or provided for, and that the Old Securities subject to said plan of readjustment are the outstanding bonds and interest coupons shown in the table on page 5 hereof; that said resolutions provided that the holders of Old Securities who should join in said plan should deposit the same or otherwise give satisfactory assurances that the Old Securities held by them would be subjected to said plan; that said resolution further provided that any balance of the loan to be authorized that might not be required for paying for Old Securi-

ties so -deposited might be applied either to the
payment of costs incurred in connection with such
refinancing or to the payment of any sums that it
might prove advisable to advance in order to avoid
the necessity of the issuance of new bonds having
a principal of less than $1,000, as might be deter-
mined by the Chief or Acting Chief of the Drainage, Levee and Irrigation Division of said Reconstruction Finance Corporation, called in said resolution and hereinafter referred to as "the Division Chief"; that said resolution also provided that
the loans to be made thereunder should be conditioned upon the authorization by said district of refunding bonds having a principal amount sufficient,
in the opinion of the Division Chief and Counsel
for said Reconstruction Finance Corporation, to
insure the completion of the proposed refinancing,
which said bonds should bear interest at the rate of
4% per annum payable semi-annually; that said
resolution further provided that the amounts to be
loaned by said corporation thereunder should be
sufficient to provide for the purchase of all of the
out- [11] standing bonds of said district at the
rate of 48.82 cents for each dollar of principal
amount thereof, provided that all of said bonds had
been deposited as provided in said resolution for
acceptance of said price at the time when said corporation should make its first loan thereunder; that
it was further provided in said resolution that said
price of 48.82 cents for each dollar of principal
amount of bonds deposited as provided in said

resolution should be paid for the bonds so deposited in case said district was unable to procure the deposit of all of its outstanding bonds, but should procure as large a proportion thereof as should be required or approved by the Division Chief; that said resolution further provided that payment would be made for any of said outstanding bonds not thus deposited at the time when the first loan should be made under said resolution, but subsequently deposited, at the rate of 46.82 cents on each dollar of principal amount of said bonds, provided they should be deposited within such time or times as might be fixed or approved by the Division Chief; that said resolution also provided that each of the bonds deposited as aforesaid should be accompanied by such of its appurtenant coupons, if any, representing interest accrued on or before February 1, 1933, as might be required by the Division Chief and should also be accompanied by all coupons representing interest payable thereon after said date, and that, in case any such bond or bonds should not be accompanied by any coupon required by the Division Chief representing interest accrued on or before February 1, 1933, the amount payable on such bond or bonds should be reduced in such amount as might be determined by the Division Chief, but that such reduction should not be less than 44.79 cents for each dollar of the face amount of such missing coupons, and that if any bond should be presented with any coupon or coupons missing that had ma-

tured or were to mature after the aforesaid date,
the Division Chief might refuse to accept the same
or deduct from the price to be paid for said bond
the full face amount of such missing coupon or
coupons, but if any such bond should be [12] deposited without all the required coupons and for
that reason a reduction should be made in the price
of such bond and thereafter such missing coupon or
coupons should be deposited as prescribed or approved by the Division Chief, there should be paid
for such coupon or coupons an amount equal to
the sum originally deducted on account thereof,
but that in no event would any payment be made
from said loan for any interest coupons, but that
the payments to be made under said plan for Old
Securities are to be made for bonds only, and the
full amount to be paid for any bonds under said
plan can be obtained only by surrendering with
said bonds all interest coupons appertaining thereto
and maturing on or after July 1, 1932, and that no
allowance is provided for in said plan for counsel
fees or any other expenses of any creditors of said
district appearing herein to contest said petition
or otherwise objecting to or taking any measures
to prevent the carrying out of said plan.

IV.

That pursuant to said plan the American Trust
Company, a banking corporation, was selected as a
depositary for Old Securities referred to in said
resolution of the Reconstruction Finance Corpora-

tion; that bonds of said district of the total face value of $459,600, with the unpaid interest coupons appertaining thereto and maturing on or after July 1, 1932, have been deposited with said American Trust Company for acceptance of the price offered therefor under said plan as aforesaid; that the only creditors of said district affected by said plan were and are the holders of the outstanding bonds of said district, towit, bonds of the total face value of $631,-925, and the unpaid interest coupons appertaining thereto, as shown in said table on page 5 hereof; that said petition was accompanied with written acceptances of said plan by creditors of said district owning not less than 30 per centum, to-wit, in excess of 66 2/3 per centum, [13] in amount of the bonds, notes, and certificates of indebtedness of said district affected by said plan, excluding bonds, notes, or certificates of indebtedness owned, held, or controlled by said district in a fund or otherwise; that said petition was also accompanied with a list of all known creditors of said district, together with their addresses so far as known to said district and description of their respective claims, showing separately those who had accepted said plan of readjustment, together with their separate addresses.

V.

That upon the filing of said petition, an order of the Court was duly made and entered herein approving it as properly filed in good faith under Chapter IX of the Bankruptcy Act, and thereupon an order was duly made and entered herein fixing a time and place within 90 days after the approval of said petition for the purpose of considering the plan of readjustment filed therewith and any changes therein or modifications thereof which might be proposed, and prescribing a form of notice of said hearing, and said order did require said district to give notice of said hearing in substantially the form so prescribed, by publication of such notice for at least once a week for three successive weeks in The Waterford News, which said The Waterford News was and is a newspaper of general circulation printed and published in said County of Stanislaus, and said order did also require said district to mail a copy of said notice, enclosed in a sealed envelope with postage thereon fully prepaid, to each creditor named in the list of creditors accompanying said petition at the respective addresses given in said list; that notice of said hearing in the form prescribed in said order was given by publication in said The Waterford News for at least once a week for three successive weeks and by mailing copies thereof to the known creditors of said district as required in said order as aforesaid; that said matter [14] came on regularly to be heard at the time and place fixed in said order and said notice; that thereupon the Respondents above named appeared by their respective Counsel above named and controverted certain facts sets forth in said petition; that thereupon said matter was continued until a date more than 90 days after the first publication of said notice; that no other creditors of said district appeared herein, and thereupon said matter was referred by this Court to Stephen N. Blewett, Esq., of Stockton, California, as Special Master to take testimony in support of said petition and in opposition thereto; that such testimony was duly taken before said Special Master and a transcript of such testimony and the exhibits submitted to said Special Master and the report of said Special Master thereon and twelve exceptions of Counsel for Respondents to said report were filed with and duly considered by the Court, and that Counsel for the Respondents moved the Court to strike from said report of said Special Master the summary of the testimony taken before said Special Master as set forth in said report and to substitute therefor a certain summary of said testimony submitted by Counsel for the Respondents.

VI.

That less than one-half of the land within said district is suitable for irrigation; that water for irrigation purposes has been available for use in said district since the year 1919 and the greatest quantity of land within said district which has been irrigated in any year is 5,650 acres, or only about 40% of the total area of said district; that the dependable water supply available for the use of said district is not sufficient for the irrigation of more than about one-half of the area thereof; that, by reason of the location of said district between the

Tuolumne River along or near the Southerly boundary thereof and a natural watercourse known as Dry Creek along or near the Northerly boundary thereof, the lands within said district are drained rapidly [15] and to an excessive amount, making necessary the application of larger amounts of water for the proper irrigation of said lands than are required for the irrigation of similar lands in other irrigation districts in that vicinity, and making necessary the application of fertilizing materials in larger amounts than are necessary in the farming of similar lands in other irrigation districts in that vicinity; that diligent efforts have been made to colonize said district and bring the lands therein under cultivation for irrigated crops, but, by reason of the facts aforesaid, it has not been and will not be possible to increase materially the irrigated area in said district; that said district has exercised due diligence in the levying and collection of assessments and otherwise to obtain revenue to meet its obligations under its outstanding bonds and to provide for the expenses of the operation and maintenance of its irrigation works, but it has been impossible for said district to collect sufficient sums, by assessments or otherwise, to enable it to pay its debts as they matured or to maintain in proper condition it irrigation works; that said district is now in default in the payment of all of its outstanding bonds which matured January 1, 1932, and of all of said bonds which have matured since said date and is also in default in the payment of

all interest which has accrued on said outstanding
bonds since the 1st day of January, 1932; that the
works of said District are in need of repair; that
in the year 1929 said District levied an assessment
on all of the land therein at the rate of $5.90 on each
$100 of assessed valuation, according to the equal-
ized assessment book of said District for said year,
for the purposes of providing for payment of interest on its outstanding bonds and for the payment
of such bonds due or to become due before the end
of the next succeeding year and for the payment of
the general expenses of said District and the cost
of the operation and maintenance of its irrigation
works, which [16] said assessment amounted to
$63,675.57; that the assessments of said District are
payable in two installments, one thereof to become
delinquent if not paid on the last Monday in December of the year in which the assessment is levied,
and the other thereof to become delinquent on the
last Monday in June of the next following year;
that 23.7 per cent of said assessment was delinquent
after the last Monday in June, 1930; that in the
year 1930, said District levied as aforesaid, an
assessment on all the lands therein at the rate of
$6.90, which said assessment amounted to $74,471.27,
and that 21.2 per cent of said assessment was delinquent following the last Monday in June, 1931; that
in the year 1931, said District levied as aforesaid,
an assessment on all the lands therein at the rate of
$5.75, which said assessment amounted to $63,113.94,
and that 40.8 per cent of said assessment was delin-

quent following the last Monday in June, 1932; that
in the year 1932, said District levied as aforesaid,
an assessment at the rate of $4.50 on each $100 of
assessed valuation; that said rate was reduced below
the rates in said preceding years because the Board˙
of Directors of said District estimated that large
amounts of revenue would be received from the redemption of lands sold in previous years for delinquent assessments; that the total amount so levied
was $49,214.70, but that 61.2 per cent thereof was
delinquent following the last Monday in June, 1933;
that by reason of the aforesaid delinquencies in the
payment of assessments, said District was unable to
meet all of the bond interest and bond principal
maturing January 1, 1933, and had defaulted and
had, until the time for levying an assessment in the
year 1933, continued to default on its bond interest
and principal to the extent of more than 20 per cent
of the amount then due and that in said year, said
District was authorized by the California Districts
Securities Commission, in accordance with the provisions of Seeton 11 of that certain statute of the
State of California [17] approved June 19, 1931,
and known as and hereinafter called the "California
Districts Securities Commission Act," to levy and
did levy as aforesaid. an assessment upon the lands
within said District at the rate of $4.00 upon each
$100 of assessed valuation of land therein, except
certain lands that had been deeded to said District
for delinquent assessments; that the Board of Directors of said District found that said rate of assess-

ment was all that it would be reasonably possible for the lands in said District, taken as a whole, to pay without exceeding a delinquency of 15 per cent, and said finding was approved by said Commission; that the total amount of assessment levied at said rate on the lands within said District in said year was $43,000.12, and that after the last Monday in June, 1934, 61.2 per cent of said assessment was delinquent; that by reason of the delinquencies aforesaid, said District continued to be in default in the payment of interest and maturing principal of interest and maturing principal of its bonds and in 1934 was again authorized by said Commission to levy as aforesaid, and did levy, an assessment on all the lands in said District at the rate of $4.00 upon each $100 of assessed valuation of land therein, except certain lands which had been deeded to said District for delinquent assessments, which said assessment was found by said Board of Directors to be all that it would be reasonably possible for the lands in said District, taken as a whole, to pay without exceeding a delinquency of 15 per cent, which said finding was approved by said Commission; that the total valuation of the lands in said District, according to its equalized assessment book for the year 1934, was $1,010,923, which said valuation does not include any valuation of improvements on said lands; that on the 30th day of September, 1934, the assets and liabilities of said District, as shown by its books, were as follows: [18]

ASSETS

Cash:

General Fund	$2,212.96	
Bond Fund	7,048.56	
Construction Fund	10,878.10	$20,139.62
Assessment Sale Certificates		77,800.41
Sundry Debtor		415.57
Modesto Canal rights		254,000.00
Preliminary Survey and Organization Expense		18,934.39
Construction and Equipment		268,514.31
La Grange Mining Ditch Right		170,000.00
Assessment Lands		12,129.06
TOTAL		$821,933.36

LIABILITIES

Warrants payable	2,693.91
Unpaid matured bond interest coupons	87,939.43
Bond interest accrued but not yet payable	8,281.69
Bonds outstanding	631,925.00
TOTAL	$730,840.03

. VII.

That because of the facts aforesaid, particularly the insufficiency of the water supply of said District, the rapid drainage of the lands therein, and the large areas which have not been irrigated and which it is not and will not be practicable to irri-

gate, said District will not be able to collect sufficient sums, by assessments or otherwise, to pay its
existing debts as they mature or to raise, by assessments or otherwise, more revenue than will be necessary to provide for the operation and maintenance
of the works of said District and the general expenses of said District and to pay the amounts to
be required under the refunding bonds provided for
in said plan of readjustment; that the market value
of the outstanding bonds of said District is now
less than the price offered for said bonds under said
plan of readjustment, and unless said plan is carried out, the delinquency of the land within said
District in the payment of assessments thereof will
increase, the revenues of said District will be diminished and the [19] value of the outstanding bonds
of said district will be greatly decreased, and that it
will be for the best interests of the creditors of
said district if said plan of readjustment is consummated.

VIII.

That all of the creditors of said district are of
one class, to-wit, the holders of the outstanding
bonds of said district and of the unpaid matured
interest coupons thereof.

IX.

That said plan of readjustment is fair, equitable
and for the best interests of the creditors of said
district and does not discriminate unfairly in favor
of any class of creditors.

X.

That said plan complies with the provisions of Subdivision (b) of Section 80 of the Bankruptcy Act, in that said plan modifies and alters the rights of all holders of outstanding bonds of said District and interest coupons appertaining thereto and maturing or to mature on or after July 1, 1932; that no creditor of said District is affected by said plan of readjustment except the holders of such outstanding bonds and interest coupons and that, in the signing of the written acceptances of the plan of readjustment on file herein, the creditors of said District so accepting such plan acted in person and not through any committee, organization, group or individual.

XI.

That said plan has been accepted and approved as required by the provisions of Subdivision (d) of said Section 80 of the Bankruptcy Act, to-wit: that it has been accepted in writing filed in this proceeding by or on behalf of creditors of said District holding more than 66 2/3 per centum in amount of the claims of all classes of said District affected by said plan, but excluding claims owned, held or controlled by said District, and that said plan has been accepted and approved by said District in a writing [20] filed in this proceeding, signed in its name by an authorized authority, to-wit, the petition on file herein, which is signed in the name of Waterford Irrigation District by E. Whitney, President of its Board of Directors, and by C. W.

Quinley, Secretary of its Board of Directors, and that such signing of said petition was duly authorized by resolution of said Board unanimously adopted at a meeting thereof duly called and held on the 14th day of July, 1934; that said written acceptances of said plan of readjustment were signed by the holders of bonds of the First Issue of the bond of said District aggregating in face value $308,200, and the unpaid interest' coupons appertaining thereto, being more than 69 per centum in amount of the total amount of the outstanding bonds of said First Issue and the unpaid interest coupons appertaining thereto, and that such written acceptances were signed by the holders of bonds of the Second Issue of the bonds of said District aggregating in face value $151,400, and the unpaid interest coupons appertaining thereto, being more than 81 per centum in amount of all of the outstanding bonds of said Second Issue, and the unpaid interest coupons appertaining thereto.

XII.

That all amounts to be paid by said District for services or expenses incident to the readjustment of its indebtedness as proposed in said plan have been fully disclosed herein and are reasonable, which said amounts are as follows:

Escrow fee for deposit of Old Securities...$ 300

Printing escrow agreements and
 receipts 50

Typing and mailing letters and postage...... 100

Fee of Orrick, Palmer & Dahlquist,
 bond counsel 624

Balance of fee of Hankins and Hankins,
 attorneys for the District 1,000

Expenses of California Districts
 Securities Commission 100

Cost of printing refunding bonds
 (estimated) 400

Filing fee, cost of publication of notices,
 and incidental expenses in this
 proceeding 250

[21]

Miscellaneous expenses for meetings, con-
tacting bondholders, legal expenses not
specified, including cost of this proceeding not otherwise provided for, and
other incidental costs $1,600
 _____

 TOTAL $4,674

XIII.

That the offer of said plan and its acceptance as
aforesaid were and are in good faith.

XIV.

That the filing of said petition herein was legalized, ratified, confirmed and declared valid to all
intents and purposes, and the power of the Peti-

tioner herein to file such petition and take such other proceedings under or in contemplation of proceedings under Chapter IX of the Bankruptcy Act was ratified and confirmed by that certain act of the Legislature of California, adopted at the special session thereof in September, 1934, and entitled "An act in relation to relief from special assessments and in relation to financial relief therefrom, and of taxing districts, as defined in Chapter IX of the act of Congress entitled " 'An act to establish a uniform system of bankruptcy throughout the United States," approved July 1, 1898, as amended, validating petitioners and proceedings under or in contemplation of proceedings under, said Chapter IX, and authorizing contribution by cities and counties toward the payment of such assessments, and declaring the urgency thereof, to take effect immediately," approved and effective September 20. 1934, and designated as Chapter 4 of the Statutes of said Extra Session.

XV.

That within the meaning of Subdivision (k) of said Section 80 of the Bankruptcy Act, the California Districts Securities Commission was at all times herein referred to a state agency, duly existing and organized under an act of the Legislature of said State of California, designated as the California Districts Securities Commission Act, approved June 19, 1931 (Cal. Stats. 1931, p. 2263), [22] as amended, and that said Commission was at the time of the filing of the petition herein authorized to exercise supervision and control over the fiscal affairs of Petitioner, and had assumed such supervision and control over Petitioner; that said petition was accompanied by the written approval of said Commission, and that said Commission's written approval of the aforesaid plan of readjustment of the indebtedness of Petitioner is on file herein.

XVI.

That said District is authorized by law upon confirmation of said plan of readjustment to take all necessary action to carry out said plan, to-wit: that said District is authorized by the laws of the State of California to contract said loan with said Reconstruction Finance Corporation and issue refunding bonds of said District to evidence its obligations under said loan; that by provisions of said Chapter 4 of the Statutes of said Extra Session of the Legislature of California, said District is required, before a final decree or order of this Court confirming said plan of readjustment shall become effective to bind said District, to file with this Court a certified copy of a resolution of said District, adopted by the Board of Directors thereof, consenting to the plan of readjustment set forth or referred to in such final decree or order, and upon the filing of such certified copy of such resolution, said District is authorized by said statute to do all things necessary to be done by it to carry out said plan.

XVII.

That the summary of the testimony taken at the hearing of said matter as set forth in said report of said Special Master is fair and sufficient, and that the order heretofore made herein affirming said report and overruling said exceptions was intended to and did deny said motion to amend said report.

XVIII.

That the hearing of said matter before said Special Master [23] was held for the convenience of the parties herein in the City of Modesto, County of Stanislaus, State of California, and required the taking of testimony on five separate days; that said Special Master resides in the City of Stockton, County of San Joaquin, State of California, and that a reasonable sum to be allowed said Special Master for traveling expenses in attending the hearing of said matter is the sum of Thirty Dollars ($30.00), and a reasonable sum to be allowed said Special Master for stenographic services in connection with the preparation and transcription of his report to this Court is the sum of Seventy-five Dollars ($75.00), and that a reasonable sum to be allowed said Special Master as his fee for the conducting of said hearing and the preparation of his said report is the sum of Five Hundred Dollars ($500.00).

XIX.

That the respondents herein are respectively the owners and holders of outstanding bonds of said District in the total principal amounts set opposite their respective names as follows:

George F. Covell	$90,000
George H. McKaig	100
David F. Selby	1,000
E. A. Covell	8,000
Nellie L. Covell	25,000
N. O. Bowman	17,000
Alice Dennett	5,000
Eleanor Dennett	500
Total	$146,600

That no interest accruing on any of said bonds since January 1, 1932, has been paid, and the Respondents aforesaid are respectively the owners and holders of all interest coupons appertaining to their said respective bonds and maturing or to mature on and after July 1, 1932.

XX.

That for the consummation of said plan of readjustment it is necessary that the Reconstruction Finance Corporation be authorized and permitted to buy all of the outstanding bonds of said district now on deposit or which may be hereafter deposited [24] with the American Trust Company in accordance with said Plan of Readjustment or which may be offered directly to said Reconstruction Finance Corporation for sale under said plan, and that said American Trust Company be authorized and permitted to sell to the Reconstruction Finance Corporation in accordance with said plan, all bonds deposited with it thereunder, and that all owners of outstandng bonds of said district not now so deposited be authorized and permitted to deposit their bonds under said plan, or sell them to said Reconstruction Finance Corporation in accordance with said plan; that said District be authorized and permitted to issue refunding bonds in the total amount of the loan to be obtained by it from said Reconstruction Finance Corporation and to exchange for its outstanding bonds purchased by said Reconstruction Finance Corporation the refunding bonds of said District in an amount or amounts equal to the amount or amounts expended by said Reconstruction Finance Corporation in the purchase of such outstanding bonds, and to sell to said corporation such of said refunding bonds at their par value and accrued interest as may be necessary to enable said District to provide for the purchase, in accordance with said plan, of such of its outstanding bonds as may not be purchased by said Reconstruction Finance Corporation.

That further to carry out said plan of readjustment it will be necessary for this Court to designate and appoint a disbursing agent, with which all holders of outstanding bonds of said district who have not deposited or who may not deposit their said bonds with said American Trust Company as aforesaid may deposit their bonds for acceptance of the amounts to be paid therefor as provided in said Plan of Readjustment, and that said District be authorized and required to deposit with said Disbursing Agent, from the proceeds of the sale of its refunding bonds to said Reconstruction Finance Corporation, a sufficient [25] amount of money to pay for all bonds not theretofore deposited with said American Trust Company for acceptance of the price provided for in said plan or sold directly to said Reconstruction Finance Corporation; that a reasonable time to be allowed said District for making such deposit with such disbursing agent is ninety days from the time when a decree is entered herein, and a reasonable time to be allowed for the deposit of such outstanding bonds with said disbursing agent is the period ending with the 1st day of June, 1936, and that it will be necessary and proper to require said disbursing agent to pay into the registry of this Court immediately after June 1, 1936, all money deposited with it by said District and not paid out by it on or before said date for the purchase of outstanding bonds of said District, and that the Clerk of this Court be authorized, as is or may be provided by the rules of this Court, to purchase, in accordance with said plan, any of the bonds of said First or Second Issue of said District not purchased by the Reconstruction Finance Corporation, and that a reasonable time to be allowed for the presentation of bonds of said District to the Clerk of this Court for purchase in accordance with said plan is the period ending with the 1st day of June, A. D. 1937. [26]

CONCLUSIONS OF LAW.

From the foregoing Findings of Fact, the Court now draws the following Conclusions of Law:

1. That said Petitioner, Waterford Irrigation District, is a taxing district within the meaning of Chapter IX of the National Bankruptcy Act.

2. That said District is entitled to a decree confirming the plan of readjustment set forth in its petition on file herein and as summarized in the foregoing findings, provided that said District shall have filed with this Court, as provided in Chapter 4 of the Statutes of the Special Session of the Legislature of California held in 1934, a certified copy of a resolution of said District consenting to said plan of readjustment as set forth or referred to in said findings.

3. That said decree should forever enjoin and debar all owners or holders of any outstanding bond or bonds of said District or any interest coupons appertaining thereto from making or attempting to enforce any claim or claims against said District for or on account of any of said outstanding bonds or interest coupons except as provided in said plan of readjustment, and should forever enjoin and debar said District, its officers,

agents and representatives from making any settlement with the owner or holder of any of said
bonds or interest coupons for or on account of said
bonds or interest coupons except as provided in
said plan.

4. That said District should pay to said Special
Master the sum of $605.00 in full compensation
for the traveling expenses and for stenographic
services incurred by him and as his fee as such
Special Master.

5. That said decree should authorize and permit
the Reconstruction Finance Corporation to buy any
of the outstanding bonds of said District in accordance with said plan of readjustment [27] and
any holder of such bonds to sell the same to the Reconstruction Finance Corporation in accordance
with said plan, and should authorize and permit
said District to issue its refunding bonds in the
total amount of the loan to be obtained by it from
said Reconstruction Finance Corporation and to
exchange, for its said outstanding bonds purchased,
or to be purchased, by said Reconstruction Finance
Corporation, its refunding bonds in an amount or
amounts equal to the amount or amounts expended
by said Corporation in the purchase of said outstanding bonds, and should authorize said District
to sell and said Reconstruction Finance Corporation to buy the refunding bonds of said District
not so exchanged at a price not less than par and
accrued interest; that said decree should provide for

the appointment of a disbursing agent and should require said District to deposit with said disbursing agent an amount in cash sufficient for the purchase, in accordance with said plan, of all of its outstanding bonds, not purchased by said Reconstruction Finance Corporation, and should require all holders of such outstanding bonds not sold or deposited for sale to said Reconstruction Finance Corporation to deposit their said bonds with said disbursing agent for sale in accordance with said plan; that said decree should further provide that if any money deposited by said District shall remain with said disbursing agent after the first day of June, 1936, said disbursing agent shall pay all such money into the registry of this Court and should provide that the Clerk of this Court may, as is or may be provided by the rules of this Court, purchase for said District in accordance with said plan any of the bonds of its First or Second Issue not theretofore purchased by the Reconstruction Finance Corporation at any time during the period beginning with the first day of June 1936, and ending with the 1st day of June, 1937, but that any of the outstanding bonds of said District not purchased [28] by the Reconstruction Finance Corporation or delivered to said disbursing agent or to the Clerk of this Court in accordance with said decree, shall become and thereafter be null and void, and that all owners and holders and all persons having any claim to or interest in such bonds, or any of them, be forever barred from claim-

ing or asserting as against said District, or any
property therein, or the owners of any such property, any claim for, or lien of, on account of, or
arising out of, any of said bonds not so deposited
or not purchased by the Reconstruction Finance
Corporation.

6. That said decree should provide that said
Petitioner do have and recover as costs from the
above-named creditors appearing herein, the sum
of Sixty Dollars ($60.00), being five dollars for
each overruled exception to the report of said Special Master.

In pursuance of an order heretofore made herein,
these Findings of Fact are signed this 12th day of
February, A. D. 1936, but are hereby ordered to be
filed herein as of the 30th day of July, A. D. 1935.

HAROLD LOUDERBACK,

Judge of the District Court.

[Endorsed]: Filed Feb. 13, 1936. [29]

[Title of Court and Cause.]

DECREE CONFIRMING PLAN OF READ-
JUSTMENT, AUTHORIZING AND DI-
RECTING PROCEDURE FOR CONSUM-
MATION OF SAID PLAN, AND ENJOIN-
ING ATTEMPTS TO ENFORCE CLAIMS
FOR OR UNDER OUTSTANDING BONDS
EXCEPT IN ACCORDANCE WITH SAID
PLAN.

The above-entitled matter having come on duly
for hearing at a stated term of the Northern Division of the United States District Court for the
Northern District of California, on the petition of
Waterford Irrigation District for the confirmation
of a certain Plan of Readjustment of its outstanding bonded indebtedness, the Petitioner being represented by Messrs. Hankins & Hankins, of San Francisco, California, and certain creditors of [30] said
District, to-wit, Geo. F. Covell, Geo. C. McKaig,
David F. Selby, E. A. Covell, Nellie L. Covell and
N. O. Bowman, having appeared herein in opposition to said petition and being represented by W.
Coburn Cook, Esq., of Turlock, California, and certain other creditors of said District, to-wit, Alice
Dennett and Eleanor Dennett, having appeared
herein in opposition to said petition and being represented by Messrs. Dennett and Zion of Modesto,
California, which said creditors so appearing did
controvert certain allegation of said petition, and
said matter having been referred to Stephen N.

Blewett, Esq., of Stockton, California, as Special
Master to take testimony upon the issues raised by
said creditors so appearing, and said Special Master
having taken oral and documentary evidence in
respect to said issues and having submitted to the
Court his report thereon, wherein he found the existence of all facts and circumstances prescribed by
law as conditions precedent to the confirmation of
said plan and found that the best interests of said
District and of its creditors required the confirmation of said plan, and Counsel for said creditors so
appearing having duly filed herein twelve exceptions
to said report of said Special Master and prayed for
a certain amendment of said report, and the Court
having, on the 3rd day of July A. D. 1935, affirmed
said report of said Special Master except as to the
amount of his fee, and having overruled all of said
exceptions to said report and confirmed said plan,
and having heretofore signed and filed herein its
Findings of Fact and Conclusions of Law, and having found that said plan provides for the purchase
of the outstanding bonds of said District for a price
equal to 48.82 cents on each dollar of principal
amount of said bonds, provided that all of said bonds
are offered for sale at said price and that all interest coupons appurtenant to such bonds and maturing or to mature on or after July 1, 1932, be surrendered therewith, and having found that outstanding bonds of said District in the total [31]
principal sum of $459,600 have been deposited with
the American Trust Company, a corporation, under
a certain agreement for acceptance of said offer of

purchase, and, inasmuch as the confirmation of said plan by this decree makes the same binding upon all holders of outstanding bonds of said District, whether so deposited or not, and said District having heretofore filed with this Court a certified copy of a resolution of said District, adopted by the Board of Directors thereof, consenting to said plan of readjustment as set forth and referred to in said findings; now, therefore,

IT IS HEREBY ORDERED, ADJUDGED, AND DECREED as follows:

1. That said plan of readjustment of the bonded indebtedness of said District as more fully set forth in the petition originally filed herein be, and the same hereby is, confirmed and approved and declared binding upon said District and upon all owners and all holders of any of its outstanding bonds and upon all holders and all owners of any interest coupons appurtenant to any of said bonds and maturing or to mature on or after July 1, 1932, and that the owners and the holders of any of said outstanding bonds, and the owners and holders of any such interest coupons be, and hereby are and each of them hereby is, forever enjoined and debarred from making or attempting to enforce any claim or claims against said District for or on account of any of said outstanding bonds or coupons, except in accordance with this decree, or such other decree as may hereafter be made herein, and that said District, its officers, agents and representative be, and they hereby are,

and each of them hereby is, forever enjoined and debarred from making any settlement with the owner or holder of any of said outstanding bonds or coupons for or on account of said bonds or for or on account of any interest accrued or to accrue thereon after January 1, 1932, except in accordance with this decree or such other decree as may hereafter be made herein, but [32] nothing contained in this decree shall be construed to prevent said District from paying, or any person from presenting for payment, any interest coupons which matured on or prior to January 1, 1932, or to prevent said District from paying, or any person from claiming, interest on the purchase price of bonds deposited under the aforesaid agreement, at the rate of four per cent (4%) per annum from November 1, 1934, or from the date of deposit of any bonds so deposited after said date, until payment is made for said bonds.

2.   That the liabilities of and claims against said District which are affected by said plan of readjustment are and consist of its outstanding bonds, of two certain issues, designated respectively as First Issue and Second Issue, of the aggregate principal amount of $631,925, and all interest thereon which has accrued or is to accrue from and after January 1, 1932.

3.   That to provide for the retirement of outstanding bonds of said District, hereinafter referred to as "old bonds", except such of said old bonds

as may be purchased by Reconstruction Finance
Corporation as hereinafter provided, the American
Trust Company, a corporation, be, and hereby is,
appointed the disbursing agent of this Court, and
that said District be, and hereby is, directed and required to deposit with said disbursing agent, within
ninety days after this decree is entered herein, such
sum or sums as may be necessary to provide for the
payment for such old bonds as may be deposited
with said disbursing agent at the price specified in
said plan of readjustment, to-wit 48.82 cents for
each dollar of principal amount of such bonds, excluding all interest due or to become due on said
bonds and all interest due or to become due on any
matured bonds or coupons which have been presented
for payment and not paid, for which said interest no
payment shall be made, and that all holders of any
of said old bonds, except such as may have been
or may be deposited for sale, [33] or otherwise
offered for sale, to Reconstruction Finance Corporation in accordance with said plan, be and hereby are authorized and required to deposit their
said bonds, together with all interest coupons appertaining thereto and maturing or to mature on
or after July 1, 1932, with said disbursing agent
for sale at said price, provided that if any such
bond or bonds be so deposited, and any interest
coupon or coupons appertaining thereto and maturing or to mature on or after July 1, 1932, are missing,
the disbursing agent shall deduct from the amount to

be paid on such bond or bonds amount equal to the full face value of such missing coupon or coupons, except that if any such bond or bonds shall have been registered with said District to insure payment thereof and of the interest thereon to the registered owner of said bond or bonds and the missing coupon or coupons shall have been detached from such bond or bonds by the District and cancelled, as provided by the statute authorizing such registration, or if any such missing coupon or coupons shall have matured more than four years prior to the time of the purchase of such bond or bonds and the Treasurer of said District shall certify that such missing coupon or coupons have never been presented for payment and have never been registered as not paid because funds were not available for the payment thereof, as provided in Section 52 and Section 61a of the California Irrigation District Act, then no deduction shall be made for such missing coupon or coupons; that in case any deduction shall have been made by said disbursing agent or by the Clerk of this Court from the price of any bond on account of any such missing coupon and such missing coupon shall thereafter be offered to said disbursing agent on or before June 1, 1936, or to the Clerk of this Court after said date and before June 1, 1937, payment shall be made therefor in an amount equal to the amount which was deducted on account thereof from the price of the bond to which such coupon appertains; that payment as aforesaid shall [34] be made on the

surrender of such old bonds and appurtenant coupons
to said disbursing agent, if or as soon as sufficient
funds have been deposited therefor by said District as
hereinbefore provided, and said disbursing agent
shall cancel all such bonds and all coupons attached
to or accompanying such bonds by punching the
signatures on such bonds and the signature on
such coupons and stamping the word "cancelled"
on each such bond and each such coupon, provided
that if at any time said District shall not have
deposited with said disbursing agent sufficient
money to pay for any bond or bonds so deposited,
the amount herein required to be paid for such
bond or bonds shall bear interest from the date
of the deposit of such bond or bonds at the rate of
four per cent (4%) per annum, payable semi-annually on the first day of January and the first day
of July of each year until .paid, and said District
shall in such event, prior to each such interest
payment date, deposit with said disbursing agent an
amount of money sufficient to pay such interest
to the persons entitled thereto, and whenever said
District shall deposit with said disbursing agent
sufficient money to provide for the purchase of old
bonds then deposited with said agent, payment of
the amount due for said bonds as herein provided,
with any unpaid interest thereon as aforesaid to
the date of such deposit of said money by said District, shall be made promptly by said disbursing
agent to the persons entitled thereto in the order
in which said bonds were so deposited.

4. That the said American Trust Company as the disbursing agent of this Court shall immediately after the first day of June, 1936, make and file with this Court a verified report of all money received by it and all bonds deposited with it and all bonds purchased by it, as herein provided, and that the Court may at any other time call for a report from said American Trust Company of all of its transactions as the disbursing agent of this Court, which [35] said report or reports shall be subject to confirmation by this Court; that said disbursing agent shall, when so authorized by order of this Court, deliver to the Treasurer of said District all bonds and coupons theretofore purchased by it as such disbursing agent; that if any of the old bonds of said District remain outstanding after said first day of June, 1936, said disbursing agent shall, unless otherwise directed by this Court, forthwith pay into the registry of this Court any money theretofore deposited with it by said District and not expended as hereinbefore provided, and after said first day of June, 1936, unless otherwise hereafter provided by order of this Court, all holders of said old bonds then outstanding shall be required to present such bonds to the Clerk of this Court for purchase in accordance with the provisions of this decree, and the purchase price therefor shall be paid from the registry in accordance with the rules and orders of this Court.

5. That during the pendency of these proceedings the Reconstruction Finance Corporation be, and

hereby is, permitted to buy any of the old bonds of said District and that any and all holders of such bonds be, and hereby are permitted to sell such bonds to said Reconstruction Finance Corporation for a price equal to 48.82 cents for each dollar of the principal amount of the bonds so purchased, provided that all interest coupons appertaining to said bonds respectively and maturing or to mature on or after July 1, 1932, are missing, there shall be deducted from the purchase price of such bond or bonds an amount equal to the full face value of such missing coupon or coupons, except that if such bond or bonds shall have been registered with said District to insure payment thereof and of the interest thereon to the registered owners of said bond or bonds and the missing coupon or coupons shall have been detached from such bond or bonds by the District and cancelled, as provided by the Statute authorizing such regis- [36] tration, or if any such missing coupon or coupons shall have matured more than four years prior to the time of the purchase of such bond or bonds and the Treasurer of said District shall certify that such missing coupon or coupons have never been presented for payment and have never been registered as not paid because funds were not available for the payment thereof, as provided in Section 52 and Section 61a of the California Irrigation District Act, then no deduction shall be made for such missing coupon or coupons; that in case any deduction shall have been made from the price of any bond so purchased by the Reconstruction Finance Corporation on account of any such missing coupon and such missing coupon shall thereafter be offered to said Reconstruction Finance Corporation, payment may be made therefor in an amount equal to the amount which was deducted on account thereof from the price of the bond to which said coupon appertains; that any bonds with appurtenant interest coupons so purchased by Reconstruction Finance Corporation may be held by it and enforced at their full face value as security for the repayment of any money expended for the purchase thereof, with interest thereon at the rate of 4 per cent per annum from the time or the respective times of such purchase or purchases, such interest to be paid semiannually on the first day of January and the first day of July of each year upon the surrender to the Treasurer of said District in the order of their maturity, of matured interest coupons of such old bonds then held by Reconstruction Finance Corporation equal to the respective amounts of 4 per cent interest due on such dates; that said District and said Reconstruction Finance Corporation be, and hereby are, further authorized to exchange old bonds purchased by Reconstruction Finance Corporation as aforesaid for refunding bonds of said District in an amount or amounts equal to the amount or amounts expended by Reconstruction Finance Corporation in the purchase of the old bonds so exchanged, [37] and if it shall not be possible for the District to deliver the exact amount of refunding bonds which should be delivered in exchange for such old bonds, it shall deliver as many of such refunding bonds as the denomination thereof will permit and pay to the Reconstruction Finance Corporation the difference in cash, and any difference in accrued interest on the amount or amounts so expended by Reconstruction Finance Corporation and the accrued interest on the refunding bonds delivered therefor shall be adjusted in cash.

6. That for the purpose of the consummation of said plan and the payment of necessary expenses thereof, said District be, and hereby is, authorized to issue its refunding bonds in the total amount of $312,500 bearing interest at a rate not exceeding Four per cent (4%) per annum, payable semi-annually on the first day of January and the first day of July of each year until the maturity of the respective bonds, and otherwise in such form as may be provided by the Board of Directors of said District and in accordance with the laws of the State of California, and to exchange said refunding bonds for outstanding bonds of said District purchased or to be purchased by Reconstruction Finance Corporation, as hereinbefore provided, and said District is further hereby authorized to sell to Reconstruction Finance Corporation in accordance with the laws of the State of California, its refunding bonds not so exchanged at a price not less than par and accrued interest, and the Reconstruction Finance Corporation is hereby author-

ized to purchase such refunding bonds at such price, but in making such sale the matured interest coupons, if any, attached to the refunding bonds so sold shall be detached therefrom and cancelled by the District before the delivery of such refunding bonds, and the accrued interest on said bonds shall be computed only on such coupons thereof as are to mature at the next interest payment date following the delivery of said bonds.

7.   That all old bonds of said District which have not been [38] purchased by the Reconstruction Finance Corporation or have not been delivered to said disbursing agent of this Court or to the Clerk of this Court for purchase in accordance with the terms of this decree, or such decree or order as may be hereafter made, and all unpaid interest coupons appertaining to old bonds of said district and not delivered or deposited for delivery to Reconstruction Finance Corporation or to said disbursing agent or to the Clerk of this Court as hereinbefore provided, shall on and after the first day of June, 1937, become and thereafter be null and void, and any money remaining in the registry of this Court for the purchase of such old bonds shall be offered, as may then be provided by the Court, to the Reconstruction Finance Corporation for the purchase for said District of any refunding bonds of said District held by the Reconstruction Finance Corporation, at a price of par and accrued interest, and any of said money not paid to the Reconstruction Finance Corporation for the purchase of such bonds shall be

returned to said District as the Court may direct.

8. That the Clerk of this Court shall cause to be published in the Modesto Bee, a newspaper of general circulation published at Modesto, California, and in the San Francisco Chronicle, a newspaper of general circulation, published at San Francisco, California, for two successive issues of each of said newspapers, a notice to the holders of the outstanding bonds of said District not deposited with said American Trust Company under said Deposit Agreement, directing and requiring every holder of said bonds, except bonds sold or deposited for sale to Reconstruction Finance Corporation, to deposit such bonds so held by them respectively, together with all unpaid coupons appertaining thereto and maturing or to mature on or after July 1, 1932, with the American Trust Company as disbursing agent of this Court on or before the first day of June, 1936, or thereafter [39] with the Clerk of this Court, for purchase in accordance with the terms of this decree and the plan of readjustment of the outstanding bonded indebtedness of Waterford Irrigation District, and notifying owners and holders and all persons having any claim to or interest in such bonds, or any of them, that any of such bonds not purchased by the Reconstruction Finance Corporation or not deposited with said disbursing agent or with the Clerk of this Court, as provided in this decree, shall on and after said first day of June, 1937, be-

come ānd thereafter be null and void, and that all
such persons shall be forever barred from claiming
or asserting as against said District, or any property therein or any of the owners of any such property, any claim for or lien of or on account of or
arising out of any of said bonds not so deposited
or so purchased by the Reconstruction Finance
Corporation; provided, however, that nothing contained herein shall preclude the Reconstruction Finance Corporation from asserting its rights and
claims, under the old bonds purchased by it as herein provided, to the extent or amount expended by
it in acquiring such bonds, together with interest
thereon at the rate of 4 per cent per annum payable
semi-annually on the first day of Jannary and the
first day of July of each year until said District
shall have delivered to the Reconstruction Finance
Corporation its refunding bonds in form satisfactory
to said Reconstruction Finance Corporation in the
aggregate principal amount of the money so expended by it in acquiring said old bonds, and provided further, that in case the Court shall make
an order extending the time for the deposit of
bonds with said disbursing agent, it shall provide for
such notice of such extension as it may deem proper.

9.   That Petitioner shall pay all costs of the
procedure herein provided for and that Petitioner
do and have recover as costs from the above-named
creditors appearing herein, the sum [40] of Sixty
Dollars ($60), being Five Dollars ($5) for each
overruled exception to the report of said Special
Master.

10. That the Court will retain jurisdiction of this proceeding until the entry of a final decree herein, as provided in Subdivision (g) of Section 80 of the Bankruptcy Act, for the purpose of making such orders or further decrees herein as to the Court may seem necessary or proper.

This decree is made this 21st day of February, 1936, as of the 30th day of July, 1935, and, pursuant to an order heretofore made by this Court, the Clerk is hereby authorized and directed to enter it as of the 30th day of July, 1935.

HAROLD LOUDERBACK,
Judge of the District Court.

[Endorsed]: Fled Feb. 21, 1936. [41]

[Title of Court and Cause.]

PETITION FOR ORDER ALLOWING APPEAL.

To the Above Entitled Court and the Honorable Judges Thereof:

WHEREAS, George F. Covell, George H. McKaig, E. A. Covell, Nellie L. Covell, N. O. Bowman, Alice Dennett and Eleanor Dennett, respondents and objecting creditors in the above entitled proceeding, consider themselves aggrieved by the order and decree of the above entitled court rendered in the above entitled proceeding, which decree is entitled "Decree Confirming Plan of Readjustment, Authorizing and Directing Procedure for Consum-

mation`of Said Plan, and Enjoining Attempts to
Enforce Claims for or Under Outstanding **[42]**
Bonds Except in Accordance With Said Plan''
and is dated February 21st, 1936, at 3 P. M. and
is signed by the Hon. Harold Louderback, for the
reasons and because of the errors set out in the
Assignment of Errors presented and filed with this
Petition.

NOW, THEREFORE, the said respondents and
objecting creditors do hereby appeal from the aforesaid order and decree to the United States Circuit
Court of Appeals for the Ninth Circuit upon all
of the grounds and for the reasons specified in the
Assignment of Errors filed herewith, and pray that
said appeal may be allowed and that a citation
in due form shall be issued herein directed to the
petitioner, Waterford Irrigation District, in the
above entitled proceeding, demanding it to appear
before the said Circuit Court of Appeals to do
what may be adjudged to be done in the premises,
and that a transcript of the record, proceedings and
papers upon which order and decree was made shall
be duly made and authenticated and sent to the
aforesaid Circuit Court of Appeals, and that such
other and further order may be made as may be
proper.

Dated: March 9th, 1936.

W. COBURN COOK,
Attorney for Respondents
named in the above Petition.

ORDER ALLOWING APPEAL.

In the above entitled case (mentioned in the petition to which this order is attached), it is ordered that the appeal therein prayed for shall be and the same is hereby allowed, and the court hereby fixes the amount of the cost bond to be given by the appellants, the respondents named in said petition, in the sum of $250.00.

Dated: March 9th, 1936.

HAROLD LOUDERBACK,

United States District Judge.

[Endorsed]: Filed Mar. 9, 1936. [43]

[Title of Court and Cause.]

ASSIGNMENT OF ERRORS.

The appellants in this proceeding in connection with their petition for an order allowing an appeal, make the following assignment of errors, which they aver occurred at the trial and determination of this proceeding and in the rendering of the final decree appealed from.

1. The court erred in making and rendering the "Decree Confirming Plan of Readjustment, Authorizing and Directing Procedure for Consummation of Said Plan, and Enjoining Attempts to Enforce Claims for or Under Outstanding Bonds Except in Accordance with Said Plan" in this cause dated February 21st, 1936, from which the appeal is taken and in not holding to be unconstitutional [44] and

void under the United States Constitution those
provisions of Section 80 added on May 24, 1934,
to the Act entitled "An Act to establish a uniform
system of bankruptcy throughout the United States"
approved July 1, 1898, and thereafter amended which
purported to confer jurisdiction upon the district
court to make and render the said decree.

2. The court erred in holding it had jurisdiction to render said decree.

3. The court erred in holding that Waterford
Irrigation District was a person or legal creation
of such a character as that the court had power
to enforce as against said district or impose upon
said district the plan of debt readjustment mentioned in said decree.

4. The court erred in applying said so-called
bankruptcy law to said district in that said district
had no power to surrender its property to its
creditors in settlement of its debts or to surrender
its property to the court for valuation in order to
determine a fair composition of the debts of said
district. Said district's property is not leviable and
is held in a public trust. Assuming power to make
a bankruptcy law applicable to political subdivisions, municipal corporations or state agencies under some state laws, there is no such power where
the state law withholds the public agency's property from its creditors.

5. The court erred in finding and ruling that
said District was a political agency of the State
of California or taxing district within the meaning

and intent of Subdivision (a) of said Section 80, and in not holding and ruling that said Waterford Irrigation District is an arm or agency of the State of California for governmental purposes.

6. The court erred in holding that the power of Waterford Irrigation District to levy taxes on the lands or property of private individuals is property within the meaning of a true [45] bankruptcy law.

7. The court erred in ruling that this taxing power was not the sovereign power of the State and the court erred in ruling that it had jurisdiction to determine in this proceeding how such power should be exercised and in controlling the exercise of such power.

8. The court erred in holding that the Waterford Irrigation District does not exercise such governmental functions as did prevent the court from confirming the plan of debt readjustment set out in its decree.

9. The court erred in holding said Section 80 is a bankruptcy act within the meaning of the word "bankruptcies" as used in the Constitution of the United States.

10. The court erred in not holding said Section 80 is not a bankruptcy act which Congress could make applicable to Waterford Irrigation District.

11. The court erred in holding that Waterford Irrigation District was not a state agency created for the purpose of exercising, and exercising, powers of sovereignty conferred upon said district by the Laws of the State of California to carry out

public governmental purposes, and it erred in holding that the confirmation of said plan of debt readjustment was not a void and illegal interference with the exercise of said sovereign powers so conferred upon said district.

12. The court erred in not holding that Waterford Irrigation District was engaged in the exercise of governmental functions.

13. The court erred in holding it had jurisdiction to confirm the plan of debt readjustment set out in said decree in favor of Waterford Irrigation District, a California irrigation district.

14. The court erred in holding it had jurisdiction to confirm said plan of debt readjustment as against the appellants who are bondholders of Waterford Irrigation District. [46]

15. The court erred in not holding that neither said Section 80 nor the amendatory statute of which it is a part is a bankruptcy act in that it:

(a) Permits a partial bankruptcy.;

(b) Is not a uniform bankruptcy law;

(c) Restricts judicial power;

(d) Violates "The Due Process" clause of the United States Constitution;

(e) Permits the taking of private property for public use without just or any compensation;

(f) Permits the confirming of a plan of debt readjustment which impairs or changes the obligations of bonds of Waterford Irrigation District without impairing or changing the obligations of other public bonded indebtedness payable through taxation of the very lands which are taxed to pay the bonds of Waterford Irrigation District and yet the law does not make the tax lien created to pay said other bonds superior to that created to pay irrigation district bonds;

(g) Permits the confirming of a plan of debt readjustment which impairs and changes the obligations of bonds of Waterford Irrigation District without impairing or changing the obligation of private mortgages on lands and private deeds of trust on lands subject to taxation to pay the bonded indebtedness of the Waterford Irrigation District and yet the tax lien created to pay said bonds is superior to the lien of said mortgages and deeds of trust.

In this case, the uncontradicted evidence shows that the plan of debt readjustment confirmed by the court accomplishes the discrimination and confiscation defined in the aforesaid paragraphs (f) and (g).

16. Said plan is unfair in that it compels no surrender of any property of said district and it wholly fails to measure the new obligations of said district to pay by any valuation of any [47] assets or property of said district.

17. The court erred in sustaining the application of a bankruptcy act as constitutional in the situation in an irrigation district organized under the laws of the State of California, inasmuch as Section 52 of the California Irrigation District Act provides for priority of right of payment from

the bond and bond interest funds of the district, inasmuch as the application of said bankruptcy act here results in the destruction of the right of priority under Section 52 as between creditors of the same class, inasmuch as all creditors are under the "plan" to be paid an equal amount based upon the principal of their bonds without reference to whether or not the bonds were due or without reference to the maturity of the bonds, and without taking into consideration the relative values of a bond which is past due and one which may become due in, for example, ten years, or which may become due in, for example, twenty years, and which bear rates of interest exceeding those which can now be obtained on sound investments, and discriminating further between creditors of the same class in that some of the past due bonds and coupons are, under Section 52 of the California Irrigation District Act, entitled to priority of payment.

18. Said plan of debt readjustment is in its essentials unfair, for it discriminates between bondholders having the right of payment through taxation of the same land, in that it discriminates against the bondholders having county and school district bonds as against those having irrigation district bonds.

19. Said plan of debt readjustment is unfair in that it impairs bond obligations and sacrifices the interest of bondholders for the benefit of and advantage of the holders of private mortgages and deeds of trust.

20. The court erred in confirming a plan of debt readjustment in that said plan provides for the use of funds which were in [48] legal effect trust funds and for property which was in legal effect trust property, in that funds which may have been collected as the result of levies for bond interest or principal are trust funds belonging to the bondholders, and that the tax certificates which have not been collected by the district represent assets which likewise belong in part to the bondholders, and as the right of the appellant bondholders in these funds and properties are taken from them without just compensation and as the right of the bondholders are not equal in those trust funds, by reason of the fact that some have bonds which are due and some have bonds which are not due and some have bonds which have been presented under Section 52 of the California Irrigation District Act and others have bonds which have not been presented, the plan is discriminatory, unfair in its essential nature, and violates unconstitutional inhibitions against such discrimination. Delinquent revenue represented moneys for taxes levied for the particular purpose of meeting the bonds which had become payable long before the adoption of any resolution for the filing of the petition herein; in other words, matured interest coupons and bonds belonging to the objectors had been duly presented for payment long prior to the adoption of any plan of debt readjustment pursuant to said Section 80.

21. 'The court erred in confirming said plan of debt readjustment notwithstanding it impairs the obligations of the bonds held by the objectors.

22. The court erred in upholding and sustaining Section 80, notwithstanding it accords no fair or reasonable hearing to creditors.

23. The court erred in holding that said Section 80 was not void, notwithstanding it delegated restricted judicial powers.

24. The court erred in not holding that said Section 80 was unconstitutional because it denies and did deny in this case the [49] equal protection of the law and was violative of the equal protection clauses of both the Federal and the State Constitution.

25. Said Section 80 of this court's decree contravene the following provisions of the Constitution of the United States.

(a) Article X of the amendments;

(b) Article XI of said amendments;

(c) Article I, Section 10 of said Constitution;

(d) Section 1 of Article XIV of the Amendment to the United States Constitution;

(e) Section 14, Article I of said Constitution;

(f) Section 16, Article I of said Constitution;

(g) Section 1 of Article III of said Constitution;

(h) Other provisions of said Constitution.

26. Where any of the preceding or following assignments use the word "holding" or the word "finding", each assignment is repeated using the

other word, that is to say, "finding" or "holding".

27. The court erred in failing to grant the motion to dismiss made by the appellants.

28. The court erred in not holding that said Section 80 does not violate the Fifth Amendment to the Constitution of the United States.

29. The court erred in not holding that under the facts of this case the confirming of the "plan of readjustment of debt" violates the Fifth Amendment to the Constitution of the United States in the following respects:

(a) It takes the trust property of which the appellants are beneficiaries in that it takes the bond and bond interest funds and the tax certificates from them.

(b) It transfers rights from the appellant bondholders to bondholders of other taxing agencies, such as the County of Stanislaus, the Oakdale Union High School District, and the other [50] school districts.

(c) It transfers property from the appellants to the landowners within the district.

(d) It transfers property from the appellants to the mortgage holders and deed of trust holders within the district.

(e) It takes property from the appellants without due process of law, inasmuch as the testimony and findings show that the assets of the Waterford Irrigation District greatly exceed its liabilities.

30. The court erred in holding that the district is authorized by law upon confirmation of the plan

to take all action necessary to carry out the plan.

31. The court erred in confirming the plan, inasmuch as it is a limitation or impairment of the power of the State of California to control by legislation or otherwise the Waterford Irrigation District in the exercise of its governmental powers, including expenditures therefor.

32. The court erred in holding that any state agency, authorized to exercise supervision or control over the fiscal affairs of the district, did or could lawfully consent to the plan proposed.

33. The court erred in not holding that Assembly Bill #12 of Extra Session Laws of 1934 of the State of California was an unconstitutional enactment, and in not holding that the same was void as violating the provisions of the Constitution of the State of California prohibiting the impairment of contract by legislation and as violating Section 10 of Article I of the Constitution of the United States, and as violating Article I, Section 16, Article I, Section 21, and Article XIII, Section 6 of the California Constitution, and as being otherwise unconstitutional and void.

34. The court erred in holding that it had jurisdiction to [51] enter its decree in this cause on the 21st day of February, 1936.

35. The court erred in confirming a plan for readjustment of debts which provided for payment of 48.33% of principal of creditors claiming when the appellee's assets greatly exceed its liabilities.

36. The court erred in finding that the appellee was unable to pay its debts as they mature in view of Section 11 of the District Securities Commission Act of the State of California, and in view of Section 52 of the California Irrigation District Act of the State of California, and in view of other provisions of said last mentioned act.

37. The court erred in holding that it had jurisdiction to make any of the orders it made in the case.

38. The court erred in that it entered a decree contrary to equity, fairness and constitutional principles, a decree which provided that the appellants should be and were restrained from asserting any rights under their bonds and in adopting a plan which provided for the surrender of the evidences of obligations held by the appellants when the Waterford Irrigation District is not in possession of funds with which to pay the same, and no bondholder can obtain payment of his bonds upon surrender of the same unless the Reconstruction Finance Corporation of the United States, an agency of the United States, shall within its own discretion and without being subject to any order or direction of the court, voluntarily within such time as it may deem desirable to it solely furnish such funds to the Waterford Irrigation District, and when this court is without any authority or jurisdiction, by decree or otherwise, to compel the Reconstruction Finance Corporation to furnish such money or to compel the Waterford Irrigation District, unless the

district shall receive the same upon the voluntary action of the Reconstruction Finance [52] Corporaton in furnishing such moneys to pay the same to the bondholders, and that said plan in that regard violates the due process clause of the Constitution of the United States.

WHEREFORE, appellants pray that the decree of the District Court appealed from shall be reversed.

Dated: March 9th, 1936.

W. COBURN COOK,

Attorney for Appellants named
in the above Petition.   [53]

[Title of Court and Cause.]

7 St. Paul Street   NEW AMSTERDAM
Baltimore, Md. CASUALTY COMPANY

60 John Street
New York

UNDERTAKING ON APPEAL.

KNOW ALL MEN BY THESE PRESENTS:

That GEORGE F. COVELL, as Principal, and NEW AMSTERDAM CASUALTY COMPANY, a Corporation, duly organized and existing under the Laws of the State of New York, and authorized to do business in the State of California, as Surety, are held and firmly bound unto the petitioner in the above entitled proceeding, hereinafter referred to as Appellee, in the sum of TWO HUNDRED

FIFTY and no/100ths ($250.00) DOLLARS to be paid to the said Appellee, for the payment of which well and truly to be made we bind ourselves jointly and severally by these presents.

Sealed with our seals this 6th day of March, 1936.

WHEREAS, the above entitled court did in the above entitled proceeding render its decree, which decree is entitled "Decree Confirming Plan of Readjustment, Authorizing and Directing Procedure for Consummation of said Plan, and Enjoining Attempts to Enforce Claims for or under Outstanding Bonds Except in Accordance with said Plan", and is dated February   , 1936, and signed by Hon. Harold Louderback, District Judge, and which said decree confirms the plan of debt readjustment set out in the petition filed in the above cause on August 6th, 1934; and

WHEREAS, George F. Covell, Geo. H. McKaig, E. A. Covell, Nellie L. Covell, N. O. Bowman, Alice Dennett and Eleanor Dennett (the parties last named being all designated herein as appellants) have obtained an order allowing them to appeal to the United States Circuit Court of Appeals for the Ninth Circuit, for the purpose of reversing the aforesaid decree; and

WHEREAS, the citation directed to said Appellee citing and admonishing it to be and appear at a session of the United States Circuit Court of Appeals for the Ninth Circuit, to be held at the City of San Francisco, California, to show cause why said decree should not be reversed has been duly issued.

NOW, THEREFORE, the condition of this obligation is such that if the said appellants prosecute their appeal to effect and answer and pay all costs of appellee if they fail to make their plea good, then the above obligation to be voided, otherwise to remain in full force and effect [54] thereon, mentioned in rule 34 of the District Court.

The Surety further undertakes and agrees that in case of a breach of any conditions hereof, the above entitled Court may upon notice to said Surety of not less than ten days proceed summarily in this proceeding to ascertain the amount which the undersigned Surety is bound to pay on account of such breach, and render judgment thereon against said Surety and award execution therefor.

Dated: March 6, 1936.

[Seal]   GEORGE F. COVELL,
                    Principal.

NEW AMSTERDAM
          CASUALTY COMPANY,
By WALTER W. DERR,
          Agent and Attorney in Fact.

State of California
City and County of
San Francisco.—ss.

On this sixth day of March in the year one thousand nine hundred and thirty six, before me CON

T. SHEA, a Notary Public in and for the said County and State, residing therein, duly commissioned and sworn, personally appeared WALTER W. DERR, known to me to be the duly authorized Agent and Attorney-in-Fact of the NEW AMSTERDAM CASUALTY COMPANY, the corporation whose name is affixed to the foregoing instrument; and duly acknowledged to me that he subscribed the name of the NEW AMSTERDAM CASUALTY COMPANY thereto as Surety and his own name as Attorney-in-Fact.

IN WITNESS WHEREOF, I have hereunto set my hand and affixed my official seal the day and year in this certificate first above written.

[Seal]   CON T. SHEA,

Notary Public in and for said
County and State.   [55]

State of California,
County of Stanislaus—ss.

On this 9th day of March, in the year One Thousand Nine Hundred and thirty-six before me, W. Coburn Cook, a Notary Public, in and for the County of Stanislaus, personally appeared George F. Covell known to me to be the person whose name is subscribed to the within instrument, and acknowledged to me that he executed the same.

In Witness Whereof, I have hereunto set my hand and affixed my Official Seal, at my office, in the

County of Stanislaus, the day and year in this certificate first above written.

[Seal]   W. COBURN COOK,

Notary Public in and for the
County of Stanislaus, State of
California.

Approved 3/9/36

HAROLD LOUDERBACK

U. S. Dist. Judge.

[Endorsed]: Filed Mar. 9, 1936. [56]

[Title of Court and Cause.]

AGREED STATEMENT FOR APPEAL.

It is hereby stipulated by counsel for petitioner and for the respondents appearing herein in the above entitled cause, that the following shall constitute a statement of the case, as provided in Equity Rule 77 for the record on appeal and that no other record need be certified to the Circuit Court of Appeals upon the appeal of this case other than this statement, and a certain Order Continuing Proceeding In Effect, an Order Amending Minutes of the Court and Authorizing Entry of Findings of Fact and Conclusions of Law and Formal Decree as of July 30, 1935, and Findings of Fact and Conclusions of Law, and Decree Confirming Plan of Readjustment, Authorizing and Directing Procedure for Consummation of said Plan, [57] and Enjoining Attempts to Enforce Claims for or Under Outstanding Bonds Except in Accordance with Said Plan, entered herein.

BE IT REMEMBERED that the Waterford Irrigation District, the petitioner herein, an irrigation district organized under "the California Irrigation District Act" filed its petition herein on the 6th day of August, 1934, in the following words, except for exhibits:

The Petition

"PETITION FOR CONFIRMATION OF PLAN OF READJUSTMENT OF DEBTS.

To the Honorable Judge of the District Court of the United States for the Northern District of California:

The petition of Waterford Irrigation District of Stanislaus County, located in the Northern Division of the Northern District of California, with its principal office at Waterford, Stanislaus County, California, hereinafter referred to as 'Petitioner', respectfully represents:

1. That petitioner is an irrigation district duly formed, organized and existing in accordance with and under and by virtue of the provisions of that certain act of the Legislature of the State of California designated as 'the California irrigation district act' (approved March 31, 1897, Stats. 1897, P. 254, as amended), and is a taxing district within the meaning and intent of an act of the Congress of the United States, approved May 24, 1934 amending an act entitled 'An Act to establish a uniform

system of bankruptcy throughout the United States'
approved July 1, 1898, and acts amendatory thereof
and supplementary thereto, by adding thereto a
new chapter designated Chapter IX thereof. That
said district comprises approximately 14,000 acres
of land and is located wholly in the County of
Stanislaus, State of California and within the territorial jurisdiction of the above entitled court.

2.   That petitioner is insolvent and unable to meet
its [58] debts as they mature and it desires to effect
a plan of readjustment of its debts.

That petitioner's debts, which it desires to readjust, consist of two issues of bonds, duly issued
under the provisions of 'the California irrigation
district act', together with matured and unpaid
interest thereon, described as follows, to-wit:

An issue of bonds designated as FIRST IS-
SUE in the aggregate principal amount of
$465,000.00 bearing interest at the rate of 6%
per annum, payable on the 1st day of January
and the 1st day of July of each year, all dated
January 1, 1917 due serially from 1928 to 1947
(both inclusive) payable January 1 of each
year of which bonds $446,000.00 of principal
amount are now outstanding.

An issue of bonds designated as SECOND
ISSUE in the aggregate principal amount of
$205,000.00 bearing interest at the rate of 5½%
per annum, payable semi-annually on the 1st
day of January and the 1st day of July of
each year all dated July 1, 1919, due serially

from 1927 to 1946 (both inclusive) payable
July 1, of each year, of which bonds $188,525.00
of principal amount are now outstanding.

Matured and unpaid interest on the aforesaid
bonds amounting to approximately the sum
of $87,661.98 represented by interest coupons
attached to said bonds.

That a plan of readjustment has been prepared,
accepted and approved by petitioner and is filed
and submitted with this petition, which plan is as
follows, to-wit: the payment in cash of the sum of
48.82 cents for each dollar of principal amount
of the said outstanding bonds of petitioner, said
amount to be obtained through a loan from the
Reconstruction Finance [59] Corporation, an agency
of the United States, as more fully appears in the
resolution of said Reconstruction Finance Corporation, dated January 29, 1934, authorizing such loan
and the resolution of the petitioner accepting the
same, copies of which resolutions being attached
hereto, made a part hereof for all purposes and
marked Exhibit 'A'.

That a copy of the resolution of the Board of
Directors of petitioner adopting a plan for the refunding and readjustment of its outstanding indebtedness pursuant to the requirements of said Reconstruction Finance Corporation is attached hereto, made a part hereof for all purposes and marked
Exhibit 'B'.

3. That pursuant to the provisions of 'the California irrigation district act' and an act of the Leg-

islature of the State of California, entitled 'an act
to authorize irrigation districts to cooperate and
contract with the United States etc.; to provide for
the borrowing or procuring of money from the
United States or any agency thereof and the entering into contracts, and/or the issuance of bonds, warrants or other evidence of indebtedness for the repayment thereof' (approved May 5, 1917, Stats.
1917 p. 243 as amended, Stats. 1933 p. 2394), petitioner duly submitted to the California Districts
Securities Commission, successors to the California
Bond Certification Commission, for its approval,
the said plan for the readjustment of the debts of
petitioner, and the same was duly approved by said
Commission; that a copy of the order of said Commission approving said plan is attached hereto, made
a part thereof for all purposes and marked 'Exbibit C'.

4. That creditors of petitioner owning not less
than 66-2/3 per centum in amount of the bonds
of petitioner, excluding bonds, notes or certificates
of indebtedness owned, held or controlled by petitioner in a fund or otherwise, have accepted said
plan in [60] writing, which written acceptances
accompany this petition, are attached hereto, made
a part hereof for all purposes and marked 'Exhibits
D-1 to D 107 Inc.'

5. That a list of all known creditors of petitioner, together with their addresses, so far as
known to petitioner, and description of their re-

spective claims is attached hereto, made a part hereof for all purposes and marked 'Exhibit E'.

That a separate list of the aforesaid creditors who have accepted the plan of readjustment, together with their separate addresses, is attached hereto, made a part hereof for all purposes and marked 'Exhibit F'.

That all of said creditors are holders of the aforesaid bonds of petitioner and the accrued and unpaid interest thereon and petitioner has no creditors except the holders of said bonds of the face amount of $631,925.00 and accrued and unpaid interest thereon in the approximate sum of $87,661.98.

6. That in conformity with the said plan of readjustment and the requirement of the Reconstruction Finance Corporation the creditors accepting said plan have deposited their bonds, in escrow, with the American Trust Company, a banking corporation, under all the terms and conditions set forth in the letter of transmittal and deposit, a copy of which is attached hereto, made a part hereof for all purposes, and marked 'Exhibit G'.

7. That no contract or agreement has been entered into between any committee, organization, group, or individual and the creditors of petitioner, except said escrow agreement aforesaid, and no compensation is to be received directly or indirectly by any such agent or committee, save and except that the payment of the costs and expenses of carrying out said plan of readjustment will be paid by

petitionèr, the amount of which cost and expense is set forth in the schedule attached hereto, [61] made a part hereof for all purposes and marked 'Exhibit H'.

8. That within the meaning and intent of paragraph 'K' of said Chapter IX of the said Bankruptcy Act, as amended May 24, 1934, the California Districts Securities Commission, a state agency, duly existing and organized under an act of the Legislature of the State of California, entitled 'the California districts securities commission act' approved June 19, 1931 Stats. 1931 p. 2263, as amended, authorized to exercise supervision and control over the fiscal affairs of irrigation districts organized under the laws of the State of California, has assumed such supervision and control over petitioner, and petitioner is now under such supervision and control and subject to regulation by said commission.

That said commission, in writing, has duly approved of the filing of this petition which said written approval accompanies this petition, a copy of which is attached hereto, made a part hereof for all purposes and marked 'Exhibit I'.

9. That this petition is filed pursuant to and under authority of a resolution of the Board of Directors of petitioner, duly and unanimously adopted at a meeting thereof duly called and held on the 14th day of July, 1934, copy of which resolution is attached hereto, made a part hereof for all purposes and marked 'Exhibit J'.

WHEREFORE, your petitioner prays:

(a) That this court make its order approving this petition as properly filed in good faith under the provisions of said Chapter IX as added by said amendment approved May 24, 1934 to an act entitled 'an act to establish a uniform system of bankruptcy throughout the United States' approved July 1, 1898, and acts amendatory thereof and supplementary thereto.

(b) That the court order notice to the creditors of petitioner be given and published as in said Chapter IX of said [62] Bankruptcy Act provided.

(c) That the court allow and give such hearings and make such orders, decrees, confirmations and final determinations as may be proper and necessary in the premises.

> WATERFORD IRRIGATION
> DISTRICT
> By E. WHITNEY
> President of its Board of
> Directors
> By C. W. QUINLEY
> Secretary of its Board of
> Directors
> HANKINS & HANKINS
> Attorneys for Petitioner
> 918 Pacific Bldg.
> San Francisco, Calif.''

(Duly verified)

The following exhibits were attached to the petition, namely:

Exhibit A was a copy of the resolution of the Reconstruction Finance Corporation of January 29, 1934, authorizing the loan, pertinent and material portions of which read as follows:

"(Form 1/5/34)   Meeting of
RECONSTRUCTION FINANCE
CORPORATION
AMENDED RESOLUTION
Re: WATERFORD IRRIGATION DISTRICT
Docket No. Ref. 204

WHEREAS Waterford Irrigation District Stanislaus County of Waterford, California (Post Office Address) a political subdivision duly organized under the laws of the State of California (herein called the 'District'), has applied to this Corporation for a loan to enable it to reduce and refinance its outstanding indebtedness, pursuant to the provisions of Section 36, Part 4, of the Emergency Farm Mortgage Act of 1933, as amended, and

WHEREAS the District has represented that prior to May 12, [63] 1933, it had completed a project devoted chiefly to the improvement of lands for agricultural purposes and that in connection with such project it had incurred and now has outstanding indebtedness in approximately the following amounts:

Nature of Debt	Principal Amount	Interest Unpaid on Feb. 1, 1933	Total Out-standing
Bonds	$634,925.00	$53,525.93	$688,450.93

Such indebtedness, together with all interest accrued and unpaid thereon as of Feb. 1, 1933, is hereinafter referred to as the 'Existing Debt' and the bonds and coupons or other instruments evidencing such debt are hereinafter referred to as the 'Old Securities'; and

WHEREAS this Corporation has caused an appraisal to be made of the property securing or underlying the Old Securities and has determined that the project of the District is economically sound, and now desires to make a loan to enable said District to reduce and refinance all or by far the greater part of such Existing Debt on the basis of payments to holders of its Old Securities, or to Committees or other (for 1/27/34) representatives of such holders, at the rates herein set forth,

NOW, THEREFORE, BE IT

RESOLVED, that there is hereby authorized a loan of not exceeding $312,500.00, to or for the benefit of said District, subject, however, to the following terms and conditions:

1. Time Limits. All loans hereunder shall be disbursed on or before June 30, 1934, but the Chief or Acting Chief of the Drainage, Levee and Irrigation Division (hereinafter referred to as the 'Division Chief') may fix any shorter time within which such loans must be disbursed.

2. Deposit of Old Securities. The holders of Old Securities who join in this plan of refinancing shall deposit the [64] same with one or more committees,

depositaries, or other responsible representatives satisfactory to them, which shall consent to the plan of refinancing contemplated by this resolution (hereinafter referred to as 'Owners' Agents'), or shall otherwise give this Corporation satisfactory assurances that the Old Securities held by them will be subjected to such plan, in which latter case they are hereinafter referred to as 'Consenting Owners'. Old Securities deposited with Owners' Agents or held by Consenting Owners are hereinafter referred to as 'Deposited Securities.' Each Owners' Agent shall be duly authorized to receive all moneys payable to the holders of Old Securities deposited with it, to surrender the Deposited Securities and do all other acts and things necessary to enable the District to effect a reduction in its indebtedness to the extent and in the manner contemplated by this resolution.

No loan shall be made hereunder (a) unless all of the Old Securities shall be thus deposited or (b) unless the Division Chief shall deem that such a large proportion of such securities has been deposited as will satisfactorily accomplish the purposes of this Corporation in authorizing this loan. In this latter event, as hereinafter more fully provided, lesser amounts may be payable on the Deposited Securities than in case all of the Old Securities are deposited.

3. Payments on Deposited Securities. The amounts to be loaned by this Corporation hereunder shall be sufficient to provide for payments of differ-

ent amounts of money on account of the Deposited Securities, as follows:

(a) 48.82 cents for each dollar of principal amount of [65] Deposited Securities, provided that all of the Old Securities shall have been deposited at the time when this Corporation makes its first loan hereunder.

(b) 48.82 cents for each dollar principal amount of such Deposited Securities, in case the District is unable to procure the deposit of all of such Old Securities but shall procure the deposit of such large proportion thereof as shall be required or approved by the Division Chief. (Form 1/5/34)

(c) 46.82 cents for each dollar principal amount of Old Securities that are not thus deposited at the time when the first loan is made pursuant to the provisions of subparagraph (b) of this section, but which are subsequently deposited within such time or times as may be fixed or approved by the Division Chief.

Each Deposited Security shall be accompanied by such of its appurtenant coupons, if any, representing interest accrued on or before February 1, 1933, as may be required by the Division Chief and shall also be accompanied by all coupons representing interest payable thereon after such date. In case any such security shall not be accompanied by any coupon required by the Division Chief

representing interest accrued on or before the aforesaid date, the amount payable thereon shall be reduced in such amount as may be determined by the
Division Chief, but such reduction shall not be less
than 44.79 cents for each dollar of the face amount
of such missing coupons. In case any Old Securities
shall be presented with any coupons missing that
mature after the aforesaid date, the Division Chief
may refuse to accept the same, or if such security
is accepted there shall be deducted from the amount
to be paid on account thereof a sum equal to the
full face amount of such missing coupons. [66]

In case any Old Security shall be deposited without being accompanied by all the required coupons
and if because of such missing coupons reductions
are made in the amounts payable on account of such
Old Security, but thereafter such missing coupons
are deposited within such time or times as may be
prescribed or approved by the Division Chief. there
shall be paid on account of such coupons subsequently deposited amounts exactly equal to the sums
which were originally deducted from the sum paid
on account of such Old Security to which such
coupons appertained.

5.   *   *   *   *   *   *   *

How Loans are to be Effected. Unless the Division Chief shall direct otherwise, loans made hereunder shall be conditioned upon the authorization
by the District of new 4% bonds (herein referred to
as 'New Bonds') having a principal amount sufficient in the opinion of said Division Chief and

Counsel for this Corporation to insure completion of the proposed refinancing. Such loans shall be effected in any of the following ways as said Division Chief and Counsel shall direct:

(a) If the Division Chief shall deem it advisable to have the Deposited Securities canceled immediately upon issuance of the New Bonds, such loans may be advanced directly to the District or to the Owners' Agents and consenting owners at the time of the surrender and cancellation of the Deposited Securities but only upon receipt by this Corporation of New Bonds having a principal amount equal to the amount of the loans it has made hereunder.

(b) In the event that the Division Chief shall deem it necessary to keep any or all of the Deposited Securities alive for a greater or lesser length of time in order to [67] maintain a parity of rights as between the holders of the Deposited Securities and the rights of the holders of Old Securities who did not deposit same, or for any other purpose, then such loans may be made directly to the Owners' Agents and consenting owners. All such loans shall be represented by the notes of such consenting owners or Owners' Agents and the Deposited Securities shall be pledged as security therefor. When executed by Owners' Agents, such notes may provide that the makers thereof shall not be individually liable thereon. Each such note shall give this Corporation authority at any time to surrender all or any part of the pledged securities to the District in exchange for New Bonds and shall also authorize this Corporation, upon first having requested payment of such note and payment having been refused, to purchase the pledged securities at such sale as may be provided for by such note.

Each such note shall bear interest at the rate of 4% per annum, payable as nearly as practicable on the interest payment dates borne by the major part of the Deposited Securities. The District shall not be a party to such note but in case it shall pay the interest thereon promptly when and as the same falls due, the Corporation will accept such interest payments and will thereupon give credit to the District for payment of the interest for such period on all the Deposited Securities at that time held by this Corporation, it being expressly provided, however, that nothing contained in this resolution shall be deemed to limit the right of this Corporation to enforce full payment of interest or principal on Deposited [68] Securities it may hold, at any time when it may deem it advisable to do so in order to protect its rights as holder of the Deposited Securities against any rights claimed by the holders of Old Securities that have not been deposited.

As a condition precedent to the making of any such loan in the manner provided in this subparagraph, the Division Chief and Counsel for this Corporation may require the District to execute or agree to execute such amount of its New 4% Bonds as they may specify and when executed, to deliver such Bonds to a trustee or custodian satisfactory to this Corporation. Such trustee or other custodian shall be irrevocably bound to exchange such New Bonds for the Deposited Securities held by this Corporation at any time when it shall so request, but the New Bonds thus to be delivered to this Corporation shall not exceed in principal amount the sums then owed to this Corporation on account of the advances which it has made hereunder, together with any interest then accrued and unpaid thereon.

(c) In the event that Counsel for this Corporation shall have any doubt as to the legal authority of the District to issue New Bonds in exchange for some part or some class of the Deposited Securities, provision shall be made for delivery to this Corporation of New Bonds having a principal amount equal to the sums owed to this Corporation on account of the advances it has made or is then making hereunder, upon the surrender and cancellation of only such part of the Deposited Securities as such counsel deems the District can lawfully accept in exchange for New Bonds. Promptly after . effecting any such exchange of a part of [69] the Deposited Securities for New Bonds, the

Treasurer of this Corporation shall surrender
or assign to the District without charge all of
the Deposited Securities then held by this Corporation that were not previously exchanged
for New Bonds.

*   *   *

7.   Date, Maturities and Interest of New Bonds.
Such New Bonds shall bear such date as shall be
satisfactory to Counsel for this Corporation. No
part of the principal thereof shall mature during
the first three (3) years after their date and such
bonds shall mature thereafter in annual instalments
over a period of thirty (30) years, commencing at
the end of the fourth (4th) year from the date
they bear according to a maturity schedule satisfactory to the Division Chief. If the District may
legally (Form 12/20/33) do so, such annual maturities, so far as practicable, shall be such that the
totals of the sums payable for interest and for the
retirement of bonds shall be approximately the same
in each year during which there is a maturity.
Interest on New Bonds is to be paid semi-annually
unless the Division Chief shall otherwise direct.

*   *   *   *   *   *   *   *

FURTHER RESOLVED, that when said District, Owners' Agents and Consenting Owners have
complied with the provisions, terms and conditions
of these resolutions and of any contracts that may
have been executed by the Corporation in this matter to the satisfaction of the Division Chief and of

the designated counsel for this Corporation, the Treasurer of this Corporation is authorized and directed to execute all such instruments, make all loans, payments and exchanges of securities and take any other action so approved by the Division Chief and by said Counsel.

*   *   *   *   ⚓   ⚓   ⚓   ⚓

I. G. R. COOKSEY, Secretary of the RECON-STRUCTION FINANCE [70] CORPORATION do hereby certify that the foregoing is a true and correct copy of the resolutions of its Executive Committee duly adopted at a meeting thereof, regularly convened and held on the 29th day of January, 1934, at which a quorum was present and acting throughout.

IN WITNESS WHEREOF I have hereunto set my hand and the seal of this Corporation this 1st day of February, 1934.

> G. R. Cooksey
> Secretary"

Exhibit B was a copy of the resolution of the Board of Directors of petitioner adopting a plan for the refunding and readjustment of its indebtedness, reading as follows:

"RESOLUTION ADOPTING REFUNDING PLAN

WHEREAS said Waterford Irrigation District has heretofore duly authorized and issued an issue of its bonds designated as 'issue No. 1' or 'first issue' in the aggregate principal amount of $465,000. bearing interest at the rate of 6% per annum, payable semi-annually, on the 1st day of January and the 1st day of July of each year, all dated January 1st, 1917, due serially from 1928 to 1947 (both inclusive) payable January 1st of each year having denominations of $575, $500, $450, $400, $325, $300, $250, $200, $150, and $100, of which bonds $446,400 of principal amount are now outstanding, and

WHEREAS said district has heretofore duly authorized and issued an issue of its bonds designated as 'issue No. 2' or 'second issue' in the aggregate principal amount of $205,000, bearing interest at the rate of 5½% per annum, payable semi-annually on the 1st day of January and the 1st day of July of each year, all dated July 1st, 1919, due serially from 1927 to 1946 (both inclusive) payable July 1st of each year, having denominations of $1000. $300, and $125.00 [71] of which bonds $188,525. of principal amount are now outstanding, and

WHEREAS on the 18th day of September, 1933 said Waterford Irrigation District (hereinafter designated as the 'district') duly filed with the Reconstruction Finance Corporation (hereinafter designated as the 'Corporation') its application (Docket No. File 204) for a loan for the purpose of reducing and refinancing the outstanding indebt-

edness of said district under the provisions of the
Emergency Farm Mortgage Act of 1933, and

WHEREAS on the 29th day of January, 1934
the said Corporation authorized a loan to or for
the benefit of said district of not exceeding $312,500
under all the terms and conditions set forth in the
resolution adopted by said Corporation, hereinafter
referred to, and

WHEREAS on the 10th day of February, 1934 the
Board of Directors of said district, by resolution,
duly accepted said loan and agreed with said Reconstruction Finance Corporation, to comply with,
fulfill and carry out all the provisions, terms, conditions and requirements set forth in said resolution, to be by said district carried out and fulfilled,
and

WHEREAS, the Board of Directors of said district desires the California Districts Securities Commission to approve a plan of reducing and refinancing the outstanding indebtedness of said district and
the authorization and issuance of bonds as provided for and subject to the terms and conditions
of the said resolution of the Reconstruction Finance Corporation dated January 29, 1934 (hereinafter designated as the 'Corporation Resolution').

NOW THEREFORE, BE IT RESOLVED AND
ORDERED that the following plan for the refunding of the bonds of said district and [72] reducing
and refinancing the outstanding indebtedness of said
district, in compliance with the requirements of said

Corporation Resolution, be and the same is hereby adopted, to-wit:

1. The proceedings for the issuance of said refunding bonds under and pursuant to and in accordance with said Corporation Resolution shall be taken in compliance with and under the provisions of "the California irrigation district act" and also the provisions of an act of the Legislature of the State of California, entitled:

An Act to authorize irrigation districts to cooperate and contract with the United States under the provisions of the Federal reclamation laws for a water supply, or the construction, operation or maintenance of works, including drainage works, or for the assumption by the district of indebtedness to the United States on account of district lands; and to provide the manner and method of payments to the United States under such contract, and for the apportionment of assessments, and the levy thereof, upon the lands of the district to secure revenue for such payments, and to provide for the judicial revenue and determination of the validity of the proceedings in connection with such contract, and to provide for construction of works by the district; to provide for the borrowing or procuring of money from the United States or any agency thereof and the entering into contracts, and/or the issuance of bonds, warrants or other evidence of indebtedness for the repayment thereof, (approved May 5, 1917, Stats. 1917, p. 243, as amended) and all of said refunding bonds when issued shall contain such terms and conditions and shall be payable in such manner [73] and from such source or sources of income and/or revenue as may be agreed upon between said District and the Reconstruction Finance Corporation, and the District shall be obligated to do and perform all of the obligations imposed upon it pursuant to the terms of said Corporation Resolution.

2. That a refunding issue of bonds of said district (designated as "New Bonds" in the said Corporation Resolution) in the aggregate principal amount of $312,500 shall be authorized. No part of the principal thereof shall mature during the first three (3) years after their date and such bonds shall mature thereafter in annual installments over a period of thirty (30) years commencing in the fourth (4th) year from the date they bear according to a maturity schedule satisfactory to the Chief of the Division of Drainage, Levee and Irrigation of the Reconstruction Finance Corporation and approved by the California Districts Securities Commission. Said bonds shall bear interest at the rate of four (4%) per cent. per annum, such interest being payable semi-annually.

3. As provided for in said Corporation Resolution, the District hereby promises, covenants and agrees with said Reconstruction Finance Corporation to the effect that so long as any of said new bonds or any of the old securities pledged with or

acquired by said corporation remains outstanding
said district will duly and fully fulfill, comply with
and carry out all the terms and conditions on its
part to be fulfilled, complied with and carried out
under the terms and conditions of said Corporation
Resolution and further that said District will at
all times levy and collect sufficient assessments to
pay all expenses of operating, maintaining and re-
pairing its works, all sums necessary for payment
of interest and principal on the bonds and any
other indebtedness at any time owed by the District,
plus such additional amounts as the [74] Division
Chief and Counsel for the Reconstruction Finance
Corporation may deem necessary for assurances
against delinquencies in payment of taxes and the
creation of a reserve fund, and in addition thereto
the District shall furnish said corporation with such
assurances as may be required by the Division Chief
and its Counsel that so long as any of the bonds
remain outstanding such assessments cannot or will
not be reduced below the amount above required
by any action of the California Districts Securities Commission or by any other governmental officer or Board. The District shall be obligated and
bound for the payment of said Refunding Bonds
in accordance with the terms of this plan and all
of the terms and conditions on the part of the District to be kept and performed are hereby incorporated herein and made a part hereof.

AND BE IT FURTHER RESOLVED AND
ORDERED that the said Board of Directors deem

it desirable that said refunding bonds in the aggregate principal amount of said $312,500. shall be
made available for the purposes specified in Section
9 of "the California districts securities commission
act", approved June 19, 1931, as amended.

AND BE IT FURTHER RESOLVED AND
ORDERED that the said district be authorized to
make such expenditures and incur such indebtedness and to issue warrants of said District therefor as may be required in order to pay the costs
and expenses incident to the carrying out of said
plan or in connection with the reducing and refinancing of its outstanding indebtedness and the issuance of refunding bonds for such purpose.

AND BE IT FURTHER RESOLVED AND
ORDERED that this Board of Directors submits to
the California district securities commission, this,
the proposed plan of said district to [75] reduce
and refinance its outstanding indebtedness and the
refunding of its said bonds under the terms and
conditions of said resolution and the President and
Secretary of this Board of Directors be and they
are hereby authorized and directed for and on behalf of the Waterford Irrigation District, to sbumit
to the California Districts Securities Commission
the aforesaid plan and to request the approval of
said Commission thereto, to sign and execute such
applications, petitions, reports and other documents, and to submit to and file with said Commission and said Reconstruction Finance Corporation,
such records, files and reports of said district as

may be necessary or proper or be requested or required in obtaining the approval of said commission and of the Reconstruction Finance Corporation
to said plan and to take any and all steps and to do
any and all things which may be necessary or proper
to carry this resolution and said plan into effect and
to fully comply with and carry out all the terms
and conditions of the said resolution of the Reconstruction Finance Corporation authorizing the said
loan to this district.

AND BE IT FURTHER RESOLVED AND
ORDERED that upon said proposed plan being approved by said commission and the Reconstruction
Finance Corporation, an election be called in said
district for the purpose of authorizing said contract
with the Reconstruction Finance Corporation set
forth in said Corporation Resolution and the issuance of such Refunding Bonds, as provided by law.''

Exhibit C was a copy of Order 12 of the California Districts Securities Commission approving the
plan.

Exhibits D-1 to D-107, inclusive, consisted of the
acceptances in writing of the plan by certain creditors of said district named in Exhibit F. [76]

Exhibit E was a list of all creditors of petitioner,
together with their addresses and a description of
their claim, consisting of the known bondholders
of petitioner.

Exhibit F was a separate list of the creditors mentioned in Exhibit E who had accepted the plan, together with their addresses.

Exhibit G was the form of letter of transmittal and deposit used by the consenting creditors.

Exhibit H was an itemization of the expenses incident to carying out the readjustment plan in the total sum of $4,674.00.

Exhibit I was a copy of an order of the California Districts Securities Commission approving the filing of the aforesaid petition.

Exhibit J was a copy of a resolution of the Board of Directors of the Waterford Irrigation District, authorizing the filing of said petition and accepting and approving said plan of readjustment.

Proceedings Upon Approval of Petition.

Upon the filing of the petition, Hon. A. F. St. Sure made an order approving the petition as properly filed in good faith, and at the same time Judge St. Sure signed an order fixing the first day of October, 1934, at Sacramento as the time and place for hearing upon the plan, and requiring that notice to creditors be given by publication, as provided in the act.

Thereafter notice was given by publication, the first date of publication being August 9th, 1934, and due proof of publication was made and filed in the proceeding.

At the time set for the hearing, the hearing was regularly continued to the 12th day of November, 1934.

Prior thereto and within 90 days from the first publication of the notice to creditors, certain creditors of the district, to-wit: George F. Covell, George H. McKaig, David F. Selby, E. A. Covell, Nellie L. Covell, N. O. Bowman, Alice Dennett and Eleanor [77] Dennett, filed a motion to dismiss the petition and an answer.

Motion to Dismiss.

In the motion to dismiss it was set forth that the respondents owned the bonds which were credited to them in the petition, aggregating $146,600.00, together with interest due thereon and unpaid in the sum of $20,110.00. The motion was based upon the following grounds:

1. That the court is without jurisdiction to entertain and hear the petition or determine the cause, for the reason that Section 80 of the bankruptcy act under which the petition was filed violates Section 8, Article I, of the Constitution of the United States; that it violates the Fifth Amendment to the Constitution of the United States; that no power has been delegated to Congress to pass legislation such as this regulating the rights of the interveners against the State of California, that it violates the Tenth Amendment to the Constitution and that it attempts to submit a state governmental agency to the jurisdiction of the Federal Court contrary to the plan and scheme of government, as set forth in the Constitution, and that it violates other provisions of the Constitution of the United States. The motion was based upon the further grounds that the Waterford Irrigation District is without legal capacity

to make its petition, for the reason that Article I, Section 16, of the Constitution of the State of California prohibits the impairment of obligation of contract; that Article I, Section 21, of the California Constitution prohibits discrimination between classes; that Article 13, Section 6, provides that the power of taxation shall never be surrendered or suspended by any grant or contract to which the state shall be a party, and that the district is not one of the agencies permitted under Section 80 of the act to file such a petition; and lastly upon the grounds that the petition does not state facts sufficient to constitute a good and sufficient petition under Chapter IX of the Bankruptcy Act of 1898. [78]

The motion to dismiss was accompanied by points and authorities and was submitted to Hon. A. F. St. Sure on November 12, 1934, at which time Judge St. Sure denied the motion to dismiss and the respondents' exception to the ruling was allowed.

Answers of Respondents.

That the answer of the respondents was in the following words:

[Title of Court and Cause.]

"ANSWER TO PETITION FOR CONFIRMATION OF PLAN OF READJUSTMENT OF DEBTS.

Now come George F. Covell, George H. McKaig, David F. Selby, E. A. Covell, Nellie L. Covell, N. O. Bowman, Alice Dennett, and Eleanor Dennett, creditors of the above entitled Irrigation District and answering the petition for confirmation of plan of readjustment of debts herein admit, deny and allege as follows:

I.

Admit and allege that they own severally the bonds credited to them in the petition for confirmation of plan of readjustment of debts on file herein aggregating $146,600, par value of bonds of the Waterford Irrigation District of the first, and second issue as set forth in the petition on file herein, together with interest thereon due and unpaid.

II.

Deny that petitioner Waterford Irrigation District is insolvent or unable to meet its debts as they mature.

III.

Respondent creditors have no information as to whether the plan of readjustment has been accepted or approved by petitioner, or whether a resolution of the Board of Directors adopting the plan was made and, basing their denial on that ground, deny the same. [79]

IV.

Respondents have no information as to whether the said plan was approved by the California District Securities Commission and, basing their denial on that ground, deny the same.

V.

That respondents have no information as to whether the creditors *owing* less than 66-2/3% or any other amount of the bonds of petitioner have accepted the plan in writing and, basing their denial upon that ground, deny the same.

VI.

That respondents have no information as to whether the creditors accepting the plan have deposited their bonds in escrow and, basing their denial upon that ground, deny the same.

VII.

That respondents have no information as to whether any contract or agreement has been entered into between any committee, individual or creditor of petitioner and whether any compensation is to be received by any agent or committee and, basing their denial upon that ground deny the same.

VIII.

Deny that the California District Securities Commission is authorized to exercise supervision over the fiscal affairs of said district insofar as this petition is concerned, and that respondents have no information as to whether or not said commission has approved the said petition and, basing their denial upon that ground, deny the same.

IX.

That respondents have no information as to whether said petition is filed pursuant to a resolution of the Board of Directors of petitioner and, basing *its* denial upon that ground, deny the same.

WHEREFORE, respondents pray that said petition be dismissed [80] and for respondents' costs of suit and such other relief as may be just.

W. COBURN COOK,
> Attorney for George F. Covell, George H. McKaig, David F. Selby, E. A. Covell, Nellie L. Covell and N. O. Bowman.

L. L. DENNETT,
> Attorney for Alice Dennett and Eleanor Dennett."

[Duly Verified.]

That on the 12th day of November, 1934, by leave of Court the said respondents filed a supplemental answer in the following words:

[Title of Court and Cause.]

"SUPPLEMENTAL ANSWER

Come now George F. Covell, George H. McKaig, David F. Selby, E. A. Covell, Nellie L. Covell, N. O. Bowman, Alice Dennett and Eleanor Dennett and by leave of court first had and obtained file this supplemental answer and allege:

I.

That this Court is without jurisdiction to entertain the petitioner's petition and the plan of readjustment filed therewith or to hear and determine this cause because this proceeding and the Act of Congress, approved May 24, 1934, being an amendment to the Bankruptcy Act, under which this proceeding is brought, is unconstitutional and void and affects the property rights of these interveners for the following reasons, to-wit:

(1) Under Section 8, Article I of the Constitution of the United States, Congress has power to pass uniform laws on the subject of bankruptcies throughout the United States and said Act is not a uniform law on the subject of bankruptcies throughout the United States.

(2) Under said Act private property may be taken for public use without just compensation, contrary to the provisions of [81] Amendment V of the Constitution of the United States, and the petitioner's petition and the plan of readjustment filed therewith propose to take interveners' property without just compensation.

(3) Under the Constitution of the United States and the plan of government set forth therein the Federal Government is a government of delegated powers and no power has been delegated to Congress to pass legislation such as the said Act of Congress approved May 24, 1934, regulating the rights of citizens and particularly these interveners against the states or state governmental agencies in the manner therein provided.

(4) Said Act was passed in violation of the reserved rights of states of the United States as guaranteed to the states by amendment X to the Federal Constitution and because the passage of said Act is a violation of the rights of the citizens, and particularly these interveners, guaranteed and re-

served to them by Amendment X to the Constitution.

(5) Said Act attempts to subject State Governmental Agencies to the jurisdiction of Federal Courts contrary to the plan and scheme of government, as set out in the Constitution of the United States.

(6) Said Act in other respects violates the Constitution of the United States.

II.

That the petitioner herein, the Waterford Irrigation District, is without legal capacity to make its petition for the following reasons:

(1) Under Article I, Section 16 of the Constitution of the State of California, no law impairing the obligations of contract shall ever be passed.

(2) Article I, Section 21, of the Constitution provides [82] that no citizen or class of citizens shall be granted privileges which upon the same terms shall not be granted to all citizens.

(3) Article XIII, Section 6, provides that the power of taxation shall never be surrendered or suspended by any grant or contract to which the state shall be a party.

(4) The Waterford Irrigation District is not one of the agencies permitted under Section 80 of the Act to file such a petition.

III.

That said petition is not filed in good faith because the said Waterford Irrigation District has the capacity to pay all of its debts.

IV.

That respondents are creditors of the bankrupt within the meaning of the Act of Congress approved May 24, 1934, being an amendment to the Bankruptcy Act by which Chapter IX was added thereto, and that this answer is made on behalf of all of the creditors named herein and of all other creditors of said petitioner who desire hereafter to join herein; that the plan proposed is not fair, equitable or for the best interest of the creditors; that the Waterford Irrigation District is not in point of fact the real debtor but is merely a trustee or intermediary for the payment of the obligations of the land owners; that the land owners are the debtors insofar as they own the lands embraced within the Waterford Irrigation District, and that the plan submitted discriminates against the respondents and others of the same class, for the reason that other classes of bond holders holding bonds against the lands of said district, such as county bonds, school bonds and the owners of deeds of trust mortgages and other liens against the lands of the District are not included, and that under the Constitution and [83] laws of the State of California and the United States the bonds of respondents are a lien upon the lands of the District prior to many of these other classes of lien holders, whose liens would be strengthened at the expense of the land owners and of bond holders in the class of respondents.

WHEREFORE, respondents pray that:

1. That this Court find and determine that said Act of Congress approved May 24, 1934, under which these proceedings were commenced, is unconstitutional and void.

2. That the Court refuse to confirm the plan of reorganization and readjustment proposed by the Bankrupt and any settlement made or to be made thereunder, and that it refuse to confirm any plan of reorganization or adjustment or any settlement of debts due the District which does not make proper provision for the payment of the debts due the respondents and recognition of the priority of such debts.

3. That in the alternative this Court make and enter an order expressly providing that neither the bankruptcy proceedings nor any order made or thing done in or pursuant thereto shall affect in any way the rights of the respondents or remedies given them by law for the enforcement of such rights, to the end that respondents may prosecute their rights to final judgment in any court of competent jurisdiction and enforce such judgment in the manner provided by law.

W. COBURN COOK,
Attorney for George F. Covell, George H. McKaig, David F. Selby, E. A. Covell, Nellie L. Covell, and N. O. Bowman.

DENNETT & ZION,
Attorneys for Alice Dennett and Eleanor Dennett."

[Duly Verified.]

Order of Reference.

That on November 12th, 1934, Judge St. Sure on motion of counsel for petitioner made an order of reference to a Special Master in the following words [84]

[Title of Court and Cause.]

"ORDER OF REFERENCE TO A SPECIAL MASTER

It appearing that the Waterford Irrigation District of Stanislaus County, California, an irrigation district duly formed, organized and existing in accordance with and under and by virtue of the provisions of that certain act of the Legislature of the State of California designated as 'the California irrigation district act' and a 'taking district' within the meaning and intent of an act of the Congress of the United States approved May 24, 1934, amending an act entitled 'an act to establish a uniform system of bankruptcy throughout the United States' approved July 1, 1898 and acts amendatory thereof and supplementary thereto, by adding thereto a new chapter designated Chapter IX thereof and consisting of sections numbered 78, 79 and 80, has filed a petition in this court stating that said district is insolvent and unable to meet its debts as they mature, and that it desires to effect a plan of readjustment of its debts as provided for in said amendment to said Bankruptcy Act, and

IT FURTHER APPEARING that said plan of readjustment of the debts of said district was duly

set forth in said petition and that said plan had
been duly accepted in writing by the creditors of
said district owning more than sixty-six and two-
thirds (66 2/3) per centum in amount of the bonds,
notes and certificates of indebtedness of said district affected by the plan, which acceptances accompanied said petition and such plan has been
accepted and approved by said taxing district in
a writing signed in its name by an authorized authority and filed in this proceeding and that said
petition contained all other matters and things required by said amendment to said Bankruptcy Act,
and

IT FURTHER APPEARING that this court
has heretofore and on [85] the 6th day of August,
1934 duly made and filed its order approving the
said petition for the confirmation of the plan of
said district for the readjustment of its debts,
as properly filed, and ordered notice to be given to
the creditors of said district as provided by law, and

IT FURTHER APPEARING that said notice
has been duly given as provided for by law and
the order of this court, and said matter has duly
come on for hearing on this 12th day of November,
1934, and

IT FURTHER APPEARING that George F.
Covell, George H. McKaig, David F. Selby, E. A.
Covell, Nellie L. Covell, N. O. Bowman, Alice Dennett and Eleanor Dennett, creditors of said district
holding more than five (5) per centum in amount of
the bonds of said district have appeared in said
proceeding and controverted the facts alleged in
said petition, and

IT FURTHER APPEARING that it is necessary to refer all matters set forth in said petition to a special master, for consideration and report upon the issues raised by said petition and the said objections thereto,

NOW, THEREFORE, IT IS HEREBY ORDERED, that the issues hereinafter specified, made by said petition and objections thereto be and they are hereby referred to Stephen N. Blewett of Stockton, California, as Special Master, under rule of Court, to ascertain and report the facts, with his conclusions thereon.

That said specified issues are as follows:

(1) Is said plan of readjustment of the debts of said district fair, equitable and for the best interests of the creditors, and does it discriminate unfairly in favor of any class of creditors?

(2) Does said plan comply with the provisions of subdivision (b) of Chapter IX of said amendment to the Bankruptcy Act? [86]

(3) Has said plan been accepted and approved as required by the provisions of subdivision (d) of said Chapter IX of said amendment to the Bankruptcy Act?

(4) Have all amounts to be paid by the taxing district for services or expenses incident to the readjustment been fully disclosed and are reasonable?

(5) Are the offer of the plan and its acceptance in good faith?

(6) Is the taxing district authorized by law, upon confirmation of the plan, to take all action necessary to carry out the plan?

WITNESS our hand this 12th day of November, 1934.

> A. F. ST. SURE,
>> Judge of the United States District Court.''

Hearings on Plan Before Master.

That thereafter upon notice duly given the matter came up for hearing before Stephen N. Blewett, Special Master, appointed herein, and hearings were conducted in Modesto, California, on December 12, 13, 14, 15, 1934, January 10 and 15, 1935, and February 8, 1935, Homer N. Hankins, of Hankins & Hankins appearing as counsel for the Waterford Irrigation District, and W. Coburn Cook and Dennett & Zion appearing as counsel for the respondents.

Narrative Statement of Testimony.

The following is a narrative statement of the testimony produced at the hearing, and including all testimony produced.

Seven farmers were called as witnesses by petitioner and testified as to their experience in farming in the district and their returns therefrom.

W. F. BEARD

testified that he has been President of Waterford Development Company since 1921, engaged in col-

(Testimony of W. F. Beard.)

onizing and farming. They had around 6000 acres—
they sold around 3000 acres in acreages of about 20
acres. The acreage sold was the better land. What
remained is largely composed of rolling land, poor
land [87] from an irrigation standpoint. The company has abandoned 700 acres to the district. There
are other lands to which the district can take a deed.
There are other lands of the Development Company
at least two years delinquent. The total loss in operations was $532,911.71. The chart showed this loss.
The net annual losses shown on the chart in evidence includes losses from land sales as well as
operating expenses. The land was set up on the
books at the cost or value at the time it was taken
over by the company, and as canals and roads were
built they were added to the various pieces of land,
and if it was sold for more than the book value,
it was given as net revenue, or, if at a loss, of course,
it would show the opposite. Commissions and office
expenses were included. An inventory was taken at
the end of every year. In addition to the $50.00 an
acre average assessment, we have mortgages on the
land and we are still protecting some of the lands.
That was his answer to the question as to whether
or not the land was worth more than the assessment.
Some of the land has a $20.00 per acre mortgage, in
particular one tract of 1000 acres. There is a bond
loan on 1700 acres amounting to $32,000.00. The
gross mortgages are about $130,000.00. The last
payment on interest on mortgage indebtedness was

(Testimony of W. F. Beard.)

in 1933. Since that time there have been payments represented by releases. The character of the land in the Modesto district, where the soil and depth of the soil is the same, is identical. The soil between Modesto and Waterford in the Waterford and Modesto districts is practically the same and it would average with the best type of soil in this area. The production in the Waterford and Modesto districts is practically the same where conditions are the same. The main difference is in the burdens against the land. The good land in the Waterford District that we operate brings in about the same amount of income as similar lands under similar crops brings in the Modesto district. The approximate selling price was $165.00. [88]

ALBERT CRESSY and ARCH L. TAYLOR testified as to quotations for Waterford bonds as shown by the Master's report.

AMOS A. GALT,

member of the committee, testified that he is President of the Bank at Hughson; that he has been in the banking business 20 years, was president of the Commercial and Savings Bank of Waterford. Patronage was around Waterford. Most of the loans were made to people living in the vicinity of Waterford. The business was transferred to the Modesto Trust and Savings Bank. On January 23, 1933, the Superintendent of Banks demanded that some

(Testimony of Amos A. Galt.)

action be taken, so he sold out to the Modesto bank. The Modesto bank took over the assets and met the liabilities to the depositors, but the Waterford stockholders had to guarantee $20,000 in order to protect them against losses in liquidating the assets. The bank had a number of mortgages. Some of them were foreclosed and it looks like some more of them will have to be taken. Rentals from lands taken haven't been enough to pay the taxes. The loans did not exceed 50% of the appraisement. He said that he would be benefited personally by the R. F. C. loan. The bank held as much as $11,000.00 in warrants about 1932. Those warrants were paid in full. He thinks the district is a great deal better off with the irrigation system than without it; there would be a material difference in the value and in the production without the irrigation district. He said that generally in 1932 prices did not equal the cost of production.

WILLIAM RODDEN

testified that he is a banker of Oakdale connected with the First National Bank and Stanislaus County Savings Bank; that his bank owned bonds of the Waterford district and that he has control of other bonds of the Waterford district; that the loan of 48.82 per cent represents the reasonable value of the district's bonds; that this was a fair value in his opinion. He would think that 90%

(Testimony of William Rodden.)

of the land not irrigated could not be **[89]** prepared for irrigation at a reasonable price, it is
too rolling. He thinks that 100¢ on the dollar would
be the reasonable value of the bonds of the Oakdale
High School District, the same applies to the bonds
of the County of Stanislaus. He expressed the opinion that the lands in the district, freed of all indebtedness, would probably be worth from $30.00 to
$50.00 an acre. He thought, but was not sure, that
the landowners could meet the new schedule of
payment and also pay their mortgages and deeds
of trust. The Waterford district didn't have enough
water supply to profit by Ladino clover.

R. K. WHITMORE

testified as to the written acceptances of creditors.

WILLIAM LEHMKUHL,

Engineer and Superintendent of the Waterford
district, testified that the district contains 14,110
acres of land along the Tuolumne River for a distance of about 16 miles. The width of the district
averages two miles. The district contains 46 miles
of canals and laterals. The water is taken into the
system at points along the canal. The water is carried under contract with the Modesto Irrigation District. He described the bond issues. It would cost
$35,000 to extend irrigation to approximately 1500
additional acres of land. Topography of the district

(Testimony of William Lehmkuhl.)

in the western portion is level excepting bluffs bordering along the river and Dry Creek. The portion of the district east of the town of Waterford is rolling excepting in the north arm of the district, which is quite level, except for some ravines. The remaining portion of the eastern part of the district is all rolling with small *acreas* of flat land between the hills. There are 4,449 acres of level land, well located, with medium soil; 2,928 acres of level land, but poorly located, with medium soil, and 1,125 acres general sloping and slightly rolling land, with medium soil. The total on the assessment roll was 13,237 acres. The general type of soil in the district is some form of sandy [90] loam, except 700 acres in the north which is adobe. The water percolates into the soil rapidly and drains off, leaching the soil, causing frequent irrigation and frequent leaching. The general elevation of the land is about 100 feet above the river and about 50 feet above Dry Creek.

The area irrigated in 1933 was 5,650 acres. They generally purchased water from the Turlock Irrigation District, but in 1931 and 1934 there was none available for that purpose. The district has 66 second feet of water rights which is the first right in the Tuolumne River. As to further claims for appropriations, they have not been adjudicated. An appropriative right was procured through posting notice in 1913 and yields water usually up to a date sometime in June, after which the district must rely entirely on its 66 second feet. At the present time the water available is insufficient for the

(Testimony of William Lehmkuhl.)

present devlopment. It would cost $2.50 to $3.00 per acre foot to pump water. The average duty of water over a period of years is 5.5 acre feet per acre. The number of real estate holdings is shown by Exhibit No. 68. There are eight landowners in the district that own 51.6 per cent of the land and fourteen landowners own 63.6 per cent of all the land. Map No. 3 shows that on November 1, 1934, there were 1468 acres that had been deeded to the district; 1470 acres that were delinquent four years, having been sold in 1931; 4,767 acres that were delinquent three years; 5,865 acres delinquent two years; and 6,561 acres delinquent one year, having been sold in 1934. Exhibit 72 is the crop report for 1934. The farmers who testified were selected by the Board of Directors, with the Secretary and the Engineer. The upper works of the district cost $74,000.00, to serve an area 3300 acres, of which only about 168 acres has been irrigated. There is a 1900 foot tunnel in that division. That was a rather expensive development. Dependent upon the winter supply the 700 acres of the adobe land referred to produces an average good crop of rice. [91]

He said that he had placed an item in the budget for structural replacement work; that they could get along with less by using old lumber and patching, but that if he was able to get the money which he asked that it would put the works in very good shape, and the rest would be just a matter of ordinary repairs. It would be possible to spread this re-

(Testimony of William Lehmkuhl.)

placement work over a period of years, although it would be some extra cost for additional expenditures of patching, but that has been the procedure for the past several years. The facts set forth in Exhibit 31, application of the Waterford district to the R.F.C. were prepared to a large part by Mr. Lehmkuhl. The facts set forth were true and correct to the best of his knowledge. He represented it to be when he drafted the report. As set forth in Exhibit 70, being a tabulation prepared in 1927 of the estimated assessments necessary for future years, the estimated rate for 1934 was $7.36 a hundred, which was estimated to produce $18,500 for maintenance and operation and $55,600 for bond service. The actual levy made for that year was $34,000, which was about $16,000 more than required for maintenance and operation. The total expenditures were very much less than the levy. The difference is accounted for by the delinquency. In other words the $34,000 levy was not collected; so in last year the levy was $43,000 while the amount needed was $18,000.

The amount actually paid out of the general fund in 1933 was $15,036.10, ending June 30, 1934. In 1933 the maintenance rate was $3.00 per hundred. It was higher than it had been in previous years. Maintenance and operation cost would not vary to any great extent. The average rate in early years for general funds was from $1.50 to $2.00 per hundred. Mr. Lehmkuhl stated that spreading the re-

(Testimony of William Lehmkuhl.)

construction over a period of several years and assuming absence of litigation and a delinquency of not more than 15% and no additional purchase of water, the tax rate for the general fund would not need to exceed $2.00 per hundred. The larger holdings were the first to [92] go delinquent and when they went delinquent that had a remarkable effect upon the increased rate for the next succeeding year. He did not think that a farmer was on the average making a living on a farm smaller than 24 acres. There are 83 holdings from 10 to 24 acres in the Waterford district. He does not think that the 46 that have farms from 5 to 9 acres can make a living, they mostly work out to make their living. The district took title to 412 town lots (of the town of Waterford), but none of them have buildings on them. Small holdings are not in default. It is the farming class that is in default, except as to large holdings in town.

He then alluded to the soils of the district. Mr. Lehmkuhl testified that in the area between Tuolumne River and Dry Creek, about two miles in width, the water level was from 17 to 55 feet. He said that from 7 to 9 feet was ideal for general crops. He thought the drainage was a great disadvantage, the moisture left the soil rapidly and carried substances away with it, although they have no alakli. In the Waterford district, it costs so much to fertilize it doesn't pay. We have some instances where gypsum or lime and sulphur will last only

(Testimony of William Lehmkuhl.)

two or three months. In other districts they last two years. They irrigated more frequently than in surrounding districts on account of rapid drainage. Around five irrigations on peach crops. They don't cultivate as much as they used to. Mr. Lehmkuhl did not agree that the district could not irrigate more than 10 per cent of the unirrigated land. He disagreed with the statement made by Mr. Rodden in this respect that there is no feasibility of placing any more land under irrigation under present financial conditions, and said that with the present indebtedness of the district, it could not finance any further water supply, but if they had additional water, there is other land that could be irrigated, and it would be financially and economically good judgment to place it under irrigation. The [93] district had looked into the matter of further water supply, but they found that they could not finance the project that would be necessary on the Tuolumne.

There are 2700 acres of nominally assessed land of the district which pays only a few cents an acre, classed as non-irrigable.

The alfalfa used to last longer. Five years is the limit now; the first crops that were put in lasted 7 or 8 years, and they took 7½ tons to the acre a season. Water is being furnished to all of the landowners, regardless of their condition as to the payment of their taxes, except that those that are delinquent four years have received no water since

(Testimony of William Lehmkuhl.)

their four year period was up. In August 1934 was
the first time the district took a deed to those lands,
and since that they haven't received any water.
Some of those lands are not subject to deed, however, because some of them had made a payment under the Moratorium Act. There are 956 acres subject to deed. The owners are still in possession of
those parcels. Practically all of that land belongs to
the Waterford Development Company and they are
now trying to finance the taxes, and they also have
had conferences with the Board of Directors and
negotiations are going on with the hopes that they
will take up the taxes.

The net water duty in the Waterford district is
3.6 acre feet per acre, the net water duty in the
Turlock Irrigation District is 2½, the gross water
duty in the Waterford district is about a foot and
a half more than it is in the Turlock and Modesto
districts. Mr. Lehmkuhl said that too much irrigation causes leaching of soil. Tree roots in the Waterford district go down about 4 feet. Irrigation in
the Waterford district takes the earth moisture
down to the ends of the tree roots, until the end
of the season. It has been found that excessive
water is really harmful. Mr. Lehmkuhl recognized
as authoritative (if a bit old) [94] a book of R. D.
Marsden, on Economy of Farm Drainage, in which
he said that the drained clay neither remains sat-
urated so long nor dries out so thoroughly as before drainage, but retains a film of capillary water

(Testimony of William Lehmkuhl.)

about each soil grain, *which* the gravitational water passes out and is replaced by air. This is the soil condition necessary for a healthy growth of the usual cultivated crops, and so the looser soil is much more easily worked, and through it the plant roots spread more freely to a larger supply of nourishment. The presence of air and the higher temperature induce the growth of bacteria that release certain food elements from insoluble compounds and make them available for the use of plants. In this way does drainage increase the fertility of soils. A drained soil offers a deeper feeding ground for the plants. Mr. Lehmkuhl did not entirely agree with the latter part of this. He said that on land that has been irrigated, it is impossible to grow a crop of grain, because he said the plant life has been washed out. Also, he agreed with statements in the publication of the U. S. Department of Agriculture entitled "Drainage of Irrigated Lands in the San Joaquin Valley," where it is stated that it is the experience of past irrigation the world over that drainage and irrigation go hand in hand.

In the district is possibly 2,000 acres that would be adaptable to Ladino clover. If they had the water supply, it would be a big help. Also there are some young trees that haven't come into bearing yet, 134 acres of peaches, 43 acres of almonds, 5 acres of cherries and 185 acres of walnuts, all non-producing young trees. The farm crops in the Waterford district are very much diversified. Dairying

(Testimony of William Lehmkuhl.)

is an important industry, and during the past two years, a considerable area has been devoted to irrigated pasture. Some of the principal crops are deciduous fruits, figs, grapes, nuts, alfalfa and beans. Peaches are the principal deciduous fruit. Crop yields are generally satisfactory. [95] The depth and fertility of the soil in the district is satisfactory for the growing of practically any crop grown anywhere in California, with satisfactory production yields. In the district there is of Fresno sandy loam, 1400 acres; Fresno fine sandy loam 2100 acres; Oakdale sandy loam 1080 acres; Hanford fine sandy loam, 200 acres. Approximately 60% of the land irrigated in 1933 was Fresno sandy loam. Of good level land, well located, assessed at $101.00 to $200.00 an acre, there is 4,449 acres. Other land assessed at $76.00 to $100.00, 2,928 acres. Other land assessed at $51.00 to $75.00, 1,125; $26.00 to $50.00, 1,092; $1.00 to $5., 2711. A filing was made for water rights on February 27, 1913, for 13,000 inches, and later, in 1913, for 16,000 inches. It is now generally understood and agreed by all interested parties, that the district is entitled to 250 cubic feet per second under these filings. This water lasts each year to sometime in June or occasionally first part of July. A very valuable addition was made to the water rights when, on January 14, 1919, it entered into an agreement with the Sierra and San Francisco Power Company to purchase perpetual right to divert a minimum of 60 cubic feet per second,

(Testimony of William Lehmkuhl.)

with a maximum of 66 cubic feet per second. Since 1930 the Waterford district has augmented its water supply by acquiring additional water from the Turlock Irrigation District. This has been accomplished by defraying the expense of pumping into the canals of the Turlock Irrigation District with that district's drainage pumps, and diverting an equal amount of Turlock district's stored water, by gravity, at La Grange Dam. The cost of this water is a dollar per acre foot, but this supply is not assured except by verbal arrangement from year to year when the water is available.

Last year the district diverted 23,498 acre feet of water; in 1933, 31,155. That water at a fair average is worth a dollar an acre foot. The water right of the district purchased from the [96] power company for $170,000.00 is worth more than that amount. The right in the use of the canals of the Modesto district cost $254,000.00. Besides that they used something over $60,000.00 for construction work that did not come out of bond money, went into permanent pipe lines, structures, and so forth. The State Emergency Relief Administration is doing a lot of canal lining now. In normal years the farmers have water from March 15 to October 15. The first application to the R. F. C. was for $415,000.00. The district represented to the government that they would sustain the burden of carrying an obligation of $415,000.00.

C. W. QUINLEY,

Secretary, Tax Collector, and Treasurer of the
Waterford district since 1927 and Assessor since
1931, identified various records and exhibits. Mr.
Quinley thought that if the assessments were reduced by the amount that they could be reduced
if this loan were granted, a large number of the
landowners could take advantage of the ten year installment plan of redemption and pay their taxes.
Some portion of the land he believes would not be
redeemed under any circumstances. He did not
think the rate will be materially different than it
is at the present time. Under the refinancing plan
the rate would be kept at about $4.00. He thinks
they will redeem their land from pyramided taxes,
because they have the hope that they can retain
their ranches and be able to pay the assessments
under the new rate. Up to the time when the district
went under Section 11 of the District Securities
Commission Act, the officers of the district took
every legal means of enforcing payment of assessments. The district has not taken a deed to certain
land to which it can take a deed, because they think
that it may be redeemed. The district considered
collecting tolls for water, but abandoned the idea
because there was so much unirrigated land that
the district would lose rather than gain revenue by
that plan. [97] As Assessor of the district he has
appraised the lands of the District for four years.
He assessed the land of the Waterford Irrigation
District in 1934 at $1,010,923.00 and this refers to
the land only and not the improvements. He ex-

(Testimony of C. W. Quinley)

plained that he merely tried to equalize assessments rather than follow cash value.

Referring to Exhibit 52, he explained that the item of $10,878 in the Construction Fund came from the sale of bonds and is cash on hand. There is $7,048.56 in the Bond Fund.

In explanation of the entries in this Exhibit with regard to the assessment sale certificates and assessment lands, he said that the entry for assessment lands represents the amount of assessments that have been transferred from assessment sales to the land account for the years in which the deeds were taken. One year before the district went under the District Securities Commission Act, they levied only a partial rate for interest, depending upon possible redemption to make up the difference. For the past two years they have levied rates under the District Securities Commission Act. He verified the application to the Reconstruction Finance Corporation, and stated that it is true and correct to the best of his knowledge and belief; that the average assessed valuation per acre of land for county ad valorem tax purposes in 1929 was $20.70; the average fair and reasonable value was $60.00. In 1933, average county assessed value was $16.10; the average fair and reasonable value was $45.00.

Motion for Judgment.

Thereupon petitioner rested and respondents moved for judgment for insufficiency of the evidence. The motion was denied by the Master and exception allowed respondents.

Thereupon the respondents put on their case and called:

Several farmer witnesses were called and examined by the respondents and testified as to farming conditions in the district.

M. R. PITTS

testified that he has been in the title business for 19 years in Stanislaus County. The total amount of mortgages and deeds of trust against lands in the district, [98] according to the county records, is $1,010,612.00, some of which mortgages and deeds of trust are further secured by lands outside of the district.

GEORGE F. COVELL

testified that he was one of the respondents, that he owned certain bonds of the Waterford district. Drainage is beneficial to deciduous fruit. He has bought and sold irrigation bonds, is familiar with the market value of irrigation bonds. There are not many people buying Waterford bonds under the present conditions. When a district goes into default and they do not pay their interest, there is some of these bonds that have been left in estates and widows' funds, and they are sold for anything

(Testimony of George F. Covell.)

that they can get for them, all the way from a few cents to above. He has known of irrigation bonds selling for four and a half cents and the purchaser, within two weeks, got that much out of the district, happened to be a little money in the fund, in the treasury in the district, so it is pretty hard to tell. He thinks the district will work out and the bonds are worth at least 90¢. He has seen land at Stockton drop to as low as $2.50 an acre in a depression, and afterwards raise to $1,000 an acre. He bases the value on the future of the district. He does not think that California is going to be wiped off of the map. This litigation is very detrimental. Palo Verdes went down to three or four cents, Terra Bellas he has seen them listed at four and a half. The directors don't levy assessments. He thinks he heard the Supreme Court ask Mr. Hankins the other day if there wouldn't be a tendency to make members forget to pay their taxes. South San Joaquin on their Melones took a 25% drop after the fund was tied up here last summer by Mrs. Morris in a law suit. Bankruptcy has had an effect upon the value of the bonds, that doesn't affect the real value behind the bonds, because he knows a great many bondholders that are scared to death, afraid they are going to lose their bonds. The reason that he puts a 90 cent value on [99] the bonds is because he thinks the district can pay it out. The worse thing the district has got is the mortgage debt against them, which is paying a much higher rate of interest and it is a pretty serious obligation on the Waterford district, as quite a number of these wit-

(Testimony of George F. Covell.)

nesses testified here at this hearing. If the district should proceed with the program of foreclosure on its lands, the sale of the lands of the district would bring in sufficient returns to pay the bonded debt, no doubt every dollar of it. That would free the lands also of their mortgage debt.

———

J. R. MASON

testified that for 20 years he was in the investment banking business in California, and that he purchased over $50,000,000 of California irrigation, reclamation and drainage bonds. He stated that the value of Waterford bonds was 100¢ on the dollar as long as the property in the district had a so-called market value of even as much as $1.00. He says that although Waterford bonds are quoted nominally at 36 bid, that he knows of other quotations of bonds of other California irrigation districts where the bid price offered is 11, although bonds have actually exchanged hands recently at 90, and that in his opinion a nominal bid price of an uncurrent inactive security, such as Waterford bonds, is not a test of the true value. He also commented upon the influence of bankruptcy litigation upon the sale of bonds, and in his opinion Waterford bonds were worth much more than the present offer.

Petitioner's Exhibits in Evidence.

Certain exhibits were introduced into the evidence at this hearing by the petitioner as follows:

Exhibits 1 to 15. Various pleadings, papers and documents on file in the proceeding.

Exhibit 16. Map of the Waterford district.

Exhibit 17. Tabulation of figures showing the amount that it would be necessary to levy for 1935, $332,000.00 in assessments, if the levy were made in accordance with Section 39 [100] of the California Irrigation District Act.

Exhibit 18. Form of tax receipt used by the district.

Exhibit 19. Statement of the Stanislaus County Auditor showing the tax rate in the county to be $1.70 per hundred, and showing also the rate of assessments for the Oakdale High School bonds and for the Waterford and other school districts within the Waterford Irrigation District; showing that the bonds of these school districts are obligations for which taxes are levied upon land within the Waterford Irrigation District.

Exhibit 20. Chart showing the loss and gain statement of the Waterford Development Company for the years 1913 to 1933, showing losses in the operation of lands within the district in the total amount of $532,911.71.

Exhibit 21. Graph illustrating the losses of the Waterford Development Company during this period.

Exhibits 22 and 23. Quotation sheets by Elworthy & Co. quoting prices for Waterford District bonds from 20 flat on December 28, 1933, to 35½ flat on December 12, 1934.

Exhibit 24. Schedule of county taxes and irrigation district assessments from 1924 to 1933 on property of various farmers witnesses.

Exhibit 25. Copy of order establishing the Waterford Irrigation District by the supervisors of Stanislaus County.

Exhibit 26. Copy of the resolution of the board of directors of the district authorizing the first bond issue of $465,000.00.

Exhibit 27. Same with reference to the second bond issue of $205,000.00.

Exhibit 28. Resolution changing the denomination of the bonds of the second issue.

Exhibits 29 and 30. Petition for, and order of California Securities Commission approving a former plan to refinance the [101] indebtedness of the district.

Exhibit 31. Application of the Waterford Irrigation District to the R. F. C. requesting a loan of $415,000.00.

Exhibit 32. Amended resolution of the Reconstruction Finance Corporation granting the district a loan of $312,500.00 upon which the present plan is based.

Exhibits 33 and 34. Transcript of various resolutions, agreements and letters of the district issued in pursuance of its efforts to refinance.

Exhibit 35. Order of the District Securities Commission approving the present plan of refinancing.

Exhibits 36, 37, 38, 39, 40, 41, 42. Copies of letters to the bondholders urging them to accept the plan and reporting the progress thereof.

Exhibit 43. Resolution of the directors, July 14, 1934, authorizing the filing of the petition.

Exhibit 44. Order of the District Securities Commission authorizing the filing of the petition.

Exhibit 45. Itemized statement of expenses incurred in the proceeding.

Exhibit 46. Resolution of the directors of May 13, 1933, requesting the District Securities Commission to approve a rate of assessment for 1933 of $4.00 per $100.00 assessed valuation under Section 11 of the California District Securities Act.

Exhibit 47. Order of the Commission approving said assessment rate for 1933.

Exhibit 48. Resolution of the directors adopted August 11, 1934, applying to the Commission under Section 11 for approval of the same rate for 1934.

Exhibit 49. Tabulation showing the assessments levied and statement of delinquent tax rolls of the district. For the year 1934 it showed 511 assessments, the assessed valuation of the land [102] of the district at $1,010,923.00, the rate of assessment at $4.00, the amount of the levy $40,436.92. For the year preceding the figures were—number of assessments 566, assessed valuation $1,075,003.00, rate $4.00, amount of levy $43,000.12, delinquent

last Monday in June $24,717.30, or a delinquency
as to 57.5%. The amount delinquent on November
1st, 1934, was $17,662.04. The acreage still remain-
ing delinquent on November 1st, 1934, was 6,561.4
acres. This tabulation also showed that for the
assessment in 1917 the percentage of delinquency
the last Monday in June of the following year was
51.6%; 1918, 24.8%; 1919, 3.1%; 1920, 35.6%; 1921,
25.7%; 1922, 29.3%; 1923, 24.2%; 1924, 30.8%; 1925,
7.8%; 1926, 8.6%; 1927, 7.1%; 1928, 1.4%; 1929,
23.7%; 1930, 21.2%; 1931, 40.8%; 1932, 61.2%; in
1930 the land delinquent on November 1st was 1469.6
acres.

Exhibit 50. Tabulation showing properties deeded
to district. By 1934 the total assessed value of all
property deeded was $107,911.00, the area being
1468 acres, in addition to which there are 956 acres
subject to deed, to which deeds had not been taken.

Exhibit 51. Tabulation showing the two bond
issues of the district and the amounts maturing and
delinquent each year. On November 1, 1934, the interest in default was $87,939.43 and the principal
was $65,974.00. This exhibit showed that for the
year 1931 bond principal in the sum of $14,425.00
became due and $14,425.00 was paid.

Exhibit 52. Trial balance sheet of the district for
September 30, 1934.

Exhibit 53. Statement showing cash on hand and
estimated revenues and total liabilities for the year
1934/35.

Exhibit 54. Copy of resolution of Board of Directors of Waterford Irrigation District fixing the assessment rate for the year 1931/32. The rate was fixed at $5.75. It provided for [103] interest that would fall due upon the bonds of the district, but made no provision for payment of principal which would become due during that year.

Exhibit 55. Resolution for the same purpose for the year 1932/33, fixing the tax rate at $4.50 per hundred. The resolution declared that it was necessary to raise the sum of $5,763.68 to pay the principal of all bonds of the district that had matured or will mature before the close of the next ensuing calendar year, and the sum of $13,386.64 to pay the interest due or that would become due on all outstanding bonds of the district on the first day of the next ensuing Jannary and the first day of the next ensuing July. (An explanation was made by Mr. Quinley to the effect that it was calculated that moneys received from redemptions would be sufficient in addition to the amount of the assessment made to pay the interest and bond principal falling due.)

Exhibit 56. Copy of resolution of Board of Directors of Waterford Irrigation District adopted September 9, 1933, levying assessments for the year 1933/34. This assessment was made in accordance with the provisions of Section 11 of the District Securities Commission Act and not in accordance with Section 39 of the California Irrigation District Act, and was not calculated to nor did it levy an assessment sufficient to pay the interest on bonds that would become due nor the principal of bonds that would fall due during the year.

Exhibit 57. Copy of resolution of Board of Directors of Waterford Irrigation District fixing the assessment rate for the year 1934/35, the assessment being made in accordance with the provision in Section 11 of said District Securities Commission Act and not in accordance with Section 39 of the California Irrigation District Act, and was not calculated to nor did it levy an assessment sufficient to pay interest upon bonds of the district which would mature nor the principal of bonds which would mature during [104] the year for which the assessment was made. The resolution stated that the aggregate assessed value of the property in the district, as it appeared on the assessment roll for the year 1934, is the sum of $1,010,923.00.

Exhibit 58 to 61, inclusive. Affidavits of publication of delinquent list for the years 1930 to 1933 and delinquent lists for those years.

Exhibit 62. Tabulation showing the original expenditures of the district of the moneys obtained from its bond issue.

Exhibit 63. Classification of the lands of the district.

Exhibit 64. Graph showing a cross section of the district giving underground water level.

Exhibit 65. Tabulation showing the crops grown in the district for the years 1919 to 1934, the main crops being alfalfa, field crops, vines, deciduous fruits, nuts, figs, berries, garden, of which main varieties the total irrigated area in 1930 averaged slightly over 5,300 acres, the remainder of the land being dry pasture or dry farmed approximating 8,000 acres not irrigated. The water diverted each year in acre feet was in 1930, 25,507; 1931, 18,120; 1932, 32,830; 1933, 31,155; 1934, 23,498. The duty of water acre feet per acre ranged from 14.3 feet in 1919 down to 4.7 feet in 1924, from where it varied from 3.4 feet in 1931 to a high of 6.1 feet in 1932. The irrigation season commenced in February and March and continued to dates ranging from September 17th to October 30th, except for the year 1931, when it ended on August 17.

Exhibit 66. Map No. 2 showing the irrigated area of the district in 1933, the peak year of irrigation, there being 5,650 acres irrigated that year.

Exhibit 67. Graph showing the development of irrigated [105] areas in the district.

Exhibit 68. Tabulation showing the real estate holdings in the district from 1918 to 1934, the figures showing 1932, 323; 1933, 336; 1934, 318.

Exhibit 69. Tabulation showing the acreage and various sized holdings in the district on November 1, 1934, showing that 8 landowners owned 51.6% of the land; 14 landowners owned 63.6% of the land. It also showed that of the 318 holdings that year one had 1614 acres, two had 1468 acres, three had 1338 acres, the eight largest having an average acres of 885. Also that 83 had 17.6; 46 had 6.7; 35

had 2.2 and 13 had 0.5 acres; that there were 76 town lots included in the total of 318.

Exhibit 70. Tabulation showing the payment that would become due under the old bond issue upon final maturity and the necessary taxe rate assuming a 15% delinquency.

Exhibit 71. Map No. 3 showing in color the condition of delinquency on March 1, 1934.

Exhibit 72. District crop report for 1934. It showed the county valuation of district lands at $356,858.00, general county tax rate at $1.20, general county taxes on district lands at $4,282.29, in addition to which it showed the school district taxes. It also showed the district assessed value at $1,010,-923.00. It showed rental from district owned land at $2,925.00, no income from sales of district land; it showed the total value of crops for the year 1934 at $221,391.40, which the Engineer explained did not include dairy production, as this was considered an industry, not a crop production.

Exhibit 73. Tabulation showing the estimated amount required for operation, maintenance and replacement for July 1, 1934 to July 1, 1935.

Exhibit 74. Tabulation showing the same for the calendar year 1935. [106]

Exhibit 75. Tabulation showing the assessments that have been levied and paid in the sum of $320,-774.01 on land which had never been irrigated.

Exhibit 76. Two certificates of extension of escrow by two bondholders.

Exhibit 77. Certificate by escrow agent setting forth a list of creditors represented by the American Trust Company.

Exhibit 78. Photostatic copy of a bond of the first issue of the district, in the following form:

"UNITED STATES OF AMERICA
State of California

Number $500

21

WATERFORD
IRRIGATION DISTRICT
First Issue

The Waterford Irrigation District, of Stanislaus County, State of California, an irrigation district duly organized and existing under and in pursuance of the laws of the State of California, is indebted to, and promises to pay to the bearer hereof, for value received, the sum of

FIVE HUNDRED DOLLARS,

on the first day of January, A. D. 1931 with interest thereon from the date hereof, until paid, at the rate of six per cent per annum, payable semi-annually, on the first day of January and July of each year. Said principal sum and interest are payable only in Gold Coin of the United States of America at the office of the Treasurer of said district, the same being at Waterford, in the County of Stanislaus, State of California, and said interest is payable only on presentation and surrender of the proper interest bearing coupon thereto attached.

This bond is one of an issue, being the first of the bonds of the Waterford Irrigation District, of 936 bonds, numbered [107] consecutively from 1 to 936, of which 917 bonds are each for the sum of $500.00, 1 for the sum of $550.00, 2 each for the sum of $575.00, 2 each for the sum of $100.00, 2 each for the sum of $150.00, 1 for the sum of $200.00, 1 for the sum of $250.00, 1 for the sum of $300.00, 2 each for the sum of $325.00, 5 each for the sum of $400.00, and 2 each for the sum of $450.00, amounting in the aggregate to $465,000.00, which bonds are issued in Twenty Series, each series being payable at the time and in the amount prescribed by statute.

This bond is issued by authority of an act of the legislature of the State of California, approved March 31st, 1897, entitled, 'An Act to provide for the organization and government of irrigation districts and to provide for the acquisition or construction thereby of works for the irrigation of lands embraced within such districts, and, also, to provide for, the distribution of water for irrigation purposes,' and of the acts amendatory thereof and supplementary thereto, and pursuant to a vote of the electors of said district at an election duly called and held therein in conformity with the requirement of said statute.

It is hereby certified, recited and declared, that this bond is issued in strict conformity with the constitution and statutes of the State of California, and of proceedings of the said irrigation district authorizing the same and that all acts, conditions, and things required to exist, happen and be performed precedent to and in the issuance of this bond have existed, happened and been performed in regular and due time, form and manner as required by law; and this bond, together with all the other indebtedness and obligations of said irrigation district, does not exceed any limit prescribed by the constituton or statutes of said State.

IN WITNESS WHEREOF, the said Waterford Irrigation District [108] has caused this bond to be signed by the President and Secretary, and the seal of its Board of Directors to be affixed hereto, and has caused all of the coupons hereto, to be signed by the Secretary, and said Secretary has caused his signature to be lithographed upon all of said coupons and hereby adopts said lithographic signature as his own.

Dated at Waterford, California, the 1st day of Jannary, 1917.

WATERFORD IRRIGATION
DISTRICT,
By J. L. Pverey

President.

Attest:

[Seal]   C. C. Horsley

Secretary.

STÂTE CONTROLLER'S CERTIFICATE.
Sacramento, California
Feb 21 1917

I, JOHN S. CHAMBERS, Controller of the State of California, hereby certify that the within bond No. 21 of the First Issue of the Waterford Irrigation District, issued Jan. 1, 1917, is, in accordance with an act of the Legislature of California, approved June 13, 1913, a legal investment for all trust funds and for the funds of all insurance companies, banks, both commercial and savings, trust companies, the state school funds and any funds which may be invested in county, municipal or school district bonds, and it may be deposited as security for the performance of any act whenever the bonds of any county, city, city and county, or school district may be so deposited, it being entitled to such privileges by virtue of an examination by the state engineer, the attorney general and the superintendent of banks of the State of California in pursuance of said act.

The within bond may also, according to the Constitution of the State of California, be used as security for the deposit [109] of public money in banks in said State.

JOHN S. CHAMBERS
Controller of the State of California''

Exhibit 79. Photostatic copy of a bond of the second issue of the district.

Exhibit 80. Communication from Emil Schram of the Reconstruction Finance Corporation extending the time of the loan to Jannary 31, 1935.

Respondents' Exhibits in Evidence.

Certain exhibits were introduced into evidence by the Respondents, as follows:

Exhibits A and B. Reconnaissance Soil Survey of the lower San Joaquin Valley together with map. The map is a soil map showing the character of the soil in the Waterford District and surrounding country.

Exhibit C. Report by the District Securities Commission showing the crop report for 1933, total crop produced for that year being $154,308.00 for comparison with Exhibit 72 of the petitioner.

Exhibit D. Statement from the Stanislaus County Auditor's office showing the outstanding bonded indebtedness of the county and of various school districts overlapping Waterford Irrigation District, as follows: County Highway bonds, $971,000.00; Oakdale High School bonds, $24,000.00; Waterford School District bonds, $16,000.00; Empire Union, $39,500.00; Robert Ferry Union, $1,000.00.

Exhibit E. Bulletin 21 of the Division of Water Resources of the State of California, page 177, containing a short history of the Waterford Irrigation District dated 1929, as follows:

"History—This is one of the few active irrigation districts in California that have been promoted chiefly by large landowners. The individual who was most active in its formation controlled some 6000 acres. He had been a member of the board of directors of Modesto Irrigation District during [110] the early years of the use of water there, and his experience there showed him the advantage of changing over from dry farming to irrigation farming. The lands included are susceptible of irrigation from Modesto Canal, and when Modesto District was formed proposals were made to include these lands in that district. but this was not done.

Obviously, the chief difficulty in connection with making a successful project of Waterford District was acquirement of a water supply. Prior rights of Modesto and Turlock irrigation districts and of San Francisco in connection with its municipal supply apparently left only flood waters of Tuolumne River available to the new enterprise.

A filing of 13,000 inches measured under a 4-inch pressure was made on behalf of the contemplated district February 27, 1913. and conveyed to the district after organization. Later, on November 13, 1913, the district made an additional filing of 16,000 inches. Both of these were prior to the effective date of the Water Commission Act of 1913, and they both covered only flood waters, or at least waters available at La Grange Dam in excess of diversions by Modesto and Turlock Irrigation districts. A very valuable addition was made to the water rights of the district when, on Jannary 14, 1919, it entered into an agreement with Sierra and San Francisco Power Company to purchase from that company for $170,000 a perpetual right to divert a minimum of 60 and a maximum of 66 cu. ft. per sec. belonging to the old La Grange mining ditch, this being the first right on the river. This right is subject to certain rights for La Grange and vicinity, not to exceed 6 cu. ft. per sec. for a 6 months' period. Certain matters connected with the amount of the reservation for La Grange and vicinity, as well as other minor features of the contract with Sierra and San Francisco Power Company, are involved impending [111] litigation with Modesto and Turlock irrigation districts.

Next to acquiring a water right, the chief problem of Waterford District was to bring the flood waters appropriated to the lands to be irrigated. An arrangement by which Modesto Irrigation District should transport this water was the obvious solution, and arrangement to that end was made through friendly suit against Modesto Irrigation District under Chapter 429, Statutes of 1915. This act amended section 1240 of the Code of Civil Procedure to permit one irrigation district to condemn property of another irrigation district when not inconsistent with its use by the latter. Acting pursuant to law, it was planned that the Railroad Commission should fix the price to be paid in this condemnation, but before the suit came to trial the two districts reached an agreement, and for a consideration of $254,000 Modesto Irrigation District agreed to enlarge and line the upper portion of its canal, and to convey to Waterford District a perpetual carrying right in such canal. The two districts share operation and maintenance costs in proportion to the amounts of water carried. Subsequent to entering into this agreement, that is, August 31, 1916, Waterford Irrigation District supplied itself with funds by voting bonds in amount of $465,000, and used the proceeds to pay Modesto District and to build a system of laterals.

Some water was diverted in 1918, but the first complete year operation was in 1919, when about 15,400 acre-feet was used on 1023 acres. It was subsequent to this that, as previously indicated, the district purchased the old La Grange ditch right from Sierra and San Francisco Power Company. At the time of the construction of Don Pedro Dam, Modesto and Turlock districts succeeded to the rights of Sierra and San Francisco Power Company under its agreement with Waterford [112] Irrigation District.

Waterford Irrigation District, after building its lateral system, has gone forward with its development, and in 1927 some 45 per cent of the net irrigable area was under irrigation.

Soils and topography—Waterford District lies mainly in the lower rolling foothills. Immediately about Waterford the soils are Fresno sandy loams, similar to adjacent lands in Modesto Irrigation

District. The main soils in the district, however, are classified as Altamont loams and clay loams and Altamont sandy loam. The district is practically separated into eastern and western parts by Warner-Dallas Reservoir of Modesto District. The eastern part extends from the upper main canal of Modesto District to the bluffs above Tuolumne River. Here the land is rolling, but it becomes flatter adjacent to Modesto District west of Waterford. The elevation at Waterford is 170 feet. Because of ample natural drainage, artificial drainage is not required. The land in the district most suitable for irrigation is already under irrigation.

Development—In 1927 there were 325 individual farm holdings, but there was still one large holding of 2687 acres. In the flatter lands alfalfa is the principal crop, but more than one-third of the entire area is in fruit-tree plantings, mainly deciduous. Being more favorably situated as to frost than the valley land, a wide range of truck and horticultural products are grown. For instance, the 1927 crop report shows eight varieties of grapes, six different deciduous fruits, three varieties of figs, walnuts, almonds, persimmons, nursery stock, and ten different field and truck crops. The entire area can be reached with the present irrigation system.

The total population of the district is about 800, of whom [113] about 220 are in the town of Waterford. A paved highway connects Waterford with Empire and Modesto. The land in the district is assessed for city and county purposes at approximately $750,000.

Water supply—The nature of the water rights of the district was mainly set forth under 'History.' The engineer of the district estimates that the annual requirements are about 45,000 acre-feet. Since 1919 the amounts diverted for the district have ranged from 15,443 acre-feet, in that year, to 29,438 acre-feet, in 1927. The Division of Water Rights has recently allowed an application of Waterford Irrigation District for water stored on the Tuolumne River system by San Francisco, on the theory that such water is foreign water and subject to appropriation. Modesto and Turlock districts have refused to recognize this allowance and a suit has recently been filed in an attempt to establish this right.

Works—Waterford District diverts from Modesto Canal, first, near lower Dominici Gulch about 15 miles east of Waterford, and again, above the Davis drop, about one mile east of the main outlet of Warner-Dallas Reservoir. The district operates 40.25 miles of unlined and 1.5 miles of lined canals; also 1.50 miles of concrete pipe line 12 inches to 42 inches in diameter.

Including the amount paid to Modesto Irrigation District for enlargement of Modesto Canal and for carriage rights, and the amount paid for the La Grange mining ditch water right, Waterford District had expended to December 31, 1927, $696,-

651.57 on capital investment. Of this, all but $50,017, raised by general district assessment, was obtained from bond issues.

Use and delivery of water—Water is served on a rotation basis, the land receiving an irrigation about every 20 days. [114] Measurements of deliveries to individuals are not made, but a record is kept of the amount diverted from the canal, and this has been referred to. The gross duty of water in acre-feet per acre for the past three years has been as follows: 1925, 5.77; 1926, 5.14; 1927, 6.05. Since the district has no storage, the amounts available in dry years may not exceed, during part of the season, the 60 cu. ft. per sec. obtained under the La Grange mining ditch right, and in such cases use will be materially restricted. Heretofore, there has been no incentive to conserve water, but if the area irrigated is to be increased, the present use on the land will need to be materially decreased. In this connection it should be remembered that Waterford District has been delivering water less than 10 years.

Waterford District does not undertake to deliver water beyond its main skeleton system, leaving it to the landowners to make necessary connections.

Bonds—Two bond issues have been put out, totaling $670,000. Bonds amounting to $4,375 have matured and have been paid to January 1, 1928, leaving $665,625 outstanding. Other bonds onstanding against lands in the district total about $49,000 as

follows: elementary and high school bonds, $30,000;
general county bonds, $19,000.

Assessments and water tolls—All income in the
district is derived from district assessments. Land
is assessed for district purposes at its cash value.
A strip one-half mile around Waterford is assessed
at $200 per acre, but the usual rate within the dis-
trict is $120 per acre, with a low limit of $5 per
acre. Land within the townsite of Waterford was
assessed in 1927-28 for $59,671. The total assessed
valuation for district purposes in 1927-28 was
$1,069,751, the amount levied for 1927-28 being
$66,695. During the past five years [115] the annual
assessment rate per $100 of valuation has ranged be-
tween $4.95 and $5.30."

Exhibit F. List of mortgages and deeds of trust
of record against lands in the Waterford Irrigation
District, the Master permitting M. R. Pitts of the
Pitts Title Company to testify that the total amount
was $1,010,612.00.

Exhibit G. Letter from George F. Covell, respondent, explaining his opposition to the plan.

Exhibit H. Report of the County Agricultural
Extension Service showing the value of the crops
for 1934 in Stanislaus County being $22,546,655.00,
an increase of over $2,000,000.00 over 1933 and over
$5,000,000.00 over 1932.

Certain Objections by Respondents.

Upon the commencement of the introduction of
testimony by petitioner, the respondents made ob-

jection to the introduction of any testimony upon the grounds set forth in the answer, namely, the unconstitutionality of Section 80 and the unconstitutionality of Assembly Bill 12 of the Extra Session Laws of 1934, of the Legislature of the State of California, and upon the grounds that the petition does not state facts sufficient to constitute a good and sufficient petition. These objections were overruled by the Master and an exception allowed to respondents.

Also at the conclusion of the testimony introduced by the petitioner, the respondents made a motion for judgment, based upon the insufficiency of the evidence. This motion was denied by the Master and the exception of the respondents was allowed. **[116]**

Master's Report.

At the conclusion of the testimony before the Special Master, the matter was submitted to him, and he made his report to the court May 15, 1935.

In the Master's report, he held that Section 80 of the Bankruptcy Act was constitutional and then reviewed the facts which he stated were established to his satisfaction. A summary of this review follows:

The greatest area under irrigation in any year was 5,650 acres out of a total of 14,110 acres. The District put out two issues of bonds. The water right purchased with part of the proceeds of the

second bond issue is the principal right upon which
the district depends for water. The district has
other water rights which are of a secondary nature
and relate principally to flood waters, and the
water from such source ceases about June of each
year. The district also purchases water from the
Turlock Irrigation District, but during very dry
seasons this source cannot be depended upon. The
Western portion of the district is good level land,
but the Eastern part is rolling. Only about 40 per
cent of the land is suitable for irrigation. The principal character of the soil is sandy loam. The level
portions compare very favorably with that of the
highly successful neighboring districts of Modesto
and Turlock. The drainage situation is not altogether favorable. While good drainage is considered an advantage to irrigated areas, in the case of
Waterford it is detrimental, for the district lies
between the Tuolumne River and [117] Dry Creek
and, owing to the sandy soil, the water percolates
freely and the soil dries out rapidly, requiring a
greater quantity of water for irrigation and ex-
pensive fertilization.

Owing to the insufficiency of the water supply, together with the rapid drainage and the large acreage which it would be economically unsound to irrigate, the District has been adversely affected in
its development for a number of years past. Great
efforts to colonize were made, but sales fell off since
1931, due to the increasing taxes and competition
from other districts.

The Master referred to the fact that the District has operated for two years under Section 11 of the California Districts Securities Commission Act, under which the annual assessments of the District may be such as it will reasonably be possible for the lands in the District to pay without exceeding a delinquency of 15 per cent and that such assessments have been levied with the approval of the Commission, but he pointed out that at the expiration of the Act, it would again become necessary to make the full levies provided by Section 39 of the California Irrigation District Act.

The Master stated that he felt that the "patient" had gotten beyond the possibility of relief from "palliatives" and could only be cured by a "major operation" such as is proposed in the plan, and that abundant testimony was produced to show the very serious financial stress of the District; that the testimony was most convincing that the land is not now or will in the future be able to pay the assessments necessary to retire the present bond issues with accruing interest; that typical farmer witnesses had portrayed graphically the plight of the landowners, telling of earnest but futile effort to make a living from their lands and carry the burden of assessments of the District.

The Master stated that he was convinced that an increase in assessment such as would be necessary to retire the bonds with [118] interest would be prohibitive and would result in wholesale aban-

donment of lands in the District by their owners
and bring a complete collapse of the District's
finances, adding "It appalls one to imagine the dis-
tress that would ensue if these consequences were
permitted to take place." He specified damage to
the physical structures of the District and loss to
the holders of the bonds as among these consequences.

He commented upon the fact that the District had
endeavored for a considerable time to work out its
financial salvation through a refunding plan, but
had been unable to obtain sufficient acceptances on
the part of the holders of the District's bonds, and
he was of the opinion that the present plan offered
the only hope. It provides for a reduction of the
bonded indebtedness to $312,500, with interest at the
rate of 4 per cent per annum, which might possibly
be lowered to 3 per cent under a bill pending in
Congress. He said that it is reasonably possible for
the District to emerge successfully under this plan
to a sound financial basis.

The Master reviewed the testimony of various
witnesses as illustrative of the necessity for the
early approval of the plan.

The Master referred to the evidence offered as
to the market value of the bonds, showing that
these bonds were quoted by dealers at certain prices,
but he commented that these bonds were not listed
on any regular exchange and, as there was no general market for the bonds and but few sales, he did

not consider the evidence of great weight, except as showing the general public appraisal of their market worth.

After reviewing the testimony and exhibits and the procedure for the deposit of bonds for acceptance of the plan and the requirements of the loan to be made by the Reconstruction Finance Corporation, the Master reported that all necessary action by the District with respect to the loan had been taken and approval had been granted by the California Districts Securities Commission [119] both to the plan of readjustment and to the budget of expenses for refinancing and that the bondholders had been fully informed from time to time of the progress of the refinancing operations.

The Master stated that the District had become subject to the jurisdiction of the California Districts Securities Commission in 1933 and had proceeded in accordance with its orders since that time in the matter of levying assessments, and that the Commission had required that all moneys derived from the assessments levied be paid into the General Fund regardless of the fact that the Board of Directors had allocated certain portions to bond service, any such allocation being considered as made for budgeting purposes.

He then gave a tabulation showing that the plan had been approved by creditors holding a total of 72.73 per cent of the outstanding indebtedness.

Then the Master reviewed certain questions of law, reporting his conclusions that Section 80 is constitutional; that all of the creditors are of one class; and, without determining whether the District was insolvent within the provision of Section 80, that it was unable to meet its debts as they matured. On the latter point he said:

> "Counsel for Respondents ably argued that exhibits introduced by Petitioner show that the assets of the District exceed the amount of the outstanding indebtedness and therefore the District is not insolvent within the meaning of Section 1, Paragraph 15, of the Bankruptcy Act. However in the opinion of the Master the District comes within the terms of the alternative provision that it is unable to meet its debts as they mature."

Touching upon the application of funds on hand, the Master was of the opinion that under instruction from the California [120] Districts Securities Commission, all assessments were properly placed in the General Fund and not in the Bond Principal or the Bond Interest Fund, and that consequently all funds on hand must be deemed to be in the General Fund and not subject to call for either matured bonds or interest coupons.

The Master referred to the bond issues of other taxing agencies within the boundaries of Waterford Irrigation District, including the bonds of the County of Stanislaus, but he declined to consider this evidence for the reason that these bond issues were not debts of Waterford Irrigation District, particularly as the District did not create the indebtedness and Section 80 of the Bankruptcy Act concerns only creditors of the taxing district.

Referring to the question of the fairness of the plan, the Master declared that, considering all of the conditions confronting the District, from the general economic point of view as well as its inherent fundamental inadequacies, the sum of 48.82 cents per $100 is the fair and reasonable present value of the bonds and that a failure to consummate the plan would result in a substantially lower value for the bonds ultimately.

The Master further reported that the petition stated facts sufficient to entitle Petitioner to relief under Section 80; that the plan of readjustment was within the purview of the Act, and then reviewed the proceedings subsequent to the filing of the petition and held them sufficient.

From the foregoing, the Master reported his conclusions as follows:

(1) That said plan of readjustment of the debts of said district is fair, equitable and for the best interests of the creditors, and that it does not discriminate unfairly in favor of any class of creditors.

(2) That said plan does comply with the provisions of subdivision (b) of Chapter IX of said amendment to the bankruptcy [121] act.

(3) That said plan has been accepted and approved as required by the provisions of subdivision (d)

of said Chapter IX of said amendment to the Bankruptcy Act.

(4) That all amounts to be paid by the taxing
district for services or expenses incident to the readjustment have been fully disclosed and are reasonable.

(5) That the offer of the plan and its acceptance
are in good faith.

(6) That the taxing district is authorized by law,
upon confirmation of the plan, to take all action
necessary to carry out the plan.

He then reported with reference to his fees and
expenses and appended a list of the papers handed
to the court.

Exceptions to Master's Report.

Thereafter and within 20 days after the filing of
the Master's report, said respondents served and
filed their written exceptions to the report of the
Special Master. These exceptions were twelve in
number and while they were in greater detail and
in greater length, the following is a brief summary
and description of those of which the respondents
make a point upon this appeal:

SECOND EXCEPTION. That the objection to
the introduction of any testimony upon the grounds
that Section 80 is unconstitutional and that Chapter
IV, Extra Session Laws of 1934 of California, is unconstitutional, and for the reason that the said act
of the State of California does not confer jurisdic-

tion upon said court, and for the reason that the petition does not state facts sufficient to constitute a petition under the terms of Section 80 of the Bankruptcy Act of 1898, should have been sustained. Under this objection the respondents referred to their motion to dismiss and their answer, setting forth the constitutional objections to the jurisdiction of the court.

THIRD EXCEPTION. That the motion for judgment at the con- [122] clusion of petitioner's case for insufficiency of the evidence should have been sustained.

FIFTH EXCEPTION. That the Waterford Irrigation District was not shown and is not a bankrupt within the meaning of bankruptcy as defined by the Constitution and laws of the United States. In this exception the respondents referred to their claim that the assets of the bankrupt exceed the liabilities; that Exhibits 54, 55, 56, and 57 show that the district never levied assessment rates sufficient to cover the bond service obligations of the district and that the bankrupt's failure to perform the duties and obligations imposed by Section 39 of the California Irrigation District Act is a form of constructive fraud. Under this exception the point was also raised that the district is operating under Section 11 of the California District Securities Commission Act.

SIXTH EXCEPTION. That the plan is unfair, inequitable, and not for the best interests of the creditors and that it discriminates in favor of certain classes of creditors.

SEVENTH EXCEPTION. That the bonds of overlapping taxing districts should be considered as relevant.

EIGHTH EXCEPTION. That the mortgages and deeds of trust against the lands of the district should be considered as relevant.

NINTH EXCEPTION. That the plan does not provide for the application of trust funds to respondents' claims.

TENTH EXCEPTION. That the plan was not presented in good faith because overlapping bonds of other districts are not scaled down, mortgages and deeds of trust are not scaled down, the assets of the district exceed its liabilities, the district can take advantage of Section 11 of the District Securities Commission Act, and for other reasons.

ELEVENTH EXCEPTION. That Section 80 and its application to the facts of this case violates the Constitution of the United [123] States, and the court is without jurisdiction to enter a decree herein, as particularly specified in the motion to dismiss.

TWELFTH EXCEPTION. That the district is not authorized by law to carry out the plan, specifying constitutional objections detailed in the answer and motion to dismiss with respect to the enabling act of the State of California.

Master's Report Affirmed.

On the 24th day of June, 1935, the Master's Report and the exceptions of the respondents thereto were submitted to Hon. Harold Louderback of San Francisco, California, upon written briefs submitted by both parties, and order of submission having been made, the Clerk entered a minute order on the 3rd day of July, 1935, as follows:

"Special Master's report and exceptions thereto having been submitted and being now fully considered, it is ordered that the said report be and the same is hereby affirmed and exceptions thereto are hereby overruled. Further Ordered that fees of Special Master shall be determined by Court at hearing to be had thereon, said hearing to be noticed to all parties interested."

Motion for Continuance and to Amend Minutes Nunc Pro Tunc.

On January 29th, 1936, petitioner presented to the court a petition of said district for an order continuing said proceeding in effect to and until the 24th day of May, 1936, unless said proceeding should be sooner terminated by final decree entered therein. Notice of presentation of the petition was waived by the respondents. There was presented therewith consent in writing to such continuance by creditors of said district holding more than one-half in amount of all claims affected by said plan.

An order relating thereto was thereafter made by the court.

At the same time there was presented to the court on behalf of the petitioner a petition for an order amending the minutes of the court and authorizing the entry of Findings of Fact and Con- [124] clusions of Law and Formal Decree as of July 30, 1935, and thereafter an order in relation thereto was made by the court.

STIPULATION.

It is hereby agreed and stipulated by and between appellants and appellee that the within and foregoing statement of the case and narrative statement of the evidence at the hearing before the Special Master may be allowed and approved and the same ordered filed as the statement of the case, including the record and all evidence produced, to be included in the record on appeal in the above entitled cause from the findings and decree confirming the plan, all in accordance with the provisions of Equity Rule 77.

Dated this 18th day of March, 1936.

W. COBURN COOK
Attorney for Appellants, George F. Covell, George H. McKaig, David F. Selby, E. A. Covell, Nellie L. Covell, N. O. Bowman, Alice Dennett and Eleanor Dennett.

HANKINS & HANKINS
Attorneys for Appellee, Waterford Irrigation District.

ORDER.

It is so ordered.

Dated this 19th day of March, 1936.

HAROLD LOUDERBACK

United States District Judge

[Endorsed]: Filed Mar. 20, 1936. [125]

PRAECIPE.

To the Clerk of the above entitled Court:

Please prepare in the above cause a transcript of the record to be transmitted to the United States Circuit Court of Appeals of the Ninth Circuit in pursuance to the appeal heretofore taken in said cause by all those certain parties named in the first paragraph of the petition for an order allowing appeal, which has been filed in this cause, being the same parties who are represented by the undersigned attorney, and include therein the following:

  1. Agreed Statement for Appeal.

  2. Findings of fact and Conclusions of Law.

[126]

  3. Petition for and Order Allowing Appeal.

  4. Assignment of Errors.

  5. Citation on Appeal.

  6. Clerk's Certificate to Record.

  7. Bond on Appeal.

  8. Order continuing Proceeding in Effect.

  9. Order Amending Minutes of the Court and Authorizing entry of Findings of Fact and

Conclusions of Law and Formal Decree as of July 30, 1935.

10. Decree confirming plan of readjustment, Authorizing and Directing Procedure for Consummation of said Plan, and Enjoining Attempts to Enforce Claims for or Under Outstanding Bonds except in accordance with said Plan.

11. Praecipe.

Dated: March 19, 1936.

W. COBURN COOK

Attorney for Respondents and objecting creditors named in the above petition for order allowing appeal.

Receipt of copy of the foregoing admitted this 19th day of March, 1936.

Counter praecipe is hereby waived.

HANKINS & HANKINS

Attorneys for Appellee.

[Endorsed]: Filed Mar. 19, 1936. [127]

CERTIFICATE OF CLERK U. S. DISTRICT COURT TO TRANSCRIPT ON APPEAL.

I, Walter B. Maling, Clerk of the United States District Court for the Northern District of California, do hereby certify that the foregoing 127 pages, numbered from 1 to 127, inclusive, contain a full, true and correct transcript of certain records and proceedings in the matter of Waterford Irrigation District, No. 5552 in Bankruptcy, as the same now remain on file and of record in this office; said transcript having been prepared pursuant to and in accordance with the praecipe for transcript on appeal, copy of which is embodied herein.

I further certify that the cost of preparing and certifying the foregoing transcript on appeal is the sum of Eighteen and 70/100 ($18.70) Dollars, and that the same has been paid to me by the attorney for the respondents and objecting creditors herein.

Annexed hereto is the original citation on appeal.

In Witness Whereof, I have hereunto set my hand and affixed the seal of said District Court, this 21st day of March, A. D. 1936.

WALTER B. MALING, Clerk

[Seal]   By F. M. LAMPERT, Deputy Clerk.

[128]

[Title of Court and Cause.]

CITATION.

UNITED STATES OF AMERICA, ss.

TO THE WATERFORD IRRIGATION DISTRICT, PETITIONER IN THE ABOVE ENTITLED PROCEEDING, AND TO ALL ATTORNEYS AND SOLICITORS OF RECORD OF SAID PARTY:

You are hereby cited and admonished to be and appear at a session of the United States Circuit

Court of Appeals for the Ninth Circuit, to be held
at the City of San Francisco, in the State of California, on the 8th day of April, 1936, pursuant to
the appeal duly obtained and filed in the office of
the Clerk of the above entitled court and in the
above entitled cause, in which said appeal the following persons are appellants: [129] George F. Covell, George H. McKaig, E. A. Covell, Nellie L.
Covell, N. O. Bowman, Alice Dennett and Eleanor
Dennett, and in which said appeal the Waterford
Irrigation District is appellee, and you are required to show cause, if any there be, why the decree in said appeal mentioned should not be corrected and speedy justice should not be done to the
parties in that behalf.

WITNESS, the Honorable Harold Louderback.
United States District Judge, for the Northern
District of California, this 9th day of March, 1936,
and of our independence the 160th.

                    HAROLD LOUDERBACK
                        United States District Judge.

Receipt of a copy of the within citation is hereby
admitted this 14th day of March, 1936.

                    HANKINS & HANKINS
                        Attorneys for Waterford
                        Irrigation District.

[Endorsed]: Filed Mar. 19, 1936. [130]

[Endorsed]: No. 8141. United States Circuit Court of Appeals for the Ninth Circuit. George F. Covell, George H. McKaig, E. A. Covell, Nellie L. Covell, N. O. Bowman, Alice Dennett and Eleanor Dennett, Appellants, vs. Waterford Irrigation District, Appellee. Transcript of Record. Upon Appeal from the District Court of the United States for the Northern District of California, Northern Division.

Filed March 23, 1936.

PAUL P. O'BRIEN,

Clerk of the United States Circuit Court of Appeals for the Ninth Circuit.

In the United States Circuit Court of Appeals, for
the Ninth Circuit.

No. 8141.

In the Matter of

WATERFORD IRRIGATION DISTRICT,

An Insolvent Taxing District,

GEORGE F. COVELL, GEORGE H. McKAIG,
E. A. COVELL, NELLIE L. COVELL, N. O.
BOWMAN, ALICE DENNETT and ELEA-
NOR DENNETT,

Appellants,

vs.

WATERFORD IRRIGATION DISTRICT,

Appellee.

PETITION FOR APPEAL

To the Honorable, the Judges of the United States
Circuit Court of Appeals, for the Ninth Circuit:

Petitioners, George F. Covell, George H. McKaig,
E. A. Covell, Nellie L. Covell, N. O. Bowman, Alice
Dennett and Eleanor Dennett, conceiving themselves
and each of them conceiving himself aggrieved by
the decree of the United States District Court for
the Northern District of California, Northern Division, rendered by Honorable Harold Louderback,
one of the Judges thereof, and entered on the 21st
day of February, 1936, whereby said court entered
a "Decree Confirming Plan of Readjustment, Authorizing and Directing Procedure for Consummation

of Said Plan, and Enjoining Attempts to Enforce Claims for or Under Outstanding Bonds Except in Accordance With Said Plan'' after the entry of Findings of Fact and Conclusions of Law, and after having confirmed the report of Honorable Stephen N. Blewett, a Special Master, theretofore filed in said proceeding, and confirmed and approved the plan of reorganization filed by the debtor Waterford Irrigation District in the above entitled proceeding and denied motions to dismiss the proceeding theretofore filed by these petitioners, file this their petition to appeal from said decree of said District Court, and in that behalf said petitioners state as follows:

I.

That on the 6th day of August, 1934, the Waterford Irrigation District, an irrigation district organized and existing under the provisions of ''The California Irrigation District Act'', the debtor named in said proceeding, filed its petition in the United States District Court for the Northern District of California, pursuant to Section 80 of the National Bankruptcy Act, for the confirmation of a plan for readjustment of its debts, and thereafter on said day said petition was approved by order of said District Court as properly filed under said Section.

II.

That said petition recited that said irrigation district is insolvent and unable to meet its debts as they mature and desires to effect a plan of readjustment of its debts, consisting of two issues of bonds issued under the provisions of said "The California Irrigation District Act", together with matured and unpaid interest thereon, namely, an issue of bonds designated as "first issue" in the principal amount of $465,000.00, bearing 6% interest per annum, dated Jannary 1, 1917, of which bonds $446,-000.00 are outstanding, and an issue of bonds designated as "second issue" in the amount of $205,-000.00, bearing interest at 5½% per annum, dated July 1, 1919, of which bonds $188,525.00 of principal amount are outstanding, there being unpaid in matured interest the approximate amount of $87,661.98 represented by interest coupons attached to said bonds. Said petition further set forth that a plan of readjustment had been prepared, accepted and approved by said petitioner. The plan provided for the payment in cash in the sum of 48.82 cents per each dollar of principal amount of said outstanding bonds, said amount to be obtained through a loan from the Reconstruction Finance Corporation, an agency of the United States. Said petition further recited that creditors owning not less than 66 2/3% in amount of the bonds of said district, including bonds, notes or certificates of indebtedness owned, held or controlled by petitioner in a fund or otherwise, had accepted said plan in writing.

III.

Thereafter and within 90 days from the first publication of notice to creditors, your petitioners filed a motion to dismiss the petition and also an answer, wherein it was set forth that your petitioner (and one David Selby, who has not joined in this appeal and who had a bond of said district amounting to $1,000.00) owned in the aggregate $146,600.00 principal amount of bonds of said district, together with interest due thereon and unpaid in the amount of $20,110.00.

IV.

The motion to dismiss was based upon the following grounds, namely, that the court was without jurisdiction to entertain and hear the petition or to determine the cause for the reason that Section 80 of the bankruptcy act violates Section 8, Article I of the Constitution of the United States; violates the Fifth Amendment to the Constitution of the United States; violates the Tenth Amendment to the United States Constitution; that Congress has no constitutional authority to pass legislation regulating the rights of said district; that said Section 80 pretends to submit a state agency to the jurisdiction of the Federal Court, contrary to the plan and scheme of government as set forth in the Constitution; and that it violates other provisions of the Constitution of the United States; and upon the further ground that the appellee was without legal capacity to make its petition for the reason that Article I, Section 16 of the Constitution of the State of California prohibits the impairment of obligation of contract, and Article I, Section 21 of the California Constitution prohibits discrimination between classes, and that Article XIII, Section 6 thereof, provides that the power of taxation shall never be surrendered or suspended by any grant or contract to which the state shall be a party, and that the appellee is not one of the agencies permitted under Section 80 to file such a petition, and upon the grounds that the petition did not state facts sufficient to constitute a good and sufficient petition under said Section 80.

V.

The motion to dismiss was accompanied by points and authorities and was submitted to Honorable A. F. St. Sure, Judge of said court, on November 12, 1934, at which time the said Honorable District Judge denied the motion to dismiss, and your petitioners exception to the ruling was allowed.

VI.

The answer of respondents placed in issue the material allegations of the petition and again set forth the aforesaid constitutional objections to the proceeding.

VII.

On November 12, 1934, the Honorable A. F. St. Sure, Judge of said court, made an order of reference to Hon. Stephen N. Blewett of Stockton, California, as Special Master, to determine the issues.

VIII.

Subsequently, hearings were had before the said Special Master during which testimony was introduced on behalf of the appellee and on behalf of the appellants.

IX.

Upon the commencement of the introduction of testimony at these hearings the appellants made objection to the introduction of any testimony upon the grounds set forth in the answer, namely, the unconstitutionality of Section 80, and the unconstitutionality of Assembly Bill #12 of the Extra Session Laws of 1934 of the Legislature of the State of California, and upon the grounds of the insufficiency of the petition. These objections were overruled by the Master and an exception was allowed to the appellants.

X.

At the conclusion of the testimony introduced by the appellee, the appellants made a motion to dismiss and for non suit, based upon the insufficiency of the evidence. This motion was denied by the Master and the exception of the respondents was allowed.

XI.

At the conclusion of the testimony before the Master, the matter was submitted to him and he made his report to the court on May 15, 1935.

XII.

In his report the Special Master sustained the constitutionality of the bankruptcy act and said statute of the State of California and he found in favor of the appellee upon the issues raised and recommended confirmation of the plan to the District Court.

XIII.

Thereafter and within twenty days after the filing of the Master's report, the appellants served and filed their written exceptions to the report of the Special Master. These exceptions were twelve in number, amongst which were the following:

Second Exception. The objection to the introduction of any testimony should have been sustained.

Third Exception. That the motion for judgment for insufficiency of the evidence should have been sustained.

Fifth Exception. The Waterford Irrigation District is not a bankrupt within the meaning of bankruptcy as defined by the Constitution of the United States.

Sixth Exception. The plan is not fair, equitable, nor for the best interests of creditors and that it discriminates unfairly in favor of certain creditors.

Seventh Exception. That the bonds of overlapping taxing districts should be considered.

Eighth Exception. That the mortgages and deeds of trust against the lands of the district is a relevant matter and should be considered.

Ninth Exception. That the plan does not provide for application of trust funds.

Tenth Exception. That the plan was not presented in good faith.

Eleventh Exception. That Section 80 of the Bankruptcy Act of 1898 in its application to the facts of this case violates the Constitution of the United

States, and that said court was without jurisdiction to enter a decree for the reasons heretofore referred to and set forth in the motion to dismiss and answer of the appellants.

Twelfth Exception. That the district is not authorized by law to carry out the plan.

XIV.

That on the 24th day of June, 1935, the Master's report and the exceptions of respondents were submitted to Honorable Harold Louderback, and on the 3rd day of July, 1935, the following minute order was made:

"Special Master's report and exceptions thereto having been submitted and being now fully considered, it is ordered that the said report be and the same is hereby affirmed and exceptions thereto are hereby overruled. Further Ordered that fees of Special Master shall be determined by Court at hearing to be had thereon, said hearing to be noticed to all parties interested."

XV.

Thereafter the appellee presented a petition for an order amending the minute order of July 3rd, 1935, to provide for confirmation of the plan in the minute order and also for an order continuing the proceedings as provided by Section 80 and presented therewith the written consent of more than 50% of the creditors affected by the plan, to all of which the appellants objected, whereupon upon submission of the matter, the Honorable Harold Louderback, United States District Judge, granted the said petition and entered an order nunc pro tunc amending the minute order as requested by appellee and continuing the proceeding, and thereafter signed findings of fact and conclusions of law, and in accordance with the conclusions of law the said Honorable Harold Louderback, United States District Judge, did on the .... day of February, 1936, enter a decree denominated "Decree Confirming Plan of Readjustment, Authorizing and Directing Procedure For Consummation of Said Plan, and Enjoining Attempts to Enforce Claims for or Under Outstanding Bonds Except in Accordance With Said Plan", which said decree, except for title of court and cause, is in the following words and form:

[Printer's Note]: The Decree Confirming Plan of Readjustment, filed in the Circuit Court of Appeals for the Ninth Circuit, is identical to the Decree filed in the District Court, and is set forth at pages 39 to 53 of this printed transcript, and is not reprinted here for purpose of economy.

XVI.

That the petitioners refer to the Assignment of Errors filed by them herewith setting forth the errors made by the court below and giving the grounds for this appeal and make said Assignment of Errors a part hereof.

WHEREFORE, petitioners pray and each of them pray that an appeal be allowed to this Honorable Court under Section 24 (b) of the National

Bankruptcy Act (USCA Sec. 47b) from said decree of the District Court dated and entered February 21st, 1936; that a citation be issued directed to Waterford Irrigation District, debtor, as appellee, citing and admonishing it to be and appear at a United States Circuit Court of Appeals for the Ninth Circuit to be holden at the City of San Francisco, State of California, and directing it to show cause, if any there be, why the said order rendered against petitioners and each of them should not be corrected and why speedy justice should not be done to the parties in that behalf, and that a transcript of all the records and proceedings in said proceeding in the said District Court, duly authenticated, be transmitted to said United States Circuit Court of Appeals for the Ninth Circuit, and that the amount of bond for costs on such appeal be fixed.

Dated: This 9th day of March, 1936.

GEORGE F. COVELL
GEORGE H. McKAIG
E. A. COVELL
NELLIE L. COVELL
N. O. BOWMAN
ALICE DENNETT
ELEANOR DENNETT

Petitioners.

By W. COBURN COOK

Their Attorney.

W. COBURN COOK
Attorney for Petitioners.

State of California
County of Stanislaus—ss.

GEORGE F. COVELL, being duly sworn, says:
That he is one of the petitioners above named; that he has read the foregoing Petition for Appeal, knows the contents thereof and that the same is true of his own knowledge, except as to such matters as are therein stated upon information and belief and as to such matters that he believes it to be true.

GEORGE F. COVELL

Subscribed and sworn to before me this 9th day of March, 1936.

[Seal]   W. COBURN COOK,
Notary Public in and for the County of Stanislaus,
    State of California.

[Endorsed]: Filed Mar. 10, 1936. Paul P. O'Brien Clerk.

———

[Printer's Note]: Assignment of Errors, filed in the Circuit Court of Appeals for the Ninth Circuit on March 10, 1936, is identical to assignment of errors filed in the District Court, and is set forth at pages 55 to 66 of transcript, and is not reprinted here for purpose of economy.

———

At a Stated Term, to wit: The October Term A. D. 1935, of the United States Circuit Court of Appeals for the Ninth Circuit, held in the Court Room thereof, in the City and County of San Francisco, in the State of California, on Monday the sixteenth day of March in the year of our Lord one thousand nine hundred and thirty-six.

Present:

> Honorable CURTIS D. WILBUR, Senior Circuit Judge, Presiding,
>
> Honorable FRANCIS A. GARRECHT, Circuit Judge,
>
> Honorable BERT E. HANEY, Circuit Judge.

[Title of Cause.]

ORDER ALLOWING APPEAL.

Upon application of Mr. Coburn Cook, counsel for appellants in the above entitled cause, and good cause therefor appearing,

IT IS ORDERED that the petition of George F. Covell, George H. McKaig, E. A. Covell, Nellie L. Covell, N. O. Bowman, Alice Dennett and Eleanor Dennett for allowance of an appeal under section 24b of the Bankruptcy Act, filed March 10, 1936, from the order of the District Court of the Northern District of California, entered herein on the 21st day of February, 1936, be, and hereby is allowed:

IT IS FURTHER ORDERED that a cost bond in the sum of $250.00 be filed within ten days from date and that for such purpose the cost bond approved by the United States District Judge upon allowance by the District Court of an appeal herein shall suffice as the cost bond upon the allowance of this appeal.

[Title of Court and Cause.]

CITATION ON APPEAL

United States of America, ss:

The President of the United States of America, to Waterford Irrigation District, Debtor, Greeting:

You are hereby cited and admonished to be and appear at a session of the United States Circuit Court of Appeals for the Ninth Circuit to be holden in the City of San Francisco, State of California, within 30 days from the date hereof, pursuant to an order allowing an appeal of record in the Clerk's office of this court, wherein George F. Covell, George H. McKaig, E. A. Covell, Nellie L. Covell, N. O. Bowman, Alice Dennett and Eleanor Dennett are appellants and you are appellee, to show cause. if any there be, why the order of the United States District Court for the Northern District of California, Northern Division, made, rendered and entered therein on the 21st day of February, 1936, wherein amongst other things the court approved and confirmed the plan of readjustment of debt filed by said debtor Waterford Irrigation District in the above entitled proceeding, should not be corrected and why speedy justice should not be done to the parties in that behalf.

WITNESS the Honorable CURTIS D. WILBUR, United States Circuit Judge for the Ninth Judicial Circuit this 16th day of March, 1936.

CURTIS D. WILBUR
Judge of the United States
Circuit Court of Appeals.

Receipt of a copy of the foregoing admitted this 19th day of March, 1936.

HANKINS & HANKINS

Attorneys for Appellee.

[Endorsed]: Filed Mar. 23, 1936. Paul P. O'Brien, Clerk.

[Title of Court and Cause.]

STIPULATION AS TO RECORD ON APPEAL.

It is stipulated between the parties to this appeal that the record on this appeal may consist of the following records brought up from the District Court; namely,

1. Agreed statement for Appeal.
2. Order Continuing Proceeding in Effect.
3. Order Amending Minutes of the Court and Authorizing entry of Findings of Fact and Conclusions of Law and Formal Decree as of July 30, 1935.
4. Findings of Fact and Conclusions of Law.
5. Decree Confirming Plan of Readjustment. Authorizing and Directing Procedure for Consummation of said Plan, and Enjoining Attempts to enforce Claims for or under Outstanding Bonds except in accordance with said Plan.
6. Petition for and Order Allowing Appeal.
7. Assignment of Errors.
8. Citation on Appeal.

9. Clerk's Certificate to Record.

10. Bond on Appeal.

11. Praecipe.

The record on appeal shall consist further of the following records and matters in the Circuit Court of Appeal:

1. Petition for Appeal.

2. Order Allowing Appeal.

3. Citation.

4. Minute Order of Court.

5. This stipulation.

6. Clerk's Certificate to Record.

It is further stipulated that inasmuch as the assignment of errors filed in the Circuit Court of Appeals is the same as that filed in the District Court, that the same need not be reprinted, and, further, that brief in support of petition for appeal may be omitted from the record, and that that portion of the petition for appeal to the Circuit Court of Appeals which consisted of the copy of the decree confirming plan of readjustment, etc., may be omitted from the printed record, as well as title of court and cause and verifications where convenient.

Dated: March 19th, 1936.

W. COBURN COOK

Attorney for Appellants

HANKINS & HANKINS

Attorneys for Appellee

[Endorsed]: Filed Mar. 23, 1936. Paul P. O'Brien, Clerk.

No. 8141

IN THE

United States Circuit Court of Appeals

For the Ninth Circuit

GEORGE F. COVELL, GEORGE H. McKAIG, E. A.
COVELL, NELLIE L. COVELL, N. O. BOWMAN,
ALICE DENNETT and ELEANOR DENNETT,

Appellants,

vs.

WATERFORD IRRIGATION DISTRICT,

Appellee.

Appeal from the District Court of the United States
for the Northern District of California,
Northern Division.

BRIEF FOR APPELLANTS.

W. COBURN COOK,
Berg Building, Turlock, California,
Attorney for Appellants.

FILED

APR 22 193

PAUL P. O'BRIEN,
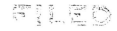

PERNAU-WALSH PRINTING CO., SAN FRANCISCO

Subject Index

	Page
Statement of the Case	1
The appellee	1
Dissolution of district	8
The Districts Securities Commission	9
The appellants	12
The petition filed August 6, 1934	12
Sections 78, 79 and 80 of the National Bankruptcy Act	12
The State Enabling Act	15
The petition	16
Proceedings taken	17
Specifications of Error	21
Argument	33
Preliminary statement regarding economic background of California irrigation districts	33
Mortgages are inferior	35
The Questions Involved	37
Summary of Argument	38

I.

The bankruptcy power of Congress does not extend to the states nor to their agencies nor mandatories	38
The bankruptcy power of Congress	45
Analogy of the sixteenth amendment	47
It is a well recognized principle of construction that general statutory language does not apply to the sovereign to its disadvantage	55

II.

The consent of the state will not complement the bankruptcy power of Congress	66
The so-called Enabling Act of the legislature of the State of California, being Assembly Bill No. 12 or Chapter IV, Extra Session Laws of 1934, is unconstitutional	75

III.   Page

The bankruptcy power is subject to the fifth amendment... 91

IV.

The Waterford Irrigation District is not a subject of
bankruptcy 100

1. The Waterford Irrigation District is engaged in
    strictly governmental and not proprietary functions 100

2. As a matter of fact an irrigation district is not a
    taxing district within the meaning of Section 80.... 114

3. The Waterford Irrigation District cannot surrender
    its property 117

4. The Waterford Irrigation District is not the debtor.. 117

5. The Waterford Irrigation District cannot be a
    bankrupt 121

6. The analogy of equity receivership cases........... 123

V.

The plan of readjustment is essentially unjust, inequitable
and discriminatory 126

    Review of the findings, decree and testimony in the
    case 126

    The findings 126

    The plan of readjustment....................... 130

    A short digest of the testimony.................... 130

    The master's report 135

    The plan is unfair............................. 137

    1. It is unfair to assess value of bonds under de-
        pression conditions 137

    2. The assets of the Waterford Irrigation District
        exceed its liabilities 137

        Trust funds and trust properties.............. 138

        Overlapping tax liens 140

        Mortgages and deeds of trust................ 141

    3. Property rights are transferred from the bond-
        holders to the landowners................... 143

VI.

Exceptions taken 153

Conclusion 154

Table of Authorities Cited

Pages

Allen v. Davenport, 107 Ia. 90, 77 N. W. 532.............. 140

Ames v. Kansas, 111 U. S. 449, 28 L. Ed. 482, 4 Sup. Ct.
Rep. 437 68

Bailey v. Drexel Furniture Co., 259 U. S. 20, 66 L. Ed. 818 156

Barber v. Galloway, 195 Cal. 1, 231 Pac. 34.............. 81

Barron v. The Mayor of Baltimore, 7 Peters 240, 247, 8
L. Ed. 672, 674.................................... 51

Bates v. Gregory, 89 Cal. 387, 26 Pac. 891............... 81

Bates v. McHenry, 123 C. A. 81....................... 8

Bonds of Madera Irrigation District, In re, 28 Pac. 272, 92
Cal. 296 106

Bradford v. Fahey, C. C. A., 4th Circuit, April 2, 1935.... 50

Bradford, Re, 7 Fed. Supp. 665........................96, 97

Buffington v. Day, 11 Wallace 113, 124, 20 L. Ed. 122,
125 ....52, 63, 64

Bunn v. Willcuts, 29 Fed. (2d) 132..................... 49

6 Cal. Juris. 767...................................... 81

California Constitution:
    Article I, Section 1............................... 85
    Article I, Section 14.............................. 89
    Article I, Section 16..........................25, 66, 79
    Article I, Section 21.............................. 25
    Article IV, Section 1.............................. 85
    Article XI, Section 13............................. 2
    Article XIII, Section 6.......................25, 85, 87
    Article XIV, Section 1............................. 2
    Article XIV, Section 3............................. 2

California Districts Securities Commission Act, Statutes
1931, p. 2263 9

California Districts Securities Commission Act, Section 11
....9, 11, 122, 123

California Irrigation District Act:
    Statutes 1897, p. 254............................. 3
    Section 2 3
    Section 29 4
    Section 30 5
    Sections 30-32e 9

Pages

Section 35 5

Section 39 5

Section 39b 6

Section 39c 7

Section 45 7

Section 47 7

Section 48 7

Section 52 ....7, 16, 31, 123, 126

Section 67 8

Cameron County Water Improvement District No. 1, Re, 9
Fed. Supp. 103 45

Central Improvement Co. v. Cambria Steel Co., 210 Fed.
696, 703 (C. C. A. 8th, 1913), aff'd, 240 U. S. 166, 36 Sup.
Ct. 334 (1916) 147

Chapman v. Jocelyn, 182 Cal. 294, 187 Pac. 962........... 82

Chisholm v. Georgia, 2 Dallas 419, 470, 1 L. Ed. 440, 462
....52, 69, 70

City of Inglewood v. County of Los Angeles, 207 Cal. 697,
707 56

City of Pasadena v. Chamberlain, 79 C. A. D. 75, 78...... 55

Civil Code, Section 3450............................... 121

Clark v. Barnard, 108 U. S. 436, 28 L. Ed. 780........... 71

Cleveland v. Edward, 109 Ohio St. 598, 37 A. L. R. 1352... 87

Cohens v. Virginia, 6 Wheat. 406....................... 71

Commissioner of Internal Revenue v. Harlan, 80 Fed. (2d)
660 ....49, 72

73d Congress, 1st Session, Report No. 207............... 73

Continental Ntl. Bank etc. v. Chicago Rock Island Railway
Co., 55 Sup. Ct. 595..........................98, 153, 154

Conway v. Chicago, 237 Ill. 128, 86 N. E. 619............ 140

7 Corpus Juris 128.................................... 140

14 Corpus Juris 73.................................... 38

61 Corpus Juris 76.................................... 86

61 Corpus Juris 83.................................... 86

65 Corpus Juris 1254.................................. 73

County of Los Angeles v. Rockhold, 89 C. D. 556 (44 Pac.
(2d) 340) 95

Cowles v. Mercer County, 7 Wall. 118, 19 L. Ed. 86...... 68

Coyle v. Smith, 221 U. S. 559, 566, 570, 571, 55 L. Ed. 853,
858, 859 62

Pages

Debs, In re, 158 U. S. 564.............................. 51
Dred Scott v. Stanford, 19 Howard 393, 404, 15 L. Ed.
 691, 700 52

English v. Sacramento County Supervisors, 19 Cal. 172... 81
Fallbrook Irrigation District v. Bradley, 164 U. S. 156, 174 39

Fray v. Woodworth, 270 U. S. 669..................... 49

Gillan v. Hutchinson, 16 Cal. 153...................... 89
Guarantee Title & Trust Co. v. Title Guaranty and Surety
 Co., 224 U. S. 152, 156, 56 L. Ed. 706, 708.............. 56
Gunter v. Atlantic Coast Line, 200 U. S. 273, 50 L. Ed. 477 71

Hanover National Bank v. Moyses, 186 U. S. 181.......... 96
Hans v. Louisiana, 134 U.'S. 1, 11.....................69, 70
Heine v. Board of Levee Commissioners, 19 Wall. (86 U.
 S.) 665, 22 L. Ed. 223..............................124, 125
Hershey v. Cole, 130 Cal.'App. 683, 20 Pac. (2d) 972..75, 119, 120
Holden v. Hardy, 169 U. S. 366...................... 96
Honnold, "Supreme Court Law", Vol. 2, p. 840........... 95
Hopkins Federal Savings and Loan Association, et al. v.
 Cleary, 56 Sup. Ct. Rep. 235.........................41, 91
Houck v. Little River Drainage District, 239 U. S. 254, 261 112
Howard v. Maxwell Motor Co., 269 Fed. 292, aff'd 275 Fed.
 53 (C. C. A. 2d 1921)................................ 147

Imperial Irrigation District, Matter of the, 10 Fed. Supp... 100
Islais Land Co. Ltd. v. Matheson, Treas., 78 C. A. D. 816,
 819 79

Jewell v. City of Superior, 135 Fed. 19.................. 139
Jochpipvky v. Mercantile Trust Company, 16 Fed. (2d)
 247 126
Jones, Bonds and Bond Securities, Section 480........... 139
Jones, Bonds and Bond Securities, Section 501........... 125
Judith Basin Irrigation District v. Malott, 73 Fed. (2d) 142 119

Kansas City Ry. Co. v. Central Union Trust Co., 271 U. S.
 445, 46 Sup. Ct. 549 (1926).........................145, 148
Kansas v. Colorado, 206 U. S. 46...................... 51
Kerbaugh Empire Co. v. Borrows, 271 U. S. 170.......... 49

Pages

Kingston v. American Car Co., 55 F. (2d) 132 (C. C. A.
8th, 1932) 145

Kinnane Company, In re, 211 Fed. 762.................. 141

La Mesa, etc., Irrigation District v. Hornbeck, 216 Cal. 730 7, 35

Lane County v. Oregon, 7 Wallace (U. S.) 71............. 111

Lansing, etc. v. Lryrerson & Son, 63 U. S. (C. C. A.) 253,
128 Fed. 701, 705................................... 122

Leacroy v. Lobree, 84 Cal. 41, 49...................... 122

Liebman v. Richmond, 103 Cal. App. 354, 459........... 56

Lincoln County v. Luning, 133 U. S. 529, 33 L. Ed. 766,
10 Sup. Ct. Rep. 363................................ 69

Lloyd v. Blanding, 54 Cal. 41.......................... 80

Loeb v. Columbia Township, 179 U. S. 472, 45 L. Ed. 280,
21 Sup. Ct. Rep. 174................................ 69

Logan v. United States, 144 U. S. 263.................. 51

Louisville Joint Stock Land Bank v. Radford, 55 Sup. Ct.
854 ....92, 153

Louisville Trust Co. v. Louisville Ry. Co., 174 U. S. 674,
19 Sup. Ct. 827.................................... 145

Male v. Atchison R. Co., 230 N. Y. 158, 129 N. E. 458
(1920) 145, 150

Manati Sugar Co. v. Mock, 75 Fed. (2d) 284............ 152

Marra v. San Jacinto and P. V. Irrigation District, 131
Fed. 780 126

Marshall v. New York, 254 U. S. 380, 382, 65 L. Ed. 315,
317 58

Martin, In re, 75 Fed. (2d) 618......................98, 139

McCollough v. Maryland, 4 Wheaton 428 (316), 4 L. Ed.
607 (579) 46, 51, 54

Merchants National Bank v. Escondido Irrigation District,
144 Cal. 329, 77 Pac. 937........................... 80

Meriweather v. Garrett, 102 U. S. 472.................. 100

Metcalf v. Merritt, 14 Cal. App. 244................... 115

Meyerfield v. South San Joaquin Irrigation District, 89
Cal. Dec. 700, 45 Pac. (2d) 321..................... 141

Meyers v. City of Idaho Falls, 52 Idaho 81, 11 Pac. (2d)
626 139

Monongahela Navigation Company v. U. S., 148 U. S. 312.. 96

Mountain State Power Co. v. Jordan Lumber Co., 293 Fed.
502, certiorari denied, 264 U. S. 582, 44 Sup. Ct. 332
(1924) 145, 146

Pages

Mulcahy v. Baldwin, 216 Cal. 517......................86, 89

Nashville etc. Ry. Co. v. Walters, 55 Sup. Ct. Rep. 486.... 121
Nevada Nat. Bk. v. Bd. of Supervisors, 5 Cal. App. 651.... 79
Nevada National Bank v. Ross Irrigation District, 140 Cal.
344 117
Northern Pacific Ry. Co. v. Boyd, 228 U. S. 482, 33 Sup.
Ct. 554 (1913) 143, 144, 146, 147, 148, 151

O'Neill v. Leamer, 239 U. S. 244....................... 111

Parker v. El Paso Water Improvement District No. 1, 116
Tex. 631 110
Pasadena v. Railroad Commission, 183 Cal. 526, 192 Pac. 25 109
People v. Bond, 10 Cal. 563........................... 139
People v. McCreery, 34 Cal. 432....................... 86
People v. Reclamation District No. 551, 117 Cal. 120....... 115
People v. Sacramento Drainage District, 155 Cal. 373, 103
Pac. 207 138
People v. Tallant, 12 Cal. 300........................ 140
Perris Irrigation District v. Thompson, 116 Fed. 832....... 117
Phipps v. Chicago, Rock Island & Pacific Ry. Co. (1924),
24 Col. L. Rev. 266, 271............................. 149
Pollock v. Farmers L. & T. Co., 157 U. S. 429, 158 U. S.
601 ....48, 49

Quarg, Ex parte, 149 Cal. 79, 84 Pac. 766............... 85
Quarles, Matter of, 158 U. S. 532, 535.................. 50

Railroad Co. v. Howard, 74 U. S. (7 Wall.) 392 (1868).... 145
Randolph v. County of Stanislaus, 44 Cal. App. 322....... 115
Reclamation Dist. No. 551 v. County of Sacramento, 134
Cal. 480 55
Red River National Bank v. Fargo, 14 N. D. 88, 103 N.
W. 390 140
Rider, In re, 96 Fed. 808............................. 142
River Farms Co. v. California Gibson, 80 C. A. D. 868.... 138
6 R. C. L. 333, 334.................................. 81

St. Louis-San Francisco Ry. Co. v. McElvain, 253 Fed. 123 145
Second National Bank of Lansing v. Lansing, 26 Mich. 207 140
Selby v. Oakdale Irrigation District, 140 C. A. 171....... 7
Selby v. Oakdale Irr. Dist., 89 C. A. D. 442, 448.......... 79

Pages

Shouse v. Quinley, 37 Pac. (2d) 89...................... 136

Shouse v. Quinley, 88 Cal. Dec. 420, 39 Pac. (2d) 89...... 140

Siebold, Ex parte, 100 U. S. 371...................... 51

Skelly v. Westminster School Dist., 103 Cal. 652, 656...... 55

Smith v. Morris, 2 Cal. 534........................... 80

South Carolina v. United States, 199 U. S. 437, 452, 50
  L. Ed. 226, 266....................................... 54

Southern Pacific Co. v. Bogert, 250 U. S. 483, 39 Sup. Ct.
  533 145

State v. Commissioners, 291 Pac. 1...................... 117

State v. Hobe, 106 Wis. 411, 82 N. W. 336............... 140

Statutes 1903, p. 3...................................... 8

Statutes 1911, p. 1407.................................. 3

Statutes 1919, p. 751.................................... 9

Sturges v. Crowninshield, 4 Wheaton 122............... 81

Tarpey v. McClure, 190 Cal. 593........................ 116

Tennessee Publishing Co. v. American National Bank, 81
  Fed. (2d) 463 151

Thompson v. Allen County, 115 U. S. 550, 29 L. Ed. 472, 6
  Sup. Ct. 140 125

Thompson v. Perris Irrigation District, 116 Fed. 769...... 117

Turlock Irrigation District v. White, 186 Cal. 183, 189.... 86

Union Pac. R. R. Co. v. Peniston, 85 U. S. 5, 21 L. Ed. 791   88

United States Constitution:

  Article I, Section 8...........................48, 80, 115

  Article I, Section 8, cl. 1........................... 65

  Article I, Section 8, cl. 4........................... 54

  Article I, Section 10......................23, 25, 67, 75

  Article I, Section 14................................ 23

  Article I, Section 16................................ 23

  Article III, Section 1............................... 23

  Article III, Section 2............................... 69

  Article IV, Section 5, cl. 1......................... 75

  Fifth Amendment 27, 92, 96, 98, 153, 155

  Tenth Amendment 23, 52

  Eleventh Amendment 23, 69, 70, 72

  Fourteenth Amendment 96

  Fourteenth Amendment, Section 1..................23, 89

  Sixteenth Amendment 47, 48, 49

Pages

U. S. v. Boyer, 85 Fed. 425............................ 115

United States v. Butler, 56 Sup. Ct. Rep. 312............. 39

United States v. Herron, 20 Wall. 251, 260, 22 L. Ed. 275,
278 57

United States v. Thompson, 98 U. S. 486, 489, 490, 25 L.
Ed. 194, 195 57

U. S. v. Young, 267 Fed. 861......................... 96

Walker v. Whitehead, 16 Wall. 310, 314, 21 L. Ed. 357.... 84

Weik v. Wausau, 143 Wis. 645, 128 N. W. 429.......... 140

Welsh v. Cross, 146 Cal. 621, 106 Am. St. Rep. 63, 2 Ann.
Cas. 796, 81 Pac. 229............................... 82

Western Union Tel. Co. v. United States & Mexican Trust
Co., 221 Fed. 545 (C. C. A. 8th, 1915)............145, 147, 149

235 West Forty-Sixth Street Company, In re, 74 Fed.
(2d) 700 152

Whiteman v. Anderson-Cottonwood Irrigation District, 60
C. A. 234, 212 Pac. 706............................81, 102

Wood v. Imperial Irrigation District, 216 Cal. 748........ 116

Worthen Co., W. B., v. Kavanaugh, 55 Sup. Ct. Rep. 555.. 94

Yolo v. Modesto Irrigation District, 216 Cal. 274, 13 Pac.
(2d) 908 110

No. 8141

IN THE

United States Circuit Court of Appeals
For the Ninth Circuit

GEORGE F. COVELL, GEORGE H. McKAIG, E. A.
COVELL, NELLIE L. COVELL, N. O. BOWMAN,
ALICE DENNETT and ELEANOR DENNETT,

Appellants,

VS.

WATERFORD IRRIGATION DISTRICT,

Appellee.

Appeal from the District Court of the United States
for the Northern District of California,
Northern Division.

BRIEF FOR APPELLANTS.

STATEMENT OF THE CASE.

The appellants, bondholders of the Waterford Irrigation District of the State of California, appeal from
a decree in bankruptcy confirming a plan of readjustment of debts.

The case is not reported.

THE APPELLEE.*

The Waterford Irrigation District, appellee in this
case, is an irrigation district organized under the provisions of "the California Irrigation District Act" and

---

* (NOTE): Pages 1 to 12 show the legal status of a California Irrigation
District.

is engaged exclusively in the distribution of water for irrigation purposes. In the discussion hereafter it will be shown that this is exclusively a governmental function. The district has no electrical distribution system and is not engaged in any other functions than irrigation.

Under the provisions of Article XIV, Section 1, of the California Constitution, the use of all water for distribution is declared to be a public use and subject to the regulation and control of the State in the manner prescribed by law.

Under the provisions of Article XIV, Section 3, of the California Constitution "it is hereby declared that because of the conditions prevailing in this State, the general welfare requires that the water resources of the State be put to beneficial use to the fullest extent of which they are capable."

Article XI, Section 13, of the California Constitution provides:

"The Legislature shall not delegate to any special commission, private corporation, company, association or individual any power to make, control, appropriate, supervise or in any way interfere with any county, city, town, or municipal improvement, money, property, or effects, whether held in trust or otherwise, or to levy taxes or assessments or perform any municipal function whatever, except that the Legislature shall have power to provide for the supervision, regulation and conduct, in such manner as it may determine, of the affairs of irrigation districts, reclamation districts or drainage districts, organized or existing under any law of this State."

By the provisions of Statute 1911, p. 1407, of the State of California "irrigation in the State of California is hereby declared to be a public necessity and a public use, and the power of eminent domain may be exercised on behalf of such public use."

In 1887 California passed the first irrigation district act of general application providing for the issuance of bonds. This act known as the Wright Act, remained on the statute books until 1897, when it was rewritten and reenacted as an entirely new law, which with its amendments is now known as "the California Irrigation District Act". This act and certain related acts control the method of organization, the issuance and refunding of bonds, the levying and collection of assessments, delinquencies, penalties and redemptions, and in general the functions and operation of irrigation districts.

The California Irrigation District Act, Statutes 1897, page 254, as amended, provides in Section 1 that a majority in number of the holders of title or evidence of title to land susceptible of irrigation from a common source and by the same system of works may propose the organization of an irrigation district, or not less than five hundred petitioners may propose it; each of the petitioners must be an elector residing in the proposed district, or the holder of title or evidence of title. A guardian and other persons holding property in trust may become a petitioner.

Section 2 provides that a petition shall be presented to the board of supervisors of the county, whereupon the board shall hear the same and proceed to determine whether or not the petition complies with the statute; if so, a copy of their resolution so declaring shall be forwarded to the State Engineer, who thereupon determines the feasibility of the undertaking. If the State Engineer reports favorably three-fourths of the holders of title must petition the board.

Following sections provide for a hearing before the board of supervisors who are authorized to make findings in favor of the genuineness and sufficiency of the petition, whereupon an election is called of the qualified electors within the proposed district.

The board of directors of the district are elected at popular election to conduct the affairs of the district. The board can acquire property for the construction and maintenance of canals, works, reservoirs, can establish regulations for the distribution of water, condemn property under the powers of eminent domain. The assessor, collector, and treasurer are also elective officers. A director must be an elector and a freeholder of the district. All officers are required to execute official bonds for the faithful performance of their duties. These bonds run to the state and are for the benefit of any injured parties.

Section 29 provides that

"The legal title to all property acquired under the provisions of this act shall immediately and by operation of law vest in such irrigation district and shall be held by such district *in trust for and is hereby declared and set apart for the uses and purposes set forth in this act.* * * * The board of directors of said district may determine by resolution duly entered upon their minutes that any

property, real or personal, held by said irrigation
district is no longer necessary to be retained for
the uses and purposes thereof and may thereafter
sell" (italics ours).

Section 30 provides that for the purpose of constructing or purchasing necessary irrigation canals
and works, water rights, reservoirs, reservoir sites and
other property necessary for the purpose of said district, and otherwise carrying out the provisions of the
act, the board of directors may cause bonds to be
issued and sold. The district is required to submit
the matter to the California Districts Securities Commission for its approval. Afterwards an election is
called upon the question of the issuance of the bonds.

Section 35 provides that the assessor must in each
year assess all lands of the district, which shall include
city and town lots,

"at its full cash value. * * * Improvements on any
land within the districts shall be exempt from assessment for any of the purposes mentioned in
this act. The term improvements as used in this
section includes trees, vines, alfalfa and all growing crops and all buildings and structures of whatever class or description."

The assessments are afterwards equalized by the
board.

Section 39 provides that the board of directors shall
annually

"levy an assessment upon the lands within the
district in an amount sufficient to raise the interest
due or that will become due on all outstanding

bonds of the district" during the next ensuing calendar year; "also sufficient to pay the principal of all bonds of the district that have matured or that will mature before the close of the next ensuing calendar year; also sufficient to pay in full all sums due or that will become due from the district before the close of the next ensuing calendar year on account of rentals, or charges for lands, water, water rights or other property acquired by said district under lease or contract; also sufficient to pay in full all sums due or that will become due from the district, before the close of the next ensuing calendar year on account of contracts entered into by the district for power or fuel used or to be used for the pumping of water for the irrigation of land within the district * * *; also sufficient to pay in full the amount of all unpaid warrants of the district issued in accordance with this act and the amount of any other contracts or obligations of the district which shall have been reduced to judgment";

also such amount as may be necessary for depreciation or replacement funds and such other amount as may be needed for any of the purposes of the act.

Section 39b provides that

"If as the result of the neglect or refusal of the board of directors to cause such assessment and levies to be made in this act provided, then the duly equalized assessment made by the county assessor of the county * * * shall be the basis of assessment for the district, and the board of supervisors of the county in which the office of the board of directors of said district is situated shall cause an assessment roll of said district to be prepared, and shall make the levy required by this act."

And this section goes on to provide for the carrying out of the other functions in relation to the collection of the assessments by the county officers in event of default of the district officials.

Section 39c provides that the district attorney of the county shall see that this is done and in his default the Attorney General of the State of California. This duty has been affirmed by the Courts. (*Selby v. Oakdale Irrigation District*, 140 C. A. 171.)

Other provisions of the act provide for the details of the collection of the assessments and for sale for delinquent assessments.

Under Section 45 a certificate of sale is issued upon the sale for delinquent assessments.

Section 47 provides that a redemption of property sold may be made within three years upon payment of the amount of the assessment with costs and penalties. (The redemption period for county taxes is five years.)

. Section 48 provides for the issuance of a deed which provides that the deed conveys to the grantee the absolute title to the lands described free of all encumbrances.

It has been held that the liens of an irrigation district assessment and the liens for taxes of a county and of a city are upon a parity. (*La Mesa, etc., Irrigation District v. Hornbeck*, 216 Cal. 730.)

Section 52 of the act provides that

"Upon presentation of any matured bond of the district, the treasurer shall pay the same from the bond principal fund, and upon presentation of any matured interest coupon of any bond of the district, the treasurer shall pay the same from the bond interest fund. If money is not available in the fund designated for the payment of any such matured bond or interest coupon, it shall draw interest at the rate of seven per cent per annum from the date of its presentation for payment until notice is given that funds are available for its payment, and it shall be stamped and provision made for its payment as in the case of a warrant for the payment of which funds are not available on its presentation."

This provision has been held not to provide for pro-rata payment. (*Bates v. McHenry,* 123 C. A. 81.)

Section 67 provides

"The following funds are hereby created and established, to which the moneys properly belonging shall be apportioned, to-wit: bond principal fund, bond interest fund, construction fund, general fund."

This section was amended in 1931 to provide as indicated.

At the time the Waterford bonds were issued the bond fund and bond interest fund comprised one fund.

DISSOLUTION OF DISTRICT.

Statutes 1903, p. 3, provides for the voluntary dissolution of irrigation districts. The point to be here noted is that Section 10 provides that "Whenever all the property of such irrigation district shall have been disposed of, and all the indebtedness and obligations thereof, if any there be, shall have been discharged, the balance of the money of said district shall be distributed to the assessment payers in said district upon the last assessment roll in the proportion in which each has contributed to the total amount of said assessment, and the court shall enter a final decree declaring said district to be dissolved.''

Statutes 1919, p. 751, which provides for the involuntary dissolution of irrigation districts, contains a like provision.

THE DISTRICTS SECURITIES COMMISSION.

The Districts Securities Commission has some fiscal supervision over the affairs of irrigation districts. This supervision is provided by Sections 30 to 32e of ''the California Irrigation District Act'' and by the provisions of the California Districts Securities Commission Act itself, Statutes 1931, p. 2263, the act having been first adopted in 1913.

These acts provide that a district must submit to the Commission the plan with estimates of costs, before the issuance of bonds, and provide also for the activities of the Commission in relation to the issuance and sale of refunding district bonds.

Section 11 was repealed and added in 1933 and was amended in 1935, and provides:

"Whenever any district has levied the annual assessment required by the California Irrigation

Districts Act or any acts amendatory thereof or supplemental thereto and when the money derived from said assessment, together with any other revenue allocated to payment of bond interest and principal, is insufficient to meet the bond interest or principal when due and said district defaults on its bond principal or interest, or both, to the extent of not less than twenty per cent of the amount due, said defaulting district may become subject to this section and to the control and direction of the Commission as herein provided upon the application of such district and the approval thereof by the Commission.''

In 1933 this act provided for automatic control.

The act continues:

"Thereafter it shall continue subject to this section and to such control and direction during the effective period of this section unless and until the amount raised by its annual assessment as hereinafter provided, together with other revenue derived from any source and allocated to bond service or other outstanding obligations, shall be sufficient to meet and pay off all matured and uncanceled or unrefunded obligations of such district, bonded or otherwise, in which event it shall cease to be subject to this section and such control and direction shall terminate so long as said district does not again default as aforesaid. * * *

The board of directors of such defaulting district, in levying the annual assessment of the district, may, notwithstanding Section 39 of The California Irrigation District Act or any other provision of law governing such district, levy only for such total amount as in their judgment by a finding of fact, approved by the Commission it will be reasonably possible for the lands in said district, taken as a whole, to pay without exceeding a delinquency of fifteen per cent. In determining the amount it is possible for the lands to pay, at the time of each annual assessment, the board of directors shall consider the productivity of lands in the districts, crops growing and to be grown during the year, market conditions as well as they can be forecast, the cost of producing and marketing crops, and obligations of the land respecting taxes and public liens. Out of the money derived from such annual assessment, the board of directors of the district may set aside such sum as, in the judgment of said board, and approved by the Commission, may be necessary, in addition to other revenue allocated to that purpose, for the operation and maintenance of said district and its works for the ensuing year. The balance of said money derived from such annual assessment shall be prorated to bond interest, bond principal and to other outstanding obligations of the district in the proportion that the total amount due on each of said items shall bear to the said balance."

The act contains some interesting provisions at the close of Section 11, reading as follows:

"Nothing in this act contained shall be applicable to refunding bonds of any irrigation district issued under or pursuant to a plan of readjustment submitted to and confirmed by any United States District Court in any proceedings under the Federal Bankruptcy Act, as amended, and such refunding bonds shall be payable, as to both principal and interest, from assessments levied and collected in accordance with the terms of said bonds and the plan of readjustment pursuant to which the same are or are to be issued, anything in this act to the contrary notwithstanding."

THE APPELLANTS.

The appellants, George F. Covell, George H. Mc-Kaig, E. A. Covell, Nellie L. Covell, N. O. Bowman, Alice Dennett, and Eleanor Dennett, are bondholders of the Waterford Irrigation District.

THE PETITION FILED AUGUST 6, 1934.

On August 6, 1934, the Waterford Irrigation District filed its petition in the United States District Court for the Northern District of California, pursuant to Section 80 of the National Bankruptcy Act for the confirmation of a plan for readjustment of its debts.

SECTIONS 78, 79, AND 80 OF THE NATIONAL BANKRUPTCY ACT.

(See Appendix B.)

Chapter IX of the Act of July 1, 1898, entitled "An Act to establish a uniform system of bankruptcy throughout the United States," as approved July 1, 1898, was amended on May 24, 1934, by the addition of Chapter IX which was headed "Provisions for the Emergency Temporary Aid of Solvent Public Debtors and to Preserve the Assets thereof and for Other Related Purposes.''

Section 78 of this Chapter headed ''Declaration of Policy'' stated that there was found to exist a national emergency caused by the increasing financial difficulties ''of many local governmental units which renders imperative the further exercise of the bankruptcy powers of the Congress of the United States.''

Section 79 provided that for two years from the date Chapter IX takes effect, the courts of bankruptcy should exercise original jurisdiction for the relief of debtors as provided in Chapter IX.

Section 80 was headed ''Municipal Debt Readjustment'' and for the convenience of the Court it is printed in full in Appendix A, but in brief it provides that any municipality or other political subdivision of any state may file a petition stating that the taxing district is insolvent or unable to meet its debts as they mature, and that it desires to effect a plan of readjustment of its debts. The petition shall state that a plan of readjustment has been prepared and that 30% of the creditors in amount have accepted it in writing. Upon filing of the petition the judge shall enter an order approving it as properly filed, if satisfied that it complies with the chapter and that it has been filed in good faith. Upon approving the petition the judge shall require the district to give notice to the creditors and to publish the same. Subdivision (c) (2) provides that if a plan of readjustment is not accepted and approved within such reasonable time as the judge may fix, the time may be extended for a period not exceeding two years from the date of the filing of the petition, and if a plan is not accepted and approved within a year from the date of filing the petition, the judge after hearing may continue the proceeding for not exceeding two years from the date of filing the petition, with the written consent of creditors holding half in amount of the claims. The Court is to determine a reasonable time and manner of filing and evidencing claims and divide the creditors into classes, to cause reasonable notice of all hearings for consideration of the plan or dismissal of the proceedings to be given, may refer any matter to a Special Master, but shall not interfere with any of the political or governmental powers of the taxing district, or any property or revenues necessary in the opinion of the judge for essential governmental purposes. Any creditor may be heard upon the question of the proposed plan and 5% may appear and controvert the material allegations of the petition, whereupon it is incumbent upon debtor to prove its allegation. The plan shall not be confirmed until it has been accepted in writing by two-thirds of the creditors affected by the plan.

After hearing the objections the Court shall confirm the plan if satisfied that it is fair, equitable and for the best interest of the creditors, and that it does not discriminate unfairly in favor of any class of creditors; that it complies with the provisions of the act; that it has been accepted and approved as required; that all amounts paid by the district for expenses are reasonable; that the offer of the plan and its acceptance are in good faith; that the taxing district is authorized by law upon confirmation of the plan to take all necessary action to carry out the plan.

Subdivision (f) provides that upon confirmation the provisions of the plan shall be binding upon the taxing district and all creditors.

Subdivision (i) provides that the jurisdiction and powers of the court and the rights of creditors shall be the same as if a voluntary petition for adjudication had been filed and a decree of adjudication entered on the day when the petition of the district was approved.

Subdivision (k) provides that the act does not limit the power of a state to control any political subdivision in the exercise of its political or governmental powers, including expenditures therefor, and including the power to require the approval of any fiscal agency of the state for the filing of a petition and of any plan of readjustment, and that any state agency exercising fiscal control over the district when it has assumed such control must first approve its petition in writing.

THE STATE ENABLING ACT.

(See Appendix A.)

At the time the petition herein was filed there was no statute of the State of California authorizing or purporting to authorize the filing of such petition, but on September 20, 1934, the Governor approved Chapter IV of Extra Session Laws of 1934, enacted at a special session of the Legislature of the State of California. This statute is set forth in full under Appendix

B and purported to authorize any taxing district of the State of California to file the petition mentioned in the Federal Bankruptcy Statute. It also provided in Section 6:

> "No final decree or order of the United States District Court confirming a plan of readjustment shall be effective for the purpose of binding the taxing district, unless and until such taxing district files with the court a certified copy of a resolution of said taxing district adopted by it or by the officials referred to in Section 2 hereof consenting to the plan of readjustment set forth or referred to in such final decree and order."

Section 7a provided that when any taxing district had theretofore filed a petition under Chapter IX of the Federal Bankruptcy Statute,

> "all acts and proceedings of such taxing district and of the governing board or body and of public officers of such taxing district in connection with such petition or proceedings are hereby legalized, ratified, confirmed and declared valid."

THE PETITION.

The petition of the district recited that it was insolvent and unable to meet its debts as they matured and that it desired to effect a plan of readjustment of its debts, consisting of two issues of bonds together with the interest coupons as well as the accumulated interest as provided in Section 52 of the California Irrigation District Act. The bond issues were a first issue of $465,000.00 bearing 6% interest, dated January 1, 1917, and a second issue of $205,000.00 bearing

interest at 5½%, dated July 1, 1919, of which $446,-
000.00 of the first issue and $188,525.00 of the second
issue are outstanding, and upon which the petition
stated there were unpaid interest coupons in the
amount of $87,661.98. The plan provided for payment
in the sum of $48.82 per each dollar of principal
amount of outstanding bonds regardless of whether
the bonds were due or not, and regardless of presentation dates of unpaid bonds or unpaid coupons. The
amount to be paid was to be provided through a loan
from the Reconstruction Finance Corporation, an
agency of the United States. The resolution of the
Reconstruction Finance Corporation shows the offer
of this agency to make a loan under conditions set
forth in the resolution. (R. pp. 78 and 87.) These
conditions did not bind the Reconstruction Finance
Corporation to furnish the money under all circumstances, but left the matter largely discretionary with
the directors of the corporation whether the loan
would be granted even in the event of the entry of a
decree, such as has already been entered. None of the
pleadings nor the evidence anywhere showed that the
district upon the entry of the decree is entitled to obtain the money from the Reconstruction Finance Corporation, nor that money for payment of the amount
provided by the plan is available or can be obtained.

PROCEEDINGS TAKEN.

The appellant bondholders of the district are the
owners of $145,600.00 of the principal amount of the
bonds of the district and at the time of the petition

were the owners of interest coupons amounting to $20,110.00 which were unpaid.

The appellants appeared in the proceeding and made a motion to dismiss based upon the unconstitutionality of Section 80 of the bankruptcy act and the unconstitutionality of Chapter IV of the Extra Session Laws of 1934 of the State of California purporting to ratify the filing of the petition, and upon the further factual ground that the petition did not state facts sufficient to constitute a good and sufficient petition under Section 80. (R. p. 96.)

This motion to dismiss was accompanied by points and authorities and was denied by Hon. A. F. St. Sure, Judge of said Court, on November 12, 1934, without opinion. (R. p. 97.)

The respondents within 90 days of the first publication of notice to creditors filed an answer, placing in issue the material allegations of the petition and restating the constitutional objections to the two acts in question. (R. pp. 97 and 100.)

The matter was referred to Hon. Stephen N. Blewett, of Stockton, California, Special Master, for hearing upon the plan. (R. p. 105.)

Upon commencement of introduction of testimony at these hearings the appellants made objections to the introduction of any testimony upon the grounds set forth in the answer, namely, the unconstitutionality of Section 80 and the unconstitutionality of Chapter IV of Extra Session Laws of 1934 of the State of California, and also upon the grounds of the insufficiency of the petition. These objections were overruled by the Master and exception was allowed to the appellants. (R. p. 146.)

At the conclusion of the testimony introduced by the appellee, the appellants made a motion for judgment and dismissal based upon the insufficiency of the evidence. This motion was denied by the Master and the exception of the respondents was allowed. (R. p. 147.)

Thereupon the matter was submitted to the Master and he made his report thereon to the Court on May 15, 1935. In his report the Master recommended favorably to appellee upon the question of the constitutionality of the bankruptcy act and of said statute of the State of California and in favor of the appellee upon the issues raised by the pleadings and recommended confirmation of the plan to the District Court. (R. p. 147.)

Thereafter and within due time the appellants served and filed their written exceptions to the report of the Special Master. (R. p. 154.) These exceptions were twelve in number, amongst which (abbreviated) were the following:

Second Exception. The objection to the introduction of any testimony should have been sustained. (R. p. 154.)

Third Exception. That the motion for judgment for insufficiency of the evidence should have been sustained. (R. p. 155.)

Fifth Exception. The Waterford Irrigation District is not a bankrupt within the meaning of bankruptcy as defined by the Constitution of the United States. (R. p. 155.)

Sixth Exception. The plan is not fair, equitable, nor for the best interests of creditors and that it discriminates unfairly in favor of certain creditors. (R. p. 156.)

Seventh Exception. That the bonds of overlapping taxing districts should be considered. (R. p. 156.)

Eighth Exception. That the mortgages and deeds of trust against the lands of the district are relevant matters and should be considered. (R. p. 156.)

Ninth Exception. That the plan does not provide for application of trust funds. (R. p. 156.)

Tenth Exception. That the plan was not presented in good faith. (R. p. 156.)

Eleventh Exception. That Section 80 of the Bankruptcy Act of 1898 in its application to the facts of this case violates the Constitution of the United States, and that said court was without jurisdiction to enter a decree for the reasons heretofore referred to and set forth in the motion to dismiss and answer of the appellants. (R. p. 156.)

Twelfth Exception. That the district is not authorized by law to carry out the plan. (R. p. 156.)

On June 24, 1935, the report and exceptions of appellants were submitted to Hon. Harold Louderback, and on the 3rd day of July, 1935, a minute order was made affirming the report and overruling the exceptions. (R. p. 157.) At that time a year had not elapsed since the filing of the petition on August 6, 1934, and findings and a decree could have been entered before the lapse of that year. None was made nor were any findings or decree made until February 1936, at which time also an order was made amending the minutes of July 3, 1935, to provide for consummation of the plan and continuing the proceedings as contemplated by Subsection (c) (2) of Section 80. A decree was entered on February 21, 1936, confirming the plan of readjustment authorizing and directing the procedure for confirmation of said plan and enjoining attempts to enforce claims for or under outstanding bonds except in accordance with said plan.

Thereafter a petition for appeal was presented to the District Court and an order allowing appeal was obtained from that Court, and a petition for appeal was also presented to this Honorable Court, which petition was granted.

The pleadings, testimony and exhibits were quite voluminous, the principal hearing having taken five days, and in order to present the matter to this Court in a concise manner an agreed statement was prepared, consented to by the parties and approved by the District Court. In this agreed statement the parties purport to set forth all of the pleadings, proceedings taken and evidence introduced in concise form. (R. p. 158.)

SPECIFICATIONS OF ERROR.

(*Explanatory Note:* For convenience of the Court the principal propositions for argument are set out and briefly summarized under the various specifications of error, following which are the assignments of error supporting the same.)

Specification Of Error No. 1.

The bankruptcy power of Congress does not extend to the states nor to their agencies nor mandatories, and the District Court erred in holding that it had any jurisdiction in this case and in making its several orders, entering its findings and decree. General words in a statute never bind the sovereign.

Assignments of Error.

1. The Court erred in making and rendering the "Decree Confirming Plan of Readjustment, Authorizing and Directing Procedure for Consummation of Said Plan, and Enjoining Attempts to Enforce Claims for or Under Outstanding Bonds Except in Accordance with Said Plan" in this cause dated February 21st, 1936, from which the appeal is taken and in not holding to be unconstitutional and void under the United States Constitution those provisions of Section 80 added on May 24, 1934, to the Act entitled "An Act to establish a uniform system of bankruptcy throughout the United States" approved July 1, 1898, and thereafter amended which purported to confer jurisdiction upon the district court to make and render the said decree.

7. The Court erred in ruling that this taxing power was not the sovereign power of the State and the Court erred in ruling that it had jurisdiction to determine in this proceeding how such power should be exercised and in controlling the exercise of such power.

8. The Court erred in holding that the Waterford Irrigation District does not exercise such governmental functions as did prevent the Court from con-

firming the plan of debt readjustment set out in its decree.

11. The Court erred in holding that Waterford Irrigation District was not a state agency created for the purpose of exercising, and exercising, powers of sovereignty conferred upon said district by the Laws of the State of California to carry out public governmental purposes, and it erred in holding that the confirmation of said plan of debt readjustment was not a void and illegal interference with the exercise of said sovereign powers so conferred upon said district.

25. Said Section 80 of this court's decree contravene the following provisions of the Constitution of the United States.

(a) Article X of the amendments;

(b) Article XI of said amendments;

(c) Article I, Section 10 of said Constitution;

(d) Section 1 of Article XIV of the Amendment to the United States Constitution;

(e) Section 14, Article I of said Constitution;

(f) Section 16, Article I of said Constitution;

(g) Section 1 of Article III of said Constitution;

(h) Other provisions of said Constitution.

26. Where any of the preceding or following assignments use the word "holding" or the word "finding," each assignment is repeated using the other word, that is to say, "finding" or "holding."

27. The Court erred in failing to grant the motion to dismiss made by the appellants.

31. The Court erred in confirming the plan, inasmuch as it is a limitation or impairment of the power of the State of California to control by legislation or otherwise the Waterford Irrigation District in the exercise of its governmental powers, including expenditures therefor.

Specification Of Error No. 2.

The consent of the state will not complement the bankruptcy power of Congress. The District Court erred in holding Chapter 4 of Extra Session Laws of the California Legislature of 1934 constitutional; and that the District was authorized to carry out the plan, and that the state could consent to the impairment of its contract and to the jurisdiction of the Court.

Assignments of Error.

21. The Court erred in confirming said plan of debt readjustment notwithstanding it impairs the obligations of the bonds held by the objectors.

23. The Court erred in holding that said Section 80 was not void, notwithstanding it delegated restricted judicial powers.

24. The Court erred in not holding that said Section 80 was unconstitutional because it denies and did deny in this case the equal protection of the law and was violative of the equal protection clauses of both the Federal and the State Constitution.

30. The Court erred in holding that the district is authorized by law upon confirmation of the plan to take all action necessary to carry out the plan.

32. The Court erred in holding that any state agency, authorized to exercise supervision or control over the fiscal affairs of the district, did or could lawfully consent to the plan proposed.

33. The Court erred in not holding that Assembly Bill #12 of Extra Session Laws of 1934 of the State of California was an unconstitutional enactment, and in not holding that the same was void as violating the provisions of the Constitution of the State of California prohibiting the impairment of contract by legislation and as violating Section 10 of Article I of the Constitution of the United States, and as violating Article I, Section 16, Article I, Section 21, and Article XIII, Section 6 of the California Constitution, and as being otherwise unconstitutional and void. (Refer to Assignment of Error No. 25.)

Specification Of Error No. 3.

The bankruptcy power is subject to the Fifth Amendment, and the District Court erred in not holding Section 80 unconstitutional on this ground, and in not finding or holding under the facts of this case the acts were unconstitutional.

Assignments of Error.

14. The Court erred in holding it had jurisdiction to confirm said plan of debt readjustment as against the appellants who are bondholders of Waterford Irrigation District.

15. The Court erred in not holding that neither said Section 80 nor the amendatory statute of which it is a part is a bankruptcy act in that it:

(b) Is not a uniform bankruptcy law;

(c) Restricts judicial power;

(d) Violates "The Due Process" clause of the United States Constitution;

(e) Permits the taking of private property for public use without just or any compensation;

(f) Permits the confirming of a plan of debt readjustment which impairs or changes the obligations of bonds of Waterford Irrigation District without impairing or changing the obligations of other public bonded indebtedness payable through taxation of the very lands which are taxed to pay the bonds of Waterford Irrigation District and yet the law does not make the tax lien created to pay said other bonds superior to that created to pay irrigation district bonds;

(g) Permits the confirming of a plan of debt readjustment which impairs and changes the obligations of bonds of Waterford Irrigation District without impairing or changing the obligation of private mortgages on lands and private deeds of trust on lands subject to taxation to pay the bonded indebtedness of the Waterford Irrigation District and yet the tax lien created to pay said bonds is superior to the lien of said mortgages and deeds of trust.

In this case, the uncontradicted evidence shows that the plan of debt readjustment confirmed by the Court accomplishes the discrimination and confiscation defined in the aforesaid paragraphs (f) and (g).

29. The Court erred in not holding that under the facts of this case the confirming of the "plan of re-

adjustment of debt'' violates the Fifth Amendment to the Constitution of the United States in the following respects:

(a) It takes the trust property of which the appellants are beneficiaries in that it takes the bond and bond interest funds and the tax certificates from them.

(b) It transfers rights from the appellant bondholders to bondholders of other taxing agencies, such as the County of Stanislaus, the Oakdale Union High School District, and the other school districts.

(c) It transfers property from the appellants to the landowners within the district.

(d) It transfers property from the appellants to the mortgage holders and deed of trust holders within the district.

(e) It takes property from the appellants without due process of law, inasmuch as the testimony and findings show that the assets of the Waterford Irrigation District greatly exceed its liabilities.

38. The Court erred in that it entered a decree contrary to equity, fairness and constitutional principles, a decree which provided that the appellants should be and were restrained from asserting any rights under their bonds and in adopting a plan which provided for the surrender of the evidences of obligations held by the appellants when the Waterford Irrigation District is not in possession of funds with which to pay the same, and no bondholder can obtain payment of his bonds upon surrender of the same unless the Reconstruction Finance Corporation of the United States, an agency of the United States, shall within its own

discretion and without being subject to any order or direction of the court, voluntarily within such time as it may deem desirable to it solely furnish such funds to the Waterford Irrigation District, and when this Court is without any authority or jurisdiction, by decree or otherwise, to compel the Reconstruction Finance Corporation to furnish such money or to compel the Waterford Irrigation District, unless the district shall receive the same upon the voluntary action of the Reconstruction Finance Corporation in furnishing such moneys to pay the same to the bondholders, and that said plan in that regard violates the due process clause of the Constitution of the United States.

Specification Of Error No. 4.

Waterford Irrigation District is not a subject of bankruptcy, and the District Court erred in not so determining. The Waterford Irrigation District is engaged in strictly governmental functions; it is not a "taxing district" within the meaning of Section 80; it cannot surrender its property to the Bankruptcy Court; it is not a debtor within the meaning of bankruptcy and cannot be adjudged bankrupt nor subject to the Court's jurisdiction.

Assignments of Error.

3. The Court erred in holding that Waterford Irrigation District was a person or legal creation of such a character as that the Court had power to enforce as against said district or impose upon said district the plan of debt readjustment mentioned in said decree.

4. The Court erred in applying said so-called bankruptcy law to said district in that said district had no power to surrender its property to its creditors in settlement of its debts or to surrender its property to the Court for valuation in order to determine a fair composition of the debts of said district. Said district's property is not leviable and is held in a public trust. Assuming power to make a bankruptcy law applicable to political subdivisions, municipal corporations or state agencies under some state laws, there is no such power where the state law withholds the public agency's property from its creditors.

5. The Court erred in finding and ruling that said District was a political agency of the State of California or taxing district within the meaning and intent of Subdivision (a) of said Section 80, and in not holding and ruling that said Waterford Irrigation District is an arm or agency of the State of California for governmental purposes.

6. The Court erred in holding that the power of Waterford Irrigation District to levy taxes on the lands or property of private individuals is property within the meaning of a true bankruptcy law.

9. The Court erred in holding said Section 80 is a bankruptcy act within the meaning of the word "bankruptcies" as used in the Constitution of the United States.

10. The Court erred in not holding said Section 80 is not a bankruptcy act which Congress could make applicable to Waterford Irrigation District.

12. The Court erred in not holding that Waterford Irrigation District was engaged in the exercise of governmental functions.

13. The Court erred in holding it had jurisdiction to confirm the plan of debt readjustment set out in said decree in favor of Waterford Irrigation District, a California irrigation district.

36. The Court erred in finding that the appellee was unable to pay its debts as they mature in view of Section 11 of the District Securities Commission Act of the State of California, and in view of Section 52 of the California Irrigation District Act of the State of California, and in view of other provisions of said last mentioned act.

Specification Of Error No. 5

The plan of readjustment is essentially unjust, inequitable and discriminatory, and the District Court erred in not so finding and holding.

Assignments of Error.

16. Said plan is unfair in that it compels no surrender of any property of said district and it wholly fails to measure the new obligations of said district to pay by any valuation of any assets or property of said district.

18. Said plan of debt readjustment is in its essentials unfair, for it discriminates between bondholders having the right of payment through taxation of the same land, in that it discriminates against the bondholders having county and school district bonds as against those having irrigation district bonds.

19. Said plan of debt readjustment is unfair in that it impairs bond obligations and sacrifices the interest of bondholders for the benefit of and advantage of the holders of private mortgages and deeds of trust.

20. The Court erred in confirming a plan of debt readjustment in that said plan provides for the use of funds which were in legal effect trust funds and for property which was in legal effect trust property, in that funds which may have been collected as the result of levies for bond interest or principal are trust funds belonging to the bondholders, and that the tax certificates which have not been collected by the district represent assets which likewise belong in part to the bondholders, and as the right of the appellant bondholders in these funds and properties are taken from them without just compensation and as the right of the bondholders are not equal in those trust funds, by reason of the fact that some have bonds which are due and some have bonds which are not due and some have bonds which have been presented under Section 52 of the California Irrigation District Act and others have bonds which have not been presented, the plan is discriminatory, unfair in its essential nature, and violates unconstitutional inhibitions against such discrimination. Delinquent revenue represented moneys for taxes levied for the particular purpose of meeting the bonds which had become payable long before the adoption of any resolution for the filing of the petition herein: in other words, matured interest coupons and bonds belonging to the objectors had been duly presented for payment long prior to the adoption of any plan of debt readjustment pursuant to said Section 80.

35. The Court erred in confirming a plan for re-adjustment of debts which provided for payment of 48.33% of principal of creditors claiming when the appellee's assets greatly exceed its liabilities.

38. The Court erred in that it entered a decree contrary to equity, fairness and constitutional principles, a decree which provided that the appellants should be and were restrained from asserting any rights under their bonds and in adopting a plan which provided for the surrender of the evidences of obligations held by the appellants when the Waterford Irrigation District is not in possession of funds with which to pay the same, and no bondholder can obtain payment of his bonds upon surrender of the same unless the Reconstruction Finance Corporation of the United States, an agency of the United States, shall within its own discretion and without being subject to any order or direction of the court, voluntarily within such time as it may deem desirable to it solely furnish such funds to the Waterford Irrigation District, and when this Court is without any authority or jurisdiction, by decree or otherwise, to compel the Reconstruction Finance Corporation to furnish such money or to compel the Waterford Irrigation District, unless the district shall receive the same upon the voluntary action of the Reconstruction Finance Corporation in furnishing such moneys to pay the same to the bondholders, and that said plan in that regard violates the due process clause of the Constitution of the United States.

Specification of Error No. 6.

The Court erred in holding it had jurisdiction to make any of the orders it made and in making any of the orders it made, including the entry of the decree.

Assignments of Error.

2. The Court erred in holding it had jurisdiction to render said decree.

22. The Court erred in upholding and sustaining Section 80, notwithstanding it accords no fair or reasonable hearing to creditors.

34. The Court erred in holding that it had jurisdiction to enter its decree in this cause on the 21st day of February, 1936.

37. The Court erred in holding that it had jurisdiction to make any of the orders it made in the case.

ARGUMENT.

(Italics throughout ours.)

PRELIMINARY STATEMENT REGARDING ECONOMIC BACKGROUND OF CALIFORNIA IRRIGATION DISTRICTS.

There are about one hundred irrigation districts in California which comprise approximately 3,600,000 acres. This includes the most highly improved agricultural property in the state. A great proportion of the acreage consists of orchards, vineyards, dairies, truck gardens, and other highly specialized crops. The most valuable farm property in California is embraced within the area of these irrigation districts. Some of the districts are small; some are extremely large, such for example are the Merced and Imperial districts. These districts are as large as counties. A similar case involving these two districts has passed through the bankruptcy courts. The Imperial case is now on appeal before this Honorable Court. The Merced case is now in process of appeal. Decrees in the Lindsay-Strathmore and Palo Verde cases it is understood will be appealed as soon as entered. Numerous cities and towns and other taxing districts, including school districts, road districts, reclamation districts, and other taxing agencies are within the boundaries of irrigation districts, and the welfare of these districts depends upon the success of the irrigation district and none of their bonds rank ahead of irrigation bonds. Without irrigation and without irrigation districts there would not be much need for these other taxing agencies. Before irrigation was brought to these lands the value was insignificant. In 1928 the properties within the boundaries of these districts was estimated to be worth one billion dollars. The bondholders who invested their moneys in irrigation bonds have contributed in great measure to the growth and development of the State of California, and the decision of this court will have a tremendous influence, not only upon the future credit of irrigation districts, but upon the welfare of the State of California itself. The real question here is whether those who have made this development in California possible by the investment of their funds in irrigation bonds are to sacrifice their investment for the purpose of enabling the second group, which also has contributed to California's development by investment in mortgages on lands within the district to improve its security. Let it be noted that the irrigation bond-holder has what is in effect a *first lien* upon the lands within these districts. California courts have held that the lien of assessments levied to pay irrigation bonds are of equal rank with the levies of counties and other governmental units. (*La Mesa, etc. Irrigation District v. Hornbeck,* 216 Cal. 730.)

MORTGAGES ARE INFERIOR.

It can be said that prior to the present general attack which is being made upon irrigation district bonds by the banking and other interests having investments in mortgages and deeds of trust, that a California irrigation district bond was the most excellent municipal security on the bond market in California. This bond has been three times passed upon by the Supreme Court of the United States, a statement which cannot be made as to the bonds of any other taxing district of this state. The courts of California and the United States have repeatedly determined the exact nature and validity of the contract represented by these bonds. They are a general obligation bond, secured by the unlimited power of taxation. Lands in an irrigation district can never escape taxation, not even by sale to the district itself, for when they are again placed upon the tax rolls they become subject to assessments and in the meantime their revenue is a resource from which the bondholders can be paid. No other California municipal bond has better or stronger provisions for the protection of the bondholder.

Since the 90's the agriculturists of California and its lawmakers have studiously applied themselves to the purpose of making this bond the most desirable security upon the market. They have done that for the purpose of developing the State of California through the means of its greatest resource, agriculture, and to insure that when these bonds were placed upon the market the irrigation districts would be able to borrow money at the lowest possible rate of interest and with the least loss upon the sale of the bonds. It is truly remarkable that in face of the onslaughts that have been made upon the legal position of these bonds, not only through the enactment of the Municipal Bankruptcy Act, but by numerous state enactments which have been passed for a like purpose, that nevertheless bonds of such districts as the Turlock Irrigation District still continue to sell at a premium. This was the object of California agriculturists to place upon the market a bond which would produce most for the people of the district and enable them to advance their construction at comparatively low cost for bond service. This they accomplished, and these bonds were widely distributed and sold by all leading financial interests of the state.

A certificate bearing the Great Seal of the State of California is still affixed to each irrigation bond, irrevocably declaring it to be a lawful investment for savings banks, insurance companies, widows and orphans funds, municipal deposits. (R. p. 138.) These are the only bonds ever issued in California so certified by the state. They would thus appear to be bonds of the State of California itself secured by the land within a certain geographical territory.

THE QUESTIONS INVOLVED.

The most important questions involved are:

Can a California irrigation district, a state legislative mandatory, be subjected to the jurisdiction of a Federal bankruptcy court?

Can the State of California consent to such jurisdiction?

Does the plan confirmed, which would scale down the principal of bonds of the district to 48.82¢ on the dollar with nothing for interest, violate constitutional principles in view of (1) that trust properties are withheld from bondholders, (2) that bonds of overlapping taxing districts will be paid in full, (3) that mortgages and deeds of trust, which are junior encumbrances, will be paid in full, (4) that the landowners will have the value of their equity increased at the expense of the bondholders, (5) that the assets of the district exceed its liabilities, (6) that the district has relief under the Districts Securities Commission Act?

Can such a plan be fair and equitable?

SUMMARY OF ARGUMENT.

In the following discussion we will attempt to group the argument under a few main heads, as follows:

I. The bankruptcy power of Congress does not extend to the states nor to their agencies nor mandatories.

II. The consent of the state will not complement the bankruptcy power of Congress.

III. The bankruptcy power is subject to the Fifth Amendment.

IV. The Waterford Irrigation District is not a subject of bankruptcy.

V. The plan of readjustment is essentially unjust, inequitable and discriminatory.

I.

THE BANKRUPTCY POWER OF CONGRESS DOES NOT EXTEND TO THE STATES NOR TO THEIR AGENCIES NOR MANDATORIES.

In 14 C. J. at page 73, we find this language:

> "Giving the term a true meaning, however, it may be said that public corporations are such as are created by the people or the government, state or federal, for political or governmental purposes, such as the United States, states, cities, towns, counties, school districts, and other municipal or political corporations and such as are created for other public purposes, although not political or municipal, where the whole interest belongs to the government, as in the case of purely public banks, hospitals, educational institutions, and the like—"

It is impossible to conceive of a public corporation that is not governmental in character.

In the case of *Fallbrook Irrigation District v. Bradley,* 164 U. S. 156, 174, decided nearly 40 years ago, the court said:

> "The formation of one of these irrigation districts amounts to the creation of a public corporation and their officers are public officers—."

An irrigation district being an agency or mandatory of the state is thus the state itself. The first and probably the most important point in the case is that the bankruptcy power of Congress does not extend, and cannot extend, to the state. We quote from the opinion of the very recent case decided by the Supreme Court on January 6, 1936, *United States v. Butler,* 56 Sup. Ct. Rep. 312:

> "It hardly seems necessary to reiterate that ours is a dual form of government; that in every state there are two governments—the state and the United States. Each state has all governmental powers save such as the people, by their Constitution, have conferred upon the United States, denied to the states, or reserved to themselves. The federal union is a government of delegated powers. It has only such as are expressly conferred upon it and such as are reasonably to be implied from those granted. In this respect we differ radically from nations where all legislative power, without restriction or limitation, is vested in a parliament or other legislative body subject to no restrictions, except the discretion of its members."

The Court also said:

"From the accepted doctrine that the United States is a government of delegated powers, it follows that those not expressly granted, or reasonably to be implied from such as are conferred, are reserved to the states or to the people.

"To forestall any suggestion to the contrary the Tenth Amendment was adopted. The same proposition otherwise stated, is that powers not granted are prohibited—

"It is an established principle that the attainment of a prohibited end may not be accomplished under the pretext of the exertion of powers which are granted. 'Should Congress in the execution of its powers adopt measures which are prohibited by the Constitution; or should Congress under the pretext of executing its powers pass laws for the accomplishment of objects not entrusted to the government, it would become the painful duty of this tribunal, should a case requiring such decision come before it, to say that such an act was not the law of the land.' McCollough v. Maryland, 4 Wheaton, 316. 'Congress cannot, under the pretext of executing delegated power, pass laws for the accomplishment of objects not entrusted to the Federal government, and we accept as an established doctrine that any provision of an act of Congress ostensibly enacted under power granted by the constitution not naturally and reasonably adopted to the effective exercise of such power, but solely to the achievement of something plainly within power reserved to the states, is invalid and cannot be enforced.' Linder v. United States, 268 U. S. 5."

In another part of the decision the Court stated:

"The courts are reluctant to adjudge any statute in contravention of them, but under our frame of government no other place is provided where the citizen may be heard to urge that the law fails to conform to a limit set upon the use of the granted power."

It is our contention under the municipal bankruptcy act that although Congress has the power to enact legislation on the subject of bankruptcy, it does not have the power to invade the reserved rights of states, and that by including state agencies, and practically the state itself, within the scope of bankruptcy, it has invaded those reserved powers. It also tends to usurp the power of sovereignty exercised through the right of taxation.

In another quite recent decision (December, 1935), that of *Hopkins Federal Savings and Loan Association, et al. v. Cleary,* 56 Supt. Ct. Rep. 235, written by Mr. Justice Cardozo, one of the so-called liberals upon the Supreme Court, three cases arising under the Home Owners' Loan Act of 1933 were under consideration, and the Court said:

"The Home Owners Loan Act, to the extent that it permits the conversion of state associations into federal ones in contravention of the laws of the place of their creation, is an unconstitutional encroachment upon the reserved power of the state." U. S. Constitutional Amendment Ten.

The Court declined to express its view as to whether Congress has power to create building and loan associations, but said:

"The critical question here is something very different. The critical question is whether along with such a power there goes also the power of putting an end to corporations created by the states and turn them into different corporations created by the Nation. * * * A corporation is a juristic person organized by government to accomplish certain ends which may be public or quasi public, though for other purposes of classification the corporation is described as private. * * * This is true of building and loan associations in Wisconsin and other states. * * * The state, which brings them into being, has an interest in preserving their existence, for only thus can they obtain the ends of their creation. They are more than business corporations. They have been organized and nurtured as quasi public instruments—how and when dissolved are matters of governmental policy which it would be an intrusion for another government to regulate by statute or decision, except when reasonably necessary for the fair and effective exercise of some other and cognate power explicitly conferred. * * * By the challenged act of Congress the same associations are dissolved in other ways for other causes, from being creatures of the state become creatures of the Nation. In this there is an invasion of the sovereignty or quasi sovereignty of Wisconsin, and an impairment of its public policy, which the state is privileged to redress as a suitor in the courts so long as the Tenth Amendment preserves a field of autonomy against federal encroachment. * * * We are not concerned at this time with the applicable rule in situations where the central government is at liberty to exercise a power that is exclusive as well as paramount. That is not the situation here.''

One of the particular features of the American constitutional arrangement is the so-called "dual sovereignty" or perhaps one had better say "divided sovereignty," by which a portion of the sovereign power of the people is divided between the states and the federal government. The powers of the State of California added to the powers of the United States comprise an incomplete sovereignty entity. The term "dual sovereignty" is nevertheless descriptive, for in its own realm the state and the federal government each is supreme, neither can be invaded by the other.

A second and also extremely important feature of the American constitutional arrangement is the reservation of power in the people. The powers of the national legislature added to the powers of the state legislature do not equal the total of sovereignty. The ultimate sovereignty of the people of the United States resides in Congress and legislatures or "conventions" of three-fourths of the states.

The written Constitution of the United States with the interpretation placed upon it by the Supreme Court is the document to which we must look for the grants of the reserve powers given the national legislature. The essential characteristics of a reserved power extend also the powers of Congress. It is in that respect that it is most noticeable. For such powers as are not granted to Congress are reserved to the people or to the several states. It is important to consider this feature of our Constitution when we shall hereafter discuss the question as to whether the consent of the State of California to the municipal bankruptcy act is a sufficient method of amending the Constitution, when the things which it purports to do are expressly prohibited by that Constitution, the point being that *Congress and one state cannot amend the Constitution of the United States.* It takes 36 states to do that. Thus it is clear that there are some powers which are beyond Congress and the State of California.

Consequently, in order to understand and analyze correctly questions as to whether or not a given enactment is constitutional, we must consider the power granted to Congress by the Constitution, the power granted to the state, and the power reserved to that ultimate sovereignty, the combination of Congress and three-fourths of the states.

That document, the Constitution of the United States, granted certain powers to Congress, it granted certain powers to the state, *but nowhere did it grant to a combination of a state and Congress any greater power than was granted to both the state and Congress.* Applying that condition to the facts of this case we reach the inescapable conclusion that Section 80 of the bankruptcy act and that also Chapter IV of Extra Session Laws of 1934 of the state legislature of California are each unconstitutional.

Admittedly, Congress of the United States does not have the power to enact a bankruptcy law applicable

to the State of California or any of its governmental
agencies without the consent of the state. The Hopkins decision would appear to be sufficient authority
for that.

Admittedly, the legislature of the State of California does not have the power to enact a bankruptcy
act applicable to one of its own state agencies. It is
prohibited from so doing by that provision of the Constitution which prohibits the state from impairing the
obligation of a contract.

*Surely, since the Constitution of the United States
prohibits the State of California from impairing the
obligation of the contract, the Congress of the United
States cannot empower the state to do so.*

*Equally, if the Constitution of the United States
prohibits Congress from passing a bankruptcy act
which would apply to a state or a state agency, the legislature of the State of California cannot pass an act to
authorize Congress to do so.*

The Bankruptcy Power of Congress.

Let us first consider what power Congress has without the aid of the states' consent to enact this legislation. It is the contention of appellants that Congress
either has the power to enact this legislation without
the aid of a state statute, or it has no power to do so
whatsoever.

In, *Re Cameron County Water Improvement District No. 1,* 9 Fed. Supp. 103, a decision which has
since been reversed, Judge Kennerly held:

"The leading case under the Act of 1898 (Hanover National Bank v. Moyses, supra), while

holding Section 8, Article 1, of the Constitution to be broad in its scope, falls far short of being authority for the view that Congress may confer Jurisdiction upon this Court to readjust, in the manner provided in this Act, Bonds issued by a Sovereign State and/or its Agency, and payable out of funds provided by taxation. * * * I conclude that Congress has no such power. And that this is true, no matter for what Governmental purpose such Agency may be created. *The controlling feature is that Petitioner, as shown by its Petition, is an Agency of the State, and one through which the State is exercising its Governmental functions of levying and collecting taxes to pay these bonds issued and sold to enable Petitioner to perform a Governmental function of irrigating arid lands.*

"To hold otherwise would be not only to go far beyond the real purpose and meaning of Section 8, Article 1, of the Federal Constitution, but to strike down the long recognized rule that under our dual system of government (National and State), one Government may not by its Laws impair the sovereignty of the other. Although the National Government and the State Governments exist within the same territorial limits, they act, each in their appropriate sphere, separately and independently, and it is indispensable to their preservation and safety that the sovereignty of each be preserved." (Italics ours.)

In *McCollough v. Maryland,* 4 Wheaton 428 (316), 4 L. Ed. 607 (579), the Supreme Court speaking through Chief Justice Marshall of the right of taxation, says:

"It is obvious that it is an incident of sovereignty and is coextensive with that to which it is an incident."

Quoting further from the opinion:

"If we measure the power of taxation residing in a state, by the extent of sovereignty which the people of a single state possess, and can confer on its government, we have an intelligent standard, applicable to every case to which the power may be applied. We have a principle which leaves the power of taxing the people and property of a state unimpaired; which leaves to a state the command of its resources and which places beyond its reach, all those powers which are conferred by the people of the United States on the Government of the Union, and all those means which are given for the purpose of carrying those powers into execution. We have a principle which is safe for the states, and safe for the Union. We are relieved, as we ought to be, from clashing sovereignty; from interfering powers; from a repugnancy between a right in one government to pull down what there is an acknowledged right in another to build up; from the incompatibility of a right in one government to destroy what there is a right in another to preserve."

Analogy of the Sixteenth Amendment.

The Sixteenth Amendment to the Constitution of the United States provides:

"The Congress shall have power to lay and collect taxes on income from whatever source derived."

The language is identical with that used in Article
I, Section 8, providing in part:

"The Congress shall have power * * * to establish * * * uniform laws on the subject of bankruptcies through the United States."

We may reasonably expect, therefore, that upon a
question of invasion of sovereignty of a state, and
the question of the power placed in Congress by these
sections of the Constitution, that judicial interpretation would be identical.

Let us examine, therefore, what has been the interpretation of the power of Congress under the Sixteenth Amendment.

In the case of *Pollock v. Farmers L. & T. Co.,* 157
U. S. 429, 158 U. S. 601, it was contended that although the property or revenues of the state or their
instrumentalities could not be taxed, nevertheless the
income derived from state, county and municipal securities could be taxed. In the opinion of the Court it
was stated by Fuller, C. J.:

"We think the same want of power to tax the
property or revenues of the state or their instrumentalities exist in relation to a tax on the income from their securities. * * * It is obvious that
taxation on the interest therefrom would operate
on the power to borrow before it is exercised and
would have a sensible influence on the contract
and that the taxing question is a tax on the power
of the state in their instrumentalities to borrow
money and consequently repugnant to the Constitution."

Let it be remarked that the *Pollock* case was decided before the enactment of the Sixteenth Amendment which became effective February 25th, 1913, and upon enactment of the Sixteenth Amendment the question arose as to whether the taxing power of the United States had been extended by this amendment so as to permit the taxation by the Congress of the income derived from bonds of the various states and of the subdivisions thereof.

In the case of *Kerbaugh Empire Co. v. Borrows,* 271 U. S. 170, the Supreme Court held that the effect of the Sixteenth Amendment was not to grant power to Congress to tax income "because that power it always has had." The real purpose of the amendment as stated in that case was to alter the decision in the Pollock case in that respect in which it declared the income tax law of 1894 unconstitutional on the grounds that it was a direct tax in so far as it related to income from property, real or personal.

In the case of *Fray v. Woodworth,* 270 U. S. 669, a writ of error was dismissed where the decision in 2 Fed. (2d) 725 was to the effect that a street railway system operated by a city is a governmental function, and an employee's salary derived from such services is exempt from taxation by the Federal Government.

And so in the case of *Bunn v. Willcuts,* 29 Fed. (2d) 132, it was held that this amendment did not give power to tax income from state or municipal obligations.

In the recent case of *Commissioner of Internal Revenue v. Harlan,* decided by this Court and cited in 80

Fed. (2d) 660, this Court held that the income of the attorney for the Bridge District is exempt from Federal income tax.

Now, if Congress has the power to enact a bankruptcy procedure applicable to a municipal corporation, purporting to authorize a voluntary bankruptcy petition on behalf of the municipality, it may likewise enact a bankruptcy statute authorizing an involuntary proceeding. If it may apply such a statute to an agency of the state with the consent of the state, surely it may do so without the consent of the state, and if it may apply such a measure to an agency of the state it may apply a similar measure to the state itself.

In *Bradford v. Fahey,* C. C. A., 4th Circuit, April 2, 1935, the Court said:

"But there can be no question, we think, but that the constitutional grant vests in Congress full power to deal with the relationship existing between debtors unable or unwilling to pay their debts and their creditors. * * * All phases of the relationship between a debtor financially embarrassed and his creditors are brought under the control of Congress by the constitutional grant of power * * *"

Whatever powers thus conferred may be exercised as Congress sees fit, without the consent or indeed even over the protests of the state.

In the *Matter of Quarles,* 158 U. S. 532, 535, the Court, speaking through Mr. Justice Gray, said:

"The United States are a nation whose powers of government, legislative, executive and judicial, within the sphere of action confided to it by the Constitution, are supreme and paramount."

See also *Logan v. United States,* 144 U. S. 263;
Ex Parte Siebold, 100 U. S. 371;
In re: Debs, 158 U. S. 564;

In the case of *McCollough v. Maryland* (supra), Chief Justice Marshall said:

"We think the sound construction of the constitution must allow to the national legislature that discretion with respect to the means by which the powers it confers are to be carried into execution * * *"

In *Kansas v. Colorado,* 206 U. S. 46, the Court quoted the foregoing statement of Mr. Chief Jutsice Marshall and concluded with these words:

"A statement which has become the settled rule of construction."

The Constitution did not emanate from the states. It came directly from the people themselves acting in their sovereign capacity. This is clearly expressed by Mr. Chief Justice Marshall in *Barron v. The Mayor of Baltimore,* 7 Peters 240, 247, 8 L. ed. 672, 674, as follows:

"The Constitution was ordained and established by the people of the United States for themselves, for their own government, and not for the government of the individual States. Each State established a constitution for itself, and in that constitution provided such limitations and restrictions on the powers of its particular government as its judgment dictated. The people of the United States framed such a government for the United

States as they supposed best adapted to their situation, and best calculated to promote their interests. The powers they conferred on this government were to be exercised by itself; and the limitations on power, if expressed in general terms, are naturally, and, we think, necessarily applicable to the government created by the instrument. They are limitations of power granted in the instrument itself; not of distinct governments, framed by different persons and for different purposes.''

See:

Chisholm v. Georgia, 2 Dallas 419, 470, 1 L. ed. 440, 462;

Dred Scott v. Stanford, 19 Howard 393, 404, 15 L. ed. 691, 700.

While it is true that the sovereign power so far as the national government is concerned, is vested in the people, yet at the time of the adoption of the Constitution there were thirteen separate independent sovereign states, and the constitution was adopted through machinery set up by the states, and the states retained all power not delegated expressly or by necessary implication to the central government. So that there might be no doubt upon the subject, the 10th Amendment was added.

In *Buffington v. Day,* 11 Wallace 113, 124, 20 L. ed. 122, 125, the Court said:

"It is a familiar rule of construction of the Constitution of the Union, that the sovereign powers vested in the state government by their respective constitutions, remained unaltered and unimpaired except so far as they were granted to the government of the United States. That the intention of the framers of the Constitution in this respect might not be misunderstood this rule of interpretation is expressly declared in the 10th article of the Amendments, namely: 'The powers not delegated to the United States are reserved to the states respectively, or to the people.' The government of the United States, therefore, can claim no powers which are not granted to it by the Constitution, and the powers actually granted must be such as are expressly given, or given by necessary implication.

The general government and the states, although both exist within the same territorial limits, are separable and distinct sovereignties, acting separately and independently of each other, within their respective spheres. The former, in its appropriate sphere, is supreme; but the states within the limits of their powers not granted; or, in the language of the 10th Amendment, 'reserved', are as independent of the general government as the government within its sphere is independent of the states. The relations existing between the two governments are well stated by the present Chief Justice in the case of Lane Co. v. Oregon, 7 Wall. 76, 19 L. ed. 104. 'Both the states and the United States', he observed, 'existed before the Constitution. The people, through that instrument, established a more perfect union, by substituting a national government, acting with ample powers directly upon the citizens, instead of the confederate government, which acted with powers, greatly restricted, only upon the states. But, in many of the articles of the Constitution, the necessary existence of the states, and within their proper spheres, the independent authority of the states are distinctly recognized. To them nearly the whole charge of interior regulation is committed or left; to them, and to the people, all powers, not expressly delegated to the national government, are reserved.' Upon looking into the Constitution it will be found that but a few of the articles in that instrument could be carried into practical effect without the existence of the states.''

See:

> *South Carolina v. United States,* 199 U. S. 437, 452, 50 L. ed. 226, 266;
> *McCollough v. Maryland,* 4 Wheat. 316, 325, 4 L. ed. 579, 600.

Under this constitutional authority and the unlimited power vested in Congress, Congress, where it has any power in that behalf, may provide for involuntary, as well as voluntary, bankruptcy. Indeed, voluntary bankruptcy proceedings were unknown in the law of England at the time of the adoption of the Constitution.

> *Continental Illinois National Bank & Trust Co. v. Rock Island Ry. Co.,* 79 L. Ed. 642 (Adv. Opinions).

It then becomes important to consider whether or not the language of the Constitution expressed in Article I, Section 8, Clause 4, was intended to apply to a state or its agencies.

If it was so intended then the power is unlimited. If the power is not unlimited then the power did not exist. We find no words of limitation.

IT IS A WELL RECOGNIZED PRINCIPLE OF CONSTRUCTION THAT GENERAL STATUTORY LANGUAGE DOES NOT APPLY TO THE SOVEREIGN TO ITS DISADVANTAGE.

In *Reclamation Dist. No. 551 v. County of Sacramento,* 134 Cal. 480, it is said:

"The principle of construction was stated in Mayrhofer v. Board of Education, 89 Cal. 110, to be, 'that the state is not bound by general words in a statute which would operate to trench upon its sovereign rights, injuriously affect its capacity to perform its functions, or establish a right of action against it.' This principle has been applied, and the Mayrhofer case has been approved in a variety of cases, and we think, should rule the present case. (Bates v. County of Santa Barbara, 90 Cal. 543; Whittaker v. County of Tuolumne, 96 Cal. 100; Skelly v. School District, 103 Cal. 652; Smith v. Broderick, 107 Cal. 644; County of Colusa v. County of Glenn, 117 Cal. 434; Russ & Sons v. Crichton, 117 Cal. 695; Witter v. Mission School District, 121 Cal. 350; Estate of Rover, 123 Cal. 614; Savings etc. Society v. San Francisco, 131 Cal. 356.)"

In *City of Pasadena v. Chamberlain,* 79 C. A. D. 75, 78, the Court stated:

"The charter is subject to the rule of legislative interpretation that 'the state *and its agencies* are not bound by general words limiting the rights and interests of its citizens' unless included expressly or by necessary implication. (Kubach v. McGuire, 199 Cal. 215.) * * *". (Italics supplied.)

In *Skelly v. Westminster School Dist.,* 103 Cal. 652, 656, the Court was considering a mechanic's lien law, and said:

"The language is general, and in its usual sense would include a schoolhouse, for that is a building and a structure. But it was held that the statute did not apply to public buildings. The rule is that the state is not bound by general words in a statute which would operate to trench upon its sovereign rights, or injuriously affect its capacity to perform its functions or establish a right against it."

In *City of Inglewood v. County of Los Angeles,* 207 Cal. 697, 707, the Court said:

"But it is well settled that the state *and its subordinate agencies, including municipal corporations,* are not bound by general words used in the statute. This doctrine was expressly approved by this court in a recent decision, wherein the question, and the authorities applicable thereto, were exhaustively discussed and considered. (C. J. Kubach v. McGuire, 199 Cal. 215 (248 Pac. 676.)" (Italics supplied.)

In *Liebman v. Richmond,* 103 Cal. App. 354, 459, the Court said:

"It is settled law that in the absence of express words to the contrary the state is not included within the general terms of a statute. (Whittaker v. County of Tuolumne, 96 Cal. 100; Mayrhofer v. Board of Education, 89 Cal. 110.)"

This proposition has likewise been well established by the Federal Courts.

In the case of *Guarantee Title & Trust Co. v. Title Guaranty and Surety Co.,* 224 U. S. 152, 156, 56 L. Ed. 706, 708, the Court was considering a bankruptcy case where it was claimed that the United States was bound as a creditor in a bankruptcy proceeding and where the question here under consideration became involved, the Court reviewed authorities and quoted with approval from *United States v. Herron,* 20 Wall. 251, 260, 22 L. Ed. 275, 278, and said:

"The decision was expressly put upon the ground 'that the sovereign authority of the country is not bound by the words of a statute unless named therein, if the statute tends to restrain or diminish the powers, rights, or interests of the sovereign.' There was much reasoning to sustain the proposition, and it was especially applied to discharges in bankruptcy. Expressing the general assent to the proposition announced, the court said:

'Greater unanimity of decision in the courts or of views among text writers can hardly be found upon any important question than exists in respect to this question in the parent country, nor is there any diversity of sentiment in our courts, Federal or State, nor among the text writers of this country.' "

In *United States v. Thompson,* 98 U. S. 486, 489, 490, 25 L. Ed. 194, 195, the Court said:

"Limitations derive their authority from statutes. The King was never held to be included, unless expressly named. No laches was imputable to him. These exemptions were founded upon considerations of public policy. It was deemed important that, while the sovereign was engrossed by the cares and duties of his office, the public should not suffer by the negligence of his servants. 'In a representative government, where the people do not and cannot act in a body, where their power is delegated to others, and must of necessity be exercised by them, if exercised at all, the reason for applying these principles is equally cogent.'

When the Colonies achieved their independence, each one took these prerogatives which had belonged to the Crown; and when the National Constitution was adopted, they were imparted to the new government as incidents of the sovereignty thus created. It is an exception equally applicable to all governments. U. S. v. Hoar (supra); People v. Gilbert, 18 Johns. 227; Bac. Abr., titl. Lim. of Act; Bac. Abr., tit. Prerog., E, 5-7; 5 Com. Dig. Parliament, R. 8; Chit. L. of Prerog., 379. * * *

The United States not being named in the Statute of Minnesota, are not within its provisions. It does not and cannot 'apply' to them. If it did, it would be beyond the power of the State to pass it, a gross usurpation, and void. It is not to be presumed that such was the intention of the State Legislature in passing the Act, as it certainly was not of Congress in enacting the law of 1789. U. S. v. Hoar (supra); Field v. U. S., 9 Pet. 182. * * *''

In *Marshall v. New York,* 254 U. S. 380, 382, 65 L. ed. 315, 317, the Court said:

"* * * The single question is presented whether the state of New York has priority in payment out of the general assets of the debtor over other creditors whose claims are not secured by act of the parties nor accorded a preference, by reason of their nature, by the state legislature or otherwise.

"At common law the Crown of Great Britain, by virtue of a prerogative right, had priority over all subjects for the payment of a debtor's property of all debts due it. The priority was effective alike whether the property remained in the hands of the debtor, or had been placed in the possession of a third person, or was in custodia legis. The priority could be defeated or postponed only through the passing of title to the debtor's property, absolutely or by way of lien, before the sovereign sought to enforce his right. Giles v. Grover, 9 Bing. 128, 139, 157, 183, 131 Eng. Reprint, 563, 2 Moore & S. 197, 1 Clark & F. 72, 6 Eng. Reprint, 843, 6 Bligh, N. R. 277; 5 Eng. Reprint, 598, 11 Eng. Rul. Cas. 550; 39 L. T. N. S. 53, 26 Week. Rep. 885. Compare United States v. National Surety Co. decided by this court November 8, 1920 (254 U. S. 73, ante, 143, 41 Sup. Ct. Rep. 29.) The first Constitution of the state of New York (adopted in 1717) provided that the common law of England, which, together with the statutes, constituted the law of the colony on April 19, 1775, should be and continue the law of the state, subject to such alterations as its legislature might thereafter make. This provision was embodied, in substance, in the later Constitution. The courts of New York decided that, by virtue of this constitutional provision, the state, as sovereign, succeeded to the Crown's prerogative right of priority; and that the priority was not limited to amounts due for taxes, but extended alike to all debt due to the state, e. g., to amounts due on a general deposit of state funds in a bank. Re Carnegie Trust Co., 151 App. Div. 606, 136 N. Y. Supp. 466, 206 N. Y. 390, 46 L. R. A.

(N. S.) 260, 99 N. E. 1096. This priority has been enforced by the courts of New Yory under a great variety of cases extending over more than half a century. It has been enforced as a right, and not as a rule of administration.

"This priority arose and exists independently of any statute. The legislature has never, in terms, limited its scope; and the courts have rejected as unsound every contention made that some statute before them for construction had, by implication, effected a repeal or abridgment of the priority. The only changes of the right made by statutes have been by way of enlarging its scope in certain cases. Thus, while by the common law of England (Rex. ex. rel. Braddock v. Watson, 3 Price 6, 146 Eng. Reprint 174), and by that of New York (Wise v. L. & C. Wise Co., 153 N. Y. 507, 511, 47 N. E. 788), the priority does not obtain over a specific lien created by the debtor before the sovereign undertakes to enforce its right, the legislature of New York extended the prerogative right, so as to give certain taxes priority over prior encumbrances. An extension of this nature is found in Sec. 197 of the Tax Law, which declares in respect to the annual franchise tax, that 'such tax shall be a lien upon and bind all the real and personal property of the corporation, joint stock company or association liable to pay the same from the time when it is payable until the same is paid in full.' (Consol. Laws, chap. 60.) By reason of that provision the annual franchise tax takes priority over encumbrances on the corporate property. New York Terminal Co. v. Gaus, 204 N. Y. 512, 98 N. E. 11. Under the earlier law a debt for franchise taxes was not a 'technical lien on specific property,' and had been ordered paid out of moneys in receivers' hands. Central Trust Co. v. New York City & N. R. Co., 110 N. Y. 250, 259, 1 L. R. A. 260, 18 N. E. 92. In the case at bar the district judge relied upon Sec. 197 as justifying him in giving priority to the claim for annual franchise taxes, and in denying priority to the claim for license fees, because, in respect to the latter, no corresponding provision is to be found in the Tax Law. But he had no occasion to seek statutory support for the priority sought by the state, since here it does not seek to displace any prior lien. It asks merely to have its prerogative right enforced against property on which there is no prior lien and upon which it is impossible to levy, because the property has been taken out of hands of the debtor and placed in the custody of the court for purposes of protection and distribution.

"Whether the priority enjoyed by the state of New York is a prerogative right or merely a law of administration is a matter of local law. Being such, the decisions of the highest court of the state as to the existence of the right and its incidents will be accepted by the court as conclusive. Compare Lewis v. Monson, 151 U. S. 545, 549, 38 L. ed. 265, 14 Sup. Ct. Rep. 424; St. Anthony Falls Water Power Co. v. St. Paul Water Comrs., 168 U. S. 349, 358, 42 L. ed. 497, 501, 18 Sup. Ct. Rep. 157; Archer v. Greenville Sand & Gravel Co., 233 U. S. 60, 68, 69, 58 L. ed. 850, 853, 854, 34 Sup. Ct. Rep. 567; Guffey v. Smith, 237 U. S. 101, 113, 59 L. ed. 856, 863, 35 Sup. Ct. Rep. 526. The priority of the state extends to all property of the debtor within its borders, whether the debtor be a resident or a nonresident, and whether the property be in his possession or in custodia legis. The property is, therefore, enforceable against the property in the hands of a receiver appointed by a Federal court within the state. * * *''

This rule was recognized in the Colonies and passed on from the Colonies to the new states. As we will see, when a new state is admitted to the union, it comes into the Union on an equal footing with the original states in all respects. The sovereignty being reserved to the state, all of the states possess prerogatives of a sovereign, one of which is that the sovereign is not bound by general language which works to his disadvantage. Since a bankruptcy law which would subject the fiscal affairs of the state to an involuntary proceeding would not only be to the disadvantage of the sovereign state, but could actually destroy the independence of the state, it is impossible to conceive that the states, or the people in their sovereign capacity, intended, by the general language of the bankruptcy clause, that the independence of the states should thus be put in jeopardy.

In *Coyle v. Smith,* 221 U. S. 559, 566, 570, 571, 55 L. ed. 853, 858, 859, the Court said:

" 'This Union' was and is a union of states, equal in power, dignity, and authority, each competent to exert that residuum of sovereignty not delegated to the United States by the Constitution itself."

In *Buffington v. Day,* 11 Wall. 113, 126, 20 L. ed. 122, 126, the Court said:

"The supremacy of the general government, therefore, so much relied on in the argument of the counsel for the plaintiff in error, in respect to the question before us, cannot be maintained. *The two governments are upon an equality,* and the question is whether the power 'to lay and collect taxes' enables the general government to tax the salary of a judicial officer of the state, which officer is a means or instrumentality employed to carry into execution one of its most important functions, the administration of the laws, and which concerns the exercise of a right reserved to the states.

"We do not say the mere circumstance of the establishment of the judicial department, and the appointment of officers to administer the laws, being among the reserved powers of the state, disables the general government from levying the tax, as that depends upon the express power 'to lay and collect taxes,' *but it shows that it is an original inherent power never parted with, and in respect to which the supremacy of that government does not exist,* and is of no importance in determining the question; and further, that being an original and reserved power, and the judicial officers appointed under it being a means or instrumentality employed to carry it into effect, the right and necessity of its unimpaired exercise, and the exemption of the officer from taxation by the general government, stands upon as solid a ground and are maintained by principles and reasons as cogent as those which led to the exemption of the Federal officer in Dobbins v. Erie Canal Co., supra, from taxation by the state; *for, in this respect, that is, in respect to the reserved powers, the state is as sovereign and independent as the general government.* And if the means and instrumentalities employed by that government to carry into operation the powers granted to it are necessarily, and, for the sake of self-preservation, exempt from taxation by the state, why are not those of the states depending upon their reserved powers, for like reasons, equally exempt from Federal taxation? Their unimpaired existence in the one case is as essential as in the other. *It is admitted that there is no express provision in the Constitution that prohibits the general government from taxing the means and instrumentalities* of the states, nor is there any prohibiting the states from taxing the means and instrumentalities of that government. In both cases the exemption rests upon necessary implication, and is upheld by the great law of self-preservation; *as any government, whose means employed in conducting its operations, if subject to the control of another and distinct government can exist only at the mercy of that government. Of what avail are these means if another power may tax them at discretion?"* (Italics supplied.)

See Rose's Notes, this case.

The *Buffington* case is without doubt the leading authority upon the subject of the right of the United States to tax an agency of the state, and it is interesting to note that the Court uses the strong language used in the *Buffington* decision regarding the right of the United States to tax an officer of the state, not-withstanding the constitutional provision: "The Congress shall have power to lay and collect taxes, duties, imposts, and excises * * *'' (Art. I, Sec. 8, Cl. 1.)

If Congress has power to apply a bankruptcy statute to an agency or political subdivision of the state, it also has the power to apply a bankruptcy statute to the state itself.

The state itself is a considerable borrower. State bonds are issued for all manner of public purposes. It is not unusual to find the state capitol constructed with funds borrowed upon a bond issue, and from that purpose down through the long category of state activities. Practically all state demands are paid by warrants or other evidence of indebtedness. If Congress has the power to enact a bankruptcy statute that will apply to an agency of the state—an arm—a department of the state—then there is no doubt but that Congress can likewise enact a bankruptcy statute that will apply to all of the fiscal affairs of the state itself. The fact that Congress has not exercised its full power and might not do so is no derogation of the power itself. If Congress can do what it has attempted to do by Section 80, then it can go all of the way. If it has the power, no one can be heard to complain against the exercise of that power. We maintain that Congress does not have the power, and in the very nature of things could not have the power. The nation, being sovereign in its field, and the state, being sovereign in its field, neither can exercise a power over the other that is not expressly given or reserved to the one attempting to exercise the power, or necessarily implied. The bankruptcy clause, being in general language, it is inconceivable that the independent sovereign state or the people intended that the sovereign could, through a bankruptcy statute, enacted under this general language, be subject to a federal court of bankruptcy and have a receiver in bankruptcy put in charge of the fiscal affairs of the state.

II.

THE CONSENT OF THE STATE WILL NOT COMPLEMENT THE BANKRUPTCY POWER OF CONGRESS.

We have seen that if the Congress has power to enact a bankruptcy statute applicable to the state or its agencies, it may do so without the consent of the state. In other words, if the power exists, it is plenary and can be exercised by the Congress as the Congress may determine. If the power does not exist so that it can be exercised by Congress unimpaired and unhindered, the power cannot be conferred by the state. The state has no control over it whatsoever except by concurrent action through an amendment to the Constitution, which, of course, is in no wise involved here.

The argument that in some instances the state may waive its immunity as a sovereign has no application. In this case, clearly the bonds are solemn contracts and the law at the time the contracts were made has become a part of the contracts. The state is prohibited by its own Constitution (Art. I, Sec. 16) from impairing the obligation of contracts, and the state is further prohibited by Article I, Section 10, of the Federal Constitution, from impairing the obligation of contract. This proceeding clearly is an impairment of the obligation of contract. Therefore, it cannot prevail except under the bankruptcy clause. The consent of the state, therefore, becomes wholly immaterial, except in a procedural way which Congress may require, but it has nothing whatsoever to do with the power. If the power exists, it may be exercised. If it does not exist, the state cannot give it. Furthermore, it will be kept in mind that there is a third party. In fact, it is the third party, primarily, that the act is attempting to reach (the creditor). There is no analogy between a bankruptcy proceeding and a suit against the state. There is nothing in the Constitution of either the nation or the state that hinders the state from waiving its immunity to be sued, but both of these Constitutions prohibit the impairment of contract. We get back to the fundamental proposition that if the act is good, then the authority to enact it must be found in the bankruptcy clause. We cannot look elsewhere for it. If the authority is not there, it does not exist. Since the state has not consented in the Constitution to being treated as a bankrupt, the power does not exist and the act must fail.

We have seen that the whole power which Congress may exercise may be exercised without the consent of anyone. Therefore, if Congress has the power to legislate under the bankruptcy clause upon states, it may do so without the consent of the state. Consent is not necessary to the exercise of the power. The fact that Congress has provided for consent is a procedural limitation and does not go to the power. Indeed, since the state is prohibited from impairing the obligation of contract, its consent beyond procedure upon a subject to which Congress has full jurisdiction is void.

On March 3, 1936, the Circuit Court of Appeals of the Fifth Circuit reversed the case of *Cameron County Water Improvement District v. Ashton,* the Appellate Court holding that Congress

> "may extend the jurisdiction of the inferior Courts of the United States over the states of the Union where the state is seeking relief and a federal question is presented for decision."

We respectfully submit that in our opinion there is a vital distinction between the authorities relied upon by the Appellate Court and the case at bar. In *Ames v. Kansas,* 111 U. S. 449, 28 L. Ed. 482, 4 Sup. Ct. Rep. 437, the defendant, railroad company, claimed a right under an act of Congress and, therefore, a federal question was present, the State of Kansas commenced the suit. The Courts of the United States had jurisdiction. The question as stated was the construction of an act of Congress.

In *Cowles v. Mercer County,* 7 Wall. 118, 19 L. Ed. 86, it was held that Mercer County, Illinois, a municipal corporation, might be sued in Federal Court, the statute of Illinois providing that the county could sue or be sued, the plaintiff being a nonresident of the state.

In *Lincoln County v. Luning,* 133 U. S. 529, 33 L. Ed. 766, 10 Sup. Ct. Rep. 363, it was again held that a county might be made a defendant in a Federal Court, the Supreme Court stating:

> "The Constitution of the State of Nevada, explicitly provides for the liability of counties to suit."

In *Loeb v. Columbia Township,* 179 U. S. 472, 45 L. Ed. 280, 21 Sup. Ct. Rep. 174, action was against the trustees of Columbia Township in Hamilton County, Ohio. One of the questions presented was whether the defendant township is a corporation. The Supreme Court states:

> "Now by the statutes of Ohio, the defendant township was constituted a body politic and corporate for the purpose of enjoying and exercising the rights and privileges conferred upon it by law, and was made capable of suing and being sued, pleading and being impleaded."

The Eleventh Amendment and the decision thereunder have, we submit, no relevancy here. Its enactment arose out of a special situation. The Constitution (Art. III, Sec. 2) had declared that the judicial power of the United States should extend 'to controversies between a state and citizens of another state'. In *Chisholm v. Georgia,* 2 Dall. 419, it was held that under this provision a state might be sued, without its consent, by a citizen of another state. As Justice Bradley says, in *Hans v. Louisiana,* 134 U. S. 1, 11:

> "That decision * * * created such a shock of surprise throughout the country that, at the first

meeting of Congress thereafter, the Eleventh Amendment to the Constitution was almost unanimously proposed, and was in due course adopted * * *. This amendment, expressing the will of the ultimate sovereignty of the whole country, superior to all legislatures and courts, actually reversed the decision of the Supreme Court. It *did not in terms prohibit suits by individuals against the states,* but declared that the Constitution should not be construed to impart any power to authorize the bringing of such suits.''

In the same case, *Hans v. Louisiana,* 134 U. S. 1, 16, Mr. Justice Bradley discusses the evil intended to be corrected by the Eleventh Amendment. He points out that ''the suability of a state without its consent was a thing unknown to the law'', and cites in support of this doctrine the dissenting opinion of Mr. Justice Iredell in *Chisholm v. Georgia.* The purpose of the amendement, as he says, was to reestablish the old rule that a state could not be sued unless it voluntarily consented. He says further:

''Undoubtedly a state may be sued by its own consent, as was the case in Curran v. Arkansas, et al., 14 How. 304, 309, and in Clark v. Barnard, 108 U. S. 436, 447. The suit in the former case was prosecuted by virtue of a state law which the Legislature passed in conformity to the constitution of that state.''

In the light of the circumstances surrounding the adoption of the Eleventh Amendment, as thus explained, it is quite clear that it did not intend, by restoring the states' immunity from suit in the Federal Courts, to do away with their privilege to waive such immunity and submit to suit. The purpose of the Eleventh Amendment was simply to restore a privilege, and it did not, therefore, preclude the waiver of the privilege. As Chief Justice Marshall, in *Cohens v. Virginia,* 6 Wheat. 406, says:

> "That its motive was not to maintin the sovereignty of a state from the degradation supposed to attend an involuntary appearance before the tribunal of the nation, may be inferred from the terms of the amendment."

It was quite natural, therefore, that in *Clark v. Barnard,* 108 U. S. 436, 28 L. Ed. 780, the Supreme Court should have held that where a state was sued and "appeared in the cause and presented and prosecuted a claim to the fund in controversy, and thereby made itself a party to the litigation to the full extent required for its complete determination", it had waived its privilege and that the Federal Court might assume jurisdiction.

And so, in *Gunter v. Atlantic Coast Line,* 200 U. S. 273, 50 L. Ed. 477, it was held, in conformity with these earlier decisions that "although a state may not be sued without its consent, such immunity is a privilege which may be waived, and hence where a state voluntarily becomes a party to a cause and submits its rights for judicial determination, it will be bound thereby and cannot escape the result of its own voluntary act by invoking the prohibitions of the Eleventh Amendment."

These decisions, we submit, have not the remotest bearing on the present question. They hold simply

that the Eleventh Amendment was intended to restore to the states an optional privilege. They afford
no color of excuse for the claim that the inherent
sovereignty of the state and its right to control its
own fiscal affairs may be destroyed or impaired, or
a new power conferred upon the Federal Government, by a mere act of a state legislature.

In the case of *Commissioner of Internal Revenue
v. Harlan,* 80 Fed. (2d) 660, decided by this Court
December 19, 1935, this Court said:

> "Petitioner contends that because Section 10
> of the Bridge and Highway District Act con-
> ferred upon the Golden Gate Bridge and High-
> way District 'the power to sue and be sued', it
> changed the governmental character of the
> agency. Immunity of suit is an inherent qualtiy
> of sovereignty. The fact that a sovereign may
> waive its immunity does not alter its nature or
> effect the governmental character of the function
> its agency may be performing."

This Court avoided committing the error in logical
reasoning that was committed by the Fifth Circuit
in its decision in the case of *Cameron County Water
Improvement District No. 1 v. Ashton,* for the Court
there said:

> "If the state chooses to exercise the sovereign
> authority she has the right to do so and the act
> is without effect."

Saying also:

> "The sovereign state may not be sued by an
> individual without her consent, but Congress
> may extend the jurisdiction of the inferior courts

of the United States over the states of the Union where the state is seeking relief and a federal question is presented for a decision.''

It seems to us that the Fifth Circuit entirely missed the point, for this is not a question of whether a state can be sued, but is rather a question of whether a state can surrender its sovereignty.

But the question here, however, is whether or not the power of the state can supplement the power of Congress to enact a bankruptcy law. To hold that it could would be to hold that the Constitution of the United States can be amended by the consent of a single state.

At 65 *Corpus Juris*, p. 1254, it is said:

"The United States has no inherent sovereign powers, and no inherent common-law prerogatives and it has no power to interfere in the personal or social relations of citizens by virtue of authority deducible from the general nature of sovereignty, but it has so much of the royal prerogatives as belonged to the king of England in his capacity of parens patriae or universal trustee. It has no general police powers. *It has been said that the United States takes no power or authority from state constitutions or laws.''* (Italics ours.)

The minority views of the House Judiciary Committee on this act contain the following statement (73d Congress, 1st Session, Report No. 207):

"In our view there is no authority to enact such legislation even for municipal corporations which have received the prior consent of the state in which they are incorporated. * * *

Either Congress alone has the power to subject municipal corporations to the jurisdiction of the United States courts of bankruptcy, or else the power does not exist. * * *

We conclude, in view of the foregoing, that there is to say the least, the greatest doubt of the constitutionality of this bill, with reference to municipal corporations. We conclude, also, that as to all other political subdivisions, there is no authority whatever for Congress to subject them to the Federal bankruptcy jurisdiction, either alone or in conjunction with state enabling legislation. Therefore, we feel the bill should be rejected on its evident lack of constitutionality in this latter respect and its doubtful constitutionality as to municipal corporations."

Charles H. Weston, Special Assistant to the U. S. Attorney General, has given his opinion on this legislation in the following language (Apr. 21, 1933 in re H. R. 3083):

"But in my opinion it is beyond the power of Congress, even with state consent, to enact any bankruptcy law which is applicable to the States themselves or to political subdivisions which are merely departments or branches of the State government."

As a preliminary to this expression of opinion, Mr. Weston had said:

"It seems foreign to the conception of bankruptcy to extend its remedies and the jurisdiction of this Court to a purely governmental body. Historically, at least, bankruptcy legislation represented remedies and relief which the sovereign granted to adjust the relations between creditor and debtor when private persons, individual or corporate, became insolvent. It was never supposed that the sovereign itself could adjust its own debts through the medium of the bankruptcy court. For the United States to provide such relief for the States would seem, under our dual system of government, equally beyond the scope of bankruptcy legislation. It would, therefore, seem that Congress could bring within the scope of its bankruptcy legislation only private debtors and those other corporate bodies which, although they exercise by delegation certain governmental functions, also have a definite private or proprietary capacity, in which capacity they have many of the characteristics of a private juristic person. * * * In my opinion the Constitution did not mean to permit Congress, through the medium of bankruptcy laws, to break down the boundaries between Federal and State power even if the States gave their consent. It follows that, if the Constitution does not confer this power upon Congress, its lack of authority cannot be supplied by acquiescence of the States. The situation is entirely different where the Constitution itself provides that Congress can act only with State consent or that the States can act only if Congress consents." (See Art. 1, Sec. 10, Clauses 2 and 3; Art. IV, Sec. 5, Clause 1.)

The So-Called Enabling Act of the Legislature of the State of California, Being Assembly Bill No. 12 or Chapter IV, Extra Session Laws of 1934, is Unconstitutional.

In *Hershey v. Cole,* 130 Cal. App. 683, 688, 695, 697, 699, the Court said:

"* * * This presents the important question: Does there exist in legal effect a contract between the owners of lands upon which an assessment has been levied, and the holders of bonds purchased upon the faith of the security afforded by the unpaid portion of the assessment at the date of the issuance of the bonds?

In Rorick et al. v. Board of Commissioners of Everglades Drainage Dist. et al., 57 Fed. (2d) 1048, tried before Circuit Judge Bryan, and District Judges Sheppard and Strum, a case involving the rights of bondholders of a drainage district, the law is laid down as follows: 'Legislation by authority of which bonds are issued, and their payment provided for, becomes a constituent part of the contract with the bondholders. Such a contract is within the protection of the Constitution, article I, section 10. The obligation of the bond contract, of which such legislation is a part, cannot be impaired, nor its fulfillment hampered or obstructed by subsequent legislation to the prejudice of the vested rights of bondholders. This rule has reference to subsequent legislation which affects the contract directly, and not incidentally, or only by consequence.' (Citing a number of cases.) 'A different result would leave nothing of the contract, but an abstract right—of no practical value—and render the protection of the Constitution a delusion.' * * * An impairment occurs when the value of the contract has been diminished by subsequent legislation. The question of impairment is not one of degree, but of encroaching in any respect upon the obligation—dispensing with any part of its force. (Citing a number of cases.) Though the state cannot by contract surrender its sovereign prerogatives in the performance of essential governmental duties (citing authorities), nevertheless, when the state authorizes a taxing subdivision to contract by issuing bonds and to exercise the power of local taxation to the extent necessary to meet such obligations, the power thus given cannot be withdrawn so long as its exercise is necessary to satisfy the vested rights of bondholders. In such cases, the state and the subordinate taxing unit are equally bound. 'The power given becomes a trust which the donor cannot annul, and which the donee is bound to execute.' (Citing a number of authorities.) * * *

It also appears to be well settled that the law in force under which bonds are issued, enters into and becomes a part of the contract. This is clearly set forth in the well-considered case of Oklahoma Cotton Growers Assn. v. Salyer, 114 Okl. 77 (243 Pac. 232). We quote therefrom as follows: 'The existing statutes and the settled law of the land at the time a contract is made become a part of it, and must be read into it. All contracts are therefore to be construed in the light of the rules and principles of law applicable to the subject matter of the transaction, and those rules and principles control the rights of the parties, except where the contract discloses an intention to depart therefrom. However, from the fact that every contract, not expressly providing to the contrary, is presumed to have been made with reference to the then existing state of the law, it follows that if a subsequent change is made therein which in any degree affects such contract, such change is presumed to be excepted therefrom. (6 R. C. L. p. 855; 13 C. J. p. 247; Deweese v. Smith, 106 Fed. 438 (45 C. C. A. 408, 66 L. R. A. 971); cases in note to Union Central Ins. Co. v. Pollard, 36 L. R. A. 271.) The laws upon the subject of a contract are read into and become a part thereof to the same extent as though they were written into its terms. (Armour Packing Co. v. United States, 153 Fed. 1 (82 C. C. A. 135, 14 L. R. A. (N. S.) 400).)' * * *

To the same effect is the case of Runnells v. Oklahoma City, 150 Okl. 292 (1 Pac. (2d) 740). It is there held that existing laws under which street improvement bonds are issued become a part of the contract, so that obligations thereof cannot be impaired by subsequent changes in the law. * * *

That the law in existence at the time that bonds are issued becomes a part of the contract and cannot thereafter be changed without violating the constitutional prohibitions is held in the case of Nelson v. Pitts, Treasurer of Muskogee County, 126 Okl. 191 (259 Pac. 533, 53 A. L. R. 1137). A somewhat similar principle is involved by an act which purports to extend the time before a deed can be secured by a purchaser under a tax sale. The authorities are numerous to the effect that such an act cannot be given retroactive effect. (See Rott v. Steffens, as City Controller, etc., 229 Mich. 241 (201 N .W. 227, 38 A. L. R. 224).) * * *

As we have seen by the cases cited, the rights and obligations of the bondholder are based upon the law as it stood at the time of the issuance of the bonds, and cannot be changed so as to alter the obligations specified in the bond. It necessarily follows that the rights and obligations of the property owners are reciprocal. His obligations cannot be increased nor lessened. The portion of the assessment, or rather, the amount of the installment that is to be paid by the landowner at each annual period is fixed when the contract is completed, by the sale of the bonds. We find no negative answer to this contention of the appellants.''

In *Islais Land Co. Ltd. v. Matheson, Treas.,* 78 C. A. D. 816, 819, it is stated:

"There are unquestionably many decisions to the effect that a statute existing at the time of the issuance of bonds, which statute provides for the security of the bonds or the manner of enforcement thereof, are part of the contract with the bondholders, and a statute cannot be validly passed which either impairs a substantial right thereunder or materially alters the remedy for enforcing the security of the bonds. (County of San Diego v. Childs, 217 Cal. 109; Chapman v. Jocelyn, 182 Cal. 294.) No such situation, however, is here presented. * * *''

See:

> *Selby v. Oakdale Irr. Dist.,* 89 C. A. D. 442, 448;
> *Nevada Nat. Bk. v. Bd. of Supervisors,* 5 Cal. App. 651.

First of all, therefore, the statute of the State of California violates the provisions of the National Constitution and of the State Constitution each prohibiting the state from passing any law "impairing the obligation of contracts". Article I, Section 16, California Constitution. This applies not only to private contracts but to contracts of the state. Not only has the State of California in the exercise of its sovereign power authorized the issuance of the obligation, but it has passed legislation authorizing the assessment of special liens against real property as security for the payment of the obligation, and has enacted legislation that these assessments shall be repeatedly and continuously made until the bonds are paid, and in the event the assessments are not paid that the lands may be sold, the state having exercised its sovereign power in the issuance of the bonds. What authority did the enactment of Section 80 confer upon the state or any of its mandatories? Can Congress by virtue of Article I, Section 8, tell the sovereign State of California that it can repudiate its obligation, do something which the state itself cannot constitutionally do, or can the State of California authorize Congress to exceed its constitutional limitation? If Congress can say to the State of California and its governmental agencies that it can repudiate its obligation, can it not also authorize the state to "coin money", to "regulate commerce" or to do any other act which has been delegated specifically to the Federal Government?

A state can no more impair the obligation of a contract made by it with an individual than a contract between two citizens. (*Lloyd v. Blanding,* 54 Cal. 41.)

An act extinguishing the debts of a city is void. (*Smith v. Morris,* 2 Cal. 534.)

The provisions of the act for the organization of irrigation districts, as to the extent of the liability of the land, created a contract between the landowners and the state which could not be impaired by state legislation. (*Merchants National Bank v. Escondido Irrigation District,* 144 Cal. 329, 77 Pac. 937.)

A law providing for a tax for the payment of bonds to be issued thereunder becomes a part of the contract and cannot be repealed. (*English v. Sacramento County Supervisors,* 19 Cal. 172.)

See, also:

6 *Cal. Juris.* 767;

6 *R. C. L.* 333, 334;

Whiteman v. Anderson-Cottonwood Irrigation District, 60 C. A. 234.

A bankruptcy law which impairs a contract is void. (*Sturges v. Crowninshield,* 4 Wheaton 122.)

An act destroying the legal remedy upon a contract impairs the obligation of the contract. (*Bates v. Gregory,* 89 Cal. 387, 26 Pac. 891; *Barber v. Galloway,* 195 Cal. 1, 231 Pac. 34.)

The laws of the state under which a contract is made are considered provisions of the contract, and the contract, so defined, cannot be substantially altered by the legislature.

"It is settled that all the laws of a state existing at the time a contract is made which affect the rights of the parties to the contract enter into and become a part of it, and are as obligatory upon all courts which assume to give a remedy on such contracts as if they were referred to or incorporated in the terms of the contract. (Citing cases.) The remedy, where it affects substantial rights, is included in the term 'obligation of a contract', and the remedy cannot be altered so as to materially impair such obligations. (Citing cases, including Edwards v. Kearzey, 96 U. S. 600.) In the latter case it is said: 'The obligation of a contract includes everything within its obligatory scope. Among these elements nothing is more important than the means of enforcement. This is the breath of its vital existence. Without it, the contract, as such, in the view of the law, ceases to be, and falls into the class of those imperfect obligations, as they are termed, which depend for their fulfillment upon the will and conscience of those upon whom they rest."

Welsh v. Cross, 146 Cal. 621, 106 Am. St. Rep. 63, 2 Ann. Cas. 796, 81 Pac. 229.

The above rule and reasoning applies to bonds.

"The constitution forbids the passage of a law impairing the obligation of a contract. (Art. I, sec. 16.) It follows that a law enacted after such contract is made, and which materially alters the remedy of the bondholder to enforce his lien by means of a sale, or the rights of the owner under the law existing at the time the bond was issued, cannot apply to previous contracts and can have only a prospective effect. (Houston v. McKenna, 22 Cal. 553.) The case in this aspect is not distinguishable from Welsh v. Cross (supra), wherein it was held that a law extending the time for redemption from a foreclosure sale impaired the obligation of a mortgage executed before its enactment."

Chapman v. Jocelyn, 182 Cal. 294, 187 Pac. 962.

The 1934 Act (Assembly Bill 4, extra session 1934) removes a disability to which taxing districts were subject at the time of the issuance of the bonds; it permits a defense, an abrogation of the remedy of the bondholder, which did not exist at the time the contracts were made.

The districts had no power to file a petition in bankruptcy, of any sort, prior to the Act of 1934. It is submitted that, as to matters directly affecting contracts and their enforcement, the powers of the districts as set forth in the law by which they were created and under which they functioned, as it existed at the time of the making of the contract, became a portion of that contract; and the absence of a power, to the same extent and degree. The passage of an Act permitting taxing districts to file under Section 80 was a positive act of the state creating a new means by which such districts might defend themselves against the enforcement of contract obligations previously incurred, and a new burden upon bondholders, which would not have been available under the law as it stood at the time the contract was made, nor at any time without definite action by the state.

"The laws which exist at the time and place of the making of a contract, and where it is to be performed, enter into and form a part of it. This embraces alike those which affect its validity, construction, discharge, and enforcement.

Nothing is more material to the obligation of a contract than the means of its enforcement. The ideas of validity and remedy are inseparable, and both are parts of the obligation which is guaranteed by the Constitution against impairment.

The obligation of a contract is the law which binds the parties to perform their agreement.

Any impairment of the obligation of a contract, the degree of impairment is immaterial, is within the prohibition of the Constitution.

The states may change the remedy, provided
no substantial right secured by the contract is
impaired. Whenever such a result is produced
by the act in question, to that extent it is void.
The states are no more permitted to impair the
efficacy of a contract in this way than to attack
its validity in any other manner. Against all
assaults coming from that quarter, whatever guise
they may assume, the contract is shielded by the
Constitution. It must be left with the same force
and effect, including the substantial means of
enforcement which existed when it was made.
The guaranty of the Constitution gives it protection to that extent. Von Hoffman v. Quincy,
4 Wall. 535, 18 L. Ed. 403.''

Walker v. Whitehead, 16 Wall. 310, 314, 21 L.
Ed. 357.

It is clear from the above and many other decisions
that a law abrogating a remedy is a law impairing the
obligations of contract. And it must follow that a
law permitting a creditor to do an act which he could
not legally do before the passage of such law, the
necessary effect of which is to make available to him
a defense to enforcement of a contract which he did
not have when the contract was made, is a law impairing the obligation of contract; particularly, when
this is the only effect of the law, and the law was
passed for that specific purpose.

It is submitted, therefore, that the law permitting
taxing districts to file under Section 80 of the Bankruptcy Act, is a positive act of the state by its legislature; that it cannot be so construed as to make

this privilege available to taxing districts as to contracts entered into before the passage of said law, and that as to such contracts it is unconstitutional as permitting a defense to the rights of a creditor which did not exist when the contract was made. Inasmuch as the bonds are contracts made before the passage of said law, as to them it is unconstitutional, and the district must be held to be without right to file a petition in bankruptcy.

Second. Article I, Section 1 of the Constitution provides that the right of property includes the right to dispose of such property in such manner as the owner pleases and to sell it for such price as he can obtain in fair barter. (*Ex parte Quary,* 149 Cal. 79, 84 Pac. 766.)

Third. Article IV, Section 1 of the Constitution of the State of California relates to the initiative and referendum and limits the power of the state legislature to enact emergency legislation, and provides:

"That no measure creating or abolishing any office, or changing the salary, term or duties of any officer, or granting any franchise or special privilege, or creating any vested right or interest shall be construed to be an urgency measure."

Since the act was an urgency measure, it is ineffective as in effect it takes vested rights from bondholders and confers them upon the landowners of the district.

Fourth. The California Constitution, Article XIII, Section 6, provides:

"The power of taxation shall never be surrendered or suspended by any grant or contract to which the state shall be a party."

The power of taxation is an attribute of sovereignty and cannot be surrendered. (61 *C. J.* 76.)

We deny that a California irrigation district can be subject to bankruptcy. The Supreme Court of California has clearly shown that the property, rights and works of a district are essentially public and the property of the district is essentially property of the sovereign. (*Turlock Irrigation District v. White,* 186 Cal. 183, 189.)

Under California law to subject the property of a district to the obligation of its bonds requires the vote of its people. (*Mulcahy v. Baldwin,* 216 Cal. 517.)

However, there is no provision in the bankruptcy act which requires the irrigation district to surrender its property to the Court, and we take it that such provision would be void as an invasion of state's rights. No state can by contract or law part with its sovereignty. The power of taxation is one of the high attributes of sovereignty. (*People v. McCreery,* 34 Cal. 432.)

At 61 *C. J.* 83, it is said that the power of taxation cannot, unless the Constitution so provides, be delegated to either of the other departments of the government.

"The levying of taxes, general or special, is an act of sovereign prerogative which neither a state nor a municipality * * * can barter away. Necessarily such surrender is against public policy." (*Cleveland v. Edward*, 109 Ohio St. 598, 37 A. L. R. 1352.)

This is supported by Section 6, Article XIII of the California Constitution, already referred to.

In the event the plan of readjustment contemplates the issuance of refunding bonds, the taxing district does not have jurisdiction to adopt a resolution, unless before the adoption of the resolution it holds a hearing after notice, as is provided in Section 7 (5) (e) of the enabling act.

> "In such event before the signing of the order or decree of the Federal District Court approving the plan of readjustment, the taxing district shall cause to be given a notice, for a reasonable time and in a reasonable manner of its intention to adopt the resolution mentioned in Section 6."

The effect of these provisions, as we interpret them, is that Chapter IV of the Extra Session Laws of 1934 provide that after the district has filed its petition in bankruptcy and before the Court can enter its final decree, a further and separate resolution must be passed by the district consenting to the decree. Consequently, the Waterford Irrigation District can entirely nullify the proceeding by declining to pass the resolution.

Section 7 further provides in Subdivision (d), amongst the powers referred to:

"To assess, levy and collect taxes, special assessment taxes and special assessments and to enforce the collection thereof in the manner and with the effect provided in the plan of readjustment."

Further, Section 7 (b) (2) states that in the case of irrigation districts, the bonds shall be obligations of the district without election. Thus, the Federal Court is given power to say to the district what amount of taxes shall be levied, for unless the Court's decree is made the power does not exist to levy the tax for the bond which the creditor must accept in a case where the acceptance of a bond is involved.

"That the taxing power of a state is one of its attributes of sovereignty; that it exists independently of the Constitution of the United States, and underived from that instrument; and that it may be exercised to an unlimited extent upon all property, trades, business and avocations existing or carried on within the territorial boundaries of the State, except so far as it has been surrendered to the Federal Government, either expressly or by necessary implication, are propositions that have often been asserted by this Court. And in thus acknowledging the extent of the power to tax belonging to the States, we have declared that it is indispensable to their continued existence." (*Union Pac. R. R. Co. v. Peniston,* 85 U. S. 5, 21 L. Ed. at p. 791.)

Fifth. True bankruptcy involves capacity to have leviable property and surrender leviable property and to receive a discharge. Power of taxation is in no sense property, and that power is the sole source of debtor's income and the measure of the bondholders' rights.

> "The plan of the Irrigation District Act is that the holders of outstanding bonds of the district have the right to enforce their demands solely by an annual assessment on the lands of the district. This was their contract." (*Mulcahy v. Baldwin,* 216 Cal. 517, at p. 525.)

The fiscal management of an irrigation district is not private business conducted by private direction; it is fiscal management of the affairs of a sovereign state of the legislative and administrative governmental functions.

Sixth. Article I, Section 14 of the California Constitution provides that the legislature has no power to take the property of one person and give it to another, nor can it be taken for a public use unless compensation to the owner precedes or accompanies the taking. (*Gillan v. Hutchinson,* 16 Cal. 153; Amendment 14, Section 1, United States Constitution.)

The following article appeared in the Bond Buyer of February 9, 1935. We do not have the citation. The article itself is explanatory.

> "Jackson, Miss.—Branding the 1932 bankruptcy statute for drainage improvement districts 'a scheme for repudiation of indebtedness', the State Supreme Court sitting en banc January 28 held the act unconstitutional.
>
> 'Instead of ordering affairs of the district wound up and the district discontinued', the opinion read, 'the act permits it to remain a going concern despite its bankrupt condition.

It is difficult to conceive of the insolvency of a taxing district. Lands constituting the district are there—they cannot be lost except by tax title in the State. Furthermore, the assessed benefits of the district may be wholly insufficient to pay its obligations during the years of an economic depression and amply sufficient for many years after recovery from such depression. If the legislature has power to enact a bankruptcy law for drainage districts—one of the State's governmental units—why not for the counties, municipalities and levee districts, and if that could be done, why not a bankruptcy for the State itself?

The court's decision upheld the ruling of the Chancery Court of Calhoun County in which commissioners of Saboula Drainage District No. 2 of Calhoun and Webster counties filed bankruptcy and unsuccessfully sought to have $31,000 in bonds held by R. E. Goza and the Peoples Bank & Trust Co. scaled down in proportion to remaining assets.''

Seventh. Under this heading we wish to call particular attention to the wording of Section 6 of the State Statute, providing that no final decree of the Court confirming a plan shall be effective for the purpose of binding the taxing district unless and until the taxing district files with the Court a certified copy of a resolution consenting to the plan.

From this it appears that in any event no real jurisdiction is conferred upon this Court for the reason that after a decree has been entered, it is still necessary for the district to consent thereto. In other words the district can file its petition and after putting the appellants to the expense of a trial, the district has the authority under the act to say that the decree is not binding upon it. What kind of a lawsuit is that where one of the parties can renounce the judgment if it is not satisfactory to him?

Finally, on the subject of the state's consent, in our view the Supreme Court of the United States has already and quite recently laid the foundation for the decision which will overthrow this legislation in its entirety, for Justice Cardozo in the case of *Hopkins v. Cleary* (supra), decided last December, said:

> "*Aside from the direct interest of the state in the preservation of agencies established for the common good, there is thus the duty of the parens patriae to keep faith with those who have put their trust in the parental power. True, most of the shareholders in the cases now before us assented to the change. Even so, an important minority were not represented at the meeting, and their approval is not shown. Creditors other than shareholders have not been heard from at all. To these non-vocal classes the parens owes a duty.*"

(Italics ours.)

Thus it will be seen that the state is estopped from consenting to this so-called bankruptcy provision.

––––––––

III.

THE BANKRUPTCY POWER IS SUBJECT TO THE FIFTH AMENDMENT.

We have already indicated the importance with which we regard the case of *Hopkins v. Cleary.*

The learned Justice, in his decision, said:

"51 per cent is the minimum required here. Another act may reduce the minimum to 10%, or even one, or dispense with approval altogether. If non-assenting shareholders or creditors were parties to these suits, the question would be urgent whether property interests may be so transformed consistently with the restraints of the Fifth Amendment. The Wisconsin courts hold that the protest of a single shareholder will check 'a fundamental and radical change' in the powers and purposes of the corporation, though the change be brought about by voluntary amendment."

It is thus to be seen that for the purpose of constitutionality, the protest of one shareholder is as valid and as of great a force as the protest of all the shareholders. The Court considers that even if the state had not protested against the transformation of the building and loan association, that the state owes a duty to those who have invested their money in reliance upon the state and its statutes, and also, that regardless of such situation, the question arises as to whether property interests may be transformed consistently with the restraints of the Fifth Amendment.

In the case of *Louisville Joint Stock Land Bank v. Radford,* 55 Sup. Ct. 854, the Court held that the bankruptcy power of Congress is subject to the Fifth Amendment, the Court saying:

"No instance has been found except under the Frazier-Lemke Act—of either a statute or a decision telling the mortgagee to relinquish the property of the mortgagor free of the lien unless the debt was paid in full. * * *

It is the general rule that a holder of the equity of redemption can redeem from the mortgagee only on paying the entire mortgage debt. * * *

This right of the mortgagee to insist upon full payment before giving up his security has been deemed of 'the essence of a mortgage. * * * To protect his right to full payment of the mortgaged property, the mortgagee was allowed to bid at the judicial sale on foreclosure.

The statutes were sustained by this court when as in Homebuilders' and Loan Association v. Blaisdell, 290 U. S. 398, 54 S. Ct. 231, 78 L. Ed. 413, 88 A. L. R. 1481, they were found to preserve substantially the right of the mortgagee to obtain, through application of the security, payment of the indebtedness. They were stricken down, as in W. B. Worthen Co. v. Kavanaugh, 295 U. S. 56, 55 S. Ct. 555, when it appeared that this substantive right was substantially abridged.

Although each of our national bankruptcy acts followed a major or minor depression, none had, prior to the Frazier-Lemke amendment, sought to compel the holder of a mortgage to surrender to the bankrupt either the possession of the mortgaged property or the title, so long as any part of the debt thereby secured remained unpaid. * * *

*No bankruptcy act had undertaken to supply him capital with which to engage in business in the future. * * *

No bankruptcy act had undertaken to modify in the interest of either the debtor or other creditors any substantive right of the holder of a mortgage valid under federal law. * * *

In Continental Illinois National Bank & Trust Co. v. Chicago, Rock Island & Pacific Ry., 294 U. S. 648, 55 S. Ct. 595, 606, 'The injunction here in no way impairs the lien, or disturbs the preferred rank of the pledgees'. * * *

By the settled practice, a sale free of liens will not be ordered by the bankruptcy court if it appears that the amount of the encumbrance exceeds the value of the property.''

Further the Court held:

"Because the act * * * purports to take away rights of the mortgagee in specific property, another provision of the Constitution is controlling.''

Although the Court does discuss compositions and holds the scope of bankruptcy power is not necessarily limited to that which has been exercised, and that the Court has no occasion to decide whether the bankruptcy clause confers upon Congress generally the power to abridge the mortgagee's rights in specific property, nevertheless the Court declares illegal the avowed object of the Frazier-Lemke law which is defined to be "to scale down the indebtedness to the present value of the property", for the reason that the Frazier-Lemke act takes from the mortgagor certain property rights.

The case of *W. B. Worthen Co. v. Kavanaugh,* 55 Sup. Ct. Rep. 555, is also enlightening. The decision in this case was handed down by Justice Cardozo. A Municipal Improvement District of the State of

Arkansas had issued bonds. In 1933 the Legislature of Arkansas passed certain statutes reducing the penalty for non-payment of assessments from 20% to 3%. The rate of interest on redemption was likewise reduced and other changes were made, and the Court held:

> "To know the obligation of a contract we look to the laws in force at its making. * * * Not even changes of the remedy may be pressed so far as to cut down the security of a mortgage without moderation or reason or in a spirit of oppression. Even when the public welfare is invoked as an excuse, these bounds must be respected."

In the case of *County of Los Angeles v. Rockhold*, 89 C. D. 556, at page 569, the Court said (44 Pac. (2d) 340):

> "There can be no doubt that it is indispensable, from a constitutional standpoint, so far as bondholders are concerned, that either 100 per cent consent to the change or that the dissenting bondholders be so taken care of that no impairment of their contract ensues.
>
> The act is unconstitutional in that it fails adequately to protect the rights of dissenting bondholders."

Mr. Honnold in his work "Supreme Court Law" makes the following statement under the heading of "Due Process" (Vol. 2, p. 840):

> "The due process clause requires that State action shall be consistent with the fundamental principles of liberty and justice. It requires notice and opportunity to be heard, but not always

proceedings in court or the privilege of an appellate review. It precludes the taking of private property for private purposes, and the taking for public purposes without authority and just compensation."

He further says:

"Whether acting through its judiciary or through its legislature, the State *may not deprive a person of all existing remedies for the enforcement of a right,* which the State has no power to destroy, unless there is or was afforded to him some real opportunity to protect it."

As said in the case of *Holden v. Hardy,* 169 U. S. 366:

"There are certain immutable principles of justice which inhere in the very idea of free government, which *no member of the Union* may disregard."

The case of *U. S. v. Young,* 267 Fed. 861, suggests that the due process clause of the Fifth Amendment is broad enough to cover both the "due process" and the "equal protection" clauses of the Fourteenth Amendment.

Federal Bankruptcy Acts are not exempt from the requirements of the "due process" clause. (*Monongahela Navigation Company v. U. S.,* 148 U. S. 312; *Re Bradford,* 7 Fed. Supp. 665; *Hanover National Bank v. Moyses,* 186 U. S. 181.)

In California the controlling purpose of the irrigation law with relation to bonds is that the property within the district shall be dedicated primarily to the payment of these bonds. The dedication is more primary than the dedication in Kentucky of mortgage security in the *Radford* case for tax liens are superior to every other lien, whenever and however created.

Likewise this legislation deprives appellants of property rights just as important as the rights protected in the *Radford* case (1) the right to retain the pledge of the tax lien until the bonds are paid (2) the right to have taxes levied and collected from year to year (3) the right to have the security disposed of at public sale.

As was said by one eminent authority, Mr. S. M. Haskins of Los Angeles:

> "The failure to realize from the bonds would mean that all the property within the district could not be liquidated for the amount of the bond issue. This is the implication of the act. If the bondholder has satisfied himself as to the value of the district up to the amount of bonds issued he need have no fear as to the ultimate payment of his obligation."

The utter unreason of the law and its complete failure to protect property rights as security is made evident by comparison with the terms of the railroad bankruptcy act, amendment to Section 77. Secured creditors are there protected in subdivisions (g) and (h) either by payment in full or payment of the appraised value of their security. Two-thirds of the bondholders, confused and discouraged over the low state of public morale and frightened by public corporate bankruptcy proceedings and driven by necessity for ready money, are given the power to force the remaining one-third to a property sacrifice. Whether members of a class or not, appellants are property holders and their class-hood does not outlaw them or deprive them of their protection under the Fifth Amendment. Even the other bankruptcy amendments of 1933 protected the secured investors in the value of their security. A public bondholder secured by sovereign pledge of taxes alone is unprotected in his property.

From many aspects the Municipal Bankruptcy Act is unreasonable and arbitrary. The tax districts overlap. In this case the lands are encumbered by the liens of bonds of the County of Stanislaus and of school districts. From these secured bondholders, all with security on the same property, irrigation district bondholders alone are selected for sacrifice. This situation is inherently and necessarily true of almost any proceeding under the act and does not accord due process of law to the victim.

This bankruptcy act, therefore, was to destroy the lien of the bondholders upon the funds in the hands of the treasurer and upon the lands which have been deeded to the district upon default in payment of assessments, and no accounting is had either of these funds or of those assets in the hands of the district. Such a lien and such a trust cannot be destroyed by a bankruptcy. (*Continental Illinois Nat. Bank & T. Co. v. Chicago, R. I. & P. Ry. Co.*, 55 Sup. Ct. 595; *In re Martin* (C. C. A. 7), 75 Fed. (2d) 618.)

Let us now examine the record to ascertain what property rights the appellants had been deprived of without due process:

(1) The findings of fact (R. p. 24) show the assets of the district to be $821,993.36 and the liabilities $730,840.03, and the assessed value of land alone is over $1,000,000 (R. p. 23), whereas the plan provides for payment to the bondholder of an amount equal to $48.82 for each dollar of the principal amount of the bonds and providing nothing on account of delinquent interest. (R. p. 47.)

(2) That appellants are restrained from attempting to enforce their obligations under the laws of the State of California against the Waterford Irrigation District (R. p. 41) and the plan of readjustment is put into operation although the appellee does not have available funds with which to pay the said 48.82 cents per dollar (R. pp. 30 and 47), and provides further that the bonds of appellants shall become void on June 1, 1937, unless delivered to the Reconstruction Finance Corporation or the disbursing agent or the clerk of the Court, although there is no assurance that there will be money with which to pay the appellants. (R. p. 37.)

(3) It takes property of which the appellants are beneficiaries and it takes the bond and bond interest fund and the tax certificates from them.

(4) It transfers rights from the appellant bondholders to bondholders of other taxing

agencies, such as the County of Stanislaus, the Oakdale Union High School District, and the other school districts.

(5) It transfers property from the appellants to the landowners within the district.

(6) It transfers property from the appellants to the mortgage holders and deed of trust holders within the district.

(See Assignment of Errors 29, R. p. 63.)

IV.

THE WATERFORD IRRIGATION DISTRICT IS NOT A SUBJECT OF BANKRUPTCY.

1. The Waterford Irrigation District is Engaged in Strictly Governmental and Not Proprietary Functions.

Judge McCormick in the *Matter of the Imperial Irrigation District,* 10 Fed. Supp., held that

"the private or proprietary element of an irrigation district is sufficiently distinct and definite to bring it within the purview of the bankruptcy power of Congress. This is especially true where the state as the creator or dominant power of the district's governmental functions has given its consent. Compare Meriweather v. Garrett, 102 U. S. 472."

We have compared *Meriweather v. Garrett* and instead of finding substantiation for the opinion of the District Court in the *Imperial* case, we find the following:

"But while the charter of a municipal corporation may be repealed at the pleasure of the legislature, where there is no inhibition to its action in the Constitution of the State, the lawful contracts of the corporation, made whilst it was in existence, may be subsequently enforced against property held by it, in its own right, as hereafter described at the time of the repeal. * * *

The levying of taxes is not a judicial act. It has no elements of one. It is a high act of sovereignty, to be performed only by the legislature upon considerations of policy, necessity, and the public welfare. In the distribution of the powers of government in this country into three departments, the power of taxation falls to the legislative. * * *

We are of the opinion that this court has not the power to direct a tax to be levied for the payment of these judgments. This power to impose burdens and raise money is the highest attribute of sovereignty, * * * Especially is it beyond the power of the Federal judiciary to assume the place of a State in the exercise of this authority at once so delicate and so important.

It is certainly of the highest importance to the people of every State that it should make provision, not merely for the payment of its own indebtedness, but for the payment of the indebtedness of its different municipalities. Hesitation to do this is weakness; refusal to do it is dishonor. Infidelity to engagements causes loss of character to the individual; it entails reproach upon the State.

The Federal judiciary has never failed, so far as it was in its power, to compel the performance of all lawful contracts, whether of the individual, or of the municipality, or of the State. It has unhesitatingly brushed aside all legislation of the State impairing their obligation. * * * In some instances, where the tax was the inducement and consideration of the contract, all attempts at its repeal have been held invalid."

Judge McCormick in his decision in the Imperial Irrigation District case held that in the Rock Island Railway case "a quasi public corporate body" was the bankrupt, and that the Imperial Irrigation District "is also a public body", and held further that "the private or proprietary element of an irrigation district is sufficiently distinct and definite to bring is within the purview of the bankkruptcy power of Congress." This makes it necessary to consider the correctness of such a finding.

We find that in the case of *Whiteman v. Anderson-Cottonwood Irrigation District,* 60 C. A. 234, 212 Pac. 706, this matter has been decided by the California Courts contrary to the decision of Judge McCormick. The following is quoted from that decision:

"The parties seem to be in accord as to the principle of law that governs any possible theory of the case, but they are in disagreement as to the character of an irrigation district, and whether its functions be of a public or private character. * * *

As to the character of irrigation districts as organized under our statute, it must be conceded that they are public corporations or public agencies, but not 'municipal corporations,' as that term is usually understood. * * *

In Lindsay-Strathmore I. Dist. v. Superior Court, 182 Cal. 315, 187 Pac. 1056, referring to these districts, the court said:

'They are public agencies.' * * *

In Turlock Irrigation District v. White, 186 Cal. 183, 198 Pac. 1060, 17 A. L. R. 72, the court declares:

'* * * such a corporation is not a "municipal corporation," but a "public corporation for municipal purposes."' Fallbrook Irrigation District v. Bradley, 164 U. S. 112.'

And the court quotes with approval People v. Reclamation District No. 551, 117 Cal. 114, 48 Pac. 1016, wherein it was said that these corporations are 'state organizations for state purposes.'

In Tormey et al. v. Anderson-Cottonwood Irr. Dist. (Cal. App.) 200 Pac. 814, the Supreme Court, in denying a hearing after the decision of this court said:

'The canal is constructed for public purposes and to serve the purpose of distribution of water to public use.'

In fact, it has been consistently held by the Supreme Court from the beginning that these districts created under the elaborate scheme devised for their organization and operation by the Legislature are public agencies for the promotion of a public purpose. While the primary object is to secure the distribution of water for irrigation, and while the mere furnishing of water for irrigation might involve only the exercise of a proprietary function in the case of a municipal corporation, yet the situation and condition of the land in these districts are so peculiar and the public is so vitally interested in the project that the purpose is regarded, not only as for the advancement of the individual welfare, but for the promotion of the public interest. If appellant's contention be accepted as sound, it would follow that we have the anomalous situation of a public agency created for the mere purpose of exercising a private right or privilege. This view would necessitate the adoption of an entirely different theory from what has prevailed in this state for the justification of this legislation.

It would also destroy the foundation for the conclusion reached by the United States Supreme Court in the well-considered case of Fallbrook Irrigation District v. Bradley, 164 U. S. 112, 17 Sup. Ct. 56, 41 L. Ed. 369, which decision has been approved and followed by the Supreme Court of this state. Therein the validity of the Wright Act (St. 1887, p. 29, as amended), was assailed upon various grounds, one of which is that it provided for the assessment of lands and the taking of property for a private purpose. Manifestly, this attack challenged the intergrity of the whole scheme, and it received careful consideration at the hands of the court. In the opinion it is said:

'Coming to a review of these various objections, we think the first, that the water is not for a public use, is not well founded. * * * Is this assessment, for the nonpayment of which the land of the plaintiff was to be sold, levied for a public purpose? The question has, in substance, been answered in the affirmative by the people of 'California, and by the legislative and judicial branches of the state government.'

The court then calls attention to section 1 of article 14 of our state Constitution, section 12 of said act, as amended in 1891 (St. 1891, p. 145), and the following decisions of the Supreme Court of this state: Turlock Irrigation District v. Williams, 76 Cal. 360, 18 Pac. 379; Central Irrigation District v. DeLappe, 79 Cal. 35, 21 Pac. In re Madera Irr. Dist., 92 Cal. 296, 28 Pac. 272, 675, 14 L. R. A. 755, 27 Am. St. Rep. 106. After stating that the foregoing considerations are not necessarily binding upon the federal courts, the opinion proceeds:

'It is obvious, however, that what is a public use frequently and largely depends upon the facts and circumstances surrounding the particular subject-matter in regard to which the the character of the use is questioned. To provide for the irrigation of lands in states where there is no color of necessity therefor within any fair meaning of the term, and simply for the purpose of gratifying the taste of the owner, or his desire to enter upon the cultivation of an entirely new kind of crop, not necessary for the purpose of rendering the ordinary cultivation of the land reasonably remunerative, might be regarded by courts as an improper exercise of legislative will, and the use might not be held to be public in any constitutional sense, no matter how many owners were interested in the scheme. On the other hand, in a state like California, which confessedly embraces millions of acres of arid lands, an act of the Legislature providing for their irrigation might well be regarded as an act devoting the water to a public use, and therefor as a valid exercise of the legislative power. * * * Viewing the subject for ourselves and in the light of these considerations, we have very little difficulty in coming to the same conclusion reached by the courts of California. The use must be regarded as a public use, or else it would seem to follow that no general scheme of irrigation can be formed or carried into effect. In general, the water to be used must be carried for some distance and over or through private property, which cannot be taken in invitum if the use to which it is to be put be not public, and, if there be no power to take property by condemnation, it may be impossible to acquire it at all. The use for which private property is to be taken must be a public one, whether the taking be by the exercise of the right of eminent domain or by that of taxation. Cole v. La Grange, 113 U. S. 1.'"

A further discussion of the nature of an irrigation district in California and its legal status is found in the case of *In re Bonds of Madera Irrigation District,* 28 Pac. 272, 92 Cal. 296, from which we quote as follows:

"Whether the reclamation of the land be from excessive moisture to a condition suitable for cultivation, or from excessive aridity to the same condition, the right of the legislature to authorize such reclamation must be upheld upon the same principle, viz., the welfare of the public, and particularly of that portion of the public within the district affected by the means adopted for such reclamation. * * *

In the present case the legislature has chosen to authorize the creation of a public corporation, in the manner and with the forms specified in the act under discussion. For this purpose it has provided that a petition of 50. freeholders, or a majority of the freeholders owning lands within a proposed district susceptible of one mode of irrigation, shall be presented to the boards of supervisors of the county within which such lands are situate; and that the board of supervisors shall, upon the hearing of such petition, after notice thereof, determine whether or not it will take steps to organize an irrigation district; and that upon such determination an election shall be ordered, at which, if two-thirds of the electors within the district shall vote in favor of such organization, the district shall thereupon be organized, and its management confided to a board of directors chosen by the electors of that district, * * * and it is only when these electors have determined by a vote of two-thirds of their number in favor thereof that the district can be created. * * *

That an irrigation district, organized under the act in question, becomes a public corporation, is evident from an examination of the mode of its organization, the purpose for which it is organized, and the powers conferred upon it. It can be organized only at the instance of the board of supervisors of the county * * * the legislative body of one of the constitutional subdivisions of the state; its organization can be affected only upon the vote of the qualified electors within its boundaries; its officers are chosen under the sanction and with the formalities required at all public elections in the state * * * the officers of such election being required to act under the sanction of an oath, and being authorized to administer oaths when required for the purpose of conducting the election; and the officers when elected being required to execute official bonds to the state of California, approved by a judge of the superior court. *The district officers thus become public officers of the state.* When organized, the district can acquire, either by purchase or condemnation, all property necessary for the construction of its works, and may construct thereon canals, and other irrigation improvements; and all the property so acquired is to be held by the district in trust, and is dedicated for the use and purposes set forth in the act, and is declared to be a public use, subject to the regulation and control of the state. For the purpose of meeting the cost of acquiring this property, the district is authorized, upon the vote of a majority of its electors, to issue its bonds; and these bonds, and the interest thereon, are to be paid by revenues derived under the power of taxation, and for which all the real property in the district is to be assessed. *Under this power of taxation, one of the highest attributes of sovereignty,* the title of the delinquent owner to the real estate assessed, may be divested by sale, * * * *Here are found the essential elements of a public corporation, none of which pertain to a private corporation.* The property held by the corporation is in trust for the public, and subject to the control of the state. Its officers are public officers chosen by the electors of the district, and invested with public duties. Its object is for the good of the public, and to promote the prosperity and welfare of the public. 'Where a corporation is composed exclusively of officers of the government, having no personal interest in it, or with its concerns, and only acting as organs of the state in effecting a great public improvement, it is a public corporation.' Ang. & A. Corp. Sec. 32. 'A municipal corporation proper is created mainly for the interest, advantage and convenience of the locality of its people. The primary idea is an agency to regulate and administer the interior concerns of the locality in matters peculiar to the place incorporated, and not common to the state or people at large.' 15 Amer. & Eng. Enc. Law, p. 954. 'Public corporations are such as are created for the discharge of public duties in the administration of civil government.' Lawson, Rights, Rem. & P. Pr. 332.'' (Italics ours.)

In California the furnishing of water for purposes of irrigation has been repeatedly held to be a governmental function. We have already cited some authorities on this point and have quoted from the California Constitution. In the case of *Pasadena v. Railroad Commission*, 183 Cal. 526, 192 Pac. 25, it was held that the powers of the Railroad Commission extend only to private corporations. The Supreme Court declared that it is not true that a city is a private corporation when carrying on a municipally owned public utility, adding:

"All the decisions on the subject recognize the fact that a city does not change its character by engaging in such enterprises."

A number of decisions have been rendered on the question of the character of an irrigation district and these are conveniently summarized in the case of *Yolo v. Modesto Irrigation District,* 216 Cal. 274, 13 Pac. (2d) 908, which points out that irrigation districts have been variously denominated "public corporations" for "governmental purposes", "agents or representatives of the state in the particular locality in which they exist", etc., and the Court says that these districts "are not generally liable for torts of their agents because they are held to be state agencies performing governmental functions".

In the Waterford Irrigation District we have the situation of an irrigation district engaged exclusively, however, in irrigation.

In the case of *Parker v. El Paso Water Improvement District No. 1,* 116 Tex. 631, the Court said:

"The admitted facts stated, the extracts from the arguments of Mr. Joseph Choate, counsel for the Bradleys, appearing in the report of the case, as well as the opinion of the court itself, show that the question was squarely before the Supreme Court as to whether or not lands which the owners did not care to irrigate, or which might not need irrigation from the improvements proposed by a district, could under the Constitution be included in an irrigation district. The Supreme Court held they could be included, holding that the *irrigation of land was a public purpose,* and the use of water thereon a public use, and that irrigation districts, such as the one before us, were public corporations with power to tax any land included in the district."

So, also, in the case of *O'Neill v. Leamer,* 239 U. S. 244, which involved a condemnation proceeding instituted by a drainage district in the State of Nebraska. The Supreme Court of the United States quoted with approval the following language from the Nebraska Supreme Court:

"In our opinion, it is too late in the day to contend that the irrigation of arid land, the straightening and improvement of water courses, the building of levees, and the drainage of swamp and overflowed lands for the improvement of the health and comfort of the community, and the reclamation of waste places and the promotion of agriculture, are not all and every of them subjects of the general and public concern, the promotion and regulation of which are among the most important of *governmental powers, duties and functions."*

If this latter question requires some debate, it can hardly seem possible that the question of whether the power of taxation is a governmental function can be a subject of debate. It will, therefore, no doubt be sufficient to cite one case. It was stated in *Lane County v. Oregon,* 7 Wallace (U. S.) 71:

"Now, to the existence of the States, themselves necessary to the existence of the United States, the power of taxation is indispensable. It is an essential function of the government."

We quote further from the case, as follows:

"If, therefore, the condition of any State, in the judgment of its legislature, requires the collection of taxes in kind, that is to say, by the delivery to the proper officers of a certain proportion of products, or in gold or silver bullion, or in gold and silver coin, it is not easy to see upon what principal the National Legislature can interfere with the exercise, to that end, of this power, original in the States, and never as yet surrendered."

It would seem that the statement in the foregoing cases is conclusive, but the United States Court, speaking through Mr. Justice Hughes, went even further in the case of *Houck v. Little River Drainage District,* 239 U. S. 254, 261:

"The district is, indeed, a conspicuous illustration of the class of enterprises which have been authorized in order to secure the recognized public advantages which will accrue from reclaiming and opening to cultivation large areas of swamp or overflowed lands. Egyptian Levee Co. v. Hardin, 27 Mo. 495, 72 Am. Rep. 276; Columbia Bottom Levee Co. v. Meier, 39 Mo. 53; Morrison v. Morey, 146 Mo. 543, 48 S. W. 629; State ex rel. Compton v. Chariton Drainage Dist., 192 Mo. 517, 90 S. W. 722; Mound City Land & Stock Co. v. Miller, 170 Mo. 240, 60 L. R. A. 190, 94 Am. St. Rep. 727, 70 S. W. 721; State ex rel. Applegate v. Taylor, 224 Mo. 393, 123 S. W. 892; Squaw Creek Drainage Dist. v. Turney, 235 Mo. 80, 138 S. W. 12; Little River Drainage Dist. v. St. Louis, M. & S. E. R. Co., 236 Mo. 94, 139 S. W. 330. *It was constituted a political subdivision of the state for the purpose of performing pre-*

scribed functions of government. Mound City Land & Stock Co. v. Miller, 170 Mo. 240, 60 L. R. A. 190, 94 Am. St. Rep. 727, 70 S. W. 721; State ex rel. Applegate v. Taylor, 224 Mo. 393, 123 S. W. 892. *These drainage districts, as the supreme court of the state has said, exercise the granted powers within their territorial jurisdiction 'as fully, and by the same authority, as the municipal corporations of the state exercise the powers vested by their charters'. 248 Mo. p. 383."* (Italics supplied.)

"In view of the nature of this enterprise it is obvious that, so far as the Federal Constitution is concerned, the state might have defrayed the entire expense out of state funds raised by general taxation, or it could have apportioned the burden among the counties in which the lands were situated and the improvements were to be made. Mobile County v. Kimball, 102 U. S. 691, 703, 704, 26 L. ed. 238, 241, 242. It was equally within the power of the state to create tax districts to meet the authorized outlays. The legislature, unless restricted by the state Constitution, can create such districts directly, or, as in this case, it may provide for their institution through a proceeding in the courts in which the parties interested are cited to appear and present their objections, if any. The propriety of a delegation of this sort was a question for the state alone. And with respect to districts thus formed, whether by the legislature directly or in an appropriate proceeding under its authority, the legislature may itself fix the basis of taxation or assessment; that is, it may define the apportionment of the burden, and its action cannot be assailed under the 14th Amendment unless it is palpably arbitrary and a plain abuse. These principles have been established by repeated decisions. Harag v. Reclamation Dist., 111 U. S. 701, 709, 28 L. ed. 569, 572, 4 Sup. Ct. Rep. 663; Spencer v. Merchant, 125 U. S. 345, 353, 356, 31 L. ed. 763, 766, 767, 8 Sup. Ct. Rep. 921; Fallbrook Irrig. Dist. v. Bradley, 164 U. S. 112, 167, 168, 41 L. ed. 369, 391, 392, 17 Sup. Ct. Rep. 56; Bauman v. Ross, 167 U. S. 548, 590, 42 L. ed. 270, 288, 17 Sup. Ct. Rep. 966; Parsons v. District of Columbia, 170 U. S. 45, 52, 42 L. ed. 943, 946, 8 Sup. Ct. Rep. 521; Williams v. Eggleston, 170 U. S. 304, 311, 42 L. ed. 1047, 1049, 18 Sup. Ct. Rep. 617; Norwood v. Baker, 172 U. S. 269, 278, 43 L. ed. 443, 447, 19 Sup. Ct. Rep. 187; French v. Barber Asphalt Paving Co., 181 U. S. 324, 343, 45 L. ed. 879, 889, 21 Sup. Ct. Rep. 625; Wight v. Davidson, 181 U. S. 371, 379, 45 L. ed. 900, 904, 21 Sup. Ct. Rep. 616; Wagner v. Lesser, decided this day (239 U. S. 207, ante, 230, 36 Sup. Ct. Rep. 66)."

2. **As a Matter of Fact an Irrigation District is Not a Taxing District Within the Meaning of Section 80.**

Section 80 (a) reads:

"Any municipality or other political subdivision of any state, including (but not hereby limiting the generality of the foregoing) any county, city, * * * school, drainage, irrigation * * * or other districts (hereby referred to as a 'taxing district') may file a petition, etc."

An examination of this provision leads to the conclusion that it was the intention of Congress to authorize any political subdivision of the state to file a bankruptcy petition, but that the use of the example, such as cities, irrigation districts, etc., was merely intended to illustrate the type of political subdivisions and was not intended to enlarge the class beyond that of political subdivisions.

The principle laid down in the case of *U. S. v. Boyer,* 85 Fed. 425, that the use of the words "authorizing Congress to provide for the general welfare of the United States" contained in Article I, Section 8, does not confer upon Congress any power to enact any legislation, but should provide a rule of interpretation here.

The use of the words "irrigation district" was merely illustrative of the type of district to be included within the general provision of municipality or other political subdivision.

In *People v. Reclamation District No. 551,* 117 Cal. 120, the Court said:

> "They certainly are not municipal corporations in the strict sense."

In the case of *Metcalf v. Merritt,* 14 Cal. App. 244, the Court said:

> "It is not a municipal corporation possessing in any degree general powers of government."

In the case of *Randolph v. County of Stanislaus,* 44 Cal. App. 322, the Court said:

> "We think it does not require very much argument to demonstrate that an irrigation district formed under the laws of the State of California is not a municipal corporation."

Nor is it a political subdivision of the state, for in the case of *Tarpey v. McClure,* 190 Cal. 593, the Court states:

> "The decisions of the Idaho Court to the contrary, based upon the view that these districts are political subdivisions of the state, are out of harmony with the decisions of this state."

In the case of *Wood v. Imperial Irrigation District,* 216 Cal. 748, the Court said:

> "An irrigation district is not a political subdivision of the state or county or a political subdivision at all."

The real distinction seems to be that in the case of an irrigation district, the legislature is not dealing with elections, with suffrage or with the ballot. The formation of these districts is a function pertaining purely to the legislative branch of the government. This discussion is found in the case of *Tarpey v. McClure* (supra). It seems logical to assume that Congress intended to include only those types of organizations which were political subdivisions of the state. A well founded argument would seem to back the assumption that the Congress did not intend to include mere mandatories or agencies of the state itself. It intended only to apply the bankruptcy act to municipalities and other similar political subdivisions, who perchance might engage in private or proprietary activities.

3. **The Waterford Irrigation District Cannot Surrender its Property.**

This subject has been argued supra and will not be here enlarged upon.

4. **The Waterford Irrigation District is Not the Debtor.**

The sole remedy of the bondholders is to compel the levy of assessments upon all of the lands of the district by a writ of mandate. *Nevada National Bank v. Ross Irrigation District,* 140 Cal. 344; *Thompson v. Perris Irrigation District,* 116 Fed. 769, and *Perris Irrigation District v. Thompson,* 116 Fed. 832.

The case of *State v. Commissioners* (a Montana case), 291 Pac. 1, may not now be good law upon the question of the character of the obligation of an irrigation bond, but it is good law, it seems to us upon the question of the relationship of the juristic person, the district, to the debt—in this respect—that the district is a trustee.

We are justified, therefore, in giving consideration to the proposition that the obligations on the bonds of the Waterford Irrigation District are not debts of the district within the meaning of the bankruptcy act of 1898. It is true that the obligations on the bonds arise from the loan of money to the district, which, of itself under the English Common Law, would create an implied assumpsit. But the obligation thus created has been changed to a statutory contractual obligation and while the bond contains a promise to pay, we must take the case presented by the bonds and the statutes by its four corners, from a consideration of which we arrive at the conclusion that the obligation of the Waterford Irrigation District as a juristic person *is the obligation to carry out the duties imposed by the statutes* providing for the levy of assessments and the collection of the same and the payment of the proceeds thereof to bondholders as provided by the California Irrigation District Act.

It would appear, therefore, that the sole obligation of the Waterford Irrigation District and its officers is to *perform those duties,* and once having performed them there is no further obligation upon the district. The fact that no execution can be issued for the obligation, the fact that payment cannot be recovered from any fund other than the bond fund, the fact that the district cannot be compelled to pay, except as moneys come into the bond fund, lead to the conclusion that the bond is not a debt or an obligation in the sense and meaning of the bankruptcy act, and that in so far as the Waterford Irrigation District is concerned, there is merely a legal duty imposed upon a trustee, the irrigation district, to perform certain duties prescribed by the legislature.

This question bears upon the problem in hand in two important particulars—first, the obligations under the bonds are not debts which could be discharged by proceedings under the bankruptcy act; secondly, if there is any obligation, *the obligation is that of the landowner to meet the assessments* levied and that question bears upon the fairness of the plan, because other obligations of the landowners, such as their obligations to pay county and school bonds, and their obligations to pay assessments for other improvements, and their mortgages and deeds of trust are not scaled down or refunded in the same proportion, or at all.

It was said in the case of *Judith Basin Irrigation District v. Malott,* 73 Fed. (2d) 142, in a decision written by Mr. Justice Wilbur of this Court, in a case in which all of the property had been sold at tax sales, and in which the Court noted that the law of Montana is patterned after the Wright Act of the State of California, that:

> "It has been uniformly held that bonds of an irrigation district issued in pursuance to the Wright Act—are general obligations of the district."

and further:

> "The payment of the bonds of earliest maturity does not release any parcel of land from the lien of the bonds, and all of the lands within the district, according to the terms of the bond and of the statute, are liable for the payment of the unpaid bonds."

In the case of *Hershey v. Cole,* 130 Cal. App. 683, 20 Pac. (2d) 972, the Court said:

> "The conclusions drawn therefrom that there is no contract or quasi contract in legal effect between the landowners of the district and the purchasers of bonds of the district does not appear to be supported either in principle or by the authorities."

From one view, therefore, these debts are not debts of the Waterford Irrigation District, although they are general obligations to the effect that all of the lands within the district is forever liable as security therefor, even after tax sale. If, as has been said, equity will pierce the veil and look at the facts and in so doing will find that substantially the bond is not a debt of the Waterford Irrigation District, but is either one of two things, *either it is a debt of the landowner as such,* in accordance with the theory of *Hershey v. Cole,* that the bond is a contract between the landowner and the bondholder, *or it is a debt of the sovereign State of California.* If it is a debt of the landowner it explains why one's sense of justice and fairness is shocked by realizing that under the Municipal Bankruptcy Act this debt can be scaled down on the theory that it is a debtor of the Waterford Irrigation District, whereas the obligations of the same land to bondholders of the County of Stanislaus, of the Oakdale Union High School District, and other school districts will be paid one hundred cents on the dollar, and whereas also at the same time obligations upon the mortgages and deeds of trust of these landowners will escape reduction or scaling down altogether.

On the other hand if the view be taken that they are obligations of the sovereign, and in support of this view it is pointed out that these bonds bear the Seal of the State of California, that they bear a certificate of the State Controller, and that since the sovereign created the district and it is a state legislative mandatory, then in a true sense these are debts of the sovereign, which sovereign also created debts in favor of county bondholders and school bondholders, limited perhaps as to security to a certain geographical division of the state.

In either view taken, therefore, the Waterford Irrigation District cannot be a subject of bankruptcy, for the real debtor, whether it be the state or whether it be the landowner, is not reached in these proceedings.

Which is just another illustration of the fact that a statute which disregards sound principles of law and justice is sure to be difficult to fit into any sound system of jurisprudence.

In this case it can not be fit.

A statute valid as to one set of facts may be invalid as to another and a statute valid when enacted may become invalid by changing conditions. Nashville etc. Ry. Co. v. Walters, 55 Sup. Ct. Rep. 486.

5. The Waterford Irrigation District Cannot be a Bankrupt.

"A person shall be deemed insolvent within the provisions of this act (Section 80 is one of such provisions) wherever the aggregate of his property, exclusive of any property which he may have conveyed—with intent to defraud, hinder or delay his creditors shall not at a fair valuation be a sufficient amount to pay his debts." Bankrupt Act Sec. 1a (15).

"A debtor is insolvent within the meaning of this title when he is unable to pay his debts from his own means as they become due." Civil Code of California, Sec. 3450.

"By 'means' thus used is meant 'resources' or 'income', but resources does not necessarily mean money in hand. A debtor may have ample resources to pay all his debts as they become due and again have no money in his pocket or in banks." Leacroy v. Lobree, 84 Cal. 41, 49.

"It seems absurd to say that a man is insolvent because he has transferred some of his estate with intent to defraud his creditors, when he has an estate remaining which is abundantly sufficient to pay all his debts." Lansing, etc. v. Lryrerson & Son, 63 U. S. (C. C. A.) 253, 128 Fed. 701, 705.

The testimony and showing made in this case and the findings of the court itself abundantly show that the assets of this district exceed its liabilities. (See Findings R. p. 24.) R. p. 23 shows too that the assessed value of the property in the district is in excess of a million dollars, and that this assessment is upon the lands only of the district and not upon the improvements, vines, or orchards. The California Irrigation District Act, as has been shown, requires the assessor to assess the lands "at their full cash value". The district is, therefore, estopped to deny that the value of its assets exceed its liabilities.

Further than that the Waterford Irrigation District has for several years taken advantage of Section 11 of the Districts Securities Commission Act. (See Findings, R. p. 23.) This act, as has been shown, enables an irrigation district to levy only such assessments as the lands are able to pay; consequently, it requires no argument to show that it is solely the fault of the district officials themselves if they are unable to pay their debts as they mature, inasmuch as under the California Statute, Section 11 of the Districts Securities Commission Act, they are required to levy only such assessments as the lands are able to pay, and if they are able to pay the assessments which the officers conclude they are able to pay, how can they claim to be insolvent or unable to meet their. obligations as they mature? For if Section 11 of the Districts Securities Commission Act is constitutional, then in view of that section, together with Section 52 of "the California Irrigation District Act", which provides ample protection for the bondholder by providing 7% interest upon his obligation when it has not been paid, not only gives ample protection to the bondholder in the preservation of his rights, but equally protects the district and its landowners from assessments which they cannot pay, and so it is difficult to conceive how an argument can be made that it is unable to pay its obligations as they mature.

` Not only that, but the testimony at the hearing showed (R. p. 122) that the district is not taking title to much land in the district, because they think it may be redeemed, and when this property has been redeemed the district will then be able to pay much of the interest and principal that has matured.

6. The Analogy of Equity Receivership Cases.

Some enlightment can be obtained by considering several cases which have come before the Federal Courts in the attempts of bondholders to enforce payment of their obligations. A large part of the law upon the question of the rights of bondholders of various municipal and other public corporations is found in the cases of the Federal Courts, for the reason that the courts of the state are quite often found to be sympathetic with the local public corporations, to the great disadvantage of the creditor, and consequently many creditors have found it necessary to go into the United States Courts for the enforcement of remedies.

We wish to point out the fact that the Federal Courts have through their equity jurisdiction exercised considerable control over classes of corporations which were not amenable to the bankruptcy statutes, and it was not unreasonable to expect therefore that creditors of municipalities should appeal to the equity side of the Federal Courts and seek federal receivership for the purpose of the enforcement of their rights, particularly where the state law gave little or no remedy which was of any substantial benefit to the bondholder or creditor.

In the case of *Heine v. Board of Levee Commissioners,* 19 Wall. (86 U. S.) 665, 22 L. Ed. 223, it was said:

> "It is very clearly shown that the total failure of ordinary remedies does not confer upon the courts of Chancery an unlimited power to give relief."

> "It is possible for circumstances to arise where the equitable powers of the court may appropriately be invoked by a bondholder, but it is obvious that such is not the case when the object of the holder is merely to collect the indebtedness owed him by the corporation as evidenced by the

bonds or coupons.'' Jones Bonds and Bond Securities, Sec. 501.

In the case of *Heine v. Board of Levee Commissioners,* the Court also said:

"The power we are asked here to exercise is the very delicate one of taxation. This power belongs in this country to the legislative sovereignty, state or national. In the case before us the national sovereignty has nothing to do with it, the power must be derived from the legislature of the state. So far as the present case is concerned, the state has delegated the power to the Levee Commissioners. * * * It certainly is not vested as in the exercise of an original jurisdiction in any Federal Court. It is unreasonable to suppose that the legislature would ever select a Federal Court for that purpose. *It is not only not one of the inherent powers of the court to levy and collect taxes, but it is an invasion by the judiciary of the federal government of the legislative functions of the state government.*" (Italics ours.)

So, in the case of *Thompson v. Allen County,* 115 U. S. 550, 29 L. Ed. 472, 6 Sup. Ct. 140, the Court said:

"A court of law possesses no power to levy taxes. Its power to compel officers who are lawfully appointed for that purpose, in a case where the duty to do so is clear, and is strictly ministerial, rests upon a ground very different from and much narrower than that under which a court of chancery would act in appointing its own officer either to assess or collect such tax."

In the case of *Jochpipvky v. Mercantile Trust Company*, 16 Fed. (2d) 247, the Court said:

"Sometimes receivers are appointed for insolvent or dissolved districts on the statutory prescription, but the Federal Courts decline to appoint receivers for municipal or quasi municipal corporations, unless such an appointment is especially authorized by the state statute.

Under said situations they have no right to have a receiver appointed to do those things which it is the duty of the district's officials to do." *(Marra v. San Jacinto and P. V. Irrigation District,* 131 Fed. 780.)

V.

THE PLAN OF READJUSTMENT IS ESSENTIALLY UNJUST, INEQUITABLE AND DISCRIMINATORY.

Review of the Findings, Decree and Testimony in the Case.

The Findings.

The findings, on page 10 of the Record, set out the table of maturities of the district's bonds, and the Court found that none of the bonds or interest coupons which have matured since January 1, 1932, have been paid (note should be taken of the fact that there is nowhere any effort shown to distinguish between the amounts due creditors upon their bonds and interest, thus a creditor having past due bonds is entitled to more than one whose bonds are unmatured under Section 52 of the California Irrigation District Act); and that a plan has been filed with the petition, R. p. 12, and that it provides "for the purchase of the outstanding bonds of said district with money to be obtained by a loan to said district from the Reconstruction Finance Corporation—as set forth in a certain resolution of said Reconstruction Finance Corporation authorizing a loan of not exceeding $312,500.00 to or for the benefit of said district on certain terms and conditions set forth in said resolution"; that a resolution of the Waterford Irrigation District accepted said loan "on the terms and conditions set forth in said resolution of said Reconstruction Finance Corporation." The findings then outlined further details of the plan and then find (R. p. 20) "that said district is now in default in the payment of all of its outstanding bonds which matured January 1, 1932, and of all of said bonds which have matured since said date, and is also in default in the payment of all interest which has accrued on said outstanding bonds since the 1st day of January, 1932." In other words, the district has paid interest to July 1, 1932, and here again is a discrimination. The findings also show (R. p. 22) that in 1933 the district was authorized by the California Districts Securities Commission, under the provisions of Section 11, to levy an assessment rate of $4.00 based upon said section, and likewise in 1934; that the assets and liabilities of the district as shown on September 30, 1934 (R. p. 24), were $821,933.36, and its liabilities $730,840.03; that the assessed value of the lands in the district is over $1,000,000.00. (R. p. 23.) The Court finds that the district will not be able to collect sufficient sums,

by assessments or otherwise, to pay its existing debts
as they mature or more revenues than will be necessary to provide for operation and maintenance and
to pay the amounts required under the refunding
bonds provided in the plan of readjustment; and
"that the market value of the outstanding bonds of
said district is now less than the price offered for
said bonds under said plan of readjustment"; that
the plan is fair, equitable and for the best interests
of the creditors and does not discriminate unfairly
in favor of any class of creditors; that the plan has
been accepted by the district in a writing (R. p. 26),
filed in this proceeding, namely, by the petition (R.
p. 30); that the district is authorized by law to issue
the bonds; that Chapter 4 of the Statutes of Extra
Session of the Legislature of California requires the
district before a final decree of the Court is effective
to bind the district to file a resolution consenting
to the plan, and that upon the filing of such resolution the district is authorized by statute to do all
things necessary to be done by it to carry out said
plan; that the appellants are the owners of $145,-
600.00 of bonds and that no interest has been paid
on them since January 1, 1932 and that the appellants are the owners of the interest coupons appertaining to their bonds.

The decree (R. p. 39) confirmed the plan of readjustment and declared it binding upon the district (R. p. 41), and enjoined the creditors from enforcing any claims against the district, except in
accordance with the decree, and (R. p. 43) decreed

"that all holders of any of said old bonds * * * are * * * required to deposit their said bonds, together with all interest coupons * * * with said disbursing agent for sale at said price * * * and whenever said district shall deposit with said disbursing agent sufficient money to provide for the purchase of old bonds * * * payment * * * shall be made promptly by said disbursing agent."

Said decree also provided (R. p. 49) "That for the purpose of the consummation of said plan and the payment of necessary expenses thereof, said district be, and hereby is, authorized to issue its refunding bonds", and also (R. p. 51) that any of the bonds not deposited, as provided in the decree, "shall on and after said 1st day of June, 1937, become and thereafter be null and void." (R. p. 53.) The Court is to retain jurisdiction until the entry of final decree, as provided in Subdivision (g) of Section 80, and for the purpose of making such further orders or decree as the court may deem necessary or proper (R. p. 43), the district is "directed and required to deposit with said disbursing agent, within 90 days after this decree is entered herein, such sum or sums as may be necessary to provide for the payment of such old bonds as may be deposited with said disbursing agent at the price specified in said plan of readjustment, to-wit, 48.82 cents for each dollar of principal amount of such bonds, excluding all interest due or to become due on said bonds * * * for which said interest no payment shall be made."

The Plan of Readjustment.

We desire briefly to call attention to some of the provisions of the resolution of the R.F.C. which constitute the plan approved by the Court. This resolution was attached as an exhibit to the petition (R. pp. 78-79), the time limit is set as June 30, 1934, and presumably the R.F.C. may decline to extend a loan at this time. (R. p. 80.) No loan shall be made "unless all of the Old Securities shall be thus deposited or (b) unless the Division Chief shall deem that such a large proportion of such securities has been deposited as will satisfactorily accomplish the purposes of this Corporation in authorizing this loan".

From an examination of this resolution it appears that many things are left to the discretion of the R.F.C., for example (R. p. 85), in the event the counsel for the R.F.C. has any doubt as to the legality of the new bond issue, only a part of the old securities need be surrendered to the district in exchange for its bond issue.

But the essential point we wish to direct attention to is the fact that there is no certainty that the decree of the Court is going to be carried out. The money is not now available and *while the bondholder is required to deposit his bonds, he cannot now secure payment.*

A Short Digest of the Testimony.

The oral testimony has been reduced in an agreed statement to but 20 pages (R. p. 108) and the exhibits are summarized on 30 additional pages. (R. p. 127.)

Two bond salesmen testified as to market quotations.

Galt and Rodden, bankers, testified. Rodden stated that the value of the lands in the district, freed of all indebtedness, would probably be worth from $30.00 to $50.00 an acre. He thought, although he was not sure, "that the landowners could meet the new schedule of payment and also pay their mortgages and deeds of trust". (R. p. 112.)

Mr. Lethmkuhl, Engineer and Superintendent of the district, testified that 1468 acres had been deeded to the district (R. p. 114); that 1470 acres had been delinquent four years and 4767 acres delinquent three years. At R. page 115 he explained that the levy for maintenance and operation was made large enough so that the amount collected would be sufficient for their needs, taking into account the delinquency. He thought that $2.00 a hundred would be sufficient for the general fund levy for the future. The water right of the district purchased for $170,000.00 he said was worth more than that amount. (R. p. 121.) In 1933 the district diverted 31,155 acre feet; at a fair average he said this is worth a dollar an acre foot. (R. p. 121.) (Here let it be remarked that $30,000.00 per year at 4% is sufficient to pay the interest on $750,-000.00, which is more than the bond debt today.)

C. W. Quinley, Secretary, Tax Collector and Treasurer (R. p. 122) testified that a large number of the landowners could take advantage of the ten year installment plan of redemption to pay their taxes, if the assessments were reduced under the conditions of the loan. Under the refinancing plan the rate could be kept at about $4.00. "The district has not taken a deed to certain land to which it can take a deed, because they think that it may be redeemed." (R. p. 122.) "He assessed the land of the Waterford Irrigation District in 1934 at $1,010,923.00 and this refers to the land only and not the improvements." (R. p. 123.) There is $7048.56 in the Bond Fund. He verified the application to the Reconstruction Finance Corporation, wherein he stated that the average fair and reasonable value of the land in 1933 was $45.00.

(R. p. 124.) M. R. Pitts in the title business testified that according to county records the amount of mortgages and deeds of trust against the lands in the district is $1,010,612.00.

George F. Covell (R. p. 124) testified that he had known irrigation bonds selling at 4½¢ and the purchaser within two weeks getting that much out of the district; that he thinks that the bonds are worth at least 90¢; that he has seen land at Stockton drop to $2.50 an acre in a depression and afterwards rise to $1000.00 an acre; he bases the value on the future of the district; he does not think that California is going to be wiped off the map. This litigation was very detrimental. The Palo Verde bonds went down to three or four cents, Terra Bella bonds at four and a half. South San Joaquin's dropped 25% after the fund was tied up in a lawsuit. Bankruptcy has had an effect upon the value of the bonds, that doesn't affect the real value behind the bonds, because many bondholders are scared to death, afraid they are going to lose their bonds. The worst thing the district has is the mortgage debt which is paying a much higher rate of interest. If the district should proceed with the program of foreclosure on its lands, the sale of the lands of the district would bring in sufficient returns to pay the bonded debt. That would free the lands also of their mortgage debt.

J. R. Mason, for 20 years in the investment bond business in California, stated that the value of Waterford bonds was 100¢ on the dollar as long as property in the district had any market value. Although Waterford bonds are quoted nominally at 36 bid, he knows of other quotations where the bid price offered is 11, although bonds have actually exchanged hands at 90, and in his opinion a nominal bid from an uncurrent inactive security is not a test of true value. Bankruptcy litigation has an influence upon the sale of the bonds.

There was no other testimony on the value of the bonds except Exhibits 22 and 23 (infra).

Thereafter follows the resume of the exhibits. (R. p. 127.)

Exhibit 19 (R. p. 127) showed the tax rate in the county for Oakdale High School bonds and Waterford and other school districts, showing that the bonds of these school districts are obligations for which taxes are levied upon the land within the Waterford Irrigation District.

Exhibits 22 and 23, the quotation sheets of Elworthy & Company, quoting prices for Waterford bonds from 20 in 1933 to 35½ December 12, 1934.

Exhibit 31 (R. p. 128) is an application of the Waterford 'District to the Reconstruction Finance Corporation requesting a loan of $415,000.00.

Exhibit 50 (R. p. 130) showed the total assessed value of all property deeded to the district $107,911.00, the area being 1468 acres, in addition to which the exhibit showed there were 956 acres subject to deed to which deeds had not been taken.

Exhibit 54 (R. p. 131) showed the tax rate for 1931-32 showing that no provision for payment of principal was made during that year.

Exhibit 55 (R. p. 131) showed that an inadequate tax rate was levied for 1932-33 not sufficient to pay the principal of all bonds that would mature or sufficient to pay the interest. Mr. Quinley explained that it was calculated that moneys received from redemptions would make up the difference.

Exhibit 56 (R. p. 131) showed that the levy for 1933-34 did not levy an assessment sufficient to pay interest on bonds, nor the principal of bonds.

Exhibit 57 (R. p. 132) showed the same for 1934-35. The resolution also showed that the assessed value of the property in the district in 1934 was $1,010,-923.00.

Exhibit 72 (R. p. 134) again showed the assessed value of the district; it showed the county value of land as well.

Exhibit 78 (R. p. 135) was a photostatic copy of a bond of the first issue showing that the bond is an unqualified promise to pay, issued "in strict conformity with the Constitution and Statutes of the State of California.'' Attached to it is the State Controller's Certificate certifying that it is a legal investment for all trust funds and for the funds of all insurance companies, banks, school funds, and funds which may be invested in county, municipal or school district bonds, and that it may, according to the Constitution of California, be used as security for the deposit of public money in banks in said State.

Exhibit D (R. p. 139) was a statement from the Auditor's Office of Stanislaus County showing the overlapping bonds, the County Highway bonds, $971,-000.00; Oakdale High School, $24,000.00; Waterford School District, $16,000.00; Empire Union, $39,500.00; Roberts Ferry Union, $1000.00.

Exhibit E (R. p. 140) contained a short history of the Waterford District in Bulletin 21 of the Division of Water Resources of the State of California, to which reference is made.

The Master's Report.

A resume of this report is set forth at R. p. 147.

At R. p. 150 it is shown that the Master ''commented that these bonds were not listed on any regular exchange and, as there was no general market for the bonds and but few sales, he did not consider the evidence of great weight, except as showing the general public appraisal of their market worth'', referring to the evidence offered as to the market value of the bonds, showing that these bonds were quoted by dealers at certain prices. The Master also (R. p.

152) in discussing the question of the insolvency of the district said:

"Counsel for respondents ably argued that exhibits introduced by Petitioner show that the assets of the District exceed the amount of the outstanding indebtedness and therefore the District is not insolvent within the meaning of Section 1, Paragraph 15, of the Bankruptcy Act. However in the opinion of the Master the District comes within the terms of the alternative provision that it is unable to meet its debts as they mature."

Touching upon the application of funds on hand, the Master was of the opinion "that under instruction from the California District Securities Commission, all assessments were properly placed in the General Fund and not in the Bond Principal or the Bond Interest Fund, and that consequently all funds on hand must be deemed to be in the General Fund and not subject to call for either matured bonds or interest coupons". (R. p. 152.) This conclusion is erroneous under California decisions. If Section 11 purports to authorize that, then Section 11 is unconstitutional as violating the constitutional prohibition against impairment of contract. (*Shouse v. Quinley,* 37 Pac. (2d) 89.) On the same page, also: "The Master referred to the bond issues of other taxing agencies within the boundaries of the Waterford Irrigation District * * * but he declined to consider this evidence for the reason that these bond issues were not debts of Waterford Irrigation District, particularly as the district did not create the indebtedness and Section 80 of the Bankruptcy Act concerns only creditors of the taxing district.''

The Plan is Unfair.

The plan is unfair because (1) it is not fair to assess the value of these bonds under depression conditions, (2) the assets of the Waterford Irrigation District exceed its liabilities, (3) trust funds and trust properties belonging to the bondholders are taken, (4) the debts due the holders of county and school bonds are not included, (5) junior encumbrancers, to-wit: mortgage holders and deed of trust holders, are not subjected to these proceedings and their debts are not scaled down in just proportion, (6) property rights are transferred from the bondholders to the landowners.

1. It is Unfair to Assess Value of Bonds Under Depression Conditions.

It would seem obvious that this statement is fair and reasonable that it is not just to place an appraisal upon the bonds in a depression period when the bonds have many years yet to run, and our reason tells us conditions will improve. In fact, the Court will take judicial notice of the fact that conditions are already greatly improved over the low period of 1932.

2. The Assets of the Waterford Irrigation District Exceed its Liabilities.

This proposition has been discussed and it seems obvious that it is unjust and inequitable to give to appellants a value less than the value of the assets of the district.

3. Trust Funds and Trust Properties.

As indicated in the case of *People v. Sacramento Drainage District,* 155 Cal. 373, 103 Pac. 207, all property owned by the district is considered as property of the state—the property is taken in a trust capacity and the agency created by the state is just as much bound by the law relating to trusteeship as a private individual would be. The purpose in both cases, being the taking of the title for the purpose of executing the trust according to any contract that may have previously been executed.

In the case of *River Farms Co. v. California Gibson,* 80 C. A. D. 868, the Court said:

"* * * the county treasurer was made a trustee for a particular purpose, to-wit: To hold the lands and sell the lands for the benefit of the bond fund. This was his duty, whether he acted under the title of trustee for the bond fund, or under the title of trustee for the district. * * * While a reclamation district is only a public agency or arm of the political organization of the state, and is performing only such functions, and endowed with such privileges and powers as may be accorded by the legislature, it acts only in the capacity of a trusteeship, and never as an absolute owner or holder of the title placed in its charge. * * * All moneys collected by the treasurer, whether on account of installments, penalties, interest or sale of lands, must be by him paid into the treasury for the benefit of the bondholders."

The Court quoted the case of *Meyers v. City of Idaho Falls,* 52 Idaho 81, 11 Pac. (2d) 626, where it was said:

> "The bonds succeed to the lien of the original assessment, and the assessments thereafter levied and collected are a 'trust fund pledged by law for the payment of the bonds' ", citing *Jewell v. City of Superior,* 135 Fed. 19.

The Court further saying:

> "It follows, as hereinbefore stated, that the funds collected by the city by means of special assessments are trust funds, pledged to the payment of the bonds issued against each district."

> "The property of a public corporation acquired by it for public uses and in its capacity as a governmental agency is held in trust for the uses and purposes acquired." Section 480, *Jones Bonds and Bond Securities.*

In the case of *People v. Bond,* 10 Cal. 563, at p. 573, the Court said:

> "Having been collected and paid to the treasurer of the corporation, it stands as a trust fund, with the treasurer as the bailee of the same, to be paid to the commissioner."

In the case of *In re Martin,* 75 Fed. (2d) 618, decided February 8, 1935, it was held that under a provision of a bankruptcy act allowing priority for debt given priority by state law, the State of Illinois was held to have preferred claim against the motor fuel distributors bankrupt's estate for unpaid motor fuel taxes.

Money derived from assessments made for the purpose of paying for local improvements become a trust fund to be applied to that purpose.

> *Conway v. Chicago,* 237 Ill. 128, 86 N. E. 619;
>
> *Allen v. Davenport,* 107 Ia. 90, 77 N. W. 532;
>
> *Second National Bank of Lansing v. Lansing,* 26 Mich. 207;
>
> *Red River National Bank v. Fargo,* 14 N. D. 88, 103 N. W. 390;
>
> *State v. Hobe,* 106 Wis. 411, 82 N. W. 336.

Irrespective of statute, a fund raised by a municipality for special purposes is a trust fund. (*Weik v. Wausau,* 143 Wis. 645, 128 N. W. 429.)

The board of supervisors of San Francisco have no control over the treasurer in the payment of interest or principal of the sinking fund in that city. (*People v. Tallant,* 12 Cal. 300.)

At 7 *C. J.* 128, it is said:

> "The trustee does not acquire title to property held by the bank as the mere bailee or as the agent of another. Neither does he acquire title to property, the legal title to which is in the bankrupt as trustee."

> "By the general terms of the act a bond holder had the right to have his bonds paid upon presentation if money were available and if not to have them registered and paid in the order of presentation." *Shouse v. Quinley,* 88 Cal. Dec. 420, 39 Pac. (2d) 89.

4. Overlapping Tax Liens.

The plan discriminates in favor of bondholders of other overlapping districts. In order to illustrate our point more clearly, let us assume for the sake of argument that the Waterford District, County of Stanislaus, and the school districts all occupy the same territorial division. These bonds are substantially on an equality; they are paid from the same sources, by the same property owners.

The aim of the bankrupt law is equality between creditors and a composition must be for the best interests of all creditors and not of a special class. (*In re Kinnane Company,* 211 Fed. 762.)

In the case of *Meyerfield v. South San Joaquin Irrigation District,* 89 Cal. Dec. 700, 45 Pac. (2d) 321, the Supreme Court of California had under consideration the question as to whether a power contract entered into by the South San Joaquin Irrigation District could be assigned as security for one of the bond issues of that district. In the opinion the Court said:

> "The attempt to grant a preference to the holders of bonds of one general issue as against the holders of other bonds of the same general character would, if accomplished, grant a special privilege to one class of citizens not accorded to others similarly situated in contravention of Section 21 of Article 1 of the Constitution of this state."

5. Mortgages and Deeds of Trust.

As to the mortgage obligations whatever liens they hold are certainly secondary to the bonds, yet they are not required to scale down.

As the Court said in the *Frazier-Lemke decision,* saying through Mr. Justice Brandies:

> "Fifth. The controlling purpose of the act is to preserve to the mortgagor the ownership and enjoinment of the farm property. It does not seek primarily a discharge of all personal obligations— a function with which alone the bankruptcy act has heretofore dealt. Nor does it make provision of that nature by prohibiting, limiting or postponing deficiency judgment as do some state laws. Its avowed object is to take from the mortgagee rights of the specific property held as security; and to that end to 'scale down the indebtedness' to the present value of the property."

In speaking of composition the Court in *In re Rider,* 96 Fed. 808, said:

> "The effect of a composition is to supersede the bankruptcy proceeding and to reinvest the bankrupt with all his property free from the claims of creditors. As an abstract proposition, considered for a moment apart from the provisions of the statute, it is entirely clear that a condition so plainly in derogation of common law rights should not be permitted unless it is reasonably certain that the creditors approve and that they will fare at least as well as they would were the estate administered in the usual course. * * * A law which compels a creditor against his will to accept as discharge of his debts just what the debtor sees fit to offer should be strictly construed."

6. **Property Rights are Transferred from the Bondholders to the Landowners.**

The landowners of the district are comparable to stockholders of the corporation, and it would seem, therefore, that considerable benefit can be obtained by the discussion and consideration of reorganization of corporations where there are involved stockholders, and perhaps junior and senior bondholders; in other words, three classes, for that is the situation with the Waterford Irrigation District. We have the irrigation district bondholders, who, together with the holders of other tax liens, are the first lienholders. Then we have the group of mortgage holders and deed of trust holders; and, thirdly, we have those who have the equity, so to speak, in the corporation, who are the stockholders; namely, the landowners. In the following discussion it will be shown that under the principles of the *Boyd* case one class of creditors is not permitted to participate in the assets until the superior class has been paid in full. *There was no right in the stockholders to receive anything out of the corporation before all the creditors had been paid, and it was for that reason that there was written into the provision of the Corporate Reorganization Act a proposition that the Court must see that the plan does not discriminate unfairly in favor of any one class of creditors. That appears to be the reason and purpose of that provision.*

Now, we find the identical provision written into the Municipal Bankruptcy Act. Of course, it is quite apparent that the Municipal Bankruptcy Act is slipshod legislation and seems to have been drafted for the purpose of compelling a scale-down of municipal bonds with some attempt to give legal semblance to the proceedings, and the authors of the bill wrote the same provision in the Municipal Bankruptcy Act, and the Court must determine that the plan is fair and just and that it does not discriminate unfairly in favor of any class of creditors. The meaning of that expression under the reorganization of corporation cases is that a junior encumbrancer or a stockholder cannot be paid anything until a senior lien holder has been paid in full. But under the Municipal Bankruptcy procedure the District Court has interpreted the provision to mean absolutely nothing, for the overlapping liens are not taken into consideration and are to be paid in full, and the stockholders of the corporation are utterly disregarded on the grounds that they are not really stockholders at all, and that the only one to be considered is the juristic person, the Waterford Irrigation District. Thus equity and justice are dispensed with.

The now historic *Boyd* case establishes as a net result that if the plan of reorganization gave a benefit to the stockholders of the old corporation, old creditors who had received no offer of participation in the plan could follow the property of the old corporation in the hands of the new corporation to the extent of the benefit conferred upon the stockholders.

Northern Pacific Ry. Co. v. Boyd, 228 U. S. 482, 33 Sup. Ct. 554 (1913).

Upon reorganization the stockholders may not receive any interest or rights in the reorganized corporation in preference to the creditors. (*Railroad Co. v. Howard,* 74 U. S. (7 Wall.) 392 (1868); *Louisville Trust Co. v. Louisville Ry. Co.,* 174 U. S. 674, 19 Sup. Ct. 827 (1899).)

Objections to the fairness of a plan may arise because it discriminates unfairly either in favor of or against a part of a class of creditors or stockholders or against an entire class of creditors or stockholders.

> *Kingston v. American Car Co.,* 55 F. (2d) 132 (C. C. A. 8th, 1932);
>
> *Southern Pacific Co. v. Bogert,* 250 U. S. 483, 39 Sup. Ct. 533;
>
> *Kansas City Ry. Co. v. Central Union Trust Co.,* 271 U. S. 445, 46 Sup. Ct. 549 (1926).

A fair plan must give due recognition to security holders and creditors in order of priority of their respective holdings and claims. For this purpose, any provision is not sufficient; the provision must be adequate and equitable before lower ranking groups can participate.

> *Louisville Trust Co. v. Louisville Ry. Co.,* 174 U. S. 674, 19 Sup. Ct. 827;
>
> *St. Louis-San Francisco Ry. Co. v. McElvain,* 253 Fed. 123;
>
> *Male v. Atchison R. Co.,* 230 N. Y. 158, 129 N. E. 458 (1920);
>
> *Mountain State Power Co. v. Jordan Lumber Co.,* 293 Fed. 502, certiorari denied, 264 U. S. 582, 44 Sup. Ct. 332 (1924);
>
> *Western Union Tel. Co. v. United States & Mexican Trust Co.,* 221 Fed. 545.

Where, for example, a provision is made to pay unsecured creditors 60 per cent of their claims, either in cash or in new securities, but the actual value of their claims against the debtor corporation is 80 per cent of the face amount of the claims, the offer to such creditors is unfair. The plan must preserve the normal relation between the general creditor and the old stockholder, and the opportunity must be afforded to the creditor to fully enjoy his preference.

> *Mountain States Power Co. v. Jordan Lumber Co.*, 293 Fed. 502 (C. C. A. 9th, 1923), certiorari denied, 264 U. S. 582, 44 Sup. Ct. 332.

The *Boyd* case states the principle that any plan of reorganization which provides for the participation of stockholders without making provision for unsecured creditors is an unfair plan, and that this is true whether or not any equity exists in the property of the old company above the secured indebtedness. The principle of the *Boyd* case is really one of fraudulent conveyance. For the purpose of doing justice the veil of the corporate entity is pierced and the stockholders are treated as if they were the corporation. As a result, the conveyance of the property by the old corporation to a new one, in which the old stockholders are given an interest, is treated in exactly the same manner as if the interest awarded to the old stockholders was a payment to the old corporation. Viewed in this light, it appears that the mortgagor has sold the property to itself. Under such circumstances, the assets or securities given to the old stockholders should be, and are, reachable by the creditors of the old cor-

poration. As the new corporation was a party to the
"fraudulent conveyance", chargeable with knowledge,
the Court permits the old creditors to proceed against
the property of the new corporation to the extent of
the value given to the old stockholders on the reorganization.

> *Western Union Tel. Co. v. United States &
> Mexican Trust Co.,* 221 Fed. 545 (C. C. A.
> 8th, 1915);
>
> *Central Improvement Co. v. Cambria Steel Co.,*
> 210 Fed. 696, 703 (C. C. A. 8th, 1913), aff'd,
> 240 U. S. 166, 36 Sup. Ct. 334 (1916).

"Moreover, the property of the Belt Co. was a
trust fund. The stockholders of that Company
were trustees charged with the duty to apply that
property to the payment of the claims of the trust
company and of the other creditors of the Belt
Co. before they took to themselves any share in or
benefit therefrom."

> *Howard v. Maxwell Motor Co.,* 269 Fed. 292,
> aff'd 275 Fed. 53 (C. C. A. 2d 1921).

In the *Boyd* case the Court declared:

*"For, if purposely or unintentionally a single
creditor was not paid or provided for in the reorganization he could assert his superior rights
against the subordinate interests of the old stockholders in the property transferred to the new
company. Their original contribution to the capital stock was subject to the payment of debts.
The property was a trust fund charged primarily
with the payment of corporate liabilities. Any*

*device whether by private contract or judicial
sale under consent decree, whereby stockholders
were preferred before the creditor was invalid.
Being bound for the debts, the purchase of their
property by the new company, for their benefit,
put the stockholder in the position of a mortgagor
buying at his own sale."* (Italics ours.)

From this quotation it will be readily seen that the
Boyd case has as its underlying principle the idea
that the mortgagor is not to be allowed to participate
in any plan of reorganization which does not first
provide for all of its creditors. If it were allowed
to do so while any creditor was excluded, the result of
the foreclosure sale would be a fraudulent conveyance.

A reorganization which recognizes any rights of
the old stockholders must first secure and preserve
the rights of every creditor.

> *Kansas City Terminal Ry. Co. v. Central Union
> Trust Co.*, 28 F. (2d) 177, 184.

The Court summarized the opinion of the Supreme
Court in *Kansas City Terminal Ry. Co. v. Central
Union Trust Co.*, 271 U. S. 445, 46 Sup. Ct. 549 (1926),
as follows:

"We think the effect of this opinion may be
summarized as follows: That, in any reorganization embracing stockholders, the prior rights of
unsecured creditors against all of the property
involved must be preserved; that such reorganiza-
tions and preservation of such creditor prior
rights are practical matters; that, therefore, what
constitutes such priority of treatment depends
upon the circumstances and necessities of the par-

ticular situation; that determination thereof largely rests in the 'informed discretion' of the chancellor 'concerning the practical adjustment of the several rights'.''

Western Union Tel. Co. v. United States & Mexican Trust Co., 221 Fed. 545, 549 (C. C. A. 8th, 1915).

"Any plan or scheme threatened or executed whereby the holders of the bonds secured by the mortgage and the stockholders secure, or intend or undertake to secure, to the stockholders, by contract, foreclosure sale, or other device, an equal or a greater benefit from the property than is thereby secured to, or offered to and rejected by, the general creditors, is such a breach or threatened breach of trust as entitles any complaining creditor to relief in a court of equity. * * *''

The principles set forth are not confined to plans providing for participation by stockholders without participation by unsecured creditors. They are to be applied with equal effect to any plan which provides for participation of stockholders and at the same time makes no provision for any class of creditors secured or unsecured.

Rosenberg (Phipps v. Chicago, Rock Island & Pacific Ry. Co. (1924), 24 Col. L. Rev. 266, 271):

"The power of the Court to deal in like manner with secured creditors has not been expressly adjudicated but the theory of the Boyd case and of the Phipps case would seem to apply with at

least equal force to secured creditors as it does
to unsecured creditors."

See

> *Male v. Atchison R. Co.,* 230 N. Y. 158, 129
> N. E. 458 (1920).

That the assets of the old company do not exceed
in value the amount of the debts prior in rank to the
neglected class, does not make the plan impervious
to attack when the claim of unfairness is based on
the inclusion of the old stockholders. It is the character of such a plan which makes it unfair, for the
mortgagor should not be permitted to retain any interest in the mortgaged property unless adequate provisions has been made for its creditors. In the *Boyd*
case the Court remarked:

> "* * * *the invalidity of the sale flowed from
> the character of the reorganization agreement
> regardless of the value of the property. * * *
> If the value of the road justified the issuance of
> stock in exchange for old shares, the creditors
> were entitled to the benefit of that value, whether
> it was present or prospective, for dividends or
> only for purpose of control. In either event it
> was a right of property out of which the creditors
> were entitled to be paid before the stockholders
> could retain it for any purpose whatever."*
> (Italics ours.)

The questions which we have discussed under this
heading are both questions of fact and of law. We
suppose that the statute intended to authorize confirmation of a plan of readjustment which would do
the very things which have been done in the *Waterford*

case, otherwise the *Boyd* case would control. We take it that if this statute is constitutional that the Court has power to violate trust provisions, to single out the irrigation bondholders for scaling down of debts, and to permit the school bondholders and the county bondholders to be paid in full; to permit the holders of junior encumbrances, namely, mortgages and deeds of trust, to collect their debts in full at the expense of the bondholders; to permit the stockholders of the corporation, if the Court please, namely, the landowners of the district, to retain part of their assets when the first lien creditor has been paid less than 40% of the face amount of his obligation and the money for appellants is not now available.

As a matter of justice, fairness and equity such a thing cannot be done, but the statute purports to do it, and therefore we have treated the question as largely a legal question and we maintain that if the act permits these things to be done the act is unconstitutional. In support of this contention we cite a case recently decided by the Sixth Circuit Court of Appeals, the case of *Tennessee Publishing Co. v. American National Bank,* 81 Fed. (2d) 463, decided February 13, 1936, which was a case of a plan for corporate reorganization under the provisions of Section 77b of the Bankruptcy Act as amended. In this case it appeared from the record that the total assets of the debtor upon fair appraisal were worth less than $300,000.00, whereas the bonded indebtedness exceeded $900,000.00, and the unsecured indebtedness was more than $300,000.00, to which had to be added the cost of the receivership. The receiver had been operating at a loss, the debtor conceded that it would for sometime operate at a loss. The objectors opposed the plan on the grounds that it was not presented in good faith and that any scaling down of secured indebtedness or denial of the right of lienholders to have the mortgaged property sold at public sale, in accordance with the terms of the deed of trust, was taking property of the bondholder without due process in violation of the Fifth Amendment. The Court held that the question of good faith is not a question of honest motive or intention, but is to be determined by the feasibility of the plan and the reasonable expectation of its success, and cited *Manati Sugar Co. v. Mock*, 75 Fed. (2d) 284, and *In re 235 West Forty-Sixth Street Company*, 74 Fed. (2d) 700. Otherwise the Court said that the way is open to the exploitation of every involved corporation by visionaries whose illusory and optimistic imagination warp their business judgment and the interest of every legitimate creditor is at the mercy of debtors whose sole hope of financial salvation is an abiding faith in miracles. The Court further considered the question as to whether they should pass upon the constitutionality of the act, and remarked that obviously they should not do so unless the case required it. The Court said that it had explored carefully the possibility of avoiding the constitutional question presented. If it were to rest its decision solely upon the lack of good faith, it seemed appropriate to permit further proposals, in which event the constitutional question would remain open for ultimate decision. There was, therefore, no escape, it appeared to the Court, from present decision upon the validity of Subsection (d)(5). The Court then went on to discuss the case of *Continental*

Ntl. Bank etc. v. Chicago Rock Island Railway Co., 55 Sup. Ct. 595, and said:

> "That case, however, goes no farther in its consideration of the due process clause of the Fifth Amendment than to hold that statutory provisions permitting delay in the enforcement of contracts affect only the remedy, and deals with a statute which does not permit adjustments of liens without lienholders' consent."

Delay, the Court thought, in the application of remedies, did not destroy vested right.

> "We are here concerned only with the validity of a clause which provides for adjustment of debts without consent of creditors * * * We confine ourselves to the provisions of Subsection (b) (5) which outline a method of adjustment of claims of non-assenting creditors, and inquire as to their validity in the light of the due process clause. Upon the issue we view the decision of the Supreme Court in Louisville Joint Stock Land Bank v. Radford, 295 U. S. 555 controlling."

The Court then reviewed the right which the lienholder had, and said these rights are substantive property rights and any invasion of them under the authority of the present statute is as clearly violative of the due process clause of the Fifth Amendment as it was in the *Radford* case.

VI.

EXCEPTIONS TAKEN.

Appellants by all proper means made objections, not only by motion to forbid introduction of testimony, but for judgment upon the conclusion of the evidence, by exceptions to the Master's report, and in every stage of the proceeding and are entitled therefore to raise these objections upon appeal. (R. pp. 97, 146, 147, 154.) The Court had no jurisdiction.

CONCLUSION.

We have discussed many of the questions at great length, and we are not unmindful of the serious condition of the Court's calendar. Nevertheless, we feel justified in having given full consideration to many of the matters presented for the reason that one of the most important functions of the State of California is under consideration, that of the irrigation of its lands and the investment of the public in the means of attaining the ends desired. Of approximately 100 irrigation districts in California, with $100,000,000 of outstanding bonds, districts with half of this bonded debt have filed proceedings under Section 80—the Imperial, Merced, Palo Verde, Terra Bella, Lindsay-Strathmore, Oakdale, Waterford, South San Joaquin, East Contra Costa, Paradise, Vista and El Dorado Irrigation Districts. Some of the issues presented are vital, and they are vital not only from the point of view of the related facts, but from the point of view of the Constitution of the United States and of the State of California, and the question argued is whether by this procedure Congress of the United States can subject irrigation districts, practically the state itself, to bankruptcy procedure. Appellants contend that Congress cannot do this; that the attempt is an invasion of state's right; that the sovereign is not affected by the terms of the statute unless specifically mentioned; that the state is prohibited by the constitutional provisions cited from consenting to such invasion of its sovereignty; that the Constitution can not be so amended by the consent of one state. By the decree the provisions of the Fifth Amendment of the United States are violated. The Waterford Irrigation District cannot become a bankrupt. Its functions are governmental and not proprietary. It cannot surrender its taxing power to the bankruptcy court. It does not have leviable property. It is not a taxing district within the meaning of Section 80, but it is a legislative mandatory of the State of California. Provisions of the Constitution of the United States and of the State of California are violated, as well as principles of justice, fairness and equity, when trust properties are taken from appellants without just compensation, and when their bonds are scaled down to approximately 40%, when the assets of the district exceed its liabilities; when the irrigation district bondholders have been singled out to sacrifice amongst other bondholders of the same class, and their property has been transferred by this procedure to the deed of trust holders and landowners. The Court had no jurisdiction to render its decree even if entered within the year nor to make any of the orders which it made, nor to permit any of the proceedings to be taken by the appellee, which the appellee took.

In closing we want to say that it may be plainly seen that the purpose of this legislation is to scale down the debts of governmental units, and as the act indicates, to preserve their assets. As Chief Justice Taft said in the opinion in the child labor tax case, *Bailey v. Drexel Furniture Co.*, 259 U. S. 20, 66 L. Ed. 818:

> "A court must be blind not to see that the so-called tax is imposed to stop the employment of children within the age limit prescribed. * * * It is the high duty of this Court in cases regularly brought to its bar to decline to recognize or enforce seeming laws of Congress dealing with subjects not entrusted to Congress * * * The good sought in unconstitutional legislation is an insidious feature because it leads citizens and legislatures to promote it without thought of the serious breach it will make in the ark of our covenant or the harm which will come from breaking down recognized standards. In the maintenance of local self government on the one hand, and the National power on the other, our country has been able to endure and prosper for near a century and a half."

Wherefore Section 80 of the Bankruptcy Act and Chapter IV Extra Session Laws 1934 of California should be held unconstitutional and the District Court's decree and order reversed.

Dated, Turlock, California,
April 22, 1936.

Respectfully submitted,
W. COBURN COOK,
Attorney for Appellants.

(Appendices A and B Follow.)

Appendices A and B.

Appendices A and B.

Appendix A

An act in relation to relief from special assessments and in relation to financial relief therefrom, and of taxing districts, as defined in Chapter IX of the act of Congress entitled "An act to establish a uniform system of bankruptcy throughout the United States," approved July 1, 1898, as amended, validating petitions and proceedings under or in contemplation of proceedings under, said Chapter IX, and authorizing contribution by cities and counties toward the payment of such assessments, and declaring the urgency thereof, to take effect immediately.

[Approved by the Governor September 20, 1934. In effect September 20, 1934.]

The people of the State of California do enact as follows:

Chapter 1. Bankruptcy Relief.

Section 1. For the purpose of this act a "taxing district" is hereby defined to be a "taxing district" as described in Chapter IX of an act of Congress entitled "An act to establish a uniform system of bankruptcy throughout the United States," as approved July 1, 1898, and as amended by the addition thereto of Chapter IX, approved May 24, 1934. Said act of Congress and acts amendatory and supplementary thereto, as the same may be amended from

time to time, are herein referred to as the "Federal
Bankruptcy Statute."

Sec. 2. All powers herein granted to taxing districts may be exercised by such districts, or, in the
event that such districts have no officers of their own,
such powers may be exercised by the officers who
have the power to contract on behalf of such districts, or to levy special assessments or special taxes
within such districts.

Sec. 3. Any taxing district in the State of California is hereby authorized to file the petition mentioned in the Federal Bankruptcy Statute, and to
incur and pay the expenses thereof and any and all
other expenses necessary or incidental to the consummation of the plan of readjustment contemplated
in such petition or as the same may be modified from
time to time.

Sec. 4. Before the filing of any petition referred
to in section 3 hereof, such taxing district shall adopt
a resolution authorizing the filing thereof and
authorizing its duly and regularly elected or appointed attorney or special counsel duly appointed
for such purpose, to file the same and to represent it
in the proceedings with respect thereto in the competent United States District Court.

Sec. 5. Any taxing district is hereby authorized
and empowered to take any and all action necessary
to carry out any plan of readjustment contemplated
in said petition, or as the same may be modified from
time to time, subject only to the provisions of the

Constitution of the State of California, notwithstanding any other provisions of law.

Sec. 6. No final decree or order of the United States District Court confirming a plan of readjustment shall be effective for the purpose of binding the taxing district unless and until such taxing district files with the Court a certified copy of a resolution of such taxing district, adopted by it or by the officials referred to in section 2 hereof, consenting to the plan of readjustment set forth or referred to in such final decree or order.

Sec. 7. Upon the filing of such certified copy of such resolution, any taxing district shall have power to consummate the plan of readjustment including the following powers:

(a) To cancel in whole or in part, or remit or reduce, the moneys payable under any bonds, warrants or evidences of indebtedness or other obligations of or issued by, such taxing districts, sought to be refunded by such plan of readjustment.

(b) To issue refunding bonds to refund obligations specified in paragraph (5) of this subdivision, subject to the following:

(1) Such obligations may be those of, or issued by, such taxing district, as described in such plan of readjustment. Such refunding bonds shall have such denominations, rates of interest, and maturities, and shall be payable by taxes, special assessment taxes, or special assessments, assessed or levied in the manner provided in such plan of readjustment, except that

no such refunding bonds shall exceed in amount, or bear a higher rate of interest than the total obligation sought to be refunded.

(2) In those cases where the bonds sought to be refunded were issued pursuant to statute requiring any election of voters or electors as a prerequisite for the issuance of such bonds, it shall not be necessary to hold any election to authorize the issuance of such refunding bonds except in those cases where refunding bonds are to be issued by one of the political subdivisions mentioned in section 18 of Article XI of the Constitution. In the latter case:

(I) In the case of cities such election must be held in accordance with the procedure for the holding of an election set forth in an act of the Legislature entitled "An act authorizing the incurring of indebtedness by cities, towns and municipal corporations for municipal improvements, and regulating the acquisition, construction or completion thereof," enacted February 25, 1901, as amended.

The limitations provided by law upon the power of a city to incur a bonded indebtedness not exceeding fifteen (15%) per cent of the total assessed valuation of taxable property in such city shall not apply to any bonded indebtedness issued pursuant to the provision of this act.

(II) In the case of a county, such election must be held in accordance with the procedure for the holding of an election set forth in section 4088 of the Political Code.

(III)   In the case of school districts, such election must be held in accordance with the procedure for the holding of an election set forth in sections 4.960 and 4.1063, inclusive, of the School Code.

(3)   The refunding bonds need not be payable out of taxes or special assessments levied or assessed in the manner in which the bonds sought to be refunded were payable. By way of illustration of, but not by way of limitation upon, the powers herein granted, bonds payable by taxes levied in whole or in part according to the assessed valuation of real or taxable property in a district, may be refunded by the issuance of refunding bonds so payable or by the issuance of refunding bonds constituting specific liens upon real property described in such refunding bonds and subject to enforcement, collection and foreclosure pursuant to the plan of readjustment.

In further illustration hereof but not by way of limitation upon the powers herein granted, any city is hereby authorized to issue such refunding bonds substantially in the manner and form and with the effect provided in the Improvement Act of 1911, such refunding bonds to be payable and to entitle the holders thereof to enforce, foreclose and collect the same, as provided in said Improvement Act of 1911; provided, however, anything to the contrary herein contained notwithstanding, no refunding bonds shall be payable by the levy of taxes or special assessment taxes upon all taxable property in a district, unless the bonds sought to be refunded were payable by the levy of taxes or special assessment taxes upon all taxable property in a district.

(4) It shall be sufficient for the purposes of this act that the petition shall set forth by reference or otherwise:

(I) The procedure to be followed, respectively, in the levy and collection of taxes, special assessment taxes, or special assessments for the payment of such refunding bonds.

(II) The character and effect of, and method of enforcing the liens sought to be created by the issuance of such refunding bonds.

(III) The rights of the holders of such refunding bonds upon the issuance thereof.

(5) The refunding bonds herein authorized shall include bonds to refund bonds secured by unpaid assessments heretofore levied upon real property in a district, and shall also include bonds to fund or refund or pay any obligation of such taxing district whether reduced to judgment or not and whether represented by any written instrument or not and whether arising by contract, statute or otherwise.

(c) To adopt such ordinances as are necessary to accomplish the purposes of this act or to provide due process of law with respect to any proceedings herein authorized. The officers of such taxing district, or the officers referred to in section 2 hereof, are hereby constituted a legislative body of the taxing district for such purpose.

(d) To assess, levy and collect taxes, special assessment taxes and special assessments and to enforce the collection thereof in the manner and with the effect provided in the plan of readjustment.

(e) In the event that the plan of readjustment contemplates the issuance of refunding bonds payable by special assessment taxes, or by special assessments or reassessments, which will constitute liens upon real property, the taxing district shall not have jurisdiction to adopt the resolution mentioned in section 6 hereof unless, before the issue of the final decree or order confirming the plan of readjustment, it holds a hearing after notice thereof as herein provided. In such event before the signing of the order or decree of the Federal District Court approving the plan of readjustment, the taxing district shall cause to be given a notice, for a reasonable time and in a reasonable manner, of its intention to adopt the resolution mentioned in section 6 hereof after the issue of the final decree or order and of the fact that by the plan of readjustment it is proposed to levy special assessments or reassessments or special assessment taxes upon real property in the amounts and in the manner set forth in such plan of readjustment and of the time and place when and where all persons interested in any such assessments or reassessments or special assessment taxes will be heard by such taxing district.

(f) The taxing district shall prescribe by ordinance or resolution the manner of holding such hearing and of giving notice thereof and the effect to be given to its determination at such hearing.

(g) To cancel or reduce the taxes or special assessment taxes heretofore levied or assessed by such taxing district or in its behalf upon any taxable or real property within such district, if such levy or assessment was for the purpose of paying the principal or interest on the bonds sought to be refunded by the plan of readjustment, in the manner and as set forth in such plan of readjustment, and the powers herein granted shall include cancellation or reduction of interest, penalties and costs that may be levied or assessed upon such property within such district by reason of any previous delinquency in the payment of such taxes or special assessments.

(h) The provisions of the Special Assessment Investigation, Limitation and Majority Protest Act of 1931 shall not be applicable to any proceedings taken under this act.

(i) The above enumeration of powers shall not be deemed to exclude powers not herein mentioned that may be necessary for or incidental to the accomplishment of the purposes hereof.

Sec. 7a. Whenever any taxing district has heretofore filed or purported or attempted to file a petition under Chapter IX of the Federal Bankruptcy Statute or has taken or attempted to take any other proceedings under or in contemplation of proceedings under Chapter IX of the Federal Bankruptcy Statute, all acts and proceedings of such taxing district and of the governing board or body and of public officers of such taxing district in connection with such petition or proceedings, are hereby legalized, ratified, confirmed and declared valid to all intents and purposes and the power of such taxing district to file such petition and take such other proceedings is hereby ratified, confirmed and declared, but all such proceedings taken after the date this act takes effect shall be taken in accordance with and pursuant to this act.

Appendix B

[PUBLIC—NO. 251—73d CONGRESS]
[H. R. 5950]
AN ACT

To amend an Act entitled "An Act to establish a uniform system of bankruptcy throughout the United States", approved July 1, 1898, and Acts amendatory thereof and supplementary thereto.

Be it enacted by the Senate and House of Representatives of the United States of America in Congress assembled, That the Act of July 1, 1898, entitled "An Act to establish a uniform system of bankruptcy throughout the United States", as approved July 1, 1898, and Acts amendatory thereof and supplementary thereto be, and they are hereby, amended by adding thereto a new chapter to read as follows:

"CHAPTER IX

"Provisions for the Emergency Temporary Aid of Insolvent Public Debtors and to Preserve the Assets Thereof and for Other Related Purposes

"**Sec. 78. Declaration of policy.**—There is hereby found, determined, and declared to exist a national emergency caused by increasing financial difficulties of many local governmental units, which renders imperative the further exercise of the bankruptcy powers of the Congress of the United States.

"**Sec. 79. Additional jurisdiction.**—Until the expiration of two years from the date this chapter takes effect, in addition to the jurisdiction exercised in voluntary and involuntary proceedings to adjudge persons bankrupt, courts of bankruptcy shall exercise original jurisdiction in proceedings for the relief of debtors, as provided in this chapter of this Act.

"**Sec. 80. Municipal-debt readjustments.**—(a) Any municipality or other political subdivision of any State, including (but not hereby limiting the generality of the foregoing) any county, city, borough, village, parish, town, or township, unincorporated tax or special assessment district, and any school, drainage, irrigation, reclamation, levee, sewer, or paving, sanitary, port, improvement or other districts (hereinafter referred to as a 'taxing district'), may file a petition stating that the taxing district is insolvent or unable to meet its debts as they mature, and that it desires to effect a plan of readjustment of its debts. The petition shall be filed with the court in whose territorial jurisdiction the taxing district or the major part thereof is located and for any such district having no officials of its own the petition shall be filed by the municipality or political subdivision, the officials of which have power to contract on behalf of said district or to levy the special assessments within such district. The petition shall be accompanied by payment to the clerk of a filing fee of $100, which shall be in addition to the fees required to be collected by the clerk under other chapters of this Act. The petition shall state that a plan of readjustment has been prepared, is filed and submitted with the petition, and that creditors of the taxing district owning not less than 30 per centum in the case of drainage, irrigation, reclamation, and levee districts and owning not less than 51 per centum in the case of all other taxing districts in amount of the bonds, notes, and certificates of indebtedness of the taxing district affected by the plan, excluding bonds, notes, or certificates of indebtedness owned, held, or controlled by the taxing district in a fund or otherwise, have accepted it in writing. The petition shall be accompanied with such written acceptance and with a list of all known creditors of the taxing district, together with their addresses so far as known to the taxing district, and description of their respective claims showing separately those who have accepted the plan of readjustment, together with their separate addresses, the contents of which list shall not constitute admissions by the taxing districts in a proceeding under this chapter or otherwise. Upon the filing of such a petition the judge shall enter an order either approving it as properly filed under this chapter, if satisfied that such petition complies with this chapter and has been filed in good faith, or dismissing it, if not so satisfied. If creditors holding 5 per centum in amount of the bonds, notes, or certificates of indebtedness shall, within ninety days after the first publication of the notice provided for in subdivision (c), clause (1), of this chapter, appear and controvert the facts alleged in the petition, the judge shall decide the issues presented, and unless the material allegations of the petition are sustained, shall dismiss the petition.

"(b) A plan of readjustment within the meaning of this chapter (1) shall include provisions modifying or altering the rights of creditors generally, or of any class of them, secured or unsecured, either through the issuance of new securities of any character or otherwise; and (2) may contain such other provisions and agreements, not inconsistent with this chapter, as the parties may desire.

"No creditor shall be deemed to be affected by any plan of readjustment unless the same shall affect his interests materially and adversely, and in case any controversy shall arise as to whether any creditor or class thereof shall or shall not be affected, the issue shall be determined by the judge after hearing upon notice to the parties interested.

"The term 'securities' shall include bonds, notes, and other evidences of indebtedness, either secured or unsecured, and certificates of beneficial interests in property. The term 'creditors' shall include for all purposes of this chapter all holders of claims, debts, securities, liens or other interests of whatever character against the taxing district or its property or revenues, including claims under executory contracts and for future rent, whether or not such claims would otherwise constitute provable claims under this Act, and all holders of judgments rendered against such taxing district but excepting claims for salaries and wages of officers and employees of the taxing district.

"For all purposes of this chapter any creditor may act in person or by a duly authorized agent or committee. Where any committee, organization, group or individual shall assume to act for or on behalf of creditors, such committee, organization, group, or individual shall first file with the court in which the

proceeding is pending a list of the creditors represented by such committee, organization, group, or individual, together with a statement of the amount,
class, and character of the indebtedness held by each
such creditor, and shall accompany the same with a
copy of the contract or agreement entered into between such committee, organization, group, or individual and the creditors represented by it or them,
which contracts shall disclose all compensation to be
received directly or indirectly by such agent or committee.

"(c) Upon approving the petition or at any time
thereafter the judge (1) shall require the taxing district to give such notice as the order may direct to
creditors, and to cause publication, to be made at least
once a week for three successive weeks, of a hearing,
to be held within ninety days after the approval of the
petition for the purpose of considering the plan of
readjustment filed with the petition and of any
changes therein or modifications thereof which may be
proposed; (2) if a plan of readjustment is not accepted and approved within such reasonable period as
the judge may fix, or, if accepted and approved, is not
confirmed, the judge may, after hearing, either extend
such period not exceeding one year from the date of
the filing of the petition, or dismiss the proceedings as
the interests of the creditors may equitably require:
Provided, however, That if a plan shall not be accepted and approved within one year from the date of
the filing of the petition, the judge, after hearing, may
continue the proceeding for not exceeding two years
from the date of the filing of the petition, with the

written consent of creditors of the taxing district holding more than one half in amount of all claims affected by the plan; (3) shall require the taxing district at such time or times as the judge may direct, and in lieu of the schedules required by section 7 of this Act, to file such schedules and submit such other information as may be necessary to disclose the conduct of the affairs of the taxing district and the fairness of any proposed plan; (4) shall determine a reasonable time and manner in which the claims and interests of creditors may be filed or evidenced, and, for the purposes of the plan and its acceptance, the division of creditors into classes according to the nature of their respective claims and interests; and may, for the purposes of such classification, classify as an unsecured claim the amount of any secured claim in excess of the value of the security thereof, such value to be determined in accordance with the provisions of chapter 57, clause (h), of this Act; (5) may, with the authorized written approval of the taxing district, direct the rejection of contracts of the taxing district executory in whole or in part; (6) shall cause reasonable notice of such determination and of all hearings for the consideration of the proposed plan, or the dismissal of the proceedings, or the allowances of fees or expenses, to be given creditors by publication or otherwise; (7) may require the taxing district to open its books, records, and files to the inspection of any creditor of the taxing district during reasonable business hours; (8) may allow a reasonable compensation for the services rendered and reimbursement for the actual and necessary expenses incurred in connection with the proceeding and the payment of special masters, readjustment managers and committees or other representatives of creditors of the taxing district, and the attorneys or agents of any of the foregoing; and appeals may be taken, from the orders making such allowances, to the Circuit Court of Appeals for the circuit in which the proceeding under this chapter is pending, independently of other appeals which may be taken in the proceedings, and such appeals shall be heard, summarily; *Provided, however,* That no fees, compensation, reimbursement, or other allowances for attorneys, agents, committees, or other representatives of creditors shall be assessed against the taxing district or paid from any revenues, property, or funds except in the manner and in such sums, if any, as may be provided for in the plan of readjustment; (9) in addition to the provisions of chapter II of this Act for the staying of pending suits, the court may upon notice enjoin or stay until after final decree, the commencement or continuation of suits against the taxing district, or any officer or inhabitant of the taxing district, on account of the indebtedness of such taxing district, or to enforce any lien or to enforce levy of taxes for the payment of any such indebtedness: *Provided, however,* That the judge may enter an interlocutory decree providing that the plan shall be temporarily operative with respect to all indebtedness affected thereby and that the payment of the principal or interest, or both, of such indebtedness shall be temporarily postponed or extended or otherwise readjusted in the same manner and upon the same terms as if such plan had been finally confirmed and put into effect, and upon the entry of such decree the principal or interest, or both, of such indebtedness which has otherwise become due, or which would otherwise become due, shall not be or become due or payable, and the payment of all such indebtedness shall be postponed during the period in which such decree shall remain in force; and (10) may refer any matters to a special master, for consideration and report upon specified issues; but (11) shall not, by any order or decree, in the proceeding or otherwise, interfere with (a) any of the political or governmental powers of the taxing district, or (b) any of the property or revenues of the taxing district necessary in the opinion of the judge for essential governmental purposes, or (c) any income-producing property, unless the plan of readjustment so provides. The taxing district shall be heard on all questions. Any creditor shall be heard on the question of the proposed confirmation of the plan, and, upon filing a petition for leave to intervene, on such other questions arising in the proceeding as the judge shall determine.

"(d) The plan of readjustment shall not be confirmed until it has been accepted in writing, filed in the proceeding, by or on behalf of creditors whose claims have been allowed holding two thirds in amount of the claims of each class whose claims have been allowed and would be affected by the plan, and by creditors holding 66⅔ per centum in the case of drainage, irrigation, reclamation, and levee districts and creditors holding 75 per centum in the case of all other taxing districts in amount of the claims of all classes of the taxing district affected by the plan, but excluding claims owned, held, or controlled by a taxing district, and such plan has been accepted and approved by the taxing district in a writing filed in the proceeding, signed in its name by an authorized authority: *Provided, however,* That it shall not be requisite to the confirmation of the plan that there be such acceptance by any creditor or class of creditors (a) whose claims are not affected by the plan, or (b) if the plan makes provision for the payment of their claims in cash in full, or (c) if provision is made in the plan for the protection of the interests, claims, or liens of such creditors or class of creditors.

"(e) After hearing such objections as may be made to the plan, the judge shall confirm the plan if satisfied that (1) it is fair, equitable, and for the best interests of the creditors, and does not discriminate unfairly in favor of any class of creditors; (2) complies with the provisions of subdivision (b) of this chapter; (3) has been accepted and approved as required by the provisions of subdivision (d) of this chapter; (4) all amounts to be paid by the taxing district for services or expenses incident to the readjustment have been fully disclosed and are reasonable; (5) the offer of the plan and its acceptance are in good faith; and (6) the taxing district is authorized by law, upon confirmation of the plan, to take all action necessary to carry out the plan. Before a plan is confirmed, changes and modifications may be made therein, with the approval of the judge after hearing upon notice to creditors, subject to the right of any creditor who shall previously have accepted the plan to withdraw his acceptance, within a period to be fixed by the judge and after such notice

as the judge may direct, if, in the opinion of the
judge, the change or modification will be materially
adverse to the interest of such creditor, and if any
creditor having such right of withdrawal shall not
withdraw within such period, he shall be deemed to
have accepted the plan as changed or modified: *Provided, however,* That the plan as changed or modified
shall comply with all the provisions of this subdivision.

"(f) Upon such confirmation the provisions of
the plan and of the order of confirmation shall be
binding upon (1) the taxing district, and (2) all
creditors, secured or unsecured, whether or not
affected by the plan, and whether or not their claims
shall have been filed or evidenced, and if filed or
evidenced, whether or not allowed, including creditors
who have not, as well as those who have, accepted it.

"(g) In the event the judge shall disapprove the
plan he shall file an opinion stating his reasons for
such disapproval. If he approve the plan, the final
decree shall discharge the taxing district from those
debts and liabilities dealt with in the plan except as
provided in the plan; and upon the entry of such
decree the juridiction of the court in such proceeding
shall cease.

"(h) A certified copy of the final decree or of
an order confirming a plan of readjustment, or of
any other decree or order entered in a proceeding
under this chapter, shall be evidence of the jurisdiction of the court, the regularity of the proceedings
and the fact that the decree or order was made. A

certified copy of an order directing the transfer of any property dealt with by the plan, shall be evidence of the transfer of title accordingly, and if recorded as conveyances are recorded shall impart the same notice that a deed, if recorded, would impart.

"(i) In proceedings under this chapter and consistent with the provisions thereof, the jurisdiction and powers of the court, the duties of the taxing district and the rights and liabilities of creditors, and of all persons with respect to the taxing district and its property, shall be the same as if a voluntary petition for adjudication had been filed and a decree of adjudication had been entered on the day when the petition of the taxing district was approved.

"(j) This chapter shall take effect and be in force from and after the date of the approval of this amendatory Act and shall apply as fully to taxing districts and their creditors, whose interests or debts have been acquired or incurred prior to such date, as to taxing districts and their creditors, whose interests or debts are acquired or incurred after such date.

"(k) Nothing contained in this chapter shall be construed to limit or impair the power of any State to control, by legislation or otherwise, any political subdivision thereof in the exercise of its political or governmental powers, including expenditures therefor, and including the power to require the approval by any governmental agency of the State of the filing of any petition hereunder and of any plan of readjustment, and whenever there shall exist or shall hereafter be created under the law of any State any agency of such State authorized to exercise supervision or control over the fiscal affairs of all or any political subdivisions thereof, and whenever such agency has assumed such supervision or control over any political subdivision, then no petition of such political subdivision may be received hereunder unless accompanied by the written approval of such agency, and no plan of readjustment shall be put into temporary effect or finally confirmed without the written approval of such agency of such plans.

"(l) If any provision of this chapter, or the application thereof to any person or circumstances, is held invalid, the remainder of the chapter, or the application of such provision to other persons or circumstances, shall not be affected thereby."

Approved, May 24, 1934, 12:20 p. m.

No. 8141

IN THE

United States Circuit Court of Appeals

For the Ninth Circuit

GEORGE F. COVELL, GEORGE H. McKAIG, E. A.
COVELL, NELLIE L. COVELL, N. O. BOWMAN,
ALICE DENNETT and ELEANOR DENNETT,

Appellants,

vs.

WATERFORD IRRIGATION DISTRICT,

Appellee.

Appeal from the District Court of the United States for the
Northern District of California, Northern Division.

BRIEF FOR APPELLEE.

S. J. HANKINS,
HANKINS & HANKINS,
Pacific Building, San Francisco, California,

A. L. COWELL,
California Building, Stockton, California,

Attorneys for Appellee.

PERNAU-WALSH PRINTING CO., SAN FRANCISCO

Subject Index

                                                                Page

I.   Introduction   2

    1. Short titles of statutes........................   2

    2. The appellee   3

    3. Appellee's plan of readjustment................   5

    4. The issues on this appeal......................   7

II. The argument   8

    1. Chapter IX of the Bankruptcy Act is a uniform law
       on the subject of bankruptcies...................   8

    2. There is no express or implied limitation upon the
       power of Congress to extend the benefits of bank-
       ruptcy legislation to the states or thier agencies or
       mandatories   12

    3. It is not necessary to determine whether Congress
       could subject state agencies to involuntary bank-
       ruptcy legislation to the states or their agencies or

    4. The purpose of Chapter IX is to conserve the taxing
       district and protect the best interests of the creditors   22

    5. If there is any interference with state sovereignty
       by any provision of Chapter IX, immunity from
       such interference has been waived by the state.....   27

    6. While it is not necessary to decide the question in
       this case, the power of Congress to legislate on the
       subject of bankruptcies is superior to any rights
       of the states   30

    7. The special arguments of appellants are without
       merit   33

       a. Chapter IV of the Extra Session Statutes is
          constitutional   33

       b. The Fifth Amendment does not affect Chapter
          IX of the Bankruptcy Act....................   34

       c. Waterford Irrigation District is a ''taxing dis-
          trict'' within the meaning of Chapter IX.......   36

       d. The plan of readjustment has been found by the
          court to be ''fair, equitable and for the best in-
          terests of the creditors'', and not discriminatory
          in favor of any class of creditors..............   38

Pages

Ashwander v. Tennessee Valley Authority, ... U. S. ...,
80 L. ed. 427, 56 S. Ct. 466............................ 30

Back Bay Automobile Co., In re, 158 Fed. 679........... 35
Baltimore National Bank v. State Commission of Mary-
land, ... U. S. ..., 80 L. ed. 388, 56 S. Ct. 417........ 30
Board of Trustees of University of Ill. v. United States,
289 U. S. 48, 77 L. ed. 1025, 53 S. Ct. 509.............. 33
Bolton v. Terra Bella Ir. Dist., 106 Cal. App. 313, 289
Pac. 678 4

California Districts Securities Commission Act, Section 11
....5, 24, 26
Cameron County Water Improvement District No. 1, In re,
9 Fed. Sup. 103......................................13, 21
Chisholm v. Georgia, 2 Dall. 419, 1 L. ed. 440............ 31
Cincinnati N. O. & Texas Pac. Railway v. Interstate Com-
merce Commission, 162 U. S. 184, 40 L. ed. 935, 16 S.
Ct. 700 32
Clark v. Barnard, 108 U. S. 436, 27 L. ed. 780, 2 S. Ct. 878   30
Constitution, Article I, Section 8....................... 8
Constitution, Article III, Section 2..................... 31
Constitution, Fifth Amendment 34
Constitution, Tenth Amendment 18
Constitution, Sixteenth Amendment 19
Constitution of California, Article XIII, Section 1........ 3
Continental * * * Bank & Tr. Co. v. C. R. I. P. Ry. Co.,
294 U. S. 648, 79 L. ed. 1110, 55 S. Ct. 595............. 9, 34
59 Corpus Juris 1104................................. 16

Deering's General Laws of 1931, Act No. 3857a..........2, 5, 24
Deering's General Laws of 1931, Act No. 3854...........2, 3, 4

East Contra Costa Irrigation District, In re, 10 Fed. Sup.
175 ....13, 28, 29

Fallbrook Ir. Dist. v. Bradley, 164 U. S. 112, 41 L. ed. 369,
17 S. Ct. 56... 3, 37

Gunter v. Atlantic Coast Line, 200 U. S. 273, 50 L. ed. 477,
26 S. Ct. 252.. 30

Hagood v. Southern, 117 U. S. 52, 29 L. ed. 805, 6 S. Ct.
608 30
Hanover National Bnk. v. Moyses, 186 U. S. 181, 46 L. ed.
1113, 22 S. Ct. 857...........................9, 11, 12, 13, 36

Pages

Hans v. Louisiana, 134 U. S. 1........................... 31
Hopkins Federal S. and L. Assn. v. Cleary, 295 U. S. 721,
 79 L. ed. 1675, 55 S. Ct. 235......................... 14

Imperial Irrigation District, In re, 10 Fed. Sup. 832...... 29
Interstate Commerce Commission v. Detroit etc. Railway
 Co., 167 U. S. 633, 42 L. ed. 317, 17 S. Ct. 919.......... 32

Klein, In re, reported in a note to Nelson v. Carland, 1
 How. 265, 267 11

La Mesa * * * Ir. Dist. v. Hornbeck, 216 Cal. 730, 17
 Pac. (2d) 143 4
Louisville Joint Stock Land Bank v. Radford, 295 U. S.
 555, 79 L. ed. 1593, 55 S. Ct. 547, 97 A. L. R. 1106...... 9, 34

Madera Ir. Dist., In re, 92 Cal. 296, 28 Pac. 272, 28 Pac. 675 3
Mayrhofer v. Board of Education, 89 Cal. 110, 26 Pac. 646 15
Merchants National Bank v. Escondido Irr. Dist., 144 Cal.
 329, 77 Pac. 937...................................... 38
Morrison v. Smith Brothers, 211 Cal. 36, 293 Pac. 53...... 5

New York v. Irving Trust Co., 288 U. S. 329, 77 L. ed.
 815, 53 S. Ct. 389.................................... 32
New York v. United States (1922), 257 U. S. 591, 42 S. Ct.
 239, 66 L. ed. 385.................................... 33
Norman v. Baltimore & Ohio R. R., 294 U. S. 240, 79 L.
 ed. 885, 55 S. Ct. 407................................. 33

Pabst Brewing Co. v. Crenshaw, 198 U. S. 17, 49 L. ed.
 925, 25 S. Ct. 552.................................... 30

Reiman, In re, Fed. Cas. No. 11,673, 7 Ben. 455, 11 N. B. R.
 21; Fed. Cas. No. 11,674, 7 Ben. 505; Fed. Cas. No. 11,675,
 12 Blatchf. 562, 13 N. B. R. 128...................... 11

South Carolina v. United States, 199 U. S. 437, 50 L. ed.
 261, 26 S. Ct. 110.................................... 32

Turlock Ir. Dist. v. White, 186 Cal. 183, 198 Pac. 1060.... 3

U. S. v. Knight, 14 Pet. 301, 10 L. ed. 465.............. 16

Van Huffel v. Harkelrode, 284 U. S. 255, 76 L. ed. 256, 52
 S. Ct. 115 32

Yolo v. Modesto Ir. Dist., 216 Cal. 274, 13 Pac. (2d) 908.. 5

No. 8141

United States Circuit Court of Appeals

For the Ninth Circuit

GEORGE F. COVELL, GEORGE H. McKAIG, E. A.
COVELL, NELLIE L. COVELL, N. O. BOWMAN,
ALICE DENNETT and ELEANOR DENNETT,

Appellants,

vs.

WATERFORD IRRIGATION DISTRICT,

Appellee.

Appeal from the District Court of the United States for the
Northern District of California, Northern Division.

BRIEF FOR APPELLEE.

Appellants have presented exhaustively under five
main headings the points and authorities on which
they rely for a reversal of the judgment of the District Court confirming the plan of readjustment of
the indebtedness of Waterford Irrigation District.
Preceding the argument are 37 pages of introductory
matter, wherein certain statutory and constitutional
provisions with respect to irrigation districts are
quoted or summarized, and an outline of the proceedings leading up to this appeal is given and the assignments of error on which appellants rely are set forth.

The plan of this reply brief will be to present first a statement of the controversy and matters essential to its consideration and then submit our argument in support of the decision of the District Court.

I. INTRODUCTION.

1. Short titles of statutes.

As it will be necessary to refer to three statutes quite frequently they will be designated by short titles, as follows:

(a) "The Bankruptcy Act", meaning "an act to establish a uniform system of bankruptcy throughout the United States", approved July 1, 1898, as said act has been amended and is now in effect.

(b) "The California Irrigation District Act", meaning the act of the State of California, officially so designated as the same has been amended and is now in effect (Cal. Stats. 1897, page 254, as amended; Act No. 3854 of Deering's General Laws of 1931, as amended); said act as amended and now in effect is given in Bulletin No. 18-D of the Department of Public Works of the State of California, beginning at page 67.

(c) "The California Districts Securities Commission Act", meaning an act of the State of California, officially so designated, approved June 19, 1919, (Cal. Stats. 1931, page 2263), as amended by Cal. Stats. 1933, page 355. This act as passed in 1931 is given in Deering's General Laws of 1931 as Act No. 3857a and is given as amended in said Bulletin No. 18-D, beginning at page 36.

2. The appellee.

Appellants' brief correctly states that Waterford Irrigation District was organized under the provisions of the California Irrigation Districts Act and is engaged exclusively in the distribution of water for irrigation purposes, which is declared to be "exclusively a governmental function". Whether this be true or not need not be determined. Unquestionably the district is an agency of the state. It was held in

> *Turlock Ir. Dist. v. White,* 186 Cal. 183, 198 Pac. 1060,

that such a district is not a "municipal corporation", in the sense in which that term is used in Section 1 of Article XIII of the Constitution of California providing for taxation of certain kinds of property held by municipal corporations, but in that case it was pointed out that in

> *Fallbrook Ir. Dist. v. Bradley,* 164 U. S. 112, 41 L. ed. 369, 17 S. Ct. 56,

such a district is said to be "a public corporation for municipal purposes".

In the case entitled

> *In re Madera Ir. Dist.,* 92 Cal. 296, 28 Pac. 272, 28 Pac. 675,

it was declared that an irrigation district organized under what is commonly called the Wright Act of 1887, which has been superseded by the California Irrigation District Act, becomes "a public corporation"; that its officers become "public officers of the state", and that it is authorized to exercise the power of taxation, "one of the highest attributes of sovereignty". After further summarizing the legislative provisions for the government of such a district and the exercise of its powers, which are in all essential respects the same under the California Irrigation District Act as they were under the Wright Act, the court continued as follows:

> "Here are found the essential elements of a public corporation, none of which pertain to a private corporation. The property held by the corporation is in trust for the public, and subject to the control of the state. Its officers are public officers, chosen by the electors of the district, and invested with public duties. Its object is for the good of the public, and to promote the prosperity and welfare of the public."

In some later decisions of the California courts it has been intimated that such a district should be called "a state agency" rather than a public corporation, but there can be no question that it exercises governmental powers for public purposes, and, as pointed out in appellants' brief, it was held in

> *La Mesa * * * Ir. Dist. v. Hornbeck,* 216 Cal. 730, 17 Pac. (2d) 143,

that the liens of the assessments levied by such a district are of equal rank with county taxes. It had been previously held in

> *Bolton v. Terra Bella Ir. Dist.,* 106 Cal. App. 313, 289 Pac. 678,

that a sale of land for delinquent county taxes would not affect the lien of an irrigation district for delinquent assessments levied by it.

As an agency of the state, an irrigation district in California has been held to be exempt from liability from the torts of its agents. The cases so holding are cited and considered in

> *Morrison v. Smith Brothers,* 211 Cal. 36, 293 Pac. 53,

wherein the distinction between such districts and "municipal corporations" is fully set forth. In the later case of

> *Yolo v. Modesto Ir. Dist.,* 216 Cal. 274, 13 Pac. (2d) 908,

it was held that this immunity from tort liability did not extend to the operations of an irrigation district in the development and distribution of electrical energy.

The provisions of the State Constitution relating to irrigation districts and their operations are correctly set forth in sufficient detail for the purposes of this discussion on pages 2 to 8 inclusive of appellants' brief. The references to a provision of the act providing for the dissolution of irrigation districts on pages 8 and 9 of the brief and to certain provisions of the California Districts Securities Commission Act on pages 9 to 12 of the brief will be considered at the proper places in our argument.

3. Appellee's plan of readjustment.

The decree of the District Court from which this appeal is taken confirmed a certain plan of readjustment of the indebtedness of Waterford Irrigation District. It appears from the agreed statement herein that this district comprises about 14,000 acres of land in the County of Stanislaus, State of California.

It has outstanding certain bonds of two issues as follows:

First Issue	$446,400
Second Issue	185,525
Total	$631,925

The bonds of the first issue bear interest at the rate of 6 per cent per annum and those of the second issue at the rate of 5½ per cent per annum, the interest in each case being payable semi-annually January 1st and July 1st of each year. The only indebtedness of the district consists of the aforesaid bonds and all the interest which has matured thereon since January 1, 1932. The plan of readjustment provided for the retirement of this indebtedness by the payment for the bonds of amounts equal to 48.82 cents for each dollar of principal amount of said bonds provided that all unpaid interest coupons appurtenant to the respective bonds should be delivered therewith, provision being made for a reduction in the amount to be paid for any bond not accompanied by all of the unpaid interest coupons appurtenant thereto, such deduction to be at the rate of 44.79 cents for each dollar of the face amount of any missing coupon representing interest accrued on or before February 1, 1933, and the full face value of any such missing coupon representing interest accruing after that date. These payments are to be made from the proceeds of a loan awarded to said district by the Reconstruction Finance Corporation, an agency of the United States in an amount not exceeding $312,500.

4. The issues on this appeal.

Before entering the decree from which this appeal is taken, the District Court made elaborate findings, based on the report and recommendations of the Special Master to whom the case was referred for the taking of testimony. *There is no assignment of error to the effect that the court erred in making any of these findings or that the findings do not fully support the decree.*

The assignments of error all raise questions of the constitutionality of either Chapter IX of the Bankruptcy Act or of the California Statute authorizing irrigation districts and other public agencies in California to take advantage of the provisions of said Chapter IX, with the possible exception of a few assignments of error which may be deemed to raise questions of statutory interpretation.

The questions involved, according to appellants, are presented on page 37 of their brief. The first two are thus stated:

> "Can a California Irrigation District, a state legislative mandatory, be subjected to the jurisdiction of a Federal Bankruptcy Court?"

> "Can the State of California consent to such jurisdiction?"

These questions are not correctly stated. The question actually before the court is this:

> **Can a California irrigation district with the approval of the State invoke the jurisdiction of the Federal Bankruptcy Court to enforce on an objecting minority of its creditors a plan of re-**

adjustment which has been accepted as provided in Section 80 of the Bankruptcy Act?

As to the plan of readjustment submitted to the court by Waterford Irrigation District, there is no contention that it does not conform in all respects to the requirements of the statute. The questions raised by appellants with regard to details of the plan *are complaints against the law, rather than against the plan.* They will be considered hereafter.

II. THE ARGUMENT.

The authority of Congress to enact Chapter IX of the Bankruptcy Act is found in Section 8 of Article I of the Constitution, giving the Congress power "to establish * * * uniform Laws on the subject of Bankruptcies throughout the United States". If this is a uniform law on the subject of bankruptcies, then Congress had authority to enact it unless the broad language above quoted is limited by some other constitutional provision or principle.

1. **Chapter IX of the Bankruptcy Act is a uniform law on the subject of bankruptcies.**

In numerous briefs filed in various cases in the District Courts in support of motions to dismiss petitions filed under the provisions of Chapter IX of the Bankruptcy Act, the contention was vigorously made that it was not a law on the subject of bankruptcies. The question however, was determined conclusively by the Supreme Court in

*Continental * * * Bank & Tr. Co. v. C. R. I. P. Ry. Co.,* 294 U. S. 648, 79 L. ed. 1110, 55 S. Ct. 595,

wherein, with the concurrence of all the justices, the validity of Section 77 of the Bankruptcy Act providing for the reorganizing of railroads engaged in interstate commerce was upheld. The provisions of Section 80 are so nearly identical with the provisions of Section 77, that there can be no longer any doubt that Chapter IX is a law on the subject of bankruptcies.

Furthermore in a footnote to the opinion of the Supreme Court in

Louisville Joint Stock Land Bnk. v. Radford, 295 U. S. 555, 79 L. ed. 1593, 55 Ct. 854,

it was pointed out that the principle of composition has been applied to the interests of secured creditors by Sections 74 and 75 of the Bankruptcy Act, relating to individual debtors; by Section 77, relating to railroads; by Section 77B, relating to the reorganizing of corporations generally, "and by Section 80 * * * relating to public debtors".

That Chapter IX is a *uniform* law on the subject is equally clear from

Hanover National Bnk. v. Moyses, 186 U. S. 181, 46 L. ed. 1113, 22 S. Ct. 857,

holding that the uniformity required by the Constitution is geographical.

The provisions of Section 80 authorize a taxing district to file in the District Court of the United States a petition stating that it is "insolvent or unable to meet its debts as they mature", and to present for confirma-

tion by the court a plan of readjustment of its indebtedness. The section then prescribes certain procedure and provides that the plan cannot be confirmed
until it has been accepted in writing by creditors, in
the case of an irrigation district, holding more than
two-thirds in amount of the claims affected by the
plan, and shall be confirmed if the judge is satisfied
that

(1) it is fair, equitable and for the best interests of the creditors, and does not discriminate
unfairly in favor of any class of creditors;

(2) complies with the provisions of subdivision (b) of Section 80;

(3) has been accepted and approved as required by the provisions of subdivision (d) of
Section 80;

(4) all amounts to be paid by the taxing district for services or expenses incident to the readjustment have been fully disclosed and are reasonable;

(5) the offer of the plan and its acceptance
are in good faith, and

(6) the taxing district is authorized by law,
upon confirmation of the plan, to take all action
necessary to carry out the plan.

These are the essentials of a composition, and it can
no longer be contended that a law providing for a composition with creditors and compelling the acceptance
by all the creditors of a plan confirmed by the court in

accordance with such a law, is an act on the subject of bankruptcies.

It was long ago determined that in legislating on the subject of bankruptcies Congress is not limited to that subject as it was treated in England and the colonies prior to the adoption of the Constitution. The matter was thoroughly considered in the three cases entitled:

> *In re Reiman,* Fed. Cas. No. 11,673, 7 Ben. 455, 11 N. B. R. 21; Fed. Cas. No. 11,674, 7 Ben. 505; Fed. Cas. No. 11,675, 12 Blatchf. 562, 13 N. B. R. 128.

The first two of these cases were decided in the U. S. District Court for the Southern District of New York in 1874, by Judge Blatchford, and both were affirmed in 1875 in the third case by the Circuit Court. As the first case is cited with approval on the same point by the Supreme Court in

> *Hanover Nat. Bnk. v. Moyses* (supra), at page 187 of 186 U. S.,

it may be taken as controlling authority, and it constitutes virtually a brief on this subject.

In the opinion of the Supreme Court in the case of
> *Hanover Nat. Bnk. v. Moyses* (supra),

there is a quotation from the case of
> *In re Klein,* reported in a note to *Nelson v. Carland,* 1 How. 265, 267,

in which Mr. Justice Catron, in the Circuit Court for the District of Missouri, said that the word "bankruptcies" suggested ideas "numerous and complicated", of which Congress has "general jurisdiction". He suggested as the "least limit" of the jurisdiction on the subject all cases where the law causes the property of the debtor to be distributed among his creditors, and as the "grestest limit" the discharge of the debtor from his contracts. These limits were sufficient for the subject then in hand, but that the legislation on the subject might be even broader was intimated by the Supreme Court at page 187 of 186 U. S., where it is said:

> "The framers of the Constitution were familiar with Blackstone's Commentaries and with the bankrupt laws of England, yet they granted plenary power to Congress over the whole subject of bankruptcies and did not limit it by the language used."

2. **There is no express or implied limitation upon the power of Congress to extend the benefits of bankruptcy legislation to the states or their agencies or mandatories.**

In the brief for appellants there is no attempt to show that Chapter IX is not a uniform law on the subject of bankruptcies. It is likewise not contended that any express constitutional provision limits the power of Congress in legislating upon that subject. The only reliance of appellants, in their contention that Congress exceeded its power in the enactment of Chapter IX, is on a *theory,* expressed in the first point of their argument, that the bankruptcy power of Congress does not extend to the states, nor to their agencies or mandatories.

Against this theory may be cited the decisions of all of the District Courts which have passed upon the con-

stitutionality of this statute, except the decision of
Judge Kennerly in

> *In re Cameron County Water Improvement
> District No. 1,* 9 Fed. Sup. 103,

which decision was reversed by the Circuit Court of
Appeals of the Fifth Circuit, March 3, 1936, in

> *Cameron County Water Improvement District
> v. Ashton,*

in which it was held that Congress "may extend the
jurisdiction of the inferior courts of the United States
over the states of the Union where the state is seeking
relief and a federal question is presented for decision".

Among the decisions rendered by the District Courts
in support of this law, we call special attention to the
opinion of Judge St. Sure in the case entitled

> *In re East Contra Costa Irrigation District,* 10
> Fed. Sup. 175,

in which the following is quoted from the opinion in

> *Hanover National Bnk. v. Moyses* (supra), at
> page 188 of 186 U. S.:

> "The grant to Congress involves the power to
> impair the obligation of contracts, * * *" and, as
> was said by Blatchford, District Judge, in In re
> Reiman, 20 Fed. Cas. 490, 494, No. 11,673: "* * *
> In making laws necessary and proper to carry into
> execution the powers vested by the constitution in
> the government of the United States, congress
> possesses the choice of means, and may use any
> means which are, in fact, conducive to the exercise
> of a power granted by the constitution. U. S. v.
> Fisher, 2 Cranch (6 U. S.) 358, 396 (2 L. Ed.
> 304) ; McCulloch v. Maryland, 4 Wheat. (17 U. S.)

316, 421 (4 L. Ed. 579); The Legal Tender Cases, 12 Wall. (79 U. S.) 457, 539 (20 L. Ed. 287).''

Many pages of appellants' brief are devoted to a discussion of dual sovereignty in the governmental system of the United States. There is no room for debate on this subject. The Federal Government is a government of delegated powers and Congress has only such authority as is given it by the Constitution, or is clearly implied from constitutional provisions. On the other hand, in the exercise of power conferred by the Constitution or implied from its provisions, the power of Congress is plenary, except as limited by express constitutional provisions or by conclusive implications.

But it is argued by appellants that the doctrine of the sovereignty of the state is a limitation upon the broad language of the Constitution giving Congress plenary power to pass uniform laws on the subject of bankruptcies. Thus it is declared in a paragraph beginning at the bottom of page 44 of appellants' brief:

> ''Admittedly, the Congress of the United States does not have the power to enact a bankruptcy law applicable to the State of California or any of its governmental agencies without the consent of the State.''

As authority for this sweeping statement is cited
Hopkins Federal S. and L. Assn. v. Cleary, 295
U. S. 721, 79 L. ed. 1675, 55 S. Ct. 235,
in which the Home Owners Loan Act of 1933 was held unconstitutional to the extent that it permitted the

conversion of state associations into federal associations in contravention of the laws of the place of their creation. Of course, this case is not authority for the doctrine that the reserved powers of the states are a limitation upon the unlimited language of the Constitution with respect to legislation on the subject of bankruptcies. There is no constitutional provision authorizing Congress to pass uniform laws on the subject of savings and loan associations. The chartering of such organizations is essentially a state function, and obviously a federal law which interfered with such a function could not stand.

The only argument along this line which appellants make with any semblance of authority is that which begins at page 55 of their brief, based on the rule that general statutory language does not apply to a sovereign to its disadvantage. In line with this rule, it has been held that the general language of the Constitution conferring upon Congress powers of taxation does not authorize the taxing of the states or their agencies by the Federal Government.

But it should be noted that *this rule applies only to general provisions limiting sovereign powers,* which are presumed not to be abridged unless the intent to interfere with them is clear. The rule as to statutory construction was stated as follows in the early case of

> *Mayrhofer v. Board of Education,* 89 Cal. 110, 26 Pac. 646:
>
> "The state is not bound by general words in a statute which would operate to trench upon its

sovereign rights, injuriously affect its capacity to perform its functions or establish a right of action against it.''

If this rule should be applied to the construction of the Federal Constitution, Chapter IX of the Bankruptcy Act would not thereby be invalidated, because that chapter does not apply to any state or its agencies *to their disadvantage.* It is expressly stated in

> 59 *Corpus Juris* 1104

that the state may have the *benefit* of general laws, and that the rule does not apply to statutes made for the public good. Still less would it apply to a constitutional provision conferring upon Congress plenary power to legislate on the subject of bankruptcies.

That the sovereign may take advantage of general language in a statute which does not trench upon its sovereign rights was established in

> *U. S. v. Knight,* 14 Pet. 301, 10 L. ed. 465.

That case involved the construction of an act of Congress relating to executions and other final process issued on judgments and decrees rendered in any of the courts in the United States, with a proviso that it should be within the power of the courts to alter final process in said courts so as to conform to any change which may be adopted by the legislatures of the respective states for the state courts. It was argued that this language could not apply to judgments rendered in favor of the United States upon the ground that the sovereign was never to be considered as embraced in any statute unless expressly named, *but it was held that the rule did not apply to a statute which did not*

*divest the public of any right or violate any principle
of public policy.* Reference was made to the rule as
stated in Bacon's Abridgment under the title "Prerogative" where it is said that the general rule is that
where an act of Parliament is made "for the public
good, the advancement of religion and justice, and to
prevent injury and wrong, the King shall be bound
by such act though not particularly named therein,
but where a statute is general and thereby any prerogative right, title, or interest is divested or taken
from the King, in such case he shall not be bound".
The same principle was declared to have been decided
in New York, Massachusetts, Pennsylvania and, no.
doubt, in other states, not upon any notion of prerogative, but for the public good.

There is nothing in Chapter IX of the Bankruptcy
Act which trenches upon the sovereignty of any state
or operates to the disadvantage of any of its agencies.
Indeed, as pointed out on page 15 of appellants' brief,
subsection (k) of Section 80 provides that the act does
not limit the power of the state to control any political
subdivision in the exercise of its political or governmental powers, and it is expressly provided that when
any state agency is authorized to exercise control over
the fiscal affairs of a taxing district and has assumed
such control, the district cannot file its petition for the
confirmation of a plan of readjustment of its indebtedness without the approval of such state agency. Furthermore, subdivision (11) of subsection (c) of Section 80 forbids the court to interfere with (a) any of
the political or governmental powers of a taxing dis-

trict, or (b) any of the property or revenues of the taxing district necessary in the opinion of the judge for essential governmental purposes, or (c) any income-producing property unless the plan of readjustment so provides.

The plain purpose of Chapter IX is for the *relief* of taxing districts, and its effect is to enable them to enforce a plan of readjustment of their indebtedness that will make it possible to restore their lands to the public tax rolls and prevent them from being crushed by an unbearable burden of debt.

All that is done by the statute is to open the bankruptcy courts to taxing districts which are unable to meet their debts as they mature and to authorize such courts to exercise their broad powers *upon the creditors of such districts* to the same extent and for the same purpose that the Supreme Court has determined can be done in the reorganization of quasi-public corporations engaged in interstate commerce.

It is clear that nothing in the legislation under consideration violates the rights or affects any of the reserved powers of the states, and therefore there is no merit in the contention that Chapter IX is in conflict with the Tenth Amendment of the Constitution. Indeed, appellants do not point out wherein the legislation as now framed violates any constitutional provision or any of the implications by which state sovereignty has been protected.

This disposes of the analogy drawn in appellants' brief beginning at page 47 between the bankruptcy clause of the Constitution and the Sixteenth Amendment. It was held, as stated on page 49 of appellants' brief, that the amendment was adopted merely to remove a limitation on the power of Congress to levy direct taxes. Therefore its general language was held not to confer power to tax the states and their agencies, which would be to their disadvantage.

3. **It is not necessary to determine whether Congress could subject state agencies to involuntary bankruptcy proceedings.**

While appellants do not attempt to show that this particular legislation is in violation of the Constitution, they urge at great length and with much emphasis that if Congress has the right to authorize a voluntary proceeding by state agencies under the Bankruptcy Act, it must have power to subject a state or its agencies to the unlimited authority of the bankruptcy court without the consent and against the will of the state.

They cite no authority and give no reason for this conclusion. They merely allege it or assume it. For example, on page 54 of their brief, they say: "Under this constitutional authority and the unlimited power vested in Congress, Congress, where it has any power in that behalf, may provide for involuntary, as well as voluntary bankruptcy." This is true, of course, unless the general language of the Constitution is limited with respect to certain agencies by some other constitutional provision or principle.

In the exercise of the bankruptcy power, Congress has not deemed it necessary to apply statutory provisions for involuntary bankruptcy to all persons who are authorized to take advantage voluntarily of the protection of the bankruptcy courts. Indeed, it is pointed out on page 54 of appellants' brief that voluntary bankruptcy proceedings were unknown in the law of England at the time of the adoption of the Constitution. If voluntary bankruptcy proceedings were an innovation in American law, then it is clear that there is no inherent necessity that the power to provide for voluntary bankruptcy proceedings should include the power to provide for such proceedings against the will of the debtor.

Section 4 of the Bankruptcy Act provides that any person, except certain associations and corporations, shall be entitled to the benefits of the act as a voluntary bankrupt, *but a wage earner or a person engaged chiefly in farming cannot be subjected involuntarily to bankruptcy proceedings.* If Congress can make such a distinction and adopt a valid statute of which certain persons may take advantage, but to which they cannot be compelled to submit. then it follows that if Congress is restrained for any constitutional reason from subjecting a state or its agencies against their will to the jurisdiction of the bankruptcy court, this is no reason why Congress may not authorize a state agency to avail itself of the benefits of a bankruptcy act.

A limitation *by implication* upon the power of Congress can have no greater force than an *express* limitation to the same effect. If the framers of the Constitution, in granting to Congress the power to pass uniform laws on the subject of bankruptcies, had added the proviso that no such laws should affect any rights reserved to the states or impair the power of any state to control its taxing agencies, no one would contend that this would have prevented Congress from authorizing a taxing agency with the consent of the state, to apply voluntarily to the bankruptcy courts for such relief as is provided for in Section 80. How, then, can any implication that the power of Congress to legislate on the subject of bankruptcies is limited by the reserved rights of the states be given a greater force than an express provision to that effect would have? Consequently, there is no reason to determine in this case whether some other law might be unconstitutional. The issue before the court is *whether this particular statute* was within the power of Congress.

This was the view taken by the Circuit Court of Appeals of the Fifth Circuit in

> *Cameron County Water Improvement District v. Ashton* (supra).

After reviewing the provisions of Section 80, that court summed up its conclusions as follows:

> "We need not attempt to review the history and development of the Bankruptcy Law. The Act of May 24, 1934, is substantially similar in letter and intent to the Act of March 3, 1933, which added Chapter Eight, containing section 77, to the National Bankruptcy Act. The 1934 Act extends the benefit of the law to political corporations, making relief similar to that granted

to other corporations by the Act of 1933. In *Continental Illinois Nat. Bk. & Tr. Co. v. Chicago, R. I. & Pac. Ry. Co.,* 294 U. S. 648, the Supreme Court construed section 77 and held it to be valid.

"Of course, a sovereign state may not be sued by an individual without her consent. But Congress may extend the jurisdiction of the inferior courts of the United States over the states of the Union where the State is seeking relief and a Federal question is presented for decision, *Ames v. Kansas,* 111 U. S. 449. The immunity of a state and a suit to enforce the obligations of such corporations may be maintained in a Federal Court without the consent of the state. *Cowles v. Mercer County,* 7 Wall. 118; *Lincoln County v. Luning,* 133 U. S. 529; *Leob v. Columbia Township,* 179 U. S. 472.

"It is apparent that the Act of May 24, 1934, was not intended to interfere with the sovereign rights of any state. Full control over the liquidation of the indebtedness of any political subdivision is reserved to the state under the provisions of Sec. 80 (k) above quoted. If the State chooses to exercise her sovereign authority she has the right to do so and the act is without effect. We have no hesitancy in holding that the Act of May 24, 1934 is a law on the subject of bankruptcies within the power of Congress to enact and valid."

4. **The purpose of Chapter IX is to conserve the taxing district and protect the best interests of the creditors.**

In the brief of appellants this statute is treated as if it were solely for the relief of the landowners in taxing districts. A reading of Section 80 shows that this is not its primary purpose. It was passed in recognition of the fact that throughout the country there existed various taxing districts which by reason of their large indebtedness and the decreasing ability of the lands within them to produce sufficient income to provide for the payment of such indebtedness, great numbers of such districts were threatened with total collapse. This was particularly true in the class of districts whose outstanding bonds were general obligations secured by the unlimited power and duty of taxation. In such districts when the default in the payment of taxes or assessments exceeds the percentage of normal delinquency, the burden of taxation is increased upon the lands which still have the ability to pay, and this results in still greater delinquency as the less productive lands are unable to meet the increasing burden.

The famous doctrine of "the last faithful acre" is theoretically possible, but practically a myth. There are some districts in California in which bondholders have sought to press their claims in the hope of realizing something from the last faithful acre, but they have found that when it became obvious that a large proportion of the lands in the district could not meet their assessments, everybody quit paying, and remained on the land, cultivating and harvesting crops in reliance upon the improbability that the bondholders or anyone else would go to the expense and trouble of forcing them from their homes. Indeed. under such conditions, wholesale evictions would be hopeless. No one in his senses would buy land in a

district in which the accumulated and prospective obligations were greater than the ability of the land to
meet, and the bondholders will find that if they unite
to force from the land those whose toil and faith in
its future are the best security for the bonds, they
have robbed themselves of the most essential factor in
making possible the realization of anything on their
securities.

A graphic description of the conditions prevailing
in many of the irrigation districts in California was
given by the legislature in Chapter 60 of the Statutes
of 1933 by which Section 11 of the California Districts
Securities Commission Act was repealed and a new
section of the same number was added. The act was
declared an emergency measure necessary to meet "a
social problem of grave character" and the following
statement of facts was given to show the emergency:

"Due to the existing agricultural depression,
many districts in the State have been unable to
raise sufficient revenue to meet the annual obligations of their bonded indebtedness notwithstanding that they have levied the annual assessment in all respects as provided by section 39 of
the California Irrigation District Act and notwithstanding that they have included an estimated
delinquency of fifteen per cent as required by
section 60 of said act. The situation is rapidly
getting worse, both as to amounts of money in
default and number of districts involved. Assessments and their delinquencies have proved un-
collectible and the lands remain, subject to such
delinquencies, unredeemed. Under present conditions, land deeded to districts after the period

of redemption has expired, is in most instances unmarketable, nor can it be made to produce any substantial revenue. As a result of the foregoing, the burden of each succeeding annual assessment is falling upon a progressively lessening body of lands which in turn is forced to default in greater and greater quantities with the result that unless such process of pyramiding delinquencies is checked at once all lands in defaulting districts will soon be deeded to said districts for non-payment of assessments and it will be impossible for said districts to resell the same. No appreciable sum can, under such conditions, be collected to meet district bonds or other obligations and the fiscal machinery devised for their payment will break down. There will necessarily follow an utter collapse of such districts and their obligations representing a substantial part of the wealth and productivity of the State. The property within such district will be left unoccupied and unproductive and there will be a complete destruction of values in the cities and other territory within, or tributary to, such districts and in the bonds of the districts themselves.

"The Legislature hereby declares that the welfare of the State, the solvency of its banking institutions and the interests of the property owners and bondholders alike, require that the foregoing process of wholesale forced liquidation be stopped immediately, and for such temporary period as will permit ordinary economic processes to rehabilitate themselves and enable districts and bondholders to work out refinancing plans now under consideration before all values within the districts have been destroyed."

While the legislature provided a temporary expedient to meet the condition above described, it is obvious that if the burden of indebtedness is excessive, a radical readjustment of it will be necessary if the district is to be put in condition to meet a part of its obligations. In fairness to all the creditors, the jurisdiction of the bankruptcy courts has been extended so that when a plan has been accepted by a substantial majority and is found by the court to be fair and not discriminatory against any class of creditors, it may be confirmed and made binding upon all the creditors affected by it.

On page 37 of appellants' brief it is suggested that Waterford Irrigation District's plan of readjustment is unfair because the district had relief under Section 11 of the California Districts Securities Commission Act, which is set forth in large part on pages 9 to 12 of their brief. That section, of course, provides for only temporary relief, and the deferring of assessments under it would only make the burden of taxation more unbearable when the time came to meet the obligations postponed by authority of that section.

In such a situation, it is as much to the interest of the creditors that the indebtedness be readjusted as to the landowners within the district. The value of bonds depends, not only upon the possibility of ultimately collecting the principal in full, but also upon the promptness with which interest is paid. If the bondholders are to be disappointed by frequent defaults and harassed by the possibility of the ultimate collapse of the district, it is far better for them

to take a reasonable discount than to insist upon the
letter of their bonds. In many cases it has been demonstrated that the greater the tax levied, the less
is the revenue collected. The assessments of irrigation districts in California are not personal obligations of the landowners and their collection can only
be enforced to the extent of the ability of the land
to pay. Most bondholders recognize this and are
willing to adjust their claims to the facts, but there
is often a minority seeking to gain advantage by refusing to cooperate in a reasonable plan of settlement, hoping by holding out to gain some advantage
over the others. Without the aid of some authority
to enforce a plan of readjustment, either it will be
impossible to carry out any plan and the condition
will become progressively worse, or the reasonably
minded majority will yield and leave the district to
make the best settlement it can with the minority.
The enactment of Chapter IX of the Bankruptcy
Act was designed to promote the rehabilitation of
taxing districts on the basis of justice to all concerned.

5. **If there is any interference with state sovereignty by any
provision of Chapter IX, immunity from such interference
has been waived by the state.**

Appendix A, printed with appellants' brief, sets
forth in full Chapter IV of the statutes of the extra
session of California held in September, 1934. This
act authorizes taxing districts to file petitions and
carry through proceedings under Chapter IX of the
Bankruptcy Act and further contains the following
section:

"Sec. 7a. Whenever any taxing district has heretofore filed or purported or attempted to file a petition under Chapter IX of the Federal Bankruptcy Statute or has taken or attempted to take any other proceedings under or in contemplation of proceedings under Chapter IX of the Federal Bankruptcy Statute, all acts and proceedings of such taxing district and of the governing board or body and of public officers of such taxing district in connection with such petition or proceedings, are hereby legalized, ratified, confirmed and declared valid to all intents and purposes and the power of such taxing district to file such petition and take such other proceedings is hereby ratified, confirmed and declared, but all such proceedings taken after the date this act takes effect shall be taken in accordance with and pursuant to this act."

The petition of Waterford Irrigation District for the confirmation of its plan of readjustment was filed August 6, 1934, before the meeting of the legislature in extra session in that year. That the section just quoted was effective to legalize such petitions was held in

> In re East Contra Costa Irrigation District
> (supra).

In his opinion in that case, Judge St. Sure, after quoting Section 7a, said:

"In the light of the section just quoted, and the knowledge that all matters here under consideration deal with laws, both of the United States and of the State of California, which are remedial (made so because of the emergency element which was the compelling influence in their enactment), the contention that this court is without jurisdiction because the petition lacks the 'consent allegation' must fail. Where petitions of the character here involved were filed prior to September 20, 1934, as was the petition herein, the validating statute by its terms made unnecessary the obtaining the consent of the commission.

"In reaching this conclusion, People v. Van Nuys Lighting District, 173 Cal. 792, 162 P. 97, Ann. Cas. 1918D, 255, has not been overlooked, and is easily distinguishable from the instant case. In the Van Nuys Case a curative statute was involved, while in the case at bar the matters involved are in their entirety remedial, recognized both by the Congress of the United States and the Legislature of the state of California, as growing out of a great national emergency."

The same conclusion was reached by Judge McCormick of the Southern District of California in the case entitled,

> In re Imperial Irrigation District, 10 Fed. Sup. 832.

He quoted the first paragraph given above from the decision in the *East Contra Costa* case and held that the law "clearly manifests the approval by all governmental agencies of the state" of the filing of the petition involved in that case, which had also been filed before the enactment of Chapter IV of the statutes of the extra session.

That a state may waive its immunity from suit brought against it by an individual of another state by making a voluntary appearance has been held in the following cases:

> *Clark v. Barnard,* 108 U. S. 436; 27 L. ed. 780; 2 S. Ct. 878;
>
> *Hagood v. Southern,* 117 U. S. 52; 29 L. ed. 805; 6 S. Ct. 608;
>
> *Gunter v. Atlantic Coast Line,* 200 U. S. 273; 50 L. ed. 477; 26 S. Ct. 252.

It has been definitely held that either the state or the Federal Government may consent to legislation by the other government which would be otherwise unconstitutional. See

> *Pabst Brewing Co. v. Crenshaw,* 198 U. S. 17; 49 L. ed. 925; 25 S. Ct. 552;
>
> *Baltimore National Bank v. State Commission of Maryland,* .... U. S. ....; 80 L. ed. 388; 56 S. Ct. 417.

The latter case held that national bank shares owned by the Reconstruction Finance Corporation were subject to state taxation. The Supreme Court said that if it were assumed that the Corporation is an instrumentality of government, nevertheless, taxation by the state or a municipality "may overpass the usual limits if the consent of the United States has removed the barriers or lowered them".

6. **While it is not necessary to decide the question in this case, the power of Congress to legislate on the subject of bankruptcies is superior to any rights of the states.**

This principle was recognized in the recent case of

> *Ashwander v. Tennessee Valley Authority,* ...... U. S. ....; 80 L. ed. 427; 56 S. Ct. 466.

Likewise, general language in the Constitution was construed without reference to state sovereignty in

Chisholm v. Georgia, 2 Dall. 419, 1 L. ed. 440.

That was a suit against the State of Georgia by an individual of another state, under authority of Section 2 of Article III of the Constitution, providing that the judicial power of the Federal Government should extend to a controversy between a state and citizens of another state. Notwithstanding the general rule that a sovereign could not be sued without its consent, it was held that the general language of the Constitution overrode any doctrine of state sovereignty.

As pointed out on page 69 of appellants' brief in a quotation from

Hans v. Louisiana, 134 U. S. 1,

the decision "created such a shock of surprise throughout the country that, at the first meeting of Congress thereafter, the Eleventh Amendment to the Constitution was almost unanimously proposed and was in due course adopted". This amendment declares that the judicial power of the United States shall not be construed to extend to any suit in law or equity commenced or prosecuted against one of the United States by a citizen of another state or by citizens or subjects of any foreign state. Thus it was necessary to amend the Constitution in order to limit the application of general language in the original instrument. If the doctrine of state sovereignty had to yield in that instance, how can it now be invoked to limit the plain provision of the Constitution giving Congress plenary power to pass uniform laws on the subject of bankruptcies?

The right to levy taxes has been called "the highest attribute of sovereignty" and yet when a bankrupt is delinquent in the payment of taxes, a claim must be filed by the state or the taxing agency in the bankruptcy proceeding, or the discharge of the bankrupt extinguishes the lien of the taxes. As was said in

> *New York v. Irving Trust Co.,* 288 U. S. 329;
> 77 L. ed. 815; 53 S. Ct. 389:

"If a state desires to participate in the assets of a bankrupt, she must submit to appropriate requirements by the controlling power."

Likewise, it was held in

> *Van Huffel v. Harkelrode,* 284 U. S. 255; 76
> L. ed. 256; 52 S. Ct. 115,

that property administered in bankruptcy may be sold free and clear of the lien of the state tax.

Furthermore in the regulation of interstate commerce, the rights of the states have often been compelled to yield to the authority of Congress. See

> *Cincinnati N. O. & Texas Pac. Railway v. Interstate Commerce Commission,* 162 U. S.
> 184; 40 L. ed. 935; 16 S. Ct. 700;
> *Interstate Commerce Commission v. Detroit etc. Railway Co.,* 167 U. S. 633; 42 L. ed.
> 317; 17 S. Ct. 919;
> *South Carolina v. United States,* 199 U. S.
> 437; 50 L. ed. 261; 26 S. Ct. 110;

Board of Trustees of University of Ill. v.
United States, 289 U. S. 48; 77 L. ed. 1025;
53 S. Ct. 509;

New York v. United States (1922), 257 U. S.
591; 42 S. Ct. 239; 66 L. ed. 385.

In the recent decision in

Norman v. Baltimore & Ohio R. R., 294 U. S.
240; 79 L. ed. 885; 55 S. Ct. 407,

Congress, under its general power with respect to
money, was held to have the power to make private
obligations payable in any legal tender notwithstanding contracts under state authority that they must be
payable in gold.

7. The special arguments of appellants are without merit.

a. Chapter IV of the Extra Session Statutes is constitutional.

It is argued in appellants' brief that Chapter IV of
the Statutes of the Extra Session of the California
Legislature authorizing taxing districts to take advantage of Chapter IX of the Bankruptcy Act is unconstitutional: *First,* on the ground that it impairs
the obligation of contracts, and *Second,* that it was not
proper to enact it as an emergency measure.

The first argument is clearly without merit because
the act does not impair any obligations, but merely
authorizes taxing districts to file and prosecute in the
Bankruptcy Court proceedings authorized by Congress. To the extent that there is any impairment of
contracts, this results from the Act of Congress and
not from state law. Private corporations are creatures
of state law, but it has never been held that they
cannot file petitions in bankruptcy.

The second argument means only that the provision of Chapter IV putting it into immediate effect might be void. If so, the validity of the act was not affected. Its effective date was merely deferred until 90 days after the adjournment of the legislature. In any case, it was effective long before the decree herein was entered.

b. The Fifth Amendment does not affect Chapter IX of the Bankruptcy Act.

The argument that Chapter IX of the Bankruptcy Act is in violation of the Fifth Amendment of the Constitution is best answered by reference to

> *Continental * * * Bank & Trust Co. v. C. R. I.*
> *and P. Ry. Co.* (supra),

in which Section 77 of the Bankruptcy Act was upheld, although it is almost identical in its provisions with Section 80 and affects both secured and unsecured claims. There is no similarity between this legislation and the Frazier-Lemke Act that was held in

> *Louisville Joint Stock Land Bank v. Radford,*
> 295 U. S. 555, 79 L. ed. 1593, 55 S. Ct. 547,
> 97 A. L. R. 1106,

to violate the Fifth Amendment, because it arbitrarily deprived a mortgage holder of his security.

The only portion of the Fifth Amendment applicable to this matter is the provision that no person shall be deprived of property without due process of law. The last clause of the amendment that private property shall not be taken for public use without just compensation is inapplicable because the operation of a bankruptcy act is in no sense a taking of private property for public use.

A cursory reading of Chapter IX of the Bankruptcy Act will show that all of the requirements of due process of law have been observed in its provisions. When the petition is filed, a notice of the filing and of a time for a hearing thereon must be given by publication for at least three weeks and a hearing in court must be held on such notice within 90 days after the filing of the petition. It is further provided that at least 90 days must be allowed after the first publication of the required notice within which creditors may appear and contest the petition.

It is provided that the creditors making such appearance must hold at least five per centum in amount of the evidences of indebtedness described in the petition in order to raise a controversy requiring a decision on the issue presented, but in any event the plan of readjustment proposed is subject to confirmation by the court and any creditor may be heard on that point. This provision is well within the powers of Congress on the subject of bankruptcies.

Thus it appears from

In re Back Bay Automobile Co., 158 Fed. 679, that the Act of 1898 authorizes a bankrupt to offer a composition of his debts and that Section 55c of that act provides that the court shall call a meeting of creditors whenever one-fourth or more in number of those who have proven their claims shall request it. The requirement for a reasonable concert of action on the part of creditors in bankruptcy proceedings is common.

It was urged in

Hanover National Bank v. Moyses (supra),
that the Bankruptcy Act of 1898, as to voluntary proceedings, would deprive creditors of property without
due process of law, but the opinion, beginning at page
190 of the U. S. Report, shows that this objection was
untenable.

c. **Waterford Irrigation District is a "taxing district" within the
meaning of Chapter IX.**

Point IV of appellants' brief makes the contention
that Waterford Irrigation District "is not a subject
of bankruptcy", because its functions are essentially
governmental rather than proprietary. The Bankruptcy Act makes no such distinction, and we see no
reason for determining the question or reviewing the
numerous cases on the subject cited by appellants.
Section 80 of the Bankruptcy Act provides that any
"municipality or other political subdivision of any
state, including (but not hereby limiting the generality
of the foregoing) any county, city, * * * school,
drainage, irrigation * * * or other districts
(hereby referred to as a 'taxing district') may file
a petition", as further provided in that section. Appellants quote the foregoing and then cite California
cases holding that an irrigation district in this state
is not considered a "municipal corporation" or a
"political subdivision" and they argue that an irrigation district is not a "taxing district".

In determining this question, the court will seek to
ascertain the intent of Congress and will not be bound
by technical decisions of state courts as to the nature

of their agencies. In numerous Acts of Congress the term "political subdivision" has been used to include all kinds of districts, and in the Federal Power Act the term "municipality" is expressly defined to include irrigation districts. Likewise in

Fallbrook Irrigation District v. Bradley (supra),

an irrigation district was held to be a "public corporation for municipal purposes", and Congress must be held to have intended to use the terms "municipality" and "political subdivisions" in the broadest sense.

Furthermore, the Congressional reports show that the proponents of this law were the drainage districts of the south and middle west and the irrigation districts of the west and southwest, and, of course, Congress intended by its specific mention of such districts to include them.

Appellants also make a highly technical argument to the effect that the landowners rather than the district are the real debtors on the bonds. It is not denied that the bonds themselves declare that the district "is indebted to and promises to pay" the bearer of the bond its principal amount and the interest thereon, and that suits to enforce the obligations under the bonds must be brought against the district or its officers. Therefore it is absurd to say that the district is not a debtor.

Equally inconclusive is the contention that the district cannot be "bankrupt" or "insolvent". The law does not require it to be. It affords relief if the district is "insolvent *or* unable to meet its debts as they mature".

The assets of such a district cannot be seized or distributed for the benefit of its creditors. This was expressly held in

> *Merchants National Bank v. Escondido Irr. Dist.,* 144 Cal. 329, 77 Pac. 937.

In so far as the creditors are concerned, the only assets of such a district are its powers of taxation and the ability of the landowners to respond to tax levies. If the lands cannot pay the necessary taxes to meet the obligations of the district, it is insolvent, and if the maturities of its outstanding obligations are so arranged that the amounts to be paid are in excess of the ability of the land to meet then the district cannot meet its debts as they mature. In either event the district is entitled to such relief as may be fair and equitable to the creditors.

d.   The plan of readjustment has been found by the court to be "fair, equitable and for the best interests of the creditors", and not discriminatory in favor of any class of creditors.

The assignments of error do not challenge the correctness of this finding and it is abundantly supported by the evidence summarized in the agreed statement on appeal, set forth in the printed transcript herein.

In view of the fact that the assignments of error do not challenge the correctness of the findings, we believe it is improper for appellants in their brief to attack the plan on any question of fact. Indeed it may be said that the six particulars in which the plan is declared to be unfair raise questions of law rather than questions of fact. These particulars are presented in the brief beginning at page 137.

The first of these specifications of unfairness is that the value of the bonds should not be determined under depression conditions. The answer is that the fairness of the plan must be determined when the proceeding is before the court. It must be presumed that the court took into consideration all of the conditions affecting the value of the bonds and made its determination with due regard to the interests of the creditors.

The second specification is that the assets of the district exceed its liabilities as shown by its financial statement. This means no more than that the book value of its works and water rights is greater than the amount of its bonds and other obligations. As the district's property cannot be taken for its debts, this is wholly immaterial in view of the unquestioned fact that the lands in the district cannot pay enough to meet the outstanding bonded debt.

The third specification is that the property of the district and its revenues are held by the district in trust. This is likewise immaterial, the only question being whether the district by taxation can meet its obligations.

The fourth specification is that the plan does not require a scaling down of the obligations issued by the County of Stanislaus and certain school districts which overlap Waterford Irrigation District. The law does not require that such overlapping indebtedness be considered in a plan of readjustment of the indebtedness of a district, and obviously it could not do so. The county bonds are good because all the property in the county, both real and personal, is subject to taxation to pay them, and their total amount is but a small percentage of the assessed value of the taxable property. If the property in Waterford District should all go delinquent, there will still be plenty of property in the county that will respond to tax levies in sufficient amount to meet the county bonds. The same is true of the school district bonds covering Waterford Irrigation District. The amount of such bonds is limited to a small fraction of the assessed valuation of the taxable property within the school district, and therefore, unless the district lies wholly or largely within a defaulting irrigation district, the value of the school bonds is not usually affected by defaults of the irrigation district.

The next specification of unfairness is that the holders of private mortgages are not compelled by the plan to scale down their indebtedness. The answer is that this proceeding is not for the relief of the present owners of land, but is for the relief of the district, and the lands are considered independent of their ownership or the liens against them. The law makes no provision for bringing private parties into this proceeding, except as creditors of the district, and in determining the fairness of a plan of readjustment, the ability of the lands in the district taken as a whole must be considered. The assessments of an irrigation district are not personal obligations

of the landowners and as long as the bondholders get
what it is reasonably possible for the lands to pay
they have no concern with the private relations of
individual landowners.

There is likewise no merit in the sixth specification
that property rights are transferred by this proceeding from bondholders to landowners. As the findings
have not been attacked from the standpoint of any
question of fact, it must be presumed that the bondholders are getting in this settlement all that they
could reasonably hope to get. In the absence of an
assignment of error to the effect that the evidence
does not support the findings, this court will not go
into any details as to the operation of the plan.

Therefore, appellee prays that the judgment of the
district court be affirmed.

Dated, San Francisco, California,
　　　May 8, 1936.

　　　　　Respectfully submitted,
　　　　　　　S. J. HANKINS,
　　　　　　　HANKINS & HANKINS,
　　　　　　　A. L. COWELL,
　　　　　　　　　Attorneys for Appellee.

No. 8141

IN THE

United States Circuit Court of Appeals

For the Ninth Circuit 7

GEORGE F. COVELL, GEORGE H. McKAIG, E. A.
COVELL, NELLIE L. COVELL, N. O. BOWMAN,
ALICE DENNETT and ELEANOR DENNETT,

Appellants,

vs.

WATERFORD IRRIGATION DISTRICT,

Appellee.

APPELLEE'S PETITION FOR A REHEARING.

S. J. HANKINS,
HANKINS & HANKINS,
Pacific Building, San Francisco, California,

A. L. COWELL,
California Building, Stockton, California,

*Attorneys for Appellee
and Petitioner.*

PERNAU-WALSH PRINTING CO., SAN FRANCISCO

Subject Index

Page

I. While Section 80 has been commonly referred to as the "Municipal Bankruptcy Act" a careful study of that section shows that at the very beginning it segregates the public agencies to which it applies into two distinct classes and that this segregation is recognized throughout the section 2

II. The opinion of the Supreme Court in the Ashton case rests expressly upon the determination that the district there involved is a political subdivision of the State of Texas by reason of specific provisions of the constitution of that state................................... ‹

III. Irrigation districts in California are not political subdivisions of the state............................. 11

IV. Provisions of the California Irrigation District Act and various court decisions show that irrigation districts in this state belong in the second class of public agencies and are subject to Section 80 of the Bankruptcy Act 12

V. The decision in the Ashton case holds there is an implied limitation on the bankruptcy power to protect the sovereign rights of the states, just as there is an implied limitation upon the taxing power of the federal government, but such implied limitation in the case of a taxing power has repeatedly been held to apply to the states and their agencies only in the exercise of strictly governmental functions 14

VI. The unconstitutionality of Section 80 as applied to political subdivisions does not render it unconstitutional in toto 17

Table of Authorities Cited

Pages

Ashton et al. v. Cameron County Water Improvement District No. One 2, 14

Bettencourt v. Industrial Accident Commission, 175 Cal. 559, 561, 166 Pac. 323............................... 12
Brush v. Commissioner of Internal Revenue.............. 15

California Irrigation District Act, Section 29............ 12
City of Winona v. Botzet, 169 Fed. 321................. 16

Day v. Buckeye Water etc. District, 28 Ariz. 466, 237 Pac. 636 16

Hall v. Superior Court, 198 Cal. 373, 245 Pac. 814......... 13
Huck v. Rathjen, 66 Cal. App. 84, 225 Pac. 33............. 11

Ill. T. & S. Bank v. Arkansas City, 76 Fed. 271, 281....... 16

Lindsay-Strathmore Irr. Dist. v. Wutchumna Water Co., 111 Cal. App. 688, 296 Pac. 933...................... 13

Merchants' National Bank v. Escondido Irr. Dist., 144 Cal. 329, 77 Pac. 937.................................... 13

National Bankruptcy Act, Section 80, Chapter IX:
Subsection (c), Subdivision (11), clause (b).......... 5, 17
Subsection (d) 5
Subsection (e), Subdivision (6)..................... 6
Subsection (k) 3, 6, 18

Ohio v. Helvering, 292 U. S. 360...................... 15

Pikes Peak Power Co. v. Colorado Springs, 105 Fed. 1.... 16
Pollock v. Farmers' Loan and Trust Co., 158 U. S. 601, 635   17

San Diego v. Linda Vista Irr. Dist., 108 Cal. 189, 41 Pac. 291 13
South Carolina v. United States, 199 U. S. 437........... 15

Tarpey v. McClure, 190 Cal. 593, 213 Pac. 983........... 11

Vernon's Annotated Revised Civil Statutes of the State of Texas, Revision of 1925:
Section 52 of Article XVI........................... 11
Section 59 of Article XVI, subsections (a), (b), (c)...   8

Wood v. Imperial Irrigation District, 216 Cal. 748, 753, 17 Pac. (2d) 128 11

No. 8141

United States Circuit Court of Appeals
For the Ninth Circuit

GEORGE F. COVELL, GEORGE H. McKAIG, E. A.
COVELL, NELLIE L. COVELL, N. O. BOWMAN,
ALICE DENNETT and ELEANOR DENNETT,

Appellants,

vs.

WATERFORD IRRIGATION DISTRICT,

Appellee.

APPELLEE'S PETITION FOR A REHEARING.

*To the Honorable Curtis D. Wilbur, Presiding Judge,
and to the Associate Judges of the United States
Circuit Court of Appeals for the Ninth Circuit:*

Waterford Irrigation District, the above named appellee, respectfully petitions the court for a rehearing in the above-entitled matter, wherein the court on the 19th day of October, 1936, reversed the order of the District Court of the United States for the Northern District of California, confirming and remanding the case to said District Court for further action consistent with the opinion of this court wherein it was set forth that the Supreme Court has held that the provisions of the Bankruptcy Act relied upon by appellee are unconstitutional and that the lack of federal authority for such legislation cannot be acquired or validated by the consent of the state through its legislature.

In support of its decision in this matter, this court cited *Ashton et al. v. Cameron County Water Improvement District No. One,* decided by the Supreme Court May 25, 1936, petition for rehearing denied October 12, 1936.

Appellee, of course, concedes that this Court is bound by the decision of the Supreme Court in the *Ashton* case, but it is respectfully and most earnestly urged that the opinion of the Supreme Court is not applicable to the case at bar and that neither the conclusions nor the reasoning of the Supreme Court support the decision of this court that Section 80 of the Bankruptcy Act is unconstitutional where applied to a California Irrigation District. In support of this contention we submit the following argument:

I.

WHILE SECTION 80 HAS BEEN COMMONLY REFERRED TO AS THE "MUNICIPAL BANKRUPTCY ACT" A CAREFUL STUDY OF THAT SECTION SHOWS THAT AT THE VERY BEGINNING IT SEGREGATES THE PUBLIC AGENCIES TO WHICH IT APPLIES INTO TWO DISTINCT CLASSES AND THAT THIS SEGREGATION IS RECOGNIZED THROUGHOUT THE SECTION.

The *first class* of public agencies covered by the section comprises those specified as follows (italics ours):

"Any municipality *or other political subdivision* of any state, including (but not hereby limiting the generality of the foregoing) any county, city, borough, village, parish, town, or township, unincorporated tax or special assessment district."

The *second class* of public agencies covered by the section comprises those specified in the remainder of the first portion of the first sentence as follows:

> "*and* any school, drainage, irrigation, reclamation, levee, sewer, or paving, sanitary, port, improvement or other districts."

The classification above shown is emphasized by the fact that the various kinds of political subdivisions specified as included within the first class are separated by commas or the word *"or"*, and that each of the agencies specified in that class is clearly a political subdivision exercising general governmental powers, including the police power, or a district having no corporate form but set up by the governing body of a political subdivision for taxing purposes. On the other hand, the agencies in the second class are all districts which have an independent organization but are limited to the accomplishment of specific purposes and do not exercise general governmental functions, are not endowed with the power to make laws, and in many cases are not even political in their mode of government but choose their officers by the votes of landowners in accordance with the amount or value of the lands owned by them respectively.

In the first sentence of Section 80 it is provided that the term "taxing district" is to be used as a general term for all of the agencies theretofore referred to, and it is a striking fact that throughout the section the general term "taxing district" is used as referring to all the agencies to which the section applies, *until we come to Subsection (k), designed to protect the sovereign rights of the states,* and in that section the term "taxing district" is not used *but the sole reference is to "any political subdivision" of a state.*

It seems clear, then, that the section applies to two classes of public agencies, one of which includes "any municipality or political subdivision of any state" and the other comprising districts which do not exercise general governmental functions, but have an independent existence and are formed for specific purposes affected with a public interest but of particular benefit to the landowners within such districts.

This distinction is further emphasized by the fact that the first class includes *no districts* except "unincorporated tax or special assessment districts", which are terms commonly used to designate districts formed by the governing body of a city or a county purely for convenience in the assessment of property which may be specially benefited by proposed improvements to such an extent as to justify special assessments upon such property for all or a part of the cost of their construction. Such districts have no separate governing body and no voice in the management of their affairs and exercise no corporate functions. On the other hand, the enumeration of districts in the second class closes with the term "or other districts", which under the well established rule of *ejusdem generis* means other districts of the same general class as those specifically mentioned, thus indicating that Congress had in mind a general class of districts in a different category from the public agencies designated as political subdivisions.

This conclusion is further supported by the provision in the fourth sentence of Section 80 that the initiatory petition in the case of drainage, irrigation, reclamation, and levee districts, which are the principal districts in the second class, shall be signed by creditors owning not less than 30 per centum in amount of the bonds, notes, and certificates of indebtedness of the taxing district, while in all other cases the percentage required for a valid petition is 51 per cent of the outstanding obligations. Furthermore, in Subsection (d) of Section 80, it was originally provided that a plan of readjustment should not be confirmed until it had been accepted by creditors holding 66⅔ per centum in the case of drainage, irrigation, reclamation and levee districts and by creditors holding 75 per centum in the case of all other taxing districts of the claims of all classes affected by the plan. These provisions were modified *in the case of drainage, irrigation, reclamation and levee districts* by an amendment of Section 80 approved April 11, 1936, but the amendments serve to further indicate and emphasize the intent of Congress to provide particularly for the principal districts in the second class.

Still further demonstrating this distinction, Subdivision (11) of Subsection (c) of Section 80 specified that the bankruptcy court "shall not, by any order or decree, in the proceeding or otherwise, interfere with (a) any of the political or governmental powers of the taxing district, or (b) any of the property or revenues of the taxing district necessary in the opinion of the Judge for essential governmental purposes". This is a recognition of the fact that some of the taxing districts referred to in the section did have political or governmental powers and that Congress should not authorize any interference with such powers.

Furthermore it is provided in Subdivision (6) of Subsection (e) of Section 80 that one of the conditions of the confirmation of a plan should be that the judge must be satisfied that the taxing district is authorized by law upon confirmation of the plan, to take all action necessary to carry it out.

The segregation of public agencies or "taxing districts" into two classes as heretofore shown is conclusively confirmed by the provisions of Subsection (k) of Section 80. Prior to that subsection every reference to an agency subject to the provisions of Section 80 is by the use of the term "taxing district" but in Subsection (k) that term is not used, but instead there is a frequent reference to "political subdivisions". If Congress had intended that all "taxing districts" were to be considered "political subdivisions", then, of course, it would have used the term "taxing district" in Subsection (k) just as it had used it throughout the section. The change in terms shows conclusively that Congress believed that the districts included in the second class of agencies are not political subdivisions and that authorizing them to apply to the bankruptcy court for relief against unmeetable indebtedness did not even approach the field of state sovereignty.

THE OPINION OF THE SUPREME COURT IN THE ASHTON CASE
RESTS EXPRESSLY UPON THE DETERMINATION THAT
THE DISTRICT THERE INVOLVED IS A POLITICAL SUB-
DIVISION OF THE STATE OF TEXAS BY REASON OF
SPECIFIC PROVISIONS OF THE CONSTITUTION OF THAT
STATE.

The opinion of the Supreme Court describes the
district involved in that case as follows:

"The respondent was organized in 1914 as
Cameron County Irrigation District No. One, to
furnish water for irrigation and domestic uses;
in 1919, it became the Cameron County Water Improvement District No. One, all as authorized by
statutes passed under section 52, Art. 3, Constitution of Texas, which permits creation of
political divisions of the State, with power to sue
and be sued, issue bonds, levy and collect taxes.
An amendment to the Constitution—section 59a,
Art. 16—(October 2, 1917) declares the conservation and development of all the natural resources
of the State, including reclamation of lands and
their preservation, are 'public rights and duties'.
Most of the bonds now in question were issued
during 1914; the remainder in 1919."

In view of the foregoing description of the Texas
district, the court declared that it was plain enough
"that respondent is a political subdivision of the state,
created for the local exercise of her sovereign powers."

To understand the basis of this conclusion it is necessary to read the provisions of the Constitution of Texas
above referred to. Section 52 of Article III as set
forth in Vernon's Annotated Revised Civil Stat-

utes of the State of Texas, Revision of 1925, contains the general provision that the legislature "shall have no power to authorize any county, city, town, or other political corporation and subdivision of the state", to lend its credit in aid of any individual association or corporation, but is is provided, however, that any "political subdivision of the state or any definite district now or hereafter to be described and defined within the state", upon a vote of two-thirds majority of the resident property taxpayers voting thereon who are qualified electors of such district or territory to be affected thereby, may issue bonds or otherwise lend its credit, under certain restrictions, for various improvements, including irrigation and the construction and maintenance of works for the purposes of irrigation, drainage, and navigation or in aid thereof.

The section designated "59a" of Article XVI is usually referred to as Section 59. It was added to the Constitution in 1917 and consists of three sections being set forth in full in Vernon's Annotated Revised Civil Statutes of the State of Texas, as follows:

"Sec. 59a. The conservation and development of all of the natural resources of this State, including the control, storing, preservation and distribution of its storm and flood waters, the waters of its rivers and streams, for irrigation, power and all other useful purposes, the reclamation and irrigation of its arid, semi-arid and other lands needing irrigation, the reclamation and drainage of its over-flowed lands, and other lands needing drainage, the conservation and development of its forests, water and hydro-electric power, the navigation of its inland and coastal waters, and the preservation and conservation of all such natural resources of the State are each and all hereby declared public rights and duties; and the Legislature shall pass all such laws as may be appropriate thereto.

(b) There may be created within the State of Texas, or the State may be divided into, such number of conservation and reclamation districts as may be determined to be essential to the accomplishment of the purposes of this amendment to the constitution, which districts shall be governmental agencies and bodies politic and corporate with such powers of government and with the authority to exercise such rights, privileges and functions concerning the subject matter of this amendment as may be conferred by law.

(c) The Legislature shall authorize all such indebtedness as may be necessary to provide all improvements and the maintenance thereof requisite to the achievement of the purposes of this amendment, and all such indebtedness may be evidenced by bonds of such conservation and reclamation districts, to be issued under such regulations as amy (may) be prescribed by law and shall also, authorize the levy and collection within such districts of all such taxes, equitably distributed, as may be necessary for the payment of the interest and the creation of a sinking fund for the payment of such bonds; and also for the maintenance of such districts and improvements, and such indebtedness shall be a lien upon the property assessed for the payment thereof; provided the Legislature shall not authorize the issuance of any bonds or provide for any indebtedness against any reclamation district unless such proposition shall first be submitted to the qualified property tax-paying voters of such district and the proposition adopted. (Sec. 59, Art. 16, adopted election Aug. 21, 1917; proclamation October 2, 1917.)"

The attention of the court is especially called to the provision in Subdivision (b) of the above quoted section of the Constitution of Texas, declaring that districts formed for conservation and reclamation purposes *"shall be governmental agencies and bodies politic and corporate with such powers of government and with the authority to exercise such rights, privileges, and functions concerning the subject matter of this amendment as may be conferred by law."* With this language in mind—and it is clear that Mr. Justice McReynolds had it in mind by reason of his reference to this section—he could not well do otherwise than hold that the respondent in the *Ashton* case was a "political subdivision of the state created for the local exercise of her sovereign powers", and, of course, *the decision of the court as delivered by him, must be understood as applied and limited to public agencies within that category.*

If there are other public agencies within the scope of Section 80 which are not within this category, *then the decision does not determine that Section 80 may not be valid as applied to them,* unless the Court can say that Congress would not have enacted Section 80 at all if it had known that its provisions could not be applied to the agencies of the first class.

III.

IRRIGATION DISTRICTS IN CALIFORNIA ARE NOT POLITICAL SUBDIVISIONS OF THE STATE.

While the districts of Texas have, *by constitutional provision,* been expressly determined to be political subdivisions, the irrigation districts of California have been declared by both the Supreme and Appellate Courts of the state not to be political subdivisions. *There is no such provision in the Constitution of California as Section 59 of Article XVI of the Constitution of Texas.* The Third District Court of Appeal in *Huck v. Rathjen,* 66 Cal. App. 84, 225 Pac. 33, referred to the decision of the Supreme 'Court of the state in *Tarpey v. McClure,* 190 Cal. 593, 213 Pac. 983, which held that certain decisions under an Idaho statute to the effect that irrigation districts in that state were political subdivisions were "out of harmony with the decisions of this state". It was urged that the opinion in the *Tarpey* case to the effect that the district there considered was not a political subdivision of the state indicated that an irrigation district must be a political subdivision of a county, but the District Court of Appeal rejected this interpretation and said:

> "It is clear from the context, however, that what was meant by the language used is that an irrigation district is not a political subdivision at all."

Both the *Huck* and *Tarpey* cases were cited by the Supreme Court of California in

Wood v. Imperial Irrigation District, 216 Cal. 748, 753, 17 Pac. (2d) 128,

where it is flatly said:

"An irrigation district is not a political subdivision of the state, or county, or a political subsidiary at all".

This declaration is reinforced by the citation of numerous decisions in California to the effect that an irrigation district is not a municipal corporation, and, after referring to the similarity between irrigation districts and reclamation districts, by the quotation of the following from

> *Bettencourt v. Industrial Accident Commission,*
> 175 Cal. 559, 561, 166 Pac. 323:
> "But reclamation districts organized as was this petitioner, possess no political or governmental powers, are not organized for political or governmental purposes and are therefore not public corporations at all. Indeed, they are not in strictness corporations public or private, but governmental mandatories or agents, vested with limited powers to accomplish limited and specific work."

IV.

PROVISIONS OF THE CALIFORNIA IRRIGATION DISTRICT ACT AND VARIOUS COURT DECISIONS SHOW THAT IRRIGATION DISTRICTS IN THIS STATE BELONG IN THE SECOND CLASS OF PUBLIC AGENCIES AND ARE SUBJECT TO SECTION 80 OF THE BANKRUPTCY ACT.

Section 29 of the California Irrigation District Act expressly provides that the district holds "the legal title" to its property in trust for the uses and purposes set forth in that act, to which the property is expressly dedicated. This was held in *Merchants National Bank v. Escondido Irr. Dist.,* 144 Cal. 329, 77 Pac. 937, to mean that the landowners of an irrigation district had an equitable interest in the property of the district.

This was emphasized in *Hall v. Superior Court,* 198 Cal. 373, 245 Pac. 814, in which it was held that a Superior 'Court Judge owning land within Imperial District was disqualified to sit or act in a case in the outcome of which the irrigation district was interested, although it was not a party to the action. It was said at page 383 of the California Report that, while the landowners of an irrigation district did not occupy the precise status of stockholders in a corporation, yet they did sustain such a relation to the district "as to give them a proprietary interest in the district's property".

Likewise in *Lindsay-Strathmore Irr. Dist. v. Wutchumna Water Company,* 111 Cal. App. 688, 296 Pac. 933, it was held that while the legal title to certain water stock involved in that case rested in the irrigation district "the beneficial and equitable owners thereof are the landowners within that district whose funds have purchased the stock". It was further declared that in distributing water to the landowners within the boundaries of the district it would be applying the water "upon lands owned by the real owners of the stock in question." This is in accord with the holding of the State Supreme Court in *San Diego v. Linda Vista Irrigation District,* 108 Cal. 189, 41 Pac. 291, in which, at page 193 of the California Report it is said:

"The district when formed is a local organization to secure the local benefit to be derived from the irrigation of lands from the same source of

water supply and by the same system of works.
It is therefore a charge upon lands benefited or
capable of being benefited by a single local work,
or improvement, and from which the state, or the
public at large, derives no direct benefit but only
that reflex benefit which all local improvements
confer".

V.

**THE DECISION IN THE ASHTON CASE HOLDS THERE IS AN
IMPLIED LIMITATION ON THE BANKRUPTCY POWER TO
PROTECT THE SOVEREIGN RIGHTS OF THE STATES, JUST
AS THERE IS AN IMPLIED LIMITATION UPON THE TAX-
ING POWER OF THE FEDERAL GOVERNMENT, BUT SUCH
IMPLIED LIMITATION IN THE CASE OF A TAXING POWER
HAS REPEATEDLY BEEN HELD TO APPLY TO THE STATES
AND THEIR AGENCIES ONLY IN THE EXERCISE OF
STRICTLY GOVERNMENTAL FUNCTIONS.**

In the majority opinion in the *Ashton* case, it is
declared that the power to establish uniform laws on
the subject of bankruptcies can have no higher rank
or importance in our scheme of government than the
power to lay and collect taxes. Applying this comparison, the opinion continues as follows:

"Both are granted by the same section of the
Constitution and we find no reason for saying
that one is impliedly limited by the necessity of
preserving the independence of the states, while
the other is not. Accordingly, as application of
the statutory provisions now before us might materially restrict respondent's control over its fiscal
affairs, the trial court rightly declared them invalid."

This reasoning expressly concedes that the limitation upon the bankruptcy power is an implied limitation of exactly the same force and effect as the implied limitation on the taxing power defined in various decisions cited and quoted from in the opinion just prior to the language above quoted; but it has been repeatedly held that this implied limitation on the taxing power does not extend to the states or their agencies in matters not essential to the existence of the states. Accordingly in *South Carolina v. United States,* 199 U. S. 437, it was held that when the State of South Carolina engaged in the liquor business it laid aside its sovereignty and was subject to taxation the same as a private person.

The scope of the limitation on the taxing power was expressly declared by the Supreme Court in *Ohio v. Helvering,* 292 U. S. 360, wherein it was held that the immunity of the states from federal taxation "is limited to its agencies which are of a governmental character" and that whenever a state engages in a business of a private nature "it is not immune from the power of taxation which the Constitution vests in the Congress."

The United States Circuit 'Court of Appeals for the Second Circuit, in *Brush v. Commissioner of Internal Revenue,* decided July 13, 1936, held that the supplying of water for domestic purposes in the City of New York was not a governmental function, even though large deficits in the revenues of the water system were paid out of the general fund of the city, and that consequently the salaries of the employees of the water department are taxable by the federal government. Other cases holding that the operation of water works is not a political or governmental function are:

> City of Winona v. Botzet, 169 Fed. 321;
>
> Pikes Peak Power Co. v. Colorado Springs, 105 Fed. 1;
>
> Ill. T. & S. Bank v. Arkansas City, 76 Fed. 271, 281.

Likewise the Supreme Court of Arizona in

> Day v. Buckeye Water etc. District, 28 Ariz. 466, 237 Pac. 636,

construed the irrigation statute of that state, which was modeled after the California law, and referred to irrigation districts organized under that statute as follows:

> "Their function is purely business and economic, and not political and governmental".

Of course, a limitation by *implication* upon the power granted to Congress can have no greater force than an *express* limitation to the same effect. If the provision in the Constitution granting to Congress the power to pass uniform laws on the subject of bankruptcies contained a proviso that no such laws should effect any rights reserved to the states or impair the power of any state to exercise functions essential to its existence, Section 80 of the Bankrupcty Act would be construed with reference to such express limitation. The Supreme 'Court has held that in so far as the section applies to political subdivisions it does invade the reserved rights of the states and the act is unconstitutional. *It does not follow that the act is uncon-*

*stitutional when applied to districts which are not
political subdivisions* but are created for the purpose
of carrying out improvements of a public nature which
might be carried out and often are carried out as
private enterprises and which in their essential operations are particularly for private benefit, although
affected to a greater or less extent with public interest.

VI.

THE UNCONSTITUTIONALITY OF SECTION 80 AS APPLIED TO POLITICAL SUBDIVISIONS DOES NOT RENDER IT UNCONSTITUTIONAL IN TOTO.

In urging this petition for rehearing we rely upon
the rule stated as follows in *Pollock v. Farmers' Loan
and Trust Co.,* 158 U. S. 601, 635:

> "It is elementary that the same statute may be
> in part constitutional and in part unconstitutional,
> and, if the parts are wholly independent of each
> other, that which is constitutional may stand, while
> that which is unconstitutional will be rejected."

The purpose of Section 80 of the Bankruptcy Act
was to meet a serious situation requiring the refinancing of various public agencies. Congress obviously desired to make the act as broad as possible, but it recognized the necessity of not interfering with the reserved
rights of the states and for that reason in clause (b)
of Subdivision (11) of Subsection (c) provided that
the bankruptcy court should not by any order or decree interfere with any of the property or revenues
of a taxing district necessary in the opinion of the
judge for essential governmental purposes and also

included Subsection (k) to make it clear that nothing in Section 80 should interfere with the power of any state to control any political subdivision thereof in the exercise of its political or governmental powers. The Supreme Court has held that these provisions were not sufficient to preserve the constitutionality of the act *when applied to political subdivisions,* but there is nothing in the act to indicate that Congress would not have passed it for the benefit of the districts in the second category above defined, if it had known that it could not be made applicable to public agencies in the first category. Indeed, special provisions for the benefit of drainage, irrigation, reclamation and levee districts show that *Congress had these districts particularly in mind* and lead inevitably to the conclusion that it would have passed the act as applicable to such districts even if it had known that it could not be made applicable to governmental agencies of a political nature. Hence it must be concluded that the act was passed primarily for the benefit of such districts and if Congress had power to enact it for their benefit, the section is constitutional in so far as it applies to taxing districts that are not strictly political subdivisions.

Dated, San Francisco, California,
November 18, 1936.

Respectfully submitted,
S. J. HANKINS,
HANKINS & HANKINS,
A. L. COWELL,
Attorneys for Appellee
and Petitioner.

CERTIFICATE OF COUNSEL.

I hereby certify that I am of counsel for appellee and petitioner in the above entitled cause and that in my judgment the foregoing petition for a rehearing is well founded in point of law as well as in fact and that said petition for a rehearing is not interposed for delay.

Dated, San Francisco, California,
November 18, 1936.

S. J. HANKINS,
*Of Counsel for Appellee
and Petitioner.*

No. 8209

United States
Circuit Court of Appeals

For the Ninth Circuit.

8

JAMES A. JOHNSTON, Warden of the United
States Penitentiary, Alcatraz Island, California,

Appellant,

vs.

ALICE LAGOMARSINO and RAY LAGOMAR-
SINO, alias EDWIN MURPHY,

Appellee.

Transcript of Record

Upon Appeal from the District Court of the United
States for the Northern District of California,
Southern Division.

PARKER PRINTING COMPANY, 545 SANSOME STREET, SAN FRANCISCO   60--6-24-36

United States
Circuit Court of Appeals
For the Ninth Circuit.

JAMES A. JOHNSTON, Warden of the United
States Penitentiary, Alcatraz Island, California,

Appellant,

vs.

ALICE LAGOMARSINO and RAY LAGOMAR-
SINO, alias EDWIN MURPHY,

Appellee.

Transcript of Record

**Upon Appeal from the District Court of the United
States for the Northern District of California,
Southern Division.**

PARKER PRINTING COMPANY, 545 SANSOME STREET, SAN FRANCISCO   60-.6-24-36

INDEX

[Clerk's Note: When deemed likely to be of an important nature, errors or doubtful matters appearing in the original certified record are printed literally in italic; and, likewise, cancelled matter appearing in the original certified record is printed and cancelled herein accordingly. When possible, an omission from the text is indicated by printing in italic the two words between which the omission seems to occur.]

	Page
Appearances	1
Assignment of Errors	32
Citation	37
Clerk's Certificate	36
Commitment	19
Indictment	10
Judgment	15
Minute order, submitting return	24
Minute Order, granting discharge	29
Notice of appeal	34
Opinion	25
Order to show cause	16
Order of discharge	30
Order allowing appeal	32
Petition for writ of Habeas Corpus	1
Petition for appeal	31
Praecipe	35
Return to order to show cause	17
Statement of facts	5
Transfer order	23

For Appellant:
 H. H. McPIKE, Esq.,
  United States Attorney,
  San Francisco, Calif.

For Appellee:
 RAYMOND J. O'CONNOR, Esq.,
  Humboldt Bank Bldg.,
  San Francisco, Calif.

———

In the Southern Division of the United States District Court for the Northern District of California, First Division.

No. 2222-R

In the Matter of the Petition of ALICE LAGOMARSINO, in behalf of RAY LAGOMARSINO, alias EDWIN MURPHY, for a Writ of Habeas Corpus.

PETITION FOR WRIT OF HABEAS CORPUS

The petition of Alice Lagomarsino respectfully shows to this Court as follows:

I.

Your petitioner resides at Daly City, San Mateo County, California, and is the mother of Ray Lagomarsino, alias Edwin Murphy, who is of the age of 29 years. Your petitioner is a citizen of the

United States, and Ray Lagomarsino, alias Edwin
Murphy, her son, was born in the United States and
is a resident of the State of California; and your
petitioner, as the mother of the said Ray Lagomarsino, alias Edwin Murphy, has been authorized by
her said son to make this petition for a writ of
habeas corpus.

II.

That Ray Lagomarsino, alias Edwin Murphy, on
whose behalf this petition is filed, is a citizen of the
United States, unlawfully held and restrained of his
liberty by one, James A. Johnston, Warden of the
United States Penitentiary at Alcatraz Island, in
the City and County of San Francisco, California,
within the jurisdiction of this Court.

III.

On the 16th day of April, 1925, the said Ray
Lagomarsino, alias Edwin Murphy, was indicted in
the United States District Court for the Southern
Division of the Northern District of California and
the First Division charging a violation in five [1*]
(5) counts of the Criminal Code of the United
States, to-wit:

Count 1. That Ray Lagomarsino, alias Edwin
Murphy, and Abraham (Abe) Miller, alias
Jackson did on a certain day at a certain place
feloniously break into a certain post office with
intent to commit larceny in such building and

---

*Page numbering appearing at the foot of page of original certified
Transcript of Record.

in the part thereof so used as a post office, in violation of Section 192 of the Criminal Code of the United States; for which a sentence of five years was imposed.

Count 2. That the persons above named did at the same time and place unlawfully cut a certain mail pouch used for the conveyance of mail, in violation of Section 189 of the Criminal Code of the United States; for which a sentence of five years was imposed on the said Ray Lagomarsino, alias Edwin Murphy, to run concurrently with the sentence imposed on the first count.

Count 3. That the persons above named did at the same time and place, in violation of Section 194 of the Criminal Code of the United States, unlawfully steal from and out of an authorized depositary for mail matter, a certain parcel; for which a sentence of five years was imposed, to run consecutively to sentence imposed on counts one and two.

Count 4. That the persons above named did at the same time and place, in violation of Section 194 of the Criminal Code of the United States, unlawfully steal from and out of the same authorized depositary for mail matter, another certain parcel; for which a sentence of five years was imposed, to run consecutively to the sentence [2] imposed on count three.

Count 5. That the persons above named did at the same time and place, in violation of Section 194 of the Criminal Code of the United States, unlawfully steal from and out of the same authorized depositary for mail matter, another certain parcel; for which a sentence of five years was imposed, to run consecutively to the sentence imposed on count four.

A certified copy of the indictment and judgment is hereto attached and made a part hereof.

IV.

Your petitioner respectfully calls to the attention of this Court that the maximum sentence that may be imposed under Section 192 is five (5) years, on Section 189 is three (3) years and on Section 194 is five (5) years; that a sentence of twenty-five (25) years was imposed; that this petitioner believes that sentence imposed on counts four (4) and five (5) of said indictment is excessive, illegal and void: that the detention of the said Ray Lagomarsino, alias Edwin Murphy, in whose behalf this petition is presented by the petitioner herein, and his restraint since February 8th, 1936, has been illegal and erroneous.

WHEREFORE, petitioner prays that a writ of habeas corpus shall issue commanding the Warden of the United States Penitentiary at Alcatraz Island, in the City and County of San Francisco, California, to release the said Ray Lagomarsino, alias Edwin Murphy, from further custody.

ALICE LAGOMARSINO

Petitioner.

[Verification.] [3]

[Title of Court and Cause.]

I.

STATEMENT OF FACTS

The petition on file herein together with the certified copies of the indictment, judgment and order of sentence, annexed to said petition disclose all of the facts necessary to enable the Court to adjudicate the questions therein raised.

Lagomarsino was indicted upon five counts charging violation of the postal laws, pleaded guilty to the same and was sentenced to imprisonment for a term of five years upon each count. Counts 1 and 2 were ordered to be served concurrently and the remainder of the counts to be served consecutively. Petitioner concedes the validity of the sentences upon counts 1, 2, and 3 but contends that the sentences upon counts 4 and 5 are excessive and void.

Counts 3, 4 and 5 each charge a violation of Section 194 of the Criminal Code of the United States. Each charges that on the 10th day of April, 1925, Lagomarsino abstracted from the post office at Colma, California, an article of mail matter. Each is identical in language save and except that a different article of mail matter is described in each of these three counts.

Clearly each count was but part of a single indivisible transaction. At one and the same time Lagomarsino took from the post office three articles of mail matter, and received therefor, a sentence of five (5) years for each article so [4] taken rather than five (5) Years for the entire substantive crime.

II.

STATEMENT OF LAW

The following question of law is raised herein:

Are three consecutive sentences of five years each for the abstraction of three articles of mail matter from a post office at one and the same time legal, or does the maximum penalty of five years provided for in Section 194 of the Criminal Code of the United States cover the entire substantive crime?

Stated in another manner the question is:

Can an individual be punished by the maximum penalty provided for by Section 194 for each varied way in which a prosecutor may draught the separate counts of the same indictment for the abstraction of mail matter from a post office or was it the intention of the Congress that the maximum penalty therein provided for should cover the entire crime in its most extreme degree? If a person takes from a post office at one and the same time one hundred letters, is it competent to sentence him to five years imprisonment for each single letter, each sentence to run consecutively, making a total of five hundred years imprisonment for the crime?

The question herein presented is one of first impression, insofar as Section 194 is concerned. It appears that the precise question has never been adjudicated. However, the Courts of the United States have in cases which bear a striking analogy to the present one, ruled in a manner most favorable to petitioner's contention that the sentences imposed upon counts 4 and 5 are void.

In Braden v. United States, 270 F. 441, the defendant was charged in four separate counts with possession of certain drugs, and received consecutive sentences on each count. [5] Each count was identical in language save and except that one count specified possession of morphine sulphate, another cocaine, another heroin, and another smoking opium. The situation was exactly parallel to the present case, i. e., the crime was one transaction, but the article charged was different.

The decision of the Court upon this point follows:

"It is further contended that the sentence imposed by the trial Court is excessive. This contention is based on the fact that although defendant was convicted on 4 counts the transaction upon which said 4 counts are based was the finding of defendant in possession on the 16th day of November, 1918, in his flat in St. Paul, Minn. of the 4 different drugs mentioned in counts 6, 7, 8 and 9, said drugs being morphine sulphate, cocaine, heroin and smoking opium, all derivatives of opium except cocaine, which is a derivative of coca leaves. Counsel for the United States contend that the words "any of the aforesaid drugs" as used in Section 8 permit him to base a count upon each drug found in the possession of the defendant although the drugs were all found at the same time and place. We do not think that any such significance can be given to the word "any". The use of this word simply means that, if the defendant under the required circumstances should be found in the possession of any of the said drugs, he would be guilty. If a person steals 4 horses from the barn of another, all being of different color, it would not be competent to charge the thief with 4 different larcenies when the horses were all taken at the same time and place. Another illustration would be the larceny of articles of merchandise from a store. If 12 articles were all taken at the same time and place, we do not think it would be competent to charge the thief with 12 different larcenies * * * the judgment therefore, is affirmed as to the 6th count and the sentences on counts 7, 8 and 9 are reversed.''

Again in Parmagini v. United States, 42 F. 2nd 721, Circuit Court of Appeals, Ninth Circuit, the defendants were indicted upon several counts, the first of which charged sale of morphine, and the third of which charged distribution of opium. The Court in an opinion by Wilbur, Circuit Judge, approved the Braden case supra, and in the following language held categorically that but a single offense had been committed:

"The question as to whether or not the charges with reference to the distribution and concealment of the opium can be considered a separate and distinct offense is a more difficult one. As the Appellant points out, in the Circuit Court of Appeals of the Eighth Circuit, in Braden v. U. S. 270 F. 441, 443, a defendant was charged in five separate counts with having five distinct [6] narcotic drugs in his possession at the same time. The court held that only one offense was committed, stating:

The Court thereupon quoted the excerpt from the Braden case quoted supra, and continued:

> With reference to counts I and III, one for selling morphine and the other for distributing opium, the transaction was an entirety, the delivery of the opium was a mere incident to the delivery of the morphine, and the transaction comes clearly within the rule stated by the Circuit Court of Appeals of the Eighth Circuit in the last mentioned case. <u>If follows that the fine and punishment for distributing opium were imposed for the same offense as the fine and punishment for selling morphine * * *.</u>"

It was never the intention of the Congress that a man should be punished by a five year imprisonment for each of several letters taken from a post office at one and the same time and the statute must be so construed as to give to it its plain and rational meaning.

United States v. Lacher, 134 U. S. 624:

> "It appears to me", said Mr. Justice Story, in U. S. v. Winn, 3 Summer. 209, 211, "That the proper course in all these cases, is to reach out and follow the true intent of the legislature, and to adopt that sense of the words which harmonizes best with the context, and promotes in the fuller manner the apparent policy and objects of the legislature."

Maxwell on Interpretation of Statutes, 2nd
Ed. p. 318:

"The rule which requires that penal and some
other statutes shall be construed strictly was
more rigorously applied in former times, when
the number of capital crimes was one hundred
and sixty or more, * * * But it has lost much of
its force and importance in recent times, since
it has become more and more generally recognized that the paramount duty of the judicial
interpreter is to put upon the language of the
legislature, honestly and faithfully, its plain and
rational meaning, and to promote its objects."

Respectfully submitted,

RAYMOND J. O'CONNOR

Attorney for Petitioner. [7]

———

In the Southern Division of the United States District Court for the Northern District of California, First Division.

(16571)

(INDICTMENT)

At a stated term of said Court begun and holden
at the City and County of San Francisco within and
for the Southern Division of the Northern District
of California on the first Monday of March in the
year of our Lord One Thousand nine hundred and
twenty-five,

The Grand Jurors of the United States of
America, within and for the Division and District
aforesaid, on their oaths present: That Ray La-

gomarsino, alias Edwin Murphy, and Abraham (Abe) Miller, alias Jackson, hereinafter called the defendants, heretofore, to-wit, on or about the 10th day of April, 1925, at Colma, in the County of San Mateo, in the Southern Division of the Northern District of California, then and there being, did then and there unlawfully, wilfully, knowingly and feloniously break into a certain post office and a building used in part as a post office, at said Colma, with the intent on the part of them, the said defendants, to commit larceny in such building, and in the part thereof so used as a post office;

AGAINST the peace and dignity of the United States of America, and contrary to the form of the statute of the said United States of America in such case made and provided.

SECOND COUNT

And the Grand Jurors aforesaid, on their oaths aforesaid, do further present: That Ray Lagomarsino, alias Edwin Murphy, and Abraham (Abe) Miller, alias Jackson, hereinafter called the defendants, heretofore, to-wit, on or about April 10th, 1925, at Colma, in the County of San Mateo, in the Southern Division of the Northern District of California, then and there being, did then and there in violation of Section 189 of the Criminal Code of the United States unlawfully, wilfully, knowingly and feloniously and with intent to rob such mail, cut a certain [8] mail pouch used for the conveyance of the mail, to-wit: a mail pouch bearing the following label: "Postmaster, Colma, Calif., Special. Contents 2 #2 pouches, dated April 8th, 1925;

AGAINST the peace and dignity of the United States of America, and contrary to the form of the statute of the said United States of America in such case made and provided.

THIRD COUNT

And the Grand Jurors aforesaid, on their oaths aforesaid, do further present: That Ray Lagomarsino, alias Edwin Murphy, and Abraham (Abe) Miller, alias Jackson, hereinafter called the defendants, heretofore, to-wit: on or about April 10, 1925, at Colma, in the County of San Mateo, in the Southern Division of the Northern District of California, then and there being, did then and there, in violation of Section 194 of the Criminal Code of the United States, unlawfully, wilfully, knowingly and feloniously steal, take and abstract from and out of an authorized depositary for mail matter, to-wit, the Post Office at Colma, in the County of San Mateo, aforesaid, a certain parcel addressed to H. M. Russell, Room 255, Pacific Building, San Francisco, California, which said parcel was intended to be conveyed by mail and carried and delivered by and through and by means of the Post Office establishment of the United States to the person to whom the same was addressed:

AGAINST the peace and dignity of the United States of America, and contrary to the form of the statute of the said United States of America in such case made and provided.

FOURTH COUNT

And the Grand Jurors aforesaid, on their oaths aforesaid, do further present: That Ray Lagomarsino, alias Edwin Murphy, and Abraham (Abe) Miller, alias Jackson, hereinafter called the defendants, heretofore, to-wit: on or about April 10, 1925, [9] at Colma, in the County of San Mateo, in the Southern Division of the Northern District of California, then and there being, did then and there, in violation of Section 194 of the Criminal Code of the United States, unlawfully, wilfully, knowingly and feloniously steal, take and abstract from and out of an authorized depositary for mail matter, to-wit: the Post Office at Colma, in the County of San Mateo, aforesaid, a certain parcel addressed to Mr. Angelo Revere, Box 145, Colma, California, which said parcel was intended to be conveyed by mail and carried and delivered by and through and by means of the Post Office establishment of the United States to the person to whom the same was addressed;

AGAINST the peace and dignity of the United States of America, and contrary to the form of the statute of the said United States of America in such case made and provided.

FIFTH COUNT

And the Grand Jurors aforesaid, on their oaths aforesaid, do further present: That Ray Lagomarsino, alias Edwin Murphy, and Abraham (Abe) Miller, alias Jackson, hereinafter called the defendants, heretofore, to-wit: on or about April 10, 1925, at Colma, in the County of San Mateo, in the Southern Division of the Northern District of California, then and there being, did then and there, in violation of Section 194 of the Criminal Code of the United States, unlawfully, wilfully, knowingly and feloniously steal, take and abstract from and out of an authorized depositary for mail matter, to-wit: the Post Office at Colma, in the County of San Mateo, aforesaid, a certain insured parcel No. 17863, addressed to Harry Deller, Box 95, Colma, California, which said insured parcel was intended to be conveyed by mail and carried and delivered by and through and by means of the Post Office establishment of the United States to the person to whom the same was addressed.

AGAINST the peace and dignity of the United States of America, and contrary to the form of the statute of the said [10] United States of America in such case made and provided.

STERLING CARR
United States Attorney.

[Endorsed]: Presented in open Court and ordered filed April 16, 1925, Walter B. Maling, Clerk, by Lyle S. Morris, Deputy Clerk. Bail $1500.00. [11]

In the Southern Division of the United States District Court for the Northern District of California—First Division.

No. 16571

THE UNITED STATES OF AMERICA,

vs.

RAY LAGOMARSINO.

(JUDGMENT)

In this case the order allowing the defendant Probation having been vacated and set aside, it is ordered that the defendant Ray Lagomarsino for the offense of which he stands convicted be imprisoned for the period of five (5) years each on Counts 1 and 2 of the Indictment, terms of imprisonment to run concurrently and to commence and run from date hereof. That said defendant be imprisoned for the period of five (5) years as to the 3rd Count of the Indictment, term of imprisonment as to 3rd Count to commence and run upon the expiration and execution of the judgment imposed upon said defendant under counts 1 and 2. That said defendant be imprisoned for the period of five (5) years as to the 4th Count, term of imprisonment as to 4th Count to commence and run at the expiration and execution of the judgment imposed upon said defendant under count 3. That defendant be imprisoned for the period of five (5) years as to the 5th Count of the Indictment, term of imprisonment as to the 5th Count to commence and run at the expiration and execution of judgment imposed on defendant under Count 4.

Terms of imprisonment to be executed upon said defendant by imprisonment in the United States Penitentiary to be designated by the United States Attorney General.

Entered this 14th day of January, 1926.

WALTER B. MALING, Clerk

By C. W. Calbreath,

Deputy Clerk.

[Endorsed]: Entered in Vol. 20 Judg. and Decrees at page 89 (Certification of Clerk Attached).

[12]

[Title of Court and Cause.]

ORDER TO SHOW CAUSE

On reading and filing the petition of Alice Lagomarsino for a writ of habeas corpus on behalf of Ray Lagomarsino, alias Edwin Murphy, and said petition being verified by the petitioner herein, and good cause appearing therefor,

IT IS HEREBY ORDERED that James A. Johnston, Warden of the United States Penitentiary at Alcatraz Island, be and appear before this Court, at the Courtroom of MICHAEL J. ROCHE, Judge thereof, in the United States Post Office Building, Seventh and Mission Streets, in the City and County of San Francisco, State of California, on the 24 day of February, 1936, at the hour of 10 A. M. of that day and then and there show cause, if any he has, why a writ of habeas corpus should not issue as prayed for in the petition filed herein, and

IT IS FURTHER ORDERED, that a copy of this order and a copy of the said petition for a writ of habeas corpus be served upon the said James A. Johnston not less than five (5) days prior to the date set for hearing thereof, and that the custody of the said Ray Lagomarsino, alias Edwin Murphy, shall not be disturbed pending the final determination of the proceedings on said petition.

Dated: February 13th, 1936.

MICHAEL J. ROCHE
Judge of the United States
District Court.

[Endorsed]: Filed Feb. 13, 1936. Walter B. Maling, Clerk. [13]

[Title of Court and Cause.]

RETURN TO ORDER TO SHOW CAUSE

Comes now J. A. JOHNSTON, Warden of the United States Penitentiary at Alcatraz Island, California, and for cause why a writ of habeas corpus should not issue herein shows as follows:

I.

That the person (hereinafter called "the prisoner") on whose behalf the petition for writ of habeas corpus was filed, is detained by your respondent J. A. JOHNSTON, as Warden of the

United States Penitentiary at Alcatraz Island, California, under and by virtue of order of final commitment duly and regularly issued in criminal case No. 16571 on the 14th day of January, 1926, by District Judge A. F. St. Sure of the United States District Court for the Northern District of California, and transfer order No. 1747 issued at Washington, D. C., for the Attorney General of the United States of America by Sanford Bates, Director of Bureau of Prisons of the Department of Justice of the United States of America, dated August 15, 1934.

II.

That a certified copy of said order of final commitment, issued as aforesaid, is annexed hereto and made a part hereof as respondent's Exhibit "A".

III.

That a copy of said transfer order, issued as aforesaid, is annexed hereto and made a part hereof as respondent's Exhibit "B".

WHEREFORE respondent prays that the petition for writ of habeas corpus herein be dismissed.

J. A. JOHNSTON,
Warden of the United States
Penitentiary at Alcatraz Island,
California. [14]

(Commitment)

EXHIBIT "A"

UNITED STATES OF AMERICA

The United States District Court for the Northern District of California. First Division.

The President of the United States of America,

To the Marshal of the United States for the Northern District of California, GREETING:

WHEREAS, at the March 1925 Term of the United States District Court for the Northern District of California, held at the Court Room of said Court in the City and County of San Francisco, in said District, to-wit, on the 13th day of June, A. D. 1925, RAY LAGOMARSINO, alias Edwin Murphy was convicted of the offense of violating Sections 189, 192 and 194 of the Criminal Code of the United States committed on or about the 10th day of April, 1925, at Colma, San Mateo County, California, and within the jurisdiction of said Court, contrary to the form of the statutes of the United States in such case made and provided, and against the peace and dignity of the United States.

And Whereas, on the 14th day of January, A. D. 1926 being a day in the said term of said Court, said Ray Lagomarsino, etc., was, for the offense of which he stood convicted as aforesaid by the judgment of said Court ordered to be imprisoned for the period of Five (5) years each on COUNT ONE & COUNT TWO, said terms of imprisonment to run concurrently and to commence and run from date hereof; and to be imprisoned for the period of Five (5) Years on COUNT THREE, said imprisonment as to Count Three to commence and run upon the execution and expiration of the judgment imposed on said defendant under Counts One and Two; and to be imprisoned for the period of FIVE (5) years on COUNT FOUR, said term of imprisonment as to Count Four to commence and run upon the execution and expiration of the judgment imposed on said defendant under Count Three; and to be imprisoned for the period of Five (5) Years on COUNT FIVE, said term of imprisonment as to Count Five to [15] commence and run upon the execution and expiration of the judgment of imprisonment imposed on said defendant under Count Four.

Ad it was further ordered by the Court that said sentence of imprisonment be executed upon the said Ray Lagomarsino, etc. by imprisonment in United States Penitentiary.

NOW THIS IS TO COMMAND YOU, THE SAID MARSHAL, to take and keep and safely deliver the said Ray Lagomarsino, etc., into the custody of the Keeper or Warden, or other Officer in charge of said U. S. Penitentiary forthwith.

AND THIS IS TO COMMAND YOU, the said Keeper and Warden and other Officers in charge of the said U. S. Penitentiary, to receive from the United States Marshal of said Northern District of California, the said Ray Lagomarsino convicted and sentenced as aforesaid, and him the said Ray Lagomarsino keep and imprison for the term of Five (5) Years each on Counts One and Two, said terms of imprisonment to run concurrently and to commence and run from date hereof; and for the term of Five (5) Years on Count Three, said term of imprisonment as to Count Three to commence and run upon the expiration and execution of the judgment of imprisonment imposed on said defendant under Counts One and Two; and for the term of Five (5) years on Count Four, said term of imprisonment as to Count Four to commence and run upon the expiration and execution of the judgment of imprisonment imposed on said defendant under Count Three; and for the term of Five (5) Years on Count Five, said term of imprisonment as to Count Five to commence and run upon the expiration and execution of the judgment of imprisonment imposed on said defendant under Count Four.

HEREIN FAIL NOT.

WITNESS, the Honorable A. F. ST. SURE Judge of the United States District Court for the Northern District of California, this 14th day of January, A. D. 1926, and of our independence the 150th. [16]

WALTER B. MALING,
Clerk of said District Court.
By C. W. CALBREATH
Deputy Clerk.

[Endorsed]: I, WALTER B. MALING, Clerk of the United States District Court for the Northern District of California, do hereby certify the foregoing to be a full, true, and correct copy of the Original Commitment issued in the case of

The United States vs. RAY LAGOMARSINO, etc., No. 16571,

ATTEST, my hand and the seal of said District Court this 21st day of February, A. D. 1936.

[Seal]　　WALTER B. MALING,
　　　　　　　Clerk of the U. S. District Court, Northern District of California.

By E. H. NORMAN
Deputy Clerk.

[Endorsed]: The within warrant of commitment was received by me on the 29th day of Jan., A. D. 1926, and is returned executed this 1st day of Feb., A. D. 1926, by committing the within-named defendant to the Keeper or Warden of the United States Penitentiary, at Leavenworth, Kan.

FRED L. ESOLA,
U. S. Marshal.

By D. H. HOEN,
Deputy Marshal.

[Endorsed]: Filed Feb. 24, 1926. Walter B. Maling, Clerk. [17]

(Transfer Order)

EXHIBIT "B"

COPY

Miscellaneous Form
No. 39 (b)

DEPARTMENT OF JUSTICE
BUREAU OF PRISONS
WASHINGTON

SANFORD BATES
Director

Per Transfer Order #1747

To the Warden of the U. S. Penitentiary, Leavenworth, Kansas, or his duly authorized representative; and to the Warden of the U. S. Penitentiary, Alcatraz Island, California:

WHEREAS, in accordance with the authority contained in Section 7 of the Act approved May 14, 1930 (46 Stat. 325) the Director of the Bureau of Prisons for the Attorney General has ordered the transfer of Ray Lagomarsino #24692 from the U. S. Penitentiary at Leavenworth to the U. S. Penitentiary at Alcatraz Island, California.

NOW THEREFORE, you the Warden of the U. S. Penitentiary at Leavenworth are hereby authorized and directed to execute this order by causing the removal of said prisoner, together with the original writ of commitment and other official papers to the said U. S. Penitentiary at Alcatraz Island and to incur the necessary expense and include it in your regular accounts.

And you, the Warden of the U. S. Penitentiary at Alcatraz Island, are hereby authorized and directed to receive the said prisoner into your custody and him to safely keep until the expiration of his sentence or until he is otherwise discharged according to law.

For the Attorney General

8/15/34 /s/ SANFORD BATES

(Date) Director

ORIGINAL. To be left at institution to which prisoner is transferred.

TRUE AND CORRECT COPY.

W. F. DORINGTON,
Record Clerk,

U. S. Penitentiary, Alcatraz, California. [18]

District Court of the United States, Northern District of California, Southern Division.

AT A STATED TERM of the Southern Division of the United States District Court for the Northern District of California, held at the Court Room thereof, in the City and County of San Francisco, on Monday, the 24th day of February, in the year of our Lord one thousand nine hundred and thirty-six.

PRESENT: the Honorable Michael J. Roche, United States District Judge.

No. 22225.

In the Matter of
RAY LAGOMARSINO, alias EDWIN MURPHY,
on Habeas Corpus.

The application for a Writ of Habeas Corpus (by Order to Show Cause) came on to be heard. R. J. O'Connor, Esq., appearing as Attorney for petitioner and A. J. Zirpoli, Esq., Assistant U. S. Attorney, appearing as Attorney for Respondent. Mr. Zirpoli filed a Return to the Order to Show Cause. After hearing the Attorneys it is ordered that said application be and the same is hereby submitted.

[19]

[Title of Court and Cause.]

Habeas Corpus—on return to order to show cause why the writ should not issue.

RAYMOND J. O'CONNOR, of San Francisco, California, attorney for the Petitioner.

H. H. McPIKE, United States Attorney, and A. J. ZIRPOLI, Assistant United States Attorney, both of San Francisco, California, for the Respondent, J. A. JOHNSTON, Warden of the U. S. Penitentiary at Alcatraz Island, California.

MEMORANDUM OPINION.

After serving ten years of a twenty year sentence, Ray Lagomarsino had this habeas corpus proceeding

instituted to determine the legality of the balance
of his sentence. An indictment in five counts was
returned against him as a result of his burglarizing
a United States Post Office. Count one was for
breaking into a Post Office; count two was for cutting open a mail sack; and counts three, four and
five were for abstracting three separate parcels from
an authorized depositary for mail (namely, the mail
sack referred to in count two) in violation of section 194 of the Criminal Code. All five counts were
the result of one burglary, and as regards the last
three counts, presumably Lagomarsino abstracted
the three parcels simultaneously. He pleaded guilty
to all the counts and was sentenced to five years
on each one, the sentences on the first two to run
concurrently, and the others to run consecutively.

The terms of the sentences imposed on the first
three counts expired on February 8, 1936. The petitioner concedes the validity of these sentences, but
assails the legality of [20] the sentences imposed on
counts four and five.

The question before the Court is whether the sentence of five years imposed by section 194 should be
interpreted as the maximum that can be given for
one robbery transaction regardless of the number of
parcels abstracted, or whether the taking of each
parcel is the subject of a five year penalty even
though the parcels be abstracted simultaneously.

This issue has never before arisen in connection
with section 194, but decisions similar in principle

have laid down the rule n regard to other statutes. In the case of

Braden v. United States
270 Fed. 441

the defendant was found in his apartment in possession of certain narcotics. Subsequently he was convicted on four counts, each count dealing with the same transaction but naming a different variety of drug. The Circuit Court of Appeals for the Eighth Circuit in reversing the conviction on three of the four counts said:

"If a person steals four horses from the barn of another, all being of different color, it would not be competent to charge the thief with four different larcenies when the horses were all taken at the same time and place. Another illustration would be the larceny of articles of merchandise from a store. If 12 articles were all taken at the same time and place, we do not think it would be competent to charge the thief with 12 different larcenies . . . "

In this Circuit, the Court of Appeals approved the Braden holding when a similar question arose in

Parmagini v. United States
42 F. (2d) 721

where defendant was charged in count one with the sale of morphine and in count three with the distribution of opium, both being part of one sale and delivery. The court held it was error to assess a fine on the third count, saying:

"The question as to whether or not the
charge with reference to the distribution and
concealment of the opium can be considered a
separate and distinct offense, is a more difficult
one. [21]

*   *   *   *   *   *   *

With reference to counts I and III, one for selling morphine and one for distributing opium,
the transaction was an entirety, the delivery of
the opium was a mere incident to the delivery of
the morphine and the transaction comes clearly
within the rule stated . . . in the last mentioned
case. (Braden v. U. S., supra.)"

Mr. Justice Fuller, in laying down the test to
decide the intent of Congress in these penal statutes
in the case of

United States v. Lacher, 134 U. S. 624,

quoted the language of Mr. Justice Storey:

" 'It appears to me . . . that the proper
course in all these cases is to reach out and follow the true intent of the legislature, and to
adopt the sense of the words which harmonizes
best with the context, and promotes in the fuller
manner the apparent policy and objects of the
legislature.' "

It can hardly be seriously contended that section
194 would authorize a sentence of fifty years if a
person filched ten letters simultaneously from a mail
box—such a far fetched intent cannot be imputed
to Congress.

The foregoing decisions indicated counts three, four and five were all based in the same transaction and that Lagomarsino could receive only one sentence for abstracting the parcels in question. Therefore, counts four and five, being merely repetitions of count three, were contrary to law and void and afforded no basis for any sentence.

For these reasons the writ will issue and Lagomarsino will be discharged from custody. See: Stevens v. McClaughry 207 Fed. 18 (C. C. A.-8), cited with approval in Parmagini v. U. S. (C. C. A.-9) supra. Ebeling v. Morgan 237 U. S. 625 appears to be distinguishable.

Dated: February 25, 1936.

MICHAEL J. ROCHE

United States District Judge.

[Endorsed]: Filed Feb. 25, 1936. Walter B. Maling, Clerk. [22]

———

[Title of Court.]

AT A STATED TERM of the Southern Division of the United States District Court for the Northern District of California, held at the Court Room thereof, in the City and County of San Francisco, on Tuesday, the 25th day of February, in the year of our Lord one thousand nine hundred and thirty-six.

PRESENT: the Honorable Michael J. Roche, United States District Judge.

[Title of Cause.]

This matter having been regularly brought on for hearing upon the issues joined herein, and the same having been duly heard and submitted, and due con-

sideration having been thereupon had, IT IS BY
THE COURT NOW HERE ORDERED that the
said person in whose behalf the Petition for Writ
of Habeas Corpus was filed herein is illegally restrained of his liberty, as alleged in the petition
herein, and that he be, and he is hereby discharged
from the custody of the Warden of the United
States Penitentiary at Alcatraz, California, and that
he go hence without delay. [23]

———

[Title of Court and Cause.]
(ORDER OF DISCHARGE)

This matter having been regularly brought on
for hearing upon the issues joined herein, and the
same having been duly heard and submitted, and
due consideration having been thereon had, it is by
the Court now here ORDERED that the said named
person in whose behalf the Petition for a Writ of
Habeas Corpus was filed herein is illegally. restrained of his liberty, as alleged in the petition
herein, and that he be, and he is hereby discharged
from the custody of the Warden of the United
States Penitentiary, at Alcatraz, California. and
that he go hence without delay.

Entered this 25th day of February, 1936.
[Seal]   WALTER B. MALING,
                    Clerk
            By J. A. SCHAERTZER,
                Deputy Clerk.

[Endorsed]: Filed Feb. 25, 1936. Walter B. Maling, Clerk. [24]

[Title of Court and Cause.]

PETITION FOR APPEAL.

To the Honorable Judge of the District Court of the United States for the Northern District of California:

JAMES A. JOHNSTON, as Warden of the United States Penitentiary at Alcatraz Island, California, respondent in the above entitled matter and appellant herein, feeling aggrieved by the order and judgment made and entered in the above entitled cause on the 25th day of February, 1936, discharging RAY LAGOMARSINO, alias EDWIN MURPHY, from the custody of said respondent, does hereby appeal from said order and judgment to the United States Circuit Court of Appeals for the Ninth Circuit, for the reasons set forth in the Assignment of Errors filed herewith.

WHEREFORE, petitioner prays that his petition be allowed and that citation be issued, as provided by law, and that the transcript of the record, proceedings and documents, and all of the papers upon which said order and judgment was based, duly authenticated, be sent to the United States Circuit Court of Appeals for the Ninth Circuit, under the rules of such Court, and in accordance with the law in such case made and provided.

Dated: May 13, 1936.

H. H. McPIKE

AJZ

United States Attorney.

[Admission of Service]

[Endorsed]: Filed May 14, 1936. Walter B. Maling, Clerk. [25]

[Title of Court and Cause.]

ORDER ALLOWING APPEAL.

On motion of H. H. McPike, United States Attorney for the Northern District of California, attorney for respondent and appellant in the above entitled cause, IT IS HEREBY ORDERED that the appeal to the United States Circuit Court of Appeals for the Ninth Circuit from an order and judgment heretofore made in the above entitled cause, be, and the same is hereby allowed, and that a certified transcript of the records, testimony, exhibits, stipulations, and all proceedings be transmitted to the said United States Circuit Court of Appeals for the Ninth Circuit, in the manner and time prescribed by law.

Dated: May 14th, 1936.

MICHAEL J. ROCHE
United States District Judge.

[Endorsed]: Filed May 14, 1936. Walter B. Maling, Clerk. [26]

[Title of Court and Cause.]

ASSIGNMENT OF ERRORS.

Comes now JAMES A. JOHNSTON, Warden of the United States Penitentiary at Alcatraz Island, California, respondent in the above entitled cause, by H. H. McPike, United States Attorney, and in connection with his petition for appeal in the above entitled cause assigns the following errors, which he avers occurred upon the hearing of the above entitled cause and upon which he will rely upon appeal to the United States Circuit Court of Appeals for the Ninth Circuit from the order and judgment made by this Honorable Court on February 25, 1936:

1. The Court erred in ordering discharged the detained referred to in said petition for writ of habeas corpus.

2. The Court erred in holding that the allegations contained in said petition for writ of habeas corpus were sufficient in law to justify the granting of the order discharging the detained person referred to in the said petition for writ of habeas corpus.

WHEREFORE, said respondent and appellant prays that the order and judgment of the United States District Court for the Southern Division of the Northern District of California, made and entered herein in the office of the Clerk of said Court on the 25th day of February, 1936, discharging the said RAY LAGOMARSINO, alias EDWIN MURPHY, from the custody of JAMES A. JOHNSTON, Warden of the United States Penitentiary at Alcatraz Island, California, be reversed, and that the said RAY LAGOMARSINO, alias EDWIN MURPHY, be remanded to the custody of said Warden of the United States Penitentiary at Alcatraz Island, California.

Dated: May 13th, 1936.

H. H. McPIKE
AJZ
United States Attorney.

[Admission of Service.]

[Endorsed]: Filed May 14, 1936. Walter B. Mal-

[Title of Court and Cause.]

NOTICE OF APPEAL.

To the Clerk of the above entitled Court, to ALICE LAGOMARSINO petitioner in the above entitled matter, and to RAYMOND J. O'CONNOR, ESQ., her attorney:

YOU, AND EACH OF YOU, WILL PLEASE TAKE NOTICE that JAMES A. JOHNSTON, Warden of the United States Penitentiary at Alcatraz Island, California, respondent in the above entitled matter and appellant herein, hereby appeals to the United States Circuit Court of Appeals for the Ninth Circuit, from an order and judgment made and entered in the above entitled cause, on the 25th day of February, 1936, discharging RAY LAGOMARSINO, alias EDWIN MURPHY, from the custody of said JAMES A. JOHNSTON, Warden of the United States Penitentiary at Alcatraz Island, California, the respondent and appellant herein.

Dated: May 13, 1936.

H. H. McPIKE

AJZ

United States Attorney.

[Admission of Service]

[Endorsed]: Filed May 14, 1936, Walter B. Maling, Clerk. [28]

[Title of Court and Cause.]

PRAECIPE.

To the Clerk of Said Court:

Sir:

Please issue copies of the following papers, to be used in preparing transcript on appeal:

1. Petition for writ of Habeas Corpus, including certified copy of indictment and judgment attached thereto;
2. Order to show cause;
3. Respondent's return to order to show cause;
4. Minute order of the Court of Feb. 24, 1936, that the matter be submitted, etc.;
5. Order of discharge;
6. Memorandum opinion of the Court of February 25, 1936;
7. Notice of appeal;
8. Petition for appeal;
9. Order allowing appeal;
10. Assignment of errors;
11. Citation on appeal;
12. Praecipe for record on appeal.

H. H. McPIKE

AJZ

United States Attorney,

Attorney for Respondent.

[Admission of Service]

[Endorsed]: Filed May 15, 1936. Walter B. Maling, Clerk. [29]

District Court of the United States
Northern District of California

CERTIFICATE OF CLERK TO TRANSCRIPT OF RECORD ON APPEAL.

I, Walter B. Maling, Clerk of the United States District Court, for the Northern District of California, do hereby certify that the foregoing 29 pages, numbered from 1 to 29, inclusive, contain a full, true, and correct transcript of the records and proceedings in the matter of the Petition of Alice Lagomarsino in behalf of Ray Lagomarsino, etc. for Writ of Habeas Corpus No. 22225-R, as the same now remain on file and of record in by office.

I further certify that the cost of preparing and certifying the foregoing transcript of record on appeal is the sum of Twelve & 50/100 ($12.50).

IN WITNESS WHEREOF, I have hereunto set my hand and affixed the seal of said District Court, this 21st day of May A. D. 1936.

[Seal]   WALTER B. MALING
Clerk.

By C. W. CALBREATH
Deputy Clerk. [30]

United States of America, ss.

The President of the United States of America

To ALICE LAGOMARSINO and RAY LAGO-
MARSINO, alias EDWIN MURPHY, and to
RAYMOND J. O'CONNOR, ESQ., their at-
torney herein: Greeting:

YOU ARE HEREBY CITED AND ADMON-
ISHED to be and appear at a United States Circuit Court of Appeals for the Ninth Circuit, to be
holden at the City of San Francisco, in the State of
California, within thirty days from the date hereof,
pursuant to an order allowing an appeal, of record in the Clerk's Office of the United States District Court for the Northern District of California,
Southern Division, wherein JAMES A. JOHN-
STON, Warden of the United States Penitentiary,
Alcatraz Island, California, is appellant, and you
are appellee, to show cause, if any there be, why the
decree or judgment rendered against the said appellant, as in the said order allowing appeal mentioned, should not be corrected, and why speedy justice should not be done to the parties in that behalf.

WITNESS, the Honorable MICHAEL J.
ROCHE, United States District Judge for the
Southern Division of the Northern District of Cali-
fornia, this 14th day of May, A. D. 1936.

MICHAEL J. ROCHE,
United States District Judge.

[Admission of Service]

[Endorsed]: Filed May 15, 1936, 1 11 p. m. Walter
B. Maling, Clerk. [31]

[Endorsed]: No. 8209. United States Circuit Court of Appeals for the Ninth Circuit. James A. Johnston, Warden of the United States Penitentiary, Alcatraz Island, California, Appellant, vs. Alice Lagomarsino and Ray Lagomarsino (alias Edwin Murphy), Appellee. Transcript of Record. Upon Appeal from the District Court of the United States for the Northern District of California, Southern Division.

Filed May 21, 1936.

PAUL P. O'BRIEN,

Clerk of the United States Circuit Court of Appeals for the Ninth Circuit.

No. 8209

IN THE

United States Circuit Court of Appeals

For the Ninth Circuit

9

JAMES A. JOHNSTON, Warden of the United
States Penitentiary, Alcatraz Island,
California,

Appellant,

vs.

ALICE LAGOMARSINO and RAY LAGOMARSINO,
alias Edwin Murphy,

Appellees.

BRIEF FOR APPELLANT.

H. H. McPIKE,
United States Attorney,

ROBERT L. McWILLIAMS,
Assistant United States Attorney,

A. J. ZIRPOLI,
Assistant United States Attorney,
Post Office Building, San Francisco,

Attorneys for Appellant.

FILED

SEP 14 1936

PAUL P. O'BRIEN,
CLERK

PERNAU-WALSH PRINTING CO , SAN FRANCISCO

Subject Index

	Page
Statement of the case	1
Facts of the case	1
Assignment of errors	6
Question	6
Argument	6
Statute involved	6
Analysis of points and authorities relied upon by the petitioner and appellee in support of the granting of the writ of habeas corpus and order of discharge....	8
Points and authorities in support of respondent's contention that the three consecutive sentences imposed under Counts Three, Four and Five in the Lagomarsino indictment were proper	15
Conclusion	19

Table of Authorities Cited

Pages

Allen Chrysler v. Zerbst, 81 Fed. (2d) 975............... 12

Braden v. United States, 270 Fed. 441.................. 8, 13

Colbeck, et al. v. United States (C. C. A. 8), 14 Fed. (2d) 801 10

Ebeling v. Morgan, 237 U. S. 625..........8, 15, 17, 18, 19, 20

Logan v. United States, 123 Fed. 291................17, 19, 20

Morgan v. Devine, 237 U. S. 632................13, 16, 17, 19

Parmagini v. United States (C. C. A. 9), 42 Fed. (2d) 721. 8, 13
Poffenbarger v. Aderhold (C. C. A. 5), 20 Fed. (2d) 42.. 17
Poffenbarger v. Aderhold, 4 Fed. Supp. 542, affirmed 67 Fed. (2d) 250, certiorari denied 290 U. S. 703........ 17

Revised Statutes, Section 5469......................... 8, 10

Section 265, Title 18 U. S. C. A......................17, 19
Section 312, Title 18 U. S. C. A......................18, 19
Section 313, Title 18 U. S. C. A......................15, 16
Section 315, Title 18 U. S. C. A...................... 16
Section 317, Title 18 U. S. C. A...........6, 7, 8, 10, 13, 15, 20
Sections 1387-1388, Title 26 U. S. C. A.................. 13
Stevens v. M'Claughry, 207 Fed. 18...............8, 10, 12, 13

No. 8209

United States Circuit Court of Appeals

For the Ninth Circuit

JAMES A. JOHNSTON, Warden of the United
States Penitentiary, Alcatraz Island,
California,

Appellant,

VS.

ALICE LAGOMARSINO and RAY LAGOMARSINO,
alias Edwin Murphy,

Appellees.

BRIEF FOR APPELLANT.

STATEMENT OF THE CASE.

This appeal is from an order of the United States
District Court for the Southern Division of the
Northern District of California granting a writ of
habeas corpus and discharging Ray Lagomarsino, alias
Edwin Murphy, from the custody of appellant.
(Tr. pp. 29 and 30.)

FACTS OF THE CASE.

Alice Lagomarsino, the mother of Ray Lagomarsino, alias Edwin Murphy, a prisoner at the United
States Penitentiary at Alcatraz Island, California,

successfully sought the release of her son by petition
for writ of habeas corpus (Tr. pp. 1 to 4, incl.), which
was granted by the District Court of the United
States of America for the Northern District of California, Southern Division, on February 25, 1936.
(Tr. pp. 29 and 30.) Pursuant to said order, the
prisoner was discharged from the custody of appellant.

The petition rested upon the proposition that the
twenty year sentence imposed by the United States
District Court for the Northern District of California,
Southern Division, for violation of the postal laws of
the United States of America was excessive by ten
years, and that the prisoner, having served the valid
portion thereof, was entitled to his immediate release
on habeas corpus. To substantiate this proposition
the petitioner successfully contended that the theft
of three different pieces of mail by Ray Lagomarsino
from the same post office, and presumably the same
mail pouch, at the same time, constituted but one
offense instead of three as recited in the indictment;
for each of which he received three maximum consecutive sentences of five years.

The sentences were imposed on January 14, 1926,
following violation of probation granted after a plea
of guilty to five counts on an indictment filed on
April 16, 1925, which alleged offenses committed at
Colma, California, on or about April 10, 1925. The
indictment in substance was in the following language:

Count One:
"did then and there unlawfully, wilfully, knowingly and feloniously break into a certain post

office and a building used in part as a post office, at said Colma, with the intent on the part of them, the said defendants, to commit larceny in such building, and in the part thereof so used as a post office; * * *''

Count Two:

''did then and there in violation of Section 189 of the Criminal Code of the United States unlawfully, wilfully, knowingly and feloniously and with intent to rob such mail, cut a certain mail pouch used for the conveyance of the mail, to-wit, a mail pouch bearing the following label: 'Postmaster, Colma, Calif., Special. Contents 2 #2 pouches, dated April 8th, 1925:' ''

Count Three:

''did then and there, in violation of Section 194 of the Criminal Code of the United States, unlawfully, wilfully, knowingly and feloniously steal, take and abstract from and out of an authorized depository for mail matter, to-wit, the Post Office at Colma, in the County of San Mateo, aforesaid, a certain parcel addressed to H. M. Russell, Room 255, Pacific Building, San Francisco, California, which said parcel was intended to be conveyed by mail and carried and delivered by and through and by means of the Post Office establishment of the United States to the person to whom the same was addressed:''

Count Four:

''did then and there, in violation of Section 194 of the Criminal Code of the United States, unlawfully, wilfully, knowingly and feloniously steal, take and abstract from and out of an authorized depository for mail matter, to-wit: the Post Office at Colma, in the County of San Mateo, aforesaid, a certain parcel addressed to Mr. Angelo Revere, Box 145, Colma, California, which said parcel was intended to be conveyed by mail and carried and delivered by and through and by means of the Post Office establishment of the United States to the person to whom the same was addressed;"

Count Five:

"did then and there, in violation of Section 194 of the Criminal Code of the United States, unlawfully, wilfully, knowingly and feloniously steal, take and abstract from and out of an authorized depositary for mail matter, to-wit: the Post Office at Colma, in the County of San Mateo, aforesaid, a certain insured parcel No. 17863, addressed to Harry Deller, Box 95, Colma, California, which said insured parcel was intended to be conveyed by mail and carried and delivered by and through and by means of the Post Office establishment of the United States to the person to whom the same was addressed." (Tr. pp. 10 to 14 incl.)

The sentence of the Court imposed on said 14th day of January, 1926, by District Judge A. F. St. Sure, is as follows:

"In this case the order allowing the defendant Probation having been vacated and set aside, it is ordered that the defendant Ray Lagomarsino for the offense of which he stands convicted be imprisoned for the period of five (5) years each on Counts 1 and 2 of the Indictment, terms of imprisonment to run concurrently and to commence and run from date hereof. That said defendant be imprisoned for the period of five (5) years as to the 3rd Count of the Indictment, term of imprisonment as to 3rd Count to commence and run upon the expiration and execution of the judgment imposed upon said defendant under counts 1 and 2. That said defendant be imprisoned for the period of five (5) years as to the 4th Count, term of imprisonment as to 4th Count to commence and run at the expiration and execution of the judgment imposed upon said defendant under count 3. That defendant be imprisoned for the period of five (5) years as to the 5th Count of the Indictment, term of imprisonment as to the 5th count to commence and run at the expiration and execution of judgment imposed on defendant under Count 4.

Terms of imprisonment to be executed upon said defendant by imprisonment in the United States Penitentiary to be designated by the United States Attorney General.''

(Tr. pp. 15 and 16.)

On February 13, 1936, Alice Lagomarsino filed her petition as aforesaid. The Court concluded that Counts Four and Five of the indictment, being mere repetitions of Count Three, were contrary to law and void, and afforded no basis for a sentence in excess of the five years imposed under Count Three of the indictment. For that reason, it ordered the discharge from custody of the prisoner, Ray Lagomarsino.

ASSIGNMENT OF ERRORS.

The errors assigned and relied upon on this appeal are that:

1. The Court erred in ordering discharged the detained referred to in said petition for writ of habeas corpus.

2. The Court erred in holding that the allegations contained in said petition for writ of habeas corpus were sufficient in law to justify the granting of the order discharging the detained person referred to in the said petition for writ of habeas corpus. (Tr. pp. 32 and 33.)

QUESTION.

Does the theft of three parcels of mail at one and the same time, from the same depository, constitute three offenses within the meaning of Section 317 of Title 18 U. S. C. A.?

ARGUMENT.
STATUTE INVOLVED.

"Section 317, Title 18.—Stealing, secreting, or embezzling mail matter.

Whoever shall steal, take, or abstract, or by fraud or deception obtain, from or out of any mail, post office or station thereof, or other authorized depository for mail matter, or from a letter or mail carrier, any letter, postal card, package, bag, or mail, or shall abstract or remove from any such letter, package, bag, or mail, any article or thing contained therein, or shall secrete, embezzle, or destroy any such letter, postal card, bag, or mail, or any article or thing contained therein; or whoever shall steal, take, or abstract, or by fraud or deception obtain any letter, postal card, package, bag, or mail, which has been left for collection upon or adjacent to a collection box or other authorized depository of mail matter; or whoever shall buy, receive, or conceal, or aid in buying, receiving, or concealing, or shall unlawfully have in his possession, any letter, postal card, package, bag, or mail, or any article or thing contained therein, which has been so stolen, taken, embezzled, or abstracted, as herein described, knowing the same to have been so stolen, taken, embezzled, or abstracted; or whoever shall take any letter, postal card, or package out of any post office or station thereof, or out of any authorized depository for mail matter, or from any letter or mail carrier, or which has been in any post office or station thereof, or other authorized depository, or in the custody of any letter or mail carrier, before it has been delivered to the person to whom it was directed, with a design to obstruct the correspondence, or to pry into the business or secrets of another, or shall open, secrete, embezzle, or destroy the same, shall be fined not more than $2,000, or imprisoned not more than five years, or both."

As counsel for petitioner stated, "the question herein presented is one of first impression" in so far as Section 317 of Title 18 U. S. C. A. is concerned, or more precisely the first portion of that section which concerns itself with the theft of any mail from any Post Office or authorized depository.

Appellant respectfully submits that the theft of each and every letter or parcel from a Post Office constitutes a separate offense under Section 317, supra, and predicates this conclusion upon the language of the Supreme Court of the United States in the case of *Ebeling v. Morgan,* 237 U. S. 625, which together with other cases will be hereinafter discussed in detail. However, before so doing, it would be advisable to discuss the cases relied upon by the petitioner and appellee herein.

ANALYSIS OF POINTS AND AUTHORITIES RELIED UPON BY THE PETITIONER AND APPELLEE IN SUPPORT OF THE GRANTING OF THE WRIT OF HABEAS CORPUS AND ORDER OF DISCHARGE.

Appellee bases his position essentially upon the cases of *Braden v. United States,* 270 Fed. 441, and *Stevens v. M'Claughry,* 207 Fed. 18, both of which are cited with approval in the case of *Parmagini v. United States* (C. C. A. 9), 42 Fed. (2d) 721. Although there is a striking similarity between those cases and the instant case, nevertheless a careful analysis of them demonstrates that they are not conclusive, and that the sounder interpretation of the law is that of the Supreme Court in the case of *Ebeling v. Morgan,* supra.

The case of *Stevens v. M'Claughry,* supra, was one wherein the Court passed upon Revised Statutes 5469, which is now part of Section 317, and which provides as follows:

> "Any person who shall steal the mail, or steal or take from or out of any mail or post-office,

branch post-office, or other authorized depository for mail-matter, any letter or packet; any person who shall take the mail, or any letter or packet therefrom, or from any post-office, branch post-office, or other authorized depository for mail-matter, with or without the consent of the person having custody thereof, and open, embezzle, or destroy any such mail, letter, or package which shall contain any note, bond, draft, check, warrant, revenue-stamp, postage-stamp, etc. * * *; any person who shall, by fraud or deception, obtain, from any person having custody thereof, any such mail, letter, or packet containing any such article of value shall, although not employed in the postal service, be punishable by imprisonment at hard labor for not less than one year and not more than five years.''

The Court in considering the third, fourth, fifth and sixth counts, wherein the defendant Stevens was charged with the theft of four different registered letters deposited in the postoffice at Los Angeles by the Farmers and Merchants National Bank and addressed to the Importers and Traders National Bank of New York City, concluded as follows:

"The averments in each of the counts of this indictment that the six stealings occurred at the same time, at the same place, from a mail car described in each of them in the same words, and that the registered letters described in the third, fourth, fifth and sixth counts were such as in the usual course of business would have been in the mail pouch containing registered letters from Los Angeles to New York described in the first count, converge upon the mind with such compelling force as to leave no doubt that all these stealings were committed at the same time, were parts of a single continuous criminal transaction, and that they were inspired by the same indispensable felonious intent.'' (p. 22.)

When it is noted that the language of the first sentence of R. S. 5469 and its successor Section 317 is substantially the same, and when to that fact is added the identity of the indictment in the Stevens case with the third, fourth and fifth counts of the Lagomarsino indictment, the case of *Stevens v. M'Claughry* seems quite persuasive. It is true that each parcel referred to in the third, fourth and fifth counts in the Lagomarsino indictment bore the name of a different addressee, thus requiring separate proof in each case. Practically the same situation obtained in *Stevens v. M'Claughry,* for in the latter case there was a general reference in the first two counts to the registered mail, which included the four separate letters embodied in the later counts. But each of said separate letters, while destined for the same addressee, nevertheless bore different registered numbers, each of which required proof of identification.

As against this apparently persuasive language in the case of *Stevens v. M'Claughry,* we have in the same Circuit what appears to appellant to be a case to the contrary, *Colbeck, et al. v. United States* (C. C. A. 8, 1926), 14 Fed. (2d) 801. In that case it appears that conviction was had under six counts of an indictment charging violations of Section 317. Three sentences of five years, each to run consecutively, imposed under Counts Twelve, Thirteen and Fourteen, were challenged as void upon the ground that these counts charged one and the same offense. Count Twelve charged the felonious receiving and concealing of the contents of seventy-nine registered letters stolen from the mails and from a pouch with lock M9545, Rotary No. 113. The thirteenth count charged the unlawful possession of the same seventy-nine registered letters, and the fourteenth count charged the unlawful possession of 337 registered letters (which apparently covered the entire haul of a robbery and included the seventy-nine letters charged as unlawfully possessed in Count Thirteen). The offense in each count was laid on the same day and involved but one enterprise. The Appellate Court, in affirming the conviction and sentences, said:

"It is contended here that these three counts charge one and the same offense, that the same evidence was offered to sustain each of them, that defendants could not be punished separately on each count and that the court erred in adjudging that they be separately punished on each count and that the confinement so adjudged on each count be served consecutively. We think it entirely clear from the language of the section of the Code that both possession and concealment of United States mail which has been stolen are made criminal offenses if the person or persons possessing or concealing the same knew at the time that the same had been stolen. Possessing a thing is a different act from concealing the same thing. The former means to hold the thing, the latter to hide the thing. One may hold today and hide tomorrow. We, therefore, are of the opinion that counts 12 and 13 charge separate and different offenses. Likewise as between counts 13 and 14. Count 13 charges the possession of the contents of 79 registered letters and packages, and count 14 charges possession of the contents of 337 registered letters and packages. The proof required to sustain the charge in the thirteenth count would not be sufficient to sustain the charge in the fourteenth count. It would require additional and different proof to sustain the latter than that required to sustain the former." (p. 802.)

Thus, assuming it to be true that the seventy-nine letters charged in the thirteenth count were included in the 337 letters charged in the fourteenth count, it is reasonable to conclude that the Court affirmed, at least partly, two punishments for the same offense and that its decision with respect to said Counts Thirteen and Fourteen is contrary to the previous decision in the case of *Stevens v. M'Claughry.*

Further, the doctrine announced in the case of *Stevens v. M'Claughry* now appears to have been repudiated by the Tenth Circuit Court in the case of *Allen Chrysler v. Zerbst (Warden),* 81 Fed. (2d) 975, decided February 22, 1936. In the *Chrysler* case consecutive maximum sentences were imposed under two counts, one charging the unlawful transportation in interstate commerce of a stolen automobile, the other count charging the unlawful receiving and concealing of the same automobile. On habeas corpus instituted after serving the first sentence, it was contended that only one offense was involved, and the case of *Stevens v. M'Claughry,* supra, was urged in support thereof. The Appellate Court, however, affirmed the plural sentences, and stated that the doctrine announced in *Stevens v. M'Claughry* had been expressly rejected by the Supreme Court in *Morgan v. Devine,* 237 U. S. 632, which case will be hereinafter discussed. Thus, from the foregoing cases it is apparent that the decisions construing Section 317 are of no particular assistance in determining the question of law here involved. This brings us to a consideration of the other two cases relied upon by the appellee in support of his petition for writ of habeas corpus.

The other two cases, *Braden v. United States,* supra, and *Parmagini v. United States,* supra, involved narcotic violations. In the *Braden* case, involving violations of Sections 1387-1388, Title 26 U. S. C. A., which makes it an offense to have possession of any untax paid drug, there was a conviction under four counts, with sentence under each count to run consecutively. Each count charged possession of a different drug on the same day. On appeal the judgment was affirmed under only one count, the Court holding that the words "any of the aforesaid drugs" simply meant that if a defendant were found in possession of any of the mentioned drugs he would be guilty of one offense. The Court reached this conclusion upon the theory that the facts in the case showed that the same evidence was required to sustain each count. The facts in the *Lagomarsino* case are more closely analogous to the facts in the *Braden* case than in the *Parmagini* case. In the latter case, the first count charged the unlawful sale and distribution of morphine, the second count charged fraudulent concealment of the same morphine, and the third count charged the unlawful dispensing and distribution of opium, the fourth count charged the fraudulent concealment of the same opium, and the fifth count charged a conspiracy to commit the substantive offenses urged in the previous count. A sentence of five years was imposed for the sale of morphine and ten years for the concealment of the same morphine, to run consecutively. A sentence of five years was imposed for the distribution of opium and ten years for the concealment of the same opium, these sentences to run consecutively to each other but *concurrently with the sentence imposed under the morphine counts, making a total of fifteen years.* On appeal it was held that the transactions alleged in Counts One and Three were in entirety, and that the punishment for distributing the opium was imposed for the same offense as the punishment for sale of morphine. The Court, however, affirmed the judgments because they were made to run concurrently. These two decisions apparently convinced the lower Court in the instant case that Lagomarsino's contention, to the effect that the theft of the three parcels at one and the same time from the same depository, constituted one offense, was sound. As the lower Court said:

"The foregoing decisions indicated counts three, four and five were all based in the same transaction and that Lagomarsino could receive only one sentence for abstracting the parcels in question. Therefore, counts four and five, being merely repetitions of count three, were contrary to law and void and afforded no basis for any sentence.

"For these reasons the writ will issue and Lagomarsino will be discharged from custody. See: Stevens v. McClaughry, 207 Fed. 18 (C. C. A. 8), cited with approval in Parmagini v. U. S. (C. C. A. 9) supra. Ebeling v. Morgan, 237 U. S. 625, appears to be distinguishable." (Tr. p. 29.)

POINTS AND AUTHORITIES IN SUPPORT OF RESPONDENT'S CONTENTION THAT THE THREE CONSECUTIVE SENTENCES IMPOSED UNDER COUNTS THREE, FOUR AND FIVE IN THE LAGOMARSINO INDICTMENT WERE PROPER.

It is the conclusion of the District Court that *Ebeling v. Morgan,* 237 U. S. 625, "appears to be distinguishable". With this conclusion your appellant disagrees. The construction given by the Supreme Court to the postal statute therein involved, which is similar in language to that of Section 317, when applied to the facts of the case now before this Honorable Court, is controlling and should cause this Court to conclude that the District Court erred in ordering the discharge of appellee. Before discussing the case of *Ebeling v. Morgan,* supra, it might be well to first consider other cases construing postal statutes and a counterfeiting statute whose language is not dissimilar to Section 317.

Section 313 of Title 18, U. S. C. A., provides punishment of three years in the case of one who "shall steal, purloin or embezzle any mail bag or other property belonging to the Post Office Department, or shall appropriate any such property to his own use, or convey away any such property to the hindrance of public service." Section 315 of Title 18, U. S. C. A., provides five years imprisonment for one who breaks into or attempts to break into a post office with intent to commit any larceny or depredation.

In *Morgan v. Devine,* supra, the defendant having been sentenced to consecutive terms of imprisonment under two counts charging, respectively, the breaking into a post office with intent to commit larceny in violation of Section 315, and the stealing of stamps and postal funds in violation of Section 313, contended that the acts charged in the second count were done at the same time and constituted but one offense. The Supreme Court held that each of the mentioned sections defined a distinct offense, using the illustration that although one might successfully break into a post office with intent to steal, such intent might be frustrated or abandoned. Although the fact remains that here two offenses are charged in the indictment, "the breaking into a post office", and the "stealing of stamps and postal funds", whereas in the *Lagomarsino* case the defendant was charged in the third, fourth and fifth counts only with theft, nevertheless the following language in the said case of *Morgan v. Devine,* at page 640, is of some assistance in determining the interpretation to be placed upon the facts and law now before the Court. There the Court said:

> "the test is not whether the criminal intent is one and the same and inspiring the whole transaction, but whether separate acts have been committed with the requisite criminal intent and are such as are made punishable by the Act of Congress. See Burton v. United States, 202 U. S. 344."

In *Poffenbarger v. Aderhold* (C. C. A. 5), 20 Fed. (2d) 42, the contention that separate punishments for stealing mail bags and for taking and abstracting mail matter from such bags constitute double jeopardy was rejected upon the authority of *Morgan v. Devine,* supra, and *Ebeling v. Morgan,* supra. Incidentally, Poffenbarger raised the same contention subsequently in habeas corpus proceedings and the petition was dismissed. (See 4 Fed. Supp. 542.) The dismissal was affirmed (67 Fed. (2d) 250) and certiorari denied. (See 290 U. S. 703.)

In interpreting Section 265 of Title 18, U. S. C. A., which reads as follows:

> "Whoever * * * shall keep in possession or conceal with like intent *any falsely made,* forged, counterfeited or altered *obligation* or other security of the United States, shall be" punished in the manner provided. (Italics ours.)

the Circuit Court of Appeals for the Sixth Circuit in the case of *Logan v. United States,* 123 Fed. 291, held that under this section a defendant might be convicted of a separate offense for each one of the forged obligations he kept in possession with intent to pass. At page 293, the Court said:

> "The contention that the defendant below could not properly be convicted under the fifteenth count of keeping in his possession a certain forged note with intent to pass it, and under the sixteenth count of keeping in his possession another forged note with intent to pass it—in other words, that the keeping of two separate forged notes in his possession with intent to pass them was one act—does not appeal to us as well

founded. The keeping, just as the making and the passing, of each forged note, is, or may be treated as, a separate and distinct offense.''

But even more conclusive and controlling is the case of *Ebeling v. Morgan,* supra, which involves the construction of Section 312 of Title 18, U. S. C. A. That section provides as follows:

"Injuring Mail Bags. Whoever shall tear, cut, or otherwise injure any mail bag, pouch, or other thing used or designed for use in the conveyance of the mail, or shall draw or break any staple or loosen any part of any lock, chain, or strap attached thereto, with intent to rob or steal any such mail, or to render the same insecure, shall be fined not more than $500, or imprisoned not more than three years, or both.''

In that case, the second, third, fourth, fifth, sixth, and seventh counts of the indictment charged that on a certain date Ebeling did feloniously cut and injure a certain mail bag. Each count involved a different mail bag. There was a plea of guilty with a sentence of three years on the second count, and like sentences on the third, fourth, fifth, and sixth counts, to run consecutively with the sentence under the second count and with each other. After Ebeling had served the sentence on the second count he sought his release by habeas corpus upon the ground that the cutting of the bags constituted a single offense. In affirming the judgment the Supreme Court stated as follows (page 629):

"Reading the statute with a view to ascertaining its meaning, it is apparent that it undertakes to make an offender of anyone who shall cut, tear, or otherwise injure any mail bag, or who shall draw or break any staple or loosen any part of any lock, chain or strap attached thereto, with the felonious intent denounced by the statute. These words plainly indicate that it was the intention of the lawmakers to protect each and every mail bag from felonious injury and mutilation. Whenever any one mail bag is thus torn, cut or injured, the offense is complete. Although the transaction of cutting the mail bags was in a sense continuous, the complete statutory offense was committed every time a mail bag was cut in the manner described, with the intent charged. The offense as to each separate bag was complete when that bag was cut, irrespective of any attack upon, or mutilation of, any other bag. The words are so plain as to require little discussion or further amplification to ascertain their meaning. The separate counts each charged by its distinctive number the separate bag and each time one of them was cut there was, as we have said, a separate offense committed against the statute. Congress evidently intended to protect the mail in each sack, and to make an attack thereon in the manner described a distinct and separate offense.''

CONCLUSION.

The language of the Court in *Morgan v. Devine,* supra, and the unqualified construction placed by the Court in *Logan v. United States,* supra, upon Section 265 of Title 18 U.S.C.A., and by the Supreme Court upon Section 312 U.S.C.A. in *Ebeling v. Morgan,* supra, lead to but one conclusion, namely, that the theft of the three parcels of mail at one and the same time, from the same depository, constituted separate offenses. For if, as held in the case of *Logan v. United States,* supra, the possession of each forged note is a separate and distinct offense, and as held in the case of *Ebeling v. Morgan,* supra, the cutting of each mail bag is a separate offense, it follows that the theft of each and every parcel from a depository of mail matter is a separate offense under Section 317.

We therefore respectfully submit that the Court below erred in granting the writ of habeas corpus and ordering the discharge of Ray Lagomarsino, alias Edwin Murphy, from the custody of the appellant, and that the order appealed from should be reversed.

Dated, San Francisco,
September 14, 1936.

H. H. McPIKE,
United States Attorney,

ROBERT L. McWILLIAMS,
Assistant United States Attorney,

A. J. ZIRPOLI,
Assistant United States Attorney,

Attorneys for Appellant.

No. 8209

IN THE

United States Circuit Court of Appeals

For the Ninth Circuit /Ɔ

JAMES A. JOHNSTON, Warden of the United
States Penitentiary, Alcatraz Island,
California,

Appellant,

vs.

ALICE LAGOMARSINO and RAY LAGOMARSINO,
alias Edwin Murphy,

Appellees.

BRIEF FOR APPELLEES.

RAYMOND J. O'CONNOR,
111 Sutter Street, San Francisco,
Attorney for Appellees.

FILEt

PERNAU-WALSH PRINTING CO., SAN FRANCISCO

Subject Index

	Page
Facts of the Case	1
Question	2
Argument	3
The statute involved	4
Analysis of points and authorities relied upon by appellant in support of appeal	6
Points and authorities in support of petitioner's contention that the three consecutive sentences imposed under counts three, four and five in the Lagomarsino indictment were excessive, illegal and void	10
Conclusion	13

Table of Authorities Cited

	Pages
Braden v. United States, 270 F. 441	10, 11, 12, 13, 14
Chrysler v. Zerbst, 81 Fed. (2d) 975	8, 10
Colbeck et al. v. United States (C. C. A. 8), 14 Fed. (2d) 801	9
Criminal Code of the United States, Section 194	1, 2, 6
Ebeling v. Morgan, 237 U. S. 625	3, 6, 7, 8, 10
Logan v. United States, 123 Fed. 291	8
Maxwell on Interpretation of Statutes, 2d Ed., p. 318	12
Morgan v. Devine, 237 U. S. 632	8
Parmagini v. United States, 42 F. (2d) 721	11, 13, 14
Poffenbarger v. Aderhold (C. C. A. 5), 20 Fed. (2d) 42	10
United States v. Lacher, 134 U. S. 624	5
U. S. C. A., Title 18, Section 317	4, 7

No. 8209

United States Circuit Court of Appeals
For the Ninth Circuit

JAMES A. JOHNSTON, Warden of the United
States Penitentiary, Alcatraz Island,
California,

Appellant,

vs.

ALICE LAGOMARSINO and RAY LAGOMARSINO,
alias Edwin Murphy,

Appellees.

BRIEF FOR APPELLEES.

FACTS OF THE CASE.

Ray Lagomarsino was indicted upon five counts
charging violation of the postal laws (Tr. pp. 10 to
14, incl.), pleaded guilty to the same and was sentenced to imprisonment for a term of five years upon
each count. (Tr. pp. 15 and 16.) Counts 1 and 2
were ordered to be served concurrently and the remainder of the counts to be served consecutively.

It is conceded that the sentences upon counts 1, 2
and 3 were valid.

Counts 3, 4 and 5 each charged a violation of Section 194 of the Criminal Code of the United States.

Each charged that on or about the 10th day of April, 1925, Lagomarsino abstracted from the post office at Colma, California, an article of mail matter. Each is identical in language save and except that a different article of mail matter is described in each of these three counts.

After Lagomarsino had served ten years of his sentence, being the concurrent sentences upon counts 1 and 2 and the sentence upon count 3, his mother, Alice Lagomarsino, petitioned for and secured a writ of habeas corpus upon the ground that the charges contained in counts 3, 4 and 5 were indivisible parts of the same crime and therefore susceptible to but a single sentence. (Tr. pp. 1 to 4, incl.; pp. 29 and 30.) From the order granting the writ, James A. Johnston, Warden of the United States Penitentiary, Alcatraz Island, California, has appealed. (Tr. p. 31.)

QUESTION.

Can the simultaneous theft of three letters from a post office, a single act, be reasonably construed to be three crimes? Stated in another manner the question is: Can an individual be punished by the maximum penalty provided for by Section 194 of the Criminal Code for each varied way in which an ingenious prosecutor is able to frame the various counts of the same indictment for the abstraction of mail matter from a post office, or was it the intention of Congress that the maximum penalty therein provided for should cover the entire substantive crime in its most extreme degree?

ARGUMENT.

At the outset it is to be noted that each of counts 3, 4 and 5 charge that Lagomarsino did "steal, take and abstract from and out of an authorized depositary for mail matter, to-wit: the *post office*" a certain specified article of mail matter. It is not charged that the theft was from a package, bag or mail sack, but from the *post office*. In other words, the crime was committed when he walked out of the building with the letters in his possession. This necessarily makes the crime a single act unless a ridiculous assumption were to be indulged in, viz., that he left the building with one letter, returned and left again with the second, and then returned again and again left with the third. Clearly each count was but a part of a single indivisible transaction, involving but a single act, and, per se, but a single crime. (Italics ours.)

At the outset it is likewise to be noted that there is a vast distinction between the theft of mail and the mutilation of mail bags. Appellant bases his appeal almost exclusively upon cases similar to that of *Ebeling v. Morgan,* 237 U. S. 625, which involved the mutilation of mail bags. It is physically impossible to slit or cut more than one bag simultaneously. If more than one mail bag is mutilated, the crime necessarily involves as many separate acts as there are mail bags, and necessarily a separate criminal intent to commit each separate act. That is a far different matter from the one here presented where there was but a single act, a simultaneous taking. Appellant in his formulated "Question" concedes that but a single act was here involved when he queries "Does the theft of three parcels of mail *at one and the same time,* from the same depositary, constitute three offenses within the meaning of Section 317 of Title 18, U. S. C. A.?" (Appellant's Brief, p. 6.) (Italics ours.) There being but a single act, there could be but a single criminal intent, and but a single crime. The authorities relied upon by appellant will be fully discussed herein later, being passed now for the sake of logical order.

THE STATUTE INVOLVED.

The portion of the statute involved which is pertinent to the instant case is as follows:

"Section 317, Title 18, U. S. C. A.—Stealing, secreting, or embezzling mail matter.

Whoever shall steal, take, or abstract, or by fraud or deception obtain, from or out of any mail, post office or station thereof, or other authorized depositary for mail matter, or from a letter or mail carrier, any letter, postal card, package, bag, or mail * * * shall be fined not more than $2,000.00, or imprisoned not more than five years, or both."

The statute must be given its plain intent. The language cannot be distorted to give to it a false meaning. Congress must be presumed to know the meaning of the simple English which it used.

It is to be noted that it used certain specific terms and also one generic term in enumerating the items, the theft of which were made punishable. Congress specified "any letter, postal card, package, bag," and then generalized "or mail". In other words, Congress specifically made the simultaneous theft of several articles of mail matter but a single crime. Any other construction would render the term "or mail" meaningless.

Webster's New International Dictionary defines the term "mail" to be:

"The bag or bags, with the letters, papers or other matter contained therein, conveyed under public authority from one post office to another."

The statute necessarily, therefore, must be read: Whoever shall steal * * * any letter, postal card, package, bag, or who shall steal the bag or bags, with the letters, papers or other matters contained therein, conveyed under public authority from one post office to another * * * shall be fined not more than $2,000.00, or imprisoned not more than five years, or both.

That this is the true meaning of the statute is obvious. The lower Court stated the matter correctly and concisely when it said:

"Mr. Justice Fuller, in laying down the test to decide the intent of 'Congress in these penal statutes in the case of

United States v. Lacher, 134 U. S. 624,

quoted the language of Mr. Justice Storey:

'It appears to me * * * that the proper course in all these cases is to reach out and follow the true intent of the legislature, and to adopt the sense of the words which harmonizes best with the context, and promotes in the fuller manner the apparent policy and objects of the legislature.'

It can hardly be seriously contended that Section 194 would authorize a sentence of fifty years if a person filched ten letters simultaneously from a mail box—and such a *far fetched intent cannot be imputed to Congress.*" (Italics ours.)

Res ipsa loquitur.

ANALYSIS OF POINTS AND AUTHORITIES RELIED UPON BY APPELLANT IN SUPPORT OF APPEAL.

Appellant relies principally upon the case of *Ebeling v. Morgan,* supra, but an analysis of that case discloses that not only does it not uphold appellant's contention, but in fact it recognizes the principle that, when from its very nature, a crime consists of but a single act, there can be but one punishment.

The statute there involved provides as follows:

"Injuring Mail Bags. Whoever shall tear, cut, or otherwise injure any mail bag, pouch, or other thing used or designed for use in the conveyance of the mail, * * * shall be fined not more than $500.00 or imprisoned not more than three years, or both."

It is to be noted that in this statute Congress did not use a generic term after enumerating the specific mail containers. It used only specific terms, viz., "mail bag, pouch, or other thing." In other words it failed to specify that the injuring of a plural number of mail containers should be but a single crime. Obviously this statute cannot be compared to Section

317, Title 18, U. S. C. A., which specifically made the theft of a plural number of articles of mail matter punishable by but a single penalty.

In *Ebeling v. Morgan,* supra, at page 628 the Court very carefully limited the question involved to successive and separate acts:

> "This case raises the question whether one who in the same transaction, tears or cuts *successively* mail bags of the United States * * * is guilty of a *single act,* or of additional offenses because of each *successive* cutting with the criminal intent charged." (Italics ours.)

From the statement of the Court it is apparent that it clearly recognized the distinction between crimes consisting of but a single act, and those which are in a sense a part of a single transaction but which involves separate and distinct acts and separate and distinct criminal intents. It is likewise apparent that the Court very carefully limited its decision to those crimes which involved a multiplicity of acts and of criminal intents.

Again, at page 629, the Court recognizes the distinction between crimes involving a single act and those involving separate acts, when it said:

> "Although the transaction of cutting the mail bags was in a sense continuous, the complete statutory crime was committed *every time a mail bag was cut* in the manner described, *with the intent charged.* The offense as to each *separate bag* was complete when the bag *was cut,* irrespective of any attack upon, or mutilation of any other bag." (Italics ours.)

Again, at page 630, the Court recognizes the distinction, when it said:

"The case is not like those charges of continuous offenses where the crime is necessarily, and because of its nature, a *single one.*" (Italics ours.)

Clearly the case of *Ebeling v. Morgan,* supra, is not authority for holding that a crime which consists of but a single act can be punished by several sentences. Clearly it is authority to the contrary.

The case of *Chrysler v. Zerbst,* 81 Fed. (2d) 975, relied upon by appellant, is not in point. That case deals with two separate crimes, each *sui generis,* one being transportation of an automobile, and the other receiving and concealing the same automobile. We believe that it is so clear that transportation is essentially different from receiving and concealing as to make discussion unnecessary.

Likewise the case of *Morgan v. Devine,* 237 U. S. 632, which involved the breaking into a post office and the stealing of stamps. The two crimes charged were intrinsically different and, therefore, the decision is not applicable to the question here raised. In that case the Court said:

"the test is not whether the criminal intent is one and the same and inspiring the whole transaction, but whether *separate acts have been committed* with the requisite criminal intent and are such as are made punishable by the Act of Congress." (Italics ours.)

Logan v. United States, 123 Fed. 291, goes no further than to decide that a separate intent is necessary to the keeping with intent to pass several forged notes. In its decision the Court categorically states that a single crime cannot be doubled by changing the method of charging it.

> p. 293. "Under the first and tenth counts, the defendant below was twice convicted of the *same act* of forgery, the forgery charged in the first count being of the note, and in the tenth of the signature to the note. The same thing is true with respect to the second and eleventh counts and the third and twelfth counts. Under the thirteenth count he was convicted of passing a note charged as forged, and under the fourteenth of passing the same note, the signature being charged as forged. *These double convictions were not, in our opinion proper. The crime could not be doubled by changing the method of charging it* * * *." (Italics ours.)

Here again, in no uncertain terms, does the Court recognize that double punishment cannot be meted out for an offense which consists of but a single act.

Colbeck et al. v. United States (C. C. A. 8), 14 Fed. (2d) 801, appears to be an anomolous decision. A reading of the opinion in that case does not disclose that the seventy-nine registered letters involved in count 13, charged to be unlawfully possessed after having been stolen from a specified depositary, viz., a pouch with lock M9545, Rotary No. 113, were any part of the 337 registered letters, the unlawful possession of which was charged in count 14. Nor does it appear, as in the instant case, that but a single act and simultaneous theft was involved.

Poffenbarger v. Aderhold (C. C. A. 5), 20 Fed.
'(2d) 42, like the *Morgan* and *Chrysler* cases, ante, is
not in point for the reason that two separate and distinct crimes, each requiring a separate criminal intent,
were there involved, viz., stealing mail bags and abstracting mail matter from such bags, each requiring separate and distinct acts.

**POINTS AND AUTHORITIES IN SUPPORT OF PETITIONER'S
CONTENTION THAT THE THREE CONSECUTIVE SEN-
TENCES IMPOSED UNDER COUNTS THREE, FOUR AND
FIVE IN THE LAGOMARSINO INDICTMENT WERE EXCES-
SIVE, ILLEGAL AND VOID.**

In *Braden v. United States,* 270 F. 441, the defendant was charged in four separate counts with possession of certain drugs, and received consecutive
sentences on each count. Each count was identical
in language save and except that one count specified
possession of morphine sulphate, another cocaine,
another heroin, and another smoking opium. The
situation was exactly parallel to the present case, i. e.,
the crime was one transaction, but the article charged
was different.

The decision of the Court upon this point follows:
"It is further contended that the sentence imposed by the trial Court is excessive. This contention is based on the fact that although defendant
was convicted on 4 counts the transaction upon
which said 4 counts are based was the finding of
defendant in possession on the 16th day of November, 1918, in his flat in St. Paul, Minn., of the
4 different drugs mentioned in counts 6, 7, 8 and

9, said drugs being morphine sulphate, cocaine, heroin and smoking opium, all derivates of opium except cocaine, which is a derivative of coca leaves. Counsel for the United States contend that the words 'any of the aforesaid drugs' as used in Section 8 permit him to base a count upon each drug found in the possession of the defendant although the drugs were all found at the same time and place. We do not think that any such significance can be given to the word 'any'. The use of this word simply means that, if the defendant under the required circumstances should be found in the possession of any of the said drugs, he would be guilty. *If a person steals 4 horses from the barn of another, all being of different color, it would not be competent to charge the thief with 4 different larcenies when the horses were all taken at the same time and place. Another illustration woudl be the larceny of articles of merchandise from a store. If 12 articles were all taken at the same time and place, we do not think it would be competent to charge the thief with 12 different larcenies * * * the judgment* therefore,* is affirmed as to the 6th count and the sentences on counts 7, 8 and 9 are reversed.''

Again in *Parmagini v. United States,* 42 F. (2d) 721, Circuit Court of Appeals, Ninth Circuit, the defendants were indicted upon several counts, the first of which charged sale of morphine, and the third of which charged distribution of opium. The Court in an opinion by Wilbur, Circuit Judge, approved the *Braden* case supra, and in the following language held categorically that but a single offense had been committed:

"The question as to whether or not the charges with reference to the distribution and conceal-ment of the opium can be considered a separate and distinct offense is a more difficult one. As the Appellant points out, in the Circuit Court of Appeals of the Eighth Circuit, in Braden v. U. S. 270 F. 441, 443, a defendant was charged in five separate counts with having five distinct narcotic drugs in his possession at the same time. The Court held that only one offense was committed, stating:

The Court thereupon quoted the excerpt from the *Braden* case quoted supra, and continued:

"With reference to counts I and III, one for selling morphine and the other for distributing opium, the transaction was an entirety, the de-livery of the opium was a mere incident to the delivery of the morphine, and the transaction comes clearly within the rule stated by the Cir-cuit Court of Appeals of the Eighth Circuit in the last mentioned case. *It follows that the fine and punishment for distribtuing opium were im-posed for the same offense as the fine and punish-ment for selling morphine * * *.*"

It was never the intention of the Congress that a man should be punished by a five year imprisonment for each of several letters taken from a post office at one and the same time and the statute must be so con-strued as to give to it its plain and rational meaning.

Maxwell on Interpretation of Statutes, 2d Ed. p. 318:

"The rule which requires that penal and some other statutes shall be construed strictly was more rigorously applied in former times, when the number of capital crimes was one hundred and sixty or more, * * * But it has lost much of its force and importance in recent times, since it has become more and more generally recognized that the paramount duty of the judicial interpreter is to put upon the language of the legislature, honestly and faithfully, its plain and rational meaning, and to promote its objects."

CONCLUSION.

It has been demonstrated herein that no authority exists for the proposition that a crime which consists of but a single act, a simultaneous theft, can be split up into two or more crimes. The authorities cited by appellant, at most, only hold that when several criminal acts are committed in the course of what in a sense may be but one transaction, they may be separately punished. By reason of the separate acts they are separate crimes, but without separate acts there cannot be separate crimes. In addition, it has been shown that appellant's authorities in fact support the contention that when a crime, of its nature, consists of but a single act, there can be but a single punishment.

In our opinion, far outweighing the case attempted to be made out by appellant by inference drawn from decisions which do not deal with analogous facts, are the logical and well considered opinions in the *Braden* and *Parmagini* cases, the latter decided in this Ninth Circuit. These cases are squarely in point, the *Braden* case being almost identical as to facts. The logic of these decisions is unimpeachable, and it is especially worthy of note that appellant did not even attempt to distinguish the *Braden* case and did not seriously dispute the *Parmagini* case.

We respectfully submit that the *Braden* and *Parmagini* cases should be followed and the appeal herein dismissed.

Dated, San Francisco,
    October 14, 936.

RAYMOND J. O'CONNOR,
    Attorney for Appellees.

No. 8209

United States Circuit Court of Appeals
For the Ninth Circuit

——— //

JAMES A. JOHNSTON, Warden of the United
States Penitentiary, Alcatraz Island,
California,

Appellant,

VS.

ALICE LAGOMARSINO and RAY LAGOMARSINO,
alias Edwin Murphy,

Appellees.

APPELLANT'S REPLY BRIEF.

H. H. MCPIKE,
United States Attorney,
ROBERT L. MCWILLIAMS,
Assistant United States Attorney,
A. J. ZIRPOLI,
Assistant United States Attorney,
Post Office Building, San Francisco,
Attorneys for Appellant.

FILED

OCT 29 1936

PAUL P. O'BRIEN

PERNAU-WALSH PRINTING CO., SAN FRANCISCO

Table of Authorities Cited

Cases

Pages

Ebeling v. Morgan, 237 U. S. 625......................1, 2, 4, 5

U. S. v. Inabnet, 41 Fed. 130.............................   3
U. S. v. Lacher, 134 U. S. 624..........................   2
U. S. v. Marselis, Fed. Cas. No. 15,724...................   3

Statutes

Section 312, Title 18 U.S.C.A...........................2, 3, 5
Section 317, Title 18 U.S.C.A........................... 2, 3

case and in the case of *Ebeling v. Morgan,* indicates that there is no difference whatsoever between the statutes, despite the attempt of appellees to show that the term "or mail" is generic, whereas the term "or other thing" is specific. The pertinent portion of the statute involved in the instant case reads as follows:

"Section 317, Title 18, U.S.C.A.—Stealing, secreting, or embezzling mail matter.

Whoever shall *steal,* take, or abstract, or by fraud or deception obtain, from or out of any mail, post office or station thereof, or other authorized depositary for mail matter, or from a letter or mail carrier, *any letter,* postal card, package, bag, or mail * * * shall be fined not more than $2,000.00, or imprisoned not more than five years, or both." (Italics ours.)

The pertinent portion of the statute involved in the case of *Ebeling v. Morgan,* supra, reads as follows:

"Section 312, Title 18, U.S.C.A.—Injuring mail bags.

Whoever shall *tear,* cut, or otherwise injure *any mail bag,* pouch, or other thing used or designed for use in the conveyance of the mail, * * * shall be fined not more than $500.00 or imprisoned not more than three years, or both." (Italics ours.)

Applying the test laid down in the case of *U. S. v. Lacher,* 134 U.S. 624, wherein Mr. Justice Storey stated:

"It appears to me * * * that the proper course in all these cases is to reach out and follow the true intent of the legislature, and to adopt the sense of the words which harmonizes best with the context, and promotes in the fuller manner the apparent policy and objects of the legislature",

we find the legislature evidently intended to accomplish the same purpose in each statute.

By Section 317 of Title 18 U. S. C. A., Congress intended to protect each and every letter, postal card, package, bag or mail. By Section 312 of Title 18, U.S.C.A., Congress intended to protect each and every mail bag, pouch or other thing used or designed for use in the conveyance of mail. Further, an analysis of the various definitions given the phrase "or mail" indicates that it was not necessarily intended by Congress as a generic term. It was intended to mean not only the bag or bags with which letters, papers or other matter contained therein are conveyed under public authority from one post office to another, but was also intended to include both the whole bag of mail matter transported by postal agents, or any letter or package forming a component part of it. (*U. S. v. Inabnet,* 41 F. 130.) Another judicial definition of the term "mail" is:

> "The terms 'mail' and 'post office' seem, each of them, to bear, in the acts of congress and in general acceptation, both a generic and a specific sense. Instances are presented in sections 2, 4, 11 and 22 of the act of 1825, of the employment of the term 'mail' as embracing the whole body of mailable matter transmitted from office to office, and also the particular packets addressed from and received at different post offices."

U. S. v. Marselis, Fed. Cas. No. 15,724.

From the foregoing we must of necessity conclude that there is no difference in the language of the statutes, for one makes it an offense to *steal* from a post office *any letter,* and the other makes it an offense to *tear any mail bag* used or designed for use in the conveyance of mail. There being no difference in the statutes involved, the case of *Ebeling v. Morgan,* supra, is controlling. It follows that when a person takes three letters from the same depositary, whether he take them at once or consecutively, he commits separate offenses and not a single act, as appellees contend. This is readily apparent when we consider the language of the Supreme Court at page 629, where it said:

> "Although the transaction of cutting the mail bags was in a sense continuous, the complete statutory crime was committed every time a mail bag was cut in the manner described, with the intent charged. The offense as to each separate bag was complete when the bag was cut, irrespective of any attack upon, or mutilation of any other bag."

and revise the same to fit the facts of the instant case. By so revising it we have the following:

> Although the transaction of *stealing the letters* was in a sense continuous, the complete statutory crime was committed every time a *letter was stolen* in the manner described, with the intent charged. The offense as to each *separate letter* was complete when the *letter* was stolen, irrespective of any *theft of any other letter.* (Italics ours.)

Thus we must again conclude that the language of the Supreme Court in the case of *Ebeling v. Morgan,* supra, in interpreting Section 312 of Title 18, U.S.C.A., leads to but one reasonable conclusion, namely, that the theft of three parcels of mail at one and the same time from the same depositary constitutes three separate offenses, and that therefore the Court below erred in granting a writ of habeas corpus and ordering the discharge of Ray Lagomarsino, alias Edwin Murphy, from the custody of appellant. It is respectfully submitted that the order appealed from should be reversed.

Dated, San Francisco,
October 28, 1936.

H. H. McPike,
United States Attorney,

Robert L. McWilliams,
Assistant United States Attorney,

A. J. Zirpoli,
Assistant United States Attorney,

Attorneys for Appellant.

United States

Circuit Court of Appeals

For the Ninth Circuit.

/2/

UNITED STATES OF AMERICA, to the use of
TREVE W. BERLIN, and L. E. CLEAVER,
et al.,

Appellants,

vs.

HERBERT M. BARUCH CORPORATION, LTD.,
a corporation, HERBERT M. BARUCH,
MILTON BARUCH, UNITED STATES FI-
DELITY and GUARANTY CO.,

Appellees.

Transcript of Record

**Upon Appeal from the District Court of the United
States for the Northern District of California,
Southern Division.**

No. 8290

United States
Circuit Court of Appeals

For the Ninth Circuit.

UNITED STATES OF AMERICA, to the use of
TREVE W. BERLIN, and L. E. CLEAVER,
et al.,

Appellants,

vs.

HERBERT M. BARUCH CORPORATION, LTD.,
a corporation, HERBERT M. BARUCH,
MILTON BARUCH, UNITED STATES FI-
DELITY and GUARANTY CO.,

Appellees.

Transcript of Record

Upon Appeal from the District Court of the United
States for the Northern District of California,
Southern Division.

INDEX

[Clerk's Note: When deemed likely to be of an important nature,
errors or doubtful matters appearing in the original certified record are
printed literally in italic; and, likewise, cancelled matter appearing in
the original certified record is printed and cancelled herein accordingly.
When possible, an omission from the text is indicated by printing in
italic the two words between which the omission seems to occur.]

Page

Assignment of Errors... 79

Assignment of Errors... 82

Amended Praecipe 89

Bond on Appeal.. 86

Complaint 1

Complaint in Intervention... 41

Citation 93

Clerk's Certificate 92

Demurrer to Complaint.. 58

Demurrer to Complaint in Intervention........................ 63

Judgment 72

Minute Order Sustaining Demurrer................................ 70

Minute Order Sustaining Demurrer................................ 71

Minute Order for Judgment.. 71

Names and Addresses of Attorneys................................ 1

Notice of Entry of Judgment.. 76

Order Permitting Intervention....................................... 40

Order Allowing Appeal... 84

Petition for Leave to Intervene...................................... 38

Petition for Appeal... 78

Petition for Appeal... 80

Stipulation 96

NAMES AND ADDRESSES OF ATTORNEYS

A. BROOKS BERLIN, Esq.,
    525 Standard Oil Bldg., San Francisco, Calif.,
    Attorney for Appellants.

JULIUS MACKSON, Esq.,
    357 South Hill St., Los Angeles, Calif.,
    Attorney for Appellees.

In the District Court of the United States, in and for the Northern District of California, Southern Division.

No. 19921-L

UNITED STATES OF AMERICA, to the use of TREVE W. BERLIN,

Plaintiff,

vs.

HERBERT M. BARUCH CORPORATION, Ltd., a corporation, HERBERT M. BARUCH, MILTON BARUCH, UNITED STATES FIDELITY AND GUARANTY COMPANY, a corporation, First Doe, Second Doe, Third Doe, Fourth Doe and Fifth Doe,

Defendants.

COMPLAINT

Laborers Claims for Services Rendered

Plaintiff above named complains of defendants above named, and for cause of action alleges:

I.

That this action is brought in the name of the United States of America for the use and benefit of Treve W. Berlin, under and by virtue of the provisions of Section 270 of Title 40 of the United States Code.

II.

That at all of the times herein mentioned, Treve W. Berlin, was and now is an individual residing at San Francisco, California.

III.

That at all of the times herein mentioned, defendant Herbert M. Baruch Corporation, Ltd., was and now is a corporation duly organized and existing under and by virtue of the laws of the State of California, with principal office for the transaction of its business in the City of Los Angeles, County of Los Angeles, State of California.

IV.

That at all of the times herein mentioned, defendant United [1*] States Fidelity and Guranty Company was and now is a corporation duly organized and existing under and by virtue of the laws of the State of Maryland, and authorized to conduct, and conducting a surety business in the State and Northern District of California.

V.

That the true names of defendants sued herein as First Doe, Second Doe, Third Doe, Fourth Doe and Fifth Doe are not known to plaintiff at this time,

---

*Page numbering appearing at the foot of page of original certified Transcript of Record.

and plaintiff prays that when their true names are ascertained that the same may be inserted herein in lieu of said fictitious names.

VI.

That on the 12th day of January, 1933, the said Herbert M. Baruch Corporation, Ltd., Herbert M. Baruch and Milton Baruch made, executed and entered into a written contract with the United States of America by and through the United States Department, Veterans Administration, for the wrecking and removing of old buildings as specified under "General Information" and constructing and finishing complete for Veterans' Administration at San Francisco, California, certain veterans' buildings and hospital buildings in said City and County of San Francisco, in the Southern Division of the Northern District of California; that a true and correct copy of said contract is attached hereto as Exbibit "A", and made a part hereof as if fully set forth at length herein.

VII.

That subsequent thereto and on or about the 23rd day of January, 1933, Herbert M. Baruch Corporation, Ltd., a California corporation, Herbert M. Baruch and Milton Baruch, as principals, and defendant United States Fidelity and Guaranty Company, a corporation, as surety, made, executed and filed with the United States Treasury Department, Commissioner of Accounts and Deposits, in compliance with Section 270 of Title 40 of the United States Code, a bond on behalf of the United States

of America, with the added [2] obligation that said
principals should promptly make payment to all
persons supplying said principals with labor and
materials in the prosecution of the work provided
in said contract hereinabove referred to; that a true
and correct copy of said bond is attached hereto as
Exhibit "B" and is made a part hereof as if fully
set forth at length herein.

VIII.

That pursuant to the terms of Federal statutes
and laws made and provided for in said case, and
more particularly 46 Federal statutes, 1494, known
as the "Davis-Bacon Act, approved March 3, 1931"
and Executive orders supplementary thereto, all in
effect at the time of the execution of said contract
referred to in paragraph VI hereof, the rate of
wages under the terms of said contract and all
laborers and mechanics employed by the contractor
or any subcontractor on the public buildings
governed by said contract shall not be less than the
prevailing rate of wages for work of a similar
nature in the city, town, village or civil division of
the States in which said public buildings are located, and said wages shall be paid unconditionally
in full, not less often than once a week in lawful
money of the United States to the full amount accrued to each individual so employed at the time of
payments and without subsequent deduction or re-
bate on account.

IX.

That within two years last past, the defendants
Herbert M. Baruch Corporation, Ltd., Herbert M.

Baruch and Milton Baruch became indebted to one
A. L. Arnold in the sum of $825.00 as a balance due
and owing for work and labor done and performed
by said A. L. Arnold for said defendants at the
special instance and request of said defendants and
each of them on the Veterans Administration buildings covered by said written contract specified in
paragraph VI hereof, and located at Fort Miley,
California, a public works project in the City and
County of San Francisco, [3] in the Southern Division of the Northern District of California; and
which said sum of $825.00 represents the difference
between the sums of money actually received by said
A. L. Arnold for said work and the amounts then
due and owing to him in accordance with the prevailing rate of wages then duly established and
posted for work and labor of a similar nature in
said City and County of San Francisco.

X.

That prior to the commencement of this action,
this claimant transferred, assigned and set over by
an instrument in writing all of his right, title and
interest in and to his claim to plaintiff and plaintiff
then and there became, ever since has been and still
is the holder and owner thereof.

XI.

That no part of said sum of $825.00 has been paid,
and the whole thereof is now due, owing and unpaid
from said defendants and each of them to plaintiff
herein.

XII.

That plaintiff is informed and believes and therefore alleges the fact to be that the contract specified in paragraph VI hereof was physically completed on the 14th day of November, 1934, and finally settled on the 26th day of January, 1935; that more than six months and less than one year have elapsed between the completion and final settlement of the said contract and the filing and commencement of this action; that plaintiff is informed and believes and on such information and belief alleges that the United States of America has brought no action against defendant on the bond or contract hereinabove referred to.

WHEREFORE: Plaintiff Treve W. Berlin prays judgment against defendants and each of them for the sum of $825.00, together with costs of suit incurred herein. [4]

For a second cause of action against the defendants and each of them, plaintiff further complains and alleges:

I.

Plaintiff realleges paragraphs I, II, III, IV, V, VI, VII, VIII, X and XII of the first cause of action by reference as fully as though here repeated and fully set forth.

II.

That within two years last past the defendants Herbert M. Baruch Corporation, Ltd., Herbert M. Baruch and Milton Baruch became indebted to one Edward Russell in the sum of $423.00 as a balance due and owing for work and labor done and per-

formed by said Edward Russell for said defendants
at the special instance and request of said defendants and each of them on the Veterans Administration buildings covered by said written contract
specified in paragraph VI of the first cause of
action, and located at Fort Miley, California, a
public works project in the City and County of San
Francisco, in the Southern Division of the Northern
District of California; and which said sum of
$423.00 represents the difference between the sums
of money actually received by said Edward Russell
for said work, and the amounts then due and owing
to him in accordance with the prevailing rate of
wages then duly established and posted for work and
labor of a similar nature in said City and County of
San Francisco.

III.

That no part of said sum of $423.00 has been paid,
and the whole thereof is now due, owing and unpaid
from said defendants and each of them to plaintiff
herein.

WHEREFORE: plaintiff Treve W. Berlin prays
judgment against defendants and each of them for
the sum of $423.00 together with costs of suit in-
curred herein. [5]

Joe Brozovich	$ 157.00
G. R. Fulton	388.50
Arthur Addington	1028.00
Frank Wilson	1529.00
Max B. Miller	1283.00
Laurel Johnstone	1534.00
James V. Sullivan	342.00

William G. Riley	90.00
J. Malatesta	245.00
G. Malatesta	206.00
James Ghielmetti	726.20
Fred Melton	120.00
R. Diaz	140.00
F. Gonzales	215.00
E. Spriggs	276.00
Sam Rascon	140.00
Harry Grodberg	824.20
John Alupsky	956.50
John H. Rediger	550.00
John West	69.00
R. L. Williams	1042.60
William F. Joyce	294.26
William T. Joyce	465.51
Carl Hagstrom	193.00

WHEREFORE: plaintiff prays judgment against said defendants and each of them for the total sum of Fourteen Thousand Sixty Two and 77/100 Dollars ($14,062.77), together with interest thereon at the rate of seven per cent per annum, together with costs of suit incurred herein.

A. BROOKS BERLIN
Attorney for Plaintiff [30]

City and County of San Francisco
Northern District of California—ss.

TREVE W. BERLIN, being first duly sworn, deposes and says: That he is the plaintiff named in the foregoing Complaint; that he has read said Complaint and knows the contents thereof, and the same is true of his own knowledge except as to the matters therein stated on information and belief, and as to those matters, he believes it to be true.

TREVE W. BERLIN

Subscribed and sworn to before me this 27th day of July, 1935.

[Seal]   LULU P. LOVELAND

Notary Public, in and for the City and County of San Francisco, State of California. My commission expires December 8, 1938. [31]

EXHIBIT A.

UNITED STATES OF AMERICA.

GENERAL ACCOUNTING OFFICE

Pursuant to the Act of June 10, 1921, 42 Stat. 24, I hereby certify that the annexed documents, numbered O-1 to O-13, inc., are true copies of the official documents now on file in the General Accounting Office in the following case:

Herbert M. Baruch Corporation, Ltd.

IN WITNESS WHEREOF, I have hereunto set my hand and caused the seal of the General Accounting Office to be affixed this 4th day of March, in the year 1935, at Washington.

[Seal]   R. W. ELLIOTT

Acting Comptroller General of

VAc 336
COMP
STANDARD GOVERNMENT FORM OF
CONTRACT
(Construction) .

RECEIVED
G. A. O.
Feb. 20, 1933

VETERANS' ADMINISTRATION
(Department)

HERBERT M. BARUCH CORPORATION,
LTD.
(Contractor)
625 South Olive Street,
Los Angeles, California

GENERAL CONSTRUCTION WORK
Contract for BUILDINGS AND UTILITIES
Amount $898,810.00
Place: San Francisco, California
January 12, 1933 [33]

———

CONTRACT FOR CONSTRUCTION

THIS CONTRACT, entered into this Twelfth
day of January, 1933, by The United States of
America, hereinafter called the Government, represented by the contracting officer executing this contract, and HERBERT M. BARUCH CORPORA-
TION, LTD., a California Corporation, and HER-

BERT M. BARUCH and MILTON BARUCH, a corporation of the City of Los Angeles, in the State of California, hereinafter called the contractor, witnesseth that the parties hereto do mutually agree as follows:

Article 1. Statement of Work. The contractor shall furnish all labor and materials, and perform all work required for wrecking and removing old buildings as specified under "General Information" and constructing and finishing complete for Veterans' Administration at SAN FRANCISCO, CALIFORNIA, Administration Bldg. #1, Main Bldg. #2, Boiler House #3, Ward Bldg. #4, X-Ray Bldg. #5, Dining Hall and Attendants Quarters Bldg. #6, Recreation Bldg. #7, Nurses' Quarters Bldg. #8, Officers' Duplex Quarters Bldg. #9, Officers' Duplex Quarters Bldg. #10, Manager's Residence Bldg. #11, Garage and Attendants' Bldg. #12, Laundry Bldg. #13, Pump, Meter and Transformer House Bldg. #15, Gate House Bldg. #16, Animal House Bldg. #17, Flagpole, Connecting Corridors Nos. 1-2, 2-4, 2-5, 4-6 and 2-7, together with the revision and reconditioning of one Officers' Apartment Building (existing Bldg. #A23-24), and the moving and reconditioning of existing Bldg. #A4; including also the fences and gates, roads, walks, grading and drainage in connection with these buildings, but not including Plumbing, Heating, Electrical Work and Outside Distribution Systems, Electric and Hydraulic Elevators, and Refrigerating and Ice Making Plant; for the consid-

eration of Eight Hundred Ninety Eight Thousand
Eight Hundred Ten ($898,810.00) Dollars, in strict
accordance with the specifications, schedules, and
drawings, all of which are made a part hereof and
designated as follows: Specifications for Buildings
and Utilities for Veterans' Administration at San
Francisco, California, November 12, 1932, and the
schedules and drawings mentioned therein: Adden-
dum No. 1 dated November 26, 1932, as contemplated by Item I and Alternates (a), (b), (c), (d),
(f), (j), (k-a), (k-b), (k-c), (k-d), (k-e), (l),
(o-b), (o-c), (o-d), (o-e), and (p), under Item I
of the Contractor's proposal dated December 15,
1932, and letter of acceptance dated January 12,
1933.

The work shall be commenced within Twenty (20)
Calendar Days after date of receipt of notice to
proceed and shall be completed within Four Hundred Twenty Five (425) Calendar Days after date
of receipt of notice to proceed, except that sufficient
work in Main Building No.   and Boiler House
Building No. 3 be accomplished to permit the installation of steel stack, boilers and equipment, will
be completed 90 days prior thereto. [34]

Article 2.   Specifications and drawings. The contractor shall keep on the work a copy of the drawings and specifications and shall at all times give the
contracting officer access thereto. Anything mentioned in the specifications and not shown on the
drawings, or shown on the drawings and not mentioned in the specifications shall be of like effect

as if shown or mentioned in both. In case of difference between drawings and specifications, the specifications shall govern. In any case of discrepancy in the figures or drawings, the matter shall be immediately submitted to the contracting officer, without whose decision said discrepancy shall not be adjusted by the contractor, save only at his own risk and expense. The contracting officer shall furnish from time to time such detail drawings and other information as he may consider necessary, unless otherwise provided. Upon completion of the contract the work shall be delivered complete and undamaged.

Article 3. Changes. The contracting officer may at any time, by a written order, and without notice to the sureties, make changes in the drawings and (or) specifications of this contract and within the general scope thereof. If such changes cause an increase or decrease in the amount due under this contract, or in the time required for its performance, an equitable adjustment shall be made and the contract shall be modified in writing accordingly. No change involving an estimated increase or decrease of more than Five Hundred Dollars shall be ordered unless approved in writing by the head of the department or his duly authorized representative. Any claim for adjustment under this article must be asserted within ten days from the date the change is ordered, unless the contracting officer shall for proper cause extend such time, and if the parties can not agree upon the adjustment the dispute shall be determined as provided in Article 15 hereof. But nothing provided in this article shall excuse the contractor from proceeding with the prosecution of the work so changed.

Article 4. Changed conditions. Should the contractor encounter, or the Government discover, during the progress of the work, subsurface and (or) latent conditions at the site materially differing from those shown on the drawings or indicated in the specifications, the attention of the contracting officer shall be called immediately to such conditions before they are disturbed. The contracting officer shall thereupon promptly investigate the conditions, and if he finds that they materially differ from those shown on the drawings or indicated in the specifications, he shall at once, with the written approval of the head of the department or his representative, make such changes in the drawings and (or) specifications as he may find necessary, and any increase or decrease of cost and (or) difference in time resulting from such changes shall be adjusted as provided in Article 3 of this contract.

Article 5. Extras. Except as otherwise herein provided, no charge for any extra work or material will be allowed unless the same has been ordered in writing by the contracting officer and the price stated in such order.

Article 6. Inspection. (a) All material and workmanship (if not otherwise designated by the specifications) shall be subject to inspection, examination, and test by Government inspectors at any and all times during manufacture and (or) construction and at any and all places where such manufacture and (or) construction are carried on. The Government shall have the [35] right to reject defective material and workmanship or require its correction. Rejected workmanship shall be satisfactorily corrected and rejected material shall be satisfactorily replaced with proper material without charge therefor, and the contractor shall promptly segregate and remove the same from the premises.

(b) The contractor shall furnish promptly without additional charge, all reasonable facilities, labor, and materials necessary for the safe and convenient inspection and test that may be required by the inspectors. All inspection and tests by the Government shall be performed in such manner as not to unnecessarily delay the work. Special, full size, and performance tests shall be as described in the specifications. The contractor shall be charged with any additional cost of inspection when material and workmanship is not ready at the time inspection is requested by the contractor.

(c) Should it be considered necessary or advisable by the Government at any time before final acceptance of the entire work to make an examination of work already completed, by removing or tearing out same, the contractor shall on request promptly furnish all necessary facilities, labor, and material. If such work is found to be defective in any material respect, due to fault of the contractor or his subcontractors, he shall defray all the expenses of such examination and of satisfactory reconstruction. If, however, such work is found to meet the requirements of the contract, the actual cost of labor and material necessarily involved in the examination and replacement, plus 15 per cent, shall be allowed the contractor and he shall, in addition, if completion of the work has been delayed thereby, be granted a suitable extension of time on account of the additional work involved.

(d) Inspection of material and finished articles to be incorporated in the work at the site shall be made at the place of production, manufacture, or shipment, whenever the quantity justifies it, unless otherwise stated in the specifications; and such inspection and acceptance, unless otherwise stated in the specifications, shall be final, except as regards latent defects, departures from specific requirements of the contract and the specifications and drawings made a part thereof, damage or loss in transit, fraud, or such gross mistakes as amount to fraud. Subject to the requirements contained in the preceding sentence, the inspection of material and workmanship for final acceptance as a whole or in part shall be made at the site.

Article 7.—Materials and workmanship.—Unless otherwise specifically provided for in the specifications, all workmanship, equipment, materials and articles incorporated in the work covered by this contract are to be of the best grade of their respective kinds for the purpose. Where equipment, materials, or articles are referred to in the specifications as "equal to" any particular standard, the contracting officer shall decide the question of equality.

The contractor shall furnish to the contracting officer for his approval the name of the manufacturer of machinery, mechanical and other equipment which he contemplates installing, together with their performance capacities and other pertinent information. When required by the specifications, or when called for by the contracting officer, the contractor shall furnish the contracting officer for approval full information concerning the materials or articles which he contemplates incorporating in the work. Samples of materials shall be submitted for approval when so directed. Machinery, equipment, materials, and articles installed or used without such approval [36] shall be at the risk of subsequent rejection. The contracting officer may require the contractor to dismiss from the work such employee as the contracting officer deems incompetent, careless, insubordinate, or otherwise objectionable.

Article 8. Superintendence by contractor.—The contractor shall give his personal superintendence to the work or have a competent foreman or superintendent, satisfactory to the contracting officer, on the work at all times during progress, with authority to act for him.

Article 9. Delays—Damages.—If the contractor refuses or fails to prosecute the work, or any separable part thereof, with such diligence as will insure its completion within the time specified in Article 1, or any extension thereof, or fails to complete said work within such time, the Government may, by written notice to the contractor, terminate his right to proceed with the work or such part of

the work as to which there has been delay. In such
event, the Government may take over the work and
prosecute the same to completion by contract or
otherwise, and the contractor and his sureties shall
be liable to the Government for any excess cost oc-
casioned the Government thereby. If the contractor's
right to proceed is so terminated, the Government
may take possession of and utilize in completing the
work such materials, appliances, and plant as may
be on the site of the work and necessary therefor.
If the Government does not terminate the right of
the contractor to proceed, the contractor shall continue the work, in which event the actual damages
for the delay will be impossible to determine and in
lieu thereof the contractor shall pay to the Government as fixed, agreed, and liquidated damages for
each calendar day of delay until the work is completed or accepted the amount as set forth in the
specifications accompanying papers and the contractor and his sureties shall be liable for the amount
thereof: Provided, That the right of the contractor
to proceed shall not be terminated or the contractor
charged with liquidated damages because of any
delays in the completion of the work due to unfore-
seeable causes beyond the control and without the
fault or negligence of the contractor, including, but
not restricted to, acts of God, or of the public
enemy, acts of the Government, fires, floods, epi-
demics, quarantine restrictions, strikes, freight em-
bargoes, and unusually severe weather or delays of
subcontractors due to such causes: Provided further,

That the contractor shall within ten days from the beginning of any such delay notify the contracting officer in writing of the causes of delay, who shall ascertain the facts and the extent of the delay, and his findings of fact thereon shall be final and conclusive on the parties hereto, subject only to appeal, within thirty days, by the contractor to the head of the department concerned, whose decision on such appeal as to the facts of delay shall be final and conclusive on the parties hereto.

Article 10. Permits and care of work.—The contractor shall, without additional expense to the Government, obtain all required licenses and permits and be responsible for all damages to persons or property that occur as a result of his fault or negligence in connection with the prosecution of the work, and shall be responsible for the proper care and protection of all materials delivered and work performed until completion and final acceptance.

Article 11. Eight-hour law—Convict labor.— (a) No laborer or mechanic doing any part of the work contemplated by this contract, in the employ of the contractor or any subcontractor contracting [37] for any part of said work contemplated, shall be required or permitted to work more than eight hours in any one calendar day upon such work at the site thereof. For each violation of the requirements of this article a penalty of five dollars shall be imposed upon the contractor for each laborer or mechanic for every calendar day in which such employee is required or permitted to labor more than eight hours upon said work, and all penalties thus imposed shall be withheld for the use and benefit of the Government: Provided, that this stipulation shall be subject in all respects to the exceptions and provisions of the act of June 19, 1912 (37 Stat. 137), relating to hours of labor.

(b)   The contractor shall not employ any person undergoing sentence of imprisonment at hard labor.

Article 12.   Covenant against contingent fees.—The contractor warrants that he has not employed any person to solicit or secure this contract upon any agreement for a commission, percentage, brokerage, or contingent fee. Breach of this warranty shall give the Government the right to terminate the contract, or, in its discretion, to deduct from the contract price or consideration the amount of such commission, percentage, brokerage, or contingent fees. This warranty shall not apply to commissions payable by contractors upon contracts or sales secured or made through bona fide established commercial or selling agencies maintained by the contractor for the purpose of securing business.

Article 13.—Other contracts.—The Government may award other contracts for additional work, and the contractor shall fully cooperate with such other contractors and carefully fit his own work to that provided under other contracts as may be directed by the contracting officer. The contractor shall not commit or permit any act which will interfere with the performance of work by any other contractor.

Article 14.   Officials not to benefit.—No Member of or Delegate to Congress, or Resident Commissioner, shall be admitted to any share or part of this contract or to any benefit that may arise therefrom, but this provision shall not be construed to extend to this contract if made with a corporation for its general benefit.

Article 15. Disputes.—Except as otherwise specifically provided in this contract, all disputes concerning questions of fact arising under this contract shall be decided by the contracting officer or his duly authorized representative, subject to written appeal by the contractor within thirty days to the head of the department concerned, whose decision shall be final and conclusive upon the parties thereto as to such questions of fact. In the meantime the contractor shall diligently proceed with the work as directed.

Article 16. Payments to contractors.—(a) Unless otherwise provided in the specifications, partial payments will be made as the work progresses at the end of each calendar month, or as soon thereafter as practicable, on estimates made and approved by the contracting officer. In preparing estimates the material delivered on the site and preparatory work done may be taken into consideration.

(b) In making such partial payments there shall be retained 10 per cent on the estimated amount until final completion and acceptance of all work covered by the contract; Provided, however, That the contracting officer, at any time after 50 per cent of the work has been completed, if he finds that satisfactory progress is being made, may make any of the remaining partial payments in [38] full: And provided further, That on completion and acceptance of each separate building, vessel, public work, or other division of the contract, on which the price is stated separately in the contract, payment may be made in full, including retained percentages thereon, less authorized deductions.

(c) All material and work covered by partial payments made shall thereupon become the sole property of the Government, but this provision shall not be construed as relieving the contractor from the sole responsibility for the care and protection of materials and work upon which payments have been made or the restoration of any damaged work, or as a waiver of the right of the Government to require the fulfillment of all of the terms of the contract.

(d) Upon completion and acceptance of all work required hereunder, the amount due the contractor under this contract will be paid upon the presentation of a properly executed and duly certified voucher therefor, after the contractor shall have furnished the Government with a release, if required, of all claims against the Government arising under and by virtue of this contract, other than such claims, if any, as may be specifically excepted by the contractor from the operation of the releases in stated amounts to be set forth therein.

Article 17. Additional security.—Should any surety upon the bond for the performance of this contract become unacceptable, to the Government, the contractor must promptly furnish such additional security as may be required from time to time to protect the interests of the Government and of persons supplying labor or materials in the prosecution of the work contemplated by the contract.

Article 18. Definitions. (a) The term "head of department" as used herein shall mean the head of the executive department or independent establishment involved, and "his representative" means any person authorized to act for him other than the contracting officer.

(b) The term "contracting officer" as used herein shall include his duly appointed successor or his duly authorized representative.

Article 19. Alterations. The following changes were made in this contract before it was signed by the parties hereto:

In Witness Whereof, the parties hereto have executed this contract as of the day and year first-above written.

THE UNITED STATES OF AMERICA.
By H. L. TRIPP,

G. S.   Director of Construction,
H. B.   Veterans' Administration
J. E. W.   (Official Title)

HERBERT M. BARUCH CORPORATION, LTD.,
By H. M. BARUCH,
President.

GRATIA C. JOYCE,
HERBERT M. BARUCH,
MILTON BARUCH,
                    (Business Address)
                    625 S. Olive St.,
                    Los Angeles, Cal.

Two Witnesses:
    BESS HOLBROOK HARDMAN,
    STANLEY N. COLQUEST. [39]

(Construction Contract)

I, GRATIA C. JOYCE, certify that I am the Secretary of the corporation named as contractor herein; that HERBERT M. BARUCH who signed this contract on behalf of the contractor, was then President of said corporation; that said contract was duly signed for and in behalf of said corporation by authority of its governing body, and is within the scope of its corporate powers.

                    GRATIA C. JOYCE
[Corporate Seal]   Secretary Herbert M. Baruch
                    Corp.

I hereby certify that, to the best of my knowledge and belief, based upon observation and inquiry,
                    who signed
this contract for the
had authority to execute the same, and is the individual who signs similar contracts on behalf of this corporation with the public generally.

                    ....
                    Contracting Officer.

This contract is authorized by the acts of WORLD WAR VETERANS' ACT, 1924, as amended.

DIRECTIONS FOR PREPARATION OF CONTRACT

1. This form shall be used for every formal contract for the construction or repair of public buildings or works, but its use will not be required in foreign countries.

2. There shall be no deviation from this standard contract form, except as provided for in these directions, without prior approval of the Director of the Bureau of the Budget obtained through the Interdepartmental Board of Contracts and Adjustments. Where interlineations, deletions, additions, or other alterations are permitted, specific notation of the same shall be entered in the blank space following the article entitled "Alterations" before signing. This article is not to be construed as general authority to deviate from the standard form. Deletion of the descriptive matter not applicable in the preamble need not be noted in the article entitled "Alterations".

3. The blank space of Article 1 is intended for the insertion of a statement of the work to be done, together with place of performance, or for the enumeration of papers which contain the necessary data.

4. If it is deemed necessary to include an article on Patents the Invitation to Bidders shall so state and the following article be used:

Article—Patents.—The contractor shall hold and
save the Government, its officers, agents, servants,
and employees, harmless from liability of any nature
or kind for or on account of the use of any patented
or unpatented invention, article, or appliance
furnished or used in the performance of this contract, excepting patented articles required by the
Government in its specifications, the use of which
the contractor does not control. [40]

5. Where only one payment is contemplated,
upon completion of the contract, all except paragraph (d) of Article 16, "Payments to Contractor",
must be stricken out.

6. If approval of the contract is required before
it shall become binding, the following article must
be added:

Article—Approval.—This contract shall be sub-
ject to the written approval of...
and shall not be binding until so approved.

Contracts subject to approval are not valid until
approved by the authority designated to approve
them, and the contractor's copy will not be delivered,
nor any distribution made, until such approval. All
changes and deletions must have been made before
the contract is forwarded for approval.

7. The number of executed copies and of certified copies, designation of disbursing officer, statement of appropriation, amount of bond, designation
of place of inspection, as well as other administrative details, shall be as directed by the department
to which the contract pertains.

8. All blank spaces must be filled in or ruled out. The contract must be dated, and the bond must bear the same or subsequent date.

9. An officer of a corporation, a member of a partnership, or an agent signing for the principal, shall place his signature and title after the word "By" under the name of the principal. A contract executed by an attorney or agent on behalf of the contractor shall be accompanied by two authenticated copies of his power of attorney, or other evidence of his authority to act on behalf of the contractor.

10. If the contractor is a corporation, one of the certificates following the signatures of the parties must be executed. If the contract is signed by the secretary of the corporation, then the first certificate must be executed by some other officer of the corporation under the corporate seal, or the second certificate executed by the contracting officer. In lieu of either of the foregoing certificates there may be attached to the contract copies of so much of the records of the corporation as will show the official character and authority of the officer signing, duly certified by the secretary or assistant secretary, under the corporate seal, to be true copies.

11. The full name and business address of the contractor must be inserted, and the contract signed with his usual signature. Typewrite or print name under all signatures to contract and bond.

12. The contracting officer must fill in the citation of the act authorizing the contract as indicated at the end of the last page of the contract.

13. The Invitation, Bid, Acceptance, and Instructions to Bidders are not to be incorporated in the contract.

14. The specifications should include a paragraph stating the amount of liquidated damages that will be paid by the contractor for each calendar day of delay, as indicated in Article 9 of the contract. [41]

EXHIBIT B.

VAc 336

COMP

STANDARD GOVERNMENT FORM OF PERFORMANCE BOND
(Construction or Supply)

KNOW ALL MEN BY THESE PRESENTS, That we, HERBERT M. BARUCH CORPORATION, LTD., a California Corporation, and HERBERT M. BARUCH and MILTON BARUCH
(See Instructions 4, 5 and 7)
as Principal, and United States Fidelity and Guaranty Company, a corporation organized and existing under the laws of the State of Maryland, of Baltimore, Maryland, as Surety,
(See Instructions 2, 3, 4 and 7)
are held and firmly bound unto the United States of America, hereinafter called the Government, in the penal sum of FOUR HUNDRED FIFTY THOUSAND DOLLARS ($450,000.00) dollars lawful money of the United States, for the payment of which sum well and truly to be made, we bind ourselves, our heirs, executors, administrators, and suc-

cessors, jointly and severally, firmly by these presents.

The condition of this Obligation is such, that whereas the principal entered into a certain contract, hereto attached, with the Government, dated January 12, 1933, for wrecking and removing old buildings as specified under "General Information" and constructing and finishing complete for Veterans' Administration at SAN FRANCISCO, CALIFORNIA, Administration Bldg. #1, Main Bldg. #2, Boiler House #3, Ward Bldg. #4, X-Ray Bldg. #5, Dining Hall and Attendants Quarters Bldg. #6, Recreation Bldg. #7, Nurses' Quarters Bldg. #8, Officers' Duplex Quarters Bldg. #9 and #10; Manager's Residence Bldg. #11, Garage and Attendants' Quarters Bldg. #12, Laundry Bldg. #13, Pump, Meter and Transformer House Bldg. #15, Gate House Bldg. #16, Animal House Bldg. #17, Flagpole, connecting Corridors Nos. 1-2, 2-4, 2-5, 4-6 and 2-7, together with the reconditioning of Buildings #A23-24 and #A4; but not including Plumbing, Heating, Electrical Work and Outside Distribution Systems, Electric and Hydraulic Elevators, and Refrigerating and Ice Making Plant.

Now Therefore, If the principal shall well and truly perform and fulfill all the undertakings, covenants, terms, conditions, and agreements of said contract during the original term of said contract and any extensions thereof that may be granted by the Government, with or without notice to the surety, and during the life of any guaranty required under

the contract, and shall also well and truly perform
and fulfill all the undertakings, covenants, terms,
conditions and agreements of any and all duly authorized modifications of said contract that may
hereafter be made, notice of which modifications to
the surety being hereby waived, and if said contract is for the construction or repair of a public
building or a public work within the meaning of
the act of August 13, 1894, as amended by act of
February 25, 1905, shall promptly make payment to
all persons supplying the principal with labor and
materials in the prosecution of the work provided
for in said contract, and any such authorized extension or modification [42] thereof, then, this obligation to be void, otherwise to remain in full force
and virtue.

In Witness Whereof, the above-bounden parties
have executed this instrument under their several
seals this 23rd day of January, 1933, the name and
corporate seal of each corporate party being hereto
affixed and these presents duly signed by its undersigned representative, pursuant to authority of its
governing body.

[Seal]   ....
            (Individual principal)

            ....
            (Business Address)

[Seal]   ....
            (Individual principal)

            ....
            (Business Address)

[Seal] ....
(Individual surety)

....
(Business Address)

In presence of

....

....
Address

[Seal] ....
(Individual surety)

....
(Business Address)

HERBERT M. BARUCH
CORPORATION, LTD.

By H. M. BARUCH

President

HERBERT M. BARUCH
(Corporate principal)

MILTON BARUCH
(Business Address)

[Affix
Corporate Seal] By..

Attest:

UNITED STATES FIDELITY
AND GUARANTY COMPANY
(Corporate surety)

724 So. Spring St.,
Los Angeles, Calif.
(Business address)

[Affix
Corporate Seal] MYELIA HARGROVE

By H. V. G. JOHNS

Attorney in Fact

The rate of premium on this bond is $15.00 per thousand.

Total amount of premium charged, $13,482.15.

TREASURY DEPARTMENT
Office of the Secretary

COMMISSIONER OF ACCOUNTS AND DEPOSITS

Section of Surety Bonds Examined and Approved as to the within corporate surety.

D. W. BRILL

> Commissioner of Accounts and Deposits

Jan 28 1933

ofr

233943T

Approved:

G. W. A.

....

H. B.　　　(Address)

　Attest: H. L. TRIPP

　　　　　H. L. Tripp

J. W. S.　　Director of Construction

(The above must be filled in by corporate surety).

[43]

(Performance Bond)

CERTIFICATE AS TO CORPORATE PRINCIPAL

I, GRATIA C. JOYCE, certify that I am the secretary of the corporation named as principal in the within bond; that HERBERT M. BARUCH, who signed the said bond on behalf of the principal was then President of said corporation; that I know his signature, and his signature thereto is genuine; and that said bond was duly signed, sealed, and attested for and in behalf of said corporation by authority of its governing body.

[Corporate Seal] GRATIA C. JOYCE

Secretary, Herbert M. Baruch Corp.

———

AFFIDAVIT BY INDIVIDUAL SURETY

State of.................................

County of...............................—ss:

I,   being duly sworn, depose and say that I am one of the sureties to the foregoing bond; that I am a citizen of the United States, and of full age and legally competent; that I reside at

and that I am worth in real estate and personal property the sum of   dollars, over and above (1) all my debts and liabilities, owing and incurred, (2) any property exempt from execution, (3) and aggregate full penalties on all other bonds on which I am surety, and (4) any pecuniary interest I have in the business of the principal on said bond; that I own, unincumbered, real estate, the fee of which is in my name, worth   dollars, located in   ; that said property is not exempt from seizure and sale under any homestead law, community, or marriage law, or upon any attachment, execution, or judicial process, and that I am not surety on any other bonds, except as follows:

(State character and amount of each bond. If not on other bonds, so state)

....

(Surety's signature)

Subscribed and sworn to before me this   day of   19   .

....
....

[Official Seal] ....

(Title of official administering oath) [44]

AFFIDAVIT OF INDIVIDUAL SURETY

State of...........................
County of..........................—ss.

I,   being duly sworn, depose and say that I am one of the sureties to the foregoing bond; that I am a citizen of the United States, and of full age and legally competent; that I reside at   and that I am worth in real estate and personal property the sum of   dollars, over and above (1) all my debts and liabilities, owing and incurred, (2) any property exempt from execution, (3) the aggregate full penalties on all other bonds on which I am surety, and (4) any pecuniary interest I have in the business of the principal on said bond; that I own, unincumbered, real estate, the fee of which is in my name, worth   dollars, located in   ; that said property is not exempt from seizure and sale

under any homestead law, community, or marriage
law, or upon any attachment, execution, or judicial
process; and that I am not surety on any other
bonds, except as follows:

(State character and amount of each bond. If not on
other bond, so state)

....

(Surety's signature)

Subscribed and sworn to before me, this   day
of   19

[Official Seal] ....

(Title of official administering
oath.

———

Certificate of Sufficiency

I,   , do hereby certify that

one of the sureties named above, is personally
known to me, and that, to the best of my knowledge
and belief, the facts stated by such surety in the
foregoing affidavit are true.

....

....

(Address)

Certificate of Sufficiency

I,   , do hereby certify that

one of the sureties named above, is personally
known to me, and that, to the best of my knowledge
and belief, the facts stated by such surety in the
foregoing affidavit are true.

....

....

(Performance Bond)

INSTRUCTIONS. ·

1.   This form shall be used for construction work or the furnishing of supplies, whenever a bond is required.

2.   The surety on the bond for any bid or for the performance of the contract may be any corporation authorized by the Secretary of the Treasury to act as surety, or two responsible individual sureties. Individual sureties shall justify in sums aggregating not less than double the penalty of the bond.

3.   A firm, as such, will not be accepted as a surety, nor a partner for copartners or for a firm of which he is a member. Stockholders of a corporate principal may be accepted as sureties provided their qualifications as such are independent of their stock holdings therein. Sureties, if individuals, shall be citizens of the United States, except that sureties on bonds executed in any foreign country, the Canal Zone, the Philippine Islands, Porto Rico, Hawaii, Alaska, or any possession of the United States, for the performance of contracts entered into in these places, need not be citizens of the United States, but if not citizens of the United States shall be domociled in the place where the contract is to be performed.

4.   The name, including full Christian name, and residence of each individual party to the bond shall be inserted in the body thereof, and each such party shall sign the bond with his usual signature on the line opposite the scroll seal, and if signed in Maine, Massachusetts, or New Hampshire, an adhesive seal shall be affixed opposite the signature.

5. If the principals are partners, their individual names shall appear in the body of the bond, with the recital that they are partners composing a firm, naming it, and all the members of the firm shall execute the bond as individuals.

6. The signature of a witness shall appear in the appropriate place, attesting the signature of each individual party to the bond.

7. If the principal or surety is a corporation, the name of the State in which incorporated shall be inserted in the appropriate place in the body of the bond, and said instrument shall be executed and attested under the corporate seal as indicated in the form. If the corporation has no corporate seal the fact shall be stated, in which case a scroll or adhesive seal shall appear following the corporate name.

8. The official character and authority of the person or persons executing the bond for the principal, if a corporation, shall be certified by the secretary or assistant secretary, according to the form attached thereto. In lieu of such certificate there may be attached to the bond copies of so much of the records of the corporation as will show the official character and authority of the officer signing, duly certified by the secretary or assistant secretary, under the corporate seal, to be true copies.

9. Each individual surety shall justify, under oath, according to the form appearing on the bond, before a United States commissioner, a clerk of a United States court, a notary public, or some other officer having authority to administer oaths gener-

ally. If the officer has an official seal it shall be affixed, otherwise the proper certificate as to his official [46] character shall be furnished. Where citizenship is not required, as provided in paragraph 3 of these Instructions, the affidavit may be amended accordingly.

10. The certificate of sufficiency shall be signed by a judge or clerk of a court of record, a United States district attorney, or commissioner, or the president or cashier of a bank or trust company.

11. The date of the bond must not be prior to the date of the instrument for which it is given.

[Endorsed]: Filed Jul. 29, 1935. [47]

[Title of Court and Cause.]

PETITION FOR LEAVE TO INTERVENE.

To the Honorable, the District Court of the United States, Northern District of California, Southern Division:

The petition of L. E. CLEAVER, LEWIS L. FORBES, JOE KOHLES, GEORGE F. REEVES, HAROLD L. AUSTIN, E. K. LUKINS, RAY WILSON, WILLIAM KENLAR, GEORGE BARBER, EARSUL NEAL, GRANT BALES, J. A. HARGREAVES, W. L. SMITH, WALTER H. PASCOE, LEONARD MENDEZ, PAUL BALES, WILLARD T. HUFFAKER, E. GIGOUS, NORMAN G. ROBINSON, WILLIAM MONTAGUE, JOHN ANTCZAK, JOHN McGOUGH, JAMES

MUNEZ, RAYMOND MARCE, THOMAS FOLEY, JOSEPH SANFILIPPO, OSCAR BERKLEY, A. F. ANDRAIEFF, ALBERT JENSEN, W. M. DAVIS, M. E. STILLWELL and JAMES WHITESIDE, respectively shows:

That heretofore the above entitled action was commenced, and notice given requiring all persons who have [48] furnished either labor or materials, or both labor and materials in connection with the performance of the contract for the wrecking, removing of old buildings, and reconstruction of new buildings for Veterans Administration, at San Francisco, California, in the complaint on file herein referred to, to intervene so as to have the rights and claims for all labor and materials furnished therefor under said contract upon the bond made and given for payment thereof adjudicated in one and the same action;

That each of your petitioners furnished either labor or materials, or both labor and materials which were necessary and required and which were actually used in the performance of said contract.

WHEREFORE: Your petitioners pray that the above entitled court make its order permitting each of said petitioners to appear in the above entitled action and file a complaint in intervention therein.

Dated: November 6, 1935.

A. BROOKS BERLIN,
Attorney for Petitioners,
525 Standard Oil Building,
San Francisco, California.
Exbrook 6482. [49]

State of California

City and County of San Francisco—ss.

GEORGE BARBER, being first duly sworn, deposes and says: That he is one of the petitioners named in the foregoing Petition; that he has read the foregoing Petition and knows the contents thereof, and the same is true of his own knowledge except as to the matters therein stated on information and belief, and as to those matters he believes it to be true.

GEORGE BARBER.

Subscribed and sworn to before me this 7th day of November, 1935.

[Notarial Seal]   LULU P. LOVELAND.

Notary Public, in and for the City and County of San Francisco. State of California.

[Endorsed]: Filed Nov. 7, 1935. [50]

[Title of Court and Cause—No. 19921-L.]

ORDER PERMITTING INTERVENTION.

Good cause appearing therefor, it is ordered that L. E. CLEAVER, LEWIS L. FORBES, JOE KOHLES, GEORGE F. REEVES, HAROLD L. AUSTIN, E. K. LUKINS, RAY WILSON, WILLIAM KENLAR, GEORGE BARBER, EARSUL NEAL, GRANT BALES, J. A. HARGREAVES, W. L. SMITH, WALTER H. PASCOE, LEONARD MENDEZ, PAUL BALES, WILLARD T. HUFFAKER, E. GIGOUS, NORMAN G. ROBIN-

SON, WILLIAM MONTAGUE, JOHN ANTC-
ZAK, JOHN McGOUGH, JAMES MUNEX, RAY-
MOND MARCE, THOMAS FOLEY, JOSEPH
SANFILIPPO, OSCAR BERKLEY, A. F. AN-
DRAIEFF, ALBERT JENSEN, W. M. DAVIS,
M. E. STILLWELL and JAMES WHITESIDE,
be and each of them is hereby permitted to appear
in the above entitled action, and file a Complaint in
Intervention therein.

Dated: November 7th, 1935.

MICHAEL J. ROCHE,

Judge.

[Endorsed]: Filed Nov. 7, 1935. [51]

[Title of Court and Cause.]

COMPLAINT IN INTERVENTION.

By leave of court first had and obtained, L. E.
CLEAVER, LEWIS L. FORBES, JOE KOHLES,
GEORGE F. REEVES, HAROLD L. AUSTIN,
E. K. LUKINS, RAY WILSON, WILLIAM KEN-
LAR, GEORGE BARBER, EARSUL NEAL,
GRANT, BALES, J. A. HARGREAVES, W. L.
SMITH, WALTER H. PASCOE, LEONARD
MENDEZ, PAUL BALES, WILLARD T. HUF-
FAKER, E. GIGOUS, NORMAN G. ROBINSON,
WILLIAM MONTAGUE, JOHN ANTCZAK,
JOHN McGOUGH, JAMES MUNEZ, RAYMOND
MARCE, THOMAS FOLEY, JOSEPH SAN-
FILIPPO, OSCAR BERKLEY, A. F. AND-

RAIEFF, ALBERT JENSEN, W. M. DAVIS, M.
E. STILLWELL and JAMES WHITESIDE, file
herewith their Complaint in Intervention [52] and
complaining of the defendants above named, for
cause of action, allege:

I.

That at all of the times herein mentioned, defendant Herbert M. Baruch Corporation, Ltd., was and
now is a corporation duly organized and existing
under and by virtue of the laws of the State of
California, with principal office for the transaction of its business located in the City of Los Angeles, County of Los Angeles, State of California.

II.

That at all of the times herein mentioned, defendant United States Fidelity and Guaranty Company
was and now is a corporation duly organized and
existing under and by virtue of the laws of the
State of Maryland, and authorized to conduct, and
conducting a surety business in the State and Northern District of California.

III.

That the true names of defendants sued herein
as First Doe, Second Doe, Third Doe, Fourth Doe
and Fifth Doe are not known to plaintiffs at this
time, and plaintiffs in intervention pray that when
their true names are ascertained that the same may
be inserted herein in lieu of said fictitious names.
IV.   That on the 12th day of January, 1933, the
said Herbert M. Baruch Corporation, Ltd., Her-

bert M. Baruch and Milton Baruch made, executed
and entered into a written contract with the United
States of America by and through the United States
Department, Veterans Administration, for the wrecking and removing of old buildings as specified under
"General Information" and constructing and finishing complete for Veterans' Administration at
San Francisco, California, certain veterans' buildings and hospital buildings in said City and County
of San Francisco, in the Southern [53] Division of
the Northern District of California; that a true and
correct copy of said contract is attached hereto as
Exhibit "A", and made a part hereof as if fully
set forth at length herein; that subsequent thereto
and on or about the 23rd day of January, 1933,
Herbert M. Baruch Corporation, Ltd., a California corporation, Herbert M. Baruch and Milton
Baruch, as principals, and defendant United States
Fidelity and Guaranty Company, a corporation, as
surety, made, executed and filed with the United
States Treasury Department, Commissioner of Accounts and Deposits, in compliance with Section 270
of Title 40 of the United States Code, a bond on
behalf of the United States of America, with the
added obligation that said principals should
promptly make payment to all persons supplying
said principals with labor and materials in the
prosecution of the work provided in said contract
hereinabove referred to; that a true and correct copy
of said bond is attached hereto as Exhibit "B" and
is made a part hereof as if fully set forth at length

herein. That said bond was executed and approved
by the United States Department of Veterans Administration prior to the time the said defendants,
Herbert M. Baruch Corporation, Ltd., Herbert M.
Baruch and Milton Baruch, commenced the aforesaid work, and said bond ever since has been and
now is in full force and effect.

V.

That said contract was completed and final settlement thereon made on the 25th day of January,
1935. That the United States of America has not
brought any suit against the said defendants upon
the said bond.

VI.

That said contract was to be performed and was
performed within the territorial limits of the City
and County of San Francisco. State of California,
which said City and County of San Francisco was
at all the times herein mentioned and now is within
[54] the territory of the District Court of the
United States of America for the Northern District
of California, Southern Division.

VII.

That at the time said contract was entered into
and at the time the aforesaid work was done, Section 276A, Title 40 of the United States Code was
in full force and effect. That said section is hereby
referred to and made a part of this complaint. That
by and under the provisions of said section, every
contract of a nature similar to the contract here-

inabove referred should contain a provision therein
to the effect that the rate of wage for all laborers
and mechanics employed upon the contract or such
contract on public buildings caused by such contract,
shall not be less than the prevailing rate of wages
for work of a similar nature in the city, town, village or other civil division of the State in which
the public buildings, the subject of such contract,
are located, and a further provision that in case
any dispute arises as to what are the prevailing
rates of wages for work of a similar nature, applicable to the contract which could not be adjusted by the contracting officer, the entire matter
shall be referred to the Secretary of Labor for determination, and his decision thereon shall be conclusive on all parties to the contract.

VIII.

That during the period of a year and a half, in
which the work provided for in said contract was in
progress, a succession of disputes arose over the
classification of building trades employees and the
scale of wages paid; that said disputes could not
be adjusted by the contracting officer and that the
matter was referred to the Secretary of Labor for
her determination; that on the 19th day of October,
1934, the Secretary of Labor rendered her decision
on these disputes, deciding, among other things, as
follows, to-wit: [55]

    "(1) Carpenters are entitled to a minimum
of $7.20 per eight hour day. The term carpen-
ters embraces all men whose duties in the course

of employment requires the use of hammers, saws or other carpenters' tools.

(2)   When employed on Saturdays, Sundays or holidays, carpenters and other mechanics are entitled to a minimum of double their ordinary rates for their respective classifications. So far as carpenters are concerned the 'ordinary rate' is that fixed by paragraph (1).

(3)   Laborers employed in connection with building operations are entitled to a minimum of $5.00 per day regardless of whether they are classified as building or common laborers. This is not intended to be taken as a finding as to what the prevailing rate of wages for laborers is in San Francisco, but merely as a finding on the prevailing practice in the classification of laborers.

(4)   When employed on Sundays or holidays laborers are entitled to a minimum of double their ordinary rate. So far as laborers employed in connection with building operations are concerned 'ordinary rate' is that fixed by paragraph (3)."

IX.

That within four years last past, the defendants Herbert M. Baruch Corporation, Ltd., Herbert M. Baruch and Milton Baruch became indebted to one L. E. CLEAVER in the sum of $36.00, as a balance due and owning for work and labor done and performed by said L. E. Cleaver for said defendants at the special instance and request of said defendants and each of them on the Veterans Administration buildings covered by said written contract specified in paragraph IV hereof, and located at Fort Miley, California, a public works project in the City and County of San Francisco, in the Southern Division of the Northern District of California; and which said sum of $36.00 represents the difference between the sums of money actually received by said L. E. Cleaver for said work and the amounts then due and owning to him in accordance with the prevailing rate of wages then duly established and posted for work and labor of a similar nature in said City and County of San Francisco. [56]

X.

That although demand has been made on said defendants, no part of said sum of $36.00 has been paid, and the whole thereof is now due, owing and unpaid from said defendants and each of them to said L. E. Cleaver. [57]

And as and for a further, separate and Second cause of action against the defendants and each of them, plaintiffs in intervention further complain and allege:

I.

Plaintiffs in intervention reallege paragraphs I, II, III, IV, V, VI, VII and VIII of the first cause of action, and by reference thereto, make the same a part of this cause of action as fully as though here repeated and set forth at length.

II.

That within four years last past, the defendants Herbert M. Baruch Corporation, Ltd., Herbert M. Baruch and Milton Baruch became indebted to one Lewis L. Forbes in the sum of $328.15 as a balance due and owing for work and labor done and performed by said Lewis L. Forbes for said defendants at the special instance and request of said defendants and each of them on the Veterans Administration buildings covered by said written contract specified in paragraph IV of the first cause of action, and located at Fort Miley, California, a public works project in the City and County of San Francisco, in the Southern Division of the Northern District of California; and which said sum of $328.15 represents the difference between the sums of money actually received by said Lewis L. Forbes for said work, and the amounts then due and owing to him in accordance with the prevailing rate of wages then duly established and posted for work and labor of a similar nature in said City and County of San Francisco.

III.

That although demand has been made on said defendants, no part of said sum of $328.15 has been paid, and the whole thereof is now due, owing and unpaid from said defendants and each of them to plaintiff in intervention herein. [58]

Joe Kohles	$ 718.00
George F. Reeves	31.56
Harold L. Austin	112.00
E. K. Lukins	220.00
Ray Wilson	762.80

And as and for a further, separate and Eighth cause of action against the defendants and each of them, plaintiffs in intervention further complain and allege:

I.

Plaintiffs in intervention reallege paragraphs I, II, III, IV, V, VI, VII and VIII of the first cause of action, and by reference thereto, make the same a part of this cause of action as fully as though here repeated and set forth at length.

II.

That within four years last past the defendants Herbert M. Baruch Corporation, Ltd., Herbert M. Baruch and Milton Baruch became indebted to William Kenlar in the sum of $96.00, as a balance due and owing for work and labor done and performed by said William Kenlar for said defendants at the special instance and request of the Bryce Plumbing & Heating Company, subcontractors of said Herbert M. Baruch Corporation, Ltd., Herbert M. Baruch and Milton Baruch, and said defendants, on the Veterans Administration buildings covered by said written contract specified in paragraph IV of the first cause of action, and located at Fort Miley, California, a public works project in the City and County of San Francisco, in the Southern Division of the Northern District of California; and which said sum of $96.00 represents the difference between the sums of money ac-

tually received by said William Kenlar for said
work, and the amounts then due and owing to him
in accordance with the prevailing rate of wages
then duly established and posted for work and labor
of a similar nature in said City and County of
San Francisco.

III.

That although demand has been made on said
defendants, no part of said sum of $96.00 has been
paid, and the whole thereof is now due, owing and
unpaid from said defendants and each of them to
plaintiff in intervention herein. [64]

George Barber	$ 621.04
Earsul Neal	234.00
Grant Bales	166.98
J. A. Hargreaves	291.00
W. L. Smith	50.00

And as and for a further, separate and Fourteenth cause of action against the defendants and
each of them, plaintiffs in intervention further complain and allege:

I.

Plaintiffs in intervention reallege paragraphs I,
II, III, IV, V, VI, VII and VIII of the first cause
of action, and by reference thereto, make the same
a part of this cause of action as fully as though here
repeated and set forth at length.

II.

That within four years last past the said defendants Herbert M. Baruch Corporation, Ltd., Herbert M. Baruch and Milton Baruch became indebted to Walter H. Pascoe for the sum of $488.90, said sum representing materials furnished as well as the balance due and owing for work and labor done and performed by said Walter H. Pascoe for said defendants at the special instance and request of the Superior Metal Products Company, subcontractors of said Herbert M. Baruch Corporation, Ltd., Herbert M. Baruch and Milton Baruch, and said defendants, on the Veterans Administration buildings covered by said written contract specified in paragraph IV of the first cause of action, and located at Fort Miley, California, a public works project in the City and County of San Francisco, in the Southern Division of the Northern District of California; and which said sum of $88.90 represents the reasonable cost for materials furnished and the difference between the sums of money actually received by said Walter H. Pascoe for said work and labor and the amounts then due and owing to him in accordance with the prevailing rate of wages then duly established and posted for work and labor of a similar nature in said City and County of San Francisco.

III.

That although demand has been made on said defendants, no part of said sum of $488.90 has been paid, and the whole thereof is now due, owing and unpaid from said defendants and each of them to plaintiff in intervention herein. [70]

Leonard Mendez	$ 175.39
Paul Bales	360.00
Willard T. Huffaker	828.40
E. Gigous	307.20
Norman G. Robinson	163.35
William Montague	231.30

And as and or a further, separate and Twenty-first cause of action against the defendants and each of them, plaintiffs in intervention further complain and allege:

I.

Plaintiffs in intervention reallege paragraphs I, II, III, IV, V, VI, VII and VIII of the first cause of action, and by reference thereto, make the same a part of this cause of action as fully as though here repeated and set forth at length.

II.

That within four years last past the defendants Herbert M. Baruch Corporation, Ltd., Herbert M. Baruch and Milton Baruch became indebted to John Antczak in the sum of $196.00, as a balance due and owing for work and labor done and performed by said John Antczak for said defendants at the special instance and request of the Bryce Heating & Plumbing Company, the California Wrecking Company, subcontractors of said Herbert M. Baruch

Corporation, Ltd., Herbert M. Baruch and Milton Baruch, and said defendants, on the Veterans Administration buildings covered by said written contract specified in paragraph IV of the first cause of action, and located at Fort Miley, California, a public works project in the City and County of San Francisco, in the Southern Division of the Northern District of California; and which said sum of $196.00, represents the difference between the sums of money actually received by said John Antczak for said work, and the amounts then due and owing to him in accordance with the prevailing rate of wages then duly established and posted for work and labor of a similar nature in said City and County of San Francisco.

III.

That although demand has been made on said defendants, no part of said sum of $196.00 has been paid, and the whole thereof is now due, owing and unpaid from said defendants and each of them to plaintiff in intervention herein. [77]

John McGough	$ 175.00
James Munez	166.00
Raymond Marce	40.00
Thomas Foley	40.00
Joseph San Filippo	119.00
Oscar Berkley	679.20
A. F. Andraieff	206.17
Albert Jensen	259.20

And as and for a further, separate and Thirtieth cause of action against the defendants and each of them, plaintiffs in intervention further complain and allege:

I.

Plaintiffs in intervention reallege paragraphs I, II, III, IV, V, VI, VII and VIII of the first cause of action, and by reference thereto, make the same a part of this cause of action as fully as though here repeated and set forth at length.

II.

That within four years last past the defendants Herbert M. Baruch Corporation, Ltd., Herbert M. Baruch and Milton Baruch became indebted to W. M. Davis in the sum of $81.60, as a balance due and owing for work and labor done and performed by said W. M. Davis for said defendants at the special instance and request of the Bryce Plumbing and Heating Company, subcontractors of said Herbert M. Baruch Corporation, Ltd., Herbert M. Baruch and Milton Baruch, and said defendants, on the Veterans Administration buildings covered by said written contract specified in paragraph IV of the first cause of action, and located at Fort Miley, California, a public works project in the City and County of San Francisco, in the Southern Division of the Northern District of California; and which said sum of $81.60 represents the difference between the sums of money actually received by said W. M. Davis for said work, and the amounts then due and owing to him in accordance with the prevailing rate of wages then duly established and posted for work and labor of a similar nature in said City and County of San Francisco.

III.

That although demand has been made on said defendants, no part of said sum of $81.60 has been paid, and the whole thereof is now due, owing and unpaid from said defendants and each of them to plaintiff in intervention herein. [86]

M. E. Stillwell ....$ 228.00

James Whiteside 160.40

WHEREFORE: said plaintiffs in intervention herein pray for judgment against said defendants and each of them as follows:

1. Judgment in favor of said plaintiff in intervention, L. E. Cleaver, in the sum of $36.00.

2. Judgment in favor of said plaintiff in intervention, Lewis L. Forbes, in the sum of $328.15.

3. Judgment in favor of said plaintiff in intervention, Joe Kahles, in the sum of $718.00.

4. Judment in favor of said plaintiff in intervention, George F. Reeves, in the sum of $31.56.

5. Judgment in favor of said plaintiff in intervention, Harold L. Austin, in the sum of $112.00.

6. Judgment in favor of said plaintiff in intervention, E. K. Lukins in the amount of $220.00.

7. Judgment in favor of said plaintiff in intervention, Ray Wilson, in the sum of $762.80.

8. Judgment in favor of said plaintiff in intervention, William Kenlar, in the sum of $96.00.

9. Judgment in favor of said plaintiff in intervention, George Barber, in the sum of $621.04.

10. Judgment in favor of said plaintiff in intervention, Earsul Neal, in the sum of $234.00.

11. Judgment in favor of said plaintiff in intervention, Grant Bales, in the sum of $166.98.

12. Judgment in favor of said plaintiff in intervention, J. A. Hargreaves, in the sum of $291.00.

13. Judgment in favor of said plaintiff in intervention, W. L. Smith, in the sum of $50.00.

14. Judgment in favor of said plaintiff in intervention, Walter H. Pascoe in the sum of $488.90.

15. Judgment in favor of said plaintiff in intervention, Leonard Mendez, in the sum of $175.39.

[89]

16. Judgment in favor of said plaintiff in intervention, Paul Bales, in the sum of $360.00.

17. Judgment in favor of said plaintiff in intervention, Willard T. Huffaker, in the sum of $828.40.

18. Judgment in favor of said plaintiff in intervention, E. Gigous, in the sum of $307.20.

19. Judgment in favor of said plaintiff in intervention, Norman G. Robinson, in the sum of $163.35.

20. Judgment in favor of said plaintiff in intervention, William Montague, in the sum of $231.30.

21. Judgment in favor of said plaintiff in intervention, John Antczak, in the sum of $196.00.

22. Judgment in favor of said plaintiff in intervention, John McGough, in the sum of $175.00.

23. Judgment in favor of said plaintiff in intervention, James Munez, in the sum of $166.00.

24. Judgment in favor of said plaintiff in intervention, Raymond Marce, in the sum of $40.00.

25. Judgment in favor of said plaintiff in intervention, Thomas Foley, in the sum of $85.00.

26. Judgment in favor of said plaintiff in intervention, Joseph Sanfilippo, in the sum of $119.00.

27. Judgment in favor of said plaintiff in intervention, Oscar Berkley, in the sum of $679.20.

28. Judgment in favor of said plaintiff in intervention, A. F. Andraieff, in the sum of $206.17.

29. Judgment in favor of said plaintiff in intervention, Albert Jensen, in the sum of $259.20.

30. Judgment in favor of said plaintiff in intervention, W. M. Davis, in the sum of $81.60.

31. Judgment in favor of said plaintiff in intervention, M. E. Stillwell, in the sum of $228.00. [90]

32. Judgment in favor of said plaintiff in intervention, James Whiteside, in the sum of $160.40.

33. Together with their costs of suit incurred herein.

34. And for such other and further relief, as to this Court may be meet and just in the premises.

A. BROOKS BERLIN
Attorney for Plaintiffs in Intervention. [91]

State of California

Northern District of California—ss.

GEORGE BARBER, being first duly sworn, deposes and says: That he is one of the plaintiffs in intervention named in the foregoing Complaint in Intervention; that he has read said Complaint in Intervention and knows the contents thereof, and the same is true of his own knowledge except as to the matters therein stated on information and belief, and as to those matters he believes it to be true.

GEORGE BARBER

Subscribed and sworn to before me this 5th day of November, 1935.

[Seal]   LULU P. LOVELAND

Notary Public, in and for the City and County of San Francisco, State of California.

[Endorsed]: Filed Nov. 7, 1935. [92]

———

[Title of Court and Cause.]

DEMURRER TO COMPLAINT

COME NOW THE DEFENDANTS, HERBERT M. BARUCH CORPORATION, LTD., A CORPORATION, HERBERT M. BARUCH, MILTON BARUCH, AND UNITED STATES FIDELITY AND GUARANTY COMPANY, A CORPORATION, AND EACH FOR HIMSELF DEMURS TO PLAINTIFF'S COMPLAINT NOW ON FILE, ON THE FOLLOWING GROUNDS AND FOR THE FOLLOWING REASONS, TO-WIT:

I.

That the said complaint, or any part thereof, does not state facts sufficient to constitute a cause of action against the demurring defendants, or either or any of them.

II.

That the above-entitled Court has no jurisdiction of the subject of the action.

COME NOW THE DEFENDANTS, HERBERT M. BARUCH CORPORATION, LTD., A CORPORATION, HERBERT M. BARUCH, MILTON BARUCH, AND UNITED STATES FIDELITY AND GUARANTY COMPANY, A CORPORATION, AND EACH FOR HIMSELF DEMURS TO EACH CAUSE OF ACTION IN PLAINTIFF'S COMPLAINT NOW ON FILE, ON THE FOLLOWING GROUNDS AND FOR THE FOLLOWING REASONS, TO-WIT: [93]

DEMURRER TO FIRST CAUSE OF ACTION.

I.

That the alleged first cause of action, or any part thereof, does not state facts sufficient to constitute a cause of action against the demurring defendants, or either or any of them.

II.

That the above-entitled Court has no jurisdiction of the subject of the action.

III.

That the said alleged first cause of action is uncertain in that it cannot be ascertained therefrom, or any part thereof:

(a) How or in what manner the sum of Eight Hundred and Twenty-Fve Dollars ($825.00) claimed to be due from the defendants to plaintiff's assignors was arrived at or computed;

(b) What period of time the alleged sum covers;

(c) Whether or not the sum actually paid and received was the agreed price to be paid by defendants to plaintiff's assignors;

(d) Whether or not the alleged $825.00 represents the difference between the agreed price between plaintiff's assignors and defendants and the sum actually received;

(e) What the prevailing rate of wages was as to plaintiff's assignors in the first cause of action and how or in what manner the same was arrived at.

IV.

That the said first cause of action is ambiguous on the same grounds and for the same reasons that it is uncertain.

V.

That the said first cause of action is unintelligible on the same grounds and for the same reasons that it is uncertain. **[94]**

Demurrer to second cause of action $ 423.00
Demurrer to third cause of action...... 157.00
Demurrer to fourth cause of action 388.50

Demurrer to fifth cause of action 1028.00

Demurrer to sixth cause of action 1529.00

Demurrer to seventh cause of action 1283.00

Demurrer to eighth cause of action... 1534.00

Demurrer to ninth cause of action...... 342.00

Demurrer to tenth cause of action...... 90.00

Demurrer to eleventh cause of
action 245.00

Demurrer to twelfth cause of action 206.00

Demurrer to thirteenth cause of
action 726.20

Demurrer to fourteenth cause of
action 120.00

Demurrer to fifteenth cause of
action 140.00

Demurrer to sixteenth cause of
action 215.00

Demurrer to seventeenth cause of
action 276.00

Demurrer to eighteenth cause of
action 140.00

Demurrer to nineteenth cause of
action 824.20

Demurrer to twentieth cause of
action 956.50

Demurrer to twenty-first cause of
action 550.00

Demurrer to twenty-second cause of
action 69.00

Demurrer to twenty-third cause of
action 1042.60

Demurrer to twenty-fourth cause of
   action 294.26
Demurrer to twenty-fifth cause of
   action 465.51
Demurrer to twenty-sixth cause of
   action 193.00

WHEREFORE, the demurring defendants pray that said demurrers, and each of them, be sustained without leave to amend; that they recover costs herein; and for such other and further relief as to the Court may seem just and proper in the premises.

JULIUS MACKSON,
SAMUEL W. BLUM,
By JULIUS MACKSON
Attorneys for Demurring Defendants.

We, the undersigned, do hereby certify that the aforementioned demurrers, and each of them, are interposed in good faith, and, in our opinion, are well taken in law and are not interposed for the purposes of delay.

JULIUS MACKSON,
SAMUEL W. BLUM,
By JULIUS MACKSON
Attorneys for Demurring Defendants. [120]

[Title of Court and Cause.]

DEMURRER TO COMPLAINT IN INTERVENTION.

COME NOW THE DEFENDANTS AND DEFENDANTS IN INTERVENTION, HERBERT M. BARUCH CORPORATION LTD., A CORPORATION, HERBERT M. BARUCH, MILTON BARUCH, AND UNITED STATES FIDELITY AND GUARANTY COMPANY, A CORPORATION, AND EACH FOR HIMSELF DEMURS TO PLAINTIFF'S COMPLAINT IN INTERVENTION ON THE FOLLOWING GROUNDS AND FOR THE FOLLOWING REASONS, TO-WIT:

I.

That the said complaint in intervention, or any part thereof, does not state facts sufficient to constitute a cause of action against the demurring defendants in intervention, or either or any of them.

II.

That the above-entitled Court has no jurisdiction of the subject of the action.

COME NOW THE DEFENDANTS AND DEFENDANTS IN INTERVENTION, HERBERT M. BARUCH CORPORATION, LTD., A CORPORATION, HERBERT M. [151] BARUCH, MILTON BARUCH AND UNITED STATES FIDELITY AND GUARANTY COMPANY, A CORPORATION, AND EACH FOR HIMSELF DE-

MURS TO EACH CAUSE OF ACTION IN THE COMPLAINT IN INTERVENTION NOW ON FILE, ON THE FOLLOWING GROUNDS AND FOR THE FOLLOWING REASONS, TO-WIT:

DEMURRER TO FIRST CAUSE OF ACTION.

I.

That the alleged first cause of action, or any part thereof, does not state facts sufficient to constitute a cause of action against the demurring defendants and defendants in intervention, or either or any of them.

II.

That the above-entitled Court has no jurisdiction of the subject of the action.

III.

That the alleged first cause of action is uncertain in that it cannot be ascertained therefrom, or any part thereof:

(a) How or in what manner the sum of $36.00 claimed to be due from the defendants in intervention to the intervenor, L. E. Cleaver, was arrived at or computed;

(b) What period of time the alleged sum covers;

(c) Whether or not the sum actually paid and received by said intervenor was the agreed price to be paid by defendants in intervention to said intervenor;

(d) Whether or not the alleged $36.00 represents the difference between the agreed price between said intervenor and defendants in intervention and the sum actually received;

(e) What the prevailing rate of wages was as to said intervenor in the first cause of action, and how or in what manner the same was arrived at; [152]

(f) Whether or not the alleged $36.00 claimed to be due represents the difference between the amount received and the amount claimed as the prevailing rate subsequent to the date of the alleged decision of the Secretary of Labor, or prior thereto, or prior and subsequent to said date;

(g) Between whom the alleged dispute referred to in said cause of action over the classification of employees and the scale of wages was, and when the same arose;

(h) How or in what manner the prevailing rate of wages was established, and at what time;

(i) What kind of services were rendered by intervenor, and in what capacity, or under what classification.

IV.

That the said first cause of action is ambiguous on the same grounds and for the same reasons that it is uncertain.

V.

That the said first cause of action is unintelligible on the same grounds and for the same reasons that it is uncertain.

Demurrer to second cause of action
Lewis L. Forbes, $328.15
Demurrer to third cause of action, Joe Kohles, $718.00

Demurrer to fourth cause of action

George F. Reeves, $31.56

Demurrer to fifth cause of action, Harold
L. Austin, $112.00;

Demurrer to sixth cause of action, $220.00,
E. K. Lukins

Demurrer to seventh cause of action, Ray
Wilson, $762.80

Demurrer to eighth cause of action, William
Kenlar, $96.00

Demurrer to ninth cause of action, George
Barber, $621.04

Demurrer to tenth cause of action, Earsul
Neal, $234.00

Demurrer to eleventh cause of action

Grant Bales, $166.98

Demurrer to twelfth cause of action, J. A.
Hargreaves, $291.00

Demurrer to thirteenth cause of action

W. L. Smith, $50.00

Demurrer to fourteenth cause of action,
Walter H. Pascoe, $488.90

Demurrer to fifteenth cause of action, Leonard Mendez, $175.39

Demurrer to sixteenth cause of action, Paul
Bales, $360.00

Demurrer to seventeenth cause of action

Willard T. Huffaker, $828.40

Demurrer to eighteenth cause of action, $307.20

Demurrer to nineteenth cause of action
Norman G. Robinson, $163.35

Demurrer to twentieth cause of action, William Montague, $231.30

Demurrer to twenty-first cause of action
John Antczak, $196.00

Demurrer to twenty-second cause of action, John McGough, $175.00

Demurrer to twenty-third cause of action, James Munez, $166.00

Demurrer to twenty-fourth cause of action, Raymond Marce, $40.00

Demurrer to twenty-fifth cause of action, Thomas Foley, $85.00

Demurrer to twenty-six cause of action, Joseph SanFilippo, $119.00

Demurrer to twenty-seventh cause of action, Oscar Berkley, $679.20

Demurrer to twenty-eighth cause of action, A. F. Andraieff, $206.17

Demurrer to twenty-ninth cause of action, Albert Jensen, $259.20

Demurrer to thirtieth cause of action, William Davis, $81.60

Demurrer to thirty-first cause of action,
   M. E. Stillwell, $228.00
Demurrer to thirty-second cause of action,
   James Whiteside, $160.40

———

WHEREFORE, the demurring defendants and defendants in intervention prays that said demurrers, and each of them, be sustained without leave to amend; that they recover costs herein; and for such other and further relief as to the Court may seem just and proper in the premises.

    JULIUS MACKSON,
    SAMUEL W. BLUM,
  By JULIUS MACKSON
        Attorneys for Demurring De-
        fendants and Defendants in In-
        tervention.

We, the undersigned, do hereby certify that the aforementioned demurrers, and each of them, are interposed in good faith, and, in our opinion, are well taken in law and are not interposed for the purposes of delay.

    JULIUS MACKSON,
    SAMUEL W. BLUM,
  By JULIUS MACKSON
        Attorneys for Demurring De-
        fendants and Defendants in In-
        tervention. [200]

POINTS AND AUTHORITIES.

These demurring defendants in intervention have heretofore submitted a brief as their points and authorities attached to their demurrer to the complaint in the above-entitled action. We respectfully refer the Honorable Court to said points and authorities, and incorporate the same herein by reference as though fully stated herein as and for points and authorities to this the demurrer to the complaint in intervention.

Respectfully submitted,

JULIUS MACKSON,

SAMUEL W. BLUM,

By JULIUS MACKSON

Attorneys for Demurring Defendants and Defendants in Intervention.

[Endorsed]: Received copy of the within Demurrer to Complaint in Intervention this 9 day of December, 1935.

A. BROOKS BERLIN

Attorney for Plaintiff.

[Endorsed]: Filed Dec. 9, 1935. [201]

[Title of Court.]

AT A STATED TERM of the Southern Division of the United States District Court for the Northern District of California, held at the Court Room thereof, in the City and County of San Francisco, on Wednesday, the 13th day of May, in the year of our Lord one thousand nine hundred and thirty-six.

Present: The Honorable Harold Louderback, District Judge.

[Title of Cause.]

Demurrer to complaint and demurrers to complaint in intervention having been submitted and fully considered, it is ordered that the demurrer to the complaint be and the same is hereby sustained, it appearing that the complaint does not set forth facts which would entitle the complainant to the remedy sought, and that the demurrer to complaint in intervention of Stephen Morgan and Terrence McGuire be and the same is hereby sustained, it appearing that said complaints in intervention do not set forth facts which would entitled the complainants to the remedy sought. Further ordered that said order sustaining demurrer are made without leave to amend the aforesaid complaint and complaints in intervention. [202]

———

[Title of Court.]

AT A STATED TERM of the Southern Division of the United States District Court for the Northern District of California, held at the Court Room thereof, in the City and County of San Francisco, on Thursday, the 4th day of June, in the year of our Lord one thousand nine hundred and thirty-six.

Present: The Honorable Harold Louderback, District Judge.

[Title of Cause.]

Demurrer to complaint in intervention of L. E. Cleaver et al having been submitted, and being now fully considered, it is Ordered that the said demurrer be and the same is hereby sustained without leave being granted to amend the said complaint in intervention. [203]

————

[Title of Court.]

AT A STATED TERM of the Southern Division of the United States District Court for the Northern District of California, held at the Court Room thereof, in the City and County of San Francisco, on Friday, the 5th day of June, in the year of our Lord one thousand nine hundred and thirty-six.

Present: The Honorable Harold Louderback, District Judge.

[Title of Cause.]

Demurrers to complaint and complaints in intervention having heretofore been sustained without leave to amend, upon motion of Julius Mackson, Esq., (see letter May 15, 1936), it is ordered that Judgment be entered dismissing this case. [204]

In the `District Court of the United States of
America, for the Northern District of California, Southern Division.

No. 19921-L.

UNITED STATES OF AMERICA, to the use of
TREVE W. BERLIN,

Plaintiff,

vs.

HERBERT M. BARUCH CORPORATION, LTD.,
a corporation, HERBERT M. BARUCH,
MILTON BARUCH, UNITED STATES FI-
DELITY AND GUARANTY COMPANY, a
CORPORATION, FIRST DOE, SECOND
DOE, THIRD DOE, FOURTH DOE and
FIFTH DOE,

Defendants.

JUDGMENT.

It appearing from the files and records of this
Court that on the 29th day of July, 1935, the plain-
tiff's complaint was filed herein, and that on the
7th day of November, 1935, L. E. Cleaver, Lewis L.
Forbes, Joe Kohles, George F. Reeves, Harold L.
Austin, E. K. Lukins, Ray Wilson, William Ken-
lar, George Barber, Earsul Neal, Grant Bales, J. A.
Hargreaves, W. L. Smith, Walter H. Pascoe,
Leonard Mendez, Paul Bales, William T. Huffaker,
E. Gigous, Norman G. Robinson, William Monta-
gue, John Antczak, John McGough, James Munex,

Raymond Marce, Thomas Foley, Joseph Sanfilippo, Oscar Berkley, A. F. Andraieff, Albert Jensen, W. M. Davis, M. E. Stillwell, and James Whiteside, as plaintiffs in intervention, filed a complaint in intervention herein, (hereinafter referred to as complaint in intervention of L. E. Cleaver, et al.), and that on the 7th day of November, 1935, Stephen Morgan and Terence McGuire, as plaintiffs in intervention, filed a complaint in intervention herein, (hereinafter referred to as complaint in intervention of Stephen Morgan, et al.), and that thereafter the defendants, Herbert M. Baruch Corporation, Ltd., a [205] corporation, Herbert M. Baruch, Milton Baruch, and United States Fidelity and Guaranty Company, a corporation, filed a demurrer herein to said complaint and as defendants in intervention filed a demurrer to the complaint in intervention of L. E. Cleaver, et al., and as defendants in intervention filed a demurrer to the complaint in intervention of Stephen Morgan, et al., and that the demurrer to the complaint and the demurrer to the complaint in intervention of L. E. Cleaver, et al., came on regularly for hearing in the above-entitled Court on the 6th day of January, 1936, and that on said date it was ordered by the Court that the parties herein file briefs in the matter, and it further appearing that upon stipulation of the parties the demurrer to the said complaint in intervention of Stephen Morgan, et al., was submitted on the points and authorities to the said demurrer to the complaint filed herein, and that thereafter it appearing that all briefs having been filed, and upon motion duly made the demurrer to the complaint and the demurrer to each of the said complaints in intervention as aforesaid were ordered submitted to the Court for decision; and the demurrer to the complaint, and to each and every cause of action thereof, and the demurrer to the complaint in intervention of L. E. Cleaver, et al., and to each and every cause of action thereof, and the demurrer to the complaint in intervention of Stephen Morgan, et al., and to each and every cause of action thereof, having been submitted to the Court for deliberation and decision, and thereafter the Court on the 13th day of May, 1936, made and entered its order herein that the demurrer of said defendants to the complaint be and the same is sustained, without leave to plaintiff to amend, and on said 13th day of May. 1936, made and entered its order herein that the demurrer of said defendants in intervention to the complaint in inter- [206] vention of Stephen Morgan, et al., be and the same is sustained, without leave to said plaintiffs in intervention, Stephen Morgan, et al., to amend, and thereafter, on the 4th day of June, 1936, the Court made and entered its order herein that the demurrer of said defendants in intervention to the complaint in intervention of L. E. Cleaver, et al., be and the same is sustained. without leave to said plaintiffs in intervention, L. E. Cleaver, et al., to amend,

NOW, THEREFORE, on application of Julius Mackson, Esq., attorney for said defendants and said defendants in intervention, and by virtue of the law and by reason of the premises aforesaid,

IT IS ORDERED, ADJUDGED AND DECREED that the above-entitled action as against the said defendants, Herbert M. Baruch Corporation, Ltd., a corporation, Herbert M. Baruch, Milton Baruch, and United States Fidelity and Guaranty Company, a corporation, and each of them, be and the same is hereby dismissed.

IT IS FURTHER ORDERED, ADJUDGED AND DECREED that the complaint and action in intervention of Stephen Morgan and Terence McGuire as against the said defendants as defendants in intervention, and each of them, be and the same is hereby dismissed.

IT IS FURTHER ORDERED, ADJUDGED AND DECREED that the complaint and action in intervention of L. E. Cleaver, Lewis L. Forbes, Joe Kohles, George F. Reeves, Harold L. Austin, E. K. Lukins, Ray Wilson, William Kenlar, George Barber, Earsul Neal, Grant Bales, J. A. Hargreaves, W. L. Smith, Walter H. Pascoe, Leonard Mendez, Paul Bales, Willard T. Huffaker, E. Gigous, Norman G. Robinson, William Montague, John Antczak, John McGough, James Munez, Raymond Marce, Thomas Foley, Joseph Sanfilippo, Oscar Berkeley, A. F. [207] Andraieff, Albert Jensen, W. M. Davis, M. E. Stillwell, and James Whiteside, as against the said defendants as defendants in intervention, and each of them, be and the same is hereby dismissed.

JUDGMENT entered and recorded this 5th day of June, 1936.

WALTER B. MALING,

Clerk. [208]

[Title of Court and Cause.]

NOTICE OF ENTRY OF JUDGMENT.

To: Treve W. Berlin and to his attorney, A. Brooks Berlin, Esq.:

To: L. E. Cleaver, Lewis L. Forbes, Joe Kohles, George F. Reeves, Harold L. Austin, E. K. Lukins, Ray Wilson, William Kenlar, George Barber, Earsul Neal, Grant Bales, J. A. Hargreaves, W. L. Smith, Walter H. Pascoe, Leonard Mendez, Paul Bales, Willard T. Huffaker, E. Gigous, Norman G. Robinson, William Montague, John Antczak, John McGough, James Munex, Raymond Marce, Thomas Foley, Joseph Sanfilippo, Oscar Berkley, A. F. Andraieff, Albert Jensen, W. M. Davis, M. E. Stillwell, and James Whiteside, plaintiffs in intervention, and to their attorney, A. Brooks Berlin, Esq.:

To: Stephen Morgan and Terence McGuire, plaintiffs in intervention, and to their attorney, John F. O'Sullivan, Esq.,

YOU, AND EACH OF YOU, WILL PLEASE TAKE NOTICE that judgment in favor of said defendants and defendants in intervention was

entered in the records of the above-entitled Court
on the 5th day of June, 1936.

Dated this 8th day of June, 1936.

JULIUS MACKSON
Attorney for Defendants and Defendants in Intervention. [209]

Received a copy of the within this 10th day of
June, 1936.

A. BROOKS BERLIN
Attorney for Plaintiff.

Received a copy of the within this 10th day of
June, 1936.

A. BROOKS BERLIN
Attorney for Plaintiffs in Intervention, L. E. Cleaver, et al.

Received a copy of the within this 10th day of
June, 1936.

JOHN F. O'SULLIVAN
Attorney for Plaintiffs in Intervention, Stephen Morgan, et al.

[Endorsed]: Filed Jun. 10, 1936. [210]

[Title of Court and Cause.]

PETITION FOR APPEAL.

To the Honorable Harold Louderback, District
    Judge:

Now comes TREVE BERLIN, plaintiff above-
named, and respectfully alleges as follows:

That on the 13th day of May, 1936, the above-
entitled Court made its order and decree sustaining
the demurrer of the defendants herein to plaintiff's
complaint without leave to amend; that thereafter
and on the 5th day of June, 1936, the said Court
duly entered judgment against the said plaintiff and
in favor of the defendants; that said plaintiff feels
aggrieved by the said order and decree sustaining
defendants' demurrer to plaintiff's complaint, and
the said judgment in favor of the said defendants
and against the said plaintiff, and does hereby
appeal from the said order and decree and the said
judgment, and each and all of them, to the Circuit
Court of Appeals for the Ninth Circuit for the
reasons set forth in the assignment of errors filed
herewith. [211]

WHEREFORE: plaintiff prays that his appeal
be allowed on such terms and under such regulations and orders as this Court shall make; that a
citation be issued as provided by law, and that a
transcript of the record, proceedings and documents
upon which said decree and judgment and each of
them, was based, duly authenticated be sent to the
United States Circuit Court of Appeals for the

Ninth Circuit, under the rules of such Court in such cases made and provided.

AND YOUR PETITIONER further prays that proper order relating to the required security be required of him to be made.

Dated: San Francisco, California, June 16th, 1936.

A. BROOKS BERLIN

Attorney for Petitioner.

[Endorsed]: Filed Jun. 16, 1936. [212]

———

[Title of Court and Cause.]

ASSIGNMENT OF ERRORS ON BEHALF OF TREVE W. BERLIN.

Now comes TREVE W. BERLIN, plaintiff above named, having petitioned for an order from the above entitled Court allowing his appeal to the United States Circuit Court of Appeal for the Ninth Circuit, from an order and decree sustaining defendants demurrer to his complaint without leave to amend, and from the judgment entered thereon in favor of the said defendants and against the said plaintiff, now makes and files with the said petition the following assignment of errors herein upon which he will rely for a reversal of the said order and decree, and the said judgment, to which exception was duly taken, as follows:

That the said Court erred in sustaining the demurrer of defendants to the said complaint without leave to amend, and in entering judgment upon said order, for the reason that said complaint stated a cause of action against the said defendants and each of them, and for the further reason that it was an abuse of discretion for the said court to sustain the said demurrer [213] without leave to amend.

WHEREFORE, the said petitioner prays that the said order and decree, and the said judgment be reversed, and that the said demurrer be ordered overruled, and the said defendants given such time to answer as may be deemed proper.

A. BROOKS BERLIN

Attorney for Petitioner.

[Endorsed]: Filed Jun. 16, 1936. [214]

[Title of Court and Cause.]

PETITION FOR APPEAL.

To the Honorable Harold Louderback, District Judge:

Now come L. E. CLEAVER, LEWIS L. FORBES, JOE KOHLES, GEORGE F. REEVES, HAROLD L. AUSTIN, E. K. LUKINS, RAY WILSON, WILLIAM KENLAR, GEORGE BARBER, EARSUL NEAL, GRANT BALES, J. A. HARGREAVES, W. L. SMITH, WALTER L. PASCOE, LEONARD MENDEZ, PAUL BALES, WILLARD T. HUFFAKER, E. GIGOUS, NORMAN G. ROBINSON, WILLIAM MONTAGUE,

JOHN ANTCZAK, JOHN McGOUGH, JAMES MUNEZ, RAYMOND MARCE, THOMAS FOLEY, JOSEPH SANFILLIPPO, OSCAR BERKELEY, A. F. ANDRAIEFF, ALBERT JENSEN, W. M. DAVIS, M. E. STILLWELL and JAMES WHITESIDE, and respectfully allege as follows:

That on the 4th day of June, 1936, the above-entitled Court made its order and decree sustaining the demurrer of the defendants herein to plaintiff's complaint in intervention without leave to amend; that thereafter and on the 5th day of June, 1936, the said Court duly entered judgment against the said plaintiffs in intervention and in favor of the said defendants; that said [215] plaintiffs in intervention feel aggrieved by the said order and decree sustaining defendants' demurrer to their said complaint and by the judgment in favor of the said defendants and against the said plaintiffs in intervention, and the said plaintiffs in intervention do hereby appeal from the said order and decree and the said judgment and each and all of them, to the United States Circuit Court of Appeals for the Ninth Circuit for the reasons set forth in the assignment of errors filed herewith.

WHEREFORE: said plaintiffs in intervention pray that their appeal be allowed on such terms and under such regulations and orders as this Court shall make; that a citation be issued as provided by law, and 'that a transcript of the record, proceedings and documents upon which said decree and judgment and each of them was based, duly authenticated, be sent to the United States Circuit Court of Appeals for the Ninth Circuit, under the rules of such Court in such cases made and provided.

AND YOUR PETITIONERS further pray that the proper order relating to the security to be required of him be made.

Dated: San Francisco, California, June 16, 1936.

A. BROOKS BERLIN

Attorneys for Petitioners.

[Endorsed]: Filed Jun. 16, 1936. [216]

[Title of Court and Cause.]

ASSIGNMENT OF ERRORS ON BEHALF OF PETITIONERS L. E. CLEAVER, ET AL.

Now come petitioners L. E. CLEAVER, LEWIS L. FORBES, JOE KOHLES, GEORGE F. REEVES, HARLOD L. AUSTIN, E. K. LUKINS, RAY WILSON, WILLIAM KENLAR, GEORGE BARBER, EARSUL NEAL, GRANT BALES, J. A. HARGREAVES, W. L. SMITH, WALTER H. PASCOE, LEONARD MENDEZ, PAUL BALES, WILLIARD T. HUFFAKER, E. GIGOUS, NORMAN G. ROBINSON, WILLIAM MONTAGUE, JOHN ANTCZAK, JOHN McGOUGH, JAMES MUNEZ, RAYMOND MARCE,

THOMAS FOLEY, JOSEPH SANFILIPPO, OSCAR BERKELEY, A. F. ANDRIEFF, AL-BERT JENSEN, W. M. DAVIS, M. E. STILL-WELL and JAMES WHITESIDE, plaintiffs in intervention in the above entitled matter, and having petitioned for an order from the above-entitled court allowing their appeal to the United States Circuit Court of Appeals for the Ninth Circuit, from an order and decree of said Court sustaining the demurrer of defendants to their complaint without leave to amend, and from the judgment entered thereon in favor of said defendants and against said plaintiffs in intervention, now make and file with said petition the following assignment of errors herein upon which they will [217] rely for a reversal of the said order and decree, and the said judgment, to which exception was duly taken, as follows:

That the said Court erred in sustaining the demurrer of defendants to the complaint in intervention of said plaintiffs in intervention without leave to amend, and in entering judgment upon said order in favor of said defendants and against plaintiffs in intervention, for the reason that said complaint stated a cause of action against the said defendants and each and all of them, and for the further reason that it was an abuse of discretion for the said Court to sustain the said demurrer without leave to amend.

WHEREFORE, the said petitioners pray that the said order and decree, and the said judgment be

reversed, that the said demurrer be ordered overruled, and the said defendants given such time to
answer as may be deemed proper.

A. BROOKS BERLIN
Attorney for Petitioners.

[Endorsed]: Filed Jun. 16, 1936. [218]

[Title of Court and Cause.]

ORDER ALLOWING APPEAL.

Upon motion of A. BROOKS BERLIN, Esq.,
one of the attorneys for Treve W. Berlin, the above
named plaintiff, and one of the attorneys for plain-
tiffs in intervention L. E. CLEAVER, LEWIS L.
FORBES, JOE KOHLES, GEORGE F. REEVES,
HAROLD L. AUSTIN, E. K. LUKINS, RAY
WILSON, WILLIAM KENLAR, GEORGE BAR-
BER, EARSUL NEAL, GRANT BALES, J. A.
HARGREAVES, W. L. SMITH, WALTER H.
PASCOE, LEONARD MENDEZ, PAUL BALES,
WILLARD T. HUFFAKER, E. GIGOUS, NOR-
MAN G. ROBINSON, WILLIAM MONTAGUE,
JOHN ANTCZAK, JOHN McGOUGH, JAMES
MUNEZ, RAYMOND MARCE, THOMAS
FOLEY, JOSEPH SANFILIPPO, OSCAR BER-
KELEY, A. F. ANDRAIELL, ALBERT JEN-
SEN, W. M. DAVIS, M. E. STILLWELL and
JAMES WHITESIDE,

IT IS HEREBY ORDERED that an appeal to
the United States Circuit Court of Appeals for the

Ninth Circuit from an order and decree heretofore made sustaining defendants' demurrer to plaintiff's [219] complaint without leave to amend, and from the judgment entered thereon in favor of said defendants and against the said plaintiff be and the same is hereby allowed; that a transcript of the said complaint and the demurrer thereto, and all papers, records, documents and proceedings upon which said order and decree and the said judgment are based, duly authenticated, forthwith be transmitted to the United States Circuit Court of Appeals for the Ninth Circuit,

IT IS FURTHER HEREBY ORDERED that an appeal to the United States Circuit Court of Appeals for the Ninth Circuit from an Order and Decree heretofore made sustaining defendants' demurrer to the complaint in intervention of the above named plaintiffs in intervention without leave to amend, and from the judgment entered thereon in favor of said defendants and against the said plaintiffs in intervention be and the same is hereby allowed; that a transcript of the said complaint in intervention and the said demurrer thereto, and all papers, records, documents and proceedings upon which said order and decree and the said judgment was based, duly authenticated, be forthwith transmitted to the said United States Circuit Court of Appeals for the Ninth Circuit.

IT IS FURTHER HEREBY ORDERED that the appeal to said United States Circuit Court of

Appeals for the Ninth Circuit from an order and
decree heretofore made sustaining defendants' demurrer to the complaint of the above named plaintiff, as well as the said appeal to the United States
Circuit Court of Appeals for the Ninth Circuit
from an Order and Decree heretofore made sustaining defendants' demurrer to the complaint in intervention of the above named plaintiffs in intervention, may be consolidated.

IT IS FURTHER ORDERED that the bond on
appeal be fixed at the sum of $250.00.

Dated: San Francisco, California, June 22nd,
1936.

HAROLD LOUDERBACK

District Judge.

[Endorsed]: Filed Jun. 22, 1936. [220]

BOND ON APPEAL.

Know All Men by these Presents,

That we, TREVE W. BERLIN, as principal and
AMERICAN BONDING COMPANY OF BALTI-
MORE, as sureties, are held and firmly bound unto
HERBERT M. BARUCH CORPORATION LTD.
A CORPORATION, HERBERT M. BARUCH,
MILTON BARUCH and UNITED STATES FI-
DELITY AND GUARANTY COMPANY, A COR-
PORATION in the full and just sum of Two Hun-
dred Fifty and 00/100 Dollars, to be paid to the

said HERBERT M. BARUCH CORPORATION, LTD. A CORPORATION, HERBERT M. BARUCH, MILTON BARUCH and UNITED STATES FIDELITY AND GUARANTY COMPANY, A CORPORATION, certain attorney, executors, administrators, or assigns; to which payment, well and truly to be made, we bind ourselves, our heirs, executors, and administrators, jointly and severally, by these presents.

Sealed with our seals and dated this eighteenth day of June in the year of our Lord One Thousand Nine Hundred and Thirty-six.

WHEREAS, lately at a District Court of the United States for the Northern District of California, Southern Division, in a suit pending in said Court, between THE UNITED STATES OF AMERICA to the use of TREVE W. BERLIN, Plaintiffs vs. HERBERT M. BARUCH CORPORATION, LTD., HERBERT M. BARUCH, MILTON BARUCH and UNITED STATES FIDELITY AND GUARANTY COMPANY, A CORPORATION, Defendants, a Judgment was rendered against the said plaintiffs and said plaintiffs having obtained from said Court An Order Allowing Appeal to reverse the Judgment in the aforesaid suit, and a citation directed to the said defendants and plaintiffs citing and admonishing them to be and appear at a United States Circuit Court of Appeals for the Ninth Circuit, to be holden at San Francisco, in the State of California,

Now, the condition of the above obligation is such, That if the said plaintiffs shall prosecute said appeal to effect, and answer all damages and costs if they fail to make their plea good, then the above obligation to be void; else to remain in full force and virtue.

This recognizance shall be deemed and construed to contain the "express agreement" for summary judgment, and execution thereon, mentioned in Rule 34 of the District Court.

TREVE W. BERLIN   [Seal]

AMERICAN BONDING COM-
    PANY OF BALTIMORE [Seal]

WALTER JARDINE   [Seal]

Acknowledged before me the day and year first above written.

[Seal]   CHARLES HEMENWAY UPTON

Notary Public in and for the City and County of
    San Francisco, State of California. My com-
    mission expires Jan. 16, 1939. [221]

State of California,
City and County of San Francisco—ss:

On this 18th day of June, in the year one thousand nine hundred and thirty-six, before me, S. WALTER BURKE, a Notary Public in and for the City and County of San Francisco, personally appeared WALTER JARDINE, known to me to be the person whose name he subscribed to the within instrument as the Attorney-in-Fact of the AMERICAN BONDING COMPANY OF BALTIMORE, and acknowledged to me that he subscribed the name of the AMERICAN BONDING COMPANY OF BALTIMORE thereto as principal, and his own name as Attorney-in-Fact.

[Notarial Seal] S. WALTER BURKE
Notary Public in and for the City and County of
    San Francisco, State of Calif.

[Endorsed]: Form of bond and sufficiency of sureties approved.

HAROLD LOUDERBACK
Judge.

[Endorsed]: Filed Jun. 22, 1936.

———

[Title of Court and Cause.]

AMENDED PRAECIPE FOR TRANSCRIPT OF RECORD.

To the Clerk of the above entitled Court:

Please prepare a transcript of record on appeal to be filed in the United States Circuit Court of Appeals, pursuant to an appeal allowed in the above entitled action.

1. The Complaint of Treve W. Berlin, with memorandum of filing thereof;

2. Petition for leave to Intervene of L. E. Cleaver, et al, with memorandum of filing thereof;

3. Order permitting intervention, with memorandum of filing thereof;

4. Complaint in Intervention of L. E. Cleaver, et al, with memorandum of filing thereof;

5. Demurrer of defendants to the complaint, with memorandum of filing thereof;

6. Demurrer to Complaint in Intervention of L. E. Cleaver, et al, with memorandum of filing thereof;

7. Minute order of order sustaining demurrer to the complaint without leave to amend;

8. Minute Order of Order sustaining demurrer to complaint in intervention of L. E. Cleaver, et al, without leave to amend;

9. Minute order of Judgment for defendants;

10. Minute order of Notice of Enrty of Judgment, June 5, 1936, of complaint and complaint in intervention;

11. Petition for Appeal of Complaint of Treve W. Berlin from Order and decree sustaining demurrer to complaint without leave to amend, with memorandum of filing thereof;

12. Assignment of Errors from the Order and Judgment of Complaint of Treve W. Berlin, and memorandum of filing [222] thereof;

13. Petition for Appeal of Complaint in Intervention of L. E. Cleaver, et al, from Order and Decree sustaining defendants' demurrer to complaint in intervention without leave to amend, with memorandum of filing thereof;

14. Assignment of Errors from the Order and Judgment of Complaint in Intervention of L. E. Cleaver, et al, and memorandum of filing thereof;

15. Order allowing Appeal from the Order and Decree sustaining defendants' demurrer to complaint and complaint in intervention without leave to amend, and judgment thereon, and order consolidating appeals, with memorandum of filing thereof;

16. Cost Bond on Appeal with Order approving the same, with memorandum of filing thereof;

17. Citation on Appeal with Order of Consolidation, with memorandum of filing thereof;

18. This amended Praecipe with memorandum of service on defendants, and filing thereof.

Said transcript to be prepared as required by law, and the rules of this Court, and to be filed in the office of the Clerk of said Circuit Court of Appeal on or before the 22nd day of July, 1936, or until further date as ordered by the Circuit Court of Appeal.

Dated: July 13, 1936.

A. BROOKS BERLIN

Attorney for Plaintiff and
Plaintiffs in Intervention.

[Endorsed]: Receipt of a copy of the within Praecipe is herewith acknowledged this 17th day of July, 1936.

JULIUS MACKSON

Attorney for Defendants.

[Endorsed]: Filed Jul. 20, 1936. [223]

District Court of the United States
Northern District of California

CERTIFICATE OF CLERK TO TRANSCRIPT OF RECORD ON APPEAL.

I, Walter B. Maling, Clerk of the United States District Court, for the Northern District of California, do hereby certify that the foregoing 223 pages, numbered from 1 to 223, inclusive, contain a full, true, and correct transcript of the records and proceedings in the United States of America, ex rel Treve W. Berlin, vs. Herbert M. Baruch Corporation, et al, No. 19921-L, as the same now remain on file and of record in my office.

I further certify that the cost of preparing and certifying the foregoing transcript of record on appeal is the sum of $35.45 and that the said amount has been paid to me by the Attorney for the appellants herein.

IN WITNESS WHEREOF, I have hereunto set my hand and affixed the seal of said District Court, this 22nd day of July, A. D. 1936.

WALTER B. MALING,

Clerk.

[Seal]   J. P. WELSH,

Deputy Clerk.

[223A]

[Title of Court and Cause.]

CITATION.

United States of America—ss.

To the defendants HERBERT M. BARUCH CORPORATION, LTD., a corporation, HERBERT M. BARUCH, MILTON BARUCH, UNITED STATES FIDELITY AND GUARANTY COMPANY, a corporation, and to JULIUS MACKSON, Esq., their attorney:

You are hereby cited and admonished to be and appear at the Circuit Court of Appeals of the United States for the Ninth Circuit, to be held at the City and County of San Francisco, State of California, on the 22 day of July, 1936, pursuant to an order allowing an appeal filed and entered in the Clerk's office of the District Court of the United States, for the Northern District of California, Southern Division, from an Order and Decree of the said Court sustaining defendants' demurrer to the complaint of plaintiff, Treve W. Berlin, and from the judgment of said Court entered thereon in favor of said defendants [224] and against the said plaintiff, which said Order was entered on May 13, 1936, and which said judgment was entered on the 4th day of June, 1936, to show cause if any there be why the said Order and Decree, and the said Judgment should not be corrected and why justice should not be done to the parties in that behalf, and you are furthermore hereby cited and admonished to be and appear at the Circuit Court of Appeals of the United States for the Ninth Circuit, to be held at the City and County of San Francisco, State of California, on the 22 day of July, 1936, pursuant to an order allowing an appeal filed and entered in the Clerk's office of the District Court of the United States, for the Northern District of California, Southern Division, from an Order and Decree of said Court sustaining defendants' demurrer to the complaint in intervention of plaintiffs in intervention, L. E. Cleaver, Lewis L. Forbes, Joe Kohles, George F. Reeves, Harold L. Austin, E. K. Lukins, Ray Wilson, William Kenlar, George Barber, Earsul Neal, Grant Bales, J. A. Hargreaves, W. L. Smith, Walter L. Pascoe, Leonard Mendez, Paul Bales, Willard T. Huffaker, E. Gigous, Norman G. Robinson, William Montague, John Antczak, John McGough, James Munez, Raymond Marce, Thomas Foley, Joseph Sanfilippo, Oscar Berkeley, A. E. Andraieff, Albert Jensen, W. M. Davis, M. E. Stillwell, and James Whiteside, and from the judgment of said Court entered thereon in favor of said defendants and against the said plaintiff, which said Order was entered on June 4, 1936, and which said judgment was entered on the 4th day of June, 1936, to show cause if any there be why the said Order and Decree and the said Judgment should not be corrected, and why justice should not be done to the parties in that behalf, the aforementioned orders allowing appeal having been duly consolidated.

WITNESS the Honorable HAROLD LOUDER-
BACK, United States District Judge for the
Northern District of California, Southern [225]
Division, this 22nd day of June, 1936, and of the
Independence of the United States the 159th year.

HAROLD LOUDERBACK
United States District Judge for the
Northern District of California, South-
ern Division.

Receipt of a copy of the within Citation is herewith acknowledged this 23rd day of June, 1936.

JULIUS MACKSON
Attorney for Defendants

[Endorsed]: Filed June 26, 1936. [226]

———

[Endorsed]: No. 8290. United States Circuit
Court of Appeals for the Ninth Circuit. United
States of America, to the use of Treve W. Berlin,
and L. E. Cleaver, et al., Appellants, vs. Herbert M.
Baruch Corporation, Ltd., a corporation, Herbert
M. Baruch, Milton Baruch, United States Fidelity
and Guaranty Co., Appellees. Transcript of Record.
Upon Appeal from the District Court of the United
States for the Northern District of California,
Southern Division.

Filed July 23, 1936.

PAUL P. O'BRIEN,
Clerk of the United States Circuit Court of Appeals for the Ninth Circuit.

In the United States Circuit Court of Appeals for the Ninth Circuit.

No. 8290

No. 19921-L.

UNITED STATES OF AMERICA, to the use of Treve W. Berlin,

Plaintiff,

vs.

HERBERT M. BARUCH CORPORATION, Ltd., a corporation, HERBERT M. BARUCH, MILTON BARUCH, UNITED STATES FIDELITY AND GUARANTY COMPANY, a corporation, First Doe, Second Doe, Third Doe, Fourth Doe and Fifth Doe,

Defendants.

STIPULATION.

IT IS HEREBY STIPULATED by and between A. BROOKS BERLIN, attorney for plaintiff, Treve W. Berlin, and plaintiffs in intervention L. E. Cleaver, Lewis L. Forbes, Joe Kohles, George F. Reeves, Harold L. Austin, E. K. Lukins, Ray Wilson, William Kenlar, George Barber, Earsul Neal, Grant Bales, J. A. Hargreaves, W. L. Smith, Walter H. Pascoe, Leonard Mendez, Paul Bales, Willard T. Huffaker, E. Gigous, Norman G. Robinson, William Montague, John Antczak, John McGough, James Munez, Raymond Marce, Thomas Foley, Joseph Sanfilippo, Oscar Berkeley, A. F Andraieff, Albert Jensen, W. M. Davis, M. E. Still-

well and James Whiteside, and JULIUS MACK-
SON, attorney for defendants, with the approval of
the above-entitled Court, that the several counts of
plaintiff's Complaint are identical in form to the
second count of plaintiff's Complaint; and that the
several counts of plaintiff's Complaint in Intervention are identical in form to the second count of
plaintiff's Complaint in Intervention; therefore in
lieu of the several counts of the complaint and complaint in intervention being repeated in the transcript, the following pages shall be omitted from
the transcript, with the exception of the name and
amount of claim of the individuals, which shall be
printed:

COMPLAINT

No. of page to be omitted	Names to be printed	Amount to be printed
6.	Joe Brozovich	$ 157.00
7.	G. R. Fulton	388.50
8.	Arthur Addington	1028.00
9.	Frank Wilson	1529.00
10.	Max B. Miller	1283.00
11.	Laurel Johnstone	1534.00
12.	James V. Sullivan	342.00
13.	William G. Riley	90.00
14.	J. Malatesta	245.00
15.	G. Malatesta	206.00
16.	James Ghielmetti	726.20
17.	Fred Melton	120.00
18.	R. Diaz	140.00

19.	F. Gonzales	215.00
20.	E. Spriggs	276.00
21.	Sam Rascon	140.00
22.	Harry Grodberg	824.20
23.	John Alupsky	956.50
24.	John H. Rediger	550.00
25.	John West	69.00
26.	R. L. Williams	1042.60
27.	William F. Joyce	294.26
28.	William T. Joyce	465.51
29.	Carl Hagstrom	193.00

COMPLAINT IN INTERVENTION

No. of page to be omitted	Names to be printed	Amount to be printed
59.	Joe Kohles	718.00
60.	George F. Reeves	31.56
61.	Harold L. Austin	112.00
62.	E. K. Lukins	220.00
63.	Ray Wilson	762.80
65.	George Barber	621.04
66.	Earsul Neal	234.00
67.	Grant Bales	166.98
68.	J. A. Hargreaves	291.00
69.	W. L. Smith	50.00
71.	Leonard Mendez	175.39
72.	Paul Bales	360.00
73.	Willard T. Huffaker	828.40
74.	E. Gigous	307.20
75.	Norman G. Robinson	163.35
76.	William Montague	231.30

78.	John McGough	175.00
79.	James Munez	166.00
80.	Raymond Marce	40.00
81.	Thomas Foley	85.00
82.	Joseph San Filippo	119.00
83.	Oscar Berkley	679.20
84.	A. F. Andraieff	206.17
85.	Albert Jensen	259.20
87.	M. E. Stillwell	228.00
88.	James Whiteside	160.40

IT IS FURTHER STIPULATED that the defendants' demurrer to plaintiff's Complaint is identical in all the 26 causes of action, with the exception of the amounts and the names of the individuals; therefore, it is hereby stipulated between counsel that defendants' demurrer to the first cause of action of plaintiff's complaint be and hereby applies to the demurrer of the other twenty-five causes of action; the following pages therefore may be omitted from the transcript with the exception of the names of the different causes of action and the amounts involved:

No. of pages
to be omitted Words to be printed

95.	Demurrer to	second cause of action	$ 423.00
96.	”	”	third	”	”	”	157.00
97.	”	”	fourth	”	”	”	388.50
98.		”	fifth	”	”	”	1028.00
99.	”	”	sixth	”	”	”	1529.00
100.	”	”	seventh	”	”	”	1283.00

No. of pages
to be omitted   Words to be printed

101. ,,	,,	eighth ,,	,,	,,	1534.00
102.	,,	ninth ,,	,,	,,	342.00
103. ,,	,,	tenth ,,	,,	,,	90.00
104.	,,	eleventh ,,	,,	,,	245.00
105.	,,	twelfth ,,	,,	,,	206.00
106. ,,	,,	thirteenth	,,	,,	726.20
107.	,,	fourteenth	,,	,,	120.00
108.	,,	fifteenth	,,	,,	140.00
109. ,,	,,	sixteenth	,,	,,	215.00
110. ..	,,	seventeenth	,,	,,	276.00
111.	,,	eighteenth	,,	,,	140.00
112. ,,	,,	nineteenth	,,	,,	824.20
113.	,,	twentieth	,,	,,	956.50
114.	,,	twenty-first	,,	,,	550.00
115. ,,	,,	twenty-second	,,		69.00
116. ''	,,	twenty-third	,,		1042.60
117. ,,	,,	twenty-fourth	,,		294.26
118. ,,	,,	twenty-fifth	''		465.51
119. ,,	,,	twenty-sixth	,,		193.00

IT IS FURTHER STIPULATED that defendants' Points and Authorities and Argument attached to defendants' demurrers to complaint and complaint in intervention may be omitted from the transcript, and therefore the following pages may be omitted: page 121 to and including page 150.

IT IS FURTHER STIPULATED that the defendants' demurrer to the first cause of action of plaintiff's complaint in intervention being identical to the demurrers of all the other causes of action, with the exception of the amounts and the numbers of the causes of action, therefore, the following pages may be omitted from the transcript with the exception of the following words from each page which are to be printed:

No. of Pages
to be omitted   Words to be printed

153	Demurrer to second cause of action
154	Lewis L. Forbes, $328.15
155	Demurrer to third cause of action, Joe Kohles, $718.00
156	Demurrer to fourth cause of action
157	George F. Reeves, $31.56
158	Demurrer to fifth cause of action, Harold L. Austin, $112.00;
159	Demurrer to sixth cause of action, $220.00, E. K. Lukins
160	
161	Demurrer to seventh cause of action, Ray Wilson, $762.80
162	Demurrer to eighth cause of action, William Kenlar, $96.00
163	
164	Demurrer to ninth cause of action, George Barber, $621.04
165	Demurrer to tenth cause of action, Earsul Neal, $234.00
166	Demurrer to Eleventh cause of action
167	Grant Bales, $166.98
168	Demurrer to twelfth cause of action, J. A. Hargreaves, $291.00

No. of Pages
to be omitted   Words to be printed

169 Demurrer to thirteenth cause of action

170 W. L. Smith, $50.00

171 Demurrer to fourteenth cause of action, Walter H. Pascoe, $488.90

172

173 Demurrer to fifteenth cause of action, Leonard Mendez, $175.39

174 Demurrer to sixteenth cause of action, Paul Bales, $360.00

175 Demurrer to seventeenth cause of action

176 Willard T. Huffaker, $828.40

177 Demurrer to eighteenth cause of action, $307.20

178 Demurrer to nineteenth cause of action

179 Norman G. Robinson, $163.35

180 Demurrer of twentieth cause of action, William Montague, $231.30

181 Demurrer to twenty-first cause of action

182 John Antczak, $196.00

183 Demurrer to twenty-second cause of action, John McGough, $175.00

184

185 Demurrer to twenty-third cause of action, James Munez, $166.00

186 Demurrer to twenty-fourth cause of action, Raymond Marce, $40.00

187

188 Demurrer to twenty-fifth cause of action, Thomas Foley, $85.00

No. of Pages
to be omitted   Words to be printed

189   Demurrer to twenty-sixth cause of action, Joseph San Filippo $119.00

190

191   Demurrer to twenty-seventh cause of action, Oscar Berkley, $679.20

192   Demurrer to twenty-eighth cause of action, A. F. Andraieff, $206.17

193

194   Demurrer to twenty-ninth cause of action, Albert Jensen, $259.20

195   Demurrer to thirtieth cause of action, William Davis $81.60

196

197   Demurrer to thirty-first cause of action, M. E. Stillwell, $228.00

198   Demurrer to thirty-second cause of action, James Whiteside, $160.40

Dated: July 25, 1936.

A. BROOKS BERLIN

Attorney for plaintiff and plaintiffs in intervention

JULIUS MACKSON

Attorney for Defendants.

The above and foregoing stipulation is hereby approved this 3d day of August, 1936.

FRANCIS A. GARRECHT

Judge of the above-entitled Court

[Endorsed]: Filed Aug. 3, 1936.